MW00356327

HUGH OF SAINT VICTOR ON THE SACRAMENTS OF THE CHRISTIAN FAITH

(DE SACRAMENTIS)

English Version by

ROY J. DEFERRARI

Gardiner Professor of Greek and Latin
The Catholic University of America
Lecturer in Greek and Latin at Dunbarton College of Holy Cross
Fellow of The Mediaeval Academy of America

Wipf & Stock
PUBLISHERS
Eugene, Oregon

Wipf and Stock Publishers
199 W 8th Ave, Suite 3
Eugene, OR 97401

Hugh of Saint Victor on the Sacraments of the Chistian Faith
(De Sacraments)
By Hugh of Saint Victor
ISBN 13: 978-1-55635-447-2
ISBN 10: 1-55635-447-9
Publication date 5/1/2007
Previously published by Mediaeval Academy of America, 1951

To my wife, Evelyn Mary
and to my daughter, Mary Evelyn.

Preface

The late James Hugh Ryan, Archbishop of Omaha, proposed that I translate this work as long ago as the year 1928. He was the spokesman of the late Ralph Adams Cram, well known architect and devotee of mediaeval culture, for many years Clerk of the Mediaeval Academy of America.

As soon as I approached the task of translation, the problem of the Latin text presented itself. Obviously, no reliable text was at hand. Furthermore, Mr. Cram and the Mediaeval Academy were not at the moment interested in publishing a new Latin text. They wanted an English translation just as soon as it could be turned out. The translator soon discovered that he was constantly in a state of uncertainty as to whether the vagueness of his understanding of the text was due to the author himself or to the faultiness of the text's transmission through the ages. It soon became clear that whether a new text of *De Sacramentis* was to be published or not, a reliable text had to be constructed before any worthwhile translation could be attempted.

Fortunately Brother Charles Henry Buttimer, F.S.C., as a candidate for the degree, Doctor of Philosophy, in the Department of Greek and Latin, of the Catholic University of America, had constructed a critical text of the *Didascalicon de Studio Legendi* of Hugh of St. Victor, and had become well acquainted with the manuscript tradition of Hugh's works in general. Furthermore, the authorities of the Mediaeval Academy of America expressed a willingness to supply such manuscripts as he desired to make a critical text of the *De Sacramentis*. Such a text was duly made by Brother Charles Henry and it is earnestly hoped that the financial support necessary for its publication will soon be forthcoming. It is this text of Brother Charles Henry's upon which the present translation has been made.

The translator is well aware of the many theories as to the basic principles for translation which have appeared in recent years. He does not agree with many of them. He readily admits, however that a translation should read with all the freshness and smoothness of an original composition of at least passable value. This the translator has tried to achieve. He insists, however, that the translation must also reflect the outstanding qualities of the original composition. The translation must exhibit the literary style of Hugh of St. Victor rather than that of his translator. Hugh wrote in a very simple style. He was forceful, logical, and clear. These qualities, I hope, are evident in the translation. The translator, before he began his work, had been informed by at least one known scholar of Hugh's works that it was *impossible* to translate the *De Sacramentis* because

Hugh himself did not know what he was saying in it. This erroneous conclusion was undoubtedly reached because of the defective texts of the *De Sacramentis* then in existence. The excellent text of Brother Charles Henry has cleared up all these difficulties as if by magic, and we insist that Hugh of St. Victor, even in his *De Sacramentis,* is forceful, logical, and clear.

Few notes accompany this translation. They consist chiefly of references to the Holy Scriptures and occasionally of a warning that Hugh is departing from theological orthodoxy as well established in our own day. The translator has endeavored to make his translation its own commentary, a characteristic which, he believes, every worthy translation should possess.

Introduction

Any interested reader may become acquainted with the life and works of Hugh of St. Victor by consulting a handbook of Mediaeval culture. For his convenience we present here the barest outline.

Hugh was born in 1096 at the manor of Hartingham in Saxony and died on March 11, 1141, in the monastery of St. Pancras, at Hamerleve near Halberstadt in Saxony. Here, in spite of the opposition of his parents, he assumed the habit of the Canons Regular of St. Augustine. Because of the disturbed condition of the country and before his novitiate had been completed, his uncle, Reinhard, then Bishop of Halberstadt, advised him to go to the monastery of St. Victor in Paris. He arrived there in 1115 and there he remained to the end of his life.

In 1112, Gilduin had been elected to succeed William of Champeaux as head of the School of St. Victor, and he did much to enhance the School's reputation for piety and learning. It was under Gilduin that Hugh spent most of his mature life in study, teaching, and writing. When Gilduin died on August 20th, 1133, Hugh was elected to succeed him as head of the School. Under Hugh, the School of St. Victor achieved its most brilliant success.

Hugh of St. Victor was a renowned philosopher, theologian, and mystical writer. Because of his great familiarity with the works of St. Augustine, he is sometimes called *Alter Augustinus*. Harnack, the great Protestant theologian of the last century, called Hugh, "the most influential theologian of the twelfth century," (*History of Dogma*, tr. London, 1899, VI, 44).

The most important of Hugh's works are the following: the *De Sacramentis Christianae Fidei*, a translation of which is presented in this volume; *Eruditionis Didascaliae, libri septem*, comprising encyclopedics, methodology, and introduction to Sacred Scripture; also a treatise on how we may rise from things visible to a knowledge of the Trinity; scriptural commentaries, important both for his theological and mystical doctrines; *Commentarium in Hierarchiam Coelestem S. Dionysii Areopagitae secundum interpretationem Joannes Scota, libri X;* and many mystical works, the most important of which are: *De Arcâ Noe Morali et Mystica, De Vanitate Mundi, De Arrhâ Animae,* and *De Contemplatione et eius Speciebus.* Much discussion has arisen over the authenticity of the *Summa Sententiarum.* Although commonly ascribed to Hugh of St. Victor, the forceful arguments of Portalié appear to demonstrate that this work is not Hugh's. De Wulf and Pourrat support Portalié in this conclusion.

The *De Sacramentis Christianae Fidei*, composed about 1134, is the masterpiece as well as the most extensive work of Hugh of St. Victor. It has been called "a dogmatic synthesis similar to, but more perfect than, the *Introductio ad Theologiam*" of Abelard, which treated only the knowledge of God and of the Trinity. The following is an analysis of the contents of the *De Sacramentis* as we have received it in the manuscript tradition. It will be noted that the work is divided into two books, of twelve and eighteen parts respectively, each part containing numerous chapters.

ON THE SACRAMENTS OF THE CHRISTIAN FAITH

BOOK I

Prologue of Book I

1. What must be learned at the outset. 2. What the subject matter of the Divine Scriptures is. 3. How Divine Scripture touches upon the works of foundation to narrate the works of restoration. 4. That Holy Writ treats of its subject in a threefold manner. 5. That in Holy Writ not only words but also things have meaning. 6. How all arts are subservient to divine wisdom. 7. On the number of books of Holy Writ.

The Body of Book I

PART I

The Period of Six Days in the Work of Foundation

1. That there is one first principle by which all things have been made from nothing. 2. Whether matter was made before form. 3. The reason why God wished through intervals of time to bring His works to completion, and to make being before beautiful being. 4. Whether there could ever have been matter without form. 5. That all things, that is, visible and invisible, were created simultaneously. 6. On the first unformed state of all things; of what nature it was; and how long the world remained in it. 7. On the distinction made by form. 8. On the mystery of light; why it was made and where. 10. That visible and invisible light were made simultaneously, and equally divided from darkness. 11. That light illumines three days; and why it was made before the sun. 12. The sacrament of the divine works. 13. Why Scripture says: "God saw the light," (Gen. 1, 4.). 14. What precaution is here signified regarding good work. 15. What was done with that primal light after the creation of the sun; and whether the sun was made substantially from the same. 16. Whether God worked for six days without interval, or in some other manner. 17. On the work of the second day, when the firmament was made. 18. Of what matter the firmament was made; and of what nature it was made. 19. The sacrament of the matters mentioned above. 20. Why God is not said to have seen that the work of the second day was good. 21. How the waters were gathered together into one place that dry earth might appear. 22. How the earth brought forth plants. 23. Why Scripture does not say that those waters which are above heaven were gathered into one place. 24. That in these three days the disposition of things was made. 25. How in the three following days the world was adorned. 26. Whether from the elements themselves those things were made which were made for their adornment. 27. The sacrament why fishes and birds were made of the one matter and were not placed in one abode. 28. Why the works of foundation are recounted first, then the works of restoration. 29. That the discussion is especially concerned with the works of restoration. 30. That there are four points with which the subsequent discussion deals.

PART IV

On the Will of God Which Is Eternal and One, and on the Signs of His Will, Which Indeed Are Temporal and Are Called According to the Figure of the Will, Because They Are Signs of the Will

PART V

On the Creation of the Angels, and on Free Will, and on Other Matters Which Pertain to the Angelic Nature, Namely Its Office and Hierarchy

PART VI

On the Creation of Man

PART VII

On the Fall of the First Man

Part VIII

On the Restoration of Man

Part IX

On the Institution of the Sacraments

Part X

On Faith

Part XI

On the Natural Law

peoples and in the two peoples two powers and in each power different grades and orders of ranks, and one superior to the other. 5. That every ecclesiastical administration consists of three things, that is, orders, sacraments, precepts. 6. On earthly power. 7. How the Church possesses earthly things. 8. In how many ways justice is to be determined in secular power. 9. On royal ornaments.

Part III

On the Spiritual Power

1. On clerics. 2. On ecclesiastical tonsure. 3. How the orders are among holy monks. 4. On the seven sacred grades. 5. On porters. 6. On readers. 7. On exorcists. 8. On acolytes. 9. On subdeacons. 10. On deacons. 11. On presbyters. 12. On bishops. 13. On archbishops. 14. On the highest pontiff. 15. On the other offices which are in the clergy. 16. On archdeacons. 17. On the head-chamberlain. 18. On the treasurer. 19. When and how ordinations should be performed. 20. At what age those should be ordained who are ordained. 21. That priests are not to be ordained without a definite title. 22. Of what nature men should be who are to be elected to sacred orders and of what nature not. 23. For what reason a change of the ordained can be made.

Part IV

On Sacred Garments

1. On sacred garments. 2. On the tunic of byssus. 3. On the girdle. 4. On the linen thigh-bandages. 5. On the interior tunic. 6. On the superhumeral. 7. On the rational which in Greek is called the logion. 8. On the mitre which is called cydaris or tiara, and on the golden plate. 9. On the garments of new priesthood. 10. On the stole or the napkin. 11. On the planata or casula. 12. On the napkin or maniple. 13. On the dalmatica. 14. On sandals and half-boots of byssus or linen. 15. On the staff and the ring of the bishop. 16. On the pallium of the archbishop. 17. On the sacred vessels.

Part V

On the Dedication of a Church

1. On the dedication of a church. 2. Concerning those things which are carried on visibly in it. 3. What the mystery of the above mentioned matters is.

Part VI

On the Sacrament of Baptism

1. On the sacrament of baptism. 2. What baptism is. 3. Why the sacrament of baptism was instituted. 4. When the sacrament of baptism was instituted. 5. When man began to be obligated by the precept of receiving baptism. 6. What the difference is between the baptism of John and that of Christ, regarding the form of the baptism of John and that of Christ. 7. Whether after the precept of baptism was given anyone could be saved without actually receiving the sacrament of baptism. 8. On the sacraments of the neophytes. 9. On catechizing. 10. On exorcism. 11. On those things in baptism which follow after exorcization. 12. On godparents. 13. On rebaptizing. 14. Why baptism is celebrated in water only. 15. On the form of baptism.

PART VII

On Confirmation

1. On confirmation. 2. That the imposition of the hand is celebrated by pontiffs alone. 3. On what Pope Sylvester established—that a presbyter should anoint the baptized person with chrism. 4. Which is the greater sacrament—imposition of hands or baptism. 5. That the imposition of the hands should not be repeated, just as baptism should not, and that it should be celebrated by fastings. 6. How long those who have received the imposition of the hands should be under the discipline of chrism.

PART VIII

On the Sacrament of the Body and Blood of Christ

1. On the sacrament of the body and blood of Christ. 2. When the sacrament of the body and blood of Christ was instituted. 3. Whether at the supper He gave His mortal or immortal body. 4. Whether that was the body of Christ which Judas received through the dipped bread. 5. That the paschal lamb was the figure of the body of Christ. 6. That the sacrament of the altar is also a figure as far as pertains to the appearance of bread and of wine, and is the thing as far as pertains to the truth of the body of Christ. 7. That there are three things in the sacrament of the altar: the appearance of bread and wine, the truth of the body of Christ, spiritual grace. 8. Why Christ instituted the sacrament of His body and blood under the appearance of bread and wine. 9. Of what nature the change of bread and wine into the body of Christ is to be understood. 10. What those three portions signify which are made of the body of Christ in the sacrament of the altar. 11. That the body of Christ, when it seems to be divided, is divided according to appearance alone, but remains entire according to itself, thus entire in individual parts, just as in different places it is one and the very same. 12. That those things which seem unworthy in the body of Christ are done according to appearance only. 13. What happens to the body of Christ and its corporeal presence after taking of the sacrament. 14. That the celebration of the body of Christ is called the mass, and when and by whom it was first instituted and why it is called the mass.

PART IX

On the Sacraments That Have Been Instituted for Practice. That All Are Sanctified through the Word of God

1. On the sacraments that have been instituted for practice. That all are sanctified through the word of God. 2. On the water of aspersion which is blessed together with salt. 3. On the reception of ashes. 4. On blessing branches of palms and foliage. 5. Regarding the candle which is blessed on Holy Sabbath and regarding lambs which are blessed on the Pasch. 6. On the signs by whose sound the faithful are called together. 7. On curtains. 8. On the other sacraments that consist of deed. 9. On those sacraments that consist of words. 10. On things sacred and not sacraments.

PART X

On Simony

1. Why it is so called and what simony is. 2. On the authors of simony. 3. On those who buy or sell spiritual things. 4. On those who by buying corporeal things in the Church buy spiritual things with them and in them. 5. On the fact that corporeal things alone are sold.

Part XI

On the Sacrament of Marriage

1. On the sacrament of marriage. 2. On the origin of marriage. 3. On the twofold institution of marriage and on the twofold cause of the institution. 4. What marriage is. 5. When marriage begins to be. 6. On those who marry secretly or after they have married do some fearful things contrary to marriage. 7. That there are three blessings that accompany marriage, namely, faith, hope of progeny, sacrament. 8. Whether or not these blessings are inseparable from marriage. 9. On those who live incontinently in marriage and take care more to satisfy lust than generate progeny. 10. For what reason the ancients had several wives at the same time. 11. Whether that is to be called marriage which can at some time be dissolved. 12. On those who think that even between any illegitimate persons whatsoever mutual consent makes a proper marriage. 13. On the marriage of unbelievers. 14. On consanguinity and the degrees of consanguinity. 15. On affinity. 16. On spiritual relationship. 17. What difference there is between blood relationship or consanguinity and affinity and spiritual union. 18. Whether the ruse called substitution dissolves marriage. 19. Whether the condition of slavery, if it be unknown, afterwards dissolves marriage.

Part XII

On Vows

1. On vows; whether they are different. 2. On the five ways in which the mind treats what must be done. 3. What making a vow is. 4. What vows should not be kept. 5. What vow admits no exchange. 6. What vows permit change.

Part XIII

On Vices and Evil Works

1. On vices and evil works. 2. On virtues and good works. 3. On fear and love. 4. What fear is. 5. On the four fears. 6. On charity. 7. Why there are not three precepts of charity. 8. That he loves purely and gratis who loves God on account of himself. 9. On the measure of loving God. 10. On the measure of loving neighbour. 11. Whether charity once possessed is lost. 12. Whether all love of God is to be called charity.

Part XIV

On Confession

1. On confession. 2. On penance and the fruit of penance. 3. On those who do not fulfill penance in this life. 4. Whether penance can be repeated. 5. On those who repent at the very end. 6. That good will alone suffices, if the opportunity for operating is not given. 7. That man judges work; God weighs the will. 8. On the remission of sins and whether priests who are men can forgive sins. 9. On the question whether sins return after they have once been dismissed.

Part XV

On the Anointing of the Sick

1. On the anointing of the sick. 2. When and by whom the anointing of the sick was established. 3. Whether this sacrament can be repeated.

Part XVI

On the End of Man and Those Who Seek that End

1. On the dying. 2. On the departure of souls. 3. On the punishment of souls. 4. On the places of punishment. 5. On the nature of the torments of hell. 6. On taking care of the dead. 7. To whom there may be benefit after death or how that is of benefit which is done for them. 8. On obsequies. 9. On the sacrifice for the dead. 10. To whom it is a benefit. 11. Whether souls know what things are being done in this world.

Part XVII

On the End of the World

1. On the time of Christ's coming at the very last. 2. On the last tribulation. 3. Why the devil is now bound. 4. Why he will be freed at the very last. 5. For how long will the last tribulation be. 6. On the coming of Elias and Henoch. 7. On the quality of the person, judge. 8. On the swiftness of judgment. 9. On the swiftness of judgment, continued. 10. On the swiftness of judgment, continued. 11. On the order of rising again. 12. How what has been written: "He shall judge the living and the dead," is to be understood. 13. On the resurrection of bodies, how or of what nature they will rise again. 14. On abortions and monsters: whether they rise again and of what nature they are. 15. On the manner of the resurrection. 16. An example of the things mentioned above. 17. That the bodies of the saints will rise again without blemish and incorruptible. 18. That infants will not rise again in that stature in which they died. 19. That all will rise again in the same stature which indeed they had or were to have in the perfect or youthful age. 20. Whether the bodies of the wicked will rise again with their vices and deformities. 21. How earthly bodies will abide in heaven. 22. Of what nature the judgment will be. 23. That God uses our conscience as a witness for judging us. 24. How God judges in the present. 25. How God judges in the present, continued. 26. How God judges in the present, continued. 27. How God judges in the present, continued. 28. Where the saints will be corporeally when the world will burn.

Part XVIII

On the Renewing of the World

1. On the renewing of the world. 2. How the eternal punishment of the evil will benefit the good. 3. That the good will see the evil, not the evil the good, and on the second death. 4. That the evil will always live for this purpose, that they may always die. 5. That eternal fire will not torture all equally. 6. That eternal fire will not torture all equally, continued. 7. That eternal fire will not torture all equally, continued. 8. How it is just that eternal punishment be paid for a temporal sin. 9. How it is just that eternal punishment be paid for a temporal sin, continued. 10. How it is just that eternal punishment be paid for a temporal sin, continued. 11. How the devil is now being tormented and how he will be tormented in the future. 12. How the devil is now being tormented and how he will be tormented in the future, continued. 13. That after the damnation of the wicked, the saints recognize more fully the grace of God. 14. That, after the evil have been damned, the saints will enter upon eternal life. 15. How the just will not then have pity for the evil. 16. On the wisdom of God. 17. What is the difference between seeing and believing. 18. On the corporeal and spiritual visions in the future. 19. Whether our thoughts there will be changeable. 20. Of what nature and how great will be the future felicity and

blessedness. 21. That true blessedness consists of three things. 22. That for the saints in the future the memory of the past will conduce not to pain but to joy.

This work of Hugh's is the first complete theological treatise of the mediaeval schools, and it is likewise the most literary of all the many contemporary works dealing with the same subject. It is to be noted that Hugh of St. Victor used the word *sacramentum* in a broad sense to include natural mysteries as well as supernatural mysteries, sacramentals as well as sacraments. According to Michel, Hugh appears to have been the first to establish the distinction between sacraments in the strict sense and sacramentals. He is careful to point out the diverse senses of the term. See especially Book I, Part IX.

SELECTED WORKS ON HUGH OF SAINT VICTOR

Baltus, Urbain. "Dieu d'après Hugues de Saint-Victor," Revue Bénédictine, XV (1898), pp. 109-123: 200-214.

Bringmann, A. "Hugo von St. Victor," Wetzer und Welte's Kirchenlexikon (Freiburg im Br.: Herder, 1889), VI, cols. 392-398.

Beuchitté, H. "Hugues de St. Victor," Dictionnaire des Sciences Philosophiques, ed. M. Franck (Paris: Hachette, 1885), pp. 732-734.

Ceillier, Remy. "Hugues de St. Victor," Histoire Générale des Auteurs Sacrés et Ecclesiastiques, Nouvelle Ed., Bauzon (Paris: Vivès 1863), XIV, pp. 347-361.

The Columbia Encyclopedia, art. "Hugh of St. Victor" (New York: Columbia, 1940).

De Ghellinck, J. Le Mouvement théologique du XIIe Siècle (Paris: Gabalda, 1914).

De Wulf, M. Histoire de la Philosophie Médiévale, Sixième Ed., (Louvain-Paris: Vrin, 1934), 2 vols. English Translation: History of Mediaeval Philosophy, E. C. Messenger (New York, 1935).

Endres, J. A. Review of H. Ostler, Die Psychologie des Hugo von St. Viktor, Philosophisches Jahrbuch, XX (1907), pp. 212-214.

Grabmann, M. Die Geschichte der scholastischen Methode (Freiburg im Br.: Herder, 1911), II, pp. 249-291.

Grassi-Bertizzi, G. La filosofia di Hugo di San Vittore (Rome, 1912).

Haureau, B. Les Oeuvres de Hugues de Saint-Victor, Essai Critique (Paris: Hachette, 1886).

Kilgenstein, Jacob. Die Gotteslehre des Hugo von St. Viktor (Würzburg, 1897).

Landgraf, Artur. "Hugo von St. Viktor," Lexikon für Theologie und Kirche (Freiburg im Br.: Herder, 1933), V, p. 184.

Liebner, Albert. Hugo von St. Victor und die theologischen Richtungen seiner Zeit (Leipzig: A. Lehnhold, 1832).

Michel, A. "Sacramentaux," D.Th.C. (Paris, 1922), XIV, col. 469.

Mignon, A. Les Origines de la Scholastique et Hugues de Saint-Victor (Paris, 1895), 2 vols.

Myers, E. "Hugh of St. Victor," Catholic Encyclopedia (New York: Appleton, 1910), VII, pp. 521-523.

Ostler, Heinrich. Die Psychologie des Hugo von St. Viktor, Ein Beitrag zur Geschichte der Psychologie in der Frühscholastik (Muenster, i.W., Aschendorff, 1906), BGPM VI, 1.

Vernet, F. "Hugues de Saint-Victor," D.Th.C. (Paris, 1922), VII, cols. 240-308.

Zöckler, O. "Hugo von St. Victor," Realencyklopädie für protestantische Theologie und Kirche (Leipzig, 1900), VIII, pp. 436-445.

HUGH OF SAINT VICTOR
ON THE SACRAMENTS OF THE
CHRISTIAN FAITH
(DE SACRAMENTIS)

On the Sacraments of the Christian Faith

PREFACE

I have been forced by the zeal of certain persons to write a work on the sacraments of the Christian Faith, in which I have incorporated some writings that from time to time I had composed previously, because it seemed to me an irksome, if not a superfluous task to express them in a new form. And if perhaps the simplicity of my diction in these writings was unable to observe beauty of style, I have not thought it of great importance, as long as the same truth abides in them.

But this disturbs me more — the fact that after I had composed these same writings with some carelessness in the past (since at that time I had no plan for a future work) I gave them out indiscriminately to be transcribed, thinking then that it was enough that trifles of this sort or notes become generally known; but afterwards, when I was incorporating these writings into the text of the present work, reason kept urging me to change certain things in them, in fact to add or take away certain things. I wish the reader to be advised of this in order that, wherever he discovers these writings outside the text of the present work to be different either in content or form, he may know that the fore-going is the cause of the difference, and, if it should happen that anything has to be corrected in them, he may make changes according to the norm of the present work.

Now I have divided the present work into two books, in order that in such an abundance and richness of material this division of my exposition may prevent any weariness on the reader's part and may at the same time offer a more convenient form for those who are unable to copy the two books or who for any other reason wish to have the work divided.

Prologue of the First Book on the Sacraments

Why he has changed the reading.

Since, therefore, I previously composed a compendium on the initial instruction in Holy Scripture, which consists in their historical reading, I have prepared the present work for those who are to be introduced to the second stage of instruction, which is in allegory. By this work they may firmly establish their minds on that foundation, so to speak, of the knowledge of faith, so that such other things as may be added to the structure by reading or hearing may remain unshaken. For I have compressed this brief *summa,* as it were, of all doctrine into one continuous work, that the mind may have something definite to which it may affix and conform its attention, lest it be carried away by various volumes of writings and a diversity of readings without order or direction.

I. *What must be learned at the outset.*

Whoever approaches the reading of the Divine Scriptures for instruction ought to consider first what the nature of the subject matter is with which their discourse is concerned; because if he has knowledge of those things about which Scripture is composed, he will more easily thereafter perceive the truth or profundity of its words.

II. *What the subject matter of the Divine Scriptures is.*

The subject matter of all the Divine Scriptures is the works of man's restoration. For there are two works in which all that has been done is contained. The first is the work of foundation; the second is the work of restoration. The work of foundation is that whereby those things which were not came into being. The work of restoration is that whereby those things which had been impaired were made better. Therefore, the work of foundation is the creation of the world with all its elements. The work of restoration is the Incarnation of the Word with all its sacraments, both those which have gone before from the beginning of time, and those which come after, even to the end of the world. For the Incarnate Word is our King, who came into this world to war with the devil; and all the saints who were before His coming are soldiers as it were, going before their King, and those who have come after and will come, even to the end of the world, are soldiers following their King. And the King himself is in the midst of His army and proceeds protected and surrounded on all sides by His columns. And although in a multitude as vast as this the kind of arms differ in the sacraments and observance of the peoples preceding and following, yet all are really serving the one king and following the one banner; all are pursuing the one enemy and are being crowned by the one victory. In all these writings the works of restoration are considered, with which the whole intent of the Divine Scriptures is concerned. Worldly or secular writings have as subject matter the works of foundation. Divine Scripture has as subject matter the works of restoration. Therefore, it is rightly believed to be superior to all other writings insofar as the subject matter is the more dignified and the more sublime with which its consideration and discourse are concerned. For the works of restoration are of much greater dignity than the works of foundation, because the latter were made for servitude, that they might be subject to man standing; the former, for salvation, that they might raise man fallen. Therefore, the works of foundation, as if of little importance, were accomplished in six days, but the works of restoration can not be completed except in six ages. Yet six are placed over against six that the Restorer may be proven to be the same as the Creator.

III. *How Divine Scripture touches upon the works of foundation to narrate the works of restoration.*

Now although the principal subject matter of Divine Scripture is the works of restoration, yet, in order to approach the treatment of these more competently, it first, at the very commencement of its narrative, recounts briefly and truthfully the beginning and constitution of the works of foundation. For it could not fittingly have shown how man was restored, unless it first explained how he had fallen; nor, indeed, could it fittingly have shown his fall unless it first explained in what condition he was constituted by God. But to show the first condition of man, it was necessary to describe the foundation and creation of the whole world, because the world was made for the sake of man; the soul indeed, for the sake of God; the body, for the sake of the soul; the world, for the sake of the body of man, that the soul might be subject to God, the body to the soul, and the world to the body.

In this order, accordingly, Sacred Scripture describes first the creation of the world, which was made for the sake of man; then it relates how man when made was disposed in the way of justice and discipline; next how man fell; lastly how he was restored. First, therefore, it deals with the subject matter of man's creation and original disposition; next with his misery in sin and punishment; then with his restoration and piety in the knowledge of truth and love of virtue; finally with his true home land and the joy of heavenly happiness.

IV. *That Holy Writ treats of its subject matter in a threefold manner.*

Now of this subject matter Divine Scripture treats according to a threefold sense: that is, according to history, allegory, and tropology. History is the narration of events, which is contained in the first meaning of the letter; we have allegory when, through what is said to have been done, something else is signified as done either in the past or in the present or in the future; we have tropology when through what is said to have been done, it is signified that something ought to be done.

V. *That in Holy Writ not only words but also things have meaning.*

Wherefore, it is apparent how much Divine Scripture excels all other writings in subtlety and profundity, not only in its subject matter but also in its method of treatment, since indeed in other writings words alone are found to have meaning, but in it not only words but also things are significant. Hence, just as wherever the sense between words and things is uncertain, the knowledge of words is necessary, so in the case of that which exists between things and mystical acts done or to be done, the knowledge of things is necessary. But the knowledge of words is considered under two heads, namely: pronunciation and meaning. To pronunciation alone grammar applies, to meaning alone dialectic applies; to pronunciation and meaning together rhetoric applies. The knowledge of things is concerned with two points, form and nature. Form is in the exterior disposition; nature, in the interior quality. The form of things is considered either under number, to which arithmetic applies, or under proportion, to which music applies, or under dimension, to which geometry applies, or under motion to which astronomy applies. But the consideration of the interior nature of things belongs to physics.

VI. *How all arts are subservient to divine wisdom.*

Therefore, it is clear that all the natural arts serve divine science, and that the lower wisdom, rightly ordered, leads to the higher. Accordingly, under the sense of the significance of words in relation to things history is contained, which, as has been said, is served by three sciences: grammar, dialectic, and rhetoric. Under that sense, however, consisting in the significance of things in relation to mystical facts, allegory is contained. And under that sense, consisting in the meaning of things in relation to mystical things to be done, tropology is contained, and these two are served by arithmetic, music, geometry, astronomy, and physics. Besides these, there is above all that divine science to which the Divine Scripture leads, whether in allegory or in tropology; one division of this which is in allegory, teaches right faith, the other, which is in tropology, teaches good work. In these consist knowledge of truth and love of virtue; and this is the true restoration of man.

VII. *On the number of books of Holy Writ.*

Now that we have shown what the subject matter of the Divine Scriptures is, and how these treat of their subject matter in the three-fold sense of history, allegory, and tropology, it is now fitting to indicate of what books the work justly distinguished by the term "divine" consists. The whole body of Divine Scriptures is comprised of two Testaments: namely, the Old and the New. Both are divided into three parts. The Old Testament contains the Law, the Prophets, and the Hagiographers, which translated means holy writers or writers of holy things. In the Law are contained five works: namely, Genesis, Exodus, Leviticus, Numbers, Deuteronomy. Genesis, moreover, is so called from "generation;" Exodus, from "going out;" Leviticus, from the Levites. The book of numbers is so called, because in it are numbered the sons of Israel. Deuteronomy is the second law. In Hebrew these books are called bresith, hellesmoth, vagetra, vegedaber, adabarim.

In the division comprising the prophets there are eight works: the first, the book of Josue, who is also called Jesu Nave and Josue Bennun, that is, son of Nun; the second book, that of Judges, which is called Sopthim; the third book, that of Samuel, which is the first and second of Kings; the fourth, that of Malachim, which is translated of Kings, which is the third and fourth of Kings; the fifth is Isaias; the sixth, Jeremias; the seventh, Ezechiel; the eighth, the book of the twelve prophets which is called thareasra. These books are called prophetical because they are of prophets, although they are not all prophecies. Now a prophet is defined in three ways: by his office, by his grace, by his mission. But in the common use of the word they rather are called prophets who are prophets either by their office or by their manifest mission, just as in this place. And according to this acceptance of the word David and Daniel and many others are not called prophets but hagiographers.

In the division comprising the hagiographers nine works are contained. The first is Job; the second, the book of Psalms; the third, the Proverbs of Solomon, which in Greek are called parabolae, in Hebrew masloth; the fourth, Ecclesiastes, which in Hebrew is translated coeleth, in Latin concionator; the fifth, syra syrim, that is the Canticle of Canticles; the sixth, Daniel; the seventh, Paralipomenon, which in Latin is translated verba dierum, in Hebrew, dabreniamin; the eighth, Esdras; the ninth, Esther. All these, that is the five and the eight and the nine together, make twenty-two, the number of letters also contained in the Hebrew alphabet, so that the life of the just may be instructed to salvation by the same number of books as is that of the letters by which the tongue of learners is instructed in speech. There are besides in the Old Testament certain other books which indeed are read, but are not written in the body of the text or in the canon of authority. Such are the books of Tobias, Judith, Machabees, the book which is entitled The Wisdom of Solomon, and Ecclesiasticus.

The New Testament contains the Gospels, the Apostles, and the Fathers. There are four Gospels: those of Matthew, Mark, Luke, and John. There are likewise four books of the Apostles: the Acts of the Apostles, the Epistles of Paul, the Canonical Epistles, and the Apocalypse. These books combined with the twenty-two of the Old Testament mentioned above make thirty, and of this number the body of Divine Scripture is comprised. The writings of the Fathers are not reckoned in the body of the text, since they add nothing, but by explanation and a broader and clearer treatment they amplify the same matter contained in the books mentioned above.

HERE BEGINNETH THE FIRST BOOK

PART ONE

The Period of Six Days in the Work of Foundation.

Prevailed upon by your frequent entreaty, I am truly entering upon an arduous and laborious task, not merely by compression to reduce to a compendium the whole content of Divine Scriptures, but also by explanation to bring to light the secrets of their profundity. I, indeed, offer the beginning of this work with ready devotion; and I hopefully promise its completion.

I. *That there is one first principle by which all things have been made from nothing.*

"In the beginning God created heaven and earth." (Genesis 1, 1.) What is created is made from nothing. For what is made from something, is indeed made, but is not created, because it is not made from nothing. Therefore, God made heaven and earth; and He not only made but created them; that is, He made them from nothing. The philosophers of the pagans assumed, so to speak, a certain three principles of things without beginning: an artisan, matter, and form, maintaining that those things which were made were all fashioned from matter into form by an artisan. But they maintained that God was a maker only, not a creator. The true faith, however, declares that there is one first principle only which always was, and that by this alone was that which once did not exist made to exist. And the virtue of its ineffable omnipotence, just as it could not have anything else coeternal with it, to assist it in making, thus reposed in itself while it wished, so that what it wished, and when, and as much as it wished, might be created out of nothing. Therefore, God not only made all things that were made from matter, but He himself created the matter of all things from nothing.

II. *Whether matter was made before form.*

But it is no unimportant question whether those things that were made came into being simultaneously in matter and in form, or were first created indeed essentially through matter, and afterwards given form. I know that certain of the Holy Fathers, who, before us, skilfully examined the mysteries of the word of God, have left contradictory statements, apparently, on this question; some indeed asserting that all things were created simultaneously in matter and in form; others, however, favoring this view: that all corporeal things made should be considered to have been created as matter at the time and once, but to have been given form afterwards through the intervals of the six days. I think that, as men of wisdom, in things so obscure and doubtful and so remote from our knowledge, they did not rashly assert what they did not know, nor could they have erred in what they asserted, since it was presented with the greatest possible care. I am more inclined to believe this: that under the form of their assertion there was sometimes zeal for investigation. Those who thus wish to give a pious interpretation to the words of the saints, will neither fall into error by believing what is false, nor into pride by reprehending what is true. We, therefore, inclining to neither side by rash assertion will set forth, in so far as we are capable, that view to which our mind in the mean time has arrived. Those who contend that God made all things simultaneously in matter and form, perhaps think that their assertion is just on this account, because it seems unworthy of the omnipotence of the Creator, after the likeness of human weakness, to bring his work to perfection through intervals of time; and because also certain passages of the Scriptures are found in some measure to make the same assertion, as the following: "He that liveth for ever created all things together." (Eccli. 18. 1.) Even the book of Genesis itself, from which the first knowledge of this subject has come down to us, speaks so ambiguously about the work of the six days that it often seems to prove rather that all things were made simultaneously. Therefore, for these and similar reasons, they say that we should believe that this distribution of the six days in Genesis is mystical, while in reality every creature, from that very beginning of the time from which it began to be, began to be such and of such a form as it now is seen to have, in so far as this pertains to the disposition of the whole.

III. *The reason why God wished through intervals of time to bring His works to completion, and to make being before beautiful being.*

To us, however, with the understanding that we do not wish to define anything rashly in this matter, it does not seem at all derogatory to the omnipotence of the Creator, if He is said to have brought His work to completion through intervals of time, provided, however, that we believe without question that he could also have done otherwise, if the plan of the Omnipotent Will had so demanded. For the omnipotent God, whose will can never be separated from His goodness, just as He made all other things on account of the rational creature, so also in making all these He must especially have observed that mode which was more suited to the benefit and interest of the rational creature itself. Now this mode was that in which indeed not only homage but also example might be prepared for this same rational creature, that is, in which the latter might not only receive what it needed in the way of homage, but also through what it received might recognize what it was. Therefore, in other things matter was first made unformed and then formed, to show by this very fact that things not existing had first received their essence from that mode without which in a confused state they could not have form and order. In the same way the rational creature itself through what was being done outside itself might have understanding of itself both from that being which was, and from that being to be desired, which it was about to be; thus it might rise to render thanks for what it had received, and might open itself to the very affection of love in order to obtain what it was destined to receive. For even the rational creature itself was first made unformed in a certain mode of its own, afterwards to be formed through conversion to its Creator; and therefore matter unformed but afterwards formed was shown to it, that it might discern how great was the difference between being and beautiful being. And by this it was warned not to be content with having received being from the Creator through creation, until it should obtain both beautiful being and happy being, which it was destined to receive from the Creator through the conversion of love.

But if any one should ask what rational creation already then existed at the very beginning of the world, for which this example could be given, it may be replied easily, that the angels had already been created then, who might be admonished by this to know themselves, and to the end that there would be men, who, although they did not see this when it was done, yet being taught by the Scriptures can in no way be ignorant that this was done. If this reasoning which we have proposed will seem insufficient to anyone for proving our opinion on the creation of things, we permit him with all freedom to seek out someone else better and more subtle to prove this point more clearly; or if the doctrine asserted here does not please him, let him adopt another as he wishes. We, however, according to the plan of our undertaking shall proceed with our subject in order.

IV. *Whether there could ever have been matter without form.*

For it remains for us, if we assert that the matter of things was created unformed, to show whether or not anything could have existed without form, or what kind of essence we should believe it had before form was given. And, to explain briefly what it seems to me must be thought on this point, I certainly do not think that the first matter of all things was unformed in such a way that it had no form at all, because I am inclined to believe that no such thing can exist at all which has some being and not some form. Yet I am inclined to believe that matter can be thus called unformed without absurdity, because subsisting in a kind of confusion and mingled state it did not yet begin to have that beautiful and fitting disposition and form in which it is now seen. Therefore, before form, matter was in a broken state, yet in form—in a form of confusion, before a form of disposition. In the first form, that of confusion, all corporeal things were first created as matter simultaneously and once; in the second form, that of disposition, they were afterwards arranged through the intervals of the six days.

V. *That all things, that is, visible and invisible, were created simultaneously.*

But not even this, in my opinion, will be absurd, if we believe that there was one and the same moment of time at which in the beginning both the matter of visible and corporeal things and the essence of the invisible things in the angelic nature were created simultaneously; and that this is what Scripture means when it says that all things were created simultaneously, as we have said above: "He that liveth for ever created all things together," (Eccli. 18, 1.), because at the same moment both the matter of visible things and the nature of invisible things were created simultaneously in essence; and nothing was made afterwards of which either the matter as in bodies or the likeness as in spirits did not precede in this first beginning. For even if new souls are still created daily, yet no new creature is made, because its likeness preceded already in the angelic spirits at the time when they were created. But now two subjects present themselves to us for discussion: first, what was the nature of the unformed form of the first creation of matter; second, how it was brought from the unformed state to that form which it now has.

VI. *On the first unformed state of all things; of what nature it was; and how long the world remained in it.*

So far as I have been able to conjecture from what I have found truthfully expressed in Scripture, whether clearly or obscurely, on this mater, that first mass of all things, when it was created, proceeded then to be there where it now subsists in its formed state. And this earthly element, resting in the middle and in this same lowest place, the other elements being mingled in one confusion, was endowed with a better form; but it was so enveloped by the other elements which were spread about on all sides like a cloud, that it could not appear what it was. Now these three elements, as has been said, still mingled in one confusion or rather confused in one mixture, suspended on all sides, extended on high as far as the highest point of corporeal creation now reaches. And all this space which extends from the surface of the earth lying in a middle position to the extreme and highest limit of the circle of heaven was filled with that aforementioned cloud and darkness. And what are now the beds or channels of waters, already then at the very beginning of the nascent world had been prepared in the body of the earth as future receptacles of waters. Among these also, that great abyss, from which the streams of all waters were to be produced or derived, showed the sheer void, horrible with its mouth still open and empty. Indeed over this from above a cloud of that dark mist extended with which the whole surface of the earth was then enveloped, and this darkness, as I therefore think, Scripture testifies was over the face of the abyss when heaven and earth were created. Such an appearance of the world in the beginning before it received form or disposition is indicated by Scripture when it is said: "In the beginning God created heaven and earth. And the earth was void and empty" or, as another translation has it, "uncomposed," "and darkness was upon the face of the abyss." (Gen. 1, 1 and 2.). For by "heaven" and "earth" in this passage, I think, is meant that matter of all heavenly and earthly things from which afterwards the things which were first created simultaneously in this matter in essence were made successively in form. For there the earth was the element itself of earth, and the mobile heaven was indeed that light confusion of the remaining three elements, which moved in the middle circuit of the earth as it lay suspended; and in these two was contained the matter for forming all the heavenly and earthly bodies.

Then Scripture goes on to say: "And darkness was upon the face of the abyss." It had mentioned two things previously, that is, heaven and earth. Now it adds two others, darkness and the abyss; signifying that one, that is, the abyss, must be understood as being in the earth, and the other, that is, darkness, as in that which it had called heaven. For darkness was upon the face of the abyss on this account, because the abyss was below and the dark mistiness was above. Nor was the abyss darkness, because it was not to become light; but above the face of the abyss was the place of darkness, in that element in fact whence light was afterwards to come. For darkness could not have been save in the place of light; therefore darkness was upon the face of the abyss. "And the spirit of God moved over the waters." (Gen. 1, 2). Suddenly it mentions waters, after it had first made mention in the creation of things of earth and heaven only. But not on this account must it be believed that the waters were uncreated—because in the creation of things the name of waters is not stated, since heaven itself is darkness itself, and this is also the waters: heaven, on account of its lightness; darkness, on account of privation of light; waters, on account of movement and fluctuation.

For if the abyss was in the earth and darkness was upon the face of the abyss, then darkness was upon the earth.

But what was upon the earth? In the beginning two things were made, heaven and earth. Which of these do you think was below, or which shall we say was above? Was either the earth above and the heaven below, or the earth below and the heaven above? But must we believe that in the first creation of things the heaven was created below, and afterwards when form was given, was placed above? Perhaps, because Scripture has mentioned heaven before earth, someone for this reason may say that heaven was created below as a foundation. I think that it is so mentioned not for the sake of order but of dignity, and also because the word following must be considered as applying to the element of earth as the nearest term, as it were, and on this account last mentioned; therefore, heaven had to be mentioned first and earth afterwards. But not even the nature of created things itself would have suffered any other order of position or location than that the heavy should be arranged below and the light above. Therefore, the earth was below and heaven above, and what was above the earth was heaven. Therefore, heaven was above the earth.

And where were the waters? Under heaven or above heaven? The waters were neither under heaven nor above heaven, but the waters were in heaven, because heaven itself was the waters. All was waters and all was heaven, because the waters and heaven were the same. On the second day the firmament was made and was called heaven, and it was placed so that it made a division between waters and waters, and the waters which first were waters were made waters, the waters which are under heaven and the waters which are above heaven. And heaven was made heaven and heaven; heaven above heaven and heaven under heaven. Even to this day also heaven is above heaven, and heaven under heaven, and the whole is from one heaven and is one heaven. But before this heaven, which is called the firmament, was made from that heaven, that heaven was not heaven and heaven, but only heaven. Nor were those waters waters and waters, but only waters. Both the waters and heaven were one heaven; and that heaven and those waters were neither above heaven nor under heaven, but above earth; and there was nothing between heaven and earth because there was nothing except heaven and earth. And yet there were waters, and there was darkness, and there was the abyss: the abyss in the earth, the darkness and waters in heaven. And darkness was upon the face of the abyss, and the spirit of God moved over the waters. Therefore, the spirit of God was over all things, because all things were in the power of God, and in all things the power of God was not limited.

Perhaps it is already enough, in keeping with our plan of brevity, to have discussed these matters so far, if we shall add only this: how long a time the world existed in this confusion before its disposition was begun. For that that first matter of all things began at the beginning of time, or rather with time itself, is clear from what has been said: "In the beginning God created heaven and earth." But how long it remained in this unformed state or confusion, Scripture does not clearly indicate. But to me it seems, so far as I can conjecture, that between the creation and disposition of things an order of time, to be sure, but no delay was interposed; so that it may be truly said that this was done after that, but that between this which was made and that no delay at all intervened. And to state briefly what it seems to me we should think on this point, I think that in the first beginning of time, or rather with the very beginning of time, that is, when time itself began, there also began simultaneously the matter of all visible things, and at exactly the same moment the essence of the invisible things in the angelic nature: both in a measure in form, and both in a measure without form. For just as that matter of bodies to be formed, when it was first created, had a certain form in which it began to subsist, and yet was unformed, because it was not yet disposed and arranged, so likewise that rational nature, when it was first created in the angelic spirits, was soon formed by wisdom and discretion; but because it had not fixed itself through the conversion of love upon that highest and true good in which it was to be made happy, in a certain measure it still remained unformed. Both natures, therefore, namely, the corporeal through matter and the incorporeal through essence, came into being simultaneously, because both in the former whence they were made and in the latter which they were made, they began at one and the same moment of time to be in time equally, and with time. For the spiritual nature, since it is simple and entirely identical with that being which it is, does not have a material existence before a personal existence like corporeal nature; and so the latter, when it was first created, came into being, to be sure, through the matter from which it was made; but the former received its being at once from the first in that simple life and immortal and indissoluble essence itself in which it subsists. Yet both were made simultaneously: the one, the corporeal, in that from which it is itself; but the other, the incorporeal, in that which it is itself. Both were formed, and both unformed, just as has been said. And, indeed, on the state of the first creation, before nature came into form and disposition, we wish these words to suffice.

VII. *On the distinction made by form.*

Next, we must treat in order how this disposition itself was accomplished. In six days God disposed, and ordered, and reduced to form all that he had made. And He completed His work on the sixth day. "And" so finally "he rested on the seventh day," (Gen. 2, 1.), that is, He ceased from work. On the first day, light was made; on the second day, the firmament was made; on the third day, the waters were gathered; on the fourth day, lights were made; on the fifth day, fishes and birds; on the sixth day, beasts, cattle, and creeping things; last of all, yet on the same day, man.

Here we wish first to warn the reader of this: that as often as he hears the simple fact among these works that something was made within the six days, as for example when it is said: On the first day, light was made; on the second day, the firmament was made; on the third day, the waters were gathered; on the fourth day, the lights were made, he should not by any means think that, when first these things are said to have been made, they were created from nothing; but rather he should understand that they were formed from the matter itself which was first created from nothing. Even if sometimes he finds that the word "creation" is used as it is here: "And God created the great whales, and every living and moving creature," (Gen. 1, 21.), he should know that the reference is not to the matter by which they begin to be, but to the form by which they begin to be what they are.

VIII. *On the mystery of light; why it was made first.*

Therefore, God in beginning to accomplish His works made light first, that afterwards he might make all things in light. For He signified to us that He does not like works which are done in darkness, because they are evil: "For every one that doth evil hateth the light, and cometh not to the light, that his works may not be reproved, for they are evil." (John III, 20. The last phrase is apparently from end of John III, 19). "But he that doth truth, cometh to the light, that his works may be made manifest, because they are done in God." (John III, 21). Therefore, He himself who was to do truth, did not wish to work in darkness; but He came to light and made light, that He might make Himself manifest through light. For He did not make light that He Himself might see by light, but that He might make His works manifest by light, because they were done in God. "And" so "God saw all the things that he had made, and they were very good." (Gen. 1, 31.). It was necessary for me to state this by way of introduction to give the reason why God made light first.

IX. *Of what nature this light was made and where.*

But now it remains for us to examine the truth of the matter more diligently. The beginning of the divine works, therefore, was the creation of light, when light itself was created, not as material from nothing, but when from that first existing matter of the universe it was made in form to be light, and to have the power and property of lighting. This work was done on the first day, but the matter of this work was created before the first day. And soon with light itself day began, because before light there was neither night nor day, although there was time. If, however, it is asked of what nature this light was, whether corporeal or incorporeal, and, if corporeal, what kind of body it had, and whether circumscribed in one place or diffused everywhere, whether in motion or immobile, it may be answered quite correctly in my opinion that light, unless corporeal, could not have been fitted to illumine corporeal and visible things. Moreover, every body, however subtile and close to spiritual nature, must be circumscribed in place. And again, unless that light had been mobile, it would not have been able by any means alternately to distinguish day and night, nor in any way without motion to complete a space of time. And, in accordance with this consideration, therefore, I think it more fitting for us to believe that this light made in the beginning to illumine corporeal things was without doubt corporeal; (such perhaps any luminous body might have been by whose presence all things would be illuminated, just as now appears in the case of the sun) and that this light was made instead of and in place of the sun, so that it might meanwhile be circulated by its motion and distinguish night and day.

Because the first day had risen, I am rather inclined to believe that that light, on being made, appeared first with this day there where the sun making its daily course emerges when rising. Thus travelling around in the same path, and descending first to its setting, it might make the evening, and then, on being recalled to its rising, it might illumine the dawn, that is the morning before the rising of the following day. And, because the first day did not have a preceding dawn (since before light was created there was complete darkness, but soon with light appearing on the earth, complete day, because the work of God must have been begun from what was completed), therefore Scripture has said: "And there was evening and morning one day." (Gen. I, 5.). For it has not said: "There was morning and evening," but, "There was," it says, "evening and morning one day." Because, as we have said, the first day did not have a preceding morning, since it took its beginning from a full and perfect light, thus every dawn is of the preceding day, and day takes its beginning from the rising of the sun. And the natural day is that space of time which, in passing from the rising of the sun to its setting, includes night and day in itself. As regards the latter, since day naturally precedes night and we call the end of the day "evening," and the end of the night "dawn," it is clear without doubt that dawn must always refer to the preceding day. Therefore, that first moment of time when the nature of all things visible and invisible was created was neither night nor day; and yet there was time, because there was change. Afterwards, when light was made, darkness and light were immediately divided, and time now began to be distinguished by day and night.

X. *That visible and invisible light were made simultaneously, and equally divided from darkness.*

And, in my opinion, at exactly the same moment of time at which light was divided visibly and corporeally from darkness, invisibly also the good angels were separated from those evil angels who were falling into the darkness of sin; the former too being turned toward the light of justice and illumined by light, that they might be light and not darkness. For thus the exemplars of God's works had to be in harmony, so that those works of wisdom which were visible might follow the productions of the invisible, according as this wisdom itself, operating in both cases, in the one exercised judgment, in the other formed an example. Light, therefore, was divided from darkness; and there was visible light, and there was visible darkness; likewise, there was invisible light and invisible darkness; and a division of both was made; and the division of darkness and light was made simultaneously. And the light was called "day," and the darkness "night." God indeed divided both, and named both; but He did not also make both. For God is not the author of darkness but of light, because sin is darkness and sin is nothing: "And without him nothing was made." (John I, 3.). Light was made by Him, because justice and truth are light, and of light we have heard what God said: "Be light made." "And," straightway, "light was made." (Gen. 1, 3.). God never said: "Be darkness made." But of light He said: "Be light made. And He divided the light from the darkness. And he called the light Day, and the darkness Night." (Gen. I, 3, 4, 5.). Therefore, He did not make both; yet He divided both, and He named both. He divided by judgment, and by merit He named, judged, and disposed. Because that which was inordinate in those sinning, certainly could not be inordinate in Him judging. He called light "day," and darkness "night."

XI. *That light illumined three days; and why it was made before the sun.*

Therefore, let no one say: How could there have been day before the sun was made?, because, before the sun was made, there was light: "And God saw the light that it was good, and he called the light Day, and the darkness Night." (Gen. 1, 4 and 5). And the light itself made those first three days before the sun was made, and illumined the world. But what does it signify that the sun was not made immediately from the time that light must have been made, but that there was light, so to speak, before clear light? Very possibly the confusion was not worthy of full light; yet it received some light, that it might see how to proceed to order and disposition.

XII. *The sacrament of the divine works.*

I think that here a great sacrament is commended, because every soul, as long as it is in sin, is in a kind of darkness and confusion. But it can not emerge from its confusion and be disposed to the order and form of justice, unless it be first illumined to see its evils, and to distinguish light from darkness, that is, virtues from vices, so that it may dispose itself to order and conform to truth. Thus, therefore, a soul lying in confusion can not do without light, and on this account it is necessary first that light be made, that the soul may see itself, and recognize the horror and shamefulness of its confusion, and extricate itself, and fit itself to that rational disposition and order of truth. Now, after all relating to it has been put in order and has been disposed according to the exemplar of reason and the form of wisdom, then straightway will the sun of justice begin to shine for it, because thus it has been said in promise: "Blessed are the clean of heart: for they shall see God." (Matt. 5, 8). First, therefore, light is created in that rational world of the human heart, and its confusion is illumined that it may be reduced to order. After this, when the interior of this confusion has been purified, the clear light of the sun comes and illuminates it. For it is not worthy to contemplate the light of eternity, until it has become clean and purified, having, as it were, beauty through matter and disposition through justice.

Thus the law preceded grace; the word, spirit; thus John as a precursor, Christ; light, light; a lamp, the sun; and Christ himself first showed His humanity, that He might thereafter make manifest His divinity; and everywhere light precedes light; the light which illumines sinners to justice, that light which illuminates the justified to blessedness. Therefore, light was made before the brightness of the sun was made manifest; and there was day; and there were three days when there was light, but no sun. On the fourth day the sun shone, and that day was bright, because it had true light, and there was no darkness. Thus no soul deserves to receive the light of the sun and to contemplate the brightness of the highest truth, unless these three days precede in it. Now, on the first day, light is made, and light and darkness are divided; light is called and is made day, and darkness, night. On the second day the firmament is made and is placed between the higher waters and the lower waters; and the firmament is called heaven. On the third day the waters which are under heaven are gathered into one place; and the dry land is ordered to appear and put on its dress of plants.

Now all these things represent spiritual examples. Light is first created in the heart of the sinner, when he begins to recognize himself, so that he distinguishes between light and darkness, and begins to call light day, and darkness night, and is no longer of those of whom it is said: "Woe to them that call evil good, and good evil: that put darkness for light, and light for darkness." (Isa. 5, 20). After this, however, when he has begun to distinguish between light and darkness, and also to call light day, darkness night, that is, when he has begun truly to condemn his evils by the judgment of reason, and to choose the works of light, which are good and praiseworthy, there remains for the firmament to be made in him. This means that he must be strengthened in his good resolution to distinguish between the upper and lower waters, namely, the desires of the flesh and of the spirit, so that as an interposer and mediator he may not suffer two mutually hostile elements to be mingled or to be transposed, nor suffer what should be divided to be brought together nor what should be placed below to be above, nor what should be placed above to be below. Finally there follows in the order of disposition the work of the third day: the waters which are under the heavens are to be gathered into one place, lest the desires of the flesh should be floods, and expand beyond the bound of necessity, so that the whole man, being recalled to the status of his nature and disposed according to the order of reason, may collect into one place every desire to the end that the flesh may be subject to the spirit and the spirit to the Creator. Whoever is so ordered is worthy of the light of the sun, so that, when the mind is directed upward and the desires fixed upon heavenly things, the light of the highest truth may beam forth upon the beholder, and no longer "through a glass in a dark manner," (I Cor. 13, 12), but in itself as it is, he may recognize and know truth.

But this also, which is said, must not be passed over neglectfully: "And God saw the light that it was good; and he divided the light from the darkness. And he called the light Day, and the darkness Night." (Gen. 1, 4, and 5). For He made and saw; then He divided and called. Why did He see? He did not wish to divide before He had seen; He first saw whether it was good; and then afterwards He divided light from darkness; and He called the light day, and the darkness night. For He will bring all His work into judgment; and not only the other works which He made in the light did God see that it was good, but He also saw the light itself that it was good, and He divided the light and the darkness. For the evil angel himself at times transforms himself into an angel of light, and tries to deceive the mind, as if he were the true light. But this light is not to be divided from darkness, and is not to be called day, but night, because it has indeed the appearance of light but is true darkness. Therefore, God first saw the light, whether it was good, so that we may not at once "believe every spirit; but may try the spirits if they be of God," (I John 4, 1.); and when we have seen the light, that it is good, then let us divide the light from the darkness, and let us call the light day, and the darkness night. Therefore, we should not only desire ardently that light precede in our works, and that our works be done in the light; but the light itself also must first be seen and considered diligently; and thus at last when we have seen the light, that it is good, let us divide light from darkness, and let us call light day, and darkness night.

XIII. *Why Scripture says: "God saw the light." (Gen. 1, 4).*

But the question arises perhaps, how "God saw the light that it was good; and He divided the light from the darkness. And He called the light Day and the darkness Night." (Gen. 1, 4 and 5). For if He saw His other works in the light, that they were good, in what light did He see the light, that it was good, and did He divide the light from darkness and call light day and darkness night?

For nothing can be seen without light. But not even darkness is seen without light. How much the more is light not seen without light? What then was that light not seen without light? What then was that light by which God saw the light, that it was good, and divided the light from the darkness? Did He see by the light itself, that it was good, or did He see by another light that it was good? But how could He have seen by the light itself, that it was good, unless He had had another light by which and in which He had seen the light itself, that it was good? For, if He saw that this light was good and saw truly, He saw it in something about whose goodness there could be no doubt. Therefore, there was another uncreated light, in which this created light was seen, that it was good; because it imitated that former light, which is always good. For in that light, since it itself is only good, are seen both evils and goods; and not only evils and goods are seen in it, but also evils to be evil and goods to be good are seen in it, because it itself is truly and supremely good. For what is seen to be out of harmony with it, is seen to be evil; and what is seen to be like to it, is seen to be good; and both are not seen save in it and by it. By light, therefore, He tried light, because in the unchangeable light He saw that this changeable light in its own mode and order was good.

"And He divided the light from the darkness, and He called the light day, and the darkness night," and in this light in which He saw the light, that it was good, He also saw the other works that He had wrought, that they were good; and He saw nothing without that light, either good or evil, whether of those things which He himself made good or of those things which we ourselves have made evil, all of which He himself saw not in an evil but in a good manner. And He saw there, where He saw no evil. This is the very light by which we also should see every light, whether it is good; and we shall not be able to judge truly about light, whether it is good, until we have been illumined by that light which is truly good: "For the spiritual man judgeth all things; and he himself is judged by no man." (1 Cor. 2, 15). And if the Spirit of God truly dwells within us, the spirits of error will not be able to deceive us, even if they come to us in light, because we shall have light in us, in which it will be manifest to us regarding every light, whether it is good; and thus with assurance we shall divide light from darkness, and we shall judge not only between darkness and light, but also between light and light shall we judge; not only between night and day, but also between day and day shall we judge, and we shall judge every day. For it is not enough to judge perfectly between day and night; it is not enough to divide light and darkness, that is, to separate virtues from vices; we must know also how to judge between day and day, and know how to judge every day, that we may understand what those impulses are which come to us under the appearance of virtues, as it were, by a different light, and what those are again, which send forth the true brightness of virtues, that in these virtues themselves we may also prove not only what things are good but also what are better. "For the spiritual man judgeth all things, and he himself is judged by no man," (1 Cor. 2, 15), "for the Spirit searcheth all things, yea, the deep things of God," (1 Cor. 10), "and His unction teacheth us of all things," (Cf. 1 John 2, 27).

XIV. *What precaution is here signified regarding good work.*

Note here how much precaution you must observe with reference to good work. At the beginning of all your works see that you have light in you, so that all your works may be of light and not of darkness. Next, consider carefully whether your light is pure and not darkened; and when you have found that it is good, then finally divide it from darkness, and call the light day, and the darkness night. Then, in the case of your other works which you do in the light, see if these also are good; and do not let any work at all go by without judgment, until you know all that you have done. Thus judgment is twofold: the first judgment is that in which light is judged and seen whether it is good, so that it may be divided from darkness; the second judgment is when the works themselves which are done in light are called to judgment, and it is seen that they also are good. And thus at last God rests. Meanwhile, we have touched upon a certain few mysteries of light, passing over them in temporary fashion. Now, let us again return to the systematic exposition of our work as planned.

XV. *What was done with that primal light after the creation of the sun; and whether the sun was made substantially from the same.*

Therefore, God wished first to make light to illumine the world, before He created the sun running ahead with its vicarious aid until that should come which is perfect. And there are some who ask what was done with that light, because now no traces of it can be found, ever since the brightness of the sun shone forth. Others say that, on being dispersed through the broad spaces of the air, it lost its power of shining and illuminating, but that there are still left certain slight remnants of it which here and there periodically appear by night on the inner periphery of the firmament to those who gaze rather carefully, although by day these are hidden by the greater brightness of the sun so that they can not be seen. Thus everyone fashions his own opinions in so far as it is possible. But who knows whether that same light was not afterwards transformed into the substance of the sun, and with increased clarity received a better form, just as Jesus at the marriage feast made wine out of water, that He might show the state of change for the better and the sacrament of restoration? For there was light before the sun was made; and for this reason there was water before it was changed into wine, not that something else might be made which was displayed as preferable, but that it might be made from that same thing which before was considered cheaper. Thus in doubtful matters there is no one who can define anything with certainty.

XVI. *Whether God worked for six days without interval, or in some other manner.*

That alone still remains for investigation which has to do with the work of the first day, whether God created light at the first beginning of this day, that is of the first. Since it is read that He made nothing else on this day but light, should He be believed to have ceased from work until the beginning of the following day, when He made the firmament, although Scripture testifies that He finally rested on the seventh day? This question we shall meet with a two-fold answer; for we shall say either that God in those six days brought forth His work with such continuous industry, that during no interval of time did He cease from work, or that He so worked in the six days, that He let no day at all intervene in His work, not that He did not cease to work during any period of time. For, if indeed we wish to prove the former assertion, that His work was continuous, we shall be able to say that on the first day, at the beginning of this day, He made light; then, that by its course He might distinguish day and night, He first directed it from the east to the west, and again from the west to the east; and that His work was not only that light was made, but that, directed under His guidance and ordinance, it completed its course. In the same way it shall be said of the second day, when the firmament was made, and it received the precept and at the same time the law of perpetual revolution.

This view also regarding the third, fourth, fifth, or sixth day, in so far as reason shall dictate, will he who shall elect the assertion of the first part demand. If, however, this interpretation shall seem to anyone too obscure, especially because the assertion of the motion of the firmament is not yet definitely established, let him turn to that other explanation which we have proposed, since it is easy and more readily adapted to reason for understanding. Thus he will say that God worked for six days, and then on the seventh day rested from work, because there is no day of the six on which God did not perform a work, until the seventh day came, when He at last rested from all work. Let this much then be said about the work of the first day.

XVII. *On the work of the second day, when the firmament was made.*

"And God saw that it was good, and said: Let there be a firmament made midst the waters." (Gen. I, 4 and 6). God did not wish, therefore, to pass to the subsequent work, until He had judged the first. When, therefore, He had seen, regarding light, that it was good, then He said: "Let there be a firmament made." In so far, it seems, as the literal interpretation is concerned, the firmament was made on the second day; first indeed it was created from nothing in that matter of the universe, and then from this same matter raised to such a form and made a firmament, so that, with its circumference intervening, as it were, as a middle body, it might separate and divide that great and immense gathering of waters from one another, and of the waters might make waters and waters: that is, waters which it might comprise internally within its circumference and contain beneath itself, and waters which it might leave outside and above the circle of its boundary.

XVIII. *Of what matter the firmament was made; and of what nature it was made.*

There are many things indeed that could rouse the mind with inquiry about the nature of the firmament, if many by investigation did not see that these matters are rather to be left alone than discussed. For, whether it was made from pure fire, or from air, or even from water, or finally from two or three of these combined; and whether it has a substance solid and palpable by nature; or how great its density should be thought; and whether it itself is hot or cold; or whatever other quality it possesses, might well be investigated, if therefrom anything certain could be learned. But I do not think that much labour should be expended in the investigation of these matters, which reason does not understand and authority, to which allegiance must be given, does not approve. Only this which we read should we believe without hesitation, that the firmament was made to divide waters from waters, that is, to enclose a part of the waters within its circumference and to segregate a part outside.

XIX. *The sacrament of the matters mentioned above.*

But why it came to pass that the firmament divided the waters from one another, and that the nature of these waters consisted in part above and in part below, let him not seek outside himself, who believes that these things were made for his sake. For there is in that world which has been fashioned interiorly a certain something possessing the form and exemplar of this work, where a kind of earth placed below is the sensual nature of man, but heaven placed above, the purity of intelligence and reason animated by a kind of movement of immortal life. Now these two natures, so dissimilar in a man, are confronted by a great mass of desires, fluctuating hither and thither, and often striving alternately in opposite directions, because the flesh, pressed down by infirmity, desires one thing and the spirit, raised up by the contemplation of truth, aspires to another. But it sometimes happens that the contrary impulses beget confusion, unless reason, intervening as a mediatrix, divides them from one another, and separates inclinations and appetites, and judges between desires: for example, something, whatever it may be, coming from the flesh drags downward; something coming from the spirit yearns for heaven, seeking the highest and immortal good. For when very reason in stern judgment resolutely places itself as a kind of firmament in the midst, and on one side sets apart the waters above the heavens, but on the other those which are under the heavens, lower corruption can not infect the higher purity of the soul, nor does that integrity which is above suffer itself to incline toward those base and worthless things which are below.

XX. *Why God is not said to have seen the work of the second day, that it was good.*

But it is strange why God did not see the work of the second day, that it was good, just as it is read that He saw on all the other days; "and God saw that it was good." For either it was not His work and was not good, or, if it was His work, it was good. But if it was good and it was His work, He who could not have been ignorant of what it was, whether it was good or evil, certainly saw that it was good. Why then is it not said here: "God saw that it was good," just as everywhere else it is said: "God saw that it was good"? (Gen. 1, 4). For if, therefore, it is said elsewhere that it was so done, why also should it not have been said here whether it was so done? Perhaps, because the number two is a sign of division, which is the first to depart from oneness. Some sacrament is here commended. And second works were not praised, not because they were not good, but because they were a sign of evils. For God made His first works and "they all were very good," (Gen. 1, 31), in which corruption was not present nor was perfection lacking. But then came the devil and man, and they made their own works; and these were works second after the first, evil after good; and God did not wish to see those works because they were evil, but what He saw through wisdom, He condemned through judgment.

XXI. *How the waters were gathered together into one place that dry earth might appear.*

"God also said: Let the waters that are under the heaven, be gathered together into one place". (Gen. 1, 9). So far as the literal interpretation is concerned, the one place, where the waters that were under the heavens were gathered, is believed to be the great abyss, and this is thought from the very beginning of the world to have been made in the body of the earth of so great a capacity that it could have been the receptacle for all the waters. For the nature of the waters in the beginning was very thin and light, and dispersed like a kind of cloud. After it began, by the divine power and command, in some way to be pressed together into one mass, as I might thus describe it, and to become dense, turning downward by its very weight and falling to the lowest level, it was received by the earth, and that space, which it had occupied above up to the firmament itself, it left clear and pure. The very surface of the earth also began to appear, when all the waters had been confined wtihin their channels; at first, indeed, muddy and slimy and bare, like land that had not yet brought forth any plants with which it could be clothed and covered.

XXII. *How the earth brought forth plants.*

"God, therefore, said that the earth should bring forth the green herb, and such as might seed, and the fruit tree yielding fruit after its kind, which might have seed in itself upon the earth; and it was done." (Cf. Gen. 1, 11). Then, for watering the whole earth, from that great abyss as from a fountain, the waters deep within the bowels of the earth were conducted by hidden channels and passages, but above on the surface through their own beds, in all directions by a wonderful and tireless departure from and return to one place in accordance with an eternal law.

XXIII. *Why Scripture does not say that those waters which are above heaven were gathered into one place.*

Regarding those waters which are above heaven, Scripture has not said that they were gathered into one place, as in the case of those which were under heaven. Great are the sacraments in all these matters, and not to be explained in the present summarized treatment: that the waters which are under heaven are gathered together into one place; that the dry land appears and brings forth plants, and that at the same time the very spaces of the air finally through the contraction of the dark mist are made clear, and that the courses of the waters are scattered everywhere for irrigating and moistening the earth through its body; and that nothing was done without cause.

This seems strange, that the waters which are under heaven are gathered together into one place, and that those which are above heaven are not gathered together and no one place is assigned to them, but they are left diffused and spread out, as if the waters did not wish to be compressed or collected. What do you think this means, unless that "the charity of God is poured forth in our hearts by the Holy Ghost who is given to us"? (Rom. 5, 5). And these waters are above the inhabitants of heaven, because, says the Apostle, "I show unto you yet a more excellent way." (Cor. 12, 31). "If I speak with the tongues of men and of angels, if I should have all prophecy and should know all mysteries," (I Cor. 13, parts of 1 and 2), what is this? "It profiteth me nothing, if I have not charity". (I Cor. 13, 2). "The peace of God", he says, "which surpasseth all understanding, keep your hearts and minds". (Philip 4, 7). Now in a certain way we see why those waters which are above heaven were not to be collected and compressed into one place, since charity ought always to be spread out and extended; and the more widely it is expanded, the more highly is it elevated. But the waters that are under heaven must be gathered together and constrained into one place, so that by fixed passages and definite outlets they may be conducted from there anywhere. For unless the lower affection of the soul is constrained by a definite law, dry land can not appear, nor can it produce plants, just as the Apostle chastises his body and brings it into subjection; lest perhaps, when he has preached to others, he himself may become a castaway. (Cf. 1 Cor. 9, 27).

XXIV. *That in these three days the disposition of things was made.*

Behold these are the works of the three days, before the sun or the other lights had been made. In these first three days the frame work of this universe was arranged, and was distributed in its parts. When the firmament was spread overhead, and then the earth was uncovered, resting in the lowest place, and poised by its weight, and the masses of waters were collected within their receptacles, and the air was made clear, the four elements of the world were distinguished and arranged in their places.

XXV. *How in the three following days the world was adorned.*

Then followed the adornment of these, and this was done likewise in three successive days. On the fourth, which was the first in the three, the firmament was adorned with the sun and moon and stars. On the fifth day, which was the second in the three, the air received ornaments in the flying things; and the waters, in the fishes. On the sixth day, which was the third in the three, the earth received beasts and cattle and creeping things and the other living things that move on earth. Now man was made on this last day out of earth and on earth, yet not for earth, nor for the sake of earth, but for heaven and for the sake of Him who made earth and heaven. (Cf. Gen. 1, 1). Therefore, man was made, not as an adornment of the earth, but as its lord and possessor, so that his creation, for whose sake the earth was made, should not be referred to the earth.

XXVI. *Whether from the elements themselves those things were made which were made for their adornment.*

If anyone should inquire about the adornments of the elements, whether it should be believed that all these things were created from the elements themselves, for whose ornament and beauty they are shown to have been made,—as for example, that those things, which were made for adornment of the earth, could not have been taken except from the earth,—even if we grant this as true in the other elements, yet we can not in any way show this in the case of the element of the air, since we clearly read that flying things received origin from the waters and habitation in the air. Why it came to pass that they did not, after the fashion of the other things which were created for the adornment of the elements of the world, take their matter from the element itself in which they were to be allotted their place, one perhaps may refer to the matter of the element itself, on the ground that air did not possess, so to speak, such corporeity that the bodies of living things, which require solid matter, might be created from it. Now the nature of waters was more akin to the earth and had more corporeity, and on this account was more adapted for forming bodies. But the higher virtue of a sacrament is presented in these things.

XXVII. *The sacrament why fishes and birds were made of the one matter and were not placed in the one abode.*

There are two kinds of living things which proceed from one origin, but are not allotted one habitation. Fishes remain in their original abode. Flying things are raised aloft, and become, as it were, above what they were made. Thus from the one mass of nature, corruptible and fluctuating in its own changeableness, is derived the whole descent of the human race. But while some are justly left below in that corruption in which they were born, others are raised above by the gift of grace to the lot of their heavenly country.

XXVIII. *Why the works of foundation are recounted first, then the works of restoration.*

There are very many other things that could have been said mystically regarding these days. But we have touched upon these cursorily as if outside of our subject matter, in order that out of the preceding we might have a more convenient approach for treating the same subject, since indeed we have proposed to treat in this work, in so far as the Lord will allow, of the sacrament of man's redemption, which was formed from the beginning in the works of restoration. But since the works of foundation were first in time, we have begun our discussion with these, that thence we may make our way to the other works which follow in their order. For we call the works of foundation the creation of all things, when the latter, which were not, were made to be; but the works of restoration, wherein the sacrament of redemption was fulfilled or was figured by which those things which had perished were restored. Therefore, the works of foundation are those which were made at the beginning of the world in the six days; but the works of restoration, those which from the beginning of the world are made in six ages for the renewal of man. And to define these briefly, we say that the works of restoration are the Incarnation of the Word, and those things which the Word with all His sacraments performed in the flesh and through the flesh, whether those sacraments which preceded from the beginning of the world to figure the Incarnation itself, or those which follow after, even to the end of the world, to announce and declare it. About all these Divine Scripture speaks, and about these and for all these Divine Scripture was made; because, just as the books of the gentiles investigate and treat of the works of foundation, so the divine writings give their attention especially to the treatment and commendation of the works of restoration.

XXIX. *That the discussion is especially concerned with the works of restoration.*

Therefore, in the works of restoration the mystery of the redemption must be investigated from the beginning. And if we inquire into this carefully in all these works according to the sequence of time and the succession of generations and the dispensations of precepts, we declare with confidence that we shall have touched upon the whole sum of Divine Scriptures. But we must begin with the foundation of our first parents, and we must develop the story gradually as we proceed always to those works which follow in order. But let us sum up briefly in conclusion what has been spoken above, that we may obtain an understanding of what remains to be said.

Therefore, the works of creation, that is, this sensible world with all its elements, were made indeed in matter before any day, equally in time and with time; afterwards in six days they were disposed into form—arranged in the first three days and in the following three adorned. Lastly, on the sixth day man was made, Adam and Eve, for the sake of whom all other things were made; and he was placed in paradise, first to abide there and to work, so that, after his work was finished and his obedience fulfilled, he might be transported from there to that place where he was destined to abide forever. But, since we propose to go on with the succession of works that follow from the foundation of the first man, it is proper that at the very beginning of the book we first investigate the cause of man's creation, so that at the same time we may show that man was first rationally created by God and afterwards mercifully restored. In the one case also, when he was created, rational work was done gratuitously; in the other, when he was redeemed, the work of grace was fulfilled rationally.

XXX. *That there are four points with which the subsequent discussion deals.*

So there are four points with which the subsequent discussion should deal in order, that is: first, why man was created; then, of what nature he was created; then how he fell; finally, moreover, how he was restored.

PART TWO

I. *On the Cause of Man's Creation, and on the Primordial Causes of All Things.*

In the beginning of this work, which I have undertaken more on account of your insistence than on account of my own eagerness, I set forth the origin and disposition of this sensible world in the briefest possible discussion and one that, in keeping with our original design, may be especially suited to beginners. But now it is proper that we take up the creation of man, for whose sake the world itself was made by a word, proceeding indeed with our discussion of this in that order which the Creator of things Himself showed in his work. For, in truth, God the Creator first made the world, and then man as the possessor and Lord of the world, so that man might rule over all other things by right of his foundation, being subject with free will to Him alone by whom he had been made. Whence it is clear that the creation of man was certainly posterior in time to the creation of all visible things, but prior in cause, because all things were made for his sake who was made after all things.

The cause, therefore, of the creation of man is before all things, and we should investigate this above all and before all things which came into existence in time, and were ordained before time. For if God made all things for the sake of man, man is the cause of all, and causally man is prior to all; but that itself for whose sake man was made is prior to man, and much before all things to which man is prior causally. Now what else will that be for whose sake man was made, unless He himself by whom man was made? If, therefore, the cause of the world is man, because the world was made for the sake of man, and the cause of man is God, since man was made for the sake of God, then God was and the world was not, nor was man, and for the sake of God man, who was not, was made, and the world, for the sake of man who was not yet; and, as it were, the same cause appeared for man's being made for the sake of God, and the world, for the sake of man. For man was made that he might serve God for whose sake he was made, and the world was made that it might serve man for whose sake it was made. And, in a way, there was a sameness here and there was not a sameness, because there was not a sameness in those on account of whom he was.

God was perfect and full of complete good, nor did He have need of being helped from any other source, since, being eternal, He could not be diminished nor, being infinite, could He be increased. But man by nature was in need of another's help whereby he might either preserve what he had received as changeable, or increase what he had as not completed. Man was so placed in a middle position, that he might both be served and he himself serve, and that he himself might receive from both sides and claim all for himself, and that all might re-dound to man's good, both the homage which he received and that which he rendered. For God wished man to serve Him, in such a way, however, that by this service, not God, but man himself in serving should be helped, and He wished that the world serve man, and that from it man likewise should be helped, and that all good should belong to man, because for man's sake all this was made.

Therefore, all good belonged to man, that is, both what was made for his own sake, and that for whose sake he himself was made. But one good was below and was taken from below for his necessity; the other good was above, and was taken from above for his happiness. For that good which was placed in the creation was the good of necessity, but the good which was in the Creator was the good of happiness. And both were brought to man since both were due man, because for the sake of one, man was made, that he might possess and enjoy it; the other was made for the sake of man that he might receive it and be helped by it. To such an extent then is the foundation of the rational creature proven to be superior to all other things which were made for its sake, because it itself is the cause of all these.

Now its own cause is no other save Him from whom it is. For just as it is from this cause that it should be something, so it is for His sake that it should be in a happy state, receiving one thing from Him, that is, that it should be, the other in Him, that is, that it should be in a happy state. But someone will say: Why did God make the creature if He Himself could not have been helped by the creature? For whom else did He make that which He did not make for Him-self, when there was no other save Him Himself who made? For what was so made seems, as it were, to have been made for nothing, and to have had no cause for being made; from it the one who made was not helped, since being perfect He did not need help, nor was another helped thereby, since outside of Him Him-self who made there was no other. And this perhaps on being considered rather carefully may trouble some one. Therefore, we should investigate in a kind of general consideration the cause of the foundation of rational things, which we have placed in the sole author of things, not only with reference to man, the object of our discussion, but also with reference to the angels; for they also, just as they are participants of the same nature, so too derive their cause of origin from the same source, since in this cause is the beginning of all things that were made.

II. *On the primordial causes and their effects.*

The order and disposition of all things from the highest even to the lowest in the structure of this universe so follows in sequence with certain causes and gen-erated reasons that of all things that exist none is found unconnected or separable and external by nature. For all things, whatever there are, either are found to be the causes of subsequent effects or the effects of preceding causes. And some, indeed, are only causes of things, not also effects, just as the first cause of all things. Others are only effects, not also causes, just as the ultimate and last cause of all things. Now some are both causes to posterior things which they generate, and effects to prior things by which they are generated; and just as nothing is perceived posterior to those things which are last and effects only of prior things, so indeed nothing is found prior to those that are first and the causes only of subsequent things.

As regards intermediate things, however, whichever of these are prior are better designated causes and not effects. But whichever are posterior are rather effects and not causes, and the first things are the most causal. And the things that are first after the first are first effects; and the things that are last before the last are ultimate causes, namely, the last are generated and the first are generating. Now some first causes are created, and these are first in their kind; others are uncreated, and these are universally first. For those which are first in their own kind are first in relation to something, but are not universally first, since, although they precede all things that follow, yet they themselves also have something to which they are found to be posterior, in as much as they do not precede all things. For in this universe of all things, with all things connected causally, something is so found to be first that none of all these can be prior to it, since it itself of all things is the first of all; and yet something must be prior to it, since it belongs to all those things to which something is universally prior. To these causes which are universally first nothing is prior, since these are the first of all, nor do these prior causes have other causes, since they are the causes of all.

III. *On the production of the primordial causes.*

Now these effect without movement and produce without transference, since eternity did not fail in its state by ordaining time, nor did it minister substance from its own store by creating corruptible things, but remaining what it was it made what was not, containing in itself the power of making, not taking from itself the matter of what was made. For it did not degenerate by creating lower things, so that its nature descended into those very things to which it had given a beginning; its nature contained this very property of omnipotence—without nature to create a nature by which the things that were not might take beginning, since the work and the maker could not be the same by nature. Therefore, just as in making things eternity did not diminish itself, so in the things made immensity did not increase. But before things were made it existed complete without defect; and after things were made, it remained unfailing without movement, assuming nothing new, losing nothing old, giving all and casting away nothing. This first cause of all things performed its own work according to itself and on account of itself: according to itself, since it did not receive the form of its work from without; on account of itself, since it did not have the cause for operating from any other source. For it made to its own likeness what it disposed to participation in itself, so that from itself that which with it was to possess the same good might take the same form.

IV. *What is the first cause of the foundation of rational beings.*

From this, then, did the foundation of the rational creature take its first cause, because God in His eternal goodness wished that there be made sharers in His blessedness which He saw could both be communicated and not at all be diminished. That good, therefore, which He Himself was and by which He Himself was blessed, was induced by goodness alone, not by necessity, to communicate itself, since it was characteristic of the best to wish to benefit, and of the most powerful, not to be able to suffer harm.

V. *That both goodness and power were present to the divine will.*

For the divine will would not have been perfect through goodness alone, unless power had equally been present, since that which it willed through antecedent goodness it fulfilled through subsequent power. In the predestination, therefore, of things to be created goodness operated, but in the creation of things predestined power operated, but in the beatification of created things power and goodness operated together.

VI. *On the three things which are perfect and make all perfect.*

For there were three things, and these three were one; these three were eternal; nothing could be perfect without these three, and with these nothing was diminished. For it was clear that if these three were present, nothing perfect would be wanting; and if one of these three were wanting, nothing could be completed. And these three were power, wisdom, will; these three concur to produce every effect, and nothing is accomplished unless these be present. The will moves, knowledge disposes, power operates. And if you propose a distinction in these, being able is not the same as knowing, nor is knowing the same as willing, and yet for God being able, knowing, and willing are one. Reason distinguishes these; nature does not divide them; the Trinity which contains all comes to us undivided, and without it all is nothng. Whatever is truly said of God, or can be reverently believed to be in God, is contained in these three—power, wisdom, and goodness. And these three are equally full.

If you speak of someone as infinite, if you call him uncorrupted or eternal or unchangeable or anything else of this sort, all this belongs to power. If you call someone knowing or provident or observant or scrutinizing or deliberating or judging, all this belongs to wisdom. If you call someone gentle or mild or compassionate or kind or anything else of this sort, all this belongs to goodness. There is nothing which is not in these three; and what is in these is full and wholly complete. Moreover, these three are specifically distinguished. The Catholic faith accepted the Trinity, which it did not wish to be increased in number, lest it seem to confess something outside the three, and did not wish to confound in nature, lest it be convicted of denying something in the three. And it found that the three were in God, and that in God the three were one; that they were not three for the reason that they were one, and that they were not one for the reason that they were three. Prompted by the three it said that the three persons were the three, because they were by nature God, and one substance, and so one God; it assigned power to the Father, wisdom to the Son, goodness to the Holy Ghost, and it confessed the Trinity, Father and Son and Holy Ghost.

VII. *That these three are spoken of God according to substance.*

And the Son appeared powerful not as of Himself, because power belonged to the Father, nor the Father wise of Himself, because wisdom belonged to the Son, and neither the Father nor Son good of Himself, because goodness belonged to the Holy Ghost. If this were said, truth would suffer scandal, and unity scission; nor could one in the three be called perfect, to whom something proper would be wanting which another would have as a special prerogative. Therefore, power belonged to the Father, and it belonged to the Son, and it belonged to the Holy Ghost; it belonged substantially, and it belonged equally. Wisdom belonged to the Son, and it belonged to the Father and to the Holy Ghost, and it belonged substantially and equally. And goodness belonged to the Holy Ghost, and it belonged to the Father and to the Son, and it belonged substantially and equally. And yet there was reason for distinguishing in the persons what in substance was the same.

VIII. *Why these three, while they are mentioned as according to substance, are found in certain places as attributes proper to the persons.*

By these three faith did not signify the persons according to special characteristic, because they were according to substance, but these three it assigned to the persons according to a necessary notion, so that it might assert that they were according to a communion of nature. Father and Son had to be named in the Trinity, and the words themselves were taken from human usage to which they were first given. And what was only similar according to something had to be spoken of in all similarly. The prudence of Divine Scripture took care lest a full similarity should be believed to exist in disparate things, if in the Godhead the Father should be called prior and the Son posterior. For thus nature holds among men that there can not be a father who is not prior to a son; nor a son, who is not posterior to a father. Therefore, power was assigned to the Father, and wisdom to the Son; not because the former was more powerful, but because He could be believed to be less so.

For Holy Scripture had said that God is a Father, and man who had seen a human father but had not seen God the Father heard this. And he began to think, in connection with the man whom he had seen, of prolonged years, a long life already past, and the decline of old age. But Scripture counteracted this and called the Father powerful, lest you might believe Him impotent or less powerful, and not only powerful but also all powerful. Therefore, not because the Father alone is this was He alone said to be this, but because the Father alone was thought less likely to be this.

Again, when Scripture called the Son God, lest man who knew human things but not divine might think that there was a kind of minor degree of sense and intelligence in the Son, as if He were still short of the perfection of mature age, it added the term "wise", not because He was in particular that which was common to all, but because He was in particular the one of whom it could be doubted more whether He was this or not.

And God was also called Spirit, and God was said to have Spirit; this seemed a name of inflation and pride; the conscience of man was terrified before God for His sternness and cruelty; and Scripture followed and tempered its expression, calling the Spirit kind, lest He who was gentle be thought cruel.

And those things were distinguished in the persons which in substance were common, so that the mind of man should not learn to evaluate the truth of divine things according to human ones, when it heard certain things being said of God contrary to human usage. Therefore, God the Trinity by this threefold power completed all His works, so that perfect things followed Him who was perfect, and all things that He had made imitated their Author. For whatever appeared in time was disposed before time in eternity; and the eternal disposition itself had the coeternal cause of all things—the will of the Creator, by which it came to pass that there was made whatever was made, and it itself was not made.

IX. *That the wisdom of God, although it is indeed one in itself, receives different names among us.*

Now divine wisdom is also called knowledge, and foreknowledge, and disposition, and predestination, and providence. Knowledge is of existing things, foreknowledge of future things, disposition of things to be made, predestination of things to be saved, providence of things subject. And all this was one wisdom, and one disposition, and was itself eternal; with this the will was coeternal, and the disposition itself was according to the will, and yet was not posterior to the will.

X. *That the will of God was eternal as regards work in time.*

According to His will, then, He disposed what He was to make by His will; and His will was eternal, but the work of His will was not eternal. For He always willed to make, but He did not will to make always, but to make at some time what He always willed to make at some time. Thus His will was eternal as regards His work in time, since even time itself was in the eternal will, when that should come to pass which was to be.

Thus these two were in the Creator equally—goodness and wisdom, and these were eternal, and likewise there was present coeternal power; He willed by goodness, He disposed by wisdom, He made by power. There seems to be a kind of distinction in time and succession; goodness presents itself first to our consideration, because through it God willed; then wisdom, because through it He disposed; lastly power, because through it He made. For there seems to be an order; and the will seems to have been first; after it disposition, and lastly operation seems to have followed. For unless He had willed, He would not have disposed, and if He had not disposed, He would not have made. A great reason for this offers itself, because among men the will always precedes plan, and work follows plan. But what are we doing? Shall we dare to introduce time into eternity? For if these things are in God as in men, something in Him was prior, something posterior, and not all God is eternal. But to confess this is abominable.

XI. *That the three in God were coeternal.*

So by eternal goodness He always willed, and by eternal wisdom He always disposed what He sometimes makes by coeternal power. Goodness, wisdom, and power were always together, nor could these, which were the same in substance, be divided or separated from one another by time. From them God the Creator gave form to His work, and by them all things were completed from the age of beginning; and ordained from the beginning of eternity.

XII. *That three visible things in the world indicate the three invisible things of God.*

And the ineffable Trinity is found in these three, which indeed are one in the Creator, but through the appearance of creation present themselves separately to cognition. For the immensity of things received the form of power; beauty, that of wisdom; and utility, that of goodness. And these were seen externally and were in harmony with another image which was more perfect within.

XIII. *That the likeness of God in the rational creature is more perfect than it is externally.*

For the rational creature came, having in itself a more perfect likeness of these things in will and plan and power; and it compared what it found externally with what it had within, and it combined these two, that through the visible it might see the invisible. And it saw the power and wisdom and goodness of the

Creator by itself, on being moved to perceive them through these things which appeared externally. These things were, so to speak, the first admonition and recollection that God is threefold; but the fullness of knowledge was not yet perfect, since they were according to substance, nor could they which were one be divided singly. For power, which was of the Son and was of the Holy Ghost, was not of the person of the Father in particular; nor was the wisdom, which was of the Father and was of the Holy Ghost, in particular of the person of the Son; nor was the goodness, which was of the Father and was of the Son, in particular of the person of the Holy Ghost. But the Trinity was predicated from these, not signified in these. Yet these three things were eternal and were the cause of all things; through these all were made, and they themselves were not made. We have assigned to goodness will, and to wisdom disposition, and to power operation. There arises serious inquiry and profound investigation about the will of God, and about His foreknowledge, and providence, and disposition, and power. For all these are present in the causes of things, and offer a subject of inquiry for our proposed investigation.

XIV. *On the knowledge and foreknowledge of God, and that necessity in things seems to proceed from this.*

For the necessity of making things seems to fall upon God, as if there could not be a Creator unless there were a creature. Then from this foreknowledge and providence of God another necessity seems to proceed in things already made or to be made, as if it were impossible for what was foreseen or foreknown by God not to come to pass. These two points strike the mind with equal difficulty and troubles its reflection.

First, then, we must consider in what way the necessity of making things seems to fall upon God from His foreknowledge and providence, from His disposition or predestination of those things which were to be made by Him. For all knowledge, and foreknowledge, and providence, and disposition or predestination seem to be with reference to something, and seem to be of something. Just as all knowledge, in truth, is of something because it is in something, so it is of something because it is about something. For everyone who knows, knows something; and he who does not know something, knows nothing. To be sure, there is knowledge about nothing, and it is no knowledge. Therefore, all knowledge is about something, because if there were nothing about which there were knowledge, there would be no knowledge.

In God, therefore, there would not be eternal knowledge and foreknowledge, unless there were to be something about which it could be. If, therefore, nothing had been created or was to be created, nothing in the Creator would have been known or foreknown. And for this reason there would have been no knowledge or foreknowledge. Now, if there had been no knowledge in the Creator, it follows manifestly that not even the Creator Himself would have been, who certainly could not have been without knowledge, for whom being is the same as knowledge. That knowledge, therefore, or foreknowledge could have been in the Creator, it was necessary that there be something or would be something concerning which it could have been, since, as has been said, if it were about nothing, it would be no knowledge. For all knowledge is knowledge of something, and is about something. If, therefore, the foreknowledge of the Creator depends causally upon His creatures, that which was created will seem to be prior to Him who created it.

XV. *How all things in God were from eternity, before they subsisted in themselves, and how with Him there was not foreknowledge of them but knowledge.*

Shall we say that in the Creator from eternity all things were uncreated which were created by Him in time, and were known there where they were contained, and were known in the way in which they were contained? Shall we say that God did not know anything outside Himself who contained all things in Himself? They were not there because they were to be here, nor should the cause of those there be believed to have been from these here; they did not come here because they were there, as if those there could not have been without these here. For the former also would have been, even if the latter were not to be from them; only they could not have been the cause of the latter, if the latter were not to be.

XVI. *If things were not to be, God's wisdom would be knowledge, but it would not be called foreknowledge.*

And indeed there would have been knowledge of those things which were; but there would not have been foreknowledge of those things which were not to be. And not on this account would there have been anything else in the Creator, if there had not been foreknowledge of those things which were not to be, because what is foreknowledge would have been knowledge itself, even if there had not been foreknowledge that something was not to be.

XVII. *How both are eternal, foreknown being and future being.*

But now what is foreknown from eternity is to be from eternity, and that is not eternal which is to be, because, if it were eternal, it would not be future but present. And it was not foreknown before it was to be, but it was foreknown and it was to be before it was. Before it was, when it was still to be, it was able to be according to the contingency that it would not come into being; and this could always be, as long as it was to be so that it would not come into being, just as it was always to be that it would come into being. What was to be, looked to that which was to be; what was able to be, looked to that which was able to be and was not to be. And these two ran along together from eternity—what was to be, and what was able to be which was not to be.

XVIII. *How, if the events of things were changed, foreknowledge, nevertheless, would not be changed.*

And if that had been made which could be and yet was not to be, it would have been foreknown also that it was not to be; and the foreknowledge of this future would not have been changed but never would have been possessed, because it was not to be. But what God predestined that He would do, He disposed, nor did He predestine except what He was going to do. Now He who was not going to do certain things foreknew it, because He foreknew everything which was to be, in which were to be certain things which He was to do, certain things which He was to permit. On this account predestination seems to possess something more than foreknowledge, because foreknowledge is also regarding another's, but predestination can not be except regarding one's own.

XIX. *On the providence of God, and that the providence of God is two-fold, in His own things and in the things of others.*

Now if you ask about the providence of God, we say rightly that providence is the care of those things which must be furnished to subjects, and which it is fitting to give those under one's charge. It is written that "He hast care of all". (Wisdom 12, 13). This then is that providence whereby God cares for all that He has made. He abandons nothing of all those things that belong to Him, and which are subject to Him, but He provides for them individually, that each may have what is due and befitting it. And so according to this universal providence over all things, not only to His own which He has made good, but also to the things of others which He Himself has not made evil but has permitted, He dispenses what is due, that nothing in His kingdom may evade just regulation. For even iniquity itself has its reward through this providence, and not even evil itself could pass into forgetfulness with Him who exercises providence over all things.

Do you wish to know what are the wages of iniquity and sin? It is written: "For the wages of sin is death; but the grace of God, life everlasting". (Rom., 6, 23). The wages of sin is death, the wages of justice life. To sin is given death, to justice life, to blame punishment, to virtue glory. Each receives what is its own. This is providence. It operates in a twofold manner: with respect to its own and with respect to that of another; with respect to its own which it has made, with respect to that of another which it has permitted. All things are subject to it, and, presiding over all, it provides for all—government for creation, glorification for justice, damnation for evil.

XX. *On the divine disposition.*

Similarly the divine disposition is considered in a twofold manner. Goods indeed have their disposition from above—both that they are because they are good, and that they are so because they are ordered. But evils do not have from divine disposition what they are because they are evil, and yet they have that they are so because they are ordered. For God does not make evil, but, when it is done, He does not permit it to be unordered, since He is not the author of evil but the orderer.

XXI. *On divine predestination.*

Predestination is the preparation of grace. Therefore, God's design, in which He disposed to give grace to His elect, is itself predestination; and this is called predestination for this reason, because in it what was to be made was disposed before it was. Yet, in general, predestination can at times be understood to be the disposition itself of the things to be made, so that God may be said to have predestined from eternity whatever He was thus to make, but not to have predestined, but only to have foreknown, what He was not to make but was to permit.

XXII. *On the power of God, and that power is considered to be in God in a twofold manner; and that in both cases God is omnipotent.**

Just as we have said certain things about the wisdom of God, as far as time allowed, so also we must mention some things about His power for the instruction of our readers. His power is twofold: one power for doing something, the other for suffering nothing. According to both, God is most truly declared omnipotent, because there is nothing which can inflict corruption upon Him to suffer, and nothing which can offer impediment to His doing. He can in truth do all things except that alone which can not be done without injury to Him; and yet in this He is no less omnipotent, because, if this were possible, He would not be omnipotent. I say, therefore, that God can do all things, and He can not destroy Himself. For this power would not be power, but non-power. And so God can do all things, to be able to do which is power. And so He is truly omnipotent, because He can not be impotent.

Therefore, let them go now and glory in their opinion, who think that they can discuss divine works by reason, and confine God's power within measure. For when they say: "So far is he able and no more", what else is this than limiting His power which is infinite and restricting it to a measure? For they say: "God can not make other than He makes, nor make better than He makes. For if He can make other than He makes, He can make what He has not foreseen; and

---

*Abelard when treating of creation had replaced the freedom and omnipotence of God by a most exaggerated optimism. Hugh attacks this error vigorously in this chapter.

if He can make what He has not foreseen, God can operate without providence, because everything which He has foreseen that He would make, He makes, and He does not make anything that He has not foreseen. If, then, His providence can not either be changed, so that something may be made other than has been foreseen, or be frustrated, so that what has been foreseen may not be made, it is necessary that all which has been foreseen be made, and that nothing be made which has not been foreseen. Furthermore, it is clear that whatever is made was foreseen, and there is no doubt that whatever was foreseen is made. But if it is impossible that something be made without providence, (but everything which has been foreseen to be, must be made), it is by no means possible that anything be made other than is made. Further, whatever God makes, if He can make it better than He makes, in this very thing He does not do well, because He does not indeed make best what He makes. For He would make better, if He would make better what He makes. In truth to make, and not to wish to make better, is to make badly even on the part of one making something good. But a pious mind does not suffer this to be said against God, and on this account it seems most proper and logical that He can not make better than He makes, who so makes that He does not make badly in that which He so makes.

For causes and reasons of this kind some are induced to say that God is so restrained and bound by the measure and law of His works that, beyond what He makes, He can not make anything else or make better. And for this reason clearly they are shown to bind that infinite and immense power of divinity under limit and measure, who extend this power as far as something which indeed itself has an end, and deny that it proceeds beyond. For it is certain that every-thing that is made "in measure and number and weight," (Wisdom, 11, 21), has its lawful limit and end. And, therefore, if the Creator's power is equated with the measure and bound of work, it itself is without doubt declared to be limited by both measure and end. Accordingly, lest we may seem, either to deny assent without cause to these arguments which arise or even without consideration to accept credulously the false as true, we must reply briefly, in keeping with the present compendium, to what has been said.

First we must consider whether God in any way, without His providence being changed or frustrated, can make something other than He makes. For it is clear that all that is made was foreseen from eternity as to be, because that is to be from eternity, which itself, however, is not from eternity. And we say that it is possible that what is to be be not made. And if that were not made which will be made, and it is possible that it be not made, it never would have been destined to be nor would it have been foreseen, which, because it will be made, is both always to be and was foreseen. Therefore, no change or frustration of providence is here apparent, because, just as it has been foreseen and will be made, so, if it had not been foreseen, it would not be made. But now, they say, it has been foreseen. Very well. It has been foreseen because it is to be. And they say: "But providence can not be changed or be frustrated, but the event of the thing can be impeded, so that what is to be is not made. But if the event of a thing should be impeded, which can happen, providence would be changed or frustrated, which can not happen at all." But we reply to this, that if the event were changed, which can happen, providence would neither be changed nor frustrated, because this can not happen at all. But rather never would that have been foreseen which was never to be, and providence would be firm in this, that the thing did not come to pass, just as now it has been firm in this, that it did come to pass, providence not being changed so that it was one thing after another, but so that it never was anything else. Therefore, God can make anything other than He makes, yet in such a way that in making anything He Himself is not different. But whether He should make the same or anything else, He Himself would always be the same.

Now there remains for us to discuss whether or not God can make anything better than He makes. Here those investigators of ours, who have failed in analysing their investigations, say that they offer something new and truly new— but not so true as new! And they say that creatures, indeed, considered individually by themselves have less of perfection, but that the universe of all things has been made in so great a completeness of good that it can not be better than it is. In this I first demand that they answer me, when they say that the universe of things can not be better than it is, just how this statement of theirs, that it can not be better, is to be understood; whether on this account it can not be better, because it is so supremely good that no perfection of good at all is wanting to it, or whether on this account it cannot be better, because it itself can not contain the greater good which is wanting to it. But if it is called so supremely good that no perfection of good is wanting to it, then its work clearly would be made equal to the Creator; and either what is beneath is extended beyond limit, or what is supreme is restricted within immensity, both of which, because of like difficulty, are impossible. But if, therefore, it can not be better, because it iself can not contain the greater good which is wanting to it, then this very lack of capacity belongs to deficiency, not to completeness; and it can be better, if it is made capable of greater good, because He who makes can do this also. Therefore, in itself it can not, in God it can, because it itself can not, but God can, and in so far as He Himself can, it can not be said to have this power.

Therefore, He Himself cannot be better. But all that He has made can be better, at least if He Himself, who has the power, should so wish. And He Himself can make better what He has made, not, however, by correcting what has been made badly, but by promoting what has been made well to something better, not that He may make it better as regards Himself, but that what He has made, through His operation likewise and perseverance in respect to the same, may be made better. Therefore, He is supremely powerful who can do all that is possible, nor on this account is He less powerful, because He can not do the impossible; for the power to do the impossible would not be power but non-power. And so God can do all things, to be able to do which is power, and so He is truly omnipotent, because He can not be impotent.

Since, therefore, there are three things in God,—wisdom, power, will,—the primordial causes indeed proceed, so to speak, from the divine will, are directed by wisdom, and are produced by power. For will moves, wisdom disposes, power executes. These are the eternal foundations of all causes and the first principle, which are ineffable and incomprehensible to every creature. For just as time does not equal God's eternity, nor place His immensity, so neither does intellect equal His wisdom, nor virtue His goodness, nor work His power. On the will and providence of God many matters remain to be examined: first, whether God's foreknowledge and providence do violence to things, concerning which much has already been said; then, on the will of God, about which certain things must be said, in such a way, however, that we should look first to contemplating God Himself with the eyes of faith, in so far as this is possible for human frailty.

PART THREE

On the Trinity.

I. *How God was known from the beginning, both that He is one and that He is three.*

Scripture says: "No man hath seen God at any time". (John 1, 18). Yet faith believes what it does not see. And in this the merit of faith consists, that it has not seen and believes. Whence we have that beautiful saying: "For if you see, there is not faith." Therefore, faith believes what it has not seen, and it has not seen indeed what it believes. And yet it has seen something by which it is admonished and incited to believe what it has not seen. For God from the beginning so tempered knowledge of Himself on the part of man, that just as it could never be comprehended fully what He was, so it could never be entirely unknown that He was.

II. *Why God can neither be entirely known nor entirely unknown.*

Therefore, in truth, God from the beginning wished neither to be entirely manifest to human consciousness not entirely hidden, lest, if He were entirely manifest, faith would have no merit, nor lack of faith a place. For lack of faith would be convicted from the manifest, and faith in the hidden would not be exercised. But, if He were entirely hidden, faith indeed would not be aided unto knowledge, and lack of faith would be excused on the ground of ignorance. Wherefore, it was necessary that God should show Himself, though hidden, lest He be entirely concealed and entirely unknown; and again, it was necessary that He should conceal Himself, though shown and known to some degree, lest He be entirely manifest, so that there might be something which through being known would nourish the heart of man, and again something which through being hidden would stimulate it.

III. *By what ways the knowledge of God comes to man.*

And now this must be considered first: how first God, though hidden and unseen and concealed, was to such a degree discovered by the human heart, that it could be known that God is, or could be believed what He was. There are two modes and two ways and two manifestations by which from the beginning God, though hidden, was shown to the human heart and revealed though concealed, in part of course by human reason, in part by divine revelation. And human reason indeed discovered God by a twofold investigation; partly, to be sure, in itself, partly in those things which were outside it. Similarly, also divine revelation by a twofold indication revealed Him as unknown who was unknown or doubtfully believed in, and declared him to be partly believed in. For now by illuminating within by aspiration, it taught human ignorance; then indeed either it instructed it from without by the medium of teaching or confirmed it by the manifestation of miracles.

Both modes of divine manifestation whereby God was either known by man through human reason or was made manifest to man by divine revelation, the Apostle sets forth, saying: "That which was known of God is manifest in them. For God hath manifested it unto them". (Rom. 1, 19). And then He adds: "For the invisible things of Him, from the creation of the world, are clearly seen, being understood by the things that are made". (Rom. 1, 20). For when he says: "That which was known of God," that is knowable regarding God, He shows Him neither as entirely hidden nor wholly manifest. But when He says: "Is manifest in them," and does not say: "Is manifest to them," He shows plainly that not only by divine revelation which was made to them but also by human reason which was in them was this made known to them. Now when He adds: "For God hath manifested it unto them," He shows that human reason would have been quite unable and insufficient to investigate and understand these sublime and lofty things, unless divine revelation had been added to it as an aid and support for understanding truth. Then, after having shown that way of investigation or revelation which was within, straightway He adds at the same time a statement regarding the other mode which is without, saying: "For the invisible things of Him, from the creation of the world, are clearly seen, being understood by the things that are made." For the invisible things of God which were within and were hidden, through those things which were without and were known, either were seen visible in the creation of things by human reason, or in the government and administration of things they were made visible by divine revelation.

IV. *That God is three and one; and what in oneness and what in trinity.*

Thus then from the beginning God was shown to human consciousness, and faith aided by the evidences of truth confessed that God was, and that He was one, then that He was also three. And indeed in oneness it confessed eternity and immensity, but in eternity immutability, but in immensity simplicity, that is an eternity without time, and immensity without quantity. But in trinity it confessed communion of oneness, equality of immensity, coevity of eternity, and indeed communion of oneness without division, equality of immensity without diminution, coevity of eternity without order or succession, that is, that He was respectively, whole in oneness, full in immensity, perfect in eternity.

V. *Explanation of the distinctions proposed.*

Now we must consider cursorily one by one the propositions which have been made, how the human mind which is so far from God, was able to comprehend so much about God, either directed by its own reason, or assisted by divine revelation. And first the question of the extent to which human reason itself received power from the light of truth implanted in it is worthy of consideration, lest if all be granted to man we be convicted of denying grace, or if all be taken from him we be convicted of excusing his ignorance. And so let us take up in order both modes of human investigation, whereby the reason of man, either directed by itself or admonished by those things which were outside of it, visible in nature, strove to know truth.

VI. *On that kind of knowledge by which the rational mind can see God in itself.*

And first let us examine what was in the rational mind, because this indeed was man's first and principal mirror for contemplating truth. In this mirror, therefore, first and principally the invisible God, in so far as this was exposed to manifestation, could be seen, since it had been made nearest and most related to His image and likeness. Now this was reason itself and mind using reason whereby it had been made to the first likeness of God, so that through itself it might find Him by whom it was made.

VII. *That the rational mind sees that it itself is.*

To state what occurs to us first, (for even to those who know nothing it cannot be less), the mind can not be ignorant that it itself is something, since it sees that it is nothing nor can it be anything of all those things which it sees visible in itself, that is, in its body. Therefore, the mind separates and divides itself by itself from all that it sees visible in itself, and it sees that it is quite invisible, in so far as it sees itself, and yet it sees that it can not be seen. Therefore, it sees that there are invisible things which, however, it does not see visibly, because it sees that it itself is invisible and yet does not see itself visibly.

VIII. *And that it knows that it began.*

Since, therefore, the mind can not doubt about itself, that it is, because it can not be ignorant of itself, it is compelled of itself to believe this also, that it recalls that it once began, that it is not always, because it can not be ignorant of itself, when it is. Since, therefore, by itself and in itself it sees that it began and had a beginning, the mind can not be ignorant of this either, that, when it was not, it was not at all able to give subsistence to itself so that it might have a beginning.

IX. *That God is and that He is without beginning.*

So, then, in order that what was not might begin, it was made by another who was. And the latter himself necessarily did not begin to be from another for the reason that he who received being from another could not be the author of existence for all things. Therefore, he could not have received being from another who gave being to all things, whom it is necessary to confess always was and never began, because everything which began to be at sometime had an author through whom it began. Therefore, it is clear and can not be doubted in any way that He through whom that began which was not always, never began but always was. Now reason investigates that author and first principle of things in this way, and piety venerates him when found, and faith declares him God to be adored.

X. *Proof of the same thing externally in creatures.*

Now reason proves that this is found in itself, and in those things which it sees outside itself, because all things having origin and decline, without an author, could have neither origin nor restoration. On this account there can be no doubt that these *in toto* began at some time, because even in their parts without cessation that which is not seems to originate and that which is to pass away. But all that is mutable must at some time not have been, because what could not stand when it was present indicates that it was not at some time before it was. Thus those who are without correspond to those things which are seen within for establishing truth, and nature which shows itself to have been made by Him proclaims its author.

XI. *That God is three and one.*

And so reason through reason discovered that God was, and another reason came to prove not only that God was but that He was one and three, and first through itself, then through those things which were outside itself, made according to itself. One piety, one devotion, one adoration prove one Lord and one God. So reason said and proved in itself, lest the division of minds be turned into many principles, and there might be no certain salvation, that it was better and more consonant with truth and more in accord with nature that there be one principle and one end to which all things that existed from it might turn, and that otherwise without a head and without a principle and without a ruler there would be a disintegration of the universe. And nature cried out externally to reason and bore witness to the same truth, and one work said that there was one author, and one concord said that there was one counsel, and one administration that there was one providence. And one God was made manifest, one creator, one ruler and guide, because He was one whole and unto one whole.

XII. *That God is truly and supremely one.*

Reason approved this and acquiesced, and said that He was one, not through the gathering of diverse elements lest He form a multitude, nor through the composition of parts lest He form a mass, nor through the likeness of many lest He appear a superfluous plurality or an imperfect singleness. For every unity consisting in the likeness alone of many shows either imperfection in part, if the individual elements have too little, or a superfluous duplication in the whole, if all elements are perfect. And in all these there is not true unity, but these merely emulate unity, because in a manner they approach it, but they do not attain it, since there is not one, and because they are, they are not truly one, but they are merely united and brought into proximity with one another. And the result is that they are together, and come into one, and are one. Yet they are not truly one, since they are not so essentially, nor is what they are one whole.

But God must be one, and essentially one, and immutably one, and supremely one. For what is essentially one is truly one; what is immutably one, is supremely one. But what is good in both, is better as both than as only the one. And it is good to be essentially one, and to be immutably one, and it is better to be both. But God is the highest good, and there can not be lacking to the highest good a good which is better. And reason urges to give to the best the good which is better. And so it confesses its God and its author and its principle to be one, for this is better, namely, to be truly one, since it is so substantially, and to be supremely one, since it is invariably so.

XIII. *That God is immutable.*

And reason rises and proceeds and proves that this is so, namely, that God can not be altered and changed at all. For He can not be increased who is immense, nor be diminished who is one, nor be changed in place who is everywhere, nor in time who is eternal, nor in knowledge who is most wise, nor in disposition of mind who is best.

XIV. *That creation rightly considered aids the reason to know God.*

Creation from without proclaims and itself proves this reasoning, and urges that it is so. And the supreme beauty of the work shows that the wisdom of the founder is perfect. And the perseverance of this very splendor as well as the fact that the first good which was instituted is not diminished present themselves as further proof. Creation says that His wisdom is eternal and can not in any way be diminished, nor does the fullness of His understanding ever decrease from completeness. It proceeds from reason with another proof, and sees that the will of God is eternal; and to perceive that this is so is good. It sees that His work which does not change proves this, and that the order of the universe preserving the same does likewise.

Creation itself adds a reason to believe that there is nothing new in God, so that then or now He begins to love what before He did not know, or to forget like man His former love, so that what first had been known does not come into His memory, or begins to err thinking what is evil good, so that He loves what He should not, and then, as if repentant, changing His heart and altering His affection when He has begun to recognize His error. Because these things are not worthy of God, reason does not approve that we should think so about Him who is wise and good and perfect. No mutability is found in Him, although all kinds of mutability have been introduced for consideration, whether those which are found in bodies, or those which touch the nature of spirits.

XV. *In what ways bodies are changed.*

For every body is changed either in place or in form or in time; those which are changed in form, receive either increase, or diminution, or alteration. And, indeed, to those which receive alteration, nothing seems to be added which was not, nor is anything shown to depart which was, but what was is only altered and is otherwise disposed. And this is not done without place, since the parts change place in the same consistent whole; yet it is not done except according to place, nor yet is it called according to place on account of the whole which does not change place, but another form appears only in the whole on account of the parts which have changed place. And so this change is called according to form, since this is seen manifestly in the whole. It is not called according to place, (although, however, in the parts it is according to place), since this is not manifestly seen. Form is nothing else at all but the disposition of parts in a whole; when this is changed, because the parts change place, the form in the whole is changed, because the disposition of parts is changed, which is the form of the whole. And so change of form in a whole can not be made without the change of place in the parts. But change of place is not so called except when the whole changes place, the parts remaining consistent in the whole. Thus change of time follows change of place and form, and is never without them in body, since according to these only is order present, and succession which is called time.

We must consider likewise that of these three changes two are made extrinsically, for they do not change the being of a thing, but something about a thing, that is, change of place and time. Again the first change produces the second and the third, since it is the cause of these. But the second brings on the third, since it is the cause of this. The third, however, is only produced and does not produce, since it is an effect only. Now the change of form is alone called intrinsic, since it changes something not about a thing but in the thing itself, and yet the change itself is not made without change of place and time.

XVI. *In what ways spirits are changed.*

After these changes of bodies, to which are subject all things that are changed corporeally, we pass to the spiritual creation, considering its mutability, whether any of the above changes befit it, and whether any other change which is outside the nature of bodies befalls it. We see that spirit can neither increase at all by augmentation of parts, since it is not body, nor decrease by diminution, since it is a simple nature; and yet spirit is changed by affection and cognition. It passes from this to that, it varies, and experiences the vicissitudes of joy, grief, repentance, and wish; its knowledge increases and forgetfulness befalls it; it varies its thoughts and it knows in succession, and that change in it of knowledge and affection is, as it were, a change of form. Temporal change follows this, and it is subject to time on account of these things which are varied in it. Nor is this doubtful to anyone regarding created spirit, since it is varied in time according to those things which do not abide the same in it.

But concerning change of place great doubt arises among investigators; there are some who say that no spirit can be changed in place, since place is properly the abode of body and the capacity of body which is determined according to body, sometimes according to that which is in it, sometimes according to that in which it is itself. And place is not body, since place is not anything, nor does place posit anything but is, as it were, an empty space and void where body is or can be, and is not body itself. Yet it is not called place unless determined by body, either what is in it according to limit of dimension in which the body stops and beyond which it is not, or according to body which contains place, or according to the circumscription of body itself, since body is not the same within. So we state that there can be nothing in place except what has corporeal dimension and circumscription, since place exists according to dimension and circumscription of body; and that this can not in any way befit the spirit which is devoid of corporeal quantity; therefore, that body alone is in place and is changed in place and time, but that the spirit is not created in place; that, since it is not a body, it is not changed in place but in time; but that the creating Spirit is neither in place nor changed in place, since He is not body, nor changed in time, since He is absolutely invariable; therefore, that it is rightly assigned to body alone, and that this is something because it is defined, and that it is here somewhere because it is circumscribed, and that it is now at sometime because it is variable; indeed that it befits the created spirit; and that this is something because it is defined, and that it is now at some time because it is variable, but that it is not here somewhere because it is not circumscribed which is not capable of dimension; but that the creating spirit is neither this something because it is not defined, nor is it here somewhere because it is not circumscribed nor is it now at sometime because it is invariable; yet that it is truly and essentially present in all that is this something, and in all that is here somewhere, and in all that is now at sometime, since it is in all, and is everywhere, and is always, always without time, everywhere without place, in all without limit and definition. And we, indeed, by no means accuse of falsehood the sublime consideration of these men, yet we judge their words beyond the capacity and power of lesser minds and too great for the understanding of the simple.

XVII. *That God essentially is and truly is, in every creature or nature*
without definition of Himself, and in every place without circum-
scription, and in every time without vicissitude or change.

Now we are of the opinion and thus fully approve that it should be truly asserted much more soberly and fittingly that God substantially or essentially and properly and really is, and that He is in everything whether by nature or by essence without definition of Himself, and in every place without circumscription, and in every time without mutability. As to the opinions of certain foolish men, rather those who know the flesh alone and consider only what is of the flesh, that the defilement of corporeal filths and pollutions could touch God, if it be said that He is present essentially or substantially in all things, this is so trivial that it is not even worthy of an answer, since even created spirit itself can not be defiled by corporeal filths. For if corporeal filths touch spirits, let they themselves say how the human soul placed in flesh can be immaculate, since no greater defilement or pollution can be found than the filths of human flesh. Let them say regarding the flesh of the leper, whose contact even man can not bear without horror, how it does not defile a holy and just soul, which so lives in it without pollution that through it the flesh is even cleansed of pollution. Finally let them answer whether they think that it must rather be conceded regarding God, that God is nowhere or that He is everywhere. But if it is certainly absurd to confess that God is nowhere, they themselves are necessarily forced by their own judgment to confess that which is more suitably taken as the meaning of their statement, that He is somewhere. For those who have elected to serve words rather than truth, and think that this alone should be rejected which the ears of the multitude abhor, it is just that they in this also do not deviate from their opinion. Let them say, therefore, if they presume to spread this abroad, that God is nowhere, and let them not think that it immediately follows from this that what is nowhere is itself nothing at all.

If therefore, it can not be said fittingly that God is nowhere, who we must believe is, and is more truly than all things that are, let them say where He is. For if He is somewhere, and is not everywhere, there is where He is, and there is where He is not; and now God is made local, and He is confined by limit and boundary, which is altogether impossible. So it must be confessed and admitted without hesitation that the divine nature which because of its own immensity can be wanting nowhere is truly and essentially in every place, and that yet it is not contained in any place since it cannot in any way be circumscribed. Divine nature, therefore, is where the whole is, which contains the whole and penetrates the whole; nothing can be without it of all the things that have been made by it, and it cannot be divided because of its simplicity, nor be defiled because of its purity, nor in any way comprehended because of its immensity.

XVIII. *How created spirits are local, and how bodies.*

Certainly regarding created spirit we confess that this is more fitting to say and this more adapted for understanding, that we declare without hesitation that it is not only in place but that it is local; that it is in place, indeed, because it is perceived present here somewhere, but that it is local, because, although it is somewhere, it is not found everywhere. For everything which is defined is local according to something, since in the very fact that it has end and limit it also determines place just as it is determined in place. But body having dimension is circumscribed by place, since to it according to place are assigned beginning, middle, and end. But spirit, since it is not capable of dimension, but is limited by definition alone, does not indeed receive the circumscription of place, and yet in a certain manner is enclosed by place, since, although it is present entire here somewhere, it is not found elsewhere.

And so body is local, since it is circumscribed by place, but spirit, since it is enclosed in place through the presence of nature and operation, is iself also rightly called local. But uncreated spirit, since it is present in every place, and yet cannot be enclosed in any place or circumscribed, is truly said to be in every place, nor yet at any time is it called local. However, I am not unaware that some have wished to remove place universally from all spirit, since they have argued that there is question of place only according to dimension and corporeal circumscription. But, as we have said above, their view has departed too much from common opinion and possibility. Rather, however, are those things to be presented for the purpose of discussion, which freely adapt themselves, and bring in nothing from the outside foreign to truth.

XIX. *The reason why God is not only one but three.*

We have already said how true reason proves that God is one, and how it considers those things to be true which pertain to the Oneness of the Godhead. Then it also argues and urges that God is not only one but is also three. And of this good investigation and consideration also it has true exemplars from God. For God who could not be seen in Himself, was made manifest in His work, and human reason saw Him not in Himself because He was invisible, but in His likeness since it was made for this purpose, that God might be seen in it.

XX. *Of the extrinsic and intrinsic word.*

For just as man's wisdom is not seen except by man himself, until it goes forth and is made manifest through word, so God's wisdom was invisible and could not have been known except by Him Himself alone of whom it was, until it was made manifest through His work. And wisdom itself was word, but, as it were, intrinsic and hidden word, which could not be known at all unless it were made manifest through extrinsic word; so man's thought is his intrinsic word, which is hidden and is concealed until it is revealed through the utterance of the mouth, and the utterance itself of the voice similarly is word just as thought of the heart is word. But the word which is manifest comes forth and reveals the word which is hidden.

Thus also in God the intrinsic word was the hidden and invisible word of His heart, and wisdom was this word; it was invisible, until it became manifest through the extrinsic word made visible, which was His work. Just as through word of mouth the word of the heart is made manifest, so all nature speaks to its author, and shows what has been made to those having sense to understand their Maker.

XXI. *That the image of God is more exact in the rational creature, and that a trace of the Trinity is found in it.*

And there are in these things certain representations, as it were, signifying from afar and having likeness in part. Certain things, in truth, marked by a clear image and perfect imitation produce a clear demonstration. That of God which is invisible is more quickly recognized, therefore, in those in which it is more clearly demonstrated through manifest evidence. For those things manifest their author more perfectly, which more closely approach His likeness. Now this is the rational creature itself, which was made excellently and properly according to His likeness, which then recognizes his Creator more quickly whom it does not see, when it knows that it itself was made to His image. In this, therefore, was found the first trace of the Trinity, when the rational creature itself began to recognize what was in itself, and from this considered what was above itself. For it saw that of itself is born the wisdom which is in itself; it itself loves its wisdom, and love proceeds from itself as does its wisdom, whereby it loves the wisdom born of itself, and it does not divide this wisdom abiding in itself from itself.

Three things, as it were, appear in one—mind, wisdom, and love; mind and wisdom are of mind, and of mind and wisdom love. A kind of trinity arises, and oneness does not depart; there are simultaneously trinity and oneness according to the power and virtue of the image. Mind illuminated by these things ascends from them, and considers its Creator to be wise and to have wisdom, and that its own wisdom is from Him, and that He never was without wisdom, since He was always wise. Because He Himself always loved His wisdom, and always had love for His wisdom, His love was coeternal with the eternal and with His coeternal wisdom.

XXII. *How the three persons are one in essence and substance.*

Again, it considers that there can not be in God anything different from Himself, and that all that is is one; so indeed there is Trinity, and oneness remains. For since there is there one who is from no one, and there is there one who is from Him, and equally with both one who is from both, there is trinity. For he who is from no one can not be he who is from another, nor can he who is from both be either he who is from no one or who is from one only. Thus the Trinity is true, and oneness remains perfect, since in God there can be nothing which is not God. Undivided nature and true oneness indeed forbid scission, but distinction and peculiarity teach the Trinity.

XXIII. *On the distinction of names in the Trinity.*

And faith gave names whereby what is believed might be signified; the Father was named in the Trinity because from Him was the Son, who was of His substance. For he who begets and begets of his own substance, begets that which he himself is. And so He from whom He was and He who was with Him are the same as He Himself was. He was called Father because the Son was from

Him. But He who was from both was not the Son of both, lest there be two Fathers of one Son, and He be called Father who was Son, and the distinction of the Trinity be confused, but the Holy Ghost was of the Father and of the Son, proceeding from both Father and Son. The Catholic Faith professed Father and Son and Holy Ghost. He is Father who has Son, and Son who has Father, and Holy Ghost who is from Father and Son. And indeed the Father is Spirit since He is God. The Father is likewise holy since He is God. But faith wished to distinguish one person in the Trinity when it called Him Holy Spirit. For it is He who is given for sanctification when He is inspired into those to be sanctified. And yet He does not come without the Father and the Son, since the Trinity is undivided.

XXIV. *How the Holy Spirit is sent forth from the Father and the Son by eternal procession from them and by a coming in time to us.*

But as to His being inspired from the Father and the Son, this is His coming from the Father and the Son. And this is eternal with Him, lest He be the name of a function who is given and received according to time, because His being from the Father and the Son is not temporal but eternal. Wherefore, He is said to be given, when He comes from the Father and the Son, because it is from the Father and the Son that He has eternal not temporal being; so the Holy Spirit is the gift of God, because He is the gift of the Father and the Son. When He is given according to time, and He is given by the Father and the Son, His being given by the Father and the Son is nothing else for Him than when His being is given by the Father and the Son, from the fact that He has eternal being from the Father and the Son. In the Trinity are Father and Son and Holy Ghost; the Father from Himself, the Son from the Father alone, the Holy Spirit from the Father and the Son. And because there is one nature and one substance, there is one Trinity in one nature and one substance. When one mind considers the things that are distinct and peculiar in the Trinity, it finds three things and confesses three persons. But when it begins to note what is the same to the three, one thing is discovered.

XXV. *Why those three ineffable things in the Godhead are called three persons, and the three in man are not so called.*

Again there arises on the other hand a doubt, and it strikes the mind with the depth of obscure things; inquiry sets forth and reason asks itself why those three things which are found in the Godhead are called persons, since in that Trinity which the mind first finds in itself three things are likewise found; yet rational reflection would not suffer the rational mind to contain three persons within itself or the soul to consist of three persons. Let reason investigate diligently why this is so, since one may not doubt that it is so, nor can it be easily known how it is so.

And yet it sees something of that which it does not see entire, nor is it permitted to ignore what it is not allowed to comprehend. For it sees that the things that are in mind are not truly the same as the mind itself. For these are sometimes separated from the mind, and when they have been present, they depart; and they return again when they have gone away; they are varied in relation to the mind, nor are they truly identical with it, but as if certain affections and forms of it, which do not have this being something, but only being present in that which is this something. Therefore, since man himself is a person, but these are found to be only affections, as it were, adhering to the person and existing in relation to it, to be person is not at all proper to these, but only to be present in the person. But since those things which are in God can not be different from Himself as if neither accidents nor affections changeable according to time nor separable on account of the incommutable nature of essence, and since He is one for whom to be whole is identical with what He is, the three things are truly predicated to come together in Him; it is asserted also that there is one in three, and that this very identity is eternal and perfect. The three things are called three persons, not three essences, because the nature in the three individually is perfect and undivided in the three. And so they are called persons individually, because they are God and one God is three, because there is one Godhead in the three.

XXVI. *Why power is attributed to the Father, wisdom to the Son, goodness or benignity to the Holy Ghost.*

Power is attributed to the Father, and wisdom to the Son, and goodness or benignity to the Holy Ghost. And those things are distinguished which are common. Among these no mention, indeed, is made of what is not, but what is, is passed over in silence, lest that be believed which is not. For the Father is called powerful, and the Father is powerful, and not the Father alone, because the Father is powerful and the Son and the Holy Ghost; not three are powerful, but one is powerful, because there is one power in one nature and in one substance. And the Son is wise, but not alone, because the Father is wise and the Son and the Holy Ghost; not three are wise, but one is wise, because there is one wisdom in one nature and in one substance. And the Holy Ghost is called kind and good, and indeed the Holy Ghost is kind and good, but the Holy Ghost is not alone kind and good, but the Father is kind and good and the Son and the Holy Ghost; yet the three are not kind and the three are not good, but one is kind and one is good, because there is one benignity and one goodness in one nature and in one substance.

But Scripture had care for human conscience lest it should err thinking that in its God were things similar to men which were not in Him, since certain words had been assumed by men not for every likeness but to signify the things that were of God above men. And there was something similar there lest the imitation be different, but not the whole lest that which differed so much be regarded as the same. In the Godhead Father was spoken of, since in it there was He from whom He was who was of His substance, just as he who begets, begets of his own substance, and the very one who begets is not he whom he begets, but one is different from the other. There is not one nature for him who begets, and another for him who is begotten. And in this there was a likeness between divine and human things; so Father and Son were so called from this, because the one begot, and the other was begotten. The Father who begot is not He who was begotten Son; yet because one nature belongs to the begetter and the begotten, and one substance, the begetter is not different from the begotten, because He is God; and God is one, begetter and begotten, because one Godhead belongs to the begetter and the begotten. Therefore, they were found to be one in that they were God, because they were one all that they were. But they were not one in one, because the Father was He who was from no one, and the Son He who was from the Father, and the Holy Ghost He who was from both, who was not Son since He was from both, and was so equally. These three things were called three persons, because each of the three was this all, and was a person; yet not one person, since all this was one, but three persons, because three things were in this one and this one was all; these three things were three persons, and this one was one God; these three things were this one and three persons were one God: Father and Son and Holy Ghost.

Therefore, He was called Father because He begot the Son of His own substance, and there was the likeness in this. But lest the Father be thought prior to the Son as always among man, and it can never be otherwise than that the Father precede the Son, on this account the Father was called powerful, not because He was alone so, because the Son and the Holy Spirit were powerful, but because He alone had to be called powerful since of Him alone could there be greater doubt, as it were, of one prior and old, and enfeebled by the weight of years. The Son was called wise, not because He was alone so, but because of Him alone could there be greater doubt, as it were, of one posterior and still immature in age and not fully developed in mind. Therefore, the Father was called powerful lest He be thought prior to the Son, and the Son wise, lest He be believed posterior to the Father, and the Holy Spirit good or kind, lest God should be judged cruel; human consciousness might have been in terror before Him, if God were said to have Spirit, and there had not been added "holy" or "kind," since Spirit of itself seems to signify a kind of harshness and to mean "cruel."

XXVII. *Another reason why those things, which are mentioned according to substance and which are common, are distinguished according to persons.*

Therefore, on account of its likeness, by which it was found, the most high Trinity similarly presented this very likeness also as a trinity, a kind of trace and image of the ineffable Trinity. And in it this was so, since in the rational mind there was a kind of power and a kind of force. From this was born understanding which alone was wisdom, and without it the mind was not wisdom; lastly proceeded the love or the joy of the mind for its wisdom, and it itself was only love, because without it in the mind and wisdom there was not love.

These names were given according to peculiarity, because each was by itself, and these three things were distinguished: first, power, from which was wisdom; then, wisdom itself, which had been born of power; lastly, love which had proceeded simultaneously from power and wisdom. And these were distinguished, because these were not entirely the same, since they were separated from each other, and did not consist in one. Thus in the rational mind power was one thing, because it was prior without wisdom, and yet wisdom was not. Afterwards came wisdom, and it begins to be with power, as one thing in another. There were now two, power and wisdom, and there was added a third. There begins to be three, power and wisdom and love. And power was not from something, and from it was wisdom, but love had proceeded from power and wisdom. Power was not wisdom, because power was before wisdom and wisdom went out from it. Nor again could love be called power or wisdom, because it only proceeded from them, and they had existed sometime without it.

These three were distinguished in the soul, and in these three was found the trinity of the soul. The soul ascended from these to the most high Trinity and found there the Father who was from no one, just as power in itself, and the Son who was from the Father, just as wisdom in itself, and the Holy Spirit who was from the Father and the Son, just as love in itself had proceeded from power and wisdom. So it attributed power to the Father, because there had been a likeness of Him in itself, and wisdom to the Son, since there was this image of Him in itself which had arisen from power, and it attributed love to the Holy Ghost, because in itself love proceeded from power and wisdom, just as the Holy Ghost from the Father and the Son, who is the love of the Father and the Son.

So indeed it distinguished truth according to the image by which it had found truth, so that what was found here proper according to signification might there be called singular according to peculiarity. Yet, since for God all that is is one being, and that can not be found diverse which in a simple nature is the same, neither can that be of one which is not of the other, where one is identical with the other. For since the power of the Father is nothing else than His essence, the wisdom of the Son nothing else than His essence, and the love of the Holy Ghost nothing else than His essence, it is quite necessary where there is one essence that there be one power, one wisdom, and one love, and that it be common and entire and that it be properly and equally so. So power is of the Father, and is of the Son, and is of the Holy Ghost, and is properly and equally so; wisdom is of the Son, and is of the Father, and is of the Holy Ghost, and is properly and equally so; and love or goodness is of the Holy Ghost, and is of the Father, and is of the Son, and is properly and equally so. Because for God to have is the same as to be, and all that is in God can not be other than God, the Father is power, and the Son is power, and the Holy Ghost is power, and one power because one essence. Similarly, the Father is wisdom, and the Son is wisdom, and the Holy Ghost is wisdom, and one wisdom because one essence. The Father is love, and the Son is love, and the Holy Ghost is love, and one love because one essence. But the power is the Father, and the power is of no one because He is from no one; likewise also wisdom is the Father, and wisdom is of no one, because He is from no one. Love is the Father, and love is of no one because He is from no one. But the power is the Son, and it is the power of the Father, because He is from the Father. Wisdom is the Son, and wisdom is of the Father, because He is from the Father. The Holy Ghost is the love of the Father and of the Son, because He is from the Father and the Son. In this we should guard diligently lest what is to be distinguished be confounded in communion, and lest that which is peculiar be not distinguished by singularity; that is, when we wish to distinguish the persons in the Trinity, we should not attribute to one what is common to another, nor when we wish to prove the oneness of substance should we assign to another what is proper to one.

XXVIII. *That the trace of the Trinity is found not only in the rational creation but also in the corporeal.*

We have then pointed out some trace of the most high Trinity, in so far as human reason can from the little which it possesses and was given it and is in it, and it is little as compared to the perfect whole. For it found three things in itself, and from these it became aware of the Trinity which was above it. Nature from without bore witness to the Trinity, just as in the case of the oneness of the Godhead Three things appeared without as signs of the Trinity, but they were not an image as those which were within, and these themselves were imperfect in likeness. For power was within, and wisdom, and love. These three were the image of the Creator's power and of His wisdom and of His love, because they were here and they were there. But they were here in image, there in truth; yet they were in both places, and were the same, because that was here which was there. But what was here was image, and what was there was truth. Yet power was not without, but a sign only; nor was wisdom, but a sign only; nor was love or goodness, but a sign only; nor were the signs themselves either power or wisdom or love as within, but only signs of power, wisdom, and love. For the sign of power was the immensity of things; of wisdom beauty; of goodness utility. And the signs themselves were not power or wisdom or goodness, but only signs of these attesting to those which were peculiar within. The Trinity was proven true in its works, nor could reason add anything to these which were perfect nor take away anything from those which were distinguished.

For these are the three things which perfect every rational thing, and without them nothing is perfect. Likewise these three concur in every effect, and if any of these is lacking, nothing is accomplished; if they be present equally all things are brought to completion. These are power, knowledge, and will; and if you take away any one of these, you diminish perfection; if you establish all equally, you confess that nothing is lacking. Therefore, by these even the Creator of things Himself accomplished His works; He Himself exists as perfect, since they are perfect in Him which can not be increased in part because they are full, nor completed in the whole because they are perfect, nor divided in oneness because they are one.

XXIX. *That all things are in these three.*

Whatever things are said of God, and believed truly to be in God, are referred to these three and they consist in these three in Him; from these, as has been said, if you take anything away, what is left is not perfect; and if you try to add anything, what is amplified is not greater. For if you call Him strong and uncorrupted, and immutable, and invincible, and other like terms, all this herein is of His power; if you call Him provident, if an inspector, if a scrutinizer of secrets, and knowing, all this is of His wisdom; if you call Him pious, if kind, if merciful, if patient, all this is of His goodness. And truth can not add anything to these things, because all is contained in them which is perfect and true. Therefore, these three pointed out the Trinity in perfect likeness; they convinced that nothing should be added to the three, because this is perfect, and nothing should be taken away, since it thus exists complete. These three in God were one, and for God they were one, but were found distinct here where they were not one, and therefore they became an image of the Trinity. Consideration followed the peculiarity found here even to the ineffable Trinity, and distinguishd as peculiar there what was peculiar here only, and something different was found: there, indeed, in one was all, and one was all.

XXX. *Recapitulation of the aforesaid.*

Now, then, we have expressed how human reason first both found that God was in itself and proved this outside itself; how it judged that God is one and simple in nature, and immense, and eternal, and that He is great but not in quantity, simple but not in smallness, and that He is three without division of oneness, and one without confusion of Trinity; how the most high Trinity was found through that which was its image in us, and how it argued that the three things in us are not persons and the three things in God are persons, because they are God; how nothing can be added to the three because they are perfect, nor anything taken away because they are differentiated; how those things which are in God are distinguished even according to those which are differentiated in us, since the latter are an image for the former and point out the Trinity. These things, indeed, according to the judgment of reason we combined into one, since it approved this as truth; for, indeed, something was added from these things which rise above reason, and reason did not succeed in satisfying them, since they are formed according to reason. For some things are from reason, some according to reason, others above reason, and beyond these those which are contrary to reason.

From reason are necessary things, according to reason are probable, above reason marvelous, contrary to reason incredible. And the two extremes, indeed, are not at all capable of faith. For those things that are from reason are certainly known and can not be believed because they are known. But what are contrary to reason likewise can not in any way be believed, because they are not susceptible of any reason, nor does reason at any time give assent to them. Therefore, things that are according to reason and that are above reason are alone susceptible of faith. In the first kind, indeed, faith is aided by reason and reason is perfected by faith, since the things that are believed are according to reason. If reason does not comprehend the truth of these things, yet it does not contradict faith in them. In those things which are above reason, faith is not aided by any reason; since reason does not grasp what faith believes, and yet there is something by which reason is admonished to respect the faith which it does not comprehend. What was said, therefore, and was according to reason, was probable to reason, and it freely gave assent to them. But what was above reason was made known by divine revelation, and reason did not operate in these, but yet it was restrained lest it contend against them.

Now then we shall next show how much divine revelation added to those things which were the object of reasoning and were considered as probable, and those things which were made manifest through inspiration and those which were asserted through doctrine, and of these those which were proved by miracles, in so far as shall seem best and will be possible.

XXXI. *A brief summary of the aforesaid, with some additions.*

Before all creation the Creator, indeed, was alone, but yet not lonely, because with Him was His wisdom in which through providence were all things from eternity which were made by Him in time through essence. He was alone, therefore, since there was nothing except Himself, and yet He was not lonely, because He did not need another's society who was sufficient unto Himself, to whom nothing was lacking, because, as has been said, all was in Him through providence which was to be made by Him through essence. These two things, therefore, must be carefully distinguished from each other, and considered in themselves, namely, the Creator and the creature, lest either the creature be believed eternal or the Creator temporal. For in these two consists the whole knowledge of truth.

First, then, we must consider what is to be said or believed about the Creator. Therefore, we confess the Creator of all things as one and three, one in essence, three in persons, because the essence of the Godhead is one, and in the one essence are three persons: Father and Son and Holy Ghost. The Father is from no one, the Son is from the Father alone, the Holy Ghost from the Father and the Son. Just as in one soul are mind and understanding and joy, and mind indeed is from itself, but understanding from the mind alone, but from the mind and understanding joy, and these three according to substance, indeed, are one soul, so in one body are figure and form and beauty, these three. Figure seems to be first according to substance, then form, and from both beauty, and these three are in one body and are one body, so that in both natures the image of the Creator shines forth, in the first, indeed, according to likeness, in the second, however, according to the imitation of likeness. So, then, we confess God to be both in essence one and in persons three, and in the oneness, indeed, we recognize eternity and immensity, but in eternity immutability, in immensity, however, simplicity, that is, eternity without time, immensity without quantity. In the Trinity we confess a communion of oneness, an equality of immensity, a coevity of eternity, and indeed a communion of oneness without division, an equality of immensity without diminution, a coevity of eternity without order or succession, and that is for each, entirety through oneness, fullness through immensity, perfection through eternity.

Now we confess that three persons are nothing else than one essence, because the three have one being and one essence. Wherefore, the three are one, but the three are not one person, because, if the three were not one there would not be one essence for the three, and if the three were one person they would not be three. Therefore, the three are one being, lest their substance be divided, and the three persons are not one person, lest the persons be confused. What, therefore, the Father is, the Son is, because there is one nature of the Father and of the Son. But the Son is not who the Father is, because the person of the Father and the Son is different. Likewise, what is said of God according to substance, is said equally of Father and of Son and of Holy Ghost, because the substance of the Father and of the Son and of the Holy Ghost is one and is so equally. God is the name of the substance, and for God this being is identical with being substance. So the Father is God, and the Son is God, and the Holy Ghost is God, and not three Gods but one God, since they are one substance. Similarly other things which are said of God according to substance are so said equally. Of each person they are said singly and equally, and of all together they are said not plurally but singly and equally. When things are said of each person singly, no less is said; and when things are said of all in common, no more is proclaimed. For when it is said: "The Father is God," no less is said than when it is said: "The Father and the Son and the Holy Ghost are God." For the Godhead is entire in the Father, and entire in the Son, and entire in the Holy Ghost, and no less in the Father alone than together in the Father and the Son and the Holy Ghost. Similarly must it be understood of the Son and of the Holy Ghost.

There is one name only which is used of each person singly, yet in the sum total it is employed not singly but plurally, since, moreover, it is used according to substance. For it is said: "The Father is a person, and the Son is a person, and the Holy Ghost is a person"; and yet it can not be said simultaneously: "The Father and the Son and the Holy Ghost are a person," but "three persons." For this alone of those things which are said with reference to substance is said of each singly. In the sum total, however, it is not proclaimed singly but plurally. But the things that are said according to relation are said according to themselves, and those that are said of each singly, in the sum total, however, are proclaimed neither singly nor plurally, since they are said according to themselves, and so can not be said according to one another. Likewise what is being Father is being from Himself, what is being Son is being from the Father, what is being Holy Ghost is being from both. The Son has generation, the Holy Ghost procession, and generation is the Son's alone, not the Holy Ghost's. For what generation is, is being from another, but not into another. But what procession is, is being from something, and some times into another. For what is inspired is inspired from something, and is inspired in something. Therefore, words have been assumed to signify what had to be said of God, so that what could not be comprehended could be understood in some measure. Thus likewise from the beginning God tempered knowledge of Himself on the part of man, so that He would be neither wholly manifest nor wholly hidden. For if He were wholly manifest, faith would not be practiced and infidelity would be refuted. But if He were wholly hidden, faith would not be assisted and infidelity would be excused. Likewise, the invisible God comes to the knowledge of man by four modes, two within, two without. Within, through reason and aspiration; without, through creation and doctrine. Of these, two pertain to nature, two to grace; reason and creation pertain to nature; aspiration and doctrine to grace. Therefore, after this we must observe in doctrine those things which authority approves, because human reason unless it has been illumined by the word of God can not see the way of truth.

PART FOUR

On the will of God which is eternal and one, and on the signs of His will, which indeed are temporal and are called according to the figure of the will, because they are signs of the will.

I. *On the will of God therefore, that it is just.*

The first cause of all things is the will of the Creator which no antecedent cause moved because it is eternal, nor any subsequent cause confirms because it is of itself just. For He did not will justly, because what He willed was to be just, but what He willed was just, because He Himself willed it. For it is peculiar to Himself and to His will that that which is His is just; from Him comes the justice that is in His will by the very fact that justice comes from His will. That which is just is just according to His will and certainly would not be just, if it were not according to His will. When, therefore, it is asked how that is just which is just, the most fitting answer will be: because it is according to the will of God, which is just. When, however, it is asked how the will of God itself is also just, this quite reasonable answer will be given: because there is no cause of the first cause, whose prerogative it is to be what it is of itself. But this alone is the cause whence whatever is has originated, and it itself did not originate, but is eternal.

II. *In what ways Scripture accepts the will of God.*

We must not pass over here what Sacred Scripture in certain diverse ways is wont to say of the will of God; and the will is not diverse, but the phraseology is diverse about the will which is not diverse. For the will of God in Holy Writ is sometimes accepted as that which is truly in Him, and identical with Him, and coeternal with Him. Sometimes, however, according to a figure of speech His will is called that which according to its real nature is not His will but the sign of His will. The sign itself of will is called will, although it is not the will but the sign only, as also the signs of anger are called anger, and the signs of love designated love. God is called angry, and there is no anger in Him; but only the signs which are without, by which He is shown to be angry, are called His anger. It is a figure of speech, according to which what is said is not false, but the truth which is said is obscured out of regard for likeness. According to these figurative modes diverse wills, as it were, are attributed to God, because those things which are called His will by figure are diverse, although His will properly so called is one.

III. *The first will of God is called good pleasure.*

Therefore, the will of God which is mentioned first and principally is that which is truly His will. And this is one and is incapable of multiplicity or of mutability.

IV. *The second will is operation, and the third permission.*

Then there follow two wills, that is, two things which are called wills. And these two are mentioned regarding God, and are called wills of God, because they are signs of His will. Of these wills one is called permitting, the other doing, that is, permission and operation, because His permission is called His will, and His operation is called His will, since they are exercised according to His will and are signs of His will. These two are as if consequents of His most high will, and, so to speak, its unfolding and its effect are like to it, yet not coeternal. For whatever is in it is always in these at some time, and whatever is not in these at some time is never in it. For all that is in it is always, and all that is in these is at some time, because nothing is beyond His will nor can anything be done outside His operation or permission. Two follow one, and one is found in both, since He does not operate unwillingly, nor does He permit except willingly. Whenever anything is done, this is called the will of God, because that it was done or permitted came to pass by the will of God. By His will He made what He made, and He made well, and He made that good which He made. He permitted voluntarily what He permitted, and He permitted well and it was good that He permitted, even if that was not good which He permitted.

V. *That God made good things, permitted evil.*

For He made good things and He made well, and He permitted evils but did not make them. He made well because both were good. Therefore, He willed both, because both were good. Good things were good, and evil evil, nor were good things evil, nor evil things good, but it was good that there be both good and evil. God willed that there be both, because it was good that there be both; and not both were good, because evil was not good. Therefore, God did not will evil, when He willed that evil also exist. Yet, He did not make the latter in that which He made good, but He permitted that it be because what He willed was good. Nor was this good evil, but from evil was good; nor did He make evil good, but from evil He, who knows how to use both evil things and good things unto good, made good.

VI. *Why God permitted evil.*

It was a greater good that there be good from good and from evil than from good alone. Wherefore, the highest good willed that this should be good, and what He willed was good. Therefore, just as all that was to be could not have been unknown to His eternal wisdom, so all that was good could not have displeased His coeternal will. He saw all that was to be, and that it was good that this all should be all, and He willed that the all should be because it was good that all should be. He saw the evils that were to be far in the future with the good before they were; He considered that, with these evils added, good things might be commended and become more beautiful through comparison with evil, and that good things would be evil among the good which were not good, since good things would be adorned from these and commended and would receive greater good to the glory and beauty of all.

He regarded all things in their order; He saw good things there, and the things that were not good in His sight; He willed all things to be thus as it was good, because it was good thus as He saw and He willed what was to be. With equal judgment He weighed all things that He saw in one agreement, in which it was good and just that all be and that there be nothing else, and He willed that all be and nothing else. By this will afterwards He brought it about that those good things should be which it was good should be, just as He had seen and had willed. He permitted that those evil things should be which it was good should be, as He had foreseen would be with the good, and what He had willed should be with the good because it was good. His will, indeed, was eternal regarding both good and evil things which He willed should be, but it was not known to men, until they were completed and made, what good and evil things it was His will should be.

VII. *Why the operation and the permission of God are called His will.*

Now when He made good and permitted evil, His will appeared to us in this, because He wills to be that which He makes or permits should be; and His will which is eternal does not begin then with that which is made, but His will which is hidden is shown from that time when it is made. And so the very thing that is made is called His will, because it is a sign of His will. His will appears, as it were, now as this and now as that, because the signs of the one will are manifold.

VIII. *That there is a twofold distinction in God's will: in His good pleasure, and in the sign of His good pleasure.*

Thence there emerges for us a distinction of the Divine will to be recognized in His good pleasure and in the sign of His good pleasure. And we say that His good pleasure is His will, and the sign of His good pleasure we call His will. Both are true and both are truly said, but His good pleasure is eternal, nor can whatever is in it not be, and whatever is not in it can not be. Neither contrary to it nor outside it nor without it is anything in all that is. It is fixed and certain, nor can that which is in it at any time be frustrated. "He hath done all things whatsoever He would," (Psal. 113, 3), in this is it proven that His will is not frustrated. "For who resisteth his will," (Rom. 9, 19). In this is it proven that His good pleasure is not hindered. Thus His good pleasure is in harmony with the accomplishments of things; and the accomplishments of things themselves are not at discord with it. For all that He wills is done, and all that He does not will is not done; all that He wills He always wills to be done, but not always at the time that He wills. This good pleasure which is eternal is universal, and all things that are done in their time He approves equally with the simple assent of His justice, that they may proceed to accomplishment and be done. It is accomplished and completed and made manifest by two things which follow in time—by divine permission and operation; these themselves, indeed, embrace the universe of all things which are capable of accomplishment or subsist, corresponding to that which is one in both, and the good pleasure of the Creator is not dissimilar to all dissimilar things. So these two also are called wills. The will of God is His good pleasure, and His will is His operation, and His will is His permission.

IX. *The fourth will is in precept; the fifth in prohibition.*

There follows next His precept and His prohibition, both called His will, because, whenever He orders anything to be done, He shows that He wills that it be done, and, whenever He prohibits anything from being done, He shows that He wills that it be not done. Therefore, these are likewise called His will, because they are signs, as it were, of His will, just as His operation and His permission, but dissimilarly so, signifying in another way His will and in part signs thereof.

X. *That precept and prohibition are not similar signs of the eternal good pleasure as are operation and permission.*

For not as His operation and His permission, do His precept and His prohibition thus extend through all things, because without those nothing is done. But only these two are directed to the rational creature who alone is capable of precept and prohibition, circumspect toward both according to its innate reason. So these are signs in part, which do not pertain to all things nor do they universally bring to manifestation the highest will and all that is in it, as do operation and permission; they signify only those things which look to the very ones for whom these are done, that is precept and prohibition, since they are in the highest will and eternal good pleasure. Nor are these similar signs, as His operation and permission are certain and true signs of the eternal good pleasure.

Now these, namely, precept and prohibition, do not at all make certain what is in the eternal good pleasure, until it is proven by operation or permission when it has been done. For then it is certain, when God has done this, or if He permitted that it be done and it was done, that it was in the eternal good pleasure that it should be thus as it was done; according to this He voluntarily did or permitted that that which was done should be done, since thus it is good that it be as it is. Now when something has been commanded or prohibited, it is not yet clear what has been defined about it in the eternal good pleasure, until the accomplishment of things brings forth into evidence, either by operation or by permission, that it is good and the good pleasure that that which is to be, be before it is.

Now precept and prohibition only intimate that it is so in the will of Him who orders that it be done or not done. And they give proof that it is just and pious that he for whom it is done believe nothing else, even if there is something else in Him by whom it is done. It is often commanded that that be done which is not to be and will not be done. And it is prohibited that that be done which is to be; but it will be done, and there is nothing in the good pleasure except this alone—that that be which will be done, since it is good that it be so and nothing else than what will be done whether by the operation of God, something good, or by His permission, something evil, because all being is good. His precept and His prohibition do not correspond to His good pleasure, as do His operation and His permission, but they proceed oppositely and are dissimilarly ordered; sometimes they are not in harmony with that which is to be and will be done.

XI. *How God seems to deceive by precept or prohibition,*
intimating something other than exists in His good pleasure.

Now the precepts of God seem to be guilty of deceit and to lie about the truth, when they signify one thing about His will, and affirm to us certain foreign and extraneous things, which, indeed, were not brought out nor are they established in accord with His good pleasure which is fixed regarding all those things that will be done. The human conscience struggles seriously with two conflicting matters which do not agree: why God commanded what He did not will or why that was not done which He willed. For if there is truth in His precept, He seems certainly to have willed what He ordered; and if there is omnipotence in his good pleasure, that seems to have been done which He willed. But what He ordered was not done, and what He prohibited was done. What, then, follows according to this except that either He did not will that which He commanded, or could not have done what He willed? For what was done was done by Him, and if it was not done, yet it was permitted; if it was done, it was done voluntarily, and if it was permitted it was permitted voluntarily, because neither could He have been compelled to do anything contrary to His will, nor have been forced to permit anything without His will.

Therefore, what was done was done by His will, even if it was not done for the sake of His will, since it was done by another will which was not friendly to His will. Yet He certainly willed what was done, since it is good that it was so done as it was done, and that it be so as it is. On this account, therefore, He commanded that it should be otherwise and He prohibited it from being so, although it is good that it be so; it was to be so before it was, and it was His good pleasure because it was good that it be so and not be otherwise.

XII. *That both sound harsh: either that God commands what He does not will, or that He permits to be done what He does not will.*

We are hard pressed by such a question and we are brought into such doubt that we do not easily dare to affirm anything this way or that, either that God commanded to be done what He did not will, or that what He did not will He permitted to be done. And yet of the two we more easily approve one: that He willed the good that He commanded rather than the evil which He permitted, although, however, the good that He commanded was not done, but evil that He permitted was. For it is an easy matter, and it is said without scruple of conscience: God wills good, and when it is so said, it sounds well: God wills good.

But if it is said: God wills evil, it sounds harsh, and the pious mind does not accept this easily about the good, that He wills evil. For this alone seems to be said when it is said: God wills evil, that the good loves evil and approves what is base, and regards iniquity as friendly to Himself; He rejoices as it were at what is like to Him, and thinks good what is evil. So the pious mind opposes this, not because what is said is not said well, but because what is said well is not understood well.

XIII. *That God does not will evils, although He wills that there be evils, because this is good.*

For this is not only said but in what is said something is understood which is not said, that He wills that there be evil and does not will evil. But if this alone is to be understood in what is said, "God wills evil" ought not to be said at all, since He does not in fact approve that, nor does He think it good, but He judges evil contrary to Himself, the good, and foreign to His own; He does not desire it as being suitable and having agreement with that which He Himself is, with that which is from Himself, and with that which is like unto

Himself, but it is extraneous and remote and constituted in complete unlikeness. Yet He wills evil to be, and in this He wills nothing except good, because it is good that there be evil; He does not will evil itself, because evil itself is not good. But He wills only good, and He loves and delights in it, as in a friend and kinsman and neighbour of His. On this account it sounds well and we freely accept it when it is said: "God wills good," because not evil in which he has no participation and to which He has no likeness, but that only He loves, namely, those things which are from Him and which have likeness to Him.

So God wills good, and God does not will evil; He wills all good and does not will all evil. All this we accept and approve, and we say that all this is true: that He loves all that is His own, and does not love anything that is not His own, nor does He hate anything that is His own; all His own He loves, and all not His own He hates. And so He willed the good which He commanded, and did not will the evil which He permitted, because His own was good and from His own, and friendly to Himself and to His own; He loved and approved His own, and desired it for Himself, and loved it in Himself with eternal love. Evil which was not His own He did not love in Himself, nor did He desire it for Himself, but He rejected it and opposed its feeling of love; He did not receive it with the consent of charity that he might give it a place among His good pleasures.

XIV. *That the will of God is always fulfilled.*

But you say to me: "Therefore if He willed good, at least because He willed the good which He commanded, and He did not will the evil which He permitted, that was done which He did not will, and what He willed was not done, since what He commanded was not done, but what He prohibited was done, which He permitted. So that was not done which He willed, but what He did not will was done." On the contrary what He willed was done, and nothing was done except what He willed, because He willed that it be so done, and so be as was done, since it was good that it be so done, and be so as it was done and not otherwise. That it be so was good even in that which was [not] good. That itself which was not good He did not will, but He did will that it be, since this was good. And when it was done, that was done which He willed, since it was good and this He willed.

Yet you say: "His will held less and obtained less and was fulfilled less and remained imperfect, because the good which He willed was not done, and the evil which He did not will was done." Therefore, you do not consider that, just as He does not have the evil which was done, which He did not will, so He does not lack the good, which was not done, which He willed. For what He wills and loves, He has, and what He does not will and hates, He does not have. What He wills to be He obtains because it is done, and likewise what He wills not to be, because it is not done. Never is His will frustrated so that what He wills is not done, nor so weak at any time that what He does not will is done.

XV. *How the evil are unexcusable, although through them the will of God is fulfilled.*

But perhaps again the evil may seem excusable when they do evils, since the will of God is fulfilled even in the evils which they do. But by their will the evil are judged, because they are contrary to the will of God, not indeed by resisting His will so that what He does not will is done, because they can not, but by willing to resist because they are evil. The evil will itself is a fault whereby they will something else, but the just faculty is that whereby they can not do anything else. When they will what God wills, they are not therefore good, because not on this account do they will, because God wills. But the very thing that they will, God does not will, because they will evil and God does not will evil. For they approve and love what God hates; for this reason they are contrary to God and are evil and sinners and guilty, not indeed by doing what God justly did not will to be done, but by loving and approving what God does not love. Therefore, not in this, that what is done is done, do they hinder the will of God, but in this very thing which is done they depart from the will of God. They are evil not by performing something contrary to His will but by loving something contrary to His love. Thus indeed is the will of God always fulfilled, and the evil are not excused, because in them and through them the will of God is fulfilled, since not by their will are they directed to fulfill the will of God, but by His secret disposition, whereby they can not do otherwise, they are led to fulfill His will.

But again you say: "If God willed that all be so as was done, since it is good that all be so, and not be otherwise than was done, why then did He command what was not done and prohibit what was done, since both are good, namely that what was not done was not done, and what was done was done? Why did He not rather command that that only be done which it was good to be, and that that only be not done which likewise it was good not to be?"

XVI. *Why God commands all that He commands.*

But here we should consider more deeply the mode and the cause of command and of prohibition in the same way. For every command or prohibition is made either for his sake to whom it is made, or for his sake by whom it is made, or for the sake of another for whom it is made. Now the whole utility and good of a command whether in that which is commanded to be done or in that which is ordered to be avoided, refers to him alone for whom it is made, whether the latter be the same or different from him to whom it is made or from him by whom it is made. Now the end of the command is the fruit and the utility, the cause, and the good which follows after the accomplishment of the order. This good refers to him only for whom the command is made, and the fulfillment of the command should be his good.

XVII. *All that is called good is good either according to itself or in relation to something.*

Again we must consider that everything that is called good, either is called good according to itself or in relation to something. What is called good according to itself is called substantially good, because it is itself good. But what is called good in relation to something and not according to itself, is not called good substantially, because it itself is not good, but it is so accidentally and denominatively, since good is from it. Therefore, a certain good is good since it itself is good. But another is good since it is good for something, and it itself is not good. What, therefore, is good, good for itself, and good for another is good *in toto*. But what is good, good for itself, and not good for another is good in part, just as what is good, good for another, and not good for itself is good in part.

XVIII. *What is called good according to itself and is universally said to be truly and supremely good.*

There is still another good and one higher than other goods which is truly good, since it is good in itself, and is universally good, since it is good in relation to all and is the good of all. For what is good in itself is truly good, and what is the good of all is universal good. It is itself all good, since it is itself the good of all, and outside it there is no good. Now what is not good in relation to itself is not truly good nor true good, but it is only called good, not because it is itself good, but because good is from it and it benefits.

XIX. *On the three kinds of good.*

Therefore, the highest good is that which is itself good, and in relation to all good is good. But an intermediate good is what is itself good and is good in relation to something. Now the lowest good and, as it were, foreign and denominative only and borrowed and not peculiarly good is that which is good in relation to something and itself is not good. For what it is itself is not good, but what is from it is good. And so in some measure it is also itself good, since good is from it and it benefits. It is good that from it even that be which itself is not good, because unless that should be which itself is not good, what is good of itself would not be. Nor, therefore, do evils furnish good because good is from them, but they serve Him who furnishes and bestows, because "through them" is not "from them."

XX. *That the greater good is that from which there is a greater good.*

Now when two concur in one, namely, what is good and is not good for something, and what is not good and is good for something, both of which can not be, but one alone of the two must be, it is the greater good to be that which is good for something, even if it itself is not good, than that which is only good and is not good for something. For from that which is not good and is good for something, that also must follow which is good and is good for something, certainly a greater good than that which is good alone and not good for something. For what is not good and is good for something would not be good, unless it were from that which is good and is good for something. So what is good because it itself is good, is not good for something because from it there is no good; and what is not good because it iself is not good is good for something because there is good from it. This sometimes happens, and all things are judged in their end, whether they be good or evil, since Scripture manifestly shows that there is one good and this good itself is "to the one the odour of life unto life, to others the odour of death unto death," (2 Cor., 2, 16, not an exact quotation); for from good is evil and from evil good; and good is to the evil unto evil, and evil is to the good unto good. What is good *in toto* is greater than what is so only in part; this is proven in the following way. For every universal good is greater than that which exists in part, and what contributes more and profits more is itself rightly designated greater.

But now let us gather together and collect what has been said, since the fulfillment of every commandment is good for him for whose sake the commandment itself was made, to wit that every good is good either through itself or in relation to something; what is not good through itself and is good for something is a greater good than that which is so through itself alone, and is not good for something; that good which contributes and profits more, is rightly always judged the greater good, since in its fruit is all good, and everything is as great as is its good.

XXI. *That God commands nothing for the sake of Himself, that is, for His own utility or advantage.*

Now, then, let us see all that God commands, whether He commands for His own sake or for the sake of him whom He commands. If He commands for His own sake, what He commands is for His good, and the fulfillment of His own command is good for Him. But how does He command for His own sake who has no need of advancement in Himself, and can not be benefited by good from another, who can not be better? Scripture proclaims this, as well as the fulfiller of the commandment in Scripture: "Thou art my God, for thou hast no need of my goods," (Psal. 15, 2). Therefore, God does not command what He commands for His own sake, but for the sake of him whom He commands, since what is commanded is good for him to whom the good is commanded.

XXII. *That God has that to command to each one which is good for him whom He commands, even if it is not for the good of all.*

Since, therefore, command is made for his sake to whom the command itself is made, the good ought to belong to him to whom the command is ordered. Nothing else should be commanded except what is good for him to whom the command is given. For to no purpose would a command be made, if it were not good for him for whose sake it was made, especially since it would be commanded by the Good who should command nothing except good. For God should not be the author of evil to His creation, nor assume to Himself the causation of that evil, as if by teaching, He might corrupt what He created incorrupt. Thus He has nothing else to command to His creation except that alone which is good for it, from whom it has all which it has good and nothing which it has evil. Since, therefore, the Creator can not be the author of evil for anyone of His creation, He has alone to command what is good for it, so that His instruction is sound, just as His creation was incorrupt.

XXIII. *That God does not have to hinder the good of the whole world, even if that is not good for someone.*

But it happens that what is someone's good is his good and is not good for all; again it happens that what is someone's evil is his evil, and is the good of all, since from it is the good of all, and what is good and is good for someone is less good than what is evil and is evil for someone; for from this itself is greater good, from which is the good of all. The greater good is to be that from which is the greater good, even when that is not good for someone, since it is good *in toto*. Now in compensation for lesser good that good which is greater should not be hindered by Him who is the best. We have said that the greater good is to be good from evil and from good rather than from good alone. So evils had to be permitted to be, since it was good that they be from which good was to be. So God commanded what was good for each and permitted what was good for the whole world, since the good of the whole world which He ought not to hinder, was greater; this was not good which was evil for someone, of which He could not be the author.

So He commanded to each what was good, and what was good for him; by commanding this He signified that He willed this, and His precepts are signs of His will, and are called His will, because they are signs of His will, since He wills and approves and loves and judges as friendly to Himself the goods which He commands; the evils which He prohibits He hates and detests, and He does not find concord and friendship in them; yet these very evils which He does not will, He wishes to be for the sake of the greater good that is from them, which He wishes more. But nothing pertains to us or is demanded of us except only that we do and approve and love within ourselves what is ours and what is our good, just as God also loves and approves only the good which is in us, that we may be like Him in loving and in doing good things, just as He Himself as well only loves and does good things.

When what is our good is commanded us, it is signified to us that God wills this, and it pertains to us so to perceive and so to believe that God wills this which He commands us to do. Yet nothing is done except what He Himself wills to be done, whether we do or do not do what He commands us. If we do good, God has willed it, and He has willed it because it has been done here; He approves what has been done, and what has been done, He wills that it has been done and it is good. If we do evil He wills that we do not do good, and He approves this because it is good; He does not approve the evil which we do because it is evil, and yet He wills what has been done because it has been done, since that is good which has been done, and He himself wills what is good. His omnipotent will is established certain and firm in His good pleasure, approving goods and permitting evils for the sake of the goods; this will can neither be hindered so that what is in it may not be done, nor be weakened at any time so that what is not in it may be done.

XXIV. *That operation and permission of God are signs of what is good to be, even if that is not good; that precept and prohibition are signs of what is good, even if that is not good to be.*

After His will follow its signs, its permission and its operation, and they show what is in it, since the same thing is in them. Precepts and prohibitions are added, and these are themselves also signs and demonstrations of His highest will and eternal complacency through approbation and love; indeed not signs similar to the preceding, but demonstrations only and significations of approbation and complacency in that which is good, and not in what is good to be, whether this be good or evil. So these signify not only this indeed which is in the highest will to be done, but what is in His complacency and approbation if it be done, and yet that both are of His will, and that this is good even if it be not done, but that the other is good thus, that it be done.

XXV. *That the good pleasure of God is sometimes with reference to a thing, sometimes with reference to the doing of a thing.*

Whoever, therefore, wishes to make a distinction in speaking of the will of God, can say this. It must be considered carefully how God, indeed, wills this in one which it iself is, but in another only this, that it itself is. In this, indeed, by which He wills it itself which is, He approves the thing, but in this in which He wills it itself, that it is, He approves the doing of the thing. But in this in which He approves the thing and not the doing of the thing, He wills something and still He does not yet will to be what He wills. But in this, that He approves the doing of a thing and not the thing itself, He wills something to be, but not yet, however, does He will it itself which He wills to be. For it is not good that all be which is itself good, just as sometimes what is evil to be is itself not evil. God does not will except what is good, even when it is not good that this be. He does not will to be anything that is not good to be, even when it itself is not good. When He wills something because it is good, and does not will this itself to be because it is not good, His will is fulfilled; His will does not remain without accomplishment, even when the thing is not accomplished, because He so wills and what He wills is good. When He does not will something, because it is evil, and wills it itself to be, because it is good, His will is accomplished when the thing is accomplished, because he so wills and what he wills is good. His will is always fulfilled, and never is His good pleasure frustrated, because what He wills is always good and is always as He wills.

And these five have been presented: good pleasure, permission, operation, precept, and prohibition. Good pleasure is distinguished in this whereby the doing of the thing is approved. And operation is distinguished in this that does and in this that helps to do, because some things God does by doing what he does alone, other things by helping to do what He does not do alone. Precept is divided into that which is done extrinsically through speech and into that which is done intrinsically through aspiration. In all these it is clear what was to be said of the will of God, what is His good pleasure and the sign of His good pleasure. On this account also His wills are called many, although His will is one, because the signs of His will are many, as it is written: "Great are the works of the Lord: sought out according to all His wills," (Psal. 110, 2), on account of these signs which from it and according to it are many. We have spoken here about the will of God, since it is the first cause of all things, just as we had planned, and we have performed our task according to our understanding. There are many other things perhaps which cannot be comprehended and which escape our understanding and speech.

XXVI. *On the order of things, in the first and the second and the third.*

The order of things, therefore, is so constituted that after the first follow the next. The first of all things is the will of the Creator, since from it are all things. After it follow those things which are from it. First are those things which are in it, second are those which are from it. Those which are in it are eternal, and have neither grade nor succession, since they exist in unity and do not pass on in eternity. Those things which are from it were created by it, and they took their cause from it, not their substance in it, since divine nature did not beget substantially from itself what it created causally; for He who made and what was made cannot by nature be the same.

Those things, therefore, which were made are not one, and among these certain things are first, certain second, not first with reference to first, but first with reference to second. For what are second to the first before them are first with reference to the second from them; and the second from them are third with reference to the first. Those things in the will of God that are eternal and invisible are first of all. Those things from the will of God that are temporal and invisible are second after the first; those that are temporal and visible are third after the second. In the visible things themselves those that are rational are nearer the invisible, because the invisible in it are those that they are rational.

Therefore, in the first place there are placed in the divine mind the primordial and invisible and uncreated causes of all things to be created, in the second place the angelic nature invisible indeed but created, in the third place human nature visible and created, visible according to something and invisible according to something, in the fourth place corporeal creation *in toto* and temporal *in toto*. After the first uncreated and invisible causes, therefore, our consideration will pass on and proceed to the angelic nature rational and invisible, then to human nature visible and rational, about which it was first proposed to give full treatment. For we have indeed treated first of visible things which are last, so that from those things which are evident we might the more fittingly lead the human mind to the knowledge of hidden things.

PART FIVE

On the creation of the angels, and on free will, and on other matters which pertain to the angelic nature, namely its office and hierarchy.

I. *What must be inquired about the angels.**

After all that has been said on the beginning of the world, and that has been presented first for this reason, that we might ascend from the visible to the invisible, you now propose an inquiry into the nature of the angels, when the angels were created and of what nature they were made when they were first created, then of what nature they became when they were divided by aversion and conversion, and how they were disposed when they were sentenced to damnation and to glorification. You propose an inquiry into their number and orders and excellence and different gifts, their duties and names, the government and guidance of God in them, and many other things which follow

---

*This is the traditional heading of this section. The manuscripts of our text have nothing here.

upon these and which are contained in these. So, as best we can, we ought to develop a systematic exposition on a multitude of hidden things, but we ought not to promise what we can not carry out.

II. *That in the beginning angels were created.*

Scripture says that "Wisdom hath been created before all things," (Eccli. 1, 4), and we know that created wisdom is called rational creation, since indeed wisdom itself is as light shining from light, not an illumining light. For that wisdom which is wise is not this created wisdom, nor is it a creation, nor does it have its being from another, just as it does not have its being wise from another. But this wisdom which does not have its being wise from itself, nor its being from itself, is itself created, and has beginning.

Scripture tells when this wisdom was made, since "Wisdom hath been created before all things." Certain contradictions seem to arise from these assertions. For if wisdom hath been created before all things, all things were made after it. Heaven and earth were made after it, and it itself was made before heaven and earth. Again, if in the beginning God created heaven and earth, nothing was made before heaven and earth, nor was wisdom itself made before heaven and earth, which likewise cannot stand. On this account, lest the testimonies of holy Scriptures seem to be contradictory, which it is utterly wrong to think, we seek knowledge of the truth, since in the truth what is true is not contradictory.

III. *That the rational creation was made first of all in dignity, since to it is referred the foundation of all other things, just as its own foundation is referred to God, since it alone was made to the likeness of God.*

We say that the rational creation was made first, and after it the corporeal creation was made, yet not in time, but only in cause and retrospect and dignity. For the foundation of the corporeal creation itself is referred to the rational creation, and is perfected according to it, just as its own foundation is referred to the Creator alone, since it alone was made according to Him. Therefore the rational creation alone is reported as having been made according to the likeness of God, and it is not said that any creature save the rational alone was made to the likeness of God, although every creature had its cause and likeness in the divine reason and in the eternal providence from which and according to which it was perfected in its subsistence. But there is a great difference and a great diversity between having likeness in God, and having God Himself as a likeness. For although in God nothing can, as it were, be less than or diverse or different from God, yet it is far different to say that something has been made to the likeness of that which is in God, both in His reason and in His providence, and that something has been made to the likeness of God and is like God. For in God, indeed, all things were, before they were in Himself according to the reason and the cause and the providence from which they were to be, but individual things, so to speak, were less than perfect and each was this something and not the whole according to the reason and differentiation of each, all of which reason contained; it was greater in the whole and, as it were, superabounded in individual things.

So individually things were not this whole, but individual things were in the whole, since the whole was in relation to the whole, and individual things in relation to the individual things. Yet for God there was nothing less in the part than in the whole, because part and whole were one; but by one reason and providence those things were differentiated which were to be in part and in whole, and were to be less in the part than in the whole. So these, indeed, had less in reason, since they were to be less from reason. Yet God did not have less, who was entire in the whole and perfect and one. For this reason, therefore, not one something, either this or that, could have sufficed in the divine reason as an exemplar for the rational creature, according to whose likeness the latter should be formed; rather, in a manner of speaking, it took God entire, that it might be made the image of Him Himself, and it was represented as completely imitating His perfection, so that, just as God was spirit and was one, and in Him was the whole according to reason and providence and foreknowledge and cause, so this itself was spiritual, capable in one of foreknowledge and foresight and reason and understanding of all. There shone forth a perfect image imitating its author, and there appeared, as it were, itself in another, and one and the same.

There were found also in the second those things which were even in the first according to emulation and imitation and image and likeness, reasons and causes and likenesses and dispositions and provisions of future things which were to be made. When those things were made, which were made, they were made to the likeness of these things which had been made in the second, just as the latter were made to the likeness of those which had not been made in the first. According to reasoning and consideration of this kind corporeal creation is in the third place coming after rational creation which is second, since it was made in relation to the latter, just as the rational itself was made in relation to the first uncreated nature.

IV. *That in the first beginning were made simultaneously all corporeal things in matter and all incorporeal in angelic nature.*

But so far as pertains to moments and intervals and spaces of time, we now state this as more fitting and closer to the truth, that simultaneously at one time and at the beginning of time, when times themselves began, there was made or created equally the matter of all visible things and the nature of the invisible in angelic and spiritual creation. Nor were they in time nor was there begun one without the other, nor was one before the other, but both were simultaneous in time and with time; yet that was prior in relation to which the other was made, in which were the exemplars of wisdom, and of these exemplars the effects and expressions are those things which were founded visible. In this way wisdom was created the first of all things.

Now those who say that the angels were created before heaven and earth, and that they subsisted before all things which were made mutable, those who compute periods and years and ages during which before the establishment of the world they served God, assert that time began with the world and that there was no time before the world, since there mutability did not exist; yet, they say that the angels were without change and without time before the world was made, and that when the world began then first began time, because mutability began, and that the world was made at the beginning of time. But we on the other hand rather approve what has been said to the best of our knowledge, preserving reverence for those hidden things regarding which we think that nothing should be asserted rashly. According to this mode we have already defined that all things, both visible and invisible, were created simultaneously, as Scripture says: "He that liveth for ever created all things together," (Eccli. 18, 1).

V. *That both corporeal and incorporeal natures were made without form according to something and formed according to something.*

Therefore all things were founded simultaneously, since we believe that equally at one and the same time the matter of all visible things began, and the nature of the invisible, both unformed according to something and formed according to something. For just as the matter of all visible and corporeal things at that beginning of primary creation had the form of confusion and did not have the form of disposition, until it was afterwards formed and yielded order and disposition, so spiritual and angelic nature at its own creation through wisdom and distinction was formed according to disposition of nature; yet it did not have that form which it was afterwards to receive through love and conversion to its creator, but it was unformed without that form which was to be formed from it.

VI. *Of what nature were angels when they were first made.*

Still further on this point, of what nature were angels made, we propose a more carefully planned investigation. For we have said when they were made, that they were made in the beginning, and were the first creation, before which nothing was made, according to which there was made that, too, which was made with it. Wherefore also before all things it itself was made according to something, which is the form and cause of all. But we must show next of what nature angels were then made in that first beginning and first subsistence and commencement of their creation, in that which they began to be first, and of what nature that was which was first to have been founded in them.

VII. *That they were not made of preëxisting matter, just as corporeal things.*

For spiritual nature was not created in preëxisting matter, just as we have said that corporeal nature was founded, since it is not so, nor is it like that simple substance in which what it is and from what it is are the same, because all that it is is one and simple and undivided and immaterial. But it was made in its own nature and being, perfect in so far as pertains to spiritual substance, not as a lump or confused matter, or a rude mass or heap, or gathered accumulation or any of these things unrelated to it, but personally distinct and expressed and marked by the number of spiritual and intelligible differentiation, as a rational multitude and intelligible subsisting spirits, having inborn reason and a form of concreated wisdom and a spiritual quality of understanding, capable, according to the mode and measure of their foundation, of higher progress and of the illumination that was to come upon them, also possessing free will implanted then at the very beginning and equally innate by which without violence they could be turned of their own will to either of two things, in the one aided without compulsion, in the other abandoned without oppression.

VIII. *On the four peculiarities of the angelic nature.*

If anyone, therefore, should ask of what character spiritual nature was made or founded in its beginning, these are the four things which we have proposed and have said were attributed to the angels at their foundation, namely: first, a simple and immaterial substance; second, distinction of person; third, a rational form of wisdom and understanding; but fourth, the free power of inclining their will and choice either to good or to evil. There follows after this an important consideration, necessary for the understanding of truth, on their spiritual substance and on their wisdom and on their freedom of will and on other matters which relate to these, whether all had those things equal which were equally present in all. For equally present in all were those things which were common to all, of which nothing was expected which was not in all. But not yet is it clear whether that was equal which was equally present in them. And here we must inquire first concerning substance, afterwards concerning form, and then concerning power. For in persons there is substance, in wisdom form, in will power. Indeed to substance pertains subtlety of nature, but to form clarity of understanding, to power, moreover, intellectual motion and appetite and aptitude of the rational will.

IX. *On the difference of spiritual substance.*

This, therefore, is sought, whether those rational essences, which were spirits and simple in nature and immortal in life, were created of one subtlety or purity, whether of the same force or by whatever other name what is good essence should be signified, whether it be rightly called some better or more appropriate form. For thus the nature of bodies demonstrates itself. There are certain bodies more solid and firm; others appear purer and more cleansed and clean and bright and having, as it were, better and more worthy substance or essence or form; others light and well joined and visible and whole and more uncorrupted; and others fragile and close to corruption and infirm and feculent and gross and ponderous and unsightly. Yet in the composition and order of the universe that diversity is beautiful in which less good is not evil and different good is greater good. Therefore in this way it is reasonable that those spiritual natures also which universally were well created, received, suitable to their purity and excellence, not unworthy differences both in essence and in form, and then at the very beginning of their creation, grades, whereby some could be constituted superior and others inferior according to the regulation of the wisdom of God who creates all things good and orders them well.

X. *On the difference of knowledge.*

For those who were created more subtle in nature and more acute in wisdom were rightly constituted superior in dignity; but those who were founded less subtle in nature and less acute in wisdom were rightly given an inferior order in dignity, yet in such a way that those who were constituted as more excellent were preëminent without pride, and those who were placed lower were subject without misery.

XI. *On the difference of free will.*

But if anyone wishes to assert the freedom of the will itself as different according to the different virtue of nature and force of wisdom and knowledge and understanding, there is no one who could reasonably object, since, just as a different vigor and subtlety of nature do not prove infirmity, and less knowledge does not indicate ignorance of wisdom, so an inferior freedom does not impose any necessity on the choice of the will.

XII. *In what they were created similar, and in what dissimilar.*

Therefore that they were spirits, that they were life, that they were indissoluble or immortal, in all these they were equal. But that they were powerful in nature, that they were subtle in essence, that they were wise in understanding, and in freedom of will were ready and apt for either choice, this was not equal in all, and yet it was sufficiently in all. These invisible distinctions of invisible and intelligible beings He alone by nature could weigh, and He alone by His wisdom could comprehend the measure and the mode and the end of each by whose power all was founded and by whose providence all was ordered. But we with dim understanding timidly approach these matters, and with a realization of our weak knowledge we grope at those things which we do not comprehend with strength.

What force, therefore, and how much power belonged to invisible essences, or what wisdom, and what kind of liberty, and how much in these was common to all, and whatever thing peculiar or singular and different was granted to each, is quite ineffable and removed from human understanding. For the divine power alone and the divine wisdom is confined neither by limit nor measure, and the freedom of eternal choice and the pleasure of immutable will is never constrained by any diminution or limitation of necessity, but it is absolute and dominant, superexcellent and efficacious, and singularly perfect through the freedom of its inclination and full of its own power.

Now all that has been created is in part, that is, in part powerful and wise, and in part free, since neither is every effect subject to the power of the creature, nor is every secret manifest to its wisdom, nor does every event follow its choice, nor serve its will, but creatures have power only according to something and they are wise according to something and they are free. So their power must be determined and their wisdom determined and their freedom determined. But power pertains to operation, wisdom to knowledge, freedom to will.

XIII. *On their threefold power.*

There results at first a threefold distinction in their power, since one was the power which they had received in relation to themselves, another which they had received in relation to one another amongst themselves, but another which they had received in relation to those things which in ordered foundation had been under them. The first power belonged to virtue, the second to domination, the third to administration. In that power which they had received in themselves, they were all different, but in that which they had received among themselves some were excellent, but in that which they had received under themselves they were different and excellent. In that power which they individually had received in themselves, his own nature served each unto accomplishment. But in that which they had mutually in relation to one another the obedience of others was subject to some. But in that power which they possessed in relation to lower things, the subject creature gave service to each according to the virtue of nature and the dignity of office. These matters which have been said on the first power of rational nature furnish the first occasion for future investigation.

XIV. *On their threefold knowledge.*

In the first consideration of their wisdom also a threefold distinction is presented to us, since they were illumined in a threefold manner, and simply in relation to three things. There was a threefold knowledge in them, that they might recognize that they had been made similarly, and by whom they had been made, and with what they had been made. In this, that they were made, they had received the knowledge of good and evil, that they might know what must be sought by them or what rejected according to the power of virtue and the freedom of the will in them. But they also had received knowledge of Him by whom they had been made, that they might understand and know their beginning and end, from whom they had proceeded by foundation, and to Him they had been bound by intention to turn. But they had received knowledge of that with which they had been made, that they might know what they owed one another according to the divine dispensation and order, or to what extent in those things which by foundation had been subject to them they might exercise authority without presumption according to the power granted to them by God. In this manner those spiritual substances were founded wise and discerning and understanding, and in all these things they were as wise as was befitting incipient nature or necessary for obtaining the reward of virtue.

XV. *Whether angels were made perfect or imperfect.*

For many do not know and are ignorant, thinking that there was in them a kind of superabundant knowledge of those things which do not pertain to reality, an understanding and providence and prescience of future things, namely, those which were to come as regards themselves, that otherwise they were imperfect and ignorant, and not as they should have been complete and full, such as it was not fitting for the Omnipotent and the Perfect and the Good to make. But they do not discern that to make something with a view to perfection so that what is imperfect may be perfected, and on this account imperfect, that it may be imperfect first, but then perfect, in order that it may be perfected by Him by whom it was made imperfect that it be perfected, is not imperfection on the part of the maker nor a disgrace to what is made, since He who made could have made otherwise, and what was made ought not to have been made otherwise. But here too it must be said that it is perfect according to something, since it has all that it ought to have, even if it should not have all that it is to have.

XVI. *That "perfect" is applied in three modes.*

For perfection exists in these three modes, and is conveniently designated perfect. For there is "perfect" according to time, and "perfect" according to nature, and universally "perfect." The first perfect is, as it were, the beginning of perfection, making perfect according to time, and there follows what is greater, perfect according to nature, and the third is greatest and superexcellent, universally perfect.

XVII. *According to time.*

That is perfect according to time which has whatever time requires and is suitable to be had according to time.

XVIIII. *According to nature.*

That is perfect according to nature which has all that either was given or was due its nature.

XIX. *The universally perfect.*

That is universally perfect to which nothing is lacking. The first perfection is of a founded nature, the second perfection is of glorified nature, the third and true perfection is of a created nature.

XX. *That the angels were founded perfect according to the first perfection.*

And in this way it is not remarkable nor is it to be brought in question why angels were not founded perfect, because they were created in the first perfection, and for the second under the third, since, just as they can not reach the third, so likewise should they not have begun with the second. Otherwise, they could not have found a place for progressing and an avenue for advancing into better, unless there had been left after the first gifts of nature a means whereby they could have increased or failed.

XXI. *Whether they had foreknowledge of their future lot.*

Here the question is raised whether angels were prescient of their lot, and in the wisdom given them knew what was to befall them. For something of a twofold difficulty seems to confront us. For if those who were to be evil, foreknew their fall, and knew the punishment which had to follow their ruin and was destined not to end, forseeing such great evils threatening them, either they wished to avoid them but could not, and were wretched, or they could and would not and were foolish and perverse. But if they did not know, they were blind, and realized not whither they were going, and accidentally and fortuitously stepped forth to proceed whither they knew not. It seems, as it were, to offer something of absurdity, if this be said, and it seems to be better established and to be more fitting that they be said to have been cognizant of those things which were to be. Again another reason which we have raised against this is in opposition, and an obstacle can easily arise on either point for weak minds, unless an agreement be reached.

On this account we say that they were not prescient of their lot, nor was there given them knowledge of those things which were to be upon them, since it was not right that they should thus have free election of will without hope or fear in either choice. Therefore there was shown them what had to be done, not what was to be, so that they might not seem to be impelled by any necessity of providence, but to be directed by reason and to be turned by their own will in both. So it was good and suitable, and the work of God is thus not worthy of censure, because He so made as was good.

XXII. *Of what nature they were founded, good or evil, just or unjust, happy or wretched.*

But many other questions also are raised regarding that spiritual nature, which the curiosity of the human mind does not suffer to be at rest. They inquire whether angels were created good or evil, just or unjust, happy or wretched, and perhaps certain other things like these. And, because there are many other things which accumulate in inquiry, we can not meet all with lengthy answer. However, then in that first beginning and commencement of origin, which human consideration may accept as very brief and momentary and of a simple instant without delay and interval in the first substance, appearing from nothing into something, that human consideration may understand what the angels had first of all, we declare that this alone is discovered in founded beings which the nature of foundation conferred. For what they took they received entire. There could not be anything in them from them, since all that is from them is posterior to them. So all that they were made they themselves did not make, but they were only made and what they were made they were made entirely good. For if what they were made they were made evil, it is the fault of the Maker not the made, since they could not be anything else nor could they themselves then bring it about when they were made that they be anything other than they were made. So from the Maker, when they first were, they were all that they were, and they had received all that they were, and they had nothing from themselves who had both received from nothing that which they were, and from the Creator that they were.

But the most excellent Creator could not have been the author of evil, and so all was good that they had from Him, and all was good, since all was from Him. In this way we prove that the angels were good when they were first made, and that they all were made good, since they were made by the Good who can not make evil. So they were good and not evil, and as they were good, so also were they just and happy, but with that goodness and justice and happiness which incipient nature had received, not which it itself had made or had merited by making. For if they are called good, they were good, just as all that was good which the Good had made. If they were better, as they were, they were better in proportion as they had so been made, not in proportion as they themselves had made or were making. Similarly too as to the fact that they are called just, this alone belonged to them, that they were not unjust, and as to the fact that they are called happy, that they were not in a state of wretchedness. However, they are most truly declared neither to be just according to merit, nor unjust according to blame, just as they are not declared happy according to glorification or completeness, or wretched according to torment or punishment. Perhaps it would be clearer and more evident to the understanding for one to say that they were founded neither good nor evil, neither just nor unjust, neither turned to God nor turned away from Him, neither happy nor wretched. For who calls them good, signifies virtue; who just, merit; who turned to God, love; who happy, glorification.

XXIII. *On their free will in the first beginning of their foundation, when they began to subsist.*

Now what was first beginning was not willing or doing among them who without their willing or doing were made only to will and to do. For willing or doing has motion, and from this to that, and succession and delay. This can not belong to incipient beginning, which begins merely and no longer still is, but is first and not thereafter. But willing by will is willing, when the will is moved and presently does something; here there is this and that, and from this to that which the will preceded, from which there was willing when willing as yet was not, but the will was only in order that willing might be from this or doing which did not belong to that which begins. Therefore the simple beginning and the first origin of nascent nature is not so to be understood.

But it itself is one thing and this only and no more without space and movement and delay, all of which follow thereafter, in which there is willing and doing and procession of movements and actions after the first beginning. Now from the time that the will was moved to wish, what was moved freely was from the will because it was moved through itself and not by another's impulse. This itself was merit and was called good or evil, because it was free and was of itself. Then they began to merit from the time that they began to move by will. This was after the first beginning, and was from the first beginning; it was not in it, because it was only from it. Now from the time there was will, there was freedom, because there is freedom of the will, since it was able to move of itself so that it might go beyond hither or thither without compulsion whether aided or abandoned, since there is freedom of the will from the time that the will itself is in the very first beginning. There was free choice in them, because the will could move or be borne according to its desire in either direction.

XXIV. *What free will is.*

For spontaneous movement or voluntary desire is free will; free, indeed, in this, that it is voluntary, but will in this, that it is desire. But the power itself and the aptitude of the will is the freedom whereby it moves in either direction, and it is said to be the free choice of the will. Now moving voluntarily and being born by spontaneous desire, this is to choose with power and to judge with freedom, in which free will consists. On this account the angels were made of free choice that they might move by voluntary desire, but according to the election of the will and the inclination of their desire, without compulsion. Yet what was first in them was not to begin to move, nor to choose, nor to desire, since their first beginning was indeed simple; yet free will was already at that time, since there was will in which this was present and from which this followed, because will immediately moved from this and was lead by spontaneous desire to its own election.

XXV. *That free will always looks not to the present but to the future, not to all but to the contingent only.*

But this also must be known that free will, which we said was of the first beginning on account of the will which was in the first beginning, was not itself as regards the first beginning, since free will does not refer to present time but to those things which are to be afterwards in that which is contingent. For all that is determined can not be other than it is while it is; if it can be other, it can be other afterwards; it can not be other then when it is that which it is, but afterwards so that it ceases to be this which it is and begins to be something else which it is not. For what can be in the present, indeed can be, but can not be of the present; if it can be of the present, yet it can not be except with reference to the future. What, therefore, they themselves were first made, they were not able not to be, because they were made this entire; they themselves did not make, and they were not able not to be this when they first were, since they then were this itself and began to be only. If they had power to be something else, because there was free choice, yet they did not have power to be something else then, because they were this, but to cease to be this which they then were and to begin to be something else which they were not. For they could not be what they were not, unless they should cease first to be what they were, and then afterwards should begin to be what they were not, since free will can not be regarding the present, even if it itself is in the present, but always looks to future events, and only to those which are in that which is contingent.

Future things in truth which are to be of necessity do not follow free will, but are fixed without motion in relation to one course only, and are not susceptible to the alternate courses of what is contingent. Thus, therefore, free will was then in them, not indeed that they then might be other than they were, but, by the power which they had in that which they were, that they might cease to be this and might begin to be something else which they were not. Thus, indeed, reason answers those who rather studiously inquire regarding the first state of the angels, regarding the first beginning of their existence, of what kind they were first made, regarding their nature, regarding their wisdom, and regarding the freedom of their will as has been set forth.

XXVI. *On the aversion and fall of the evil angels, and on the conversion and confirmation of the good angels.*

After this, reflection leads us to inquire of what kind they became when they were divided by aversion and conversion. For that they were first, they were one according to some thing, because they were all good; and that they were good they were so not by their own making but by having been made so. In this, therefore, they were one, because they had been made good, and were not yet anything else than they had been made, because then they had been first made, and had not done anything before. But they began to be divided from that which they had been made, so as presently to become something else, either progressing over that so as to be good, or falling below that so as to be evil. This is conversion and aversion, whereby they who were one and good by nature were divided, so that some are good above that through justice, others evil below that through sin. For conversion made them just and aversion unjust. For both were of the will, and there was freedom of the will in both cases. And therefore both are imputed by merit and both are judged by merit, whether it be judged for good merit unto glory, of for evil merit unto punishment.

XXVII. *How in those who fall guilt averts grace; in those who stand firm grace aids merit.*

Now those who were converted to good moved voluntarily with grace co-operating without compulsion, but those who were averted from good of their own accord were cast headlong, grace abandoning them without oppression.

Those who were converted moved well because they had grace cooperating. But those who were averted were not cast headlong because they did not have grace cooperating, but were abandoned by grace because they were averted and cast headlong. Those who were averted were not averted first and then abandoned, because they did not fall with grace, and those who were converted were not converted first and then assumed because they did not advance without grace, but those who were averted were abandoned in this very act itself, and those who were converted were assumed in the very act itself, abandoned on account of aversion and assumed to conversion.

XXVIII. *That in the will alone is there both justice and injustice.*

Since, indeed, in the movement of the rational will justice and guilt were found equally, because by the movement of the will it was brought about that they were made evil on being averted from the good in which they were, and likewise by the movement of the will it was brought about that they were good on being converted from the good in which they were to the good in which so far they were not, on this account in the movement of the rational will all merit consisted in what they were, either good or evil. Therefore both good and evil must be sought there where justice and guilt are, since justice is good and guilt is evil. Guilt itself was not the will, since the will, having been given by God, was not evil; nor was movement of the will evil, since it was from the will, and was of the will, and the will had received motion from God; nor was that toward which there was movement of the will evil, since it was something, and all that was something was from God, and was good.

XXIX. *That sin is neither substance nor of substance but the privation of good.*

What, therefore, was evil there, unless that the movement of the will was not toward what it ought to have been? And it was not for this reason, because it was toward something else toward which it ought not to have been. Nor yet was it sin to be toward this but not to be toward that, because if that were not, even if this were, there would be no sin. Thus just as the rational mind had received the will, and received motion by will, so also it had received those things to which there could be motion by the will licitly; motion toward those was motion according to measure, and motion according to measure was motion according to justice. If it had moved only toward those, it would have moved according to justice and it would have been a just will, since it would have moved according to justice. But when it moved toward those things which had not been conceded, it moved outside of measure, and in this it did not move according to measure.

And there its evil was not moving according to measure. Nor was its evil moving toward what it moved, but not moving according to measure toward what it did not move, because if it had moved according to measure, it would not have moved even toward this sin. But moving beyond measure by the will was to seek what had not been granted, wherein was not moving according to measure, and this was evil, but it itself was the occasion of evil; for, since the will moved beyond measure, it did not move according to measure. Yet its evil was not moving toward what it moved, but not moving according to measure, according to which it did not move. And if this had not been, there would have been no evil. Thus this evil was done to the will averting itself and transgressing measure, because it became shameful and depraved and unordered, issuing forth and not keeping the bounds and law of its beauty. But the will that moved rightly and was fashioned according to the will of the Creator was converted to Him by whom it was controlled, and its good was not moving beyond His will from whom it was.

XXX. *How God turns all the will and power of the angels to the order and disposition of His own will.*

This also must be considered, how God governs those invisible and spiritual natures. For if they are free of will, they do what they will, and if they do what they will, how does what they do depend on the decision of God? For if we say that they do what God wills, because they neither will nor are able to will anything other than what God wills, who grants them even willing itself just as He concedes them power, although this is sometimes granted concerning the good, it is in no way approved concerning the evil. To the evil, indeed, God grants power alone not will, because, although it is by His permission that they do evil, yet it is not by His inspiration that they will the evil. For God is the orderer of evil wills, not the creator.

How then do they do anything but what God wills, who never will except what God does not will, because they always will evil which God never wills? For if they do what they will, and will what God does not will, how do they do what God wills? Again if God does not will what they do, why does He permit them to do what He does not will, although nothing can be done except with His permission or permitted except with His will? Hence we are forced to investigate rather carefully how the just regulation of God governs rational nature especially that which by its unjust will is at variance with the divine will. Hence we shall consider four general modes of divine government in these rational natures whereby they are disposed and ordered in all that they do, so that even the evils themselves which are what they are, contrary to the will of God, since they are not approved by God because they are evil, do not issue forth beyond His disposition, and in these cases it is good and pleasing that they are ordered. Therefore God regulates and rules according to His will those who by a base and unjust will strive against His will, so that they are lead and disposed according to His will, who rise against it to accomplish what pleases it to be done, by a will that displeases it.

XXXI. *That God restrains the will and the power of the evil angels in four ways.*

But this regulation, as we have said, is accomplished in four ways: either by the limit of naturally conferred power, or by the miracle of temporarily applied impossibility, or by the obstacle of difficulty offered from without, or by the judgment of disposition operating within. The limit of naturally conferred power is the extent of power naturally granted. The miracle of temporarily applied impossibility is when that natural power itself is checked by the sudden and hidden virtue of the divine presence without external impediment. The obstacle of difficulty offered from without is when by divine assent through other powers opposing from without the wills of other powers are prevented from being able to come to accomplishment. The judgment of disposition operating from within is when that divine power itself, which presides in every creature, turns even those wills which have arisen contrary to its own will, to accomplish its own will. Therefore in these four ways God disposes the base wills of angels and of men to the power of His will, so that even in that in which there is what is displeasing because it is evil, there is pleasure because it is what has been ordained.

XXXII. *On the hidden disposition of God, by which He turns even evil wills to His own will and disposes them according to His own will.*

Now regarding the manner of the divine regulation, whereby governing by hidden and invisible operation it tempers and inclines even evil wills to its own will this view must be held, that God be believed to give not corruption but order to evil wills. For every will is prior to willing, and willing indeed is always with reference to something, because everyone who wills wills something. Now will is not always with reference to something until there is willing, because not everyone who has will has it with reference to something, until by the will itself, willing and willing something begins, just as not everyone who has vision has it immediately with reference to something, until by vision itself, seeing and seeing something begins. Yet one can have vision even in darkness when he does not see, but he can not see except in light when he sees something. Thus too one can have will, and not with reference to anything, but he can not will except with reference to something. Therefore every will belongs to someone, but it is not always with reference to something, until it begins to will. But all willing also belongs to someone because it is in someone, and is with reference to something because it is concerning something.

Now every will either is good if it is so from nature or according to justice, or it is evil if it is beyond nature or contrary to justice. Therefore the evil will has vice from itself whereby it is evil, but order is from God whereby through willing the will is with reference either to this or to that. Therefore in the will is vice, and this itself is evil, and from it the will is evil. Now in willing there is vice in so far as willing is from an evil will, and there is order, in so far as it is with reference to this or to that from Him who disposes it. When willing itself is with reference to this something, it is evil which is with reference to this, because it is by an evil will. But what is rather with reference to this than to that is good, because there is order, and it is from Him who disposes well. Therefore evil will can be corrupted in itself, and be resolved through its own vice, which is not given to it from elsewhere, but it can not through willing be carried beyond itself except where a way is open to it. Whoever opens a way to it as it rushes headlong where it wills to ruin, in a certain measure inclines it, yet not by impelling but by permitting and not by holding; nor is He the author of its rushing headlong but the orderer of its course.

"The Lord," David says, "hath bid him curse," (2 Kings 16, 10), and I, he says, summoned Nabuchodonosor, my servant to destroy the earth, (Cf. Jer. 25, 9); and "in that day the Lord shall hiss for the fly, that is in the uttermost parts of the river of Egypt, and for the bee that is in the land of Assyria. And they shall come, and shall all of them rest in the torrents of the valleys, and in the holes of the rocks." In all these God is shown manifestly, in order to fulfill His just judgments, to excite to willing, the evil wills of men or demons in whatever ways and on whatever occasions He wills whether within or without, and to direct them to accomplishment, and to order them to subsistence; in all of these things that they are the evil wills is not of God, but that they are ordered. Now this eternal disposition of Him who presides invisibly is so hidden that it even escapes the notice of evil wills in which it is, who think that they are directed only by their own choice, because they feel that without compulsion they are moving by their own desire. For since they are not impelled, in no way do they understand that they are being directed, and they are unaware that they have this disposition preceding them so that they may be ordered, because they do not perceive it as it drives them back so that they may be cast headlong. On other modes of divine government we do not wish to expound at length here, because they are more evident of themselves, and they do not raise much serious inquiry.

XXXIII. *On the orders of angels; how many were founded by God in the beginning.*

On the orders of angels, authority has promulgated this, that nine orders of angels were founded by God in the beginning, namely: angels, archangels, principalities, powers, virtues, dominations, thrones, cherubim, and seraphim, so that by the addition of man the denary of celestial perfection was completed. For not as certain men think was the creation of man thus provided for the restoration of angels, as if man would not have been made, unless the angels had fallen, but man is said to have been made for restoring and replacing the number of the fallen angels because, when man on being created afterwards was conducted to that place whence they had fallen, the number of that society which had been diminished by these falling is repaired by man.

For nine orders of angels were founded from the beginning, and of these those who fell, since they all agreed simultaneously in one act of evil, made of themselves, as it were, one order of their perverted society. But tradition has it that some fell from each of the orders. Wherefore, the Apostle Paul also when he was making mention of the tyranny of evil spirits called them "principalities and powers of darkness," (Cf. Ephes. 6, 12), that he might show evidently that each now exercises the same office in evil out of perversity that he received from creation for accomplishing good. Yet nowhere in Scripture do I find the evil spirits called seraphim, since although they may still possess other gifts in evil after their fall, yet they could not in any way have had charity in the love of God.

XXXIV. *Whether more remained than fell.*

Now on the number of the fallen no certain authority is found. Yet it certainly seems probable that more remained than fell. For the prophet, when he pointed to the fiery chariots, said in consolation: "There are more with us than with them," (4 Kings 6, 16). Hence we conjecture that there are more elect angels than false. There are those who say that as many elect will ascend from men to the number of the angels as it is established that there remained elect angels, on account of Scripture which says: "He appointed the bounds of people according to the number of the angels of God."* If this is true, since there are many more false among men than elect, more false men are found than elect angels. Now if there are more false men than elect angels, since there are more elect angels than false angels, there will be more false men than false angels.

How then is it true that each one is said to have two angels detailed to him, one evil for attacking, and one good for defending, when the number of men transcends the number of angels? For if among men there are more evil than good, and among the angels there are more good than evil, since it has been stated that there will be as many elect men as there are good angels, it is established without any doubt that there are more good men than there are evil angels; and there are many more evil men than evil angels, because there are

---

*(Cf. Deut. 32, 8 which is quite different: "He appointed the bounds of people according to the number of the children of Israel").

more evil men than good, although there are more good men than evil angels; but perhaps it should be said for the reason that the human race does not subsist simultaneously, but in the succession of time some follow others, that those who among men subsist simultaneously with the angels can be compared in number, although they surpass the latter in totality. Yet since this can not be certain, it is better relegated among those hidden things in which ignorance is not blamed and presumption is rebuked.*

XXXV. *On the giving of distinctive names to angels.*

On the giving of names to spirits we think that this should especially be kept in mind here: that names have not been given them on account of themselves but on account of us. For those who are known to themselves by contemplation, become known to us by the giving of names. Therefore those gifts of graces in each are marked by the name, not those which have been given singly but excellently in participation. For in that heavenly country where there is a fullness of the good, although certain things have been given excellently, nothing is possessed singly. For all things are in all not indeed equally, because some possess certain things more highly than others, but commonly, because all have all.

Likewise it must be known that higher orders received all gifts of grace more highly and perfectly, and yet by merely taking their names from special excellences they leave the rest to the orders following after them for giving names. Thus, for example, the seraphim, which is considered the most excellent order of all, received not only love but also knowledge of the God-Head and the other gifts of virtues more highly than all others, yet taking its name from the more excellent gift, that is charity, it left the others to the orders following after it for giving names. The next order after this was called the cherubim from the next gift, that is knowledge of truth, which is likewise interpreted fullness of knowledge, just as the seraphim is called ardent or burning on account of the fire of love. This should also be the understanding regarding the orders following.

XXXVI. *Whether all heavenly spirits are sent.*

This question also is raised, whether all those spirits of heaven are sent to announce exterior things. Certain men think that there are some in that multitude who go abroad in accordance with their office to announce exterior things, and that there are others who always stand within, as it is written: "Thousands of thousands ministered to him and ten thousand times a hundred thousand stood

---

*The view that we stand between two spirits, a good one on our right hand and an evil one on our left, is an exaggerated notion of the activities of the reprobate spirits among the children of men. Cf. A. Vonier, "The Angels", The Teaching of the Catholic Church, 1.279.

before him," (Dan. 7, 10). Now the Apostle, commending the excellence of the Son above the angels, confirms that "they are all ministering spirits, sent to minister for them, who shall receive the inheritance of salvation," (Cf. Heb. 1, 4). Hence the question arises how are all sent, if certain ones always stand; and if all are messengers, how are certain ones said always to stand. If all are messengers, all are angels; and if all are angels, how is one order only among the nine orders enrolled under this name?

Some think that in that heavenly court all indeed are sent, but some by virtue of their office who are properly called angels or archangels, others on occasion and when a cause outside the common dispensation has arisen. And those themselves also, when they take up the ministry of angels on occasion, assume their name in the ministry, as it is written: "Who makest His angels spirits?" (Psal. 103, 4), since indeed those who are always by nature spirits, according to time and duty are sometimes made angels, that is messengers. Some say that the three highest orders, that is the seraphim and the cherubim and thrones, are turned to divine and interior things alone, and always stand before the Creator, but that the three lower orders are sent to do and announce exterior things, and that the three middle orders not only in dignity or place but also in office are stationed between both; these receive the divine command from the higher orders and transmit it to the lower. For the reason that the highest announce the divine command to the middle, and the middle to the lowest, and these to us, all are rightly called angels.

XXXVII. *On the angelic ministries.*

Some men by their interpretation of the ministry and offices of angels think that the whole world, that is, not only human life but all things that pertain to human life, are administered by angels according to God's dispensation, under God and according to God, but that the evil angels by virtue of office have no power, although receiving power sometimes by virtue of permission.

Sixth Part

On the Creation of Man.

I. *Why God made man of body and soul.*

What we indicated in the first part of this work was to be treated on the foundation of man, we propose now to explain in order. For four things had been proposed from the beginning: first, why man was created; second, of what nature he was created, and how he was instituted; third, how he fell; fourth, how he was restored. Indeed of these, that which was proposed first, namely, the cause of man's creation, we have already treated above to the best of our ability.

Therefore, it now remains for us to pass to the discussion of the second point which is concerned with the question of what nature man was created and how he was disposed.

Omnipotent God, whose happiness can be neither increased in any way, since it is perfect, nor diminished, since it is eternal, by charity alone, not by any necessity on His part, created rational spirit, so that He might make it a sharer in that good which He Himself was, and by which He Himself was happy. But since this pertained to the increase of its felicity, that it should recognize the grace of its Creator through whom it was to be glorified, the Creator Himself wished first to show it in its creation what He was afterwards to make in it according to its worthiness. He ordered the rational creature which He had made in part to persist in its purity; in part, joining it to corporeal coverings and earthly habitations, He caused slimy matter to quicken to the feeling of life, this, indeed, having been proposed as a pattern of the future society which was to be realized between Himself and rational spirit unto its glorification, so that in fact it might be shown that what body was to spirit then in foundation, this according to something spirit afterwards on being assumed was to be to Him according to its worthiness. Therefore, God confirmed His power and showed His grace, first by fashioning man; and this grace He was to show afterwards by glorifying man, that man might know that if God could join such different natures as body and soul in one union and friendship, by no means would it be impossible for Him to elevate the lowness of the rational creature, although far inferior, to participation in His own glory.

Again if this mortal life, which consists of the presence of the spirit in a corruptible body, is so great a joy and so great a pleasure, how great a pleasure and how great a joy would be that immortal life from the presence of the Godhead in the rational spirit? Since, then, in part, as a pattern of the whole, rational spirit was lowered even to association with earthly body, lest perhaps this very thing might seem to result in its depreciation, the providence of God added that, thereafter, with this same body glorified it should be elevated to association with those who had persisted in their purity, so that what on being founded it had received less from the dispensation of its Creator, it might afterwards through the grace of the same receive to be glorified.

Thus then God the Founder disposed the rational spirits which He had by chance made different according to the choice of His omnipotent will, establishing for those whom He had left in their purity a dwelling above in heaven, but disposing those whom He had associated with earthly bodies below in an earthly habitation; He imposed upon both the law of obedience, that the former might not fall from where they were, and that the latter might ascend from where they were to where they were not; thus when the latter had so ascended and the former had not fallen, they might pass beyond that which they had been made to that for which they had been made, and in the end might be with Him by whom they had been made. Thus God made man of a twofold substance, taking his body according to matter from the earth, but fashioning his soul without matter from nothing.

II. *How man was made to the image and likeness of God.*

Man was made to the image and likeness of God, because in the soul, which is the better part of man, or rather was man himself, was the image and likeness of God: image according to reason, likeness according to love; image according to understanding of truth, likeness according to love of virtue; or image according to knowledge, likeness according to substance; image, because all things in it are according to wisdom; likeness, because it is itself one and simple according to essence; image because rational, likeness because spiritual; image pertains to figure, likeness to nature. Now these things were made in the soul alone, because corporeal nature could not have received likeness of the Godhead, which was far from its excellence and likeness in this very fact, that it was corporeal.

III. *On the creation and origin of the soul.*

Now a great many questions are raised regarding the origin of the soul: when it was created, and whence it was created, and of what nature it was created, but we in the present compendium judge it superfluous and fruitless to pursue so many opinions, and we think that this alone will suffice for us, if we treat only those things which must be maintained and asserted. Among these, then, Catholic Faith has chosen this preferably and has judged it as more in harmony with the truth, that we believe that the soul of the first man, when it was made, was not made from preexisting material, but was created from nothing, nor was it made from the beginning when the angels were made, but afterwards, when the body itself was formed into which it was to be infused; it was made and associated with the body simultaneously by the Creator Himself. But whether it was created in the body or outside the body is the more difficult to know as it is less dangerous not to know.

And yet the genius of man should not be judged worthy of approval in this, if it persists stubbornly in those things which are difficult, but rather if it discerns prudently those things which must be known. For it is of equal folly to presume in those things which can not be known, and to fail in those of which there should not be ignorance. Therefore, in so far as suffices for sound faith, let us seek to know, and let us cease to investigate that which curiosity alone persuades us to search out.

God created the soul of the first man from nothing, and breathed it into a

body taken and formed from earth through material, giving it sense and discernment of good and evil, that it might through sense quicken the body itself
associated with it, that it might rule it through reason, and that in man himself sense might be subject to reason, reason to the Creator, and thus the body
might move according to reason through sense, but reason move through free
will according to God.

IV. *On free will.*

Moreover, there are three movements in man: the movement of the mind, the
movement of the body, the movement of sensuality. The movement of the mind
is in the will, the movement of the body in work, the intermediate movement of
sensuality in pleasure. In the movement of the mind alone is there free will;
in the movement of the body and of sensuality are those things which follow
free will. For thus was the disposition of nature, for the voluntary movement
of the mind was desire, free in the voluntary, will in desire. The mind, therefore, moves by itself, and is the first movement of the will. The movement of
the body follows the movement of the will. Thus the mind, as I have said,
has moving of itself, but ought not to move according to itself, rather according
to the will of its Creator, which is its form and exemplar and the designed rule
which it should follow. And on account of this, if it moves according to God,
this is justice; if it moves without God or contrary to God, this is injustice.

Therefore, the movement of the mind is always justice or injustice, but the
movement of the body is always obedience. For in that the mind moves, it
moves by freedom, because it moves voluntarily and moves by itself, and to it
belongs the fact that it moves, either to merit, if it moves well, or to blame, if
evilly. But in that the body moves, it moves by necessity, because it moves by
another, that is by the mind. Nor does the fact that it moves belong to itself, but
to him by whom it moves whether to merit, if it moves well, or to blame, if
evilly. Thus the movement of the mind dominates the movement of the body
subject by the law of nature, and when it abuses the latter, there is vice on the
part of him who commands, obligation on the part of him who obeys. Nor
is he who is led blamed because he is led by necessity, but he who leads is
blamed, because he abuses his liberty against a subject. Moreover, if will had
clung to justice, it would have not only an obedient movement of the body but
an acquiescent movement of sensuality.

Now, however, since it itself did not cling to its rectitude, it still indeed
through the kindness of the Creator has obedient movement of the body, but
for punishment an opposing movement of sensuality, whose violence when
weakened it sometimes follows, but when strengthened it sometimes restrains
and moderates. But if the movement of sensuality dominates the movement of
the mind, it dominates also the movement of the body which is subject to it, and

then sin begins to reign in our mortal body. But if it does not dominate, the mind uses the service of its body, and shows its members as arms of justice, and the movements of the mind and the movements of the body are together, the movement of the sensuality apart, and justice is accomplished and iniquity is restrained.

V. *On the twofold sense of the soul.*

Now the rational soul was on this account equipped with a twofold sense, that it might grasp visible things without through the flesh, and invisible things within through reason, so that both visible and invisible things might excite it to praise of the Creator. For God would not be praised in all His works by the rational creature, if all the works of God were not known by the rational creature. Therefore, that the praise of God might be perfect, the works of God were shown to the rational creature, so that it might admire Him within and without, and through admiration advance to love.

One creature was made whose sense was wholly within, and another creature was made whose sense was wholly without. The sense of the angels was within, and the sense of brute animals was without. The angels whose sense was within contemplated the things that were within, and through these those that were without. The brute animals whose sense was without attained to visible things which were without, but not through these likewise to invisible things which were within, since those who see invisible things, in these same see the visible; since visible things are recognized by the invisible, but those who see visible things do not equally see the invisible things in them, because the sense whereby invisible things are perceived in the highest comprehends the lowest, but the sense whereby visible things are attained in the lowest does not grasp the highest. Thus then there was one creature whose sense was wholly within, and another creature whose sense was wholly without. And man was placed in a middle position, that he might have sense within and without; within for invisible things, without for visible; within through the sense of reason, without through the sense of flesh, that he might go in and contemplate, and might go out and contemplate; that he might have wisdom within, the works of wisdom without, that he might contemplate both, and be refreshed from both, see and rejoice, love and praise. Wisdom was a pasture within; the work of wisdom was a pasture without. And the sense of man was permitted to go to both, and find refreshment in both, to go by cognition, to be refreshed by love.

Wisdom was a book written within; the work of wisdom a book written without. But He willed afterwards that it still be written otherwise without, that wisdom might be seen more manifestly and be recognized more perfectly, that the eye of man might be illumined to the second writing, since it had been darkened to the first. Therefore, He made a second work after the first, and that was more evident, since it not only pointed out but illumined. He assumed flesh not losing divinity, and was placed as a book written within and without; in humanity without, within in divinity, so that it might be read without through imitation, within through contemplation; without unto health, within unto felicity; without unto merit, within unto joy. Within, "In the beginning was the Word," (John 1, 1); without, "the Word was made flesh, and dwelt among us," (John 1, 14). Therefore, there was one book written once within, and twice without; first without through the foundation of visible things, secondly without through the assumption of flesh; first unto enjoyment, secondly unto health; first unto nature, secondly against blame; first that nature might be nourished, secondly that vice might be healed, and nature be blessed.

VI. *On the two goods of man.*

But since man had been composed of a twofold nature, that he might be wholly blessed, he had its two goods. His Creator from the beginning prepared one visible, the other invisible; one corporeal, the other spiritual; one transitory, the other eternal; both full, and both perfect in their kind. One belonged to the flesh, the other to the spirit, so that in one the sense of the flesh might be nourished unto enjoyment, in the other the sense of the mind might be replenished unto felicity. To the flesh belonged visible things, to the spirit invisible; to the flesh unto solace, to the spirit unto joy.

Of these goods He gave one, He promised the other; one that it might be possessed gratis, the other that it might be sought through merit. The good that was visible He gave gratis, that which was invisible He ordained should be sought through merit, so that by the gratuitous gift both the excellence of His promise and the good faith of Him who promised might be confirmed. For if that which He gave freely is of such a nature and so great, of what a nature and how great must that for which He seeks service be thought? Again, if such great goodness was in Him that He gave so many things to those who merited nothing, how could there be such malice in Him that He would not reward those who serve Him? To this it was pertinent that all visible things were given free to man, and immediately on being created he was established the lord of things.

After this, however, obedience was enjoined upon him, and a precept was given that he should merit first, then be rewarded. He could not have been rewarded in those things which had already been given him in gift, but in those things which had been proposed in reward. And yet service was not sought from man because the omnipotent Founder was in need of the service of man made by Himself, but that man himself might possess more gloriously true goods acquired through merit. And because it was more for highest goodness to give both merit and reward than reward alone without merit, man, indeed, was not obliged to serve for temporal and transitory things, lest the dignity of human foundation should be reduced to utility, if he were compelled to serve for these things which had been subject to him. On this account, invisible things as true goods are promised after merit to him who serves well, but these are added in the midst of deserving as moderate and transitory; these, meanwhile, for solace, those for joy; these for sustenance, those for glorification. Without those man cannot be blessed in his true country; without these he cannot be sustained on the way. Wherefore, man was made of such a nature that now meanwhile he might need these for the time in order that through these he might recognize his need in those, and that he might understand the things themselves, since what was good was not enough for him unless he deserved to have that good also from which he was.

Now this was good for him, that he was not sufficient to himself. Great indeed was the dignity of man's foundation, because it was made such that no good would suffice it except the highest. And again great was its liberty, because meanwhile it was dismissed through its own choice, so that it could not be forced to its own good itself, in order that it might go to that by its will alone, which it had to possess through love alone. In order, therefore, that it might learn to seek the good of the interior life, its exterior life was made of such a nature that for the time, not sufficing to stand by itself, it was in need of a sustaining good beyond and outside itself.

VII. *On the two precepts of nature and discipline.*

Good either given or promised by God would have profited man nothing, unless a safeguard had been appointed for that which had been given, lest it be lost, and a way were opened to that which had been promised so that it might be sought and found. Therefore, over the good that was given a safeguard was placed, the precept of nature, and to the good that was promised a way was opened, the precept of discipline. These two precepts have been given to man: the precept of nature and the precept of discipline.

The precept of nature was that which was infused within through nature, but the precept of discipline was that which was appointed without for discipline; within through sense, without through word. In these two commands is contained all, whatsoever is commanded to man to be done or to be avoided. In the precept of nature there are three things: ordering, prohibiting, conceding. Now by the precept of nature we understand nothing else than the natural discrimination itself which was inspired within us so that through it man might be instructed about these things which were either to be sought or to be avoided by him. For it was like giving a kind of precept to infuse into the heart of man a discrimination and understanding of what was to be done. What then was knowledge of what should be done except a kind of command made to the heart of man, and what again the knowledge of what should be avoided except a kind of prohibiting, and what indeed is to be considered the knowledge of those things which were between these except a kind of concession, so that man through his own will might be left there where, whatever way he should choose, he would not be harmed? To God, therefore, to command was to teach man what things were necessary for him, but to prohibit was to point out the harmful; to concede, however, was to indicate those which are indifferent.

VIII. *On the three kinds of things.*

For in visible things which were founded because of the lower life of man, three kinds of things are found created; some, indeed, necessary for the use of life itself to the extent that it is harmed if it does not use them, but some injurious, by which it is harmed if it uses them. Now others are intermediate, which it can use or not use without injury. For, since this lower life is the image of the higher life, it was fitting that in those things which were made for this life proof be set before man of those things which look to the higher life. Now there are some things which through these had to be indicated without, others within as harmful to the spiritual life, which it itself likewise can not use without injury, as are all vices which bring corruption on the soul. There are likewise within certain healthful and necessary things which it can not lack without injury, such as is the knowledge of God and knowledge of self, and all virtues which operate to the health of the soul and furnish it nourishment. There are likewise others which can be present and be absent without injury, and these are indifferent, because they do not hinder health as if harmful, nor do they operate as if necessary; such are knowledge of extrinsic matters and certain other things of this kind. Therefore ordering pertains to necessary and healthful things, prohibiting to harmful, conceding to intermediate.

IX. *On the twofold safeguard of the lower life.*

Reason and providence were given to man, through which he might guard this lower life of his, by this same natural providence avoiding harmful things, seeking healthful, and using intermediate indifferently. Therefore, fortified by this guard he was able to avoid negligence, he was not able to repel violence. For it was in man's providence to avoid all negligence, but it was not equally in man's power to repel all violence. Therefore, Divine Providence was added to human reason, that human reason on the one hand might watch against negligence, that Divine Providence on the other hand might take its stand against violence.

So, fortified by this twofold safeguard the city of human life would not be harmed by any adversaries, because, if human reason had not grown slack against negligence, Divine Providence would never have given a place in man to violence. Since, however, reason first through negligence deserted its place, Divine Providence afterwards justly withdrew itself from safeguarding it, so that now in the life of man violence sometimes prevails, and reason itself indeed is now forced against its will to suffer what before of its own accord it neglected to ward off.

X. *On the three states of man.*

But perhaps it may seem to some one that he should ask how man could have suffered any violence before sin, who if he had not sinned, as it seems, could not have suffered at all? If, therefore, he could not have suffered at all, violence could not have harmed him. Nor did he have need of safeguard, lest he suffer violence, who, whatever had been brought against him, would suffer nothing at all. For, if he could have suffered violence, how also was he unable to die? But if he could die, how was he immortal? For the sake of solving arguments of this kind which are raised by those who are wont to examine hidden things rather diligently, we distinguish in our first consideration three states of human life, and among these we think that it must necessarily be determined of what nature man was both in body and in soul, and how much he was changed from that which he was first made, or in what he persisted the same.

The first state of man was before sin, in that in which he was founded. The second state is after sin, (if, however, it must be called a state, and not rather ruin), into which, through sin and the punishment of sin following after sin, he fell. The third state of man will be after the resurrection from the dead, when he will be completely and perfectly freed not only from sin but also from the punishment of sin, and he will be restored not only to that in which he was created, but above that also even to that for which he was created.

In the first state God and man divided; in the second state the devil and man divided; in the third state, God will receive the whole. In the first state was praise of God, and something outside praise, yet nothing against praise of God; in the second state nothing for praise, but all against praise of God; in the third state all for praise, nothing outside praise or against praise of God; for praise of God charity, outside praise of God necessity, against praise of God iniquity; in the first state charity and necessity; in the second state necessity and iniquity; in the third charity alone.

XI. *On the first state of man before sin.*

Now many things are asked about the first state of man before sin, of what nature man was before he sinned, and of what nature he would have been, if he had not sinned, both in body and in soul, mortal or immortal, passible or impassible; on the end of the lower life, and on the transition to the higher; on the nature and mode of life, and on the propagation of children; on the life and merits of those born from him and following after him; and on many other things which, although they are sometimes asked with curiosity, yet are learned with profit, provided they be discussed with discretion. But we, especially in so many matters which are remote from our understanding and capacity, should temper our reply, and from those which are not doubtful distinguish those which are mentioned only with probability. In this way, there will be no danger in a careful investigation, if there be no presumption of rash assertion.

XII. *On man's knowledge before sin.*

If, therefore, it is asked of what nature the first man was before sin, according to his soul indeed he was rational, having discernment of good and evil, also perfect knowledge of things in so far as pertained to the beginning of foundation. For just as, so far as pertains to the perfection of the stature and the age of the human body, we believe that the first man was made perfect, so too, as far as pertains to his soul, we think that immediately on being founded he received a perfect knowledge and understanding of truth; at least he received that which was appropriate to first perfection, and he proceeded to that not by study or any teaching over periods of time, but he received it simultaneously and immediately from the very beginning of his creation by a single and simple illumination of divine aspiration. Now it is clear that the first man was instructed in a three-fold knowledge, namely, knowledge of his Creator that he might know by whom he had been made, and knowledge of himself that he might know what he had been made and what should be done by him, lastly knowledge also of what had been made with him and what was to be made by him from it and in it.

XIII. *On the knowledge of visible things.*

For of all visible things which had been made with man and for the sake of man, no one should have any doubt that man had received perfect knowledge, in so far as seemed to pertain indeed either to the instruction of his soul or to the needs of the body. For the Creator Himself did not wish names to be fashioned for every single animal by Himself or by an angel but by man for this reason, that He might show manifestly that man recognized the nature and the use and the offices of each from the reason implanted in him. For what had been created for his sake had to be ruled and disposed by him, and on this account God granted to him knowledge of all these things and left him providence. For the Apostle says: "Doth God take care of oxen?" (I Cor. 9, 9). For God left to man the care of oxen and the providence of other animals, that they might be subject to his domination, and be ruled by his reason so that for those from whom he had to receive obedience, he might know also how to provide what was necessary.

Now since man by sinning did not lose this knowledge, just as he did not lose that by which also he had to provide the comforts and the necessities of his flesh, God on this account did not afterwards care to instruct him on such matters through the Scriptures. But on the knowledge of the soul alone did man, when he was being restored, have to be instructed, since that alone did he lose before by sinning.

XIV. *On the knowledge of the Creator.*

There is no doubt, indeed, that the first man had knowledge of his Creator, since, if for perserving temporal life man received such great knowledge in transitory things, for obtaining eternal life he should have had a much more excellent and more abundant knowledge in heavenly things. Therefore man knew his Creator, not by that knowledge which is received from without by hearing alone, but by that which is ministered rather within through inspiration, not indeed by that knowledge whereby God absent is now sought in faith by believers, but by that whereby through the presence of contemplation He was then perceived more manifestly by the knowing. Yet it must be known that we should confess that that first knowledge of man which he received from his Creator, just as we truly say that it was greater and more certain than the knowledge which now consists in faith alone, so also was less than that which afterwards will be manifestly revealed in the excellence of divine contemplation.

Therefore, man knew his Creator, yet not so excellently as he would necessarily have known Him thereafter, if he had persisted. For just as the disobedience of man through subsequent ignorance took much from his first knowledge, thus, if the disobedience of man had persisted, very much would have had to be added to the same knowledge through subsequent revelation. It is difficult, indeed, to explain the mode of the knowledge of God which that first man is believed to have had, beyond that which we have mentioned, that he, taught visibly through internal inspiration, in no way could have doubted about his Creator Himself.

XV. *On knowledge of himself.*

Furthermore, we believe that the same man from his first knowledge received such a knowledge of himself that he might recognize the obligation of his obedience toward his superior, and might not be ignorant of the obligation of his providence toward his inferior. This, indeed, was to know himself, not to be ignorant of his foundation and order and obligation, whether above himself or in himself or under himself, to understand of what nature he was made and how he should proceed, what to do, what similarly to avoid. All this was to know himself.

If man had not had knowledge and discrimination of these things, he would not have known himself, nor would he afterwards have been guilty of transgression of these, if he had not before been illumined regarding knowledge of them. Now if the question is asked whether man then from the beginning had knowledge of those things which were to come about him, that is whether he foreknew his fall and ruin and all other evils that passed first upon himself, afterwards through himself upon all those who were from him; likewise if it is asked whether he foreknew the goods which he was to have had, if he had persisted in obedience, this at least seems to be probable and necessary, which looked more to the institution and form of right living, that the things to be done by him were indicated rather than that the things to be were foretold. For this would certainly seem to diminish the freedom of will and the integrity of obedience, if man himself should be said to have foreknowledge of the future before merit, because he could not have hoped for goods with a foreknowledge of evils, nor with a foreknowledge of goods could he have feared evils to come. On this account, therefore, it is judged more proper that the first man, indeed, had received knowledge and precept regarding those things which he had to do, but of those which were to be he had not foreknowledge, so that his will remained free for either choice. And, indeed, let it suffice to have said this about man's knowledge, in so far as pertains to his first state.

XVI. *On the nature of free will through three states.*

But in the present section we add something about freedom of the will, in so far as pertains to this same state. That man had free will before sin must not be doubted in any way, on account of that freedom of course by which he could incline the desire of his will either to good or evil, indeed to good with the aid of grace, but to evil, only with God permitting, not compelling. Therefore, the first freedom of the will was power to sin and power not to sin, just as the last freedom will be power not to sin and not power to sin. The first freedom, indeed, had help toward good, but infirmity toward evil, in such a way, however, that it was not forced toward good, nor held back against evil. The last freedom will have grace in good, will not have infirmity in evil, not only grace helping in good but even strengthening against evil, helping that there may be power not to sin, strengthening that there may be not power to sin.

Intermediate freedom after sin, indeed before restoration, does not have grace in good, but infirmity in evil, and on this account there is in it power to sin and not power not to sin, power to sin because it has freedom without strengthening grace, not power not to sin because it has infirmity without helping grace. Intermediate freedom after restoration, before confirmation, has grace in good, infirmity in evil, grace in good helping on account of freedom, and grace against evil helping on account of infirmity, so that there is in it power to sin on account of freedom and infirmity and power not to sin on account of freedom and helping grace, not yet, however, lack of power to sin, on account of infirmity still not perfectly removed, and on account of strengthening grace still not perfectly completed. But, when all infirmity has been entirely removed and strengthening grace has been completed, there will not be the power to sin, not because even then either freedom of will or aptitude of nature may be destroyed, but because strengthening grace, with whose presence sin can by no means exist in us, may no longer be taken away.

XVII. *On the virtue of man before sin.*

If, however, the question is raised whether there were some virtues in the first man himself before sin, and if there were virtues in him, whether in them he merited anything, since it certainly seems impossible that there be virtues without merit, we indeed reply that virtues are possessed in a twofold manner, namely, according to nature and according to grace. For virtue is nothing else than an affection of the mind ordered according to reason, and such affections are said to be very numerous according to the various inclinations of the same mind, yet having one root and origin, the will. For one will, according as it inclines itself to various things either by seeking or avoiding, forms various affections, and receives divers names according to the same affections, although, however, all these things are in one will, and are one will.

Now the will sometimes avoids by nature, sometimes is excited by grace, and is itself indeed nature by grace, but creating grace is one thing, saving grace another. By creating grace were made those things which were not, by saving grace are restored those which had perished. Creating grace first implanted certain goods in founded nature, saving grace both restores the goods which nature when first corrupted lost and inspires those goods which nature being imperfect has not yet received. Through the first goods free will is restored, through the second goods free will operates. In the first goods God operates in man, in the second goods God cooperates with man. The first goods are a gift of God, not the merit of man; the second goods are also God's through gift, and man's through merit. The first gifts are a grace, the second gifts are grace for grace. When, therefore, the will of man moves according to nature only, it does not merit outside of nature, but when it moves according to God, it merits above nature, since it deserves Him through whom and for the sake of whom it moves. For everyone who wills, wills something, and on account of something wills what he wills.

Whoever, therefore, wills something and only wills what it wills, because nature wills this, has willing according to nature, but he who wills something and wills what he wills on this account, because God wills this, has willing according to grace; in this is man's merit, that for the sake of God he wills what he wills, and for the sake of God he does what he does.

For God had to return that which is done for His sake, whether by will alone in willing or by will and work in doing. Therefore, the goods of nature and the affections ordered according to nature are natural virtues, which, even if they are praiseworthy because they are good and are from nature, are yet not worthy of that merit which is above nature, because they have nothing in themselves beyond nature. Yet it seems to me that virtues even of this kind can not properly be said to merit nothing, although they merit nothing outside these goods which were founded for the sake of nature, which are from nature alone. But the virtues which are formed by restoring grace superadded to nature, since in merit they receive something above nature, are worthy of being requited in reward also above nature, so that for those to whom love of God is the cause in work, the presence of God is a reward in requital.

But in these virtues which are through restoring grace the Holy Ghost first effects good will, then cooperates with good will which moves itself and effects. First He inspires good will that it may be, then He infuses into good will that it may move and effect so that it is not idle. First He effects it, then He effects through it. For good will is an instrument, the Holy Ghost is an artisan. Now the artisan first effects an instrument and then through the instrument; in that he first effects an instrument, he himself alone effects, but in that afterwards he effects through the instrument, he himself alone does not effect, but also the instrument itself through which he himself effects; so the Holy Ghost, in that He first effects good will in man, Himself alone effects, but in that afterwards He effects through good will, He Himself alone also does not effect, but the will too through which He effects. Yet good work is from the Spirit who effects, not from the will of man through which He effects. Indeed good is in the will itself, but is not from it. It is not from it, since it has received it from another source. Yet good is in it, since it has what it has received. And the same good itself is its own also, in so far as it has it, and not its own in so far as it does not have it from itself.

Therefore, after making such a distinction, that certain virtues are from nature alone, certain others from grace, if the question is asked whether the first man in that first state of his creation had any virtues, we think without any doubt at all that good affections and orders according to justice were implanted in his nature from his first origin; through these he was attracted by natural desire to seek out goodness and justice, and in these good affections, indeed, were natural virtues with which from the beginning the nature of man was fashioned and furnished. Now regarding those virtues which are accomplished by good will moved from divine love, we do not wish to define anything rashly about this, in so far as pertains to that first state, especially since regarding the work of His charity we have no certain argument either from authority or from reason. Even if indeed he began to love his Creator, yet this was not at all worthy of praise, because he did not persevere, since the movement of incipient virtue was extinguished and destroyed by the coolness of subsequent fault.

XVIII. *Of what nature the first man was created according to body.*

It now remains for us to consider also of what nature the first man was made according to body, that is, whether mortal or immortal, capable of suffering or incapable of suffering, and other things which seem bound to arise about the state of the human body. The first man, therefore, in so far as pertains to the nature of his earthly body was made immortal according to something, because he could not die, and mortal according to something, because he could die. For just as in that first state he had the power to sin and the power not to sin, because this was the first freedom of the will, so too in the same state he had the power to die, and also the power not to die, because this was the first immortality of the human body.

In the second state he has the power to die and not the power not to die, just as he has also the power to sin and not the power not to sin, since in this state there is the necessity both of dying and of sinning. The necessity of dying exists as long as life is present, the necessity of sinning as long as grace is absent. In the third state he will have the power not to die and not the power to die, just as also the power not to sin and not the power to sin, since the impossibility both of dying and of sinning pertains to this state. Yet both possibilities are from grace not from nature, because if grace were not present, there would not be lacking to nature on the one hand the possibility of dying, on the other that of sinning. If then the last immortality will be from grace, in which there will be no possibility of dying, how much the more was the first immortality not from nature in which there was the possibility of dying? Therefore, the first man before sin was immortal, since in his body was no corruption and no infirmity, and externally beyond other nourishments of foods whereby he was obliged to feed and sustain the life of the body he had received a special medicine in the tree of life; by this he could preserve this same life whole and uncorrupted against the decline of death, until he would be translated to the true immortality where he could no longer die, and being translated would be confirmed.

Just as, therefore, we do not say that the first man was immortal before sin, so that he could not die at all, so too by no means ought we to believe that he was incapable of suffering, as if he could have suffered nothing at all, since he had in him a nature capable of suffering. But yet if he had not sinned, just as he would not have died, so also he would have suffered nothing at all whether as regards vexation of will in the mind or as regards corruption of integrity in the body. For that the first man could not die, not according to the nature of earthly body but through the benefit of a vital food, Scripture clearly shows, where it testifies that he was cast out from that tree lest he be able to preserve everlasting life itself, saying: "Behold Adam is become as one of us, knowing good and evil: now, therefore, lest perhaps he put forth his hand, and take also of the tree of life, and live forever. And the Lord God sent him out of the place of pleasure," (Gen. 3, 23 and 24).

He who then is said to have been cast out from the tree of life lest he might live forever, is manifestly shown destined to have this from the benefit of the tree itself, if he should live forever. And thus, therefore, the first man before sin was mortal and capable of suffering by nature; however, through the anterior benefit of the Creator and by his own subsequent zeal, he could have brought it about that he would not die nor suffer corruption in life. Because, therefore, man had a nature capable of suffering, he had against suffering a necessary guard, so that in fact he might be excited by his own reason to guard against negligence, and through divine providence might be preserved unharmed against all violence; thus fortified on either side he might neither die nor suffer.

XIX. *How long man would have been obliged to remain in this lower life, if he had not sinned.*

But as to how long man would have been obliged to remain in this earthly life, no other argument can be considered except that it is altogether probable that after completing his obedience, if he had persisted in obedience itself, he would necessarily have been translated immediately to the reward of obedience itself, so that without the interposition of death he would pass from the first state where he had the power not to die to another state where he could no longer die at all.

XX. *On his nourishment.*

But meanwhile he could have nourished earthly life with earthly fruits, until he would be translated to that life where he would have no need at all of nourishment, as it is written: "The first man was made into a living soul; the second into a quickening spirit," (1 Cor. 15, 45). For since what lives has life, but what quickens gives life, it is certainly more to quicken than to live. Therefore, since the first life could not stand by itself, but the last life will have no need of being sustained from any source, the first man is said to have been made into a living soul, which indeed had life in itself, but could not give life to the body through itself alone; but the second man into a quickening spirit, which will have life in itself and will give it to the body through itself.

XXI. *On his zeal.*

Now if the question is raised with what zeal human life, if man had not sinned, would have had to be cultivated and practised, it is not unfittingly said that beyond the internal and spiritual zeals of wisdom and contemplation of God, externally also in cultivating the land, whether in ploughing or in sowing or in transplanting and in other works of this kind by which good nature on being cultivated makes progress toward the better, men at first were not for practicing labour but pleasure, so that even work was unto pleasure and example unto instruction. For thus the exterior man had to be practiced so that by zeal itself for exterior work a form might be taken for interior zeal, and that in what he should do externally he might learn what had to be done by him within. For within also in a similar manner was there a kind of land which had indeed been created good, and yet, if it were well cultivated, could be still better; when cultivated it would produce good fruits, but when neglected it would bring forth bad and harmful offshoots.

XXII. *If man had not sinned, what kind of children he would have begotten.*

After what has just been said this also, it seems, should be asked, how man could have procreated children if he had not sinned, and of what nature they would have been who were to be born of him. Now in questions of this kind, as we have already often said, we ought to consider carefully so as to distinguish those things which are stated with probability only from those which are beyond doubt. For what things authority does not approve nor reason show to be manifest are left as doubtful, yet the latter, not without utility, are sometimes admitted into question, so that either that which is true may be found or at least that which is false may not be believed.

XXIII. *Whether they would have been born just or unjust.*

Since, therefore, we read that union between male and female was instituted by God before sin, and was granted and enjoined upon them with the gift of benediction to increase and multiply, we should by no means doubt that mingling of the flesh in the generation of offspring would be without turpitude and concupiscence. Therefore, it certainly follows that those who are begotten without sin would be born also without sin, just as those who are now begotten with concupiscence, taking corruption as it were from the very vice of their root, are born with guilt.

XXIV. *Whether they would have been heirs of ancestral justice.*

This also seems worthy of question, whether the merit of ancestral obedience through incorrupt origin was obliged to pass down to all posterity, just as now the guilt of that disobedience through the same vitiated origin by diffusing itself spreads into all. If this is true, accordingly at that time there would have been original justice through the merit of parents among those born, just as now original sin is found in the same through the guilt alone of ancestral transgression. Yet it must not be asserted rashly on this account, because it does not seem similar that just as now nature through disobedience is perceived changed to corruption, so too then through observed obedience, unless it had been preserved by God to a predestined time, it would have been changed to incorruption. For to transgress once was full disobedience, but similarly there would not have been perfect obedience if man had not persisted in obedience itself to the end. Therefore, just as disobedience consummated at one time changed nature to corruption, so obedience would not have changed nature to incorruption, until it had been preserved perfect in its own time even to the end. But those who would meanwhile be begotten, would be generated by a nature still not yet transformed to true incorruption, nor would they in being born have received the merit of original justice, since even they themselves from whom they were born would still not yet have the justice of perfect obedience. But nature could not have given to those being born what it did not as yet possess in those begetting, just as those also, who are now begotten in sin, take nothing else from being born than the vice which they receive from the nature from which they are generated. And so the first man in the time of his obedience complying by chaste union with the divine command to propagate posterity would beget children without sin indeed, since they would be from a nature free from all vice, but not similarly heirs of ancestral justice, because nature itself would not yet be transformed to the reward of incorruption, which was not to be given except after obedience had been accomplished. Now after man had been transformed from earthly life to a heavenly and spiritual state, he would no longer have had to beget, just as now through disobedience he is subject to mortality and does not cease indeed from the propagation of the flesh. On this account, therefore, there does not seem to be the one condition in the two cases, since the same reason does not appear in both.

Yet there are those who believe that it must be truthfully asserted that the first man, if he had not sinned, would have begotten none but good children, and no one of all who were born of his flesh would be damned. Yet this is rightly asked whether obedience tried alone in the first man would necessarily have sufficed unto merit for all posterity to be born from him, or whether all in turn in their times after him, just as he himself first was tried, would have had to be tried by the observance either of the same or of some other command. And it can perhaps be believed without absurdity that his posterity would have had to observe the same command which was given to the first parent, so that all in turn would be tried by their own obedience, and individually in accordance with their merits would be glorified with worthy recompense, but that the observance of the first obedience would be the cause of helping grace to all following and imitating obedience itself in obeying.

XXV. *Whether they would of necessity have been translated at the same time or in succession.*

Now regarding the end of this lower life in which man was to have remained to a definite time, until he should be conducted above to the heavenly and truly immortal life, and after the fulfillment of obedience should be translated to the reward of obedience without the interposition of death, this seems more in agreement with reason and worthy of belief, that just as in this mortal life some destined to live through birth succeed others falling off through death, so also then, when those who were anterior had been translated to the life eternal after the end of this temporal life, these who would have been from them would succeed them on their departure, and they themselves also would fulfil their times and observe obedience until finally the number of those predestined to life would be filled, and the time allotted to this lower life in human kind would be accomplished.

XXVI. *Whether they would have been born perfect in stature and knowledge.*

But if it is asked what kind of children man would necessarily have begotten, if he had not sinned, whether indeed just as the first man himself was founded immediately perfect according to stature of body and sense of mind, so too those who were to have been born from him would have had to be perfect both in body and in sense at the very first beginning of their birth, we according to our opinion approve this rather, that the first man indeed, as we have said, should be believed to have been made immediately perfect both in body and in sense, but that those who would be born from him by the same law by which we perceive even now that human birth is ordered would be born small, and then over intervals of time would receive increase both in sense of mind and in corporeal stature. For thus in every kind of things we perceive that first foundation had one law, and subsequent propagation another. For all first things were made perfect, but all others that arise from them and follow after them can not arrive at perfection except by increasing over intervals of time. This we perceive in all trees and plants and shoots, this in all beasts and living things, since they all begin from what is small, and then gradually by increase in order arrive at perfection. Therefore, by no means should it be regarded as a vice of human nature, if having begun in its origin from the perfect, through subsequent propagation it proceeds from the small to greater and better things. And indeed regarding the human body, perhaps it will not be difficult, nor will it seem unfitting, to take this into consideration.

But regarding the sense and the knowledge of truth, perchance it will be considered less probable that those indeed who would be born without sin would be born imperfect in sense and intelligence of mind, for the reason that all ignorance in the rational creature seems to be from nothing save punishment of sin. But those who say this do not consider carefully enough that not everyone who does not know something or knows something less perfectly should at once be said to possess ignorance or to be in ignorance, because the term ignorance is applied only when that which ought to have been known is not known. So such ignorance is understood to be present only through the punishment of sin, when the mind shut off from the light of truth is prevented by its own vice from being able to understand those things which it ought to know. Indeed that that imperfection of sense or knowledge which seems to be present from the beginning in all creatures that are born even now, and then also is believed to have been present of necessity, belongs to nature not to fault, is manifestly clear from this, that the Lord in the Gospel, when under the figure of the soul He addressed the Samaritan woman about her secrets, testified first that she had had five husbands and also that the husband she then had was not her husband, saying: "For thou hast had five husbands: and he whom thou now hast, is not thy husband," (John 4, 18). Who are the five husbands to which the rational soul is said to have been first united lawfully, unless the five senses of the body, according to which the first age of human life is governed without discretion of reason? And if in fact it were not nature but vice for that age to proceed according to the dispositions of these senses, these very senses would by no means have been called husbands but rather adulterers. Moreover, when thereafter it was added that he whom she had was not her husband, it was clearly shown that the five which she had before were hers, that is legitimate, and not those of others. It is natural, indeed, for human nature in the first age to move and proceed according to the disposition of the senses alone.

But when it has arrived at the years of discretion, if abandoning truth it follows error, its error is then called not a husband but an adulterer. Now the fact that before when proceeding it operates according to the movement of the senses alone is not imputed to it as evil unto blame nor good unto merit. Therefore, even for infants born in sin it is not a vice to be born without knowledge, but this is a vice for them—to be born with such vice in fact by which afterwards, when they have arrived at the years of discretion, it happens that, if they do not have helping grace, they are hindered from obtaining knowledge of truth, in so far as that which pertains to salvation is concerned. And if this is true, it would not have been a vice for those who were born without sin to be born also without knowledge, because through birth they would have nothing in them by which afterwards, when they had come to the age of knowing, they could have been hindered from obtaining knowledge of truth.

And we indeed in this manner in hidden things have chosen those which seemed more probable to us, yet in such a way that in no wise do we presume to assert what is doubtful as certain. Now, so far as it was within our purpose to treat of what nature the first man was created, we wish this to suffice for the present compendium. But now it remains for us to expound also that which follows, namely, how man was instituted by God, in so far as it has meanwhile occurred to our mind and shall seem to be in harmony with our plan.

XXVII. *On the institution of the first man.*

That we can more fully understand how the first man was instituted by God and was instructed for right living, it is necessary to recall a little what has already been said above. For we said above that two goods were prepared from the beginning by God for man: one corporeal, the other spiritual; one visible, the other invisible; one transitory, the other eternal; one for the body, the other for the spirit; one for the lower life, the other for the higher, that each life might have its own enjoyment. Some things were for nourishment, others for joy; some for necessity, others for felicity; some for temporal use, others for the eternal reward. Therefore, over these goods which pertained to both lives care was enjoined upon the spirit, which presided over the flesh itself in man, that it might indeed through providence dispose one, that is corporeal good, to the use of the lower life, but through obedience might seek the other, that is spiritual good, to the reward of the higher life.

Therefore, it pertained to the rational spirit, to provide both for its flesh and itself; for its flesh, indeed, in the good which had been supplied it for the use of the same flesh, but for itself in that good which was preeminent in dignity not only over the flesh but also over itself which was superior in the flesh. Wherefore providence, indeed, pertained to preserving the lower good, but obedience was necessary for obtaining the higher good; providence being from reason, obedience from precept; providence being in the precept of nature, obedience in the precept of discipline. And so the first man was instituted, that through providence he might guard the good of the lower life, and might through obedience seek the good of the higher life. If, therefore, he had proceeded according to this institution, he would have possessed perfect justice; and just as he would have been a stranger to guilt, so also would he have remained free and immune from punishment. But as we understand more perfectly the mode of this institution in either instance, we should consider more carefully the nature and form of each life, and those goods and their use which seem to pertain to each life.

XXVIII. *On the institution of man according to the lower life.*

Therefore, God had from the beginning prepared the two goods for man which we have distinguished above, the one temporal, the other eternal, both full and perfect. The one, that is temporal good, He supplied to man immediately on his foundation; the other that is eternal good, He proposed to be given full after merit. To that which He had given, the precept of nature supplied a guard with His providence; to the other which he had proposed, the precept of discipline opened a way with His grace.

But the precept of nature contains three things: command, prohibition, concession. Natural command is natural discretion, through which there is inspired in man the things that are necessary for his nature. Prohibition, indeed, is that through which he is informed of the things that are harmful. But concession is the discernment of those things which are intermediate, that is, which it is possible to use or not to use without danger or disadvantage. If, therefore, man instructed by natural precept had wished to guard against negligence, Divine Providence would not have permitted him to be oppressed or harmed by any violence.

XXIX. *On the institution of man according to the higher life.*

Thus man was able through the precept of nature to preserve the natural good which he had, but he was not able through it to obtain the eternal good, that which he did not yet have. For he would not have merit toward obtaining the higher life, if he should either avoid things harmful to this life or should seek what are salutary, or should use things intermediate, indifferent in character, since in all these he would be attending not so much to the affection of Him commanding as to the advantage of him obeying. And so that man might merit something above this life, it was necessary that to the precept of nature the precept of discipline be added, and that in the execution of the precept itself man might be shown to embrace not merely the utility of the precept but the love of Him who made it.

But what more will there be which should be enjoined by Him to try man's obedience, since all that pertains to human life is contained in the precept of nature? For whatever things have been made for the sake of man, either are necessary to human life, and pertain to command, or are harmful and pertain to prohibition, or are intermediate and pertain to concession. Now the command of discipline could not be taken either from natural precept or from prohibition, lest, if God should either command or prohibit the same things which before He had ordered or prohibited, the one obeying, as has been said, would not have merit unto life. If, however, He should change the command in both, so that He either prohibited the necessary things or commanded the harmful, He would unjustly injure nature which was made by Him. And in the contradiction of His commands, whichever of the two would be put into effect, it would cast man into the necessity of transgression, since of two contraries he could not fulfil the one without the violation of the other. Therefore, the precept of discipline had to be taken from natural concession, because there could have been merit only where there was free will and where man could incline to either choice according to his desire. But, however, the precept of discipline had to be taken from concession itself so that concession would not be changed, that is, in order that the precept might not change the nature of the thing regarding which it was to be made, nor cause harm to human life contrary to its first institution, so that disobedience alone might harm the transgressor not the nature of the thing itself in which transgression was made.

Now, since the precept of discipline had to be formed from natural concession, it was fitting that this should be done rather according to prohibition not according to command, lest the devil be able to calumniate man's obedience, and in one thing only, not in many, lest man be able to excuse disobedience itself. For, if God had told man to eat of the tree of knowledge of good and evil, the devil would have had something which he could have said against man, that, indeed, in the execution of the command man had looked to his own advantage rather than to the precept of his Creator, and that he had been led to accomplish what had been commanded not through love of God but through delight in food. Again, if God had forbidden man many of those things, which had been conceded naturally, and had granted few, man would seem to have an excuse for his transgression against God, according as he would be shown to have been impelled to transgression more by necessity than by will.

On this account, God in instructing man by command to try his obedience granted many things and prohibited few, so that obedience itself might be free, and what he prohibited, he prohibited rather than commanded on this account, that obedience itself might be pure. "Of every tree of paradise," He said, "Thou shalt eat: But of the tree of knowledge of good and evil, thou shalt not eat," (Gen. 2, 16, 17), so that clearly He might first console the infirmity of human sense by concession, lest perchance thereafter it might be frightened at prohibition. If, therefore, man had persisted in this obedience, after the time defined by God he must of necessity have been translated without pain of death to that good which had been prepared for him in heaven, to live a heavenly life without end, together with all his progeny following after him in the society of the blessed angels.

XXX. *On where the first man was placed.*

"And the Lord God had planted," as Scripture says, "a paradise of pleasure from the beginning: wherein he placed man whom he had formed," (Gen. 2, 8). Now of what nature paradise was where man was placed to be tried and occupied, Scripture continues and says: "And the Lord God brought forth of the ground all manner of trees, fair to behold, and pleasant to eat of: the tree of life also in the midst of paradise: and the tree of knowledge of good and evil. And a river went out of the place of pleasure to water paradise, which from thence is divided into four heads," (Gen. 2, 9, and 10).

Therefore it is clear of what charm that place was in which the nature of man as yet free from corruption was to have been fostered and nourished, which is praised as being watered by fountains and rivers, as leafy and wooded with trees of all kinds, as filled with fruit beautiful to behold as well as pleasing to eat.

XXXI. *On the tree of life. (Cf. Gen. 2, 9).*

Here midst the other gifts of God prepared for the enjoyment of human life, that wonderful gift is also mentioned, which is said to be the tree of life, whose virtue is declared to have been so marvelous that taken at certain times, as long as man made use of it, it could have protected corporeal life in man unharmed not only from death but also from every decline.

XXXII. *On the tree of knowledge of good and evil. (Cf. Gen. 2, 9).*

The tree of knowledge of good and evil also is said to have been there, which indeed could not likewise by its nature give to man knowledge of good and evil, just as the tree of life could preserve corporeal life in man by its nature and the virtue granted it by God, but is called the tree of knowledge of good and evil for this reason only, because it was prepared to test man's obedience or prove his disobedience. For there were certain goods which man did not yet know through experience and there were similarly certain evils of which he was still ignorant through experience. And the tree of knowledge of good and evil was placed, as it were, in the middle, so that by it man either through obedience might pass to the taste and knowledge of goods, or through disobedience might come to feel and perceive evils. Thus, therefore, in this place he was due to receive occasion of knowing either good or evil, yet not by the nature of the tree which could not of itself have given this to man, but because in this either through obedience he received occasion of good, or through disobedience occasion of evil according to due recompense.

But if we wish to interpret the force of this term otherwise, we shall be able to say that Adam before sin knew good and evil, good indeed through knowledge and through experience, but evil through knowledge alone. After, however, he had touched the forbidden tree, then too he began to recognize evil through experience, and through experience of evil itself he knew also how strictly good should have been kept. Thus, therefore, that tree through the virtue of obedience or through the fault of disobedience was able to benefit or injure man. Now as far as pertained to its nature, this tree is believed to have been such that whether man ate or did not eat of its fruit he would not have been injured. But fittingly the tree of life of its nature gave virtue; the tree of knowledge of good and evil, indeed, furnished only the occasion of virtue, because the goods of the lower life are from nature, the goods, however, of the higher life from grace.

XXXIII. *That man was placed, not created in paradise.*

Therefore, man was placed and not created in such a place filled with such delights, that he might impute the blessing of God not to nature but to grace, as it is written: "The Lord God took man, and placed him in a paradise of pleasure," (Cf. Gen. 2, 8). For he whom He is said to have taken and afterwards placed in paradise, is clearly shown to have been created elsewhere, and to have been removed thence to be placed here.

XXXIV. *Why one was first created.*

Therefore, God created first one man, that the beginning of the human race might be one, so that in this the pride of the devil also might be confounded, and the humility of human nature glorified by the likeness of the divine image. For the devil had desired to be another beginning from God, and, that his pride might on this account be the more confounded, man received that in gift which the devil wished perversely to seize and could not obtain; so that the image of God appeared in man in this, that just as God was the beginning of creation for all things, so man would be the beginning of generation for all men, and all men, because they would know that they were from one and were one, would all love one another as if one.

XXXV. *Why woman was made from man, and why from the side.*

But afterwards as a help to generation woman was made from man himself, since, if she had been made from another source, surely the beginning of all men would not have been one. Now she was made from the side of man that it might be shown that she was created for association in love, lest perhaps, if she had been made from the head, she would seem to be preferred to man unto damnation, or, if from the feet, to be subject unto slavery. Since, therefore, she was furnished to man neither as a mistress nor a handmaid but as a companion, she had to be produced neither from the head nor the feet but from the side, in order that he might realize that she was to be placed beside him, whom he learned had been taken from his very side.

XXXVI. *Why the rib was taken from man in sleep.*

The rib, indeed, from which the body of woman might be fashioned was taken from man in sleep rather than in wakefulness, lest in this he should be thought to have felt some punishment, and that at the same time the marvelous work of divine power might be proven, which opened the side of man while asleep, and yet did not arouse him from the repose of slumber. But, so far as pertains to the spiritual interpretation, the first Adam in sleep furnished from his side the material whence his spouse might be created, because the second Adam afterwards, overcome by the sleep of death on the cross that His spouse the Church might be formed, supplied sacraments by shedding blood with water from His side.

Furthermore, that the body of woman is said to have been made from the rib of man must be understood thus, that from the substance alone of the rib itself, multiplied by the divine power in it, without any extrinsic addition, the same body is believed to have been made, by that miracle indeed whereby afterwards with five loaves of bread multiplied in the hands of Jesus by heavenly benediction five thousand men were filled.

XXXVII. *On the six modes of operating.*

Indeed, there are six works according to which all things that are done are brought into effect. The first work is to make something from nothing. The second work is out of something to make some things into a greater thing according to substance and quantity. The third work is from some things to make something into a smaller thing according to substance and quantity. The fourth work is from something to make some things, yet not into a greater thing according to substance and quantity. The fifth work is to make something from some things, yet not into a smaller thing according to substance and quantity. The sixth work is from something to make nothing.

Of these six works four are possible to God alone; only the remaining two befit the possibility of the creature. For God alone can make something from nothing, and from something make some things into a greater thing, and from some things make something into a smaller thing or from something nothing. The two remaining, that is from something to make some things not into a greater thing, as when the whole is divided into parts, or from some things to make something not into a smaller thing, just as when parts are united in a whole, the creature can do. And its work is on this account rightly said to be nothing for this reason, because through its work nothing is taken away from or added to the essences of things whether in joining what is divided or in dividing what is joined. But when something is made from nothing, something is made, because this very something is made to be in this, which, unless it were made that very thing which it is, would not be something. Again when more is made from something, something is made, because, unless something were made in that which already is something, that itself, which is afterwards more there, would not be. Again, when from some things something is made, something is made because unless that, which before was there more, had been made something in that which just now is less, that would not be at all. From nothing something was made when that which before was nothing was made to be something. But when afterwards that which before had been made small was made greater, something was made from something into a greater thing. Yet when what was made great, is sometimes made less, something is made from something into a smaller thing.

The first is the work of creation, the second is the work of multiplication, the third is the work of union or collection. In the first work something is made and from nothing. In the second work something is made and from something. In the third work something is, indeed, made but not from nothing, because what is made has matter, and not from something, because when it is made it itself has form in matter, but, when two are one, another thing is made and passes into that that it may be that, and it ceases indeed to be what it is, and yet it does not cease to be because it begins to be what it is not. And, when it is made that which it begins to be, something is made, because that is something which it begins to be and which it is made, and yet that which is made is not made from nothing, because, before this was made, something was, nor again is that made from something, which is made, because it ceases to be what it was before, when it begins to be that which it was not before.

Let us express what we mean by something as an example. All which is one is, and all which ceases to be one ceases also to be in this very thing which ceases to be one. Thus without unity nothing can subsist. But from these things which are and are one, some gather their unity out of many, such as are compounds and consist of parts, which indeed have one being but do not have it from one because they consist of many. Others have their unity from one and have it in one, because one and the same is the thing itself from which they are and the thing itself which they are, such as are all simple things and those that do not consist of parts. For compounds, therefore, being one is nothing else than being united, and on this account being one does not truly exist, since it is of many and in many. Now, those things which have simple being, truly have being one, because one is both all which it is and from which it is. But of those again which are one from simplicity, some do not derive their unity from many because they have not been compounded, nor do they diffuse their unity into many, because they can not be multiplied nor be matter. Of such a nature are corporeal spirits who neither are from matter, because they are simple, nor can they be matter, because they are not bodies. Others indeed do not likewise gather their unity from many, because they are simple, but yet they diffuse their unity into many, because they are multiplied and become matter. Of such a nature are simple bodies, which are called atoms, which indeed are not from matter, because they are simple, but yet they become matter, because in themselves they are multiplied and grow increasingly. When, therefore, simple matter or a simple atom was made, something was made from nothing. But when this simple body itself is multiplied in itself and grows multiple, something is made from something into a greater thing. Although this seems wonderful, yet to make something from nothing is greater than to make more from something.

By this mode of operating, from the substance of the rib multiplied in itself by divine power without external addition the body of woman was made. For it is not proper that we should say that the rib received addition from without, that it might increase to that size which could have sufficed for the formation of woman's body, since, if this were true, it must more fittingly have been said that the body of woman was made not from the rib indeed but from what was added beyond the rib, which certainly was much greater. For this indeed would have been greater in matter and more significant, and would have had to be called principal matter. Thus nothing was added from without to that rib, but it itself was multiplied of itself through the cooperation of divine power, just as afterwards we perceive that human nature, disseminated by our first parents into subsequent generation, was so multiplied from a little that we see that already many thousands of men have grown from it. And all this pertains to the second work since from something are made some things into a greater thing.

But when through collection and union many things return to simple essence, just as before by increasing through multiplication they went forth in great numbers from simple essence, this is a third work; whether divine power works this in the secret bosom of nature with respect to some essences, so that for example He reduces some things from multiplicity to simplicity which before He had brought forth from simplicity to multiplicity, just as we can not know this, so also we should not stubbornly deny it. Only this should be considered, that it is one work when a simple essence is multiplied, another when a multiple essence is reduced to simplicity.

After these three works which are possible for God alone, there follow a fourth and fifth work also which befit the creature, in which there is nothing else to do than to separate what are joined, or to join what are separated. A sixth work is this, to reduce something to nothing. This is possible for God alone. Whether God ever does or does not do this, yet this is quite certain, that He who could create all things from nothing could also, if He should wish, reduce created things to nothing. After these six devoted to works follows number seven, to which not work but repose is due. These works, therefore, we have distinguished on account of those who are accustomed to wonder, and what is more, to doubt how woman was made from the rib of man and how from a small paternal seed so numerous a progeny can grow.

Part Seven

On the Fall of the First Man.

I. *How man fell through the envy of the devil.**

Therefore, man by Divine Providence was established as lord of the world in a place of delights and, as it were, in a favoured position; for the preservation of the goods which he possessed he was fortified by this same providence of God added to human reason, and the precept of obedience with grace operating equipped him for seeking and obtaining those goods which he was to have; and when the devil saw this he was envious that man should ascend there through obedience whence he himself had fallen through pride.

II. *Why the devil came in the form of another.*

Because indeed he could not do harm through violence he turned to fraud, that he might overthrow man by deceit whom he could not overcome by virtue. But through fear that his fraud would be of no avail at all, if he should be clearly revealed, it was impossible for him to come in his own form, lest he should be manifestly recognized and not at all received. Again, lest his fraud be too violent, if he should be entirely hidden, and at the same time lest man should seem to suffer injury, if God should permit him to be deceived by such a fraud as could not be guarded against, he was permitted indeed to come in another's form, but in such a form that his malice would not be entirely concealed.

That, therefore, he did not come in his own form was accomplished by his will, but that he could not have another form save such as would befit his malice was ordained by the regulation of God. Therefore, the wily enemy came to man as a serpent, who, perhaps, if he had been permitted, would have preferred to come in the form of a dove. But the Holy Spirit reserved this vessel for Himself, because surely it was not worthy that the wicked spirit should make that form odious to man in which afterwards the Holy Spirit was destined to appear to him.

III. *Why he came to woman first.*

But it pleases us to consider how fearful the malice of the enemy was in the beginning for tempting man's virtue. For, as if presuming little upon his own power, he attacked human nature in that portion where it seemed weaker, so that, if perhaps he should prevail to some extent there, afterwards with greater confidence he might proceed to assault the other portion which was stronger, or afterwards to overthrow it. Knowing, therefore, what was true, although it had not as yet been said: "Woe to him that is alone, for when he falleth, he hath

---

*This heading is lacking in our mss.

none to lift him up," (Ecclesiastes 4, 10), "and if a man prevail against one, two withstand him," (Ecclesiastes 4, 12), he first carefully sought out woman by herself, and, finding her, resolved to try in her first every effort of his temptation.

IV. *Why he began by questioning.*

Consider how great is the confusion and timidity of iniquity in the sight of virtue. Standing there even in the presence of a woman the enemy proud in his malice as yet only meditated and not uttered, is confounded, and, as if fearing that he was already caught before he even spoke, he does not dare to enter upon words of persuasion until by questioning he tries out beforehand the mind of her to be tempted. "Why," he says, "hath God commanded you, that you should eat of every tree of paradise?" And the woman answered him: "Of the fruit of the trees that are in paradise we do eat: But of the fruit of the tree which is in the midst of paradise, God hath commanded us that we should not eat; and that we should not touch it, lest perhaps we die." And the serpent said to the woman: "No, you shall not die the death," (Gen. 3, 1-4). Consider the accentuations of wickedness! First, God had said: "For in what day soever thou shalt eat of it, thou shalt die the death," (Gen. 2, 17). Then woman said: "Lest perhaps we die." Lastly, the serpent said: "No, you shall not die the death." God affirmed, woman doubted, the devil denied. But by no means would the devil have presumed in the presence of woman to deny the words of God, if he had not first found woman herself in doubt. Therefore, she who doubted departed from Him who affirmed and approached him who denied. She herself, then, to some extent began malice, who gave to the tempter the boldness of iniquitous persuasion.

V. *That the precept was not given to man alone.*

Here certainly we must consider that the precept was not, as seems above, given to man alone. For woman herself here bears witness that the command was given to her also, that she should not touch the tree of knowledge of good and evil. Evidently Scripture wished to show that woman, who was subject to man, was not to receive the divine command except through the medium of man, so that God's statement was first made as it were immediately to man, then through the medium of man it came to woman also, who was subject to man and was to be instructed by man's counsel.

VI. *On the manner of the temptation.*

But we must consider this carefully, how cleverly the enemy first by denying removed the evil which woman feared, and then freely persuaded her of the evil which he himself intended. Now, lastly he added a promise to support his persuasion, and, that the same persuasion might be received the more readily he doubled the promise. For he who persuaded a single eating only, setting up two things one by one as a reward, promised likeness of God and knowledge of good and evil. So in the persuasion to food he tempted man by gluttony; in the promise of divinity and knowledge, by vain glory and avarice. For immoderate desire to eat is gluttony, and inordinate desire to excel is vain glory, and the excessive passion for holding and possessing is avarice.

VII. *What evils were in original sin.*

In original sin, therefore, there were three vices, two acts of disobedience and one sin. The three vices were: pride, avarice, gluttony; the two acts of disobedience: one in the precept of nature, the other in the precept of discipline. And all these, because they were accomplished in one act, are called one sin.

Among the vices the first was pride, the second avarice, the third gluttony. In pride and avarice, the disobedience concerned the precept of nature; in gluttony alone did the disobedience concern the precept of discipline. For nowhere is it read that God prohibited man from desiring likeness of divinity or knowledge of good and evil. Yet because by desiring this inordinately he acted contrary to his reason, he was in a certain way a transgressor of the precept of nature. Of the tree of knowledge of good and evil alone do we read that God prohibited man from touching anything, and on this account when woman in her desire touched it she incurred the guilt of disobedience as regards the precept of discipline.

VIII. *That woman through delight in the promise gave assent to persuasion.*

Now we say that pride and avarice in original sin deceived and gained possession of the mind of man before the vice of gluttony, because, unless woman had first sought what was promised, by no means thereafter would she have given assent in that which was being persuaded. But, because she first was perversely delighted in the promise, thereafter she foolishly gave her assent in persuasion. For first she sought the promised excellence through pride, then she desired the promised abundance and such as befitted such excellence through avarice. Finally, that she might deserve to obtain these two according to her wish, corrupted by the vice of gluttony she consented to taste the forbidden food. First, indeed, she consented for the sake of other things which she loved; afterwards looking and seeing something desirable she burned with desire to such a degree that already, even if there were no reward, that which she saw pleased for its own sake.

At first, then, she was, as it were, induced to consent by a reward, afterwards attracted by her own delight she descended to the act. In pride and avarice, allured by the desire of reward she sold herself, but afterwards delighted in gluttony she presently began to serve gladly without reward. For when her foolish mind was first turned by love of the promise, Scripture says: "And the woman saw that the tree was fair to see, and sweet to eat, and she took of the fruit thereof, and did eat," (Cf. Gen. 3, 6).

At first through pride and avarice she consented to see, afterwards in seeing she recognized beauty, then in beauty she perceived sweetness. Now through sweetness, she burned with the desire of gluttony; lastly overcome by desire she took and ate. Thus then first for a reward she sold herself to serve sin; afterwards overcome by her own delight she presently even began gladly to serve without reward. Thus sometimes the just mind in its own imperfection, first by some reward which is offered, is excited to serve God; then when it has begun to grow into love of goodness it is held in His service by voluntary delight alone.

IX. *On the two kinds of temptations.*

Furthermore, we must know that there are two kinds of temptations, one exterior, the other interior. There is exterior temptation, when externally an evil is suggested to us, either visibly or invisibly, to be done. There is interior temptation when through the movement of depraved delight the mind within is urged to sin. Now this temptation is overcome with greater difficulty, because opposing within it is strengthened against us from our own. On this account the devil did not deserve forgiveness, because he sinned without any temptation. But man, because he fell overcome by external temptation alone, was the more severely to be punished in proportion to the lightness of the shock by which he had been cast down, and yet, because he had some occasion, though small, for falling, grace finally raised him to God's pardon. Yet the more serious the violence of the temptation that we suffer in sinning, the lighter the expiation by which we are restored to lost grace.

X. *Which sinned more, Adam or Eve?*

Some also ask which sinned more, Adam or Eve. But as the Apostle says: "The woman was seduced, not man," (Cf. I Tim. 2, 14). Indeed, Eve was seduced because she believed that what the devil said was true. And, therefore, not only did she inordinately seek likeness of God together with knowledge of good and evil, but she is thought very probably to have fallen into such perversity that she believed that God out of envy forbade the tree of knowledge of good and evil to man, lest man himself from tasting it might have been able to advance to equality with Him. For this is that perverse likeness which does not befit the creature, and is sought not out of imitation but out of comparison. Therefore, the woman desired this puffed up into pride, and, lest she might have been able to have it, she thought that the Creator Himself through envy had forbidden this tree to be touched.

Therefore, voluntary wickedness raised itself against its Creator, perversely wishing against Him, and impiously thinking about Him. Yet Adam was not seduced, because he knew that what the devil promised was false. And he did not eat the forbidden apple on this account, as if through that eating he believed that he could be made equal to God or even wished to be made equal, but only lest by resisting her will and petition he might offend the heart of the woman who had been associated with him through the affection of love, especially since he thought that he could both yield to the woman and afterwards through repentance and supplication for pardon please the Creator. Truly then is it said that he sinned less who thought of repentance and mercy; yet he sinned because he consented to the one sinning and did not correct the sinner. And so whatever blame there is in original sin, although dissimilarly, yet it redounds entirely to both; to her, indeed, because she sinned, to him because he consented to her sinning and made her sin his sin by consenting. And in this way, indeed, was man first seduced by the devil to sin. Now if we wish to consider interiorly, how sin came to him, or even what sin itself is which vitiates good nature and takes away its beauty and integrity, we must bring into the midst of our discussion certain things about the quality of interior man which will seem necessary to this investigation.

XI. *On the desire for the just and the desire for the beneficial.*

God had placed two things in man from the beginning, by which his whole nature might be ruled and led to the fulfilment of its end. These two were desire for the just and desire for the beneficial. One, that is, desire for the just, He had given so that it might be present for the will. The other, that is, desire for the beneficial, He had given so that it might be present according to necessity. One, voluntary; the other, necessary. He wished that the desire for the just be voluntary on this account, that in it man might deserve either good, if clearly he retained it when he was able to desert it, or evil, if he deserted it when he was able to retain it. God wished that the desire for the beneficial be necessary, in order that in it man might be rewarded either unto punishment, if he should abandon the other desire, that is the desire for the just, or unto glory, if he should retain this same desire, namely, for the just. In the desire, therefore, for the just God constituted the merit of man, but in the desire for the beneficial his reward. He subjected the desire for the just only to the will of man, because there could not have been merit except in the will and in free choice.

After these two desires followed their two effects: the just and the beneficial, yet dissimilarly and in contrary order. For the desire for the just or the affection is separable, because it is present according to the will, but its effect, that is the just or justice, is inseparable from it, because the desire for the just cannot be without justice. For to seek justice itself is to some degree to have justice. Therefore the affection for the just can be separated from the will, but its effect, that is justice, cannot be separated from the affection itself. Again, the desire for the beneficial is inseparable, because it is present according to necessity, and can never be separated from the rational will. But its effect, that is benefit, is separable from it, because benefit can be longed for, even when it is not possessed. And in this consists the greatest punishment when the creature, after he has been assigned punishment, can neither disdain its benefit on account of immutable nature, nor can possess it on account of irremissible guilt. On this account, therefore, God gave affection of justice to man as something separable, and ordained that its effect, that is justice, be inseparably present to the affection itself when it was at hand.

The affection for the beneficial he granted inseparable, and its effect, that is benefit, He did not equally command to be present inseparably, so that man, indeed, having lost that desire for the just alone, might lose the effect of this and that, or having retained that alone, might retain the effect of one and the other. But man did only what he could, and, because he abandoned of his own accord the desire for the just, on this account rightly did he lose both justice and benefit, retaining only desire for the beneficial unto the increase of unhappiness. For just as there would have been an increase of glory for man persevering in justice not to be able to grow cool in love and desire for good possessed, so it is the height of misery not to be able to restrain himself from desire for good, although he can not obtain this.

XII. *Whether man unwillingly or willingly lost the desire for the just.*

But it seems strange, if man first had a desire for justice, how afterwards he lost it. Did he, indeed, abandon it unwillingly or willingly? For if he abandoned it unwillingly, or rather if he lost it unwillingly, he suffered a necessity, he did not perform an iniquity. Nor should violence be called the blame of him who suffers it but of him who employs it. But if will is said to have preceded in this, because he cast aside the affection for justice by a kind of spontaneous deliberation, then the abandonment itself of justice is denied to have been the first sin, because the evil will through which it was done preceded that.

Nor can it be found whence such a will came to man, whereby he willed to abandon the good which he had, since he neither could have the willing from himself, nor did he receive from God the willing anything except the beneficial and the just. But it must be considered that, since to seek the just is nothing else than to will justice, to abandon the desire for the just is the same as to cease to will justice. Now he who ceases to will, does not cease to will by willing but by ceasing from the will, because similarly he who ceases to do something ceases not by doing, but by stopping and resting from what he is doing. Therefore, because man in abandoning his desire for the just did not begin to will what he first did not will, but only ceased to will what he first willed, it is not necessary that he be said to have done this willingly or not willingly.

Yet he willed something, because, since he could not have willed with this, he ceased to will this which he willed. Nor indeed did he will that because he ceased to will this, but rather he ceased to will this because he willed that. Yet his sin and iniquity do not depend on this, because he willed that, but because he ceased to will this, since if he had not ceased to will this, he could never have sinned by willing that or anything else. Now what will that be said to have been which he ceased to will in willing the just, except that he willed something outside the measure in which alone was justice? For whatever is outside the measure can not be just. But what this measure was in which the will of man had of necessity to be, that it might be good and no evil be in it, this we should consider diligently.

XIII. *That justice is a measure.*

God had prepared two goods for man, one temporal, the other eternal, that he might use the temporal and enjoy the eternal. But because to use or to enjoy goods is not praiseworthy, unless you use and enjoy them well, a measure was defined for man according to which he might use his temporal goods well and enjoy the eternal well.

XIV. *On the lower measure.*

Now the mode of the measure in the use of the lower good was four-fold: first, that he might use those only which he should use; second, as he should; third, to what extent he should; fourth, when he should. And if man should pass over any of these, he would lose the measure.

XV. *On the higher measure.*

Now the mode of the measure in the fruit of the higher good was found to be only twofold: first, that man might know how he should enjoy that good; second, that he might also recognize when it befitted him to enjoy that good. For the good that was to be enjoyed there did not have to be sought, because there was no good there except the one alone. Similarly also, how much that good was to be enjoyed did not have to be sought at all, since it was established without doubt that the more anyone would enjoy it, certainly the happier he would be. But the measure of quantity is to be sought only there where there can be too little or too much. But the fruit of this good is so constituted that it is full in him who possesses less and is not superfluous in him who possesses more. Therefore, in this alone did measure consist, that it should be recognized how he ought to enjoy that good, lest he should desire to possess it inordinately, not indeed according to imitation as befits the creature, but according to equality which transcends the possibility of the creature; similarly, that he should give heed lest he hasten to snatch it up before time, since he was not to receive it before he had completed his obedience.

Therefore, just as in these goods man's benefit had been established, so his justice must have been in the measure of using or enjoying these goods. And just as the will had been given him, whereby he might seek his goods and his benefit in his goods, so too it had been implanted in his will that the measure itself according to which he should have used or enjoyed these same goods of his should not displease him. In this, therefore, that he loved his goods, we consider the desire for the beneficial. But in this that he loved the measure of the beneficial in his goods, we understand the desire for the just.

Now he would always have loved measure, if he had wished for nothing outside measure. But from the time that he began to wish for something outside measure, he ceased to wish for measure. Moreover, after he ceased to wish for measure, he failed to love justice. And he lost justice in this, wherein he lost the very love of justice. For as justice can not be lacking its lover, so it can not by any means be present to him by whom it is not loved. In this, therefore, was the injustice of man: that he extended his desire beyond measure, both according to quality, when he wished to be made like his Creator, and according to time, when he hastened to foreseize reward before merit. When, therefore, he desired the highest good, he desired good but he did not desire well, because he sought to seize this both immoderately and unreasonably.

XVI. *What evil indeed was in man.*

Behold, therefore, what evil was there. For the good that was sought was not evil, nor the will likewise by which it was sought, in so far as it was will; and in so far as it was for good, there was not evil, but what was sought without measure this alone was evil. Therefore, for the will of man, this is not evil, which is will, because it is something, and all that is something is good, nor is this evil toward which it is, because it is likewise somethng, and all that is something is good, but what is without measure this is evil. For to be this is not to be something, but not to be that which should have been is something. And, therefore, evil is nothing, since that which should have been is not.

Therefore, this evil, that is, not to be what it should have been, since elsewhere it is either punishment or for punishment, is a fault in the rational will, because as often as it is in itself, it is from itself and through itself; from itself, because it was done through free choice and through itself because it was done by its own choice, in which it recedes by a kind of perverse imitation from likeness of God, from whom and through whom and in whom it is all that it is, because, when it is made base from itself and through itself and in itself, this alone is that which is nothing. This is its sin and injustice and blame, from which it appears base and reprehensible and worthy of reprobation, because it does not have its form or comeliness or beauty, for which it should have been loved and brought to glory.

XVII. *That man sinned in desire for the just, was punished in the desire for the beneficial.*

Since, therefore, man sinned in abandoning the desire for the just, he was punished in the desire for the beneficial which he retained. For this, indeed, was thus given to him, that it might be present to rational will inseparably, so that it might either be punished in this if it departed from justice, or rewarded if it remained in justice; since surely it could suffer no punishment at all, if it were seeking no benefit. For, in truth, the non-beneficial is nothing else than what is proven to be contrary to the will or desire.

Since, therefore, man abandoned the desire for justice, desire for benefit alone remained to him unto punishment. And in this he is doubly punished, either when he is restrained from those things which he desired ordinately, or when he is given free rein to seek other benefits which can not be desired ordinately. In the one is punishment, in the other punishment and blame. Now the measure of the higher desire has been placed in free will, but the measure of the lower desire had been conceded in gift. Wherefore, to wish to possess the former would have belonged to virtue, but to be able to retain the latter to felicity. Hence, just as it was a fault not to have retained the former, so it was made a punishment to have lost it. However, in this punishment there was also blame, because here also not to retain measure was against justice. But this blame was the punishment of antecedent blame, because, unless the spirit had abandoned measure in its desire, the flesh subject to spirit would not have crossed the bound of measure in its desire against the spirit itself.

XVIII. *Why the lower desire does not keep measure.*

For God had founded the body of the first man sound and whole; sound because there was nothing in it unto corruption; whole, because there was nothing lacking to it unto perfection. But in both He had set such a condition that neither integrity nor soundness could have been preserved without support. And so among created things He ordained certain ones outside, which could have availed to preserve and guard its soundness or integrity.

XIX. *That the care of the flesh is enjoined on the spirit.*

Now He enjoined upon the spirit which presided over the body the care and the duty of providing for these things. For just as God presided over the spirit, so also the spirit presided over the flesh, and the flesh itself was the mount of the spirit. It pertained to the rider to provide fodder for his mount, lest it grow weak, and this alone perhaps could then have sufficed. For now besides fodder, he has need of a bridle and spurs; the bridle, indeed, that he may check him when fiery and violent from evil; spurs, however, that he may excite him when slothful to do good. Then, accordingly, by furnishing fodder alone, without bridle or spurs, the rider would be carried pleasantly, and if perhaps a bridle were there, by which unknowing of itself the flesh might be guided how to go, yet it would have no need of being spurred, because it would not be slothful, nor need of being restrained, because it would not be impetuous. Because, therefore, the spirit was the rider, the office was enjoined upon it of providing fodder for its mount.

Therefore, in the execution of this, if the spirit should fulfill its office through command alone, not also through love, lest the mount would be crushed by its servile condition, God gave to the spirit affection, whereby it might love its body, that, just as it loved the integrity and soundness of the latter, so also it might freely provide all things which would avail to preserve these qualities. Again, lest there might be labour in seeking these or danger in taking them, a certain measure tempered equally both want and carnal desire so that a few things could have sufficed for nourishment, and moderate amounts for satiety. And so providing for the flesh would not have been so much a task as a pleasure and exercise, if man had kept justice. But because the spirit exalted above itself did not wish to restrain its desire within measure, on this account was it brought about to its toil and misery that now in the desire of its flesh it could not keep measure. For to punish the sin of the spirit, God by mortality destroyed the integrity of the human body; and because of this it now needs more nourishment than before both for restoring soundness, in so far as it has perished, and for preserving it, in so far as it has remained. Hence that dire necessity is born to extend desire necessarily beyond the order of the first disposition, so that indeed it may not only guard nature but also expel the vice and corruption of nature itself. For the spirit, just as there was naturally granted to it to love the benefit of its flesh, so naturally possessed this characteristic also, that it can not love what is not beneficial to it.

XX. *That the necessity of desiring does not excuse, since it comes from the will.*

But we ought to know that this necessity of desiring is not, on this account, not a fault, because it is a necessity, since, that this necessity might be, necessity was not the cause but the will. But what shall we say? If man naturally possesses this characteristic, that he can not love what is not beneficial to him, nor despise what is beneficial, whatever he seeks, therefore, is beneficial to him, and he never seeks anything except what is beneficial to him. If this is true, why is he sometimes reprehended or accused for what he seeks, since he never seeks anything except what is beneficial to him, and it has been granted to him naturally to seek this to such a degree that, since nature itself consists unalterably in that which it was made, he can not seek anything else at all except what is beneficial to him?

XXI. *That what is beneficial and what is ordinate must be sought.*

But it is one thing to seek what in some mode is beneficial in that mode in which it is not beneficial, and another to desire what is beneficial in that mode in which it is beneficial. For everything that is beneficial is beneficial in some mode, and similarly all that is not beneficial is not beneficial in some mode and not universally so. Therefore, whoever seeks what in some mode is beneficial, but does not seek it in that mode in which it is beneficial, even though he thinks that it is beneficial in that mode in which he seeks it, he does not seek anything that is not beneficial; yet what he seeks is not beneficial, because he seeks what he seeks for the sake of what is beneficial, and he thinks that his benefit is in that which he seeks. Therefore, he is not deceived in this, that he seeks his benefit, because he knows that what he seeks is his benefit, but he is deceived in this, that he thinks that his benefit is where it is not, that is, in that which he seeks for the sake of his benefit.

Now, whenever one seeks what is beneficial, and in that mode in which it is beneficial, yet is not ordinate, the evil consists not in this, that he seeks what is beneficial, but in this, that he seeks what it is not ordinate. For just as it was granted to him to seek what is beneficial, so also was it forbidden him to seek what is not ordinate. When, therefore, these concur, what in some mode is beneficial and what is not ordinate, if there is desire for the beneficial in his affection, because this has been implanted in his nature, he must be restrained, nevertheless, from the effect on account of the obligation of reason to which it was not conceded to go to inordinate things. For the beauty and dignity of reason appear in this, that it checks its affection from inordinate things; because on this account there ought to have been more benefits, from which, while reason presided and restrained affection as it issued forth as much as it could, the greatness of its dignity and excellence might appear.

XXII. *That nothing is desired save benefit.*

If, therefore, we say that nature can seek nothing at all except benefit, it must not be thought false, because it seeks certain things in which its benefit does not exist, when it is deceived, or even because it seeks certain things in which there is some benefit, but in which the benefit is not ordinate, when it transgresses. We see that sometimes a sick person seeks a potion or the knife, yet he does not seek bitterness or pain but health. And there are certain sweet things which are sought and sought evilly, because thy are inordinate; yet they are not evil because they are sweet but because they are inordinate. And again there are certain bitter things that are sought and are sought well, because they are ordinate, and yet they are not good because they are bitter but because they are ordinate.

It happens sometimes that the things which are sweet have some good in themselves and generate much evil from themselves, and that the good in them is small and the evil from them great. Again it happens that those that are bitter have some evil in themselves and generate much good from themselves; the evil in them is small and the good from them great. And on this account the imprudent who see the present and do not foresee the future, avoid small evils and incur great ones, and similarly they choose small goods and lose the great. Yet in all these nothing is sought save benefit; when ordinately, indeed well; but when inordinately, evilly; yet not evilly, because it is a benefit, but evilly, because it is inordinate.

XXIII. *How necessity comes from the will.*

Now if man seems excusable for the reason that nature corrupted by the infirmity of mortality can not of itself check its affection now flowing forth of necessity beyond measure, we must consider that this necessity which the will antecedently operated can not excuse. For voluntary guilt deserved punishment, but punishment produced infirmity, and infirmity brought on necessity. And, because the will produced necessity, necessity can not excuse the will itself. Therefore, the transgression of the higher desire which was guilt only, was followed by the transgression of the lower which is both punishment and guilt. In the spirit is guilt alone; in the flesh, both punishment and guilt. The inordinate concupiscence of the spirit is guilt; the concupiscence of the flesh both punishment and guilt—punishment of the antecedent guilt, and guilt of subsequent punishment.

XXIV. *What we take through generation; what we lose through regeneration.*

When, therefore, mortal flesh through coition is sown in concupiscence to generate progeny, both punishment and guilt pass in the flesh through concupiscence to the progeny to be born. But when by the sacrament of redemption they are regenerated who were generated in punishment and guilt, from those to be cleansed through the spirit of regeneration not the punishment but the guilt is taken away in the original vice itself. For guilt is taken away, that they may be justified, but punishment remains, that they may be exercised.

XXV. *On original sin.*

On original sin many difficult questions arise, and whether they are treated better by believing than by discussing, I know not—if, indeed these questions admit of any discussion which can not have a full solution. First, it is asked what original sin is; then how it is transmitted from fathers to their children, especially from those in whom through the sacrament of regeneration it was cancelled, whether through the soul alone or through the flesh alone or through the soul together with the flesh, and, if through the soul alone, whether through creation or through transmission, but, if through the flesh alone, why that redounds upon the soul which is not from the soul.

XXVI. *In how many ways original sin may be spoken of.*

Original sin can be understood in a twofold manner, namely, either as that first disobedience of man which was the first of all sins and stands out as the origin of all subsequent sin, or as that vice with which, on being transmitted by him, all those take their beginning who are transmitted by him through the propagation of the flesh. But this vice of human origin infects nature with a twofold corruption, namely, the mind with ignorance, and the flesh with concupiscence.

These two evils, indeed, were in our first parent as the punishment of antecedent guilt and of actual guilt, but in us guilt of subsequent punishment and at the same time original guilt and punishment. When, therefore, we speak of original sin as regards the first man, we understand that first blame of his disobedience, which in his case, indeed, is called original, not because his nature took origin from that or with that, but because from that as the first guilt of all there afterwards arose and went forth all its subsequent evils. Now, since in him from the first origin no sin descended, that sin also which in him is called original was actual on his part, since certainly he who did not take sin through birth did not have sin except that which he committed by act.

XXVII. *What was actual for the first man, is original for us.*

Now, we who take our origin from him by birth have as original what was actual for him, because what in him was through act descends to us through birth alone. For our nature through birth alone has transmitted to us the corruption which it received in him through his act. And, therefore, we by birth receive the sin, which that one did not have by birth but by act from whom we are come by birth. In him, indeed, the spirit swelling with pride against the Creator did not keep obedience, and, therefore, the Creator to avenge His injury punished the spirit with ignorance indeed but the flesh with concupiscence, so that the spirit does not see in itself the good to be done but in its flesh desires to do evil. These two vices to punish man's pride are justly confirmed in him, ignorance, indeed, because the light of truth is taken from the mind, but concupiscence because the flesh is afflicted with the punishment of mortality. Therefore, nature, which was first vitiated, transfers this original corruption to posterity, furnishing ignorance to the soul but concupiscence to the flesh unto corruption.

XXVIII. *What original sin is.*

If, therefore, it is asked what is original sin in us, it is understood to be the corruption or vice which we take by birth through ignorance in the mind, through concupiscence in the flesh.

XXIX. *How original sin passes from parents to children.*

After it has been shown, therefore, what original sin is, it is fitting that we also investigate how it is transmitted from parents to children, that is, whether according to the soul alone or according to the flesh alone or according to both. Some have thought that original sin descends from parents to children not only through the flesh but also through the soul, because they believed that not only the flesh but the soul also is from transmission of matter. For just as in the generating of offspring flesh is taken substantially from parental flesh, so the soul of the one begotten is believed by these to be derived essentially from the soul of the one begetting, because just as corrupted flesh is sown from corrupted flesh, so too from a sinful soul is taken a sinful soul infected by original corruption.

XXX. *That the soul is not from transmission.*

But here certain of the learned are found to have brought forward from all sides many reasons and authorities with which they have tried to establish that not the soul but the flesh alone is from transmission. And this indeed is the first reason, because it does not befit spiritual nature either to be from matter, since it is essentially simple, or to be matter, since always consisting indivisibly in the simplicity of its unity it can not be increased or multiplied at all. For a simple nature does not accomplish propagation where a part can not be taken for that which must be propagated from that by which it is to be propagated without the whole passing over. Since, therefore, there is one between two, if the whole passes over, nothing of it remains to that from which it is. But, if the whole remains, nothing is given to that which it is. If, then, the soul is born of a soul just as flesh of flesh, let them say how that simple substance either remains entire in him who begets, if it passes into the one begotten, or passes entire into the begotten, if it remains in the begetter; perhaps they should wish to say that all souls are consubstantial and that that simple nature is indeed multiplied personally in the propagation of children but is not divided essentially, not noticing with how much inconsistency they follow this doctrine, if one and the same essence should be believed to be destined alike to blessedness and damnation, to glory and punishment.

Finally, since authority says: "And the dust return into its earth, from whence it was taken, and the spirit return to God, who gave it," (Cf. Ecclesiastes 12, 7), it is shown clearly that not spirit from spirit, but flesh from flesh is materially transmitted. For although our bodies were not taken in the first place materially from the earth, yet they are not inappropriately said to have been taken from the earth, because the body of the first man from which our bodies have descended materially from matter was taken from earth through matter. Although in the same sense this could be said about our spirits also, if indeed they were believed to be from transmission, that they were given by the Lord in that the first spirit was given by the Lord from which they descended through matter; yet it is more probably established that souls are not from transmission, because just as it is read that in the first man body was taken from earth but spirit given by God, so also reason demands that it be believed that in subsequent men also flesh indeed descends from flesh but spirit comes from the Lord. But yet when we read that rational spirit was given or inspired by the Lord, by no means ought we to believe that it was taken, as it were, materially from the divine essence or substance, but that body came from earth through matter, but spirit without pre-existing matter received being through the power of the Creator alone. Just as the body is from him from whom it has taken its matter, so spirit is from Him through whom and from whom it received its being, namely, through Him when He made it but from Him when He gave it.

Now again the Psalmist says: "He who hath made the hearts of every one of them," (Psal. 32, 15). Thus God is said to make hearts individually, that is rational spirits or souls, because he is declared to create these from nothing, not some from others, as is apparent in corporeal nature, but individually by themselves. On this account, since it is written in the Law: "If one strike a woman with child, and she miscarry, if the child be not formed, let him be punished with a fine, but if the child be formed, he shall render soul for soul," (Cf. Ex. 21, 22 and 23), it is openly declared that when flesh is generated from flesh, soul similarly is not taken from soul. For if soul is generated with flesh, why in the abortion and the unformed child should soul not be rendered for soul? Since, therefore, in the formed abortion only soul is ordered to be rendered for soul, what is shown except that in that which is still unformed, soul is not yet present, so that in truth, just as in the case of first man we read that the body was formed first, then that the soul was infused, thus too in the case of all subsequent men we may believe that the human body is formed first in the womb, then that the soul is infused? But if perhaps it should seem strange to anyone, how paternal semen in the womb before animation can grow or be quickened or even proceed to the very image of the human body, let him see how shrubs and plants and all growing things of this kind, though not possessing a soul, are quickened by verdure alone and increase, and by their own movement are made to grow into a form befitting their kind. Therefore, for these reasons and others of this kind it is rendered probable that souls are not from transmission but new souls created from nothing are daily infused for quickening into new bodies formed in the womb from the paternal semen. Yet in all this never has any reason or authority been able to prevail to such an extent as to dispel questioning doubt, with this exception alone, that the Catholic faith has chosen as rather to be believed that souls are made daily from nothing to be associated with bodies which must be quickened than that such souls are propagated by transmission according to the nature of the body and the character of human flesh.

Now, if souls were thought to be from transmission, there would not be so much questioning, because justice would be more manifest in this, that original sin is said to pass from parents to children. But if we can not by reason comprehend the hidden judgments of God, yet for solving doubtful things we ought not to assert other doubtful ones. Yet it is asked: if souls are not from transmission, how are children guilty of the sin of parents? For whatever sin is in the parent descends certainly into the son through that nature alone, which alone through generation passes from father to son. If, therefore, flesh alone is generated, surely through flesh alone is original sin transmitted. And if this is true, two necessary questions confront us: namely, one, how through flesh alone without soul sin passes from father to son; second, how the soul becomes a participant in that sin which descends through flesh alone and in flesh alone. For how can flesh have sin without soul, which flesh without soul can not sin at all? If, therefore, in flesh without soul there was no sin, how through flesh or in flesh could sin pass to soul? For what at some time was not in the flesh, that afterwards the soul did not receive from the flesh.

XXXI. *How sin passes through flesh to the soul.*

From its first corruption human nature took on two vices, from which afterwards grew the stock of all subsequent evils. Now, these were ignorance of good and concupiscence of evil; of which one, that is ignorance, infected the mind; the other, that is concupiscence, sullied the flesh. Ignorance was the punishment of pride, concupiscence the effect of mortality. Thus four evils appear in man: pride, ignorance, mortality, concupiscence. Pride is the guilt of the mind only; mortality, punishment of the flesh only; ignorance, guilt and punishment in the mind; concupiscence, punishment and guilt in the flesh. On account of pride the mind was darkened through ignorance, on account of mortality the flesh was softened through concupiscence. For since the mind was puffed up through pride against God, struck with ignorance it lost the light of truth. But since the flesh was struck with mortality, dissipated by the very infirmity of its languor it extended its desire beyond the measure of the first disposition. For this is what is called concupiscence of the flesh itself, namely, the natural desire or affection transgressing order and going beyond measure—transgressing order when it moves toward those things to which it ought not; going beyond measure, when it moves otherwise than it ought. For the desire transgresses order, when we desire those things which we ought not to desire. Now desire does not keep measure when we desire also those things which should be desired otherwise than we ought. Thus, therefore, from the first guilt and ultimate punishment two intermediates have arisen, guilt and punishment—ignorance of good, guilt and punishment in mind; concupiscence of evil, guilt and punishment in the flesh. In these consists the root of original sin.

Since, therefore, human flesh is generated from parents with mortality, in this very fact, that being generated it is subject to mortality, afterwards being quickened it is found subjected to the necessity of carnal concupiscence, because the infirmity itself of mortality is the cause which the necessity of carnal desire follows. Flesh, therefore, which is generated in concupiscence is conceived with mortality, and is born with the necessity of concupiscence. In him from whom it is generated, it has guilt and the act of guilt. In that it is generated, it has neither guilt nor the act of guilt, but the cause. In that it is born, it has the cause of guilt and guilt, but it has not the act. The cause of guilt is the corruption of mortality, guilt is concupiscence. The act of guilt is to have concupiscent desire; the cause of guilt is the root. Guilt itself is the tree; the act of guilt is the fruit. So in this, that it is generated, is the corruption of mortality; but in this that it is born, is the vice of concupiscence. Now, in this that it is moved through concupiscence, the act which begins from the movement of the will is accomplished by the movement of operation. So those being born should not be thought to be without vice, because they do not have concupiscent desire, since radically the vice of concupiscence is in them themselves, through which afterwards when they are active they have such desire.

XXXII. *How ignorance is a vice.*

Now, ignorance is not a vice in these, because at birth they do not recognize truth when they ought not, but because then, when they are born, vice is in them by which afterwards they are impeded from recognizing the truth when they ought. In fact, to be born without knowledge is nature, not guilt. But to be born in that vice by which afterwards they are hindered from a knowledge of truth is guilt not nature. But this vice is in the corruption of the flesh and in the corruption of the carnal sense; this carnal sense, if it had its integrity, promoted and exercised, would take on without labour the judgment of truth instructed by those things which were seen externally. Since, indeed, through corruption of the flesh it was deprived of its integrity, it can not drink in pure truth without confusion of error.

XXXIII. *That angels were made so that they were instructed from within, men from without.*

The angels, in truth, since they were made perfect, were instructed from within; but men, (the first man alone of course being excepted, who just as he was made perfect in his mode so also was himself instructed from within), because they had to advance to knowledge through intervals of time, had to be stimulated and instructed to knowledge of truth through the forms of temporal and visible things without. Yet this stimulation and instruction would be present to man naturally and without labor, if man's sense in mortal flesh had not been corrupted through sin, so that then full and perfect that would be established which the Apostle mentions: "The invisible things of him, from the creation of the world, are clearly seen, being understood by the things that are made," (Rom. 1, 20).

XXXIV. *Whence concupiscence arises and whence ignorance.*

In mortal flesh, therefore, from corrupted sensibility is born the vice of concupiscence, from corrupted sense the vice of ignorance, because on the one hand the desire of seeking necessity extends itself beyond the measure, on the other the instrument for conceiving truth is lacking in the vigour of integrity.

Now this raises a most difficult problem, that we do not seem to ascribe original sin except to the vice of carnal corruption alone, and yet we must confess that it extends even to the participation of the rational soul.

XXXV. *How the soul becomes a participant in original sin.*

Now how the soul which is created pure and without vice becomes a participant in that vice which is brought in through the flesh alone would be worthy of inquiry, if this could be investigated with some care. But now, since this has not been explained to human science unto knowledge, we should believe with faith, not inquire with curiosity. For, if we should say that the soul when it is mingled with the body is inclined by a kind of will to delight in sin, we already show that it is guilty not only of original but also of actual sin. But if we admit that it has been forced by some necessity into association with the body and into contact with corporeal vice, we indicate that by very necessity it has been absolved of guilt. For what is entirely of necessity is not imputable, but what is of the will is not original but proper. Therefore, it is clear that the rational soul when infused into the human body is neither corrupted by the will lest sin be actual nor is it corrupted by necessity lest vice be not imputable. Thus it has neither evil nor evil will since it has not yet received willing, nor evil operation since it has not yet been able to act well or evilly, but it has evil since it is such that, unless it be aided by grace, it can neither receive knowledge of truth nor resist the concupiscence of the flesh.

Now this evil is present in it not from the integrity of its foundation but from association with corruptible flesh. And in truth this corruption, since it is transmitted from our first parent to all posterity through propagation of flesh, spreads the stain of original sin among all men in the vice of ignorance and concupiscence. But, if it is inquired by what justice those things are imputed to the soul, which it has not received from creation nor committed from will, but has contracted from association alone with flesh, (which association, however, it has not claimed by its own choice but has received in the precept and disposition of its Creator), we must in the end confess what is true, that divine justice is in truth irreprehensible in this but is not comprehensible.

XXXVI. *The argument of some on incorporating souls.*

For there are those who say that God from the beginning had proposed to associate souls with bodies to be quickened and indeed had enjoined upon man the duty of generating bodies but had retained for Himself the power of creating souls, that a just man might generate pure bodies but that just God might create pure souls and associate them with bodies. Even if man corrupted his work, God must not have changed His purpose. And, therefore, God according to His good purpose might have created pure souls and associated them with bodies, since, in those in which they find corruption and ascribe corruption, they say that this is not from God who made souls without corruption but from man who corrupted the nature of bodies. Therefore, those who say this do not explain the plan of the divine justice, since, just as it did not pertain to the divine goodness to make souls evil, so it did not seem fitting either for it to plan to place them there where they would of necessity become evil. So we must not insist strongly that this be investigated with reason, which ought to be examined with faith rather than with reason.

XXXVII. *How sinful children are born from just parents.*

However, it is asked how they contract original sin who are begotten of those who have received remission of original sin either through the sacrament of faith or by faith alone. For how can that pass from parents into children which is not in the parents themselves? But we should realize that original sin, which through generation of flesh is transmitted from parents to children, although as regards guilt it has been remitted in those who beget, yet as regards punishment remained in them, is remitted as regards guilt since it is not imputed, is retained as regards punishment since it is not taken away. For this is what the Apostle says: "There is now no condemnation to them that are in Jesus Christ," (Rom. 8, 1), in order of course that he might show that to those who are reborn in Christ Jesus, although the infirmity of the original corruption is not taken away, yet through the intervention of the sacrament of regeneration it is not imputed unto damnation.

And in these, indeed, there can certainly be incentive to sin but sin can not dominate so long as they guard their freedom and do not lose the spirit of adoption by sinning voluntarily. For though freed from the servitude of sin we are indeed held under the corruption by necessity of mortality, but we are not subject to the dominion of sin except by our will. Wherefore, the same Apostle says: "Let not sin reign in your mortal body," (Rom. 6, 12). Our body, indeed, through mortal necessity carries the incentive to sin in the root itself of corruption, but where there is the spirit of liberty, sin itself can not rise to rule. And so original sin which in parents has been blotted out regarding guilt through regeneration, since, however, it remains unto punishment, in passing to those who are generated, not only exists unto punishment but is even imputed unto guilt, until on receiving the laver of regeneration guilt is blotted out in themselves also even if punishment remains.

XXXVIII. *Whether all the sins of preceding parents pass to the children.*

Now it is asked whether all the sins of preceding parents pass to children, just as we see that that offense of our first parent has redounded unto all who were born from him. If this is true, the later men are born, the more wretched certainly they are. Nor does it seem a fair condition that time should be prejudicial to truth, unless perhaps the more nature is corrupted, the worse it is generated. For when Scripture says: "I shall visit the iniquity of the fathers upon the children unto the third and fourth generation," (Exod. 20, 5), it is shown clearly that the sins of parents are required by their children. But why "unto the third and fourth generation" and not further it can not be easily shown, unless perhaps those things which could have been exacted through justice unto all generations are terminated through mercy in the third and fourth generation, lest perhaps judgment would become unbearable, if divine vengeance should punish all sins of those preceding in those who follow.

Now this is said in another place: "The son shall not bear the iniquity of the father, and the father shall not bear the iniquity of the son," (Ezech. 18, 20). Regarding that iniquity truly it is understood how distinct, personally and essentially, and how divided from each other the father and son operate. For since the son has been made different from the father in person and the father different from the son, just as each has to operate by his own choice, so what the one does ought not thereafter to be imputed to the other.

Now what has been said: "I shall visit the iniquity of the fathers upon the children," ought to be understood of those sins which parents committed before they were born of them unto whom their sins must have redounded. Why, then, unto the fourth generation, unless because either through mercy the rigor of justice is tempered, or by the third and fourth generation every generation is meant, or, which seems more probable, the sins of the fathers are said to be punished in the sons unto the time when the sons themselves, seeing the sins of these fathers, imitate them; thus that we may know that children are never made participants in the sins of parents, unless before by sinning they have been made imitators, so that each one is condemned for his own sin not for that of another, since he makes the sin of another his own which in loving and following he imitates?

For what is generally said is more properly understood thus: The son shall not bear the iniquity of the father, and the father shall not bear the iniquity of the son, so that never do the sins of another cause any harm except to those who imitate them by sinning. For, since against what had been said: "The fathers have eaten sour grapes, and the teeth of the children are set on edge," (Ezech. 18, 2), was opposed: "The son shall not bear the iniquity of the father, and the father shall not bear the iniquity of the son; the soul that sinneth, the same shall die," it is necessary that, if in the former statement we take the meaning to be that the sins of preceding parents pass to subsequent children, in the following assertion we understand that each one is held for his own sin and the preceding sins of parents do not redound to subsequent children. And, if this is true, it is clear that the actual sins of parents do not pass to children but only original sin, which in comparison with all the rest was so much greater, the more able it was in comparison with all the rest to change nature itself. This, indeed, sown in the same corruption passed on to posterity, with which it corrupted and infected human nature at its first root.

Part Eight

On the Restoration of Man.

I. *On the fact that three things must be considered regarding the restoration of man.*

The first guilt of man was pride which was followed by a threefold punishment. One is a punishment which is punishment only, that is mortality of the body; the remaining two are both punishment and guilt, of which one is concupiscence of the flesh, and the other is ignorance of the mind. Since, therefore, man was afflicted by such punishment, through which guilt would not be cleansed but increased, he might have descended to eternal punishment through temporal punishment, had he not afterwards been freed through grace. But, lest he should be found destined to condemnation, if he should be judged immediately, his judgment was deferred. And since divine mercy foreordained him to salvation, in this time of expectation and delay it assigned him a place for repentance and correction, in order that meanwhile through its grace it might make him such that it could judge him finally not only with mercy but also with justice unto salvation.

Therefore, three things occur here for consideration in the first place on the restoration of man: time, place, remedy. The time is the present life from the beginning of the world even to the end of the world. The place is this world. The remedy consists in three things: in faith, in the sacraments, in good works. The time is long, lest man be taken unprepared. The place is rough that the prevaricator may be punished. The remedy is efficacious that the weak may be healed.

II. *On the five places.*

There are five places: one in which there is only good and the highest good; one in which there is only evil and the highest evil; after these two others, one below the highest in which there is only good but not the highest, the other above the lowest in which there is only evil but not the highest; in the middle a place in which there are both good and evil, neither the highest. In heaven there is only good and the highest; in hell there is only evil and the highest; in paradise there is only good but not the highest; in the fire of purgatory, evil only but not the highest; in the world there are good and evil, neither the highest. Paradise is the place of those beginning and progressing into better, and there must have been only good there, since creature must not have had its beginning from evil. Yet it must not have been the highest, since if the highest were there those placed there would have no progress. Heaven is the place of the confirmed good and of those who through discipline attain to the highest progress. One good alone and the highest was placed there. Hell is the place of the confirmed evil and of those who abandon discipline irreparably, and on this account evil alone and the highest was placed there. The fire of purgatory is the place of those less corrected in the first correction and who are to be perfected in the second, and on this account it was obliged to have only evil that it might be worse than the former place, where both evil and good existed simultaneously. The world is the place of the erring and of those who are to be restored, and so good and evil simultaneously were ordered in it, that through good indeed they might receive consolation, but through evil correction. Yet the highest good or the highest evil is not there, that there may be a place where those who persist in evil can regress, and those who recede from evil can progress.

Thus then heaven is in the highest place, after heaven paradise, after paradise the world, after the world the fire of purgatory, after the fire of purgatory hell. The devil, therefore, who had fallen from the highest was thrust down into the lowest for the reason that he was not to be restored. But man, since he did not fall from the highest, was not put in the lowest but was stationed in the middle, that he might have a place where he might ascend through the merit of justice or descend through the guilt of sin.

III. *How man was disposed unto repentance.*

He, therefore, was placed in this world in a place of repentance, since a time for repenting was granted that he might correct his evils, restore his goods, so that finally coming to judgment corrected he might receive not punishment for guilt but the glory prepared for him for justice. It remains, therefore, that while there is time he seek counsel and ask help for his correction and liberation. But, since he is found sufficient of himself for neither, it is necessary that He, who by His grace postpones judgment, by the same grace meanwhile show counsel for escaping, and after counsel bring help. And thus there is need that He, meanwhile, lay aside the character of the judge, and assume first the character of counselor, then that of the helper, at least in such a way that He first leave man entirely to himself, in order that man himself may both experience his own ignorance and realize that he is in need of counsel, then also feel his lack and recognize that he has need of help.

For such a reason, therefore, in the time of the natural law man was left entirely to himself, afterwards in the time of the written law counsel was given to him when he realized his ignorance, finally in the time of grace help was furnished him when he confessed his lack. Counsel was in the reckoning of satisfaction. Help was in the effect of redemption. In order, therefore, that we may be able to know more clearly the reckoning of satisfaction which man must pay to the Creator for his sin, we must first consider man's case more attentively for a little while. This case, indeed, is prepared to be pleaded among three persons, namely, God, man, and the devil.

IV. *On the case of man as regards God and the devil.*

These three, therefore, appear in the case: man, God, and the devil. The devil is convicted of having done injury to God, since he abducted man, His servant, by fraud and held him by violence. Similarly, man is convicted of having done injury to God, since he contemned His precept and placing himself under the hand of another caused Him the loss of his service. Likewise the devil is convicted of having done injury to man, since he deceived him beforehand by promising goods, and afterwards harmed him by inflicting evils. Unjustly then does the devil hold man, but man is held justly, since the devil never deserved that he should oppress man as subject to him, but man deserved through his sin that he should be permitted to be oppressed by him. For although he did not know that what the devil promised was false, yet he was not ignorant that, even if it were true, he should not have desired it contrary to the will of the Creator.

Justly then was the man subjected to the devil, in so far as pertains to his sin, but unjustly, in so far as pertains to the devil's deception.

If, therefore, man had such an advocate that through his power the devil could be brought to court, man would justly object to the devil's dominion, since the devil had no just cause whereby he might lawfully claim his right in man. Now no such advocate could be found except God, but God was unwilling to take up man's case, since He was still angry with man for his sin. Therefore, it was necessary that man first placate God, and thus afterwards with God as advocate enter suit with the devil. But he could not placate God rationally, unless he restored the damage which he had caused and made satisfaction for his contempt. But man had nothing which could compensate God worthily for the loss incurred, since if he rendered Him anything from irrational creation for the rational which had been taken away, it would be too little. But he could not render man for man either, since he had taken away the just and the innocent and he found no one save the sinner. Therefore, man found nothing with which he could placate God toward himself, since whether he should give what was his or himself, the recompense would be unworthy.

So God, seeing that man by his own power could not escape the yoke of damnation, took pity upon him, and first He assisted him gratuitously through mercy alone, that afterwards He might free him through justice, that is, since man had not the power of himself to escape justice, God through mercy gave justice. For the rescue of man would not be perfectly reasonable, unless it were just on both sides, that is, as God had the justice of seeking man, so too man would have the justice of escaping. But man could never have had this justice, unless God through His mercy would bestow it upon him. In order, therefore, that God could be placated toward man, God gave man freely what man might duly render to God. He gave to man, therefore, a man whom man might return for man, who, that a worthy recompense might be made, was not only equal to the first man but greater. So that man greater than man might be returned for man, God was made man for man, and as man gave Himself to man, that He might assume Himself from man. God the Son of God was made flesh, and God the man Christ was given to man. Just as Isaias says: "A child is born to us and a son is given to us," (Isaias 9, 6). Therefore, that Christ was given to man was the mercy of God, that Christ was returned by man was the justice of man. For in the birth of Christ God was justly placated toward man, since such a man was found for man who not only, as was said, was equal to but even greater than man. On this account at the birth of Christ the angels announce peace to the world, saying: "Glory to God in the highest, and on earth peace to men of good will," (Luke 2, 14).

But there was still left for man that, just as by restoring damage he had placated anger, so also by giving satisfaction for contempt he should be made worthy to escape punishment. But this could not be done properly unless he should assume of His own accord and obediently the punishment which he did not owe, so that he might become worthy of being rescued from the punishment which he had merited through disobedience. But man the sinner could not pay this punishment who, whatever punishment he would assume, would in no way sustain it except worthily and justly on account of the guilt of his first contempt. Therefore, that man might justly escape the punishment due, it was necessary that such a man assume punishment for man who had owed no punishment. But none such could be found save Christ. Christ, then, by His birth paid man's debt to the Father, and by His death atoned for man's guilt, so that, when He Himself assumed death for man which He did not owe, man on account of Him might justly escape death which he owed and the devil might no longer find room for calumny, since the devil himself was not to have dominion over man, and man was worthy to be freed.

So He hath maintained our judgment and our cause, as it is written: "For thou hast maintained my judgment and my cause," (Psal. 9, 5). He hath maintained our cause because He paid the debt to the Father for us, and by dying atoned for our guilt, and He hath maintained our judgment, since descending into hell and breaking the gates of death He freed the captives who were held there. Therefore, the judgment of the devil regarding God was made from the very beginning of the world; the judgment of man regarding the devil, in the passion of Christ. The judgment of man as regards God is delayed even unto the consummation of the world. And on this account, if man shall wish first to be reconciled to God through Christ, afterwards he will await his judgment without fear of damnation.

V. *On the distinction of judgments.*

There are four judgments: according to foreknowledge, according to cause, according to operation, according to retribution. According to foreknoweldge we were judged before we were. According to cause we are judged from the time when we begin to be, when we are good or evil. According to operation we are judged, when by our works externally we show of what nature we are within ourselves. According to retribution we shall be judged, when on obtaining the reward of our works we shall know of what nature we have been in the eyes of God from eternity.

Of these four judgments two are hidden: namely, judgment according to foreknowledge and judgment according to cause; and for this reason in these human judgment is not included. Two are manifest, that is judgment according to operation and judgment according to retribution. And in one of these, namely, in judgment according to operation, power of judging in the present is given men by God. But the other, namely, judgment according to retribution, will be judged not by men but by God in the presence of men. But judgment according to foreknowledge is hidden and immutable; judgment according to cause is hidden and mutable; judgment according to operation is manifest and mutable; judgment according to retribution is manifest and immutable. Judgment according to operation is in a measure an image, and a sacrament of judgment according to retribution, since the former manifests cause and suggests foreknowledge, but the latter will manifest cause and will confirm foreknowledge.

Likewise we must consider that judgment is made in one way when sentence is pronounced, in another way when it is made known. Indeed, in pronouncing the sentence of every judgment Father and Son and Holy Ghost judge together. But in making sentence known the Son alone judges, since in His divinity with Father and Holy Ghost He had the power to pronounce the sentence of every judgment; in His humanity He alone received the power to make known the sentence of every judgment. On this account His humanity, which does not have the power to pronounce sentence, in so far as pertains to pronouncing sentence, has said: "I judge not any man," (John 8, 15), and yet, since it has the power to make known according to what has been pronounced, it adds: "As I hear, so I judge." For what it hears within, when sentence is pronounced, it judges outside when it is made known. Thus having set these matters forth briefly on the distinction of judgments, let us return now to our ordered exposition itself.

VI. *Why the God man.*

And so God was made man that He might free man whom He had made, that He, the same, might be both Creator and Redeemer of man. The Son was sent that He might show His assent in the adoption of the Father. Wisdom came that it might conquer malice, that the enemy, who had conquered by astuteness, might be conquered by prudence.

VII. *Why the passion of Christ pertained to us.*

From nature He took a victim for nature, so that the holocaust to be offered for us would be from what is ours, that in this very fact redemption might pertain to us, since the offering had been taken from what is ours. And, indeed, we are made participants in this redemption, if to the Redeemer Himself who was associated with us through flesh we are united through faith. Indeed, human nature had been entirely corrupted through sin, and on account of sin had been entirely due for damnation, and, therefore if it had been entirely condemned, there would have been no injustice. But grace came and through mercy chose certain ones from the mass of all for salvation, but through justice it abandoned certain ones to damnation. And those whom it saved through mercy, it did not save without justice, because it was in its power that it could do this justly, and yet if it had not saved them, it would have done justly, since it was in their merit that if it should do this it would not be unjust.

VIII. *On the justice of power and equity.*

For there is one justice according to the obligation of the doer, another according to the merit of the sufferer. Justice according to the obligation of the doer is of power, justice according to the merit of the sufferer is of equity. Justice of power is that by which without injustice there is permitted the doer, if he wishes, whatever is due his power. Justice of equity is that by which there is requited to the sufferer, even if he does not wish it, whatever is due his merit. When, therefore, God punishes the sinner, He does justly, since it is due His power that He can do this if He wishes, and he who suffers is justly punished, since according to his merit there is requited him what is due his merit, and in that there is just power by which God does justly and He Himself is just.

And here is the fair retribution by which the sinner justly suffers, by which, however, he himself is not just but his punishment is just. When, indeed, God justifies a sinner, He acts justly and He is just by the justice of the power by which this is permitted Him. He, indeed, who is justified is just by the justice which he receives but not in that he receives it contrary to his merit; yet he is not unjust, because he himself does not do what he receives, since he does not receive through himself but only suffers what he receives; He who does is just because He does and by the justice by which He does; he who receives is just by the justice which he receives, not, however, because he receives it, since he receives justice without his own justice through grace alone.

IX. *On suffering and compelling justice.*

Likewise it must be known that one justice is suffering, another compelling. Suffering justice is that whereby if anything be done, it is just; if it be not done, it is not unjust. Compelling justice is that whereby something is done justly in such a way that, if it were not done, it would be unjust. On this account suffering justice has dispensation, compelling justice necessity. So then God taking certain ones from the mass of the human race unto salvation uses the justice of due power, but abandoning certain ones unto perdition He uses the justice of permitted equity, in the one case according to His due, in the other according to our merit.

If, indeed, He abandoned those whom He now takes unto salvation, there would not be injustice, since they would receive the justice of equity according to their merits. But if He took those whom He now abandons, similarly there would not be injustice, since in their salvation He would use the justice of power. Therefore, whether in those who are saved or in those who are damned, there is suffering justice, through which what is done is just in such a way that, even if it were done otherwise, it would not be unjust. For even those who according to their merits are justly condemned could have been saved justly through the grace of God if God had willed. And again those who through the grace of God are saved justly, according to their merits could justly have been damned, if God had not willed to save them. Thus, then, whatever He willed, in either case was just, so that even if He had willed otherwise it would not have been unjust, since the power is in His will that without injustice He is permitted to do whatever He wills.

X. *That God could have redeemed man otherwise, if He had so willed.*

On this account we truly declare that God could have accomplished the redemption of mankind even in a different manner if He had willed; however, it was more befitting our infirmity, that God should be made man and assuming the mortality of man for man should refashion man unto the hope of His immortality; thus man might no longer despair that he could ascend to the goods of Him whom he sees had descended to bear his evils, and humanity glorified in God might be an example of glorification to men; in that He suffered they might see what they should return to Him, but in that He was glorified they might consider what they should expect from Him; He Himself might be the way in example and the truth in promise and the life in reward.

XI. *For what reason the sacraments were instituted.*

After the first parent of the human race on being driven from paradise on account of the sin of disobedience came into this world, the devil exercising the right of tyranny over him, just as he had seduced him before by fraud, so afterwards possessed him by violence. But the providence of God which disposed him to salvation so tempered the rigor of justice by mercy that He permitted him indeed to be oppressed for the time by the devil, and yet, lest he be oppressed by the latter forever, He prepared a remedy for him from the punishment itself. And so then from the very beginning of the world He proposed to man the sacraments of his salvation with which He might sign him with the expectation of future sanctification, that whoever might receive these with right faith and firm hope on account of obedience to divine institution, even though placed under the yoke might arrive at participation in freedom. And so He proposed His edict informing and instructing man, that, whosoever might elect to await Him as Saviour and Liberator, would necessarily prove the desire for this same election of his in the reception of His sacraments. The devil also proposed his sacraments with which to bind his own to himself, in order that the more clearly he separated them from those who refused his rule the more securely he might possess them.

Therefore, the human race soon began to be divided into opposing parts, some taking the sacraments of the devil, others, however, taking the sacraments of Christ. And two families were made, one of Christ, the other of the devil. For what shall I call Incarnate Word unless the king who entered this world by taking on humanity to war with the devil and to expel him thence as a tyrant and as one ruling with violence over what belongs to another? And what shall I designate all the earlier saints who were elected from the beginning, before the Incarnation unless certain excellent soldiers preceding in battle their king who was to come, fortified and protected as if by a kind of arms by those very sacraments by which they were being sanctified? What likewise shall I call those who elected after the Incarnation follow even to the end, unless other soldiers, not, however, following another with one accord and eagerly but their king himself who goes before them, they being new themselves and having new arms, yet armed by the same and ready to fight against the same? Whether, therefore, preceding or following, bearing the sacraments of the one king, they serve the one king and conquer the one tyrant, one group preceding Him who was to come, the other following Him preceding.

Wherefore it is clear that from the beginning there were Christians, if not in name yet in fact. For there are three periods of time through which the space of this world runs. The first is the period of the natural law, the second the period of the written law, the third the period of grace. The first is from Adam even unto Moses, the second from Moses even unto Christ, the third from Christ even unto the end of the world.

Similarly, there are three kinds of men, that is, men of the natural law, men of the written law, men of grace. Those can be called men of the natural law who direct their lives by natural reason alone, or rather those men are called men of the natural law who walk according to the concupiscence in which they were born. Men of the written law are those who by exterior precepts are instructed unto right living. Men of grace are those who breathed upon by the inspiration of the Holy Ghost are illumined to recognize the good which must be done, and are inflamed as they love and strengthened to accomplish good. And that we may mark this with a clearer distinction, men of the natural law are openly evil, men of the written law fictitiously good, men of grace truly good. The fictitiously good are covered; the openly evil are uncovered, who were signified by Gog and Magog, which are interpreted as covered and uncovered. And they are foretold as destined to come to persecute the people of God, since these two kinds of men always persecute the truly good. In the first kind are contained the pagans, in the second kind the Jews, in the third kind the Christians. These three kinds of men have never been wanting at any time from the beginning.

Yet the period of the natural law pertains to those openly evil since those then were more in number and more excellent in state. The period of the written law pertains to the fictitiously good since the men serving in fear purified their work, not their hearts. The period of grace pertains to the truly good who now, although they are not more in number, yet are more excellent in state and are publicly preferred on account of the grace of God even by those who oppose their life. You should know, therefore, that at no time from the beginning of the world even to the end has there been or is there anyone truly good unless justified by grace and that no one could ever have obtained grace except through Christ, so that you should realize that all whether preceding or following were saved by the one remedy of sanctification. Behold, therefore, the cause of our King and the battle lines of His army resplendent with spiritual arms; behold by what a multitude of peoples preceding and following He is surrounded as He advances.

XII. *On the time of the institution of the sacraments.*

The time of the institution of the sacraments is believed to have begun from the moment when the first parent, on being expelled by merit of disobedience from the joys of paradise into the exile of this mortal life, is held with all posterity liable to the first corruption even to the end. For from the time when man, having fallen from the state of first incorruption, began to ail in body through mortality and in soul through iniquity, God at once prepared a remedy in His sacraments for restoring man. These indeed, as reason and cause demanded, He furnished at different times and places for man's cure: some before the law, others under the law, others under grace, diverse, indeed, in species yet having the one effect and producing the one health. If anyone, therefore, seeks the time of the institution of the sacraments, let him know that as long as there is sickness, there is time for remedy.

The present life, therefore, running from the beginning of the world even to the end through mortality is a time of sickness and a time of remedy. In this life itself and on account of it were the sacraments instituted, and some from the beginning of it, which ran in their own time and availed to restore health, in so far as it had been granted to them and was to be granted through them. And these sacraments, when their time was completed, ceased and others succeeded in their place to produce the same health. Again after these others were added, as it were, last of all, to which others were not to succeed, in as much as they were perfect medicines, so to speak, which would destroy the sickness itself and restore perfect health fully. And all these things were done according to the judgment and dispensation of the Physician, who saw sickness itself and knew what kind of remedies should be applied to it on every occasion.

Furthermore, one sacrament is found to have been instituted even before man's sin. For matrimony is read as having been established even before man sinned where, with Scripture as witness, woman is mentioned as made for a help to man and as associated with him, (Cf. Gen. 2, 20 ff). Yet the cause of this institution was not at that time for a remedy but for an office, since there was no sickness in man to be cured but virtue to be exercised. On this account, of the three causes for the institution of the sacraments we find here only two, namely, instruction and exercise. For humiliation was not necessary there where there was no pride, but reason needed to be instructed to greater knowledge and virtue to be promoted to greater perfection.

Thus this sacrament is found having a singular law just as it has a singular institution. And order seems to demand that, before we proceed in our discussion to those things which must be said about the other sacraments, we present first concerning this sacrament in particular certain things which will seem to pertain to its first institution, reserving for our subsequent exposition what pertains to its second institution. For this sacrament has a twofold institution, one before sin for office, the other after sin for remedy. And according to that institution by which it was singularly instituted, it ought singularly to be treated, in order that afterwards according to that by which it is joined to others in time, it should not be separated from the others in our exposition.

XIII. *On the institution of matrimony before sin.*

The sacrament of matrimony alone of all sacraments which were instituted for man's remedy is read as having been instituted before man's sin, yet not on account of sin but for a sacrament only and for office, for a sacrament on account of instruction and for office on account of exercise. For there were these two things in matrimony: matrimony itself and the office of matrimony. And each of the two was a sacrament. Matrimony consisted in the consent of the social pact, the office of matrimony consisted in the copulation of the flesh. Matrimony was a sacrament of a kind of spiritual society which was through love between God and the soul, and in this society the soul was the bride and God was the bridegroom. The office of matrimony was a sacrament of a kind of society which was to be between Christ and the Church, through the assumption of flesh, and in this society Christ was to be the bridegroom, and the Church the bride. He who was the bridegroom in both cases was superior and his love passed through piety to His inferior. Now she, who was the bride in both cases was inferior, since she was not sufficient unto herself and was unable to stand by herself. And on this account her love was turned rather by necessity to her superior. The superior through love conferred benefit; the inferior through love received benefit. The sacrament of this society, therefore, which consisted of mutual love, was formed when matrimony was instituted as the sacrament of the one society, in the matrimony of the other society the sacrament was in the office of matrimony.

Therefore, human nature was distinguished by a twofold quality, so that in man indeed it appeared the stronger, but in woman the weaker and in need of another's help. And two were joined in one, by one love and by one society, so that they were in one love, and through one love remained in one society; man, indeed, was joined that he might be made the image of God in this sacrament, and might be inclined toward love by piety, but woman, that she might express the form of the rational soul, and might be persuaded to love rather by necessity and out of consideration for a kind of advantage; yet the two were joined in such a way that the love on both sides was voluntary, since if it were not voluntary neither could it be true love nor a sacrament of true love.

Again, that another sacrament might be formed in this society, God ordered that man and woman be joined in one flesh, so that, just as before they were one in the sacrament of matrimony through love, so afterwards in the office of matrimony they were made one through one mingling of flesh; thus it might be shown that He who before in divinity had been joined to the soul through love, afterwards by assuming flesh was joined to His Church. Again in order that the conjugal society of man and woman might not be idle, after the sacrament of matrimony there was added the office which was to have been fulfilled in the mingling of flesh, so that those joined in matrimony might be exercised through obedience unto virtue and might bear fruit through the generation of progeny. In this office, indeed, it was given to man, who was superior, to engender from his own what was to be propagated but to woman to conceive and to bear, so that in this same similitude it might be shown that in that invisible society the rational soul could in no way bear fruit unless it first received the seed of virtue from God.

There was still another thing in human nature which was to have been shown by the society of matrimony. Man in fact was so founded that a certain thing was supreme in him and nothing in man was higher, but after this something else was under it and subject to it, then another last of all established in the lowest place and subject in the other two. Reason in fact was established in man in the highest place, directing its attention to divine and invisible things alone and conforming itself to the divine will; then a certain other reason looking to corporeal and visible things, which was subject to the higher and, informed by it, dominated sensibility which was subject to it and which was established in the third and lowest place. And thus these three things were found in man: wisdom, prudence, and sensibility; wisdom, that is reason concerned with divine things; prudence, that is reason concerned with human things; and sensibility, that is affection or desire concerned with earthly things. Of these the first, namely reason, governed only and was not governed. The last, sensibility, was governed only and did not govern. Now the middle, reason, was governed by the higher and governed what was below it.

According to this similitude three animals were made outside, one rational which dominated, the second irrational which was subject, the third likewise rational which, however, was governed by the superior and with the superior dominated the inferior. Man, therefore, was the image of wisdom, woman the form of prudence, but beast the likeness of sensibility and concupiscence. On this account the serpent in persuading sin deceived woman. But woman on being deceived inclined man to consent, because concupiscence first suggests the delight of sin to the prudence of the flesh; then the prudence of the flesh deceived by the delight of sin draws reason to consent in iniquity. On account of these reasons and others of this kind human nature was distinguished so that in one portion it might be stronger but in the other might be shown weaker, so that in it one might be found to rule and another to be ruled.

Then there was added without in the flesh a distinction in the senses also, which indeed regarding the virtue of the sacrament was not necessary in matrimony but because without it in the office of matrimony the function of generating could not be fulfilled. Thus then matrimony and the office of matrimony were established before sin, both for a sacrament, so that matrimony indeed might be sanctified by the pure love of the mind, and also that the office of matrimony might be fulfilled without pollution of flesh. But now since through man's sin human flesh was corrupted, after sin indeed the mingling of flesh can no longer be made without carnal concupiscence. But perhaps someone may be moved to ask why after sin man can not fulfill this most important work without sin. But an obvious reason occurs to him who considers carefully. For as long as the rational spirit was subject to its Creator, it found no opposition in its flesh and the members of the body were subject to the dominion of the soul, so that they did not at any time move without it nor toward anything contrary to it. Now after the spirit was puffed up against his Creator through pride, it justly lost the right of its old dominion over its lower self, so that the members of the body, to avenge the injury to the Creator, now opposed its dominion since they were not to be subject to it except through the Creator. Yet since human life could not by any means subsist if the rational spirit had no power over the members of its body, God exercised His vengeance in part through justice and tempered it in part through mercy, in order that at the same time sin might be punished and nature fostered. Therefore, that disobedience might be made manifest He removed from the power of the soul one member in the human body, through which posterity was to be engendered in the flesh, so that all who should be generated through this member might know that they were children of disobedience, and from their origin might recognize their own nature and from what nature they were generated. Since, therefore, a sign of disobedience was placed on this member through which human propagation was obliged to descend, to all descending through this it is manifestly shown that they are generated with the sin of disobedience. For, just as if on an inscription itself which is inscribed on the gate through which they descend, they see whence they come and whither they go.

On this account, therefore, the other members of the body which follow the dominion of reason can operate without sin, but this member in which concupiscence especially reigns, since it does not follow the inclination of the will, does not operate without sin. This member of the body does not follow the dominion of the soul to such a degree that, just as sometimes it does not move when the soul wills, so also it often moves when the soul does not will. Accordingly then carnal intercourse should not have been practiced by man from the time when this could not have been practiced without base concupiscence and lust of the flesh. For he himself made this illicit for himself from the time when he made himself such that he could not fulfill this licitly. But since the infirmity of human flesh would flow out more basely into all concupiscence if it were not contained in some part licitly, that which first had been instituted for office alone was granted afterwards, so that while through indulgence, for the sake of avoiding greater evil, that very evil of infirmity which is present in the remedy is being committed, it may be excused through conjugal chastity. But concerning the first institution of matrimony indeed what has been said can suffice.

Part Nine

On the Institution of the Sacraments.

I. *That four things must be considered in the institution of the sacraments.*

To those who wish to treat of the sacraments, four primary considerations present themselves: first, what is a sacrament; second, why were sacraments instituted; third, what is the matter of each sacrament in which it is made and sanctified; fourth, how many kinds of sacraments are there—that is, definition, cause, matter, division? For if these four are subjected to careful discussion, they will be able to afford understanding of what is proposed. We shall begin, accordingly, with a treatment of the first.

II. *What a sacrament is.*

The doctors have designated with a brief description what a sacrament is: "A sacrament is the sign of a sacred thing." For just as in man there are two things, body and soul, and in one Scripture likewise two things, letter and sense, so also in every sacrament there is one thing which is treated visibly without and is seen, and there is another which is believed invisibly within and is received. What is visible without and material is a sacrament, what is invisible within and spiritual is the thing or virtue of the sacrament; the sacrament, however, which is treated and sanctified without is a sign of spiritual grace and this is the thing of the sacrament and is received invisibly. But since not every sign of a sacred thing can properly be called the sacrament of the same, (because the letters of sacred expressions and statues or pictures are signs of sacred things, of which, however, they can not reasonably be called the sacraments), on this account the description mentioned above should be referred, it seems, to the interpretation or expression of the word rather than to a definition. Now if anyone wishes to define more fully and more perfectly what a sacrament is, he can say: "A sacrament is a corporeal or material element set before the senses without, representing by similitude and signifying by institution and containing by sanctification some invisible and spiritual grace." This definition is recognized as so fitting and perfect that it is found to befit every sacrament and a sacrament alone. For every thing that has these three is a sacrament, and everything that lacks these three can not be properly called a sacrament. For every sacrament ought to have a kind of similitude to the thing itself of which it is the sacrament, according to which it is capable of representing the same thing; every sacrament ought to have also institution through which it is ordered to signify this thing and finally sanctification through which it contains that thing and is efficacious for conferring the same on those to be sanctified. Now it is looked upon as important, that every sacrament indeed has a similitude from first instruction, institution from superadded dispensation, sanctification from the applied benediction of word or sign.

Therefore, that we may know how these three things, which have been mentioned concerning all sacraments, are in one, we shall take the water of baptism as an example. For in it is the visible element of water which is a sacrament, and these three things are found in one: representation from similitude, signification from institution, virtue from sanctification. Similitude itself is from creation, institution itself from dispensation, and sanctification itself from benediction. The first was imposed through the Creator, the second was added through the Saviour, and the third was administered through the Dispenser. Accordingly visible water is the sacrament, and invisible grace the thing or virtue of the sacrament. Now all water has from its natural quality a certain similitude with the grace of the Holy Ghost, since, just as the one washes away the stains of bodies, so the other cleanses the iniquities of souls. And, indeed, from this inborn quality all water had the power to represent spiritual grace, before it also signified the latter by super-added institution. Now the Saviour came and instituted visible water through the ablution of bodies to signify the invisible cleaning of souls through spiritual grace. And hence water now does not represent from natural similitude alone but also signifies spiritual grace from superadded institution. But since these two things, as we have said, do not yet suffice for the perfect sacrament, the word of sanctification is added to the element and a sacrament is made; thus that visible water is a sacrament representing from similitude, signifying from institution, containing spiritual grace from sanctification. After this fashion we must consider these three things in the other sacraments also.

III. *Why the sacraments were instituted.*

Thus, since the first part of the discussion has been presented, let us pass to the second. Sacraments are known to have been instituted for three reasons: on account of humiliation, on account of instruction, on account of exercise. On account of humiliation, indeed, that, since man a rational creature by the precept of his Creator is subject to the insensible elements which were founded by nature below him, he may by this very humiliation of his deserve to be reconciled to his Creator. For man had been so made that He alone from whom he was, was his good. All other things were made under him not that his good might be in these, but that he should have service from them. For every good is greater than he of whom it is the good, because it is truly not a good unless it makes him good of whom it is the good. Therefore, everyone who is good and is good through his own good is inferior to the good itself by which he is good, because without this very good he is not good. If, therefore, the good of man was above man, He alone who was above man was the good of man. To this good, then, man was immediately joined, as long as he persevered in the order of his foundation, and hence he enjoyed it freely, because he went to it willingly and adhered to it with freedom. But after he was drawn away by concupiscence and he turned from the higher good, turning toward the lower things he fell headlong and he subjected himself to that which he made his good. So by a just recompense he who did not wish to be subjected to his superior through obedience subjected himself through concupiscence to his inferior, so that he now finds this the medium of division between himself and God, not the mediator of reconciliation. For with this dividing medium the human mind is clouded lest it be able to recognize its Creator, and it grows cold lest it seek Him through love. Therefore, it is just that man, who subjected himself to earthly things through concupiscence, first abandoning God through pride, now seeking God through humility that he may more fully declare the affection of his devotion, should incline himself to the same on account of God's precept through obedience. For just as it was a pernicious pride not to wish to be subject to a superior, so it is a praiseworthy and fruitful devotion to be inclined even to inferiors on account of a superior. And just as it was a damnable pride to despise the superior though present, so it is a praiseworthy humility to seek him though absent and with persevering love not to cease from the search until discovery, so that there is both devotion in humility and humility in devotion.

There is no one, indeed, who does not know that rational man exists superior by foundation to the mute and insensible elements, and yet when this same man is ordered to seek his salvation in these, to try the virtue of his obedience, what else is this than that a superior is subject to an inferior? This is why the eyes of infidels who see only visible things despise venerating the sacraments of salvation, because beholding in this only what is contemptible without in visible species they do not recognize the invisible virtue within and the fruit of obedience. For they do not know that the faithful do not seek salvation from these elements, even if they seek it in them, but they seek it in those out of Him and from Him by whom they are ordered to seek and they believe that they receive in these. For these elements do not contribute what is contributed through them, but He who orders to seek salvation in them offers salvation through them. In this way, therefore, what we have said must be understood, that the invisible sacraments were instituted on account of man's humiliation.

The sacraments were also instituted on account of instruction, that through that which is seen without in the sacrament in the visible species the human mind may be instructed to recognize the invisible virtue which consists within in the thing of the sacrament. For man who knew visible things and did not know the invisible could by no means have recognized divine things unless stimulated by the human. And on this account while the invisible good which he lost is returned to him the signification of the same is furnished him without through visible species, that he may be stimulated without and restored within; so in that which he handles and sees he may recognize of what nature that is which he received and does not see. For the spiritual gifts of grace are, as it were, certain invisible antidotes, and, since they are offered to man in visible sacraments in certain vessels, what else is shown by the visible species than hidden virtue? For the sick man can not see the medicine but he can see the vessel in which the medicine is given. And on this account in the species itself of the vessel the virtue of medicine is expressed that he may recognize what he receives and through this knowledge proceed to love. Thus must what we have said be understood, that the sacraments were instituted for the sake of instruction.

Similarly the sacraments were instituted for the sake of exercise, that, while the human mind is exercised and cultivated by various species of works without, it may be made fertile for the multiple fruits of virtue within. Indeed to man there belonged one good and as long as man clung to it through love he did not need this multiplicity. But after he permitted his mind through concupiscence to be divided in relation to these multiple and transitory things, he could not be stable, since just as in loving many things he is divided in these through affection so in following changeable things he undergoes change. For whatever he seeks in all these for repose and consolation, the very condition of change converts for him to toil and pain. Wherefore, it happens that just as he is compelled to go to these things lest he fail, so he is forced afterwards to go from them that he may rest, so that he appears as a second Cain, a wanderer, a fugitive upon earth, (cf. Gen. 4, 12); a wanderer seeking consolation in various things, a fugitive shunning affliction found everywhere. Man walks; if he walks always, he fails.

Therefore, he sits or stands lest he fail; yet if he always sits, he fails. We hunger and we fail, and we eat lest we fail; and yet if we ate always, we would fail; what is sought unto consolation is turned to pain. Thus every change of man has failing not progress, and we fail because we change; yet we never cease to change lest we fail. Therefore, since man's life here can not be without change, against that change which engenders failing is opposed another change which produces progress so that, since it can not stand so as always to be the same, it moves and always moves forward so as to be better. For the first good was to adhere to the highest. The second good is to ascend to higher things. And on this account changeable life, lest dissipated by its mobility to lower things it might ever fail, had to be nourished by such pursuits as those in which excited without by the variety of things and fired within by the emulation of virtues it might find occasion for progress.

Times were divided and places distinguished, corporeal species proposed, pursuits and works to be practiced enjoined, that the exterior man might prepare a medicine for the interior man and might learn to be under him and benefit him. For when human life had first run through two kinds of exercises, in the one unto necessity, in the other unto pleasure; in the one unto use, in the other unto vice, unto use for nature, unto vice for guilt; the one unto sustenance, the other unto subversion, it was fitting that a third kind of exercise also be added, so that thereby one of the two first might be put aside, since it was harmful, and the other might be perfected, since it was not sufficient. Accordingly works of virtue were proposed to man without for exercising interior edification, so that preoccupied by them he might never be free for works of iniquity nor always so for works of necessity.

Now in these pursuits of virtues by wonderful dispensation God provided multiplicity and variety and intermission, that the human mind in multiplicity might find exercise, in variety delight, and in intermission recreation. Certain places were consecrated, churches built, and certain times appointed at which the faithful should assemble together in order as a group to be urged to render thanks, offer prayers, fulfill vows. There God is now sought simply in silence, now He is praised devotedly with harmonious voices, so that in turn the hearts of the faithful are now composed for rest, not excited to devotion. Also in these divine laudations themselves the same form of praise is not always exhibited; now psalmodies fire to devotion, now hymns and songs excite to divine joy, now lessons are read for the formation of character and the instruction of a good life. Even our actions themselves in divine services do not always proceed according to the same form of institution; now erect, now prostrate, now by bending, now by turning, we express by the gesticulation of the body the state of the mind. But those very things in which the devotion of the faithful exercises itself by operating and adorns the divine worship were provided in great numbers and variety for similar reason, so that there might be numerous sacred things and sacraments to the end that faith in these might find perfect matter for exercise and a cause of restoration. For thus the faithful mind, while it is being lead without to various pursuits of holy exercise, is ever renewed more and more within from its own devotion itself unto sanctity. And in this manner, indeed, we think what has been said must be understood, that the sacraments were instituted for the sake of exercise.

IV. *On the distinction of the three works and the three operators.*

This, therefore, is the threefold cause of the institution of all sacraments: humiliation, instruction, and exercise of man. If there were not these causes, elements of themselves could not be sacraments at all, that is, signs of instruments of sacred things. For that elements are sacraments does not result from their first nature but from institution applied through dispensation and from grace infused through benediction. If elements had not received these two things after their first nature, they could not properly be sacraments. Nature first gave them the aptitude that they should be able to be this; institution second added authority that they should become this, benediction third superadded sanctity that they should be this. The first was made by the Creator, the second established by the Saviour, the third administered by the Dispenser. First the Creator by His majesty fashioned vessels, then the Saviour by institution established the same, finally the Dispenser by benediction cleansed these themselves and filled them with grace.

And it appears strange that he who was greater did what was less, and he who was less did what was greater. For sanctification contributed more than did creation, since in creation they received the nature to be, in sanctification the grace to be good and holy. If, therefore, God creates and the priest sanctifies, man seems to do more than God, which would be altogether absurd and inappropriate, if God too did not also do what man does. For God creates without man but man does not sanctify without God, so that grace in a certain measure may begin from the highest and be completed in the lowest, and in this very thing the descent of grace may be signified to us, since unless grace descended it would not raise the fallen. God first created through Himself and in His own, that is, alone and in majesty. Afterwards the Saviour instituted by Himself indeed but in ours, that is, alone and in humanity. Finally the priest sanctifies neither through himself nor in his own, since neither is he alone the one who operates nor is the virtue his which is given for sanctification. For he himself cooperates with the one who ministers, by whose virtue through the ministry of the one ministering what is to be sanctified is sanctified, that there may be truly one virtue through one work to one effect; this virtue, indeed, in the two operating simultaneously is so distinguished, since it is given by the one, ministered by the other. There is one by whom it is given, the other through whom it is sent. And when grace itself comes to us, it comes through him from whom it comes, since the author of the gift cooperates with the one who ministers; however, it does not come likewise from him through whom it comes, because he can not be the author of the gift who is only the minister of the dispensation.

Therefore, let no one say how does man sanctify, when God sanctifies through man, since man in this more truly does what God does through him. For what man does through himself and in his own he does not truly do, since he does not do truth, for through himself and in his own he does nothing except evil; similarly, then, God alone does wonderful things, as Scripture says of Him: "Who alone doth wonderful things," (Psal. 71, 18), since without Him no one does, and every one who does, does through Him and through every one who does, He himself does. Thus, He alone does, since of Him alone is what every one does who does; yet of the servant of God it is written: "For he hath done wonderful things in his life," (Eccli. 31, 9), since from God he did and through him God did and no contrariety proceeds from this. Thus God alone sanctifies and blesses, because from Him Himself is all sanctification and benediction; yet the priest, as a minister of God, sanctifies and blesses, since through him is a certain sanctification and benediction which even itself is also from God who is author in the gift and through God who is a cooperator in the ministry. Through such consideration we distinguish by reason what creation operates in all the sacraments individually, as far as pertains to the nature of the element, or what institution and sanctification operate, as far as pertains to the virtue of the sacraments; and in sanctification itself we distinguish how much is from Him who is the giver of the gift and how much from him or rather through him who is the minister only of dispensation.

Finally five things, separate and distinguished from one another, proceed to knowledge: God the physician, man the sick person, the priest the minister or messenger, grace the antidote, the vessel the sacrament. The physician gives, the minister dispenses, the vessel preserves spiritual grace which heals the sick recipient. If, therefore, vases are the sacraments of spiritual grace, they do not heal from their own, since vases do not cure the sick but medicine does. Therefore, sacraments were not instituted for this, that from them should be that which was in them, but that the physician might show his skill he prepared in that a remedy from which the sick man learned the occasion of his sickness. For since man by desiring visible things was corrupted, to be restored fittingly he had to receive an occasion of salvation in these same visible things, so that he might rise again through the same things through which he had fallen.

V. *That the institution of sacraments, in so far as pertains to God, is of dispensation; in so far as pertains to man, of necessity.*

The institution of the sacraments, therefore, in so far as pertains to God the author, is of dispensation but, in so far as pertains to obedient man, is of necessity, since it is within God's power to save man without these but it is not within man's power to attain to salvation without these. For God could have saved man, even if he had not instituted these, but man could not by any means be saved if he contemned these. For Scripture says: "He can not be saved who has not been baptized," (Cf. John 3, 3). Who does not do this or this can not be saved, and we confess that it is true. And because man can not be saved who lacks these without which salvation can not be had by man, man without these can not be saved, but God can save without these. Man in truth could be saved without these, if it were within man's power to be saved without these and if man according to his will could leave those things which were established to obtain salvation and according to his own election arrive by another way to salvation. Since this is altogether impossible for man, on this account most rightly is it said that man can not be saved at all without these.

Now God can save man without these, who can bestow upon man His virtue and sanctification and salvation in whatever way He wills. For by that spirit with which He teaches man without word, He can also justify without sacrament if He wills, since the virtue of God is not subject to elements from necessity, even if the grace of God be given according to dispensation through sacraments. Hence it is that we read that certain ones even without sacraments of this kind were justified and, we believe, were saved, just as it is read that Jeremias was sanctified in the womb and it is prophesied that John the Baptist was to be filled with the Holy Ghost from his mother's womb and those who as just under the natural law pleased God. We do not read that they had these sacraments, but about their salvation we do not doubt at all. And those of them who received these sacraments after justification had signs of their justice in these rather than its cause from them.

They, indeed, who through the spirit of God received without these whatever is conferred in them did not lack them to damnation, because the fact that they did not receive these was never due to contempt for religion but either the nature of the time did not demand it or necessity did not permit it. Therefore, let no one so establish the law of divine justice in the elements as to say that man cannot be justified without these, even if he has justifying grace, nor can be saved without these, even if he be just, when either the stress of necessity prevents him from receiving these or, as we have said, the nature of the time does not constrain him to receive them. Just as those who were just under the natural law were not imbued with sacraments of this kind, so too they were not held by precepts of this kind. Whoever, therefore, possessed the thing of the sacrament in right faith and true charity did not lack these sacraments unto damnation, because they either were not obliged to receive them on account of the time or were not able to receive them on account of imminent necessity.

What do you think, then, you who venerate the sacraments of God and when you think that you are honoring the sacraments of God are dishonoring God? You ascribe a necessity to sacraments and from the Author of sacraments you take away power and to Him you deny piety. You say to me that he who has not the sacraments of God can not be saved, and I say to you: "He who has the virtue of the sacraments of God can not perish." Either deny that there can be virtue where there is no sacrament, or if you concede the virtue deny the damnation. Which is greater, the sacrament or the virtue of the sacrament? Which is greater, water or faith? If you wish to speak the truth, say "faith."

If, therefore, the sacrament of water which is less saves certain ones who do not have faith, and they are not blamed because they have not faith, since they can not have it, how does faith, which is greater, not free those who have faith and do not have the sacrament of water? And will they not rather the more be spared in that they do not have the sacrament of water which indeed they wished to have but could not? And you say: "How then shall we understand what is written: 'Unless a man be born again of water and the Holy Ghost, he cannot enter into the kingdom of heaven.'?" (Cf. John 3, 16). And I ask you: "How do you think that which is written is to be understood: 'He that believeth in me, shall not see death forever?'" (Cf. John 3, 25 and 26). You say that he who does not do this is not saved, and I say that he who does this is not damned.

What, then, will be the middle place which receives men of this kind, neither to be saved because they have not water nor to be damned because they have faith? There is a man who has faith and with faith love; he has not water, yet does not contemn water but wishes to have water and can not. Therefore, will water by being absent damn him and not rather faith and devotion by being present save him? What then, you say, have I to do with sacraments? I have faith and love and other virtues and I shall be good and it will suffice for me. See then if you can have love of God and contemn His precepts. If then you have love of God, be zealous, work, try in so far as you can to perform His commands, and if you fall into necessity, seek piety. For if there is no necessity which may be brought forward, contemning is not excused. See, therefore, that the sacraments of God are spiritual medicines which are applied without to bodies through visible species but within heal souls through invisible truth. Indeed the institution of these, in so far as pertains to the one giving the precept, is of dispensation but the reception, in so far as pertains to the one obeying, is of necessity.

Do you wish to believe that in these visible species God does not take a remedy for healing the spiritually sick but establishes a sacrament only? Understand a sacrament from a sacrament. Ezachias fell ill and Isaias the prophet was sent to him to foretell to him an imminent death. When he heard this, terrified and struck with fear, he poured forth tears with prayer and asked and obtained mercy. Straightway, Isaias was sent back to announce that fifteen years were to be added to his life, and, for the sake of commending the virtue of the sacrament more fully, to prepare a new medicine in a new way for curing his wound. The medicine was applied without, that the hidden virtue might operate within, and there was no health from the medicine since the medicine in itself was contrary to health; so it might be shown clearly that the former was not from it which was through it. From the sacraments a great sacrament has been commended. The sick man is the human race which languishes both within through iniquity and without through mortality. To the sick man is sent a prophetic word to announce an imminent death as not only present for him but also future. Those who are terrified confess, weep, and pray, and obtain mercy. The prophetic word is sent back to make us certain of being granted a longer span of life, because the same Scripture consoles us when penitent with a promise of eternal life that terrifies those who persist in sin with the damnation of eternal death. The medicine is applied to cure our wounds. When by its quality this is shown to oppose the disease in the cure of the sick the virtue not of the medicine but of the healer is most evidently declared. The sacraments themselves are the medicine itself, and, when these are applied to us corporeally without through the ministers of sacred dispensation, the wounds of our souls are cured invisibly so that cured and healed we may be able to attain to the promise of perpetual life.

And indeed this life has been distinguished by the number of fifteen years, which begins in the present seven year period through repose of the mind and is completed in the future eight year period through mortality of the flesh. Yet this medicine, in so far as pertains to its nature, had to increase the disease not cure it, since all earthly things, as far as concerns their quality and our infirmity, are wont to purchase corruption of souls rather than their cure. Yet when God accomplishes our healing through these, what else does He clearly show than the power of His virtue, by His procuring our remedy in the same thing from which we drew the disease of infirmity and corruption? And so let not that which is administered to us through them be ascribed to these, and let us not so venerate the visible species in them that we be convicted of subordinating invisible truth to them.

From this consideration it becomes manifest to those who observe carefully, how much they owe either to that which is perceived visibly outside in the species of the sacrament or to that which operates invisibly within in the virtue of the sacrament. And indeed all these matters pertain to that which was proposed for investigation, namely, why sacraments were instituted.

VI. *On the matter of the sacraments.*

There now remains for discussion the third part of the four which had been proposed. All divine sacraments are accomplished in threefold matter, namely, either in things or in deeds or in words. For since the whole man had been corrupted, the whole that belonged to man outside had to be assumed for the sacrament that the whole may be sanctified without in the sacrament and that in the whole the virtue of the sacrament may operate a remedy within. And so sacraments had to be sanctified in things that the matter of man might be sanctified, as works in deeds, as words in speech; in that way the whole indeed may be holy, both what is man and what is of man.

In things sacraments are accomplished just as, for example, the sacrament of baptism in water, the sacrament of unction in oil, the sacrament of the body and blood of Christ, in bread and wine, and whatever other corporeal species there are in which divine sacraments are accomplished. In deeds also sacraments may be found just as, for example, when we make the sign of the cross, either opposing it as a defense against adverse powers or impressing it for sanctification on certain things to be sanctified, or when also with hands outstretched or elevated in prayer, by bending or standing erect, or by turning or by any other gesture whatever either in motion or in action, we express something sacred and the sign of a sacred thing. In speech a sacrament is found, such as is the invocation of the Trinity and others of this kind, as often as with the utterance of words we express and signify something sacred and a sacrament. Moreover, we must realize that with these three modes, sacraments are accomplished. Yet those are more properly and are principally called sacraments in which virtue is through sanctification and the effect of salvation through operation. Now that we have made this brief examination of the matter of the sacraments, let us pass on to the following.

VII. *What the three kinds of sacraments are.*

On first consideration three kinds of sacraments occur to us which must be distinguished. For there are certain sacraments in which salvation principally is established and received, for example, the water of baptism and the receiving of the body and blood of Christ. There are others which, although they are not necessary for salvation, since without them salvation can be possessed, are yet of benefit to sanctification because virtue can be exercised by these and a fuller grace can be acquired, for example, the water of aspersion and the reception of ashes and others like these. Again there are other sacraments which seem to have been instituted for this alone, that through them those things which are necessary for the sanctification and institution of other sacraments in some manner may be prepared and sanctified either about persons in performing sacred orders or in consecrating those things, or others of this kind, which pertain to the attire of sacred orders. The first sacraments, then, were instituted for salvation, the second for exercise, the third for preparation. Thus, since these matters have been treated according as reason seemed to demand, we pass to the explanation of those that remain.

VIII. *On the three that are necessary for salvation.*

There were three indeed which from the beginning, whether before the coming of Christ or after, were necessary for obtaining salvation, namely, faith, sacraments of faith, and good works. And these three so cling together that they can not have the effect of salvation if they are not simultaneous. "For faith," testifies Scripture, "if it have not works, is dead," (James 2, 17). Again, where there is not faith, good work cannot be. Likewise, those who have an operating faith, if they refuse to receive the sacraments of God, cannot be saved, since they have not love of God whose precepts in His sacraments they contemn. Yet where faith is with love, just as merit is not diminished, even if the work which is in a proposed good of devotion is not accomplished externally, so the effect of salvation is not impeded, even if the sacrament which is in true will and desire is prevented at the moment of necessity.

Now where the three can be had simultaneously, they can not by any means be absent without danger, since neither does faith have merit if, while it can operate, it is neglected, nor is good work anything if it is done without faith. And again operating faith does not suffice to sanctify man, if he contemns receiving this sanctification which is in the sacraments of God. So there are three things simultaneously, faith, sacrament, and work. In faith, fortitude is attributed to the Christian, in the sacraments, arms; in good works, weapons for him who is to fight against the devil.

PART TEN

On Faith

I. *That seven questions are to be investigated about faith.*

To those who wish to treat about faith, we propose seven questions for investigation: what is faith; in what does faith consist; on the increase of faith; on those things which pertain to faith; whether from the beginning according to the change of times the faith of believers is changed; what is the least that true faith could ever possess; on the sacrament of faith and its virtue. Let us proceed with each of these in their order.

II. *What faith is.*

"Faith is," as the Apostle says, "the substance of things to be hoped for, the evidence of things that appear not," (Heb. 11, 1). If by faith we believe that those things are signified which are believed by faith, just as through vision sometimes we receive not that vision by which we see but what we see, fittingly is faith called, "the substance of things to be hoped for," since by faith those goods which truly subsist for those who hope and await are believed to be those which are to come. According to this acceptance, not without reason is the evidence of things that appear not also mentioned, since the things that we do not comprehend with human reason we persuade ourselves by faith alone to be credible and true. But if we explain this definition in another way, we can say that faith is defined not in that which is but that which does, so that there is sense.

Faith is the substance, that is the subsistence, of things to be hoped for, that is of future goods which we hope will come and which alone are worthy of our hope and expectation since in them our good consists. Faith, therefore, is the substance of things to be hoped for, since the invisible goods which are not yet present through act presently through faith subsist in our hearts, and faith itself in these things is their subsistence in us. For although some things subsist with us either through act, when for example those present are comprehended by sense, or through intellect, when those absent or even the non-existent are grasped in their likeness or image through intellect or even through experience, when those things which are in us are felt by us, as are joy, sadness, fear, and love, which subsist in us and are felt by us, by none of these ways are the invisible things of God comprehended by us, which can only be believed, not at all comprehended. For things are present not by act so that they are comprehended by sense since they are not bodies nor do they subsist in corporeal things. Nor could they be comprehended by the mind in some likeness through image, since by the excellence of their divinity and purity they transcend by far every likeness both of bodies and of corporeal things. Nor could they be comprehended as those things are which are in us and are felt by us, since neither are minds of substance nor of those things which subsist in the mind. Therefore, by faith alone do they subsist in us, and their subsistence is the faith in them, whereby they are believed to be but are not comprehended as to their nature.

Therefore, God can be believed, by no means can He be comprehended. You say to me: "What shall I say? What is God?" I reply to you that what God is is quite ineffable. "At least," you say, "what shall I think when I wish to think what God is?" I say further that God is unthinkable. Whatever is said or is thought, is said according to something. For what cannot be said or thought according to something cannot be said and thought at all. What, therefore, will you say or will you think, when you wish to say or to think that which is God? If you think of earth, if you think of heaven, if you think of all that is in heaven and on earth, none of these is God. Finally, if you think of spirit, if you think of soul, this is not God. "I know," you say, "that this is not God, yet this is like God, and God can be demonstrated by His likeness."

See what similar thing you would show, if you should wish to demonstrate the spirit and the body, of what nature this likeness would be, and yet farther apart are God and spirit than spirit and body. For all things that are created are less distant from each other than He who made is from that which He made. What God is cannot be thought, even if it can be believed that He is, nor can it be comprehended of what nature He is. "What," said the Apostle, "eye hath not seen nor ear heard, neither hath it entered into the heart of man," (Cf. 1 Cor. 2, 9); this is what we wish to say, if, however, we can say what we cannot think. "What eye hath not seen nor ear heard," because it is not perceived by sense. "Neither hath it entered into the heart of man," since it is not comprehended by thought.

For there were certain things, three in number: body and spirit and God. The body, indeed, was the world, the soul the spirit. And the soul itself, as if it were in a certain middle place, having the world outside itself and God within itself, had also received an eye with which it could see the world outside itself and those things which were in the world, and this was the eye of the flesh. It had received another eye with which it could see itself and those things which were in itself, and this is the eye of reason. It had received still another eye with which it could see God within itself and those things which were in God, and this is the eye of contemplation. As long, therefore, as it kept these eyes open and uncovered, it saw clearly and discerned rightly, but, after the shades of sin had entered upon it, the eye of contemplation indeed was extinguished so that it saw nothing, but the eye of reason was made bleared so that it saw doubtfully. That eye alone which was not extinguished remained in its clarity and as long as this has clear light it has undoubting judgment. But the eye of reason as long as its light is cloudy cannot have certain judgment, since what does not see clearly discerns doubtfully. Hence it is that the hearts of men more easily agree with themselves in those things which they perceive with the eye of the flesh than in those things which they attain by the keenness of the mind and by the sense of reason, since where they are not cloudy in seeing they do not waver in judging. Therefore, man since he has the eye of the flesh can see the world and those things which are in the world. Likewise, since he has the eye of reason in part, he similarly sees the soul in part and those things which are in the soul. Since indeed he has not the eye of contemplation, he is not able to see God and the things that are in God.

Faith, then, is necessary by which those things may be believed which are not seen, and those things which are not yet present to us through species may subsist in us through faith. And so the substance of those things is faith, since through faith alone they now subsist in us, and similarly the proof of those is faith, since through faith alone are they proven by us. For we cannot bring forward any greater argument regarding those matters which are uncertain than that those things which are believed by faith are not comprehended by reason. For what other proof can there be for those things to which nothing can be similar and comparable, when indeed there could by no means be a proof, unless it also had some likeness with that for which there would be a proof? Therefore, by what likeness can those things which transcend all likeness and comparison be argued and proven, unless that from the faith and devotion of preceding saints we gather that we ought not to be incredulous about those goods which are predicted as to come? For great is this reason and entirely worthy of faith, since by no means would the saints and all the just by reason of their desire for the eternal life have despised the present life with such constancy, if they had not perceived beforehand something even beyond our intelligence concerning the truth of that life.

And so faith is the substance of things to be hoped for, because through it indeed in some manner the things which are to come and the proof of things which are not apparent subsist in us, since through these the things which are hidden are proven by us. But since in this description not what faith is but what faith does is shown, and since that faith is not defined which is held regarding past or present matters, if any one wishes to note a full and general definition of faith, he can say that faith is a kind of certainty of the mind in things absent, established beyond opinion and short of knowledge. For there are some who straightway repel with the mind what is heard and contradict those things which are said, and these are deniers. Others in those things which they hear select any one side whatever for consideration but they do not approve for affirmation. For although they believe one of the two as more probable, yet they do not presume to assert whether it itself is still true. These are the conjecturers. Others thus approve the other side, so that they assume its approbation even unto assertion. These are the believers. After these kinds of cognition that more perfect kind follows when the thing is made known not from hearing alone but through its presence. For more perfectly do they know who comprehended the thing itself as it is in their presence. These are the knowers. First, therefore, are the deniers, second the doubters, third the conjecturers, fourth the believers, fifth the knowers.

From this, therefore, it can be conjectured why we have called faith certainty, since when there is still doubt, there is no faith. It is clear also why we say that certainty itself which we call faith was established beyond opinion or conjecture and short of knowledge. Since without doubt to believe something is, as it were, less than to know, so also is to think more than to conjecture. I say "less," not in so far as pertains to merit but in so far as pertains to cognition. For unless to believe at some time, in so far as pertains to merit, were more than to see what is true, by no means would vision be taken away so that faith would be deserved, nor would it have been said: "Blessed are they that have not seen, and have believed," (John 20, 29). Therefore, I have said that to believe at some time is more than to see, but in so far as pertains to merit, not in so far as pertains to joy. Otherwise, in so far as pertains to the full measure of felicity and the perfection of truth it is more to see when present than to believe when absent, just as also it is more to stand firm with faith than to waiver with opinion. Thus rightly is it said: "Faith is certainly in things absent, established beyond opinion and short of knowledge," although sometimes also the certainty itself which is born of present contemplation is improperly called faith. Now, concerning that which is properly called faith, it is said: "For if you see, it is not faith."

III. *What those things are in which faith consists.*

There are two things in which faith consists: cognition and affection, that is, constancy or firmness in believing. It consists in the one, because faith itself is that; it consists in the other, because faith itself is in that. For in affection the substance of faith is found; in cognition, the matter. For faith by which there is belief is one thing; that which is believed by faith is another. Faith is found in affection; that which is believed by faith in cognition. Therefore, faith has substance in affection because affection itself is faith; it has matter in cognition since faith is regarding that and unto that which is in cognition. To believe, therefore, is in affection but what is believed is in cognition.

Now here we understand cognition as the knowledge of things, not that knowledge which is comprehended from the presence of the things themselves but that which is received from hearing only and is made manifest from the significance of words. When that which is said is also understood by him who hears as it is said, even if he knows not whether it is or is not thus as it is said, knowledge, nevertheless, exists in so far as he understands and knows what that is which is said. Now this knowledge is cognition which, just as it cannot be without that knowledge by which a thing is known to be or not to be, so it cannot be without faith by which a thing is believed to be or not to be. If faith is added to this cognition so that what was heard and understood is believed, there is credulity in cognition and there is found in credulity the substance of faith, in cognition the matter. Now there can be cognition of this without any faith but faith without any cognition cannot be, since he who hears and understands something does not always believe, but he who understands nothing believes nothing, although sometimes he can believe what he does not understand. For faith also is from faith by which that is believed which is not known, since there is belief in the knower and in the believer. For he who believes in the believer, not unfittingly is said to believe what he believes in whom he believes, and if he does not know what that is that he believes, he does know in whom he believes. Such are the simple minded in Holy Church who believe in the more perfect believers and knowers, who truly are saved in their simplicity. And they are not strangers to the merit of the former, although they do not attain to their cognition. It is written: "The oxen were ploughing, and the asses feeding beside them," (Job 1, 14). For the simple minded in Holy Church, although they are unable together with the perfect to search out the hidden things of the sacraments of God, yet, since they do not separate themselves from their society, placed as it were near them they feed themselves on the same faith and hope by operating well. Thus then faith is sometimes with cognition, when that is known which is believed; sometimes without cognition, when there is belief only in the knower and the believer.

Nevertheless, there must always be some cognition with faith which should direct faith itself through intention, since, if nothing were known of those things which are to be believed, faith would not have that by which it might direct itself through intention in good work nor by which it might excite its hope to anything by operating well. But it is one thing to transcend cognition by faith in certain things, another not to know that those things which must never be disregarded must be believed. In the one case faith has merit where even with cognition it does not discern, in the other, since it is entirely destitute of cognition, cognition itself fails and its faith ceases.

IV. *On increase of faith.*

There are two things according to which faith is said to increase: cognition and affection, that is, constancy or firmness in believing. Faith grows according to cognition, when it is instructed unto knowledge. It increases according to affection, when it is excited unto devotion and is strengthened unto constancy. The faith of certain men is great by cognition, small by affection, but of certain others great by affection, small by cognition. Some have great faith both by cognition and by affection; others small both by cognition and by affection. Yet the Lord showed manifestly that great affection in faith is more praiseworthy than great cognition when He compared faith to a grain of mustard seed which indeed is small in quantity but not in fervor. Hence to the woman of Chanan, still knowing little indeed but trusting much, it is said: "O woman, great is thy faith," (Matt. 15, 28). For that faith is reputed great with God, which, although it flourishes little by knowledge, yet is exhibited without through constancy. Therefore, when faith increases by cognition, it is assisted; when, however, it increases by affection, it is deserving of merit.

Likewise according to the increase of faith three kinds of believers are discovered. For certain men are faithful who elect to believe by piety alone what, however, they do not comprehend by reason—whether it ought to be believed or ought not to be believed. Others approve by reason what they believe by faith. Others by purity of heart and by pure conscience within already begin to sense what they believe by faith. Among the first piety alone makes the choice, among the second reason joins approbation, among the third purity of intelligence apprehends certainty. A fourth kind of men is those to whom believing is only not contradicting faith, who are called faithful by their manner of living rather than by the virtue of believing. For intent on transitory things alone they never raise their minds to reflect upon the future, and, although together with the other faithful they receive by custom the sacraments of the Christian faith, yet they do not consider why a man is a Christian or what hope there is for a Christian in the expectation of future goods. Although these are called faithful by name, yet they are in fact and in truth far from the faith. But sometimes they are visited by divine grace of this kind and are stimulated to a consideration of themselves so that they inquire why man is born, whether another life follows after this life, whether rewards have been set aside for the just and torments for sinners, and whether after the end of labor a reward of just retribution follows. When such a consideration has arisen in the heart, presently the conscience itself is struck with a great feeling of alarm over the uncertainty of mortal life, and the more he perceives that danger threatens him as he errs, the more he struggles to arrive at the cognition of truth. He reflects that in this world the opinions of men are so diverse upon those matters on which the salvation of man rests.

The pagans cut the unity of the Godhead into many parts. The Jews confess the Creator, they do not recognize the Saviour. And in all these the mind fluctuates and, unless it were held in its own piety, possibly casting truth aside it would follow falsehood. Reason is added to these at the suggestion of the Holy Spirit, since in many doubtful things, if some one thing is left aside that another may be selected, doubt is not destroyed but is changed. There is added to this another greater reason. It is better to confess one beginning than many since, where there is a multitude, there is either a superfluous plurality or an imperfect unity. Still more is it better to confess the Creator and the Saviour equally than the Creator alone. He who mentions the Creator confesses majesty; he who understands the Saviour venerates piety; and the greater good of man is that in his God he finds the majesty which he contemplates with the eye of the heart, and the humanity on which he speculates with the eye of the flesh, that the whole man may be blessed in God. The mind being comforted by these reasonings is stimulated to greater devotion of divine religion; by devotion, moreover, it is cleansed and purified so that in a way it now begins with a clean heart to obtain a foretaste of that for a knowledge of which it hastens with faith and devotion. Thus a clean conscience is instructed and made certain daily about its God by invisible proofs and by secret and familiar visitation to such a degree that already in a manner it begins to possess Him present through contemplation, and by no reason now can he be torn away from his faith and love, even if the entire world be turned into miracles. Therefore, these are the three grades of the promotion of faith by which increasing faith ascends to the perfect: first, to select through piety; second, to approve through reason; third, to apprehend through truth.

V. *On those things which pertain to faith.*

It is also asked what things pertain to faith which he who is rightly called faithful should believe. For that faith by which something is believed in this way—so that he who believes with that faith is not called faithful, does not belong to the present proposition. For it is manifest that even infidels do not live without faith for the reason that just as every man living in this life has certain things which he perceives through experience, so too he has certain things which, neither seen nor experienced, he believes by faith alone. Yet by no means is he said to have faith which is unto God except the man who believes those things by believing and loving which he deserves God. These things, therefore, are those which are said to pertain to faith, by believing which man is called faithful. If, indeed, we inquire diligently as to what these are, we find that these consist principally of two. For there are indeed two and these two are in one and these two are one. Creator and Saviour are two names and one thing; yet one name denotes Creator, the other Saviour; Creator, because He made us; Saviour, because He redeemed us. First we were not and we were made; afterwards we perished and were redeemed; and by one both were done so that all our good was from one, and all in one, and all one. To the Creator we owe that we are; to the Saviour, that we were restored. Therefore, these are the two things which as propositions of faith must be believed, Creator and Saviour, and the things that pertain to Creator and those that pertain to Saviour similarly. Creator and the things that pertain to Creator; this is one part of faith. Saviour and the things that pertain to Saviour; this is the other.

In the first part faith distinguishes between Creator and His works, in the second part faith distinguishes between Saviour and His sacraments. To the Creator pertain the works of foundation which were made in six days; to the Saviour pertain the works of restoration which are being completed in six ages. In the first part it pertains to faith to confess one Creator and that all things which have being were made by Him. In the second part it pertains to faith to venerate one Saviour and to believe that the things which were lost have been restored by Him to those to whom being blessed has been granted or is to be granted. In the first part, right faith ought so to distinguish between creator and creature that it attributes to each one of these what is his own and does not transfuse in turn the property of the one into the other, that is, neither attributes the majesty of the Creator to the creature nor ascribes the infirmity of the creature to the Creator, neither concludes God by time nor extends the creature by eternity. Thus faith, if it attributes to each what is his own, rightly bestows; if it distinguishes well between both, rightly does it separate and does not sin. But if it fails in any of these, faith indeed must suffer loss. For those who have cherished the creature before God, deceived by a two-fold error, have believed either that the creature is eternal or God temporal. What else must they be said to have done than to have attributed the excellence of the Maker to the work and the infirmity of the creature to the Creator? Again, the philosophers of the pagans, although they distinguished rightly between the Creator and His work, yet by no means should be called faithful since they did not have faith in the Saviour. Thus next follow those things which we have placed in the second part, where first in the Saviour we recognize the redemption, in His sacraments, the preparation of the redemption. The first part of faith looks to the debt of nature, the second part to the debt of grace. The former we ought to believe, since through nature we were founded; the latter we ought to believe, since through grace we were restored.

VI. *Whether faith was changed according to the changes of time.*

From here those two matters follow which we proposed in the first division of this treatise should be followed up in the fifth and sixth places after those four which have been treated thus far. One of these is whether according to the change of times from the beginning the faith of believers has changed, whether the form of faith is one and the same and exists in those saints who were from the beginning and who even to the end are to be believers. The other, indeed, is what that is which from the beginning right faith could never have had to any less degree, that is, what that is which could never have been deprived of anything that right faith might be established, even if something could have been added that it might increase. These two cling together by reason and on this account demand to be investigated inseparably. And let us not think that there is need of slight consideration in a question of this kind, where there are so many opinions among men and there is discussion about right faith by such diverse faith, nor must it be thought that this danger is small. For how can we perceive well regarding those things which must be believed with faith, if we perceive badly regarding faith itself? Therefore, every individual thing that is said must be considered carefully that we may say and perceive those things in which, while we struggle to assert right faith, we may not be convinced to oppose sound faith.

There are men who, as it were, by a kind of piety are made impious toward God, and, since they perceive beyond that which is in truth, offend against truth itself. Now this ignorance produces many errors as well regarding goodness as regarding truth. Some say that it is not befitting divine goodness that He be said to be cruel toward His works and that He permit any of those things which He made to perish, who made nothing for this purpose, to perish. Thus, while they think that they honor goodness, they offend truth. For He who was so pious as to create non-existing things is so just as to judge the erring and the delinquent.

Some say that it pertains to the justice of man to live in this life without struggle, although on the other hand he cannot be just if he does not struggle. For it does not pertain to the justice of this life not to be tempted but not to be overcome by temptation, and not that he who is good never falls but that when he has fallen he rise again. Similarly there are those who say that he is not faithful who either believes certain things differently, since through infirmity he cannot comprehend just how truth itself stands, or does not believe all things, since through ignorance he cannot grasp how great truth is. And these think that true faith must be blessed in the quantity of cognition rather than in the magnitude of devotion, although divine piety does not consider with how much cognition there is belief but rather with how much devotion that which is believed is cherished.

We recall this for this reason, because we realize that there are some less discreet who know not the measure of man's power, since they do not consider their own power, and if they do, they think that all must be endowed with the greater folly according as they see that they themselves have received something more than others. They affirm that he must by no means be called faithful who does not know, as it were, the great and numerous and sublime sacraments of faith and who has not grasped within his mind the disputation, the profundity, the series of accomplishments of certain men on the majesty of the Creator and on the humility of the Saviour. They propose also the nature itself of the Godhead for explanation to minds untrained and scarcely sufficient for those things which they see, and by a kind of subtle consideration propose the corporeal nature to be distinguished from incorporeal nature.

But they also say that those things which have already been made manifest to the world about the sacraments of our redemption in the nativity and in the passion and in the resurrection and in the ascension of our Saviour were clear to all the just and the faithful, both the greater and the lesser, from the beginning as things to come by the same cognition as that by which they are now recognized by us as having passed. Otherwise, it cannot be said truly that those who did not know these things had faith in all these. Moreover, he thinks that he proves that they both believed and knew all these things which were completed in the sacrament of our redemption not only by this reasoning—that, just as we now would not attain to that redemption unless we knew all these things as already done and believed them as known, so indeed they would not have been saved through these unless they knew that all these things were to be done and believed them as known, but also because several times the Scriptures bear witness that no one from the beginning has been saved without the faith of Christ. Blessed Augustine speaking on this very subject said: "The same faith of the Mediator made the just saved, the small men among the ancients together with the great, not the Old Testaments which generates unto servitude, not the law which was not so given that it might be able to vivify, but the grace of God through Jesus Christ." For just as we believe that Christ came into flesh, so they believed that He would come; just as we believe that He died they believed that He would die; just as we believe that He has risen, so they believed that He would rise; and both they and we believe that He will come to the judgment of the living and the dead.

If these things are true, just as they are thought by those and just as they seem to be affirmed by the above mentioned authorities, either salvation was very rare in ancient times or perfection very common on the part of those for whom indeed to know anything at all is to exceed the bounds of discretion. But if it seems more tolerable, in fact even judged more worthy of God, that He filled and enriched the world with a great number of the perfect rather than was content with so few of those to be saved, that many then became saved and all none the less filled with prophetic spirit already then penetrated the mysteries not yet revealed, if, I say, this is accepted, indeed we bless God in His gifts but we do not see what is reserved for the time of grace; but perhaps we will admit that that rather was to be called the time of grace according to knowledge, in which so many and such great riches of the Spirit of God flowed upon the people that, moreover, what Moses desired when he said: "Who will give that all may prophesy?" (Cf. Num. 11, 29), was considered filled with incredible felicity. I ask: "What similar thing has the Gospel brought forth?" To no avail does Paul boast about the first fruits of the Spirit which he thinks that he has received with his companions, his fellow apostles, when he was able to find no such things in his days. Finally he said: "Are all prophets?" (1 Cor. 12, 29). In vain, I say, does he boast of his own Gospel, since not from man nor through man did he receive that but, as it were, by a kind of special prerogative through the revelation of Jesus Christ, although even before him it had been revealed through the Spirit even to the peoples. But, neither ought the Apostle Peter to have turned that prophecy to his own times: "I will pour out of my spirit upon your sons and your daughters; and your sons and your daughters shall prophesy," (Cf. Joel 2, 28; Acts 2, 17), if already a more abundant effusion of the Spirit had preceded in past ages. Surely, either the prophet or rather God in the prophet if, when he spoke here, he was looking truly upon those apostolic times, ought to have said not simply: "I shall pour forth," but "I shall take more from my spirit." Why then? If we make all the just of antiquity equal in knowledge to the sons of the Gospel, must we not confess consequently that all are not superior in grace, all of whom indeed not reading, as in our case, or prediction but unction itself instructed about all things?

However, let it be; let us endure our injury, and the apostles also theirs, that even to them also, the least of the ancient just may be compared in knowledge and may be set forth in grace. But there is something, indeed, which we do not endure with merit in any way at all, namely, that the Lord of glory is perceived either to have been able to be deceived at some time or to have wished to deceive, and indeed He himself protested that there hath not risen among them that are born of women a greater man than John the Baptist, (Matt. 11, 11). Now see if we are not truly forced to confess this testimony of truth as false, if we attribute to the ancients so much as we can not claim for John. Surely no injury is done John, if he is believed or is said to have been ignorant of something, which indeed even he himself did not disavow. But if what we deny to the herald of truth we give to another contrary to the proclamation of truth, not only is there injury but blasphemy and clearly contradiction not of John but of truth.

Why, then, does the friend of the Betrothed doubt and ask: "Art thou he that art to come, or look we for another?" (Matt. 11, 3). And we by our lie confirm to thousands of men certainty on all things. Nor can we observe to a few that the ancients themselves so felt about themselves. Moses writes that God addressing him spoke as follows: "I am God to Abraham, and God to Isaac, and God to Jacob, and my name Adonai I did not show them," (Exod. 6, 2); you understand this as if addressed to you. He shows, therefore, that he received from the knowledge of God something more than the preceding fathers. David also more than his teachers and elders boldly assumed unto himself the gift of understanding, speaking thus: "I have understood more than all my teachers, because thy testimonies are my meditation," (Psal. 118, 99), and again: "I have understood more than the elders." But the prophet Daniel also said: "Many shall pass over, and knowledge shall be manifold," (Dan. 12, 4), even himself, indeed, promising greater knowledge to posterity. If, therefore, as also the holy Pope Gregory said, according to the increase of time the knowledge of the spiritual fathers increased, and the nearer they existed to the coming of the Saviour, the more fully did they receive the mystery of salvation, there is no doubt but that to those also were present the display of the things themselves and the presence of the displayer contributed much more. Finally too they hear: "Blessed are the eyes that see the things which you see," (Luke 10, 23), likewise: "But I have called you friends: because all things whatsoever I have heard of my Father, I have made known to you," (John 15, 15). "Many prophets and kings," he said, "have desired to see the things that you see, and have not seen them; and to hear the things that you hear, and have not heard them," (Luke 10, 24). Why? Indeed, in order that they might perceive more clearly and fully what they felt before with difficulty, slightly, and obscurely.

Yet what need was there to see the flesh without and to hear conversations of the flesh, if already by the Spirit within they had been perfectly instructed on all things, especially when the Lord says: "The flesh profiteth nothing: it is the spirit that quickeneth,"? (Cf. John 6, 64). But if the prophets and those who seemed more illustrious among that people were not at all able to know all things any time equally, but some more, others less, according as the spirit granted, dividing for each according as He wished, and this without prejudice to His sanctity and perfection, how much the more were the more simple and those who were just without detriment to salvation unable to know the time of salvation, the mode, and the order, to which salvation, however, they held most firmly with certain hope and faith, as it had been promised. Just as many today indeed among Christian people are of eternal life and of the future world which they unhesitatingly believe in and hope for and ardently desire, yet do not even consider its form and state or know it slightly; thus, therefore, many before the Saviour's coming, holding to and loving omnipotent God, the gratuitous promiser of their salvation, believing Him faithful in His promise, hoping for Him who most certainly pays, were saved in this faith and expectation, although when and how and in what order salvation was promised they did not know. For even to the apostles themselves, and there is no one who doubts that they were just, when the Saviour was present and the light already manifest was predicting the kingdom of heaven, the mystery of the passion is read to have been so unknown and hidden that, when the Lord himself openly proclaimed and predicted it, they were unable to understand what was being said. Those two disciples also to whom Christ appeared on the way as they went and who doubted, urged to question Him, are reported among other things to have said: "We hope that it was he that should have redeemed Israel," (Luke 24, 21). In this they show openly that they did not believe that the redemption of Israel would come through the passion of Christ, they who at the passion itself despaired of redemption. On this account it is said to them in the same place: "O foolish, and slow of heart to believe. Ought not Christ to have suffered these things, and to have risen from the dead, and so to have entered into his glory?" (Cf. Luke 24, 25 and 26).

Finally, this mystery was concealed from the ages, and lest perhaps it be thought concealed from the evil alone, He added in very recent times what was revealed to the saints. If all the good knew this from the beginning, how could the evil indeed have been ignorant of this, especially when it could not have been discerned by the good themselves, who had perceived this, what persons were truly good or evil, from whom this was to be veiled or concealed? And in this way we know manifestly that it follows that, if we confess that these things were revealed to all the good, we do not doubt that they were not unknown to the evil also. Furthermore, if this will have to stand, who will not see how ineffably those earlier times must be preferred to later ages, when the faith which here is received from without by hearsay only, there was read within by all through contemplation of prophetic aspiration in the full and manifest light of truth? What must our faith be called in comparison with the faith of those except, so to speak, not faith but a kind of opinion? They, we know, were so much more certain about the future than we about the past, since they knew through the spirit what they did not see in fact and we accept by hearing alone through word what we do not see. If this is true, who does not see that the coming of Christ not only brought enlightenment to the faithful but took away more certain and better knowledge? Wherefore, reflecting upon faith, let us confess things more befitting salvation and nearer truth, and, just as at one and the same time according to the different capacities of various people we recognize the cognition of those things which pertain to faith, so also let us not doubt that from the beginning through the succession of the times faith has grown in the faithful themselves by certain increases.

Yet that the faith of the preceding and the subsequent was one and the same, in whom, however, there was not the same cognition, we thus unhesitatingly confess, just as in these whom we recognize as faithful in our time we find the same faith and yet not the same cognition of faith. And so faith increased in all through the times so that it was greater but was not changed so as to be different. Before the law God was believed Creator and from Him salvation and redemption were awaited through whom indeed in some manner the same salvation was to be fulfilled and accomplished. With the exception of few to whom it had been granted by special favor to know this, it was not known by the other faithful also. But under the law the person of the Redeemer was predicted as to be sent and was expected as to come. Now whether this person himself was man or angel or God was not yet made manifest. They alone knew this, who individually through the spirit were enlightened unto this. But under grace both the mode of redemption and the quality of the person of the Redeemer are already manifestly predicted to all and are believed. Yet in the Church of God we always believe that faith and cognition of the incarnation and passion of Christ were from the beginning, since from the beginning they who knew this never were lacking. Others were saved because they were joined to the simple perfection of these by faith and they by operating well followed these.

VII. *What is the least that faith could ever have possessed.*

These things are the least that right faith could ever have possessed from the beginning, namely, to believe that there is one God, Creator of all things, Lord and Ruler of the universe, that in truth He is not the author of evil, yet that He would be the Redeemer of those who in their evils sought and expected His mercy. These things, we believe, sufficed in the beginning for the faith of the simple minded by whom, although nothing more was added unto cognition, much, however, was contributed unto devotion. These, indeed, believed that the Redeemer would come in the flesh and would die in the same flesh, would arise and ascend, even if they manifestly did not know certain other things which were hidden in those times. And yet we say that they most truly had faith in the nativity and passion, or in His resurrection and ascension, in that they clung to those who believed and knew these things with faith and devotion under hope and expectation of the same redemption, although similarly they did not know the manner of this same redemption of theirs. So, therefore, as Blessed Augustine says, we think it should be understood that the same faith in the Mediator made the ancient just safe, the small with the great, since the ancient just, the small with the great, had the same faith in the Mediator, some, indeed, believing and knowing the things which were to come as about to come, but others not indeed knowing but, by believing and desiring, clinging to those who knew and believed. And this, indeed, he added: that just as we believe that He would come in the flesh, so they believed that He would come; just as we believe that He died, so they believed that He would die, etc. Indeed, it is not to be referred to all but to them only to whom it was granted individually to know beforehand those things which are to come, so that all, indeed, are said to have had the same faith but not the same cognition of faith; however, if this is understood to have been said of all, all who believed that there would be redemption are not improperly affirmed to have believed those things in which redemption consisted. For in so far as they believed that that very redemption would come which contained all these things, they believed these things, although all in believing did not have the same cognition of them. In this manner, therefore, it can be said with sound sense that all the just from the beginning had faith in the Saviour and that all were justified in their faith in the redemption to come, since either they knew that the same redemption would come or they believed in those who knew and believed; they acceptd with this faith unto sanctification the sacraments of redemption itself which had been instituted from the beginning and in themselves already carried this same redemption of theirs as if in shadow and figure.

This those two men well signified who carried the grape suspended on a pole from the land of promise into the desert to the sons of Israel. The grape on the pole, indeed, is Christ on the cross, the mystery of which two people carry in the sacrament. Those who preceded, carried but did not see, since preceding His coming they all truly carried the sacraments of His passion through faith but not all through cognition deserved to understand what they carried. But those who follow both carry and see, since the faithful who follow in the flesh after His coming both accept the sacrament of His passion through faith and now through revealed cognition know it. Wherefore Bede says on the same question: "The prophets and Moses knew and proclaimed one and the same victory of the Lord's cross before the apostles but the prophets proclaimed this on several occasions in figurative and veiled speech, but the apostles and the successors of the apostles always proclaimed it openly in the visible light of the Gospel, so that now all Christian people should know and confess the faith which at that time only a few and all the more perfect knew, although all people of God even then carried figuratively the mysteries of the same faith in legal ceremonies."

VIII. *Recapitulation of what has been said before.*

Therefore, true faith rests in two: Creator and Redeemer. One does not suffice for you without the other. Know both, confess both. If you believe in the Creator you know also that you were made; if you confess the redeemer you know that you were restored. Creator and redeemer are one. In His own He made you; in your own He remade you, and one made both. If He himself had made you, and another had remade you, you would owe to the one that you were made and you would owe to the other that you were remade. So your attention and love and your obedience would be divided and you would not belong entirely to one. And of the two you would love him the more from whom you had the more. He who created you gave you being, He who redeemed you gave you being blessed. Therefore, lest a certain one be loved more as redeemer by you than the Creator Himself, the Creator himself wishes to be the Redeemer and He underwent your passion that He might purchase your love.

A son by nature was sent for those to be elected, since without Him strangers necessarily would not have been introduced into the heredity. Wisdom came that the enemy might be overcome not by power but by reason, and in all these your faith rests in one and unto one and one, because, when two are named, one is signified, since Creator and Redeemer are one, Creator as to nature, Saviour as to grace. All and one are in these two, that is, in that from the beginning the faith of the believers is one; although in the same faith, in some cognition of these things was greater, in others less, according to the diversity of the times, just as at one and the same time cognition of these very things is found greater in some and less in others according to the capacity of persons. Thus although faith increased so as to be greater at some times and in some persons, yet it was not changed so as to be different. But all with one faith believed in one; all were justified by one faith who deserved to be justified. "For," as the Apostle said, "without faith it is impossible to please God," (Hebr. 11, 6), and just as blessed Augustine says: "Where there was not faith, there was not good work."

IX. *On the sacrament of faith and on virtue.*

The sacrament of faith can be understood in a twofold manner. For by the sacrament of faith either faith itself is understood which is a sacrament or the sacraments of faith are understood which must be received with faith and have been prepared for the sanctification of the faithful. For certain sacraments are called military sacraments by which soldiers are obligated by their promise to preserve faith with their general, and infidels also have certain sacraments. These last are called sacraments although they are neither sacred nor signs of a sacred thing but rather execrations and abominations by which men are not sanctified but are polluted. Yet to distinguish these the so-called sacraments of faith can be understood as those which are employed by the faithful and which are accepted with faith for sanctification.

First then let us consider by what reason faith itself is called a sacrament or is understood to be a sacrament of something. The Apostle says: "We see now through a glass in a dark manner, but then face to face," (1 Cor. 13, 12). Surely now when we see through faith we see through a glass in a dark manner, but then when we shall see through contemplation we shall see face to face. What is seeing through a glass? Seeing the image. What is seeing face to face? Seeing the thing. Imagine that someone is behind you or above you, you are turned away from him and you do not see face to face, with your face into his face. For your face is turned away from him and, if by chance he looks back at you, you nevertheless will not similarly look at him. Therefore, as long as you will be thus, you will not be able to see him face to face. Hold out a glass and place it before you, straightway you will see in it the image of him who is at your back or above your head and you will say: "I see you." What do you see? Indeed you see something but only an image. You see him but in his image, not yet in his face. You do not yet recognize as you are recognized; you do not yet see as you are seen. You are seen in yourself; you see in image. He who sees you looks back at you, but you are turned from him. Turn toward him and place your face before his face and you will see now not an image but the thing itself. You have seen him before but in his image; now you see him in his face. Yet when you begin to see the thing itself, you recognize that that which was seen in image had some likeness to that which is seen in the thing. What is seen in the image is a sacrament, what is seen in the thing is the thing of the sacrament. What, therefore, we see now through the glass in a dark manner is the sacrament with respect to that which we shall see face to face in manifest contemplation.

But what is a dark manner and what is a glass in which the image is seen until the thing itself can be seen? The dark manner is Sacred Scripture. Why? Because it has obscure meaning. The glass is your heart, if, however, it be clean and clear and clarified. The image in the glass is the faith in your heart. For faith itself is image and sacrament. But future contemplation is the thing and the virtue of the sacrament. Those who have not faith see nothing, those who have faith already begin to see something but only the image. For if the faithful see nothing, there would be no enlightenment from faith nor would the faithful be called enlightened. But if they already saw the thing itself and did not await something more to be seen, they would not see through a glass in a dark manner but face to face. Therefore, those who see through faith see the image, those who see through contemplation see the thing. Those who have the faith have the sacrament; those who have contemplation have the thing. Faith, then, is the sacrament of future contemplation, and contemplation itself is the thing and the virtue of the sacrament, and we now receive meanwhile the sacrament of sanctification that sanctified perfectly we may be able to take the thing itself. If, then, the highest good is rightly believed to be man's contemplation of his Creator, not unfittingly is faith, through which he begins in some manner to see the absent, said to be the beginning of good and the first step in his restoration; this restoration, indeed, increases according to increases of faith, while man is enlightened more through knowledge that he may know more fully, and is inflamed with love that he may love more ardently.

So, therefore, the just, as long as during his existence in this body he wanders away from the Lord, has to live according to faith just as, when he has been led out of this work house and introduced to the joy of his Lord, he will have to live according to contemplation. But by a wonderful dispensation of God it is brought about that now meanwhile the malice of the ancient enemy for persecuting and attacking the faithful is relaxed in order that this may be reputed to man according to merit, if now walking through faith even unattacked he does not desert the way of truth, who formerly strengthened by the vision of God in person had been laid low by persuasion alone. Now, that in this battle he may be able to stand unconquered and guard his good unharmed, there are given him, as it is said, arms in the sacraments with which he may fortify himself, missiles in good works with which he may lay the enemy low, so that with love of faith and with hope combined he may meanwhile both be strengthened and live.

PART ELEVEN

On the Natural Law.

I. *On the sacraments of the natural law.*

After faith we must treat of the sacraments of faith. Sacraments were instituted from the beginning for the restoration and guardianship of man, some under the natural law, some under the written law, some under grace. And among these those which have been posterior in time are always found more worthy of the effect of spiritual grace. For all those sacraments of earlier time, whether under the natural law or under the written, were signs, as it were, and figures of those which now have been set forth under grace. And the spiritual effect which they operated in their own time when placed before these, they operated by that virtue and sanctification which they assume from these. If anyone, therefore, should deny that prior sacraments had the effect of sanctification, he would not seem to me to think rightly.

II. *On the first difference between preceding and subsequent sacraments.*

Yet in this we unhesitatingly prefer the dignity of the subsequent because the former were both visible and the signs of the visible, but these indeed, although they themselves are in truth visible, are yet signs and sacraments of invisible grace. Thus sacraments of grace first take in themselves through benediction the virtue of sanctification and then they confer the sanctification which they contain in themselves so that out of sanctification these sanctify and confer out of sanctification, which is their own and has been placed in them divinely, what those were accustomed to confer through these out of only the signification of these. For the passion of the Saviour, which in the first place sanctifies sacraments of grace to effect salvation, through the medium of these sanctified also those sacraments of earlier time so that salvation was the same both for those who by right faith venerated the signs of the future in the earlier sacraments and for those who receive the effect of salvation in these.

III. *Another difference.*

We perceive that there is this difference also between those sacraments of the earliest time which were under the natural law and those sacraments which were instituted either under the written law or under grace—that the former seem to be more of the will, the latter of necessity; the former celebrated from vow, the latter from precept. For it must not be thought that those first sacraments of the natural law, whether indeed tithes or sacrifices or oblations, were so imposed upon man from necessity that he who had not performed them incurred the guilt of prevarication, just as he who faithfully cherished them found the merit of his devotion. For nowhere do we read that before the written law God said to a man who did not give tithes, who did not offer sacrifices, as He afterwards said through the law: "The male, whose flesh of his foreskin shall not be circumcised, that soul shall be destroyed out of his people," (Gen. 17, 14), and as He under grace thundered forth terribly: "Unless a man be born again of water and the Holy Ghost, he cannot enter into the kingdom of God," (John 3, 5).

Accordingly we conjecture that those first sacraments were rather set forth to exercise devotion than imposed to obtain salvation. For whence was he who possessed nothing to offer tithes? What sacrifices and what oblations could he offer who had nothing? And Jacob made a vow saying to God: "If my Lord God shall be with me," (Gen. 28, 20), and then he added: "Of all things that thou shalt give to me, I will offer tithes and peace-offerings to thee," (Gen. 28, 22). Therefore, he shows clearly that he promised that he would do this from vow, that he did not owe this from the necessity of a command.

IV. *That man was instructed by God to offer tithes.*

Yet it is altogether probable that man was instructed and taught by God from the beginning to exercise these things that by zeal of subsequent devotion he might destroy the guilt of the first contempt, and he who had been stubborn in himself might become accustomed afterwards to obey in his own. For whence could man have known that a tenth of his things rather than a ninth or an eighth or any other part must be offered, unless he had been taught by God? Therefore, we conjecture that God indeed instructed man with counsel from the beginning to exercise these but He did not obligate by precept until He afterwards found those things in which man capable of precept showed disobedience and learned to guard against prevarication. First, therefore, before the law He nourished the young by counsel. Then He tried by precept those exercised under the law. Finally, He permitted those perfect under grace to walk in the freedom of the spirit. Thus, that we may call to mind briefly what was said above, let us consider what the difference is between sacraments of the New Testament and those which were to be considered sacraments either under the natural law or under the written law.

V. *The first difference.*

The first difference, then, is that the sacraments of the New Testament are in the first place signs of spiritual grace and were instituted principally to confer grace on those to be sanctified by infusing benediction. But those of the Old Testament were only signs of these of the New Testament and through the medium of these of which they were the signs, lest they should be without salvation who preceded the time of redemption, conferred grace as sustenance.

VI. *The second difference.*

The second difference is that the ancient just who were imbued with these sacraments were not yet able to enter the gates of the kingdom of heaven until the Saviour by assuming flesh ascended heaven and opened the way to all who believed in Him and followed Him.

VII. *The third difference.*

The third difference is that the sacraments of the natural law do not seem to have been imposed from precept but to have been proposed from counsel with reference to vow, but the sacraments of the written law and of grace seem to introduce a certain necessity of execution, especially because they are known to have been instituted not only from counsel but from precept.

VIII. *Why the first were changed through the second.*

But a question not to be contemned arises as to why indeed, if grace conferred the same effect of salvation through the preceding as through the subsequent, divine command abolished the rite of the ancient through the institution of the subsequent. For if the same virtue was in those sacraments, why was it necessary that the former cease and the latter succeed? But it must be realized that the order and plan of the divine dispensation demanded this—that just as from the beginning with the progress of time the coming of the Saviour approached nearer and nearer, so always the effect of salvation and the knowledge of truth increased more and more, because the signs themselves of salvation had to be changed one after the other through the succession of times in order that when the effect of divine grace increased unto salvation, at the same time sanctification might appear more evident in the visible signs themselves.

There was indeed the same Saviour, the same grace, the same faith in the former in what was to come, in the latter in what was shown. But since He himself through whom salvation was given was far away, the signs of the same salvation had to be obscure. Afterwards, indeed, as his coming gradually approached, it was necessary that in the same order both faith in cognition and grace in salvation increase and that the same grace in the sacraments outside and in its signs manifest itself more evidently. Wherefore, first through oblation and afterwards through circumcision, finally through baptism it was ordained that the sacrament of expiation and justification be formed, since the form and the likeness of the same cleansing is found obscurely indeed in the oblation, is expressed indeed more evidently in circumcision, but is declared manifestly through baptism. For man received the first institution that as remedies of exterior salvation he might offer part of the substance to God, might retain part for his own use, in order that in this deed he might learn to attribute to God those things which were intrinsically good and to impute to himself what were truly evil.

Ten indeed, since it is the perfect number, is a sign of goodness and virtue which are attributed to God and are recognized by God in man. Now nine, since it falls short of the perfect number, signifies the lack, the wickedness, and the corruption which is rightly allotted mankind. On this account then man is ordered to give a tithe to God, to retain nine for himself, that he may confess that what is good in him is from God but what is evil is from himself. But this sign taken as it were from afar taught man rather what was than what was done. Therefore, when the time had come in which truth had of necessity to be declared, a remedy was given through the sacrament of circumcision in which, while from the interior substance of man no part indeed as naturally superfluous is cut away but something of his that is superfluous, as a figure, now that circumcision of sin which grace alone accomplishes in the interior man is demonstrated more manifestly. But since circumcision cut away the exterior squalors and the enormities which are without but ablution cleanses the interior stains, then fittingly when truth was manifested in the coming of Christ should circumcision have ceased, so that that sacrament might succeed that which could declare the perfect cleansing of man and the interior lustre of the soul, obtained in the sacrament itself and through the sacrament itself. Now furthermore, since circumcision indeed takes away squalors but inflicts pains, while ablution cleanses the iniquitous without pain, on this account circumcision was given to the earlier people serving in fear and labouring under the law, but ablution was given to the new people walking in grace through charity. Therefore, those first sacraments which preceded under the natural law seem as it were a kind of shadow of the truth; those indeed which followed afterwards under the written law seem, as it were, a kind of image or figure of the truth, but these which follow last under grace not indeed a shadow or image but a body of truth, in which the effect of salvation, since it both proceeds perfectly and is shown evidently, just as the spirit in a living body, is set forth by exterior motion. Thus in these the life of invisible grace is demonstrated very clearly. The first sacraments then were a shadow, the second an image, the third a body, after which in fourth place follows the truth of the spirit.

These words, we think, suffice for the present regarding the sacraments of the natural law which indeed then, as it has already been said above, we believe were so joined with justifying faith that in them was the exercise of devotion, not the necessity of obtaining salvation. For by faith alone operating from love they then were justified who through grace were preserved for participation in the future redemption. But since we have already said certain things temporarily regarding those first sacraments by which the devotion of the faithful was then exercised, we think that something should also be said about works.

IX. *On the three kinds of works.*

There are three kinds of works: some are so good that they can never be passed over licitly, some so bad that they can never be practiced licitly, but some are between these and according to time and place can be carried on or omitted. Therefore, the natural law prohibited only those which are such that they can never be performed licitly but commanded those alone which can never be omitted licitly, leaving all between for either side.

Concerning those which are to be prohibited He wrote one precept in man's heart: "See thou never do to another what thou wouldst hate to have done unto thee," (Tob. 4, 16). Concerning those which are to be ordered, similarly one precept: "Whatsoever you would that men should do to you, do you also to them," (Matt. 7, 12), so that clearly man might learn from consideration of himself of what nature he should maintain himself toward his neighbour. But afterwards when the law entered and proposed a narrower discipline of living, it excepted certain of those which had been midway; and of them some through precept, others through prohibition it deflected to the other side, so that just as to the first man in paradise God by a natural concession had expressed one prohibition as a precept of discipline, so now for his sons, who do not stand in one truth but are dissipated through various errors, He formed not one precept of discipline respecting natural concession for those, as it were, to be approved but many for those, as it were, to be corrected and restored; so the more they learned to restrain themselves in the things midway, the more easily would they be able to avoid those things forbidden. There many were conceded, few were prohibited; here many are prohibited, few are conceded. There it was told man that he should not eat of the tree of knowledge of good and of evil, not because it was an evil tree but because obedience was to be proven. Here it was said that they should not eat meat with blood that they should learn to abhor cruelty; that they should not eat pork that they should detest uncleanness; that they should not plough with ox and ass that they should know laziness and foolishness as harmful to prophesy, and all other similar things which were midway.

But those which under the natural law had been included in two precepts, afterwards through the written law were set forth and distinguished in these seven which were published in the second table, of which the first was: "Honour thy father and thy mother, that it may be well with thee, and thou mayest be long-lived upon the land," (Cf. Exodus 20); the second: "Thou shalt not kill;" the third: "Thou shalt not commit adultery;" the fourth: "Thou shalt not steal;" the fifth: "Thou shalt not bear false witness;" the sixth: "Thou shalt not desire thy neighbour's wife;" the seventh: "Thou shalt not desire thy neighbour's goods." Among these also that is not to be passed over negligently which alone of these seven was given according to precept, the six remaining being according to prohibition. For the first sin of man was disobedience and on this account this life which is conceded to man for repentance is wholly imputed for obedience. Since, therefore, man in doing evil is distracted out of his own desire to diverse things, in doing good the rule of obedience alone governs. On this account in finding the evils which he has from himself and can do through himself, he had to be instructed singly, but for doing good he had only to be recalled to obedience, that here he might learn more soundly through the opinion of another what he should have done by himself. For when man is ordered to give honour to father and to mother not only is this to be referred to parents of the flesh but rather is this given to him in order that he who at one time contemned God in His precepts now on account of God may not disdain to show obedience and honour to a superior man.

Part Twelve

On the Written Law.

I. *On the oneness of the faithful people.*

The first state from Adam to Abraham is more properly determined. For although the written law was given through Moses, nevertheless the observance of the law took its beginning before Moses in circumcision. That first age under the natural law had passed, as it were, in a kind of confusion and those who had existed as the faithful in that age, like some few grains dispersed among the human race and separated from each other, had been united within by faith alone.

Therefore, that an exterior unity might be founded to commend the interior unity, and that the form of faith might be manifest to which those who had to be called out of their dispersion might be invited, one was set forth to whom, in accomplishing one, all who had afterwards to be assumed might be gathered. The one out of many was called Abraham, the unity the beginning of oneness, so that to his bosom might be gathered whoever after him might be joined with him by faith and devotion. He was called, therefore, that he might go out of his land and withdraw from those with whom he had been united, not that he might be joined with those to whom he was going. And form was given him which he might transmit to all who were to be born from him and to all who were to be one in the one form itself so that, although the number of the faithful might be increased, yet the unity of the faith might not be multiplied, so that first they might be one in his form who were born from him, afterwards also that they might be made one who were associated with him in the same faith.

Afterwards, therefore, the unity of the people of God began and the unity of faithful conversion which was marked first by the sacrament of circumcision, later to be marked by the sacrament of baptism. First the mark was in the flesh under which those who were one in the flesh were to be united. Circumcision had been given only to the seed of Abraham, that they might be marked in the flesh who were united in the flesh. But after they entered upon this oneness who were not from him according to the generation of the flesh, a mark of oneness was placed outside the substance of the flesh, because they were made one by spirit and by faith who were not so in the flesh.

II. *On circumcision.*

So God commanded Abraham to cut the skin of his prepuce as a sign for himself, as an example for posterity, adding so much to his former state that through this mark the people of God might be separated from infidels until He should come who would collect the faithful not only from the sons of Abraham but from all nations and that through this, as was said, they might be separated no longer through the sign of the flesh in race but through the sign of baptism in sanctification. Surely meanwhile whoever of the faithful were not of the seed of Abraham were not subject to this command nor were they held by any obligation to receive circumcision which had been imposed on the seed of Abraham only, but by faith operating through love just as formerly under the natural law, before circumcision was instituted, the just who were without circumcision were saved.

Now the mode of circumcision was as follows. The precept was that the male child on the eighth day from his nativity should be circumcised in the flesh of his foreskin, (Cf. Gen. 17, 11). And there are those who think that there should be added, "with a knife made of stone" which, however, they prove by no other authority than that Sephora, the wife of Moses, terrified by the angel is said to have taken a sharp stone and with it to have cut the foreskin of her son, (Cf. Exod. 4, 25), and Josue, when about to enter the land of promise, is said to have introduced the sacrament of circumcision with stone knives a second time among the people of Israel, (Cf. Josue 5, 2 ff.). But in the one case indeed it is thought not unfittingly to have been done rather on account of haste and fear but in the other on account of a type and signification of the true Jesus rather than through custom. Therefore, that the sacrament of circumcision might be shown not like former sacraments as proposed to the will but to be executed of necessity, the precept is confirmed by a threat when it is said: "The male, whose flesh of his foreskin shall not be circumcised, that soul shall be destroyed out of his people," (Cf. Gen. 17, 14). The cause also is brought in when it is said: "because he hath broken my covenant." If, therefore, by the broken covenant of God we understand the prevarication of our first parents when the uncircumcised is said to be destined to perish on account of the prevarication of the covenant, manifestly it is granted to be understood that the sacrament of circumcision was instituted for this, that through it man might be liberated from the debt of the first prevarication. For, likewise, as an aid to salutary care circumcision cooperated in the law against original sin just as baptism now, except that the first fathers were not able to enter the gate of the kingdom of heaven because the death of Christ was necessary to open up the avenue of life.

There are indeed three circumcisions. One is external only in the flesh, which is a sacrament. There are two others which are things and the virtue of a sacrament: the one which takes place in the present when the soul is circumcised by the laying aside of iniquity, the other which will take place in the future when through the laying aside of corruption the body will be circumcised. The first then is in the flesh, the second in the mind, the third in the body. But the eighth day in Sacred Scripture sometimes signifies the time of the resurrection to follow after the present life which runs within seven days, sometimes the time of grace, in which, as it were, after the sabbath of the law the eternal goods are promised to those who serve God. Worthily, therefore, was that first circumcision which was the sacrament of those two ordered to be done on the eighth day that it might be shown that hearts were to be circumcised in the time of grace through the cleansing of iniquity and in the time of the resurrection the bodies through the laying aside of corruption. Thus, then, circumcision of the flesh was given to males only, because Sacred Scripture is accustomed to signify the soul through the masculine sex but flesh through the feminine, so that it was clearly shown that the exterior circumcision conferred sanctification on souls but did not take away corruption from the flesh. The knife made of stone signifies Christ of whom the Apostle says: "And the rock was Christ," (Cf. 1 Cor. 10, 4).

Of Him it was written: "Behold the Lamb of God, behold him who taketh away the sin of the world," (Cf. John 1, 29). It was ordered to be done in the flesh of the foreskin, because it was given as a remedy against original sin which we contract from our parents on being propagated by that member.

Furthermore, females among the people were saved by faith alone in circumcision, purified by sacrifices and oblations and other ceremonies of the law, accepting circumcision itself also by faith and participating by venerating with those who accepted it in the flesh. Males, who prevented by death were not able to reach the eighth day and on this account departed from this life without the sacrament of circumcision, are thought not improbably to have been saved by the faith alone of parents, by the intervention of oblations and sacrifices, for the reason that the precept of circumcision does not seem to have been imposed except on males coming to the eighth day; they do not seem to have been guilty of prevarication who had not been contemners of the precept, because it had been given only to those who came to the eighth day, especially lest this sex appear more wretched and there be prejudice against it in that from which the other sex is acknowledged to have been entirely absolved. But rightly is it inquired whether those, who by the negligence or contempt of parents passed the eighth day without the sacrament of circumcision, afterwards by receiving the same sacrament obtained the effect of salvation when the divine precept imposed that this sacrament must be celebrated only on the eighth day. And perhaps it can be believed not unreasonably that, just as regarding nations those which came to the practice of the law received this sacrament in any age unto salvation, so also, if some under the law had not received it in their own time, yet the remedy would have operated for them unto salvation if by receiving it afterwards they corrected the prior negligence.

Thus then the sacrament of circumcision was given to the seed of Abraham alike for sanctifying and for marking, for sanctifying that it might be justified, for marking that it might be distinguished from the rest of nations in order that it might remain alone and the generation from which Christ was born be distinguished. Wherefore then it is gathered as probable that circumcision was imposed only upon the seed of Abraham by precept from which Christ was to be born, as for example after Abraham upon Isaac, after Isaac upon Jacob, and then upon the twelve tribes who arose from Jacob. For Job also is believed according to some to have been from the stock of Esau who, however, is not read to have been circumcised.

III. *On the preparation of the law.*

The sacrament of circumcision was given before legislation and through it a certain preparation was made to accept the law. For just as now in the New Testament man after first being washed by the water of baptism receives the sign and the name of his profession and then associated with the number of the faithful and instructed by divine precepts he proceeds to fulfil his profession, so that ancient people first indeed were marked through circumcision, then were informed through the law.

IV. *On the sacraments of the written law.*

The written law contains three things: precepts, sacraments, promises. In precepts there is merit, in promises there is reward, in sacraments there is assistance. Through precepts it had been necessary to go to promises. But since man was weak by himself the sacraments came midway between precepts and promises, to assist him both to perform precepts and to obtain promises. Under the natural law there were few sacraments; under the written law both were multiplied, namely, the precepts and the sacraments. For when God the physician first proceeded to cure sick men, disease had seized him entirely whom health had left entirely. And He placed in the body of the human race first of all a few antidotes for a few members, that is for a few persons, in order that gradually disease might fail and health increase. Afterwards under the written law He brought together more remedies, and He restored more.

There were two precepts under the natural law and three sacraments. The two precepts: "See thou never do to another what thou wouldst hate to have done to thee," (Cf. Tob. 4, 16); and, "All things whatsoever you would that man should do to you, do you also the same to them," (Cf. Matt. 7, 12). Three sacraments: tithes, oblations, and sacrifices; tithes in portions, oblations in things, sacrifices in animals. Under the written law there were many precepts and many sacraments. For the precepts of the written law were in part movable, in part immovable. Movable are those which from dispensation are ordained for the time. Immovable are those which come from nature and are either so evil that at no time can they be performed without blame or so good that at no time can they be dismissed without blame.

V. *On the immovable precepts.*

Therefore, the natural law had the immovable alone included in the two precepts, in the one by commanding good things, in the other by prohibiting evil. But these two precepts of the natural law were extended further by the written law and were distinguished through those seven precepts which the second table contained. In these it is shown of what nature man should present himself toward his neighbour, just as in the three preceding it is demonstrated of what nature man should present himself toward God. Wherefore too it was called the first table since it contains the higher mandates which pertain to the love of God. Now the second was so called because it contains the lower precepts and those next after these which pertain to love of neighbour. Or the first table is so called because in it are contained the precepts which recommend faith, the second because in it are contained the precepts which instruct unto good operation. In the first table there are three precepts because the Trinity which is believed by faith is God. In the second table there are seven precepts because in the present life which revolves within a cycle of seven days are shown the duties of man toward his neighbour.

Now the three and the seven complete the ten, since right faith and good operation make perfect. The first precept of the first table pertains to God the Father, just as the first precept of the second table pertains to man the father, so that in both cases paternity is honored by the authority of the beginning. In the first table there is a command and a prohibition, similarly in the second, so that you may be eager both to do what you ought and to guard against what you ought not to do. For if you offend in the one, there is sin by neglect, but if you offend in the other, there is sin by act. For it is a sin by act to do what should not be done, but not to do what should be done is a sin by neglect.

VI. *On the three precepts of the first table. The first precept.*

"Hear, O Israel, your God is one God, him shalt thou adore, and him only shalt thou serve," (Cf. Deut. 6, 4, and 13). This is not all that is said regarding the precept, since before the precept through admonition the mind of the hearer is prepared for obedience. "Hear, O Israel," note obedience here; "your God", note grace here; "is one God," note the teaching here, as if it were said: "Show obedience, understand grace, recognize truth." What you hear, this is the obedience which you exacted; that He is your God, is the grace by which you have arrived; that He is one God, is the truth by which you are illumined and are made perfect. Hear your God who had already shown mercy to you and still had not yet received service from you, that you may know that both are from Him, namely, that He exacts work of virtue from you and that He promises you the reward of retribution. "Hear, O Israel," that is, listen and acquiesce. For every virtue begins from obedience, just as every vice proceeds from disobedience. For in vain would grace be given to the disobedient or teaching to the stubborn or precept to him who understandeth not. On this account He says first: "Hear, O Israel," that you may be obedient; "your God," that you may be devoted; "is one God," that you may know truth.

Then follows the precept: "Him shalt thou adore." This pertains to faith. And "him only shalt thou serve." This pertains to operation. For faith operating out of love makes perfect, since neither work without faith nor faith, to which time suffices, without work was accepted. Therefore, adore rightly by believing, serve well by operating. Now it can be asked whether that which He said, "him only," is to be referred to both so that it is said: "Him only shalt thou adore and him only shalt thou serve." But how can this be, since often in the Old Testament we read that holy men not only adored angels but also men, and yet on this account we do not find anywhere that they were reprehended. And also in the New the Apostle especially urges the faithful to serve their superiors and those placed over them. Thus, it must be realized that men in one way, God in another is ordered to be adored. For according to an old custom all superiors were said to be adored by inferiors when reverence was shown them by these with the bending of the knee or with the bowing of the head. Now to adore God is to submit the whole mind to Him through humility and devotion, and to believe Him the beginning and end of all good. There is no one of sound mind who doubts that we owe this to him alone. Wherefore, He himself also through a prophet testifies about Himself saying: "I will not give my glory to another nor my praise to graven things," (Cf. Isai. 42, 8).

Now concerning service exactly this can be understood fittingly: that everyone truly is said very rightly to serve God alone who subjects himself humbly also according to God to a superior man and where the cause of God is impugned opposes courageously, who is on his guard solicitously lest in his service he either through fear of man does something against God or through fear of earthly retribution intentionally places gain before heavenly reward. But in Greek the idea is expressed more clearly. For the Greek expression distinguishes divine service from the human by a special word which the Latin does not have. For in it service of God is latria (λατρεία) and the human is called dulia (δουλεία). And on this account they were called idolaters who showed to idols that service which they owed to God. But the Latin language includes both services under the same noun and thus the meaning has become rather obscure when it is said: "Him alone shalt thou serve," which in Greek is not ambiguous. But since the precept pertains to the Father, why is it said: "Him alone shalt thou serve," as if service is not to be rendered also to the Son and to the Holy Spirit? But the fact that "to Him alone" is said does not exclude the communion of the Son and the Holy Spirit but whatever is not God. But Father and Son and Holy Ghost are one God; He alone is to be adored and to Him alone and to no other is service to be rendered, namely, with that service which is due to Him alone. For also in the Gospel, when it is said: "No one knoweth the Father but the Son," (Cf. Matt. 11, 27), surely the Holy Ghost is not excluded from knowledge of the Father when He himself according to the testimony of the apostle searcheth the deep things of God, (Cf. 1 Cor. 2, 10). But the manner of speaking is this, that by "no one" is meant all except Him of course who is that which He is.

VII. *The second precept.*

Having passed over these matters briefly let us pass on to a discussion of the next command which is as follows: "Thou shalt not take the name of thy God in vain," (Cf. Exod. 20, 7; Deut. 5, 11). According to the simple meaning of the letter this should be understood thus, that man should not take the name of God in vain, that is either to affirm a lie or to venerate an idol, namely, that he should neither honor idols by the divine name nor associate the divine name with falsehood. Now mystically to take the name of God in vain is to consider the Son of God made visible through humanity a creature. In vain then does he take the name of God who believes that the eternal Son of God began from time, since by the name of the Father the Son is meant because in the Son and through the Son the invisible Father is made manifest not only when the world was made by Himself but also when man was redeemed by Himself. Surely those who confess that the Son of God was made man by no means take the name of God in vain, since Him whom they believe man through that which He assumed from time they know as the true God through that which He was from eternity. The expression, "Thou shalt not take the name of thy God in vain," can still be understood otherwise. For they take the name of God in vain who contemn the son of God sent to them and made flesh for their salvation. Therefore, what does it mean to say: "Thou shalt not take the name of thy God in vain," except just as you venerate and adore Him on this account, because you were made by Him, so adore and venerate on this account, because you were redeemed by Him, since no less did He contribute to you when he redeemed than when He created. To the same sense points the fact that the Son Himself in the Gospel says to the disciples and through the disciples to all who believe in Him: "You believe in God, believe also in me," (John 14, 1). Moderate words indeed as befitted a pious person, advising us by implication that we should understand that He is to be adored by us not only in His divinity by which He created but also in the humanity by which He redeemed!

VIII. *The third precept.*

The third precept is "Keep holy the sabbath day," (Cf. Exod. 20, 8). Scripture seems to make mention of four Sabbaths: first, that on which God is said to have rested after having finished His works; the second, that which the sons of Israel are commanded to observe in the flesh; the fourth, that Sabbath which God in promise offers for a Sabbath to His lovers. Therefore, there are two Sabbaths externally, one of God and one of man, and two internally, one of God and one of man. The Sabbath of God by which He is said to cease from work externally is the sacrament of that internal Sabbath of His in which His eternal and immortal eternity enjoying undisturbed bliss is never fatigued by any labour. The Sabbath of man which is accepted to be kept by him visibly and externally is the sacrament of the interior Sabbath where the holy mind through a good conscience resting from the service of sin delights in the joy of the Holy Spirit. Whoever in the present life shall keep this Sabbath so as to consent to no evil will arrive in the future life at that eternal Sabbath of God where He will percieve no evil just as was said: "And there shall be month after month, and sabbath after sabbath," (Isa. 66, 23). Thus that precept seems to refer specially to the person of the Holy Spirit when it is said: "Keep holy the sabbath day," that we may indeed accept Him in the present and guard Him within us unto the joy of a good conscience, in order that we may deserve to accept and possess Him in the future unto the joy of life. These, therefore, are the three precepts of the first table in which especially the love of God is commended and the entire Trinity is ordered to be adored and cherished equally as one God.

IX. *On seven other precepts of the second table.*

The second table contained seven other precepts which instruct man unto love of neighbour, and they are distinguished by the number seven because in the present life only which revolves within seven days our charity is exercised by works of piety toward neighbour, which afterwards, when our works have been completed and labours finished, through contemplation equally with neighbour is to be blessed unto God. Love of neighbour, therefore, is both temporal as far as it pertains to the display of work and eternal as far as it pertains to the effect of love.

X. *The first precept.*

The first precept of the second table pertains to man the father, just as the first of the first table to God the Father. In both cases paternity is placed first; in both cases it is honoured with the dignity of the beginning, because in a certain manner we so have the beginning of being born through generation from man the father as we have received the beginning of being through foundation from God the Father; the paternity of man is a sacrament and so also is the image of the divine paternity, that the heart of man in this beginning which he sees may learn what he owes to that beginning from which he is and which he does not see. Thus then is it said: "Honour thy father and they mother that it may be well with thee, and thou mayest be longlived upon the land," (Cf. Exod. 20, 12). Just as it was said above in the first precept of the first table, so also this which is set forth does not pertain wholly to the injunction; but there what was in addition to the precept is passed over; here it is added: "Hear, O Israel, your God is one," (Deut. 6, 4). All this is placed before the precept; the precept itself is added afterwards when it is said: "Thou shalt adore him, and shalt serve him alone," (Cf. Deut. 6, 13). Here the precept came first: "Honour thy father and thy mother," (Cf. Exod. 20, 12), then is added: "That it may be well with thee, and thou mayst be longlived upon the land," (Cf. Exod. 20, 12).

Why is it then that there before the precept the cause of the precept is passed over, here after the precept it is added, unless because God is to be loved on account of himself and man on account of God? For love of parents, if it has regard for flesh alone, does not acquire spiritual reward. From God, therefore, there is in us first that on account of which He is afterwards to be loved by us, since our love is preceded by His grace, and our love excited through His grace follows. Now if in the fathers of our flesh our love extends to that benefit alone by which in the flesh our merit is anticipated by these, because it does not go beyond the affection of the flesh and above regard for flesh, it does not reach the perfection of spiritual reward. Thus the author of temporal life is to be loved on account of eternity, so that indeed He may be loved not because we receive this life from Him, rather through Him, but because through this life we are about to enter upon that life. Therefore, when it was said: "Honour thy father and thy mother," well was the reason added, "that it may be well with thee, and thou mayst be longlived upon the land," (Cf. Exod. 20, 12), that is of the living, since we ought to love in the author of this life the fact that by Him through this life we have been initiated to the future life. And to one who honours his beginning well, a long life is promised, since those who cling to God through love merit eternity. Indeed, in so far as pertains to the sense of the letter, we ought to honour our parents in two ways, both by obeying them indeed in all things except those in which the love of God the Father is offended and by assisting them in so far as our power permits.

XI. *The second precept.*

The second precept of the second table is: "Thou shalt not kill," (Exod. 20, 13). Homicide is by many ways: by hand, by tongue, by consent. It takes place by hand when one actually deprives another of life or casts him into a place of death where he is deprived of life as into jail or into some other such place. It takes place by tongue in two ways, that is, by ordering or by suggesting. The Jews indeed killed Christ in that they suggested to the judge that He be killed. By consent, similarly, homicide takes place in two ways, either when we desire and wish the death of another or if, when we can liberate him from death, we neglect his life, that is, we do not go to his assistance.

XII. *The third precept.*

The third precept of the second table is: "Thou shalt not commit adultery," (Exod. 20, 14), that is, thou shalt not fornicate. Fornication is any illicit copulation. And fornication is twofold: of the soul, whereof the prophet says: "All those who fornicate you have thrown away from thyself," (Cf. Psal. 72, 7); of the body, which the present discussion is about. For this precept and certain others were established only under the old law, that is, not fully but partially granted, on account of the infirmity of the hearers, which afterwards with the advent of grace were completed. For the law says: "Thou shalt not commit adultery," prohibiting only corporeal adultery. Christ says: "Whosover shall look on a woman to lust after her, hath already committed adultery with her in his heart," (Matt. 5, 28), forbidding all illicit concupiscence of the soul as well as of the body.

XIII. *The fourth precept.*

The fourth precept is: "Thou shalt not steal," (Exod. 20, 15). Stealing is accepted in this place as any illicit usurpation of another's property, whether secret or manifest. For He who prohibited stealing did not concede rapine, since the sin is greater, as the saints bear witness, to seize openly and violently than to take secretly, because it excites greater anger and wrath. Under stealing usury also is included.

XIV. *The fifth precept.*

The fifth precept of the second table is: "Thou shalt not bear false witness," (Exod. 20, 16). Therefore, that it may be clearer what false witness is we must begin more deeply, that is, from a lie. For a simple lie is one thing in false witness, another in perjury, another in a vow when someone will vow what he does not pay. About all these we must speak but first about the simple lie. Thus a description of a lie must be set down.

XV. *On lying.*

Some think that a lie should be defined thus. A lie is a false expression with the desire of deceiving, which is either present at the moment or comes afterwards. For if anyone should promise another that he will give something, having the desire to give when he promised, yet afterwards changing his desire would not wish to give, there would be a lie not because the heart was twofold in the promise but because he by promising made the heart twofold afterwards. Thus then can that which has been said be understood. A lie is a false expression, that is, speech or statement through which he who speaks intends and expects to express a falsehood to his listener. For, even if it be true, that is, if it should be as he says, yet he lies who speaks with the expectation and intention of deceiving. Humorous lies and irony and parables are not lies. Otherwise saints would be found blameworthy, since they have said much in parables and in irony. But Christ himself spoke to the multitudes in parables which surely He would not have adopted in His speech if there had been a lie among them. There is this difference only, that humorous lies even if they do not fall in with the charge of falsehood, yet do not escape blame for levity.

There is still another kind of lie, when someone seems to lie as if for the sake of humility, namely, when he calls himself a sinner and yet does not so believe as he says. About him most truly was it said that when anyone so lies, if before he lied he was not a sinner, by lying he becomes what he was not, since he who calls himself a sinner and does not so believe, in him there is no truth.

There is another kind of lie when one lies to save the health and life of another, which itself is also by no means to be approved. For by lying evilly he saves life in the body of another, who through the lie extinguishes truth in his own heart. Yet in a matter of this kind sometimes truth can be concealed without blame when for the sake of our own safety or the utility of another reason demands. For it is one thing to conceal what is true and quite another to assert what is false. For Truth Himself says: "I have many things to say to you, but you cannot bear them now," (John 16, 12), which surely He would not have said, if it were always a fault to conceal the truth.

XVI. *On false testimony.*

False testimony is when anyone by the lie of another presents testimony regarding the truth, who is made guilty not only by lying but also because he tries to defend the lie itself against the truth. And if indeed he does this wittingly, the malice is altogether damnable, but if unwittingly, the negligence is blameworthy.

XVII. *On taking oath.*

Not every oath is evil and yet every oath with truth as witness is without evil. For when anyone swears to the truth for the necessity of his neighbour or for utility, when indeed he to whom the oath is sworn either cannot believe on account of ignorance or refuses to believe on account of malice, an oath of this kind indeed is not evil for him who swore, since he bore witness to the truth out of necessity; yet it is without evil for him to whom the oath is sworn, that is, either if he cannot believe otherwise from infirmity or if he contemns believing from perversity. Now whoever swears without cause, even if he swears the truth, is not without blame, because either he is censured for levity or he is condemned for arrogance. Whoever swears that he will do evil sins, in which case, however, it would be better to break an oath than to fulfil it, so that he should beware of the evil which he swore and nevertheless understand the guilt in that he swore evilly.

XVIII. *On perjury.*

Perjury is a lie confirmed by introducing sacrosanct testimony. For whoever swears to something false perjures himself or commits perjury, in which the first evil is the guilt of the lie when that which is false is spoken but the second is the fact that the testimony of truth is taken irreverently to protect falsehood. Whoever sees another swear to a falsehood willingly becomes a participant in the sin, if he consents and if, in so far as he can with saving truth, he does not by contradicting and admonishing prevent the evil from being accomplished. Now here we must consider that, although we cannot approve the sin of a brother, we should not publish it, lest perhaps we seem to be willing not to correct our neighbour but to defame him. On this account admonition should be given sinners when convincing testimony cannot be brought to them as they deny.

XIX. *On taking a vow.*

A vow is a voluntary promise of the spirit. Whoever shall make a vow to God should repay what he vows, according to the words of the prophet: "Vow ye and pay to the Lord," (Psal. 75, 12). Now Scripture says: "The vows of the foolish should be broken," (Cf. Eccle. 5). Wherefore by the vows of the foolish we understand all vows that either are evil, or, if they are good, are not ordained, and greater is the evil which is from them than the good which is in them. For example, if a wife against the will of her husband or a husband against the will of his wife should vow continence or a subject without the counsel and permission of the one placed over them should propose inordinate abstinence, vows of this kind, since they would be manifestly foolish, should by no means be maintained. Whoever shall vow something good, if afterwards either he could not fulfil the vow or in order to perform a greater good would be unwilling to fulfil it, according to the permission of those by whom dispensation was entrusted to him his vow can either be relaxed or changed, so that it does not rest with his will either to dismiss that which he vowed to do or to do something else in its place, even if what he did not vow is greater.

XX. *The sixth precept.*

The sixth precept which is also the ninth is: "Thou shalt not desire thy neighbour's wife," (Cf. Exod. 20, 17).

XXI. *The seventh precept.*

The seventh precept which is also the tenth is: "Thou shalt not covet thy neighbour's goods," (Cf. Exod. 20, 17). Here it seems that there must be opposition to what was said above in that precept which was presented above on avoiding fornication. "Thou shalt not commit adultery," shows that only corporeal adultery was prohibited, but afterwards through that which Christ says in the Gospel: "Whoever shall look at a woman to desire her, already has he committed adultery in his heart," it is shown that all adultery, corporeal as well as spiritual, is forbidden. For how did the Gospel complete what the written law before had to a less degree, when that which the Gospel is believed to have added is found already written in the law? For He who said: "Thou shalt not commit adultery," prohibiting corporeal adultery, afterwards said: "Thou shalt not desire," showing that even spiritual adultery should by all means be avoided. What then did the new law supply which the old did not have? The law prohibited corporeal adultery; it prohibited desire. What more did the Gospel have which one should do? But it must be known that the old law, although it repressed the desire of man from the property of another, yet did not check him at all in his own, since He who said: "Thou shalt not covet thy neighbour's wife and property," did not at all forbid a woman and property to be coveted but showed that desire should be restrained only from another's. But the new law taught that there should be moderation even in one's own affairs, so that it excluded all illicit desire. Now it can also be expressed fittingly in another sense that the old law did not signify that desire for another's wife or property, which is carried on by the will only, but the ambition and the design which by a kind of zeal and energy is exercised externally with work to fulfil desire and to obtain that which is in desire. Now the new law condemned not only illicit desire outside in the zeal of work but showed that it was also damnable within in the desire of the will.

XXII. *On the order of the precepts of God.*

Now we should not pass over without consideration the order of these precepts of God. For if there is an order of living, surely there is also an order of commanding. First then consider what is said to you, that you should adore thy God and serve him, (Cf. Deut. 6, 13). This is the first precept. In adoration know faith; in service understand good operation. After this follows the second precept, that you should not take the name of thy God in vain, (Cf. Exodus 20, 7), in order that the word of truth may be in your mouth for the sake of truth, that after the faith of the heart may follow the confession of the mouth. First, devotion unto good conscience; afterwards, example of work unto good fame; lastly, the word of proclamation unto teaching. Then follows the third precept and it is said to thee that you keep holy the Sabbath, (Cf. Exodus 20, 8), that is, that you guard the quiet of your mind so that you be not disturbed regarding truth by the adverse things that occur without but that you learn to be calm even among those who hate peace. You should proclaim truth and not overlook charity. These are the three precepts of the first table regarding those matters which pertain to God.

Afterwards there follows a second table on those matters which look to one's neighbour. The first precept of the second table is that in which you are ordered to honour your beginning that you can have a long life, (Cf. Exod. 20, 12), since he who does not honour him from whom he is, is unworthy of being able to retain that which he is. The second precept is: "Thou shalt not kill," (Exod. 20, 13). Fittingly indeed he to whom in the preceding order a long life is promised, here is prohibited from putting out the life of another, so that the one is from charity of God, because honouring his beginning he is eager for the life which knows no end, the other, however, from charity of neighbour, because from no hatred of cruelty does he release himself to end another's life. Then follows the third precept: "Thou shalt not commit adultery," and the fourth: "Thou shalt not steal," (Cf. Exodus 20, 14 and 15). "Thou shalt not commit adultery," this pertains to one's own life. "Thou shalt not steal," this pertains to the life of another. For above man was ordered to preserve both his own and another's life; here he is ordered not to harm his own and another's life. For it is just that on the way of life he beware of corruption who awaits the uncorrupted life in the homeland and who now does not oppress the life of a neighbour by open violence, also that he do no harm through hidden violence in those matters which were given him for the use of living, and not only that he should not harm through himself but that he should not presume to establish confidence or foundation either for those who harm or desire to harm. For this is forbidden in the following command when it is said: "Thou shalt not bear false witness," (Exod. 20, 16). And since he cannot check himself for long from the work of harm, who does not check his mind from the intention and will of harming, these words follow: "Thou shalt not desire thy neighbour's wife, nor shalt thou desire thy neighbour's goods." That you may not commit adultery, you should not desire thy neighbour's wife; that you may not commit theft, you should not desire they neighbour's goods.

These are the ten precepts which unfold the way of the first perfection and the path of righteousness. For the first perfection directs man in himself through good operation. The second through charity toward neighbour unfolds to the side. The third through the charity of God raises on high, since the tenth day extends the line of the first perfection. The hundredth day unfolds the width of the second. The thousandth day raises the highest perfection on high. Now let these words suffice for the present in the exposition of the precepts of the law.

XXIII. *On the movable precepts and those that have been superadded.*

There follows another group of precepts which are called movable, since according to dispensation they were added to the natural commands for the time either for exercise or for meaning; for exercise, indeed, in order that there might be a great many things in which the obedience of those to be taught might be proven and their devotion cultivated; for meaning, indeed, in order that in them the signs of the future truth might be prepared and through them those things might be demonstrated which were ordered to be done corporeally and those things which were to be done and believed spiritually. Now all these were taken from the middle, that is, from those which in their nature were neither so good that they had inevitably to be done nor so evil that they had of necessity to be avoided. For these are all that have been set forth in commands of this kind, in so far as they were such with reference to their nature, which according to the will of the agent could be done without blame and again be omitted without blame. Now this additional command deflected those things to either side, which were in themselves middle and held to both, whether by ordering or by prohibiting, so that now those things which were prohibited could not be done without blame nor again those things which were ordered could by any means be omitted without blame. This, however, the nature of the thing does not do but the force and the obedience of the command. The law prohibited flesh with blood from being eaten, not because this was evil in so far as this pertained to the nature of the thing but because that was evil which was of necessity signified in this. For when anyone is delighted at a deed of fury and cruelty it is as if flesh is eaten with blood. The same law also demanded the abstaining from the meat of swine, signifying indeed that deeds of uncleanness should be avoided. In this manner the law also excluded man from eating certain of the other animals, not only birds but fish and those which traverse on land. And many others which the first foundation did not make harmful, the second disposition commanded us to avoid as harmful.

Now there were certain others of these middle things which the written law proposed rather through concession than through command and prohibition, which possibly would have been evil in themselves if a concession had not been made. For example, the law says that if anyone should find some uncleanness in his wife and on this account should hold her in hatred, he should write for her a bill of divorce and so should dismiss her, (Cf. Deut. 24, 1), because indeed it was better that being held in hatred she should be dismissed according to his will than being retained against his will she should be killed. It is also said in the law: "That shalt offer your oath to the Lord and shall swear by the Lord," (Cf. Deut. 10, 20), not because indeed it is good to swear or to swear by the Lord but oath was conceded to the imperfect on this account, that perjury might more easily be avoided, also at the same time that they might learn to venerate the name of God, when they received it more frequently into the assertion and the testimony of their words, and might not be forced to take the names of false gods to confirm their oaths. And to these not only was it permitted but ordered to invoke the name of the Lord as testimony if the reason for confirming the truth should demand. A similar example also was this, that they were permitted for an injury inflicted to render retaliation in kind, lest perhaps burning with rather vehement fury they should try to return greater evils than those inflicted.

There are many other kinds of precepts which are contained in the written law, befitting indeed exterior conversation and at the same time suited for spiritual meaning. Therefore, in all these we note that the difference which the Apostle laid down was signified in the elements of the exordium of God's sermon. For these are three: elements, exordia, sermon. In the elements is sound but there is not sense. Wherefore, they are not called exordium because sense does not begin in them. Phrases are exordia of the senses. Wherefore they are also called phrases as if indeed they said something, and they are the first parts of an oration because the beginning of understanding arises from them. In elements, therefore, there is sound and not sense; in the exordium there is sense but it is not complete; in the sermon there is sense and it is perfect. Behold these three similar things in the Scripture of God. Scripture said: "Thou shalt not eat meat with blood," (Cf. Deut. 12, 16 and Levit. 7, 15 and 26). This is the element. Afterwards it added: "Thou shalt not kill," (Exodus 20, 13). This is the exordium. Afterwards also it completed the statement, prohibiting wrath, (Cf. Matt. 5, 22). Likewise it said that the meat of swine should not be eaten, (Cf. Matt. 14, 8). In this was the element. After this it added: "Thou shalt not commit adultery," (Cf. Exodus 20, 14). In this was the exordium. Lastly it appended: "If anyone shall look on woman to lust after her, hath already committed adultery in his heart," (Cf. Matt. 5, 28), etc. In this was the completion of the sermon. Thus the precepts added with reference to time were elements; the precepts of the decalogue, exordia; the precepts of the New Testament, sermon; the first, from the institution of discipline; the second, from the truth of nature; the third, from the perfection of grace.

The immovable precepts are by nature prior. The movable precepts, as has been said, precede in meaning because in these goodness is first formed, which afterwards is begun in them and finally through grace is completed. Of the precepts which were superadded and were movable certain ones even now in time of grace have been retained for exercise, for example, the observance of fasts. And certain others which were instituted in earlier times have, however, been reserved providentially for the instruction of the present, and those especially which look to the exercise of spiritual zeal are reserved in a time of grace, those being abolished which pertain to carnal observances.

XXIV. *That there are three kinds of sacraments in the law.*

Three kinds of sacraments are found to have been written under the law, certain ones especially for remedy, certain ones indeed for obedience, certain ones for divine worship. The first pertain to the remission of sins, the second to exercising devotion, the third to fostering piety.

The first were instituted, as it were, for necessity, that man might be sanctified in them, such as was circumcision; there were victims for sin by commission and for sin by neglect, and there were others. There were certain ones which were especially instituted for cleansing and remission.

Now the second were proposed as it were for exercise, that in them the devotion of the faithful might be exercised and merit might be increased, such as were the victims of the pacific which were offered by the faithful to reconcile divine grace to themselves.

The third were instituted for a kind of preparation, in order that certain sacraments might be instruments, as it were, for treating and sanctifying the other sacraments, such as was the atrium and the tabernacle and all the utensils which were contained in them, and also the sacred vestments of those who minister and all the other things which were instituted to adorn the divine worship. Likewise there were other sacraments which were sanctified unto cleansing, others which were treated unto devotion, the third which were exercised unto veneration. The first were of necessity, the second of virtue, the third of laudation. The first were taken up unto sanctification, the second were treated unto devotion, the third were exercised unto laudation.

Again some sacraments were in certain sanctified things, others in sacrifices and oblations, others in divine ministries. Thus the same thing can be distinguished in many ways for evidence. It was called sacrifice when the immolation was made with respect to animals. It was called oblation, indeed, of certain other things. There are three kinds of sacrifices; for some are holocausts, others simple sacrifices, others pacific. That was called holocaust which, offered either from a debt or from the will, was burned entirely. That was called sacrifice which offered for the debt of an institution, was partly cremated, partly preserved. Those were called pacific which were offered of the will, whether for the action of grace or for the fulfilment of a preceding vow or for voluntary and spontaneous devotion. A holocaust was made sometimes from herds, sometimes from flocks, sometimes from fowl. An oblation was made sometimes from wheat flour, which was called a crude sacrifice; sometimes with a stove, sometimes with a frying pan, sometimes with a gridiron, which was called a cooked sacrifice. Some sacrifices were for the sin of commission, others for the sin of omission; for the sin of commission indeed that the sin of commission might be expiated; for the sin of omission, that the sin of omission might be expiated. There is sin of commission when that is done which ought not to be done; there is sin of omission when that is not done which ought to be done. And indeed of all these did the sacraments consist.

Now we must understand that we ought not to believe that all these are sacraments in the sense defined above, that sacraments properly so called should be sacraments, but among these certain sacraments of this kind also have been called sacraments only because they were signs of sacred things. Thus then one thing is a sacrament only by signifying sanctification and by sanctifying through sanctification; another, not by sanctifying but by signifying only. And indeed regarding the sacraments of the written law let what we have said thus far suffice; it was not a part of the present proposal to treat about the promises which we laid down in the third part of the first division. There are, therefore, three things which the written law contained: precepts, sacraments, promises.

Here endeth the first book.

Prologue of the
Second Book on the Sacraments

The depths of spiritual meaning in the Sacred Scriptures are great but, since the same grace of understanding has not been given to all, Sacred Writ has certain things within itself by which it feeds the faith of the simple minded, and these indeed joined with the higher things form one rule of truth. Therefore, in the treatment of Sacred Writ the same form of expression must not be kept everywhere, since the higher sacraments of faith must be treated reverently with a higher diction and a diction worthy of sacred things, but the lower instruments of the divine sacraments must be explained according to the capacity of the simple minded in a minor kind of expression, that what is written may be clear "in gilded clothing surrounded with variety," (Psal. 44, 9). For, just as the Holy Church of the elect is adorned beautifully with a variety of good morals and virtues, so Sacred Scripture, whence Holy Church herself takes the form of living, is interwoven in its diction with beautiful variety. In this, however, variety is itself apt, that it may not generate schism and diversity, concordant that it may not produce adversity. For in Sacred Scripture neither do the great things despise the moderate nor again are the moderate deemed unworthy to be associated with the great, but they adorn each other in one truth, all of which please on account of truth. Therefore, let no one wonder if after the great, and in the midst of the great sacraments of faith, mention is made of those things which in their own order seem inferior, since things that are one in truth are not at all abhorrent to each other. For God himself deigned to be humbled, descending to human things, that afterwards He might raise man up to the divine.

HERE BEGINNETH THE SECOND BOOK

*On the Incarnation of the Word and the Fulfilment of God's
Grace, from the Sacraments of the New Testament to the
End and Consummation of All.*

PART ONE

I. *On the Incarnation of the Word.*

In the earlier part of this work I presented summarily the foundation of all things from the first beginning, together with the fall of man, and those things which were afterwards prepared for restoration, even to the coming of the Word. Now I would like to arrange in order those things which follow, even to the end and the consummation of all. The time of grace took its origin from the coming of the Son of God into the flesh, just as it is written: "Grace and truth were made through Jesus Christ," (Cf. John 1, 14). Grace of God then is the redemption of mankind, and, while this redemption is being accomplished through the coming of Christ, the truth of God's promise is being fulfilled in the exhibition of His grace.

II. *Why the Son was sent rather than the Father or the Holy Spirit.*

Now the Son, not the Father nor the Holy Spirit, was sent, because it was not fitting that the Father who was not from another should be sent by another. For if He were sent by another, He would have to come from another by whom He was sent, and He would have, as it were, a kind of beginning from Him by whom He was sent. Therefore, the Father does not have to be sent by another, because He does not have to be from another.

Now the Son, who is from the Father alone, was sent first, then also the Holy Ghost, who is from Father and Son. First the Son came that men might be freed; then the Holy Spirit came that men might be blessed. First the one freed from evil, then the other recalled to goods. The one took away what we were enduring, the other returned what we had lost. The natural Son came sent by the Father that He might call those to be adopted into inheritance, and that He might confirm His consent in the grace of adoption. For not without the consent of the Son were strangers to be led by the Father into inheritance. Thus the Father sent in behalf of sons; the Son came in behalf of brothers, since in the Father and in the Son is established the name of paternity and filiation, so that those to be adopted may receive the name of son both through Him of whom He was and from Him from whom He was. Wisdom came that the enemy might be overcome by reason and that it itself might vindicate its habitation which malice possessed. For whoever had overcome with astuteness, it was just that he be overcome not by fortitude but by prudence, that in the same way in which he had raised himself up as victor he might be overcome and laid low.

The Son of God was made Son of Man that He might make sons of men sons of God, and that the name of son might not pass over to another person, and there be two sons in the Trinity and the distinction of the Trinity be confused. For if the Father had assumed flesh, He himself likewise might be both Father and Son: Father of the Son whom He generated out of eternity and Son of the mother from whom He had been generated out of time. Now if the Holy Spirit had assumed flesh, there would be two sons in the Trinity: the one, Son of the Father without mother; the other, son of the mother without father. Therefore, in order that an incommunicable name might not be divided, the Son alone took on flesh that He, the one and the same, might be both Son of God and Son of man: son of God, born from the Father according to divinity; son of man, born from a mother according to humanity.

III. *How the Son alone could take on flesh.*

But perhaps there will be some who say: "If the works of the Trinity are inseparable, then whatever the Son does, the Father does. Now if all that the Son does, the Father does also, then, if the Son assumed flesh, the Father also assumed flesh, since the Son without the Father could not have assumed flesh, if He could do nothing without the Father. But here we must consider first that, when the Son is said to do all that the Father does, we must think especially of that operation in which God, the Founder and the Maker, founds and rules and disposes His creature. In this operation the Father and the Son and the Holy Spirit cannot at all be separated, since in the one divinity in which and through which they operate they are one.

Now then we distinguish these things concerning divine operation lest anyone contrary to what has been said, namely, "What things soever he doth, these the Son also doth," (John 5, 19), should think that this is to be said in opposition, that the Father begets, which the Son does not do, and the Son is begotten, which the Father does not do. For if the Son like the Father should beget, He would be Father, and if the Father like the Son should be begotten, He would be Son. And so lest anyone, because the Son does not beget, which the Father does, should think that the Son does not do whatever the Father does, we say that this must be understood about the operation in which either He operates the creature, that what was not may begin to be, or He operates in the creature, that what was made in that which was made may subsist. For therein the whole Trinity operates inseparably, where in operation neither the Father is separated from the Son, nor the Son from the Father, nor the Holy Spirit from both. In work, therefore, operation is properly defined. For in that which is not made, which is God, He himself does not make but only is. But in that which is made, all that is made is surely made by him by whom it is made. Here, therefore, all that the Father makes, the Son also makes similarly. So in this operation in which the assumption of flesh is found, just as this befits the Son alone and not the Father, not unfittingly is the question asked. For when it is said that the Son assumed flesh, surely the work is signified which the Son did, and if the Father is excluded from this work, the Father does not operate all things that the Son does.

Or perhaps, since it is not said: "All things that the Son does, the Father does," but: "Whatever the Father does, these the Son also does," must it be thought that the Son indeed does all things that the Father does, but that the Son does certain things which the Father does not do? Far be it from the truth! But all things that the Father does, the Son does, and all things that the Son does, the Father does, since, in as much as they are one in Godhead, they cannot be separated in operation. Therefore, all that the Son does, the Father does, since in the divinity by which the Son is of the Father, because He is one with the Father, He does nothing without the operation of the Father. He did certain things in humanity according to which the Son was not of the Father, since by being born He had not received humanity from the Father. These things then are referred only to the person of the Son, since these are the things which He did in that nature and according to that nature which He did not have in common with the Father but which He alone received individually as His own from time.

Yet all things which He did in divinity He did not do alone, because He was not alone in divinity, but He did the same with Him who was the same with Him. If, therefore, the Son in divinity assumed humanity, how did the Father in the same divinity not do the same thing with Him, who was the same with Him? Or perhaps, when it is said: "The Son assumed flesh by force of a hidden relation," by which it is understood that He united with Himself, the same is not said of the Father, because if the same were said, would it not be understood as the same but different? For if it should be said: "The Father assumed flesh," it would be understood similarly, that the Father joined flesh to Himself, which indeed would not be the same but different. Therefore, it would be different, if flesh were said to have been united with the Father rather than being said to have been united with the Son, since just as the Father is one in person, the Son another, so it is meant differently when the Son is said to have become incarnate than it would be meant, if the Father should be said to have become incarnate. So it does not follow that, if the Son assumed flesh, on this account the Father also assumed flesh, just as it does not follow that, if the Son united flesh with Himself, the Father also united flesh with Himself. But it does follow that if the Son united flesh with Himself, the Father also united the same flesh with the Son himself, since, while one operation is shown on the part of both, neither the Son is proven to have operated without the Father nor the Father without the Son. But if the Father had put flesh upon Himself and the Son upon Himself, this would not be the same but different, because in that very act the operation would be proven not to be the same, since the relation in both cases would be proven not to have been made with reference to the same one.

But now the Father also operated assumption or union of flesh, since He endowed the Son with flesh and the Son operated, since He endowed Himself with flesh, and there was one union and one operation: one union, because what was united was united to one; one operation, because what was done was done in one. Three persons were operating and not three things, but they operated one thing, and what was done was both of one, in so far as it was done with reference to Him alone, and of three, in so far as it was done by them.

It is read in the Book of Judges (14) that Manue received a wife for Samson his son, and yet he who received a wife for his son did not receive a wife for himself. And afterwards the son asked the father to receive a wife for himself, as if by himself alone he could not do this, and there is no one who would argue that he should say: "If the father received a wife for his son, then the father received the wife," and would contend that the father was married, since he received a wife for the son. So why should the Father be said to have become incarnate, because He united flesh with His Son, just as the Son himself is said to have become incarnate because He joined flesh with Himself? So the flesh of the Word was promised, and the Word assumed it for Himself; the Father of the Word similarly united it with His own Word, and the two operated one, and there was in the one one operation of the two. On this account it says: "Whatever the Father does, these the Son also does likewise;" these things, it says, the Son also does likewise. What is "these things?" Not other things. What is "likewise?" Not otherwise. The unity of operation could not have been demonstrated more perfectly. Not other things, not otherwise; the same things, in the same manner. If He should operate the same things and should not operate in the same manner, there would not be one operation because there would be another. If He should operate in the same manner and should not operate the same things, there would not be one operation because there would be another. But now He operates both the same things and in the same manner, so that there is nothing either different or otherwise in His operation.

Show me something that the Father does, if indeed we must inquire what He does who does all. But set down for example some one thing of all that the Father does; I mean that very thing that the Son does. Not even so do I mean "that very thing" as similar to that, but the very same thing. For when I say: "I do the same thing that you do," because I happen to build a house just as you build a house and, although your house which you build is different and my house which I build is different, yet I say that I do the same thing that you do, since what I do according to something is similar to what you do. In this manner I do not understand when I say that the Son does the very thing that the Father does. Now if I should build a house and you should build the same house with me, I say that you would be doing the same thing that I do, even more truly one thing, since it is the thing itself and not another, and yet not truly still one thing, since you do one part and I the other; you with your instruments, I with my instruments; you with your hands and arms, I with mine; finally, you with your strength, I with mine, and yet not truly one but in another and through other things.

So what do I mean when I say that the Son does this very thing that the Father does? Therefore, the hand of the Son is one, and the hand of the Father another, the arm of the Son one and the arm of the Father another, the power of the Son one and the power of the Father another, although the Son himself and the hand and the arm and the power are of the Father. Just as that is the same that man does with the hand and that the hand of man does, and that man does with the arm and that the arm of man does, and that man does with fortitude and that the fortitude of man does, so is that the same that the Father does and that the Son does, since everything that the Father does He does through the Son. If there is one essence, one nature, one fortitude, one will, how is there not one operation? You say that the Father does this, and I say that the Son does this same thing. This very thing the Father does; this very thing the Son. The whole thing the Father does and the whole thing the Son. The doing itself is of the Father and of the Son. Do not weigh, as it were, two actions, one greater and one smaller or perhaps two equal actions of similar weight. Unity is there; you could multiply nothing. There is one action on the part of two, rather one action on the part of three, just as one Godhead, and in one action the three are not three agents but one agent, just as in one Godhead the three are not three gods but one God. Father and Son and Holy Ghost are three persons but are not three gods nor three creators nor three makers, since in that they are one they cannot be divided. Whatever, therefore, the Father does, this the Son also does likewise. What could be more alike than unity? How can that be divided which cannot be multiplied? Or how can that recede from itself, which is one? So do not wonder if the assumption of flesh which is referred to the Son alone, the Son alone did not operate, but with the Son, the Father also and the Holy Spirit. Do not speak of the three incarnate because the three operated the incarnation of the one, since both the unity of nature made the operation inseparable and the peculiarity of person made the assumption applicable to one.

IV. *On the distinction of the three persons in the one Godhead.*

Since indeed the weakness of human intelligence does not suffice to comprehend these things that it is ordered to believe, it must be supported meanwhile by the authority of Sacred Writ which is not to be discussed by human reason. Therefore, I would like to bring out into the open those things which have already been expressed by the holy fathers on the distinction of the three persons in one Godhead, according to the strength of Catholic truth, adding nothing from our own, especially since we are found unequal to those things which have been spoken by them.

Augustine, against the impiety of Arius: The fathers created a new name, Homousion, but by such a name they did not signify a new thing. For this is called Homousion which reads: "I and the Father are one," (John 10, 30), namely, of one and the same substance. The same:* All Catholics who have written on the Trinity before me aimed to teach this according to the Scriptures, that Father and Son and Holy Ghost, of one and the same substance, by inseparable

---

*De Trin. 1, 4. 7.

equality made known divine unity. And so there are not three gods but one God, although the Father begot the Son, and on this account He would not be the Son who is the Father. The Son might be begotten by the Father, and so He who would not be the Father who is the Son. The Holy Spirit also would be neither Father nor Son but only the Spirit of the Father and of the Son, coeternal with both the Father and the Son, Himself coequal and pertaining to the unity of the Trinity and yet not to that Trinity born of the Virgin Mary but to the Son only. And he says that the same Trinity did not descend in the likeness of a dove but only the Holy Ghost, and the same did not say from heaven: "This is my beloved Son," (Matt. 3, 17), but that it was only the voice of the Father to the Son although, just as the Father and the Son and the Holy Ghost are inseparable, so they operate inseparably. For by what understanding does man grasp God, who does not yet grasp his own understanding by which he wishes to grasp Him? But let us understand God, if we can and to the extent that we can, as good without quality, great without quantity, creator without want, present without site, containing everything without appearance, entire everywhere without place, eternal without time, making changeable things without change in Himself, and suffering nothing. Whoever so thinks of God and can not yet in any way find what He is, is piously on his guard, in so far as can be, lest he perceive something about Him which does not exist. Yet there is without doubt substance or, if this is better so called, essence, which the Greeks call ousia (οὐσία).*

The same in his book against Maximinus:† Let there be no division of the parts in the unity of the Godhead; God the Father and the Son and the Holy Ghost are one, that is, the Trinity itself is one God. For the Father and the Son and the Holy Ghost are three persons, and these three, since they are of one substance, are one and entirely one where there is no diversity of natures, no diversity of wills. Now if they were one in nature and not in agreement, they would not be entirely one. If indeed they were unlike in nature, they would not be one. Therefore, because these three are one on account of the ineffable conjunction of the Godhead with which they are ineffably joined, they are one God. But Christ is one person of twofold substance, and yet God cannot be called a part of this person; otherwise God the Son before He took on the form of a servant was not whole, and He created when man was added to His divinity. But if it is said absurdly that God in one person can not be a part of that thing, how much the more can He not be a part of the Trinity who is one in three? In the Trinity then, which is God, the Father is God, and the Son is God, and the Holy Ghost is God, and these three together are one God. Nor is the third part of this Trinity one, nor are two a greater part than one therein, nor are all something greater than one individually, because the magnitude is spiritual, not cor-

---

*De Trin. 5, 1. 2. 3.
†Contra Maxim. 2, 10. 2.

poreal. "He that can take, let him take it," (Matt. 19, 12); he that cannot, let him believe and let him pray that he understands what he believes. The Father and the Son and the Holy Ghost on account of individual Godhead are one God, and because of the peculiarity of each are three persons, and on account of the perfection of each are not parts of one God. Power is Father, power is Son, power is the Holy Ghost.

The same* in the book, On the Trinity: If the Son alone understands for Himself and for the Father and for the Holy Ghost, it follows that the Father is not wise of Himself but of the Son, nor could wisdom have begotten wisdom but the Father would be said to be wise by that wisdom which He begot. For where there is not understanding, neither can there be wisdom. And thus, if the Father himself does not understand for Himself but the Son understands for the Father, surely the Son makes the Father wise. If for God this is to exist, namely to be wise, and this is that essence, namely, wisdom, the Son has not essence from the Father which is true but rather the Father from the Son, which is false. Therefore, God the Father is wise by that wisdom of His own which He is Himself, and the Son by the wisdom of the Father, from the wisdom that is the Father from whom the Son was born. Thus the Father is intelligent by that intelligence of His which He is Himself, but the Son by the intelligence of the Father, born from the intelligence which is the Father.

The same:† Not because God is the Trinity is He on this account to be thought threefold, otherwise He would be less in each than in the three together. In this Trinity also, when we speak of the person of the Father, we mean nothing else than the substance of the Father, since the person of the Father is nothing else than the Father Himself. For person is mentioned with reference to Himself, not to the Son, nor to the Holy Ghost as God, and the like. For this name alone is that which, when it is mentioned of individual things with reference to themselves, is finally accepted in the plural not in the singular. For we say that the Father is a person and the Son a person and the Holy Ghost a person. Yet the Father and the Son and the Holy Ghost are not one person but three. But when we speak of three persons as one essence, we declare it neither as a genus regarding species nor as a species regarding individuals. It seems that it can be said that three men are one nature but two men are more than one, but the Father and the Son are not greater in essence than the Father alone or the Son alone. And these three persons, if they are so to be called, are equal individually, which the sensual man perceiveth not, (Cf. 1 Cor. 2, 14). Why then did the Latin set this down so strangely, unless because it wished this one name to serve for this meaning, by which the Trinity‡ is understood; we should not entirely overlook either

*Cf. De Trin. 7. 5.
†De Trin. 6. 7, 9.
‡Cf. De Trin. 7. 4, 9.

the fact that there are three when we confess that there are three by which name it did not wish that the diversity be understood, yet was unwilling that the individuality be understood. So too those three things seem to be determined by each other, and in themselves they are infinite; so they are individual things in individuals and all things are in all individuals and individual things in all and all things are one.

The same: Finally, if God has any participation with others in some name, surely a different meaning must without doubt be understood. But we must show this with clearer reason. If it is not susceptible of any accident, how is divine nature called just or wise or anything of this kind? But it is certain that it is the highest nature, because it is whatever it is through itself, yet nothing is just except through justice. Therefore, if this highest nature is not just except through justice, and it cannot be just except through itself, what is more fitting than that the same be the justice itself through which it is just? Wherefore, if it be asked what is highest nature itself, what can be answered more rightly than justice? And when a creature is called just in this, that it is of what nature it is, because it possesses justice, it itself is not properly spoken of as having justice but as being justice. So not in that it is of what nature it is, but in that it is called what it is and there is no difference in it, whether it be called just or justice, because indeed it is seen to be a valid example of justice, the intellect through reason is constrained to believe this concerning all things which are similarly said to be of the highest nature. Whatever of these things then be said of it, there is shown not of what nature it is or how great it is but rather what it is. For whatever it is, of what nature or how great, there is also in it something else which it is, whereby it is not simple but composed. For when some person is called body and rational and human, he is called these three not in one way or in one consideration; for he is body according to one and rational according to another, and each of these is not entirely what man is. That highest essence, highest life, highest justice, highest wisdom, highest magnitude, highest eternity, and other things similarly, whatever are manifold in words, do not signify many but one.

The same: Neither the person of the Father nor the person of the Holy Ghost, but the person of the Son alone took on flesh, and that you may understand this I shall use comparisons, so that from the creature you may understand the Creator. Reason is in the soul, and, although they are one, the soul does one thing, the reason another. By the soul we live, by reason we are wise; so also is it with the Father and the Son and the Holy Spirit, although they are one substance; the whole Trinity operated man whom He assumed, and the whole Trinity did not assume him, but only the person of the Son. Likewise in the fifth book on the Trinity: Something cannot be accidental to God. He is mentioned* with reference to something, just as Father with reference to Son and Son with reference to

---

*De Trin. 5. 5, 6.

Father, which is not accidental, since He is always Father and He is always Son. But if Father were said with reference to Himself, it would be said according to substance. Likewise, although it is different to be Father and to be Son, yet there is no different substance, since these are not said according to substance but according to relation; this relation, however, is not accidental, since it is not changeable. Likewise, not according to this which is said wtih reference to the Father is the Son equal to the Father. It remains, therefore, that He be equal according to this which is said with reference to Himself. Now whatever is said with reference to Himself is said according to substance. It remains, therefore, that He be equal according to substance. Therefore, the substance of both is the same. But when the Father is said to have been engendered, He is said to be not what He is but what He is not. Now when the relation is denied, it is not denied according to substance, since the relation is not mentioned according to substance.

Likewise the same:* What are the three? Indeed human speech labours with great deficiency. It is called three persons not that that may be said but that it may not be passed over in silence. Likewise the same: The Trinity can in no way be called the Son. Likewise the same: It must be confessed that the Father and the Son are the beginning of the Holy Spirit. Likewise the same: The Son by being born possesses not only that He may be Son, which is said relatively, but entirely that He may be substance itself. Likewise the same:† When human deficiency in speaking tried to set forth what it understands about the Lord God, it feared to say three essences lest any diversity be understood in that highest equality. Likewise the same: On this account we say three persons, not that any diversity of essence may be understood, but that indeed by one word an answer can be given when it is said: "What three persons?" or "What three things?"

Jerome:‡ We confess one God in three persons; we distinguish three persons expressed under propriety, not only words but also proprieties of words, that is, persons or, as the Greeks express it, by hypostases (ὑποστάσεις); that is, we confess subsistencies; nor does the Father at any time exclude the person of the Son or the Holy Spirit; nor again does the Son or the Holy Spirit receive the name and the person of the Father but the Father is always Father, the Son is always Son, the Holy Spirit is always Holy Spirit. So they are one in substance; they are distinguished by persons and names.

Ambrose on the Trinity:§ The assertion of our faith is this, that we say there is one God, not two or three. He says there are three Gods, who separates the divinity of the Trinity. Now we confess that the Father and the Son and the

---

*De Trin. 7. 9, 10.
†De Trin. 7. 4, 9.
‡Pseudo-Jerome, P.L. 39, col. 2182.
§Cf. De Fide 1. 1, 6-10.

Holy Spirit are one God, so that in the perfect Trinity there is both fullness of divinity and unity of power. For God is one. God is a name of magnificence, not of power. If, therefore, one God; one name, one power, one Trinity. Finally He says: "Go, baptizing in the name of the Father, and of the Son, and of the Holy Ghost," (Cf. Matt. 28, 19). And so "in the name," not "in the names." There is one name where there is one substance, one divinity, one majesty. This is the name whereby all must be saved, (Cf. Acts 4, 12).

The same: "I and the Father are one." He said "one" lest a distinction of power be made; He added "we are" that we may recognize the persons. For not the Father himself is He who is Son but the Son born of the Father. From God is God; from full is full. These, therefore, are not bare names but indications of power. Fullness of divinity in the Father, fullness in the Son, but that which is one is not different or confused nor is that multiple which is without difference.* It is impossible to know how the Son was born from the Father; the mind fails; the tongue is silent not only on the part of men but also of angels. He is above angels, above cherubim, above seraphim, above all sense; we are ordered to believe, we are not permitted to discuss. Away with arguments where faith is sought. We believe in one God, the Father and the Son and the Holy Spirit; the Father, because He has the Son; the Son, because He has the Father; and the Spirit, because He is from the Father and the Son. The Father, therefore, is the beginning of divinity who, just as He was never not God, so He was never not Father. From the Father the Son was born; from Him indeed and from the Son proceeded the Holy Spirit. The Father is eternal, because He has an eternal Son whose Father is eternal. The Son is eternal, because He is coeternal with the Father and the Holy Spirit. The Holy Spirit is eternal, because He is coeternal with the Father and the Son. Not confused, as Sabellius says, the Trinity is in one person; and not separated or divided in the nature of divinity, as Arius blasphemes, but the Father is different in person, the Son is different, the Holy Spirit is different; God the Father and the Son and the Holy Spirit are one in nature.

Likewise the same: The Father did not assume flesh nor did the Holy Spirit but only the Son, so that He who was in Divinity the Son of God the Father, Himself became in man the Son of man, lest the name of Son pass to another who was not Son by nativity. Therefore, the Son of God by nativity was made the Son of man; born the Son of God according to the truth of nature from God, and the Son of man according to the truth of nature from man, so that the truth of Him begotten not by adoption and not by name but in each nativity had the name of Son by being born, and was true God and true man, one Son.

Likewise the same:† Thus we do not speak of two Christs nor two Sons

---

*Cf. De Fide 1. 2, 17.
†Cf. Ambrose, De Spiritu Sancto 3. 7, 71-74.

but God and man, one Son whom we therefore call only begotten, remaining in two substances, just as the truth of nature conferred upon Him, not with confused or intermingled natures. For thus the Son assumed man so that He who assumed and what He assumed might be one in the Trinity. For when man was assumed no quaternion was made, but the Trinity remained, that assumption ineffably making the truth of one person in God and in man, since we call Christ not only God and not only man but true God born from God the Father and true man born from a human mother. Nor do we say that His humanity by which He is less than God took anything away from His divinity, in which He is equal to the Father. Therefore, each of these is one Christ, who also said according to God: "I and the Father are one," and according to man: "The Father is greater than I," (John 14, 28). From the time when He began to be man, He began to be nothing else than the Son of God, and He was the only begotten and on account of God He was the Word, because when He was taken up He was made flesh, so that just as man indeed is one person, namely, rational soul and flesh, so Christ is one person, Word and man.

Likewise the same: Christ Jesus is the Son of God and is God and is man; God, because He is the Word of God; man, because in the unity of person there is added to the Word of God rational soul and flesh. And He who is the only Son of God is also the Son of man, Himself the same, both from both, one Christ, one Son of God, at the same time Son of man; not two sons, God and man, but one Son. Likewise the same: God assumed man; man passed over into God, not by the mutability of nature but by the dignity of God, so that neither was God changed into human substance by assuming man nor was man glorified into divine substance unto God, since change or mutability of nature makes either diminution or abolition. The Trinity is believed by us to have been joined without confusion, distinguished without separation.

Likewise the same: Nothing created or servile must be believed in the Trinity, nothing unequal, nothing equal to grace, nothing anterior or posterior, or less, nothing extraneous or attendant on another, nothing invisible to itself, nothing visible to creatures, nothing diverse in character or in will, nothing withdrawn from the essence of the Trinity to the nature of creatures, nothing peculiar to office nor communicable to another, nothing confused but all perfect, since it is all from one, and one, yet not solitary.

Likewise the same: Of like substance, therefore the same in the Divinity of the Father is the Son; of like substance with the Father and the Son is the Holy Spirit; of like substance with God and man is one Son, remaining God in his man, in the glory of the Father, desirable of being seen by angels, just as the Father and the Holy Spirit are adored by angels and by every creature, not man on account of God or Christ with God, but man unto God and God in man.

V. *That the Word assumed flesh with punishment, without fault; with mortality, without iniquity.*

Many ask about that flesh which the Word assumed, how it was clean of sin and how without sin it bore the punishment of sin. And about this indeed, how it was either clean or cleansed of sin, we ought not to pass over the opinion of certain men, lest perhaps, if that opinion were not set forth, it would not be seen, and, if what it is were not seen, what it is not might be believed. Some think that that flesh which was thus assumed by the Word, from the beginning and in the first parent, when the entire mass of human nature was corrupted through sin, was preserved unsullied by contagion and corruption of sin, and, from the first parent himself even to the taking on of flesh by the Word, was free from all sin and was brought forth clean; so it was never under sin and on this account was not freed but was free. For they say that that part of human nature must not have been under sin, through which human nature itself after it had been exposed to sin was to be freed from sin. To prove this same opinion they adduce what the Apostle said when he asserted that the new priesthood was to be preferred to the old. Melchisedech who bore the type of Christ himself and of the new priesthood showed that he had received tithes from Abraham, (Cf. Hab. 7), and in this payment of tithes Levi also from whom without doubt the ministers of the old priesthood descended approved the payment of tithes; on account of this the old priesthood which gave tithes in Levi was inferior but the new which received tithes in Melchisedech, who is the form of Christ, is superior and is to be considered more worthy. Yet when we say that Christ, who then according to the flesh just as Levi was in the loins of Abraham, did not pay tithes, let us not by similar reasoning be convinced that the new priesthood also which is in Christ gave tithes there. Now as to how Levi who was then according to the flesh in the loins of the Father gave tithes and Christ who according to the flesh was there did not pay tithes, they think that no other reason can be found except that the flesh of Levi was there with sin, the flesh of Christ was not; therefore what was submissive to sin needed expiation, but what was clean and free from sin did not. By such reasoning then they think that they prove that that flesh which was assumed by the Word was never submissive to sin but from the beginning, whether in that from which He descended or in those through whom He descended, was kept clean of sin so that on one occasion He could be the victim for sin.

But the definition of Catholic truth asserts that the Son of God, who was born for and in behalf of sinners from flesh submissive to sin, assumed flesh free from sin and free, because it had been freed; free, not because it was never under it but because it ceased at some time to be under it. When it was assumed, it was cleansed. Therefore, through the same grace human nature was cleansed so that free from sin it was united to the Word of God; through the Word the Christian is freed from sin, that he may be associated with the same nature in Christ his Head and that, as blessed Augustine says, grace may so appear to us in our Head, whence according to the measure of each one it diffuses itself through all his members. This grace takes place from the beginning of his faith; whatever man is a Christian, by what grace that man was made Christ from His beginning, from the Spirit himself this one was also reborn from Him from whom that one was born. The remission of sins takes place in us by the same Spirit by which it was effected that He had no sin. Thus then it was effected through grace that that flesh was cleansed of sin, under which it was from its origin, and that, cleansed in Him who was to be free from all sin in it, it was assumed free from sin; so grace did not cause prejudice to the corruption of nature nor did the corruption of nature impede grace.

How is it then, they say, that Christ did not pay tithes in the loins of Abraham, if His flesh there was subject to sin? But it must be known that, although the flesh of Christ just as the flesh of Levi was still under sin in the loins of Abraham, yet the sin itself was not His under which His flesh was. For this alone was His there which therefrom was to be His. Wherefore Levi there had both the nature and the sin because thence through the propagation of origin he was to take both nature and sin. Since, therefore, Christ had nature alone in the loins of Abraham, since He was to receive it alone therefrom, without doubt He did not need the sacrifice which was not necessary for that which alone was His there. For the oblation is offered not for nature but for sin, since if there were no sin, nature would have no need of a sacrifice. Thus then Levi paid tithes in the loins of Abraham, since he had both nature and sin there, who was to receive both nature and sin therefrom. But Christ did not pay tithes who, because He was to receive nature alone therefrom, did not have that sin there even then, since the nature itself which was to be His without sin was not subject to sin in its origin.

VI. *That the Word assumed rational soul with flesh, and of what nature that soul was in wisdom and virtue and justice and goodness and merit.*

There were certain heretics who thought that a rational soul had not been assumed by the Word with the flesh in Christ, but that the flesh alone had been united to the Word, that the divinity itself of the Word had vivified the flesh in place of the soul, and that the same divinity had receded from the flesh, when it died on the cross, and again, when it was resuscitated, had returned to vivify and resuscitate. But the Catholic faith holds that God assumed all that was man's except fault, since He could not otherwise have been true man, unless He had assumed all that pertained to the truth of human nature. Therefore, with flesh and in flesh He took on a rational soul which quickened the flesh and made it sensible to life and according to free will ejected sin and pursued justice; to these also the alliance with divinity contributed that it should do good with spontaneous freedom, but could indeed have declined to do evil from no necessity or weakness. Thus blessed Augustine says: "From the Holy Spirit and the Virgin Mary was born the only Son of God, not from desire of the flesh but from the gift of God alone." In Him was free will and it was greater as He was the more unable to serve sin.

Now many questions are asked about the rational soul, of which one is whether it had knowledge equal with divinity; regarding these questions I have given a fuller discussion in another work that is entitled "On the Soul of Christ." But here it is enough to recall this alone, that just as the same soul had united with it the full and perfect wisdom of God, so fully and perfectly from wisdom itself and through wisdom was it wise; yet its nature was not equal to wisdom, since it is one thing to be wise with wisdom and far different to be wisdom. As a result of this then divinity was joined with humanity; from divinity itself humanity received through grace all that divinity had through nature, so that according to that ineffable union all that was of humanity was God's in His humanity and all that was of divinity was man's in his divinity. Thus then we believe that the humanity of the Word in the rational soul from its first conception received from the ineffable union of divinity full and perfect wisdom and power and virtue and goodness; we confess that, just as it remained inseparably in the union of divinity, so in the fullness of virtue itself which was from the union of divinity it remained unchangeable.

For God did not wish to live as man among men, that, proceeding as it were through the intervals of time with wisdom and virtue, He might prepare merit for Himself and become better than Himself, but rather that by that wisdom and goodness, which He himself always had full and perfect in His divinity and had received once and at the same time full and perfect in His humanity, He might complete the dispensation of human salvation according to His ineffable ordination. Therefore, what the Evangelist says, that Jesus advanced in age, wisdom, and grace, (Cf. Luke 2, 40), is not accepted as if He had become better in Himself, but that the wisdom and grace which He himself had and kept concealed He disclosed to men ever more and more, according as the reason of the times demanded. Thus He himself was advancing before men, when men themselves advanced in knowledge of Him. Now He advanced before God in that, until He showed Himself full of the wisdom and grace of God, He summoned them ever more and more to the praise of God the Father from whom He testified that this was.

Also regarding the merit of Christ it must not be passed over that some are accustomed to say less considerately that surely Christ the man could not have otherwise arrived at the glory of immortality, unless He had first by meriting endured death through His passion. For these do not note that the fact that God was a mortal person, was not of necessity but of the will. For if the first man had been able to arrive at immortality without death, if he had wished to protect himself from the fault of disobedience, how much the more would Christ the man, who not only was a just man without sin but was God above man, have been able to give the glory of incorruption to His flesh which He at conception had raised to association with Godhead, even if He had been unwilling to humiliate it to the endurance of passion and death? For if Christ was unable to come to the glory of resurrection except by dying, then Christ died for Himself and He held it necessary to die that He might be able to live.

Now what does He say? "I come," He says, "to sacrifice myself for you." Hear this: "I come to sacrifice myself for you." Why do you not say: "And for yourself?" For if He died for us, where is "for yourself?" Hear then. Christ says that He died for us and we say that He died for Himself. We deny the blessing, since we are unwilling to return thanks. If He died for Himself, what do we owe Him? Let Him congratulate Himself. He endured for Himself. He received for Himself. Or perhaps for both Himself and for us? Why then did He pass over Himself and mention you? Possibly He was ashamed of the necessity and gloried in the piety? Then He himself was ashamed to make it manifest; you are not ashamed to reproach. But they say: "If Christ through the endurance of His passion did not merit the glory of the resurrection, why is it that the Apostle says: 'Christ for us became obedient to the Father even unto death, even to the death of cross; for which cause God also hath exalted him, and hath given him a name which is above all names,'" (Cf. Philip. 2, 8 and 9). Behold the Apostle says manifestly that on this account through the glory of the resurrection Christ deserved to be exalted, since first through the obedience of His passion He did not refuse to be humbled even unto death. If then He was exalted because He was humbled, then because of exaltation there was humiliation. Therefore, in humiliation He merited, who in exaltation received the reward of humiliation. Now if by meriting He came to glory, how could He have come to it, if He had not merited? Thus then to argue this they come from a proposition of error to a conclusion of falsehood.

Indeed they are deceived because they do not discern the name of merit. And, therefore, because they do not dare to say that Christ deserved nothing, lest perhaps they seem to say that His deeds were of no virtue or reward before God, while they fear to fall they cast themselves headlong as they assert that Christ by suffering merited glory, so that if He had not suffered He neither could nor should have deserved it. For if we say that He merited nothing, they think that it follows that He did no works of virtue or of justice. But if we say that He merited, they infer at once that by operating He obtained something not due Him before, which is to say that Christ either did no good works or by operating deserved something which was not due to Him before. But behold how foolish this assertion is. For why is it so? Then God cannot do good work because He cannot merit what is not due Him? Or would He not merit by operating, because it is due Him, even if He should not operate? When God expends benefits on us and bestows gifts of munificence, by doing these very things does He not deserve to be loved and to be praised by us for His benefits? Or because He merits, was He not worthy first or was He less worthy, and by temporal work did the merit of God increase and was God made better than Himself? Is it not better and much better that we say that by the eternal goodness which never increased in Him, because it was always full and perfect in Him, He was always fully and perfectly good and worthy to be praised and to be loved? And when He does a temporal deed and does us a benefit, He deserves to be loved and to be praised by us, and the eternal merit of the work is in Him, which is exhibited to us temporarily. He does not merit now, because He was worthy before, nor, because He merits now, was He not worthy before. Therefore, there is merit in the work because what is done is the work of goodness, and yet merit itself does not begin with the work and in the worker, since even before the exhibition of the work goodness belonged to the worker.

Similarly God is man who in His humanity from first conception received full and perfect goodness, just as he had perfect goodness in His divinity from eternity; moreover, was Himself perfect goodness. He did not then at first begin to have the obedience of suffering and of dying when He began to suffer and to die. Behold, we concede that Christ was exalted by the Father because He was made obedient to the Father. Behold, we concede that obedience is merit, exaltation reward. Why then, if obedience is merit, did merit not begin from the time that obedience began? He was made, He says, obedient. Who was made? Christ. According to what was He made? According to humanity. According to humanity He was made obedient; according to divinity He could not have been below in what He was equal. Scripture says somewhere: "He learned obedience by the things which he suffered," (Heb. 5, 8). He learned what He did not know. What did He not know? Obedience. He did not know how to be below; He was not able, in that He was equal, to be inferior. He learned what He did not know, because that which He had not experienced unto the excellence of the Godhead through inferior nature He assumed unto experience. He was made obedient. From the time that he was made man He was made obedient. From the time that He began to be man He began to be subject. In so far as He was man in dignity, so far was He good in will. Here is merit. If will always was perfect, merit also was perfect. From the time God began to be man, man also began to be God. God began to be subject man, and man began to be perfect God. If God was humbled in so far as it was possible in man, was not man raised on high in so far as it was possible in God? If God, in that He began to be man, began to be capable of suffering and mortal, man also, in that he began to be God, began to be just and good and perfect. For just as God, when He began to be man, took on what was of man, so also man, when he began to be God, took on what was of God. Accordingly, just as God is perfect wisdom and power and goodness, so man, in that he was made God, is made perfectly powerful and wise and good in God.

Or do you think that Christ as man first received full and perfect power of divinity then, when He said: "All power is given to me in heaven and in earth"? (Matt. 28, 18). So why did He first command the demons, did He have angels as ministers, did He incline the elements to the nod of His power? Or was it perhaps because you think that by praying, as if with prayers of the law, He obtained what before He could not? "Father," He says "glorify thy Son (your name)," (Cf. John 17, 1). "And behold a voice came from heaven saying: I have both glorified it and will glorify it again," (Cf. John 12, 28). You have heard the Son asking, the Father assenting. Do you think that He obtained by prayers what He would not have obtained, if He had not poured forth prayers? Hear what follows: "This voice," He says, "came not on account of me, but for your sakes," (Cf. John 13, 30). If the response was not made on account of me, neither was the demand made on account of me. Therefore, just as I do not receive the response of the Father, that I may understand myself when heard, so do I not pour forth prayers to the Father, that I may obtain what I cannot. For I am all powerful. All that the Father can do, I can do who am the Son of the Father. For all things that the Father does, these the Son also does likewise, (Cf. John 5, 19ff.). For thus I, the Son of God the Father, took it upon myself to be man; I took upon myself all the power that God the Father has. You see, therefore, how Christ the man, in that He was the Son of God and because He was the Son of God, had divine wisdom and power and goodness, and had it fully and perfectly because He was fully and perfectly.

And was this not so from the beginning, because He did not say this from the beginning? "I told you not these things," He said, "from the beginning," (John 16, 5). Therefore, Christ was man from the beginning, ever since He began to be man, not God because from the beginning, ever since He began to be man, He did not say this? Long had Christ been man among men before He pronounced Himself and proved Himself God, and when He began to say this He said it with great modesty and reverence, lest they who wondered should be scandalized, and lest they who did not understand should not accept.

Thus He reverently suggested Himself; He did not hastily bring Himself forward. "Whom," He says, "do men say that the Son of man is?" (Matt. 16, 13). He did not proclaim but He questioned. He wished to be mentioned but He did not wish to mention, lest He should seem not to teach the truth but to seek glory. "You believe in God, believe also in me," (John 14, 1). Consider how modestly He added Himself, because He knew that it was beyond man's intelligence that a man be believed God. Thus man was still below human intelligence and He had not yet ascended in man's faith so that He might be believed God. So He said to the doubting and the loving: "Do not touch me, for I am not yet ascended to my Father," (John 20, 17). On this account then, because He knew that in the human conscience He was below and that it was foreign and strange to the same conscience that He should be believed equal, He gradually fostered that conscience so as to become accustomed to the truth, so that the truth might illumine it, the novelty not scandalize it. Thus Christ the man by dwelling among men according to dispensation showed through intervals of time what was befitting human salvation and was at the same time in Him, and more and more, according as it was fitting, He disclosed through certain advances of revelation to human knowledge that He had what He himself had full and perfect from the beginning.

But they say: "If in Christ the man from the beginning as a result of obedience there was merit for undertaking the passion, in this very thing then it is clear that if He had intended to suffer from the beginning, He could not have had the merit of obedience in suffering. For if there had not been a passion, there would have been no obedience in suffering. If there had been no obedience, there would not have been the merit of obedience." Thus then to obtain the glory of incorruption they try to bring forward the necessity of the passion. But they consider less that by the same goodness by which He offered Himself spontaneously to the obedience of the passion, because He wished to suffer, He would have been just and good and worthy of glory, even if He had not wished to suffer; for, if He had not wished to suffer, He would not have been obedient unto suffering, yet He would not have been disobedient, because by not wishing this He would not have contradicted the will of the Father, since the Father himself also would not have wished it. For just as He was obedient because being willing He agreed with the willing, so without doubt He would have been obedient, if He himself being unwilling had agreed with the Father who likewise did not wish this. And so He would always have been obedient, even if He had not suffered, and nothing would justly have been diminished in Him, even if He did not humble Himself to the passion which He undertook not out of a debt but out of dignity.

Yet, they say, there is one thing which Christ obtained through his passion, which surely He could not have obtained if He had not suffered. Indeed by suffering He became an example of suffering to all who believe, just as by rising again He became a form of glorification to all who suffer. This, therefore, He gained by suffering, that they all follow Him as master and teacher who suffer well. What great gain did He achieve? What benefit is this to Him? He preceded and all follow. Whose good is this? I found them wandering. I preceded that I might show the way. All followed. What benefit is it to me? I knew the way; through myself I was able to move forward, but there was no cause for proceeding, if there were no compassion for rendering aid. "O foolish and slow of heart to believe, ought not Christ to have suffered these things, and so to enter into his glory?" (Luke 24, 25 and 26). Listen! So, he says, Christ should have suffered and so should have entered upon His glory. Why is this so? Through passion, after passion, glorification. What? Then was Christ not able to enter upon glory, unless He passed through punishment? For why is the "ought to have," unless because He could not have otherwise? How then "His own," if "ought to have;" and how "ought to have," if "His own?" If glory was His, how ought He to have suffered that He might enter upon it? But "His own" on account of Himself, "ought to have" on account of us. Indeed Christ was able, if He had wished, to enter upon His glory in another way, and, just as He wished to have received it, in this way, if He wished, He would never have lacked it but would always have had it. But He wished on account of us to go through punishment unto glory, that dying He might destroy the fear of suffering, rising He might render hope of glorification. He wished to go by this way, because we ought to have gone by this way who were not able by another way. We wish but we cannot. He himself was able but did not wish it, because, if He had gone otherwise, He would have arrived but would not have rendered aid. He, therefore, who asserts that Christ merited something in the passion, so that he contends that by the same passion He obtained something good for His own convenience or utility or glory, which He could not have justly had, if He had not suffered, clearly leads Christ into the necessity of the passion and likewise is convicted of diminishing the grace of redemption which was exhibited in His death, or rather of rendering it void— he who tries to prove that the cause of His passion was not our necessity but rather His.

So Christ did not merit as if acquiring something not due Himself, and yet He merited by performing a work of virtue worthy of remuneration. For not because He himself was worthy before, was the work of virtue afterwards shown not remunerable, nor again, because He is said to have been remunerated for the work of virtue, is He denied to have been worthy even before He operated. Accordingly, in so far as pertained to the virtue of the work, He merited because according to the work He was worthy of remuneration, and yet He did not so merit, as if He had not been worthy, even if He had not operated. The father of a family labours in his vineyard and afterwards when he comes to refection he asks for food; he says that he well merited what he is about to receive. But the hireling merits in one way, the master in another. The hireling merits because it would not be due him, if he did not operate. Now the master, even if he does not operate, devours his bread because it is his, and he has no work if he wishes to labour for it, because it is his own even without work. There are many things which could have been said upon these matters but let this suffice for the present summary.

Lastly they ask regarding that rational soul which the Word assumed with the flesh unto unity of person, whether, just as we say that He received from the ineffable union the perfect wisdom of divinity and virtue and goodness, so also we should say that from the beginning, before He put on the glory of resurrection through the immortality of the flesh from the same union of divinity, He also had full blessedness. If we grant this, they object that that soul before resurrection sustained sufferings and pains and on this account there could not have been full blessedness where there was punishment and pain. But they do not notice that that soul in one respect was joined to flesh and in another to divinity. Now in this, that it was united to flesh, flesh itself was life. Now in this, that it was united to divinity, divinity was its life. But in this, that it was joined with flesh, when it receded, flesh itself died. But in this, that it was joined to divinity, even when receding from the flesh, it was not separated from divinity itself. Therefore, the soul, which in the feeling of the flesh endured pain temporarily, in the society of the Godhead possessed full and perfect joy always. For when it was joined perfectly, it was fully and perfectly blessed. Now when temporarily it had less from dispensation, afterwards there was fulfilment in glorification. Yet so that the true good which it had in the higher part might not be returned sometime, because it was never lost, nor completed, because it was from whom it was given, it always remained perfect.

VII. *On the flesh which the Word assumed; of what nature it was according to capability of suffering and feeling and affection.*

On the flesh of the Word we should first mention this, that we believe that from conception it was so cleansed by the operation of the Holy Ghost that the Word indeed assumed it free and immune from all sin but with the punishment of sin remaining, by the will not by the necessity of Him who assumed it; thus, while it suffered in the Saviour without sin, that which had been subject to punishment for sin in those to be saved, was freed. And so regarding this punishment of capability of suffering or mortality some ask how it was in the flesh of the Saviour. But it is easy to know how that flesh, as long as it was in the mass of human kind under original debt, of necessity endured also the punishment of prevarication by which it was held entirely in the whole itself. Now after it was divided singularly from the whole itself so that it neither was in itself nor participated with itself in the cause, it then owed no punishment because it had no guilt. And thus, in so far as was in itself, it was not obliged to endure punishment, since then it had no guilt. Thus justly was the Saviour able in the flesh, which He assumed without sin, not to have assumed the punishment of mortality also and the infirmity of capability of suffering; rather, He assumed this flesh not only beyond the fact that we are mortals, because He was not a sinner, but beyond the fact also that He was the first man before sin, because He did not have to be proven to have put on the glory of immortality from first conception.

Indeed the first man, because He had to be proven, had to be such as could have both sinned and not sinned, so that both belonged to the will not to necessity. For merit could not have been for the obedient nor sin for the disobedient, unless both obedience and prevarication had been voluntary. And so, since His will was awaited in either case for proof, in either case possibility was present to Him. Since indeed He had the possibility of sinning and of not sinning, it was fitting that He should have the possibility both of dying and of not dying. For if immortality had been of necessity, even the prevaricator and the sinner could not have died, and so disobedience would not have due punishment nor would the sinner sometime recognize himself if, dead within, he always lived without. Likewise if He had been mortal of necessity, even though persisting in obedience, He should have died and unjustly would He be punished without blame, if though not sinning He died. Therefore, because He had to be proven and it was awaited whether He should persist in obedience, His flesh also was both mortal according to something, because indeed He was able to die, and was immortal according to something, because He was not able to die; so, according as He was able to die, He would die if He should sin, and similarly according as He was not able to die He would not die if He should persevere in obedience. Now Christ as man, because He was perfect and proven from the beginning, was not awaited unto perfection or unto proof. And thus, just as He had free will and yet not so that He could sin, so too He had to have immortality according as it was in Him and so that He could not die at all. Therefore it is established that to Christ the man from the beginning not only was this immortality due, which the first man had before prevarication, but also that which the second man now has after the resurrection, in order that, just as from participation in the Godhead He had been confirmed by the Spirit unto truth so that He could not sin, so also from merit of virtue He might have been confirmed unto incorruption so that He could not die. But because flesh, the sinner, could not have been freed from the punishment of sin, unless His flesh which was without sin suffered, He retained by power the infirmity of capability of suffering and mortality in the flesh which had been assumed, sustained it by will, and did not suffer by necessity.

Now on the feeling of suffering in the flesh of Christ some are found to have thought wrongly, asserting that the flesh in all those instances which have been displayed in it and about it as kinds of suffering took on indeed a likeness of suffering and pain, but endured no pain or suffering at all. But they do not notice how great an absurdity follows an assertion of this kind. For how was there true compassion in Christ, if there was not true suffering? How will that which the prophet says stand: "Surely he hath borne our infirmities and carried our sorrows"? (Isa. 53, 4). If Christ had not suffered pain on the cross, why did He ask so much that the chalice of suffering be transferred from Him? (Cf. Matt. 20, 39). What did the exuding blood mean which bore witness to the distress of imminent death? What did it mean that Christ himself setting forth both the weakness, according to which the flesh feared suffering, and the will, according to which the spirit was willing, said: "The spirit indeed is willing, but the flesh is weak"? (Matt. 26, 41, Mark 14, 38). Those, then, who deny that there was true suffering according to the weakness of the flesh, in so far as is in them are convicted of denying that redemption which was made through the passion of Christ.

There are others who with no less madness regarding the human affections in Christ, which according to the truth of nature He took on with humanity and in humanity, have not feared to utter certain blasphemies not only false but even horrible. For, since the Apostle says: "We have not a high priest, who cannot have compassion on our infirmities, but one tempted in all things," (Cf. Hebr. 4, 15), they assert that human affection in Christ felt also the movements of vices, yet without the consent of reason, according to that infirmity of concupiscence by which we, who are sinners from that original corruption which we carry, even against our will are accustomed to feel illicit appetites and movements of surging concupiscence and the delight of tempting vice; moreover, they assert that Christ endured these movements in His flesh voluntarily on this account, that, as it were, by resisting those temptations He might stand out as victor; thus by overcoming the temptation of vices He might both acquire the reward of justice for Himself, and for us when placed in temptation He might form in Himself an example of resisting and conquering. But far be it from Christian feeling either to say or to believe that there was in any way in that sacrosanct flesh of the immaculate lamb a titillation of inordinate delight and of illicit concupiscence, because if we should say that there was in it either some root of depraved delight or inordinate movement of concupiscence surely we would deny that it was free from all vice.

Now how would He cleanse vice, if He carried vice? Accordingly, the inordinate movement from the infirmity of concupiscence, surging with only the corruption itself from which it arises, is not only punishment but blame; but this is not imputed unto damnation in the baptized, since it is excused through the grace of the new regeneration. Just as the Apostle says: "There is now no condemnation to them that are in Christ Jesus," (Rom. 8, 1). Yet this corruption through the grace of the sacrament does not indeed accept that there is no sin but that it is not damnable, since if there were no sin at all, it would not have to be excused, since it would not need to be imputed. So we say truly that Christ with the assumption of flesh assumed only that infirmity of human nature which is punishment; but that which is punishment so that it is also sin, we affirm without hesitation that He by no means admitted. For we do not wish so to call Him the victor over vices that we say that He sometimes carried and felt the very vices which He conquered. For through punishment alone He consented to be weakened, that those who were sick both in sin and in punishment He might first vindicate from blame, afterwards liberate from punishment.

VIII. *How we must understand that it was written: "He was conceived of the Holy Spirit."*

Since, just as has been said above, the Father at the same time as the Holy Ghost operated the incarnation of the Son with the Son himself, worthily is it asked why in Sacred Scripture conception is mentioned particularly regarding the Holy Ghost. These things, indeed, just as other things also which are mentioned about Him, human intelligence touches upon timidly, but the devotion of faith presuming more fully according to a pure conscience inquires faithfully. And so it must be asked especially how the statement that the Blessed Mary was conceived of the Holy Ghost should be understood. For we know and we all have already learned from the very frequent experience of nature that when a woman is said to conceive by a man she is declared to have received nothing else than the substance of flesh for the generation of flesh through the coition of flesh. And, indeed, this substance of flesh transfused from the flesh of man through the coition itself of flesh is made one flesh with the flesh of the woman, so that what is about to be born from the substance of both truly taking origin from him is through this also generated from this. Accordingly, a woman conceives from a man when from the flesh of a man through coition she receives the seed of flesh for generating flesh. And she conceives nothing else than he is from whom she conceives or she herself is who conceives, and what she conceives to this she gives birth.

What then shall we say? Did the Holy Spirit from His own substance infuse the seed of the child within the womb of the virgin? How then was the spiritual substance able to provide the seed of flesh? Or perhaps it was not the seed of flesh which was conceived, but what was born was flesh. What shall we say? How did Mary conceive from the Holy Spirit? And if she conceived from the Holy Spirit how was the Holy Spirit not the Father of Christ? All these matters need great consideration, lest perhaps in a difficult and very obscure affair human sense presume something more than is within its power. We must not doubt about these things because they are obscure, nor must we give any definition rashly because they must be believed. Let us seek then what Mary conceived.

Either she did not conceive flesh and did not give birth to flesh, or if she gave birth to flesh she conceived flesh. For what she conceived, to this she gave birth. But how could flesh not have provided flesh, or flesh not have given birth to flesh? Let us consider how this intricate question or manner of inquiry can be understood soundly and competently. And first let us examine into that conception which is accomplished according to the customary and usual operation of nature, how the work of the same nature is fulfilled.

In parents generating by flesh and fashioning flesh to be born from flesh through coition of flesh, nature provides substance on both sides for creating the fetus, so that from the flesh of both proceeds that flesh which is to be formed only in the flesh of one. Yet this contribution which nature imposes as something due, according to the plan of the Creator, to complete the fabric of the human body is so required by it without necessity or coertion that except by love alone and so to speak by spontaneous esteem it is not inclined to contribute this. For there is nothing except love alone which can extort this debt from nature but, when it has been persuaded by spontaneous esteem, then surely it occurs to it on both sides mutually to consummate the work gladly and joyfully. In truth whatever is seized violently from one who is unwilling is shown indeed to be unfitting and inefficacious for the accomplishment of a cause of this kind. Therefore it is love alone which can persuade nature and in a manner force the willing to sow the fetus. And indeed in the woman love of the man but in the man love of the woman is accustomed to accomplish the same, so that, since nature alone is not sufficient to itself in the one, the other comes to its aid through love, so that what was possible in neither by itself is possible in one through itself with the other. Accordingly, the seed of the human fetus is thought to be formed by the woman alone, although it is sown alike by the man and the woman, which indeed, as has already been said, nature operates in woman through love of man and in man through love of woman.

On this account also woman is not said to conceive except from man, although she receives as much from herself as from the man from whom she is made fruitful. And rightly does she conceive from man alone, because what she conceives is indeed assumed in the one from the flesh of the man but is provided in the other through love of the man. So not only does she conceive from man this which she receives from him, but she also conceives from him this which she receives from herself by love of man. This we wished to set forth because of the statement that Mary conceived of the Holy Spirit. Therefore, Mary conceived of the Holy Spirit not because she received the seed of the fetus from the substance of the Holy Spirit, but because through the love and operation of the Holy Spirit nature provided the substance for the divine fetus from the flesh of the virgin. For since in her heart the love of the Holy Spirit was especially ardent, on this account in her flesh the virtue of the Holy Spirit worked marvelous things. And love of Him in her heart did not take an associate, whose operation in her flesh had no example. Therefore this alone did the virgin conceive, which she received from her flesh through the love and operation of the Holy Spirit, from whom alone also without the admixture of virile seed she gave birth to a son.

Accordingly, the lust of flesh did not operate conception in the virgin who neither received seed from the flesh of man nor conceived from her own flesh through love of man, but through the love and operation of the Holy Spirit. Nor is the Holy Spirit himself to be called father of Christ, because His love operated the conception of the virgin, since He did not contribute the seed of the fetus of His own essence to the virgin, but He provided substance to the virgin herself from her own flesh through His love and virtue. Christ, therefore, was both born from the virgin because He received the substance of flesh from the flesh of the virgin, and conceived of the Holy Spirit because the virgin herself from her flesh alone without the admixture of virile seed conceived Him through the operation and love of the Holy Spirit. Hence it is that to the same virgin about to give birth it is said through the angel: "The Holy Ghost will come upon thee, and the power of the Most High shall overshadow thee," (Luke 1, 35). For the Holy Spirit came upon the virgin that, through His operation, the flesh of Christ might be formed of the flesh of the virgin; and the power of the Most High overshadowed her, lest in providing the substance of flesh she might enjoy concupiscence of the flesh.

IX. *On the union of Word, soul, and flesh.*

It is also asked whether the Word assumed flesh and soul at the same time or flesh before soul or soul before flesh. But most truly and without any doubt it is believed that ever since God assumed man He assumed him entire, because ever since He assumed man, just as God was man, so was God also true man. Now He would not have been true man in flesh alone or in soul alone, because man is both flesh and soul. So when He assumed man, at the same time He assumed both. Now He assumed flesh and soul, that is man, nature not person. For He did not assume man the person but He assumed man into person. Therefore, then, He assumed man because He assumed human flesh and human soul. Indeed, He did not assume person because that flesh and that soul, before they were united to the Word into person, had not been united into person. There was one union and the union was unto one, of Word and of flesh and of soul. Not the Word first and the flesh, nor the Word first and the soul, nor the soul first and the flesh, but at the same time Word and soul and flesh. But Word indeed before this union was person, because it was the Son who was person, just as the Father was person and the Holy Spirit was person. And the person was eternal just as the Word was eternal and the Son was eternal. Nor did the Word begin to be person when He began to be man, but He assumed man that man might begin to be person and no other person than was that one who received Him.

And so the person received Word, man, not person but nature, that He who received and what He received might be one person in the Trinity. For when man was assumed, a quaternion was not made but the Trinity remained, because ever since assumed man began to be God He began to be no other person than that one who received Him. He, therefore, who denies that assumed man is a person denies that man was assumed into person. For if He were never to be that, in vain would He ever have been assumed unto that. Now then assumed man is a person and no other than that very person by whom He was assumed, because both the assumer and the assumed are one person. God is man but He is on account of His humanity. Man is God but He is on account of His divinity. God took on humanity, man received divinity. And God is man on account of the humanity which He took on and possesses, and man is God on account of the divinity—not of two is this said but of one, because God and man are not two but one, Jesus Christ.

But you say: How one? Tell me of what nature the union is and I shall tell you how one. If the union of God and man is truly ineffable, they are not ineffably two but one, God and man. Yet they are by no means two, God and man, but one Jesus Christ. He who is God is Himself man, and He who is man is Himself God, not one and the other, but Himself one and the same. What does man signify? Nature. Whom does man signify? Person. If you ask what man signifies, man signifies one thing and God another. For man signifies humanity, God signifies divinity. If you ask whom man signifies, he signifies the same one as God, because both man and God are the same. What is man? If you seek His nature, body and soul. I say well that this is man. This being is of man because this being makes man. What is man? If you seek His person, He is God. Why is man God? Because humanity was united to divinity through person. The nature of God is divinity, the nature of man is humanity, and divinity indeed is not humanity, yet God is man. Diverse nature, one person. Now since nature was united, person is one, and since the person of God and man is one, God and man are one. Therefore, what God does man does, and what man does God does, since they are not two but one, God and man. "No man hath ascended into heaven, but he that descended from heaven, the Son of man who is in heaven," (John 3, 13). He spoke on earth and testified that He was in heaven. For He was in both, on earth through humanity, in heaven through divinity. He who was in heaven was the same on earth, through humanity on earth and only on earth, through divinity in heaven and on earth. "If they had known it, they would never have crucified the Lord of glory," (1 Cor. 2, 8). It is a wonder. Man was Lord in heaven and God died on the cross. If man was able, having been placed on earth through humanity, to be in heaven through divinity, God also was able while reigning in heaven through divinity to die on earth through humanity.

But you say: How was God able to die? How is God, who is immortal, dead? This I knew, that there were those who said this. God was not able to die; man died; God did not die. Why then do you deny that God died? Because, they say, divinity cannot die. If, therefore, God did not die, because according to divinity He did not die, then God was not born from the virgin, because according to divinity He was not born from the virgin, nor did God dwell among men, because according to divinity He did not dwell among men and all the other things which the Saviour operated in the flesh. If then God did not do these things, who was he who did these things? We thought that God did all these things. You say that God did not do these things. Then say: Who was he who did these things? Christ, they say, did all these things. Then Christ did these things and God did not do them; then Christ was not God. "Touch ye not my anointed: and do not evil to my prophets," (Psalm 104, 15). You touch Christ and you do evil to the prophet. You do not say that Christ is not God and you say that if it were true, Christ would not be God. Therefore, you touch Christ. You do not deny openly but you kill secretly. We do not, they say, deny or kill but we say that God did not die, because according to divinity Christ did not die. Accordingly, you say, when Christ walked on earth He was not the son of man in heaven, because according to humanity He was not in heaven. Now if man was not in heaven, when Christ walked on earth, because according to humanity He was not in heaven, neither did God, when Christ hung on the cross, die, because according to divinity He did not die. For what reason? If according to this or that He is not, then is He not? If according to this He is not, yet He is because He is according to something else. You wish authority? Hear the lamp, if you do not believe in the light. Augustine says: If God died on account of man, is not man going to live with God? Is not the mortal going to live to eternity for whose sake He who lives to eternity died? But how did God die? For what reason did He die? And can God die? From you He received the reason why He died through you. Again the same one says: The Word was crucified but was not changed into man. And again: Therefore through the fact that He was man, God died, and through the fact that He was God. And whatever man suffered, God cannot be said to have suffered because God was assuming man but was not changed into man.

Give heed to this. Who was He who said: "Before Abraham was made, I am"? (John 8, 58). Was He not man? Who was He who said: "And now glorify thou me, O Father, with glory which I had before the world was with you"? (Cf. John 17, 5). Was He not man? Therefore the man said truly: Before Abraham was made, I am. Therefore the man said truly: With glory which I had before the world was with Thee. Why? Does this scandalize you? This moves you which moved those who said: "Thou art not yet fifty years old, and hast thou seen Abraham?" (John 8, 57). Why not? Did not they who said this say the truth? A little before the Evangelist had said: "Jesus himself was beginning about the age of thirty years," (Luke 3, 23). Little time had passed from then until this. Not yet had forty years been fulfilled; how much the more were they not fifty? Or perhaps he said the truth, who said that He was thirty years of age, because thus it was; and they did not say the truth who said that He was not yet fifty years old, since He is both this and more. For he who named thirty did not deny what was more. Now those who did not believe fifty years did not believe what was much more. Why then, when the Evangelist named thirty years, did he wish to determine nothing for us as certain regarding the extent of the age of Jesus, that is, of Christ the man, up to the point where our thought should go and proceed no further? If He had more, in that He had this, why did the Evangelist not say more? But He did not have more in that He had this. Jesus was thirty years of age, the man was thirty years of age, because the age of the man was thirty years. Thirty years had now passed and no more since He had begun to be man. Therefore the man was thirty years of age and no more. And why? If man was only thirty years of age, was not God similarly only thirty years of age, who as man was only thirty years of age? How young is God? How small an age does God have? Truly small because He was made small. A small age in a small being, a great eternity in a great being. Yet He had no more time when He was temporal. For when He was eternal, neither was He thirty years of age nor twenty nor ten nor five nor one. For there He was not annual but eternal. Now when He was temporal He was no more. When He was eternal, what shall I say? Was He more? This is not enough. For time cannot by any means approach comparison with eternity. Therefore, He was eternal and He was only thirty years of age; He began in time, and was before time, and in that He began in time He was made man, and in that He was before time He is God the Maker. And although He began to be man in time, yet He did not begin as if He had not been before. Similarly although He was made man, yet He was not made as if He had not existed before. Accordingly, the Catholic faith condemned those who said that Christ was a creature, because, although Christ began to be in time, yet He did not begin to be at all, because the same God himself was above time and before time.

Now to be a creature is this, to be something from nothing, that is to be something and to have been nothing. But no one who begins to be something begins to be because he begins to be something, just as he who ceases to be something does not cease to be because he ceases to be something. For he does not cease to be something so that he is nothing but only so that he no longer is that which he ceases to be. Thus not always does he who begins to be something begin to be something in a way, as if he were beginning to be with the result that he now is, but with the result that he begins to be something which he was not before, so that he now is. Thus Christ when He began to be man, began to be something and yet He did not so begin to be something as if He had not been something before, because even before He was that which He began to be at sometime He was something which He always was and never began. And so God was made man and yet God is not a creature, since He was made what He was made before this, because He assumed temporarily what He did not always have but He did not receive from time what He always had. Yet after God was made man and man God, He was one and not two, man and God. And on account of this ineffable union by which God and man were one, just as God through His humanity displayed Himself truly temporal, so too man through his divinity did not falsely proclaim that he was before time. If eternal God was at one time only thirty years of age on account of humanity, why similarly was not temporal man eternal on account of divinity?

Therefore, they say, man was from eternity and man created the world and man was before He was man. You are children and still you have been unable to free yourselves from the coverings of childhood. Not yet have the senses that have been exercised in you so developed that they have no need of milk but of solid food. For what are the coverings of words except certain coverings of the intelligence? And as long as the human sense is covered with these never is the eye of the heart opened perfectly to the light of truth. You ask whether man was before time and I question you whether God began in time. If the eternal one was made temporal, was not the temporal one made eternal? Or possibly God on account of humanity was in time for the reason that He was man when man was in time, but man on account of divinity was not before time for the reason that when God was before time man was still not God. Perhaps there will be some reason because of which you should beware of statements of this kind, the integrity of Christian faith being preserved, however, so that you believe that He is one and the same who both in time was man on account of His humanity and before time was God on account of His divinity. And for this reason He himself likewise said truly both that He came in time as man and before time was God.

Now when He said this and that, not one and another said it, but He said it according to one and another. What God said man said, and what man said God said, because both man God and God man were one. When I say "man," I mean human nature, that is soul and flesh. When I say "God," I mean divine nature, that is, the divinity of the Word. Likewise when I say "man," I mean person according to soul and flesh. Likewise when I say "God," I mean person in divinity. Man denotes no more in nature than soul and flesh nor in person than according to soul and flesh. Nor does God denote in nature more than divinity nor in person more than in divinity, and yet in Christ person according to soul and flesh, and person in divinity are not two persons but are one person. What is the nature of man? Humanity. What is the nature of God? Divinity. From humanity is man, from divinity is God. What man is, He is according to soul and flesh, that is, His being, because it is His nature. What man is, He is according to that which is of man. What God is, He is according to that which is of God. For what God is, He is according to divinity; this being is His because it is His nature. And on this account what God is, He is according to that which is His own. What man is, He is according to that which is of man. Therefore, because God and man, according to that which is of man, are man, and man, according to that which is of God, is God, surely both God is man and man is God. Likewise, since man is not God from any other but God, and God is not man from any other but man, God and man are not any other but the same. Yet what man in His own is by foundation, God in the same is by dignity, and what God in His own is through nature, man in the same is through grace. And so in Christ we say that one is human nature and the other divine, but we do not say that one is man and the other God, but that God and man are one Jesus Christ.

What is Jesus? Saviour. What is Christ? Anointed. Jesus denotes one thing, Christ another, and yet Jesus signifies no one else than Christ because Jesus Christ is one. Augustine says: One significance has Jesus, another significance has Christ, although Jesus Christ our Saviour is one. Yet Jesus is His proper name, just as Moses was called by his proper name, as Elias, as Abraham. Thus as a proper name also our Lord Jesus Christ is indeed the name of a sacrament, just as if He should be called prophet, as if He should be called priest. Read the sermon of Augustine on the Epistle of John. There you will find this. Likewise in the work, "On the Predestination of Saints:" He, he says, made us believe in Christ, who made Christ for us in whom we believe. And so Augustine says this: Then do you wish to hear still more fully how or according to what our Lord Jesus Christ was made or unmade? Ambrose in the book which he writes "On the Trinity" speaks thus: We say, therefore, he says, that man was made and that this is to be referred to man. Finally too you have elsewhere: "Who was made to him of the seed of David, according to the flesh," (Rom. 1, 1). Surely, according to the flesh of the seed of David was He made. Now God before the ages was born of God. Yet that He was not made is always referred to creation. For it is written: "Lord thou hast been our refuge," (Psal. 89, 1). And a little later: Therefore, if to have been made is frequently referred to something, not to nature, also to have been created is referred to a cause. On this account we understand what is written about the incarnation of the Lord: "The Lord created me the beginning of his ways, in his works," (Cf. Prov. 8, 22). It signifies that the Lord Jesus was created of the Virgin to redeem the works of the Father. Likewise in the same: Paul, he says, prohibits me from serving a creature and advises that Christ must be served. Christ, then, is not a creature. Paul, he says, "a servant of Christ," (Rom. 1, 1), and a good servant who recognizes the Lord. He himself prohibits us from serving a creature. How then would He serve Christ, if He thought Christ a creature? See then how he affirms that Christ was both made and created according to something whom, however, He denies to be a creature. Likewise in the same book he testifies that Christ was not the adopted but the natural son, saying: Through adoption we are called sons, He through the truth of nature. Therefore, just as He was from nothing who made all things from nothing, so should we according to the testimony of Scripture form the marks of faith, that we may join the purity of sincere confession to correct belief.

X. *On the separation of soul and flesh in Christ.*

Some thought that in death divinity receded from Christ the man and that the death of the man was nothing but the separation of divinity from flesh. For they find certain words in which it seems to have been stated thus, and finding words of this kind they cling to the letter, not attaining to the spirit. Blessed Ambrose seems to say something similar in the exposition of that psalm which the Lord himself in the passion shows was written about Himself saying: "O God, my God, why has thou forsaken me?" (Cf. Matt. 27, 46; Mark 15, 34; Psal, 21, 2). Thus upon this passage Ambrose says: Man on the point of death, because of the separation of divinity, cries out, and certain other things confronted Him, as if to test Him, namely, that God is life and where life was, death could not have been. And therefore, unless life had first receded, death could not have come. Surely it is written that Jesus crying out with a loud voice said: My God, My God why hast thou forsaken me? Man cries out that he has been forsaken by God, and complains that God has receded from Him and that He will die, as it were, because God has receded from Him. Therefore, He said that man, on the point of death because of the separation of divinity, cries out. But behold what is said. For if there is a question about that separation of divinity, for which Christ the man cried out on the cross, surely that had already taken place. For he bore witness, not that he was to be forsaken, but that He had already been forsaken, saying: My God, why hast thou forsaken me? If then there is a question about that separation of divinity, God had already receded when as man hanging on the cross He cried out that He had been forsaken by God. And surely Christ was still living in the flesh, when God had thus receded from Him.

Let them reply then. If death could not have been unless life departed, how could life have remained after life had receded? For already God had thus receded, and still Christ was hanging alive on the cross when He pleads that He has been forsaken. If then in this recession of God and in this separation of divinity they say that that union of person which existed between divinity and humanity was dissolved, there was some time when Christ was still living man and was not God. But who would say this? Who being in agreement with sound faith would not shudder to impose upon God the belief that while accompanying assumed man He brought Him indeed even unto death and in death, when with a greater danger threatening greater aid was necessary, He deserted Him? Why then does He reproach so much the hirelings, who, when the wolf comes, flee and desert the sheep which they should have guarded, when He himself at the approach of the wolf deserted that one sheep, namely, that lamb the son of the virgin sheep, whom He received not only to guard but also to glorify? The sheep before secure in its shepherd did not fear when the wolf came, saying: "The prince of this world cometh, and in me he hath not anything," (John 14, 30). But now forsaken by His shepherd, pleading and complaining, He cries out: Why have you forsaken me? He was man alone and was not God, and now He was not God the man, because God had already receded from man, nor was He man the God who, hanging still alive on the cross, was forsaken by God. Already then not only in death but also before death divinity had receded from man, when man still complained that God had receded from Him, and on this ground, so they say, He was not God. Who would say this?

How, they say, are we to understand that Christ cries out that He was forsaken by God and that Scripture affirms that man cried out that He would die because of the separation of divinity, if God had not receded from man? What then? Was divinity unable in any degree to have deserted humanity, in so far indeed as it did not defend it when temporarily exposed to the power of the enemy, and in any degree unable not to have deserted it, in so far indeed as even then it did not recede from it through the presence of its majesty? It forsook for them, it did not forsake for itself. It forsook because it did not contribute aid, but it did not forsake because it did not take away presence. It withdrew protection but it did not separate the union. It separated itself without, that it might not be present for defense against enemies, but it did not separate itself within, that it might be lacking to it for union of person. Thus then it forsook that it might not assist, but it did not forsake that it might recede. I go over the way; you proceed with me; we walk together. I am secure, since I have as it were a friend with me. My enemy comes and rushing upon me unarmed and unable to resist inflicts wounds. You, perceiving that I am being beaten, do not move but you endure it patiently, and you stand near as if not caring for my wounds, and I say: Why hast thou forsaken me? Still you stand near me, and I plead that you have receded from me. You are near in place but far away in assistance. You were near when you showed your presence in love. You became far away when on my being placed in dangers you withdrew yourself from compassion. Thus then humanity cried out that it was forsaken by divinity in the passion, because it had given it over to the power of enemies to be crucified, as it is written: "Thou shouldst not have any power against me unless it were given thee from above," (John 19, 11). Yet because He sustained this death, hanging on the cross, not for his own iniquity but for our redemption, He asks why He is forsaken, not as if murmuring against God for the punishment, but showing us His innocence in the punishment; He who knew not sin asked the cause.

XI. *That Christ, His soul separated from flesh and person, was both God and man.*

It is written: "And Jesus crying with a loud voice, yielded up the Ghost," (Matt. 27, 50). Who yielded? Jesus. What did He yield? The ghost. To whom did He yield it? To the Father. The Jew did not cast it forth nor did the Father draw it forth, but He himself of His own accord yielded it. It was not taken away violently, but it was given of His free will. "I have the power," He says, "to lay my soul down, and I have power to take it up again," (Cf. John 10, 18). The soul itself, He himself is the ghost. Therefore, the soul itself was sent forth by the power of Him dying, not by the violence of him killing. The soul is sent forth. He sent it forth of whom it was. From where did He send it forth? From the flesh. Where did He send it? To the Father. The soul receded and the flesh died. Christ died because the flesh of Christ died. Just as God died because the humanity of God died, so man died because the flesh of man died. Flesh alone died and in the flesh man died, to whom the flesh belonged; God also died because God was man. The separation of soul was death of the flesh. Flesh alone died from which the soul was separated; the soul did not die nor did divinity die, but flesh alone died, because the soul was separated from that life of His.

The soul descended into hell; the flesh lay in the sepulchre; divinity remained with both. For flesh and soul, when separated, were not able to destroy person which they, even when joined, had not made. The word was an eternal person. He did not begin to be a person then when He received soul and flesh into person. He received soul and flesh, that they might be person in Him, not that they might make Him person. Since, therefore, soul and flesh received being person in Him, because they began to be united by the Word of person, always indeed did they remain one and the same person with the Word, because never thereafter did they recede separated from the Word or each other. Accordingly, the Word was eternal person on account of eternal divinity, and person itself was God on account of divinity and was man on account of humanity united with the Word. So Christ the person descended into hell, but according to the soul alone, because the soul alone descended into hell, and Christ the person lay in the sepulchre according to flesh alone, but flesh alone lay in the sepulchre, and Christ the person was everywhere according to divinity alone, because divinity alone was everywhere.

The soul did not lie in the sepulchre, nor did the flesh descend to hell, and neither the flesh nor the soul was everywhere. The body alone lay in the sepulchre, and on account of that part of man did Christ the man lie in the sepulchre. Some writings say this, that when Christ is said to have lain in the sepulchre, the whole is stated for the part, since not the whole man lay in the sepulchre but one part of man, the body only. Pay attention here. Not the whole man but a part of man. Who was man? Christ. All man, all Christ. Part of man, part of Christ. Christ lay in the sepulchre; the whole is stated for the part. Therefore, not the whole lay but the part. What is the whole? Christ. What is the part? Body. Thus, indeed, Christ did not lie in the sepulchre, if Christ is said to have lain in the sepulchre, and this is the figure of speech whereby the whole is stated for the part, and in the whole the part is understood. Then Christ did not truly descend into hell but part of Christ only, the soul alone.

Something of scrupulosity comes upon us. For these matters have been taken up by Catholic truth, and it does not accept or approve that it be said that Christ did not truly lie in the sepulchre and that He did not truly descend to hell. For what reason, then? If He did not truly lie in the sepulchre because the body alone lay in the sepulchre, He did not truly descend to hell, because the soul alone descended to hell, and therefore He did not truly die, because the flesh alone was dead, not the soul or divinity. What is it that was written? That when Christ is said to have lain in the sepulchre the whole was stated for the part? Or is it one thing for the whole to be stated for the part and another for the whole to operate in the part? For when the whole is stated for the part, indeed the whole itself is named, but it is not understood but its part alone for which it is stated. When, indeed, the whole is said to operate in the part, whatever is mentioned is understood, and nothing else is understood in place of what is mentioned, although it is understood to operate according to something else, that is, according to part. For when the whole operates in a part, then truly the whole operates, since both the whole is with the part and the part is in the whole, when both the whole and the part operate. When they are together, they can operate together. Then in as much as the operation of the part is rightly said to be of the whole, when it is of the whole, the part which operates is also in the whole. When indeed the whole has been destroyed and now the whole is not, it is not properly said to be of the whole, because the part only operates outside the whole.

What then? According to this shall we say that, when the flesh of Christ died, Christ did not truly die, because man in His part endured the passion; that, when indeed the body of Christ lay in the sepulchre, Christ did not truly lie there, because the part itself which lay there was already divided from the whole? Accordingly, Christ truly died but was not truly buried. Far be it from the truth! But He truly died and was truly buried. He truly descended into hell and truly ascended into heaven. How then was the whole stated for the part, when it was written that Christ had lain in the sepulchre? What is the whole and what is the part? For the whole is mentioned with reference to the parts and the parts are referred to the whole. Then perhaps you are thinking, as it were, that some three things—divinity, soul, and flesh, composed Christ and that Christ is a kind of whole composed of three parts—divinity and flesh and soul. Then the third part of Christ is the Word. Far be it from the truth! For the Word is not a part of Christ but Christ himself is the Word. He is entirely the Word, just as He is entirely God. Not a half part of Christ is the Word and a half part man but the whole Christ is the Word and the whole Christ is man, since the very same one is God and man. Do you understand what I say? If you do not understand, nevertheless believe. It can be believed, if it cannot be understood.

Yet it is true that Christ his very self was both God and man, and not a third part of Christ was Word nor was He something entirely composed of flesh and soul and Word, as it were, of parts, because He was entirely the Word himself. Where then was the whole composed of parts? Where were the parts in the whole and where was the whole composed of the parts? Now divinity was not a part so that of itself it was the whole greater than itself, nor was a part in itself so that in itself something was less than itself. In humanity alone do we find parts and does the whole consist of parts. Man is a kind of whole consisting of two parts, soul and flesh. There are the two parts of man and of these two parts the whole man consists. Divine nature is simple; human nature is twofold; there-fore, there are two parts of man since in the nature of man there are two, soul and body. Where these two are, the whole man is. Where one of these is, part of man is. On this account, therefore, the Word assumed the whole man, since it assumed all that belonged to man, soul and flesh.

Now the whole man did not lie in the sepulchre, but part of man only, that is, flesh. For if the whole man were said to have lain in the sepulchre, surely the dead soul would be denied to have receded from the flesh. Similarly, if the whole man were said to have descended to hell, surely the flesh in like manner with the soul would be declared to have descended there. Thus part of man only lay in the sepulchre, and not the whole man, and when Christ is said to have lain in the sepulchre on account of the flesh alone which lay there, this is proven to be true. For when Christ is said to have been in the sepulchre, the whole man is said to have been in the sepulchre, since when Christ is mentioned the whole man is mentioned, because Christ is the whole man. And it is true that Christ lay in the sepulchre and yet not the whole man lay in the sepulchre, although Christ was the whole man. On this account, therefore, Christ was the whole man, because soul and flesh were united with the Word into person. Now Christ truly lay in the sepulchre because His flesh lay there. And therefore the Word could not have been lacking person where the flesh was which had been united personally with the Word itself. And thus Christ was in the sepulchre when His flesh was there, and yet the whole man was not there, since not soul and flesh alike were there but flesh alone.

Now that man is called man, and that person is called man, is said on account of the whole man and on account of all that belongs to man. Now I do not mean this, that man is named from the part assumed from the earth, but when man is mentioned and person is understood as all that man is, He is mentioned from all that belongs to man. Truly it is one thing when man is said to be that which is man, and another when He is said to be that which is in man. For when He is said to be man He is said to be on account of the whole man, that is, soul and flesh. But when He is said to be that which is in man, He is mentioned on account of a part of man, that is, on account of the soul alone or on account of the flesh alone. When man is called man, He is called person; when he is called that which is in man, he is called what is in person. For man is called wise and yet he is so called not on account of the whole that is man but on account of the part which is in man, because wisdom is not in soul and in flesh but only in the soul. Likewise when man is called white or black, he is so called not on account of the whole which is man but on account of the part which is in man, because whiteness and blackness are not in soul and flesh but only in the flesh. And if perhaps the whole man is said to be this, yet he is not so called as if this were all that there is of man, but because that which should be so in man may be this entirely. The whole man in truth is called white when the whole body of the man is white, not because all that is of man is white but because of all that can be white in man is white. And so too Christ, when He is called man, is so called on account of all that is man, that is, soul and flesh. Now when He is called mortal or dead or buried, He is so called on account of the part of man, that is, flesh alone, because flesh alone was also mortal when it carried the corruption of capability of suffering, and it alone died when on the cross the soul hung without its life.

And flesh alone was buried, since the soul was not with it as it lay dead in the sepulchre. Yet Christ truly himself did all this which flesh alone did, who through His divinity was present in person in the flesh and with the flesh which did this. Similarly when Christ is said to have exulted in spirit or is said to have had affection or desire or fear, He is understood to have had this according to soul alone, because soul alone had this, and He himself through the soul truly had it, to whose divinity the soul itself had been united in person. Indeed that soul had, according to the affections of nature with which it had been assumed, desire and joy and pain and fear of suffering according to its flesh, all of which were rationally admitted temporarily by the power of the maker and the will of the sufferer. When He feared punishment of His flesh and fled pains, He did so according to the affection of nature, because of which no one has possessed his flesh with hatred whose injury sometimes He can endure from reason but never can love. So in Christ, according to the affection of nature which the soul had in the flesh and for the flesh, there was a certain will in accordance with which He is said truly to have abhorred death and pain and suffering and not to have wished them. Yet a superior will of the spirit which was ready for obedience to the Father's command directed this will. For the will of the spirit, established in Christ as in a kind of middle place, moderated the subject will of the flesh through reason and was subject to the superior will of the Father, saying: "Not my will, but thine be done," (Cf. Luke 22, 42).

Thus then, in so far as Christ is mentioned, He is mentioned at times according to person, at times according to that which was in person, and similarly, in so far as He is mentioned, according to man, at times He is mentioned according to man himself, at times according to that which was in man. Now in the nature of divinity where there is no multiplicity or diversity, person and that which is in person cannot be different. In humanity alone, where multiplicity is found, is the whole shown to be one thing and the part another. The whole is person; the part is in person. The whole is soul and flesh; the part is soul alone or flesh alone. Now Scripture says: "As rational soul and flesh are one man, so God and man are one Christ." See the likeness. I say rightly: Soul and flesh are man, and again I say rightly: Man is person. And again I say rightly: Soul and flesh are one person. Now I cannot say similarly: The soul alone is man or flesh alone is man. And, therefore, I cannot say: The soul alone is person or flesh alone is person. But in Christ I can say: God and man are Christ, and I can say similarly: God is Christ and again man is Christ. And again I can say: God and man are one person, and likewise God is person and man is person.

Of what nature then is this likeness when it is said: Just as the rational soul and flesh are one man, so God and man are one and Christ? For if there is altogether a likeness, in view of which, just as in Christ, Christ is called God and man, and man is called Christ and God Christ, is it not also so said in man: just as flesh and soul together are man, so also flesh alone by itself is man or the soul alone by itself is man, or just as in man soul indeed and flesh together are called man and not soul alone by itself is called man nor flesh by itself is called man, so in Christ God and man together are called Christ, yet so that neither man alone by himself nor God alone by Himself is called Christ?

There is a great accumulation of words about these things, and man labours on his own, knowing how to understand almost nothing except this and according to this which he knows how to put in words. These men ask daily what must be said and rarely what must be believed. They ask whether that phrase is good and whether that phrase is to be accepted and whether that phrase is to be approved. They have been placed in a mint of words and a great multitude of conversations, and infinite perplexity occurs, since they wish to draw the judgment of the spirit from the letter, not the judgment of the letter from the spirit. For they do not know that the spirit should judge the letter, not the letter the spirit. As it is written: "The spiritual man judgeth all things; and he himself is judged of no man," (1 Cor. 2, 15). Therefore, they labour in the judgment of words, since they do not have the spirit of understanding. They wish to have judgment and they do not wish to have the spirit without which they cannot judge rightly. Accordingly, they labour in words, and different words come to be expressed about Him, to the effect that He must be understood as one.

They ask what is person and then they adduce a definition of person as it has been made and proved by certain people, that person is the individual element of rational substance. Well, let us say on our part that person is this. What person is has been well defined on our part. On our part let us speak thus. We cannot by any means express what is above us. It is something that cannot be expressed since it is incomprehensible. On our part let us say: Person is the individual element of rational substance. What is rational substance if not rational spirit? For rational substance is properly this—spiritual substance which is alone capable of reason because only in it can reason exist. For if man is said to be rational substance, he is so called not on account of the whole but on account of the soul alone which is properly called rational substance. For man according to soul is only rational, since he himself has rational soul. Now the soul is rational according to itself, because it has reason or rationality in itself, that is, capacity for reason. And thus rational substance properly and according to itself exists only as a rational spirit which is truly the individual element and, in so far as a simple nature exists, not having a composition of parts and not containing several things of the same peculiarity, is of a simple nature. Thus the rational spirit here is properly called "person," both distinguished in number and distinguishing by reason. For thus some wished that "person" be described, as it were, speaking by itself and, as it were, distinguishing peculiarly, so that in so far as it is distinguished by itself in number and in so far as it distinguishes by reason, we understand it as speaking or pronouncing or judging. Behold then according to this definition we properly say that rational spirit is person distinguishing itself through itself. There is no great question here nor ambiguity of understanding, where what is whole is one.

Now in man the same reason does not occur, where indeed there are two, and yet there are not two persons but person, flesh and soul. But here some are found to rave in so many ways, clinging to words only so that not easily could the twisting of words have been judged, had not error shown itself manifestly in the end. They say that man is a certain whole composed of soul and body, entirely different and diverse from soul and body, so that this whole is neither soul nor body nor similarly soul and body; for they say that the whole is not these things but is of these things. This, therefore, they think is the whole man, and the man himself who is this whole, is rational by the rationality which is in the whole itself, different from reason or from rationality of a part, that is, of the soul, just as the whole itself is different from the part. Finally they say that all things which are in the whole are entirely different from those things which exist in the parts, just as the whole itself is different from the parts. And so, just as the rationality of man is different from the rationality of the soul, since one is of the whole and is in the whole, the other is of the part and is in the part, so too they say that the goodness of the whole, which is in the whole, is different and the goodness of the part is different, because it is of the part and in the part only. Similarly also they say that the malice of man is different, because it is in the whole, and the malice of the soul is different, because it is in the part. Finally, they say that as often as the whole acts and the part acts, although they work together, yet the one is the action of the part, which is in the part, and the other is the action of the whole, which is in the whole, just as the whole itself is one thing and its part another. In this manner, then, as often as man sins or does well, they contend that sin or justice is in man, which happens to the whole according to propriety, and again that sin or justice is in the soul, which happens to the part according to propriety. Wherefore they say that when man dies and the soul is separated from the flesh, when the parts are divided, the whole itself which had been composed of them is now nothing and through this man himself, who was this whole, is similarly nothing and is not anywhere, and now meanwhile neither is his sin punished nor his justice rewarded; only his soul is in judgment, so that man according to his merit receives either punishment or glory, when finally at the very last, as the soul returns to the body, man again begins to be and then according to his merit he himself also receives reward.

Such ways of speaking do men devise for themselves and through false fictions of discussions they are led to true deceptions of errors. For what is more foolish than to say that man ceases to be then when he truly begins to be? And surely it is the more true as that is more true in which he begins to be. No, they say, but it is a figure when the saints are said to be with Christ. Very well. When they are with you it is truth and when they are with Christ it is a figure. You believe yourselves in this. For we do not believe you. We know that Christ is truth. Those who go to Christ do not go to a figure, but they go to truth and avoid a figure. Why indeed did the holy men desire to die, if after death they were to be nothing? I desire, says the Apostle, to be dissolved and to be with Christ, (Cf. Philip 1, 23). What do you desire? To die and to be with Christ? No, to die and to be nothing. They say this because you will be nothing after death. If you believe them, you do not long for death unless perhaps you desire not to be. If good men after death are to be nothing, how is this truly said regarding unjust and evil men: They desire to be nothing and yet they cannot be? Accordingly, let both the good cease to hope and the evil to fear now, because they will not be anything when they have departed from this world, and therefore unable to feel either evil or good things. But well do they say: Let them hope and let them fear although not for themselves but for their souls, since when they themselves will not be, their souls will be, which will either boast of justice or will be tortured for sin. On this account, then, they say, let them hope and let them fear for their souls. Would that you spoke as rightly as the right you speak! For you speak well, when you say that man must hope and fear for his soul, if, however, you understood that man never fears better or more truly for himself than when he fears for his soul. For what is man more than soul?

You did not think these things, whoever you are, who had fortified yourself with the figures of speech. Something new was brought to your ears when it was said that this was man which is rather of man. So, listen: You a Christian do not know what that pagan testified. The mind, he says, of everyone, *is* everyone. Therefore, that pagan was more religious than you a Christian, who confessed the truth which you deny. Thus, you say, is man soul? What? Do you not say that man is body and do you fear to say: Man is soul? A little before you opposed the argument that every man is body. Every man is animal and every animal is body. Therefore, every man is body. You think that there is no contradiction here. For authority says this: You produce pagan authors to prove that every man is body, and with pagan authors you do not wish to believe that every man is soul, perhaps because it pleases you more that man is this rather than that, because this pleases you more than that. But I, you say, speak about the whole, when I say: Every man is body, not with reference to a part of the whole which is body nor with reference to a part which is soul, for this whole is man, not some part of him. Accordingly, with reference to this whole which is body do I speak. Tell, therefore, why you say that this whole is body rather than soul, when it consists alike of soul and body? If on account of one part, because it is body, the whole itself is called body, ought it not rather to be called soul on account of the other part which is soul? For if the whole is said to take its nature and name from a part, without doubt it will more rightly be said to take both nature and name from that part which is worthier and better.

But ordinary speech, you say, does not hold that man be called soul. I yield to ordinary speech. Say anything, yet so that you may according to the rule of believing perceive what ought not to be denied. Ordinary speech was invented by men and for men, and on this account man should rather have that form in speaking which human feeling has in perceiving and in recognizing things. We know certainly that only that is one which is one by unity; for reason truly discerns this alone as one, in which it finds the whole to be that which is one.

Therefore, whatever are many in number, although sometimes they are united, yet truly they cannot be one, since indeed those things which are united in one composition in some manner approach each other and draw near each other so that, in so far as they can, they imitate unity. Thus in a certain way those things also which have been joined together are said to be one. For just as reason in perceiving that which is truly one does not divide, so also sense in perceiving does not discern what has been joined together and united. And just as reason does not divide essence there in that which is wholly one, so also sense does not divide form here in this which is wholly united. There reason perceives at once what is one, because in it there is not one thing and another, but here sense at once perceives what is united, because sense is not in it in one place and in another. But several things which have been united are not truly one, although they come together and in a manner approach unity; they are not so, truly and properly. For what can be more proper to itself than unity? Accordingly, when several things are called one because they have been united, they are not properly so called, because they are not truly that which they are called but only in a way are they similar. But we must know that in one way those things are united which come together equally to make a union, so that from the time that they begin to be together they begin in a manner to be one, but in another way those things are united where unity preceded before unity, and what was added from the remainder advanced to unity itself through union. It is one thing indeed for some things to be placed together through union unto unity and another for some things to be added to unity through union. For when some things are placed together unto union through union, the parts cannot share the name of the whole, since apart singly they have not a union in themselves which they make together of themselves. But when some things are added through union to something which has its own unity, they pass over into participation with that to which they are added, so that they also begin to participate in the name with that, just as they begin to participate through its union in unity with that.

For example, a wall, a roof, and a foundation are three definite things and no one of these is by itself a house. Therefore, when they come together so that they begin to be this, the three are placed together at once, no two are added to the third. Now the body and the soul have not been so united. The soul indeed, in so far as it is rational spirit, of itself and through itself has to be person and when the body is associated with it, it is not so much placed with it unto person as it is added into person so that, in that through union in a manner it is one with it, it begins to be with it the same person which it is itself. In so far, then, as body is united with soul, it is one person with soul, but yet the soul has to be person of itself, in so far as it is rational spirit. But the body has it from the soul, in so far as it was united to rational spirit. Since, however, the sense of man in living man perceives body and soul together, human speech is accustomed to speak not of soul by itself or of body by itself but of soul and body together as person. Now this person, which indeed in the soul is properly one through unity but between the body and the soul one through union, according to ordinary speech is called by different names. Of these some were assumed from the part, some indeed from those things which are in the part. For in as much as rational man is called person, either soul or body is a word assumed from merely a part, since in man only his body is found to be body and to have been assumed from earth and to have been endowed with sense by conjunction with the soul. These words, therefore, have been assumed from a part of man.

Now when a man is said to be white or black or large or small, the words are taken from those things which are in a part, since only in the body of man and not in the soul are properties of this kind found. Now when a man is called rational or wise or just, the names are assumed with reference to the whole from those things which are only in a part, since not the body of man but only the soul is found to be rational and wise and just. And so the name of man is sometimes assumed from the body, sometimes from those things which are in the body, but sometimes it is assumed from those things which are in the soul; in no case, however, is it assumed from the soul, for human speech formed very special words for man from that part of man which human sense first and chiefly knew in man. Indeed man should have assumed a better name from his better part, except that speech could not have been of service to man's intelligence, unless first it had retained that method of speaking which human sense had of perceiving. So, since that which was from earth seemed more evident in man, man was called rather from that. Thus indeed out of infirmity of perception, confusion in speech arose; and because of usage in speech we should preserve the mode of speaking and yet because of custom in speaking we should not withdraw from the truth of believing. For because of this, Sacred Scripture, lest the words of man cause you to err in the truth of God, testifies that person itself is properly rational spirit itself. Although this person, because of that which is assumed from the earth, is called man, yet most truly, even when person is associated with it, person alone operates well or poorly and, when person is separated from it, alone is remunerated in punishment or glory. And just as when placed in the body it does some things by cogitation and will without the body, some things after the will and according to the will in operation through the body, so also according to merits it receives reward first separated from the body without body, afterwards united to the body in the body.

Behold then we say: Man is animal. It is true, because in man the endowment of sensation is caused by the soul. Man is body. It is true, because that which was endowed with sensation in man and was assumed from earth is the body itself. Man is person. It is true, because that which was assumed from the earth was joined to the soul in the person. All this ordinary speech holds and, according to this manner in which it is truly said, it can be received without inconvenience as the truth. Again we may say: Man is a soul. Ordinary speech, which is formed on the mode of sense experience, does not accept this designation. For only the body is seen in man and only in the body is man seen; for this reason the name is assumed for man from the body, since man is so called on account of the body. Again, since in that which is seen there is perceived to be another thing which is not seen, two things are understood to be in man, namely, body and soul, and since these are found to be joined together and united they are called parts of the same union, body and soul. Well then let us concede what usage of speech brings forth. Man is body and man is not spirit. Man is animal and man is not soul. Then similarly shall we concede that a dead man is not man, for a living man is man? Now if a dead man is not man, then man when he ceases to live ceases to be man. But what is it that ceases to live except what dies? Now what dies except the body alone which is deserted by the soul? For the soul does not die nor does it cease to live even when it ceases to vivify. Therefore, the body alone dies.

But man, you say, that is, person itself dies. What is person? Is it not the individual element of rational substance? If then person is the individual element of rational substance, surely rational spirit which is both one in simplicity and by nature capable of reason properly has to be person of itself, in so far as it is rational spirit, indeed through itself when it is without body. Now when the body is united with it, in so far as it is one with body, it is one person with body. When in truth it is separated from body, it does not nevertheless cease to be person and the very same person which it was before, since the body withdrawing from association with the spirit does not endure being person to the same spirit, just as before, when it was joined with it, it did not grant it to be person. And so the soul remains separated from the flesh, the same person of the rational spirit, which, although perhaps it cannot now be called man according to ordinary speech, since it has not now united with itself that which had been assumed from earth, yet on this account is no less person and the same person that it was before, when it also had that united with itself and on account of that union was one person with it. Therefore, just as body joined with rational spirit does not grant it to be person, but joined with it receives from it that it itself be one person with it, so humanity joined with the word indeed granted it to be person but united to it, received from it, that it be one person with it.

Indeed it must be considered that since word and man are one person in Christ, yet rightly through itself do we say that word is person and again rightly through Himself do we say that man is person. And rightly do we say that man and Word together are not two but one person. For since the Word, even before man was assumed, was person and after man was assumed does not cease to be person, for this reason rightly do we say that by itself Word is person; since again between assumed man and the Word there was a greater and more excellent union than between soul and body, nevertheless rightly do we say that by Himself man is person. For man, that is, body and soul joined together, has to be person, yet not different from Word, since man and Word are one person. Certainly the union makes them one. For flesh and soul joined together would have been person, if they had not been one person with the Word, and if they had not been united to the person, the Word. Therefore, we say rightly that Word is also person, and again we say rightly that man is person, and similarly that Word and man are not two but one person. Again we say rightly that Word, ever since He was made man, never afterwards ceased to be man, since in the death of His flesh He never divided Himself from assumed humanity. Wherefore, Christ also in the death of His flesh did not cease to be God, since He remained immortal in true Godhead, and did not cease to be person since He was Word, and did not cease to be man since His divinity did not withdraw from His humanity. Only the soul was divided from the flesh temporarily but divinity was separated neither from soul nor from flesh. Christ then also truly died on account of dead flesh and He truly remained alive on account of immortal divinity, and true God was also at the same time true man on account of the inseparable union of divinity and humanity.

XII. *That through man united with the Word all who are His members are united with God.*

The Apostle says: A mediator is not of one: but God is one, (Gal. 3, 20). For God and man were two, diverse and adverse. God was just; man was unjust; in this note them adverse. Man was wretched, God blessed; in this note them diverse. Thus then man was adverse to God through injustice and diverse from God through wretchedness. For this reason man held it as necessary that first he be justified from fault in order to be reconciled, afterwards that he be liberated from wretchedness in order to be reformed.

In this, therefore, man needed a mediator before God in order to be reconciled to Him and be led back to Him; but He who was not by any friendship of society and of peace related to both, could not take up the pleading of the cause of dissenters. On this account then the Son of God was made man, so that between man and God He might be a mediator of reconciliation and of peace. He took on humanity through which He might approach men. He retained divinity through which He might not withdraw from God. Being made man He sustained punishment that He might show affection; He preserved justice that He might confer the remedy. The Word indeed, which was one with God the Father through ineffable unity, was made one with the assumed man through a wonderful union. Unity in nature, union in person. With God the

Father one in nature, not in person; with assumed man, one in person, not in nature. What is more one than unity? What is one by unity is one to the highest degree. The Word and the Father were one in unity, since they were one in nature, and the Word Himself wished to become one with us to make us one in Himself and through Himself and with Him with whom He himself was one.

Therefore, He assumed our nature from us that He might associate it, which had not been associated through unity in nature, to Himself through union in person; thus then through that indeed which He had made one with Himself from our own He might unite us to Himself, that we might be one with Him through that which as our own had been united to Him and through Him himself also be one with the Father who was one with Him. "Holy Father," he says, "keep them in thy name whom thou has given me: that they may be one, as we also are," (John 17, 11). "And not for them alone do I pray, but for them also who through their word shall believe in me, that they also may be one in us; that the world may believe that thou has sent me. And the glory which thou hast given me, I have given to them; that they may be one, as we also are one: I in them, and thou in me; that they may be made perfect in one; and the world may know that thou hast sent me," (Cf. John 17, 20-23). Unity prays for union. The Word with the Father, one in nature; man with the Word, one in person. The members with the head, one first in justice, afterwards in glory. For that they may be one in justice, "the world may know that thou hast sent me;" but that they may be one in glory, "I will that where I am, they also may be with me, that they may see my glory which thou hast given me, because thou hast loved me before the creator of the world," (Cf. John 17, 24).

XIII. *That Christ according to humanity is now in heaven, according to divinity is everywhere.*

You ask how can we belief that the mediator of God and man, the man Christ Jesus, (Cf. I Tim. 2, 5), is now in heaven or you question that, because God is everywhere, man also who is in God is diffused everywhere, wishing to understand from this also that He who is everywhere was able to be in heaven. So do not doubt that man Jesus Christ is now there from where He is to come. Also cherish mindfully and retain faithfully the Christian confession: "He arose from the dead, ascended into heaven, sitteth at the right hand of the Father." And only from there is He to come to judge the living and the dead, and thus is He to come according to the words of the angel: "Just as He was seen going up to heaven," (Cf. Acts 1, 10), that is, in the same form of flesh and in substance. To whom indeed He gave immortality, from Him He did not take away nature. He is not to be thought diffused everywhere, according to this form. For we must beware lest we so build up the divinity of man that we take away the truth of body. For it does not follow that what is in God is thus everywhere just as God. For the most true Scripture says concerning us: "In him we live, and move, and are," (Cf. Acts 17, 28), and yet we are not everywhere as He is, but on the one hand man is in God, since on the other also God is in man in a certain peculiar and singular way. For one person is God and man, and both are one Jesus Christ, everywhere through that which is God but in heaven through that which is man.

Therefore, God is diffused through all things. For He himself says through the Prophet: "I fill heaven and earth." (Cf. Jeremias 23, 24). But a little before I set this down regarding His wisdom: "She reacheth therefore from end to end mightily, and ordereth all things sweetly," (Wisdom 8, 1). Likewise is it written: "The spirit of the Lord hath filled the whole world," (Wisdom 1, 7), and it is said to Him in a certain psalm: "Whither shall I go from thy spirit? or whither shall I flee from thy face? If I ascend into heaven, thou art there: if I descend into hell, thou are present," (Psal. 138, 7 and 8).

But thus is God everywhere diffused through everything, so that He is no quality of the universe but substance, creator of the universe, ruling without labour and containing the universe without burden. Yet He is not over expanses of place as when a mass is diffused, so that in half the universe He is half in body and half in another half and thus whole through the whole, but in heaven alone whole and on earth alone whole and in heaven and on earth whole and contained in no place but in Himself everywhere whole. Thus Father, thus Son, thus Holy Spirit, thus Trinity, one God. But this is much more wonderful, that although God is everywhere whole, yet He does not live in all things. For what the Apostle said cannot be said to all or what I already said or even this: "Know you not, that you are the temple of God, and that the Spirit of God dwelleth in you?" (1 Cor. 3, 16). Therefore, on the contrary the same Apostle says of certain ones: "Now if any man have not the Spirit of Christ, he is none of his," (Rom. 8, 9). Who, moreover, would dare to think, unless he were thoroughly ignorant of the inseparability of the Trinity, that the Father can dwell in someone, or the Son, in whom the Holy Spirit does not dwell, or the Holy Spirit in someone in whom both the Father and the Son do not?

Accordingly, we must confess that God is everywhere through the presence of divinity but not everywhere through the grace of divinity and of habitation. For on account of this habitation, where without doubt the grace of His love is recognized, we do not say: "Our Father who art everywhere," although this also is true, but: "Our Father who is in heaven," (Cf. Matt. 6, 1), that in prayer we may rather recall His temple which even we ourselves ought to be, and to the extent that we are, to such an extent do we belong to His society and family of adoption. Therefore, although He who is everywhere does not live in all, even in those in whom He dwells He does not dwell equally. For how is it that

Eliseus asked that the Spirit of God be made in him twofold what He was in Elias? (Cf. 4 Kings 9). And how is it that among all the saints some are more saintly, unless it is that they have God as a dweller more abundantly? How then is that true which we said above, that God is everywhere whole, when He is more in some, in others less? But what we have said is not to be looked upon carelessly: In Himself He is everywhere whole, not therefore in them because some take Him more, others less. For He is said to be everywhere, because He is absent to no part of things; He is whole, because not to one part of things does He furnish His part in presence and to the other part the other part but equal to the equal, to the less indeed less, and to the greater greater. Not only to universal creation but also to every part of it He is present equally whole.

Furthermore also what we thought could not be understood strictly, when we said that God was everywhere whole, unless we added "in Himself," must on this account be set forth more carefully. For how "everywhere in Himself"? "Everywhere" surely, because He is nowhere absent, but "in Himself," because He is not contained by those to whom He is present, as if He could not be without them. Now just as He is not absent from him in whom He does not dwell and is wholly present, although he does not possess Him, so too to him with whom He dwells He is wholly present, although he does not take Him wholly. For He does not divide Himself to dwell through the hearts or bodies of men, assigning one part of Himself to this one, another to that one, just as the light through the entrances and windows of houses but rather it is just as if, although sound is a corporeal and transitory thing, a deaf person does not receive any of it, a person hard of hearing does not receive it entirely; of these who hear, when they approach it equally, the one whose hearing is more acute receives it that much more, and the one whose hearing is more obtuse receives it that much less, although the sound does not resound in the air more or less but is present equally in that place where they all are. How much more excellently is God incorporeal nature, both immutable and alive, who like sound cannot be extended and divided through spaces of time and does not need airy space as His place to be at hand for those present; rather He Himself of eternal stability remaining in Himself can be present wholly to all things and wholly to each, although those in whom He dwells have Him according to the diversity of their capacity, some more, others less; those more whom He himself builds as a most loving temple for Himself because of His goodness.

On this account God is said to dwell also in men still animals, not yet spiritual, because in them He works secretly that they may be His temple, and this He accomplishes in those who make progress and persevere in making progress. Therefore, God who is present everywhere does not dwell everywhere wholly in all but only in them whom He makes His most blessed temple or most blessed temples, snatching them from the power of darkness and transferring them to the kingdom of His light which begins with regeneration. When, then, you consider His habitation, consider the unity and the congregation of the saints especially in heaven where He is said particularly to dwell, because there His will is made perfect in them in whom obedience dwells, at length in the land where He dwells building His home to be dedicated at the end of time. Now as for Christ our Lord the only begotten Son of God, equal to the Father, and the same Son of man, in as much as the Father is greater, do not doubt that He also is present everywhere wholly just as God; He is present in the same temple of God wholly just as the indwelling God and in some place of heaven after the manner of a true body.

Second Part

On the Spirit and Graces and on the Unity of the Church and the Distribution of Ecclesiastical Administration and on Those Things Which Pertain to its earthly power.

I. *On the grace which is given through Christ, and on the spirit which is diffused from the head into the members.*

It is written that the law brought no one to perfection, (Cf. Hebr. 7, 19). For the law was able to teach ignorance, was unable to aid infirmity. These were the two evils in man and from these all his other evils proceeded. One was ignorance, the other concupiscence; ignorance of good, concupiscence of evil. From ignorance comes crime, from concupiscence sin. Therefore, these two were in man from the beginning, but that man might know his sickness it was dismissed entirely from him lest perhaps he judge grace superfluous, if first he should not know the defect of his weakness. Thus then, the time of the natural law was set that nature might operate by itself, not because it could do anything by itself but that it might recognize that it could not. So left to itself it began to wander from truth through ignorance and was convicted of blindness; afterwards it was also to be convicted of weakness.

The written law was given to illuminate ignorance but not to strengthen weakness, so that man might be aided in that part by which he recognized his defect. Now when he thought that he stood by himself, he might have been abandoned. Therefore, having received knowledge of truth through the law, he began to try to accomplish but being pressed by concupiscence, because he did not have assisting grace, he failed of the work of virtue. Accordingly, he was convicted in both, because indeed by himself he can neither recognize truth nor accomplish good. Thus, after this, grace was fittingly given both to illuminate the blind and to cure the weak; to illuminate ignorance, to cool concupiscence; to illuminate unto the knowledge of truth; to inflame unto love of virtue. Therefore, the Spirit was given in fire that it might have light and flame; light unto knowledge, flame unto love.

Furthermore, just as the spirit of man through the medium of the head descends to vivify the members, so the Holy Spirit comes through Christ to Christians. For Christ is the head, the Christian the member. One head, many members, and one body consists of head and members and in one body is one spirit whose fullness in the head is, indeed, participation in the members. If then the body is one and the spirit one, which is not in the body itself, it cannot be vivified by the Spirit, as it is written: "He who has not the Spirit of Christ, is none of his," (Cf. Rom. 8, 9). For he who has not the Spirit of Christ is not a member of Christ. In body is one spirit. Nothing dead in the body, nothing alive outside the body. Through faith we are made members, through love we are vivified. Through faith we receive union, through charity we receive vivification. Now in the sacrament through baptism we are united; through the body and blood of Christ we are vivified. Through baptism we are made members of the body, but through the body of Christ we are made participants in vivification.

II. *On the Church; what the Church is.*

Holy Church is the body of Christ vivified by one Spirit, united by one faith and sanctified. All of the faithful exist individually as members of this body, all one body on account of one spirit and one faith. Now just as in the human body all members individually have their own proper and separate offices and yet each one does not do what it alone does, for itself alone, so in the body of Holy Church the gifts of graces have been distributed, and yet each one does not have for himself alone even that which he alone has. For the eyes alone see, and yet they do not see for themselves alone but for the whole body. Now the ears alone hear and yet they do not hear for themselves alone but for the whole body. The feet alone walk, and yet they do not walk for themselves alone but for the whole body. And in this way whatever everything has alone in itself, it does not have only account of itself, since according to the disposition of the best dispenser and most wise distributor they individually belong to all and all belong to the individuals. Whoever, therefore, has merited to receive the gift of the grace of God, let him know that what he has does not belong to him alone.

Thus by this likeness Holy Church, that is, the aggregate of the faithful, is called the body of Christ on account of the Spirit of Christ which it received, and man's sharing in it is designated when he is called Christian from Christ. Thus this name designates the members of Christ sharing in the Spirit of Christ, so that each is anointed by the Anointed, who is called Christian from Christ.

Christ indeed is interpreted as the Anointed, that is, with all that oil of joy which before all His sharers He received according to fullness and transfused to all His sharers as the head to the members according to the sharing. "Like the ointment on the head, that ran down from the head upon the beard and then even to the skirt," (Cf. Psal. 132, 2), that is, it flowed down to the extremity of the vestment so that it flowed forth upon the whole and vivified the whole. When, therefore, you are made a Christian, you are made a member of Christ, a member of the body of Christ sharing in the Spirit of Christ. What then is the Church but the multitude of the faithful, the aggregate of Christians?

III. *On the two bulwarks of the Church, laics and clerics.*

Now this aggregate embraces two orders, the laics and clerics, as it were, two sides of one body. For, as it were, on the left are clerics who attend to the necessity of the present life. I do not say "on the left" in the sense that they shall be placed on the left to whom it shall be said: "Depart from me, you cursed, into everlasting fire," (Cf. Matt. 25, 41). Far be it from me to presume to place the good laics there! For those who will be good, whether laics or clerics, will not be there and those who will be evil, whether laics or clerics, will be there. Not, therefore, on that left do I place Christian laics who are true Christians but on that left of which it is said: "Length of days in her right hand, and in her left hand riches and glory," (Prov. 3, 16). For that which is on the left hand of the body is of the body and is good, although it is not the best. Therefore, laic Christians who treat earthly things and the necessities of the earthly are the left part of the body of Christ. The clerics, indeed, since they dispense those things which pertain to the spiritual life are as it were, the right part of the body of Christ. But the whole body of Christ which is the universal Church consists of these two parts.

Laic is interpreted as *popularis,* for Greek λαός (laus) is said to be Latin *populus.* Wherefore also βασιλεύς (basileus) is thought to have meant *rex,* as if βάσις λαοῦ (basis laou), that is, "support of the people." Cleric is said to be from the Greek κλῆρος which interpreted in Latin means "lot," whether because he was elected by lot by God for the service of God or because God himself is his lot and because a cleric should not have another portion on earth but God and those things that look to the part of God, to whom it was agreed that support be given by the tithes and oblations which are offered to God. Therefore, the faithful Christian laics are allowed to possess earthly things, but to clerics spiritual things only are committed, just as once among that earlier people the other tribes which preferred the form of laics received portions in heredity. The tribe of Levi alone, which represented clerics, was supported by tithes and oblations and victims of sacrifices.

IV. That there are two lives and, according to the two lives, two peoples and in the two peoples two powers and in each power different grades and orders of ranks, and one superior to the other.

For there are two lives, the one earthly, the other heavenly; the one corporeal, the other spiritual; one by which the body lives from the soul, the other by which the soul lives from God. Both have their own good by which they are invigorated and nourished, so that they can subsist. The earthly life is nourished by earthly goods; the spiritual life is nurtured by spiritual goods. To the earthly life pertain all things that are earthly, to the spiritual life all goods that are spiritual. Now, that in both lives justice may be preserved and utility flourish, at first those have been distributed on each side who would acquire the goods of each according to necessity or reason by zeal and labor.

Then there are others who by the power of the office committed to them dispense according to equity, that no one may step over his brother in business but justice may be preserved inviolate. On this account powers were established in both peoples distributed according to both lives. Indeed, among the laics, to whose zeal and providence those things which are necessary for the earthly life belong, is earthly power. But among the clerics to whose office look those things which are the goods of the spiritual life is divine power. Thus the one power is said to be secular; the other is called spiritual. In both powers are diverse grades and orders of powers; yet in both they are distributed under one head and, as it were, deduced from one beginning and referred to one. The earthly power has as its head the king. The spiritual power has the highest pontifex. To the powers of the king pertain all things that are earthly and made for the earthly life. To the power of the highest pontifex pertain all things that are spiritual and attributed to the spiritual life. Now the more worthy the spiritual life is than the earthly and the spirit than the body, so much does the spiritual power precede the earthly or the secular in honor and in dignity.

For spiritual power has also to establish earthly power in order to exist, and it has to judge it, if it has not been good. Indeed, it itself was established first by God and when it goes astray it can be judged by God alone, just as it is written: "The spiritual man judgeth all things; and he himself is judged of no man," (1 Cor. 2). Now, it is manifestly declared among that ancient people of the Old Testament where the priesthood was first established by God that spiritual power, in so far as it looks to divine institution, is both prior in time and greater in dignity; afterwards indeed royal power was arranged through the priesthood at God's order. Wherefore, in the Church sacerdotal dignity still consecrates regal power, both sanctifying it through benediction and forming it through institution. If then, as the Apostle says, "He who blesses is greater, and he who is blessed less," (Cf. Hebr. 7), it is established without any doubt that earthly power which receives benediction from the spiritual is thought inferior by law.

V. *That every ecclesiastical administration consists of three things, that is, orders,*
sacraments, precepts.

Every ecclesiastical administration consists of three things: orders, sacraments, precepts. We consider orders in the persons of prelates, sacraments in their ministry, precepts in the conversation of subjects. These need special consideration individually. Regarding orders, this first must be considered, that some are according to different grades, as are deacon and priest, others in the same grade according to eminent power, as deacon and archdeacon. One grade is in the sacrament, yet there is not one power in the ministry. For the deacon ministers to the priest in the sacrament of the body and blood of Christ. Now the archdeacon has more than this, because in addition to the ministry of the altar under the bishop and in place of the bishop he has care of churches and examines ecclesiastical cases and dispenses ministries. Similarly the priest and pontifex or highest priest are one grade in the sacrament, yet different power in ministry, because, although both have in a manner the dignity of consecrating the body and blood of Christ, baptizing, catechizing, preaching, binding, loosing, yet a special power was granted to the pontifices of dedicating churches, making orders, imposing hands, consecrating holy chrism, making common benediction over the people. And so there is a difference of grades in the sacred orders; there is a difference of dignities in the same grade. But there is one order in earthly and secular power and another in spiritual power.

VI. *On earthly power.*

Earthly power pertains to earthly life, and all things that look to the earthly life are subject to earthly power. All these things pertain in a twofold manner to the law of earthly power, so that indeed earthly power itself distributes these according to justice, even to those who possess them, and defends them against the injustice of those who attack them. Now just as it is the duty of prelates to dispense justly to subjects things that are to be possessed and to defend them against injustice, so it is the duty of subjects, according to the institutes of the laws and rational customs, to show service to prelates both in themselves and in their own.

Now one service has been determined, such as census and tribute which are executed annually. Another is fortuitous, which indeed is exacted according to the faults which happen by chance. And although even this itself is determined by the laws according to the measure of sin, in this, however, to some extent it is not determined, because its event is not certain and it cannot be exacted by law except when the fault occurs for which it must be paid. This then is the discretion of the earthly power, that it may be known what prelates must show to subjects or what subjects to prelates for the earth itself or earthly substance about which a debt is paid to both.

VII. *How the Church possesses earthly things.*

Now regarding these earthly goods pertaining to earthly life, which either prelates possess in subjects or subjects possess from prelates, some have been conceded to the churches of Christ by the devotion of the faithful to be possessed, with, however, the preservation of the right of earthly power. For thus it is reasonable and good, because our God is a lover of peace, and true justice cannot approve anything inordinate. Because spiritual power does not preside, so as to give judgment in its own right to earthly power, just as earthly power itself never usurps without sin what is due to spiritual power, thus then when matters of the kind that look to earthly power are conceded to the churches of Christ, they indeed who are the dispensers of the gift can concede only in that which they possess, since neither subjects can transfer that which is due their superiors to another power nor prelates can bring in strange possessors in these things which are justly possessed by subjects; that is, prelates do not attribute what belongs to subordinates to others, nor do subjects presume to change what belongs to prelates.

Yet it must be noted that earthly rulers in earthly possessions, which they possess among subjects or without subjects, sometimes concede only utility to the Church, sometimes both utility and power. They concede utility without power when they decide, indeed, that the fruit of the possession be transferred to the use of the Church, but they do not permit the power of exercising justice in the possession itself to pass over to its jurisdiction. Sometimes they attribute both power and utility together wherein, however, careful attention must be had because, although the Church receives the fruit of earthly possession for its use, yet it cannot exercise the power of exercising justice through ecclesiastical persons or secular judgments; yet it can have as ministers lay persons through whom it may exercise laws and judgments pertaining to earthly power according to the tenor of laws and the obligation of earthly law; this is in such a way, however, that that itself which has power may recognize that it has it from the earthly ruler and may understand that the possessions themselves can never be so estranged from royal power; rather, if reason and necessity should demand, power itself should owe them support and the possessions themselves in necessity should owe obedience. For just as royal power cannot give to another the support which it owes, so also possession itself obtained by ecclesiastical persons can not deny the obedience which is due royal power for support by law. Just as it is written: "Render to Caesar the things that are Caesar's; and to God, the things that are God's," (Cf. Matt. 22, 21).

VIII. *In how many ways justice is to be determined in secular power.*

Surely it must be known that that justice which was given to earthly power among subjects is determined in five ways, according to person, according to cause, according to mode, according to place, and according to time. For what is permitted in one way is not straightway permitted in every way, and justice itself, unless it has been justly exhibited, loses the name of justice. Wherefore, what is permitted must be examined carefully as to how it is permitted, and the modes must be considered by which the form of justice is determined. According to person something is permitted and something is not permitted; just as to the secular judge it is permitted to lay hand upon a laic person if he has sinned, it is not permitted him to do so upon a cleric. According to cause justice is determined so that, for example, secular affairs are examined by earthly power but spiritual and ecclesiastic by spiritual power. According to mode or measure justice is determined when, for example, some fault is punished by a penalty congruous and fitting to it, so that private love does not subtract anything of equity in the penalty nor does private hate add to the severity due. According to place and time justice is determined if, where and when it is fitting, judgment is exercised and a sentence of truth is proffered. According to person then justice would be violated, if a secular judge should lay hand upon an ecclesiastic person; according to cause, if he should take up ecclesiastical affairs for examination; according to measure, if he should punish lying and malediction by hanging; according to place, if he should presume to violate sacred places, that is, if he should attempt to visit violence inordinately upon defendants who fled to these places when about to be condemned for their crimes; according to time, if he should not show reverence to sacred and solemn days, when even they must be spared to whom punishments are due for their faults. In these ways then secular power should exercise justice, following the institutes of the laws and approving nothing in their judging that is contrary to justice and truth. Now secular power has as its head the king or emperor, descending from him through subject powers, dukes and counts and prefects and other magistrates, all of whom, however, take authority from the first power in that they are placed over subjects.

IX. *On royal ornaments.*

Now secular power has certain ornaments of its dignity, by which both the excellence of the order is shown and the sacrament of the ministry is represented.

The ring designates faith, the bracelet good operation, the sceptre justice, the sword punishment, the purple reverence, the diadem glory. And indeed let these words suffice for the present on secular power.

Part Three

On the Spiritual Power.

I. *On clerics.*

Spiritual power in the cleric is arranged with different grades and orders of dignity. The first sign of the cleric is the crown by which he is marked for a part of the lot of the divine ministry, serving in which is ruling. The crown indeed signifies kingly dignity. Thus the blessed apostle Peter says: "You are a chosen generation, a kingly priesthood," (Cf. 1 Peter 2, 9). On this account, therefore, the hair of the head of a cleric is cut in the manner of a crown and the very top of the head is made bare from above and is uncovered so as to grant as understood through this that it is assumed unto kingly power in Christ, and that between him and God then there should be no veil, so that with face revealed and with mind pure he may contemplate the glory of his Lord. The top of the head is the top of the mind. The baring of the head signifies the illumination of the mind.

A cleric indeed should not be ignorant of the secrets of God, because he is His messenger to the people. For the hairs of the head are shorn even to the opening and unveiling of the senses, that is, of the eyes and of the ears, that occupation with earthly things, which are signified by the hair, may not impede him from hearing and understanding the words of God. Now after one has been made a cleric, he should then be sustained by the stipends of the Church and be taught in the divine science and ecclesiastical discipline under the tutelage and custody of spiritual masters, in order that, when reason demands, he may be able worthily to enter upon the sacred orders of the divine ministry. One is to be assumed to the clerical order only under a certain title. For those who have no head are acephalous not clerics.

II. *On ecclesiastical tonsure.*

Now the practice of ecclesiastical tonsure is thought to have originated with the Nazareans who, although they used to keep their hair, afterwards shaved the head on account of the continence of their lives and placed the hair in the fire of sacrifice. Then the practice was introduced by the presbyters that whoever are given over to divine worship and are consecrated to God as the Nazareans, that is, the holy ones, should be found with hair removed, as it is said to Ezechial: "Thou, son of man, take thee a sharp knife that shaveth the hair: and cause it to pass over thy head and over thy beard." (Ezech. 5, 1; cf. Acts 18, 18). We read also in the New Testament that those Nazareans, Priscilla and Aquila, in the Acts of the Apostles, did this first; also Paul of the Apostles and certain of the disciples of Christ who in worship of this kind are to be imitated, that is to say, so that by this sign vices growing in the heart and in deed may be taught to be destroyed.

III. *How the orders are among holy monks.*

Some are of the opinion that the crown is sometimes to be accepted as a sign of repentance, just as in the order of monks to whom the other sacred orders which are proper to the cleric are conceded by indulgence. For they cannot preside over people nor receive the care of spiritual dignity in the Church until they are assumed among the clerics. On this account what is in them of the sacred sign is as a matter of indulgence, not according to the power of choice among the people of God, but lest they be not able, even in the very habit of penitence, with which of their own accord they secluded themselves on account of God, to have sacrosanct communion with the body and blood of Christ or lest they be compelled to seek an impediment to their quiet externally. Therefore, that inwardly they may live more quietly, the orders of the divine ministry are conceded to them through indulgence, not to exercise preference among the people of God but to celebrate inwardly the communion of the sacrament of God, which, however, they say was not so in the beginning. For monks, even when dwelling in the wilderness, are read to have once had presbyters.

IV. *On the seven sacred grades.*

Therefore, the first sign of the cleric is the crown by which he is assigned to a part of the sacred ministry. Then follow seven promotions in grades, by which through spiritual power he ascends ever higher to carry on sacred things. The first grade is of porters, the second of readers, the third of exorcists, the fourth of acolytes, the fifth of subdeacons, the sixth of deacons, the seventh of priests. This last grade has different dignities in the same order. For after the priests are the higher rulers of the priests, that is bishops. Above these again are the archbishops and above these those who are called primates, above whom some wish to establish patriarchs; others call the same ones primates and patriarchs. Yet we find that only four according to the ancient custom of the Church were called patriarchs: first, of Alexandria; second, of Jerusalem; third, of Antioch; fourth, of Aquileia, who afterwards was called the Great; unless perhaps according to the peculiarities of tongues the same ones were called patriarchs in one place, primates in another. After all these follows the highest pontifex whom ecclesiastical usage has decreed to call Pope, that is, Father of fathers. This last is the principal and greatest successor of the apostolic see in the Roman Church, wherefore the Holy Church is accustomed to call him especially "apostolic," to whom presiding in place of Peter, chief of the Apostles, every ecclesiastical order should give obedience, who by privilege of dignity has the keys of binding and loosening everything upon earth.

These sacred orders then are being distributed in different places through the world, wherever the body of Holy Church is diffused, not only by the voluntary ordination of spiritual fathers but also according to the very practice of paganism, with the assumption of reason, since in those cities where once the pagans were accustomed to establish their flamens, there now bishops have been appointed. Where indeed archflamens had been disposed, archbishops succeeded. Read the book of Clement. There you will find how blessed Peter instituted that the rulers of the churches be disposed through the different places of the world. Therefore, the seven grades of spiritual offices were distributed in the Holy Church in like manner, according to the seven forms of grace which the Lord Jesus Christ having a plenitude of the same spirit exhibited all in Himself. And to His body, that is, the Church, He left all to be imitated, and to this Church He conceded participation in the Spirit itself.

V. *On porters.*

Among these seven grades of spiritual office the first is of those who are called porters, who in the Old Testament were once called door-keepers. To the office of porter belong the keys of the church, that he may close and open the temple of God at fitting hours and guard all things which are within and without, receive the faithful, eject the excommunicated and the infidels. When the porter is ordained, after he has been instructed by the archdeacon as to how he should live in the house of God, at the suggestion of the archdeacon the bishop gives him the keys of the church from the altar, saying to him: So act as if about to render an account to God for those things which are disclosed by these keys. This office the Lord assumed in His person when, making a whip of ropes, He ejected those who were selling and buying in the temple. For He himself, as a porter, says: "I am the door. By me, if any man enter, he shall be saved: and he shall go in, and go out, and shall find pastures," (Cf. John 10, 9).

VI. *On readers.*

The second grade is of readers who received form and beginning from the prophets. For readers are those who announce the word of God, to whom it is said: "Cry, cease not, lift up thy voice like a trumpet," (Isai. 58, 11). When these are first ordained according to their lives and faith and character, the bishop speaks to the people, then as the people look on a book of divine readings is given them by the bishop and it is said to them: Receive and be reporters of the Word of God, you who, if you fulfil your duty faithfully and usefully, are to have a part with those who have ministered the word of God. Therefore, from this they have the power to recite in the church in the presence of the people prophetic and apostolic readings. Those, indeed, who are promoted to this grade should be instructed in the knowledge of letters so as to understand the sense of that which they read; in pronunciation let them recognize the force of accents; let them read distinctly, lest by confusion of pronunciation they destroy the understanding of listeners. Let them consider what is to be read in the indicative, what is to be pronounced as an interrogation, where there is a distinction in speech or a middle distinction is to be made, since these matters when poorly observed disturb the intellect and provoke those who are of the stamp of grammarians to laughter. The voice of the reader should consult his ears and heart, not his eyes, lest by undisciplined motion or gesture on his own account he make spectators rather than hearers, equally avoiding broken and effeminate sounds as well as coarse and rustic sounds. For readers were once called heralds and proclaimers because they utter voice among the people. The Lord showed this office in His own person when, in the midst of old men, opening the book of Isaias the prophet He read distinctly for understanding: "The Spirit of the Lord has sent me to preach the gospel to the poor," (Cf. Luke 4, 18; Isai. 61, 1). Therefore, readers are granted to understand that they who announce the word of God to the people should shine with spiritual grace.

VII. *On exorcists.*

In the third place there follows the order of exorcists who perform the sacrament of opening over catechumens and have spiritual power over unclean spirits so as to eject them from obsessed bodies. Now he ought to have a clean spirit who orders unclean spirits, so that his life should not disagree with his office, and through cleanliness of life he should expel from his own heart the evil which, through the office that he has received, he expelled from the body of another. When these are ordained, they receive from the hand of the bishop a book of exorcisms and it is said to them: Receive and commend to memory and have the power of placing hands upon those possessed of the devil or upon catechumens.

Exorcists were established in the order and ministry of the Church according to the offices which had been disposed in the temple of Solomon, which were later distributed by Esdras. For under Esdras it is read that the sons of the servants of Solomon were managers of the temple, who had the business of the entire temple under their care or served the sacred oblations. And although they were of an order in the ministry of the temple, yet they were far from the office of the altar of God. For neither the psalmists, that is the cantors, nor the porters nor the servants of sacred things were permitted to attain to the duties of the altar, only the Levites. Therefore, the exorcists are, as it were, spiritual managers of the temple of God among the people of God, who from the substance of their Lord restore what was given over to them among spiritual gifts and what had collapsed among spiritual edifices, and prepare what has been dissipated. The Apostle refers to exorcists when he says: "Have all the grace of healing?" (Cf. 1 Cor. 12, 30). God used this office when with his saliva He touched the ears and tongue of the deaf and the dumb, saying: "Ephpheta, which is, Be thou opened,"

(Mark 7, 34), teaching by this example that we should spiritually open the ears of the hearts of man to understand, and mouths to confess, so that, when the demon has been expelled, the Holy Spirit may receive His vessel. Similarly He showed this office when He ejected seven demons from Mary Magdalene, (Cf. Mark 16, 9; Luke 8, 2).

VIII. *On acolytes.*

In the fourth place come acolytes, who in Latin are called candlebearers because they carry lighted candles while the gospel is being read or while the sacrafice is being offered, not that they may illumine the darkness of the air of this kind but that just as they bear a visible light in their hands, so they may show the works of light to their neighbours and in the manner of light furnish guidance to wanderers on the road in the enticing shadows. When these are being ordained, after they have been taught by the bishop how they should act in their office, they receive from the archdeacon a *ceroferarium,* that is, a candelabrum with wax, that they may know that they are assigned to furnish lights. They receive also an empty pitcher to pour wine in the chalice, in which the blood of Christ is to be consecrated, wherein there may be a commemoration of the blood flowing from Christ's side and of the water proceeding from it. These two are mixed in the chalice, because we have been redeemed by the blood of Christ and washed of sins by the water of baptism. The Lord testifies that He has this office in the Godhead saying: "I am the light of the world: he that followeth me, walketh not in darkness, but shall have the light of life," (John 8, 12).

IX. *On subdeacons.*

In the fifth place is the order of subdeacons, who among the Greeks are ὑποδιάκονοι. These are those who in Esdras are called Nathanei, that is, serving the Lord in humility, of whose order was that Nathanael who in the Gospel confesses the Saviour and by Him merited to be praised when the Lord said: "Behold an Israelite indeed, in whom there is no guile," (John 1, 47). These give service to the Levites, and they present the vessels of the body and blood of Christ at the altar to them and bear them back again.

Concerning these, indeed, it has pleased the Fathers that those who come in contact with the sacred mysteries observe the law of continence, as it is written: "Be ye clean, you that carry the vessels of the Lord," (Isa. 52, 11). These receive oblations from the peoples in the temples of the Lord. To provide these it is their duty to place on the altar as much of the oblations as can suffice for the people of God. Similarly, they themselves should wash the corporeal mantles and spreadings and prepare the water for baptism, also hold the pitcher and the water, the cloth and the towel for bishop and presbyter, and before the altar to furnish deacons with water to wash their hands. When these are ordained, just as priests and deacons, they do not receive the imposition of the hand but only the empty chalice and empty dish from the hand of the bishop.

From the hand of the archdeacon, indeed, they receive the pitcher with water, the cloth, and towel, with which the priest and deacon should cleanse their hand when about to handle the divine sacraments. The Lord performed this office when, after supper with the disciples was done, He girded himself with a towel and putting water into a basin washed the feet of the disciples and wiped them with the towel, (Cf. John 13, 4 and 5).

X. *On deacons.*

The order of deacons follows in sixth place, sixth not without some mystery, in which on account of their own perfection the perfection of works is signified. This order in the Old Testament has its origin from the tribe of Levi. For the Lord gave orders to Moses that after the ordination of Aaron and his sons the tribe of Levi again should be ordained for the ministries of divine worship and should be consecrated to God, and that they should do service for Israel in the presence of Aaron and his sons in the tabernacle of God; they themselves should bear the ark and the tabernacle and all its vessels and they should establish quarters in the neighbouring region of the tabernacle; in transporting the tabernacle they themselves should place it down and should put it together again. Now after twenty years and more they were ordered to serve in the tabernacle. This rule also the holy Fathers in the New Testament established, since this age is strong for carrying burdens, and this burden was established for that order by Moses. This also is represented in the New Testament when a stole is placed on the left shoulder of deacons and a chasuble is wound about the same shoulder on days of fasting, since whatever labour and patience we endure in this life we bear on the left, as it were, until we have rest on the right, that is, in eternity. This order in the New Testament took its beginning from the Apostles, for we read the following in the Acts of the Apostles. The Apostles selected for this office "seven men of good reputation full of the Holy Ghost" (Cf. Acts 6, 3), and "they praying imposed hands upon them," (Cf. Acts 6, 6).

And then the apostles and their successors decreed that in the entire Mother Church seven deacons of the higher rank assist around the Altar of Christ like columns of the altar, also not without some mystery in the number seven. In this it is represented that they, shining with the spirit of sevenfold grace, should be holy in body and spirit. These are the seven angels in the Apocalypse playing on the trumpet, (Cf. Apoc. 8, 2). These are the seven golden candlesticks, (Cf. Apoc. 1, 12). These are the seven voices of thunders, (Cf. Apoc. 4, 5). For they themselves with clear voice in the manner of a herald advise all either to pray or to bend knee or to sing the Psalms of David or to read and to hear the word. They themselves proclaim the gospel; they themselves dispense the sacraments of God. Without them the priest has name but not office. For just as in the priesthood there is consecration, so in the ministry there is dispensation of the sacrament. For priests themselves on account of presumption are not permitted to take the chalice of the Lord on the table, unless it has been given them by the deacon. The Levites place the victims upon the altar; they themselves arrange the table of the Lord. The Levites cover the ark of the testament, since not all should or can see the deep mysteries which are covered by the Levites. They themselves clothed in white vestments assist at the altar, so that the whiteness of their vestment signifies the cleanness of their lives and they approach the victims bright and immaculate. For the Lord should have for His ministers the kind of men who are not being corrupted by any contagion of flesh but shine with perfect chastity of mind and body.

For the Apostle teaches very fully when he describes to Timothy, (Cf. 1 Tim. 3, 8ff), the kind of men that should be ordained as deacons. For when he had first spoken of the election of bishops, straightway he added: The deacons likewise irreprehensible, that is without crime; chaste just as bishops, that is continent of lust; not double tongued, lest they disturb those who have peace; not given to much wine, because where drunkenness is there lust and fury dominates; not greedy for filthy lucre, lest from a heavenly service earthly gains be pursued. And after this he added: "And let those also first be proved; and so let them minister, having no crime." And so these just as bishops should be proved before ordination and, if they should be found worthy, thus at last admitted to the sacred ministry. When these are ordained, the bishop alone places hands upon them. Because they are attached to the ministry, not to the priesthood, the bishop places a napkin upon them, that is, a stole on their left shoulder, that by this they may know that they have received the yoke of the Lord in order to endure bravely all adversities pertaining to the left, that is, the present life, and in order to subject them to divine fear. They also receive the text of the Gospels from the hand of the bishop, through which they understand that they are heralds of the Gospel of Christ. For just as the readers are commanded to preach the Old Testament, so the deacons are commanded to preach the New, especially the Gospel which they alone may pronounce in the church.

It is their duty to assist the priests and to minister in all things which are done in the sacraments of Christ, namely, in baptism, in anointing, in dish, and in chalice, also to bring the oblations and dispose them on the altar, also to arrange and to clothe the table of the Lord, to carry the cross and to preach the Gospel and the Apostle. Their duties also include the office of prayers and the recitation of names. They themselves admonish ears unto the Lord, they themselves exhort to prayer. They themselves cry out and announce peace. The Lord used this office when, after the supper, by His own mouth and by His own hands He dispensed the sacraments which had been accomplished, and when He roused the sleeping apostles to prayer, saying: "Watch ye, and pray that ye enter not into temptation," (Matt. 26, 41).

XI. *On presbyters.*

In the seventh place follows the order of presbyters, who in the Old Testament took their beginning from the sons of Aaron. For those who were then called priests, are they who are now called presbyters, and those who were then spoken of as rulers of the priests are now termed bishops. Now the presbyters are interpreted as elders, because the Greeks call the elders presbyters. For the presbyters should be the elders among the people of God, not so much in age of body as in prudence of character and in maturity of good conversation, as it is written: "Venerable old age is not that of long time, nor counted by the number of years, but the understanding of a man is grey hairs. And a spotless life is old age," (Wisdom, 4, 8 and 9). Now there is this one difference between pontifices and priests of this time, that to the pontifices alone was attached the ordination of clerics, the dedication of basilicas, the consecration of sacred chrism, the imposition of the hand, and the common benediction over the people. Now in other sacraments, whether, for example, of catechizing or of baptizing or of celebrating mass and of consecrating the body and blood of Christ or of speaking in the church, both had common dispensation. Therefore, the privileges named above were reserved to the highest priests individually for this reason, lest the same authority of power indeed claimed by all alike would render the inferiors insolent toward those placed over them and create scandal by this loose bond of obedience.

Presbyters are the successors and vicars of the seventy disciples who preceded the Lord Jesus into every city and place where He himself was to go, (Cf. Luke 10, 1). Thus indeed the presbyters, who are assistants of the bishops, initiate pagans by catechizing the people, incorporate them into the unity of the church by baptizing, and in all the sacraments even to the imposition of the hand minister to the people of the Lord. The bishops indeed are the successors of the Apostles, who out of necessity for assistance and for the fulfilment of their office in so great a multitude seek for themselves the ministry of priests for ruling peoples, just as Moses in the desert chose seventy wise men with whose counsel and assistance he might rule more easily over so great a multitude. Whether they are priests of the lower or the higher order, that is, whether presbyters or bishops, they perform the duty of the highest pontifex when they call delinquent peoples to repentance and heal with the remedy of their sermons. Wherefore, the Apostle says: "God was in Christ, reconciling the world to himself, and he hath placed in us the word of reconciliation. For Christ, we beseech you, be reconciled to God," (Cf. 2 Cor. 5, 19 and 20). In this then priests function as mediators, that they entreat God for the sins of the people and by absolving reconcile the penitents. Therefore, it is fitting that as good mediators between men and God they both bring the precepts of God to the people by preaching truth and offer the prayers of the people to God by interceding for sinners.

"Now a mediator," as the Apostle says, "is not of one," (Gal. 3, 20), because he who is not in concord with both sides by the peace of association and the bond of friendship cannot reconcile the discordant, but on this account the priests should have peace with God through excellence of sanctity and should preserve concord with neighbours through a feeling of compassion. Therefore, the Apostle writing to Titus indicates the kind of nature that presbyters should have, saying: "For this cause I left thee in Crete, that thou shouldst ordain priests in cities as I appointed thee. If any be without crime, the husband of one wife, having faithful children, not accused of riot or unruly. For a bishop must be without crime," (Cf. Titus, 1, 5-7). In this statement he also shows that presbyters are classed under the name of bishops. Thence too he writes to Timothy on the ordination of a bishop and deacon, being silent about presbyters, whom he leaves to be understood under the name of bishops. Therefore, such also does the Apostle assert should be established presbyters in the Church just as bishops, and the canons following apostolic authority so testify.

When presbyters are being ordained, while the bishop blesses them and holds his hands over their heads, all the presbyters who are present raise their hands together with the hand of the bishop over their heads, and invoke the Holy Spirit upon those who are being ordained. The hands of presbyters, as of bishops, are anointed that they may know that they are receiving in this sacrament the grace of consecrating and should exercise in accordance with their strength works of mercy toward all. The anointing of the head especially pertains to a bishop, that he may understand that he is the vicar of Him about whom it is written: "God, thy God, hath anointed thee with the oil of gladness," (Psal. 44, 8). These, after the invocation of the Holy Spirit, receive a stole upon both shoulders, which in the manner of supports fortify the right and left sides, that from this they may understand that they, through the arms of justice, are fortified by the right and the left so that adversities may not break them nor prosperities exalt them. They receive both a chalice with wine and a basin with hosts from the hand of the bishop, in order that by these instruments they may realize that they have received the power of offering hosts pleasing to God.

To them it belongs to perform the sacrament of the body and blood of the Lord on the altar of God, to give sermons, and to bless the gifts of God. Our Lord Jesus Christ performed this office when, after the supper, He changed the bread and wine into His body and blood. When dying He appointed the apostles, that they might do likewise in memory of His passion. He also showed this, excellently fulfilling His office, when He himself as priest and victim offered Himself on the altar of the cross for the sins of mankind, and entering upon holy eternity by His blood pacified the heavenly and the earthly. In this it appears how great the excellence of the sacerdotal office is, through which the passion of Christ is celebrated daily on the altar, and every defendant being turned from sin is reconciled to God. After all these matters regarding the sacerdotal office have been treated briefly, the priests of Christ are to be admonished in order that, just as they excel by the dignity of their order, so they may excel by the sanctity of life, so that the people committed to them and taught by their teachings may obey them gladly and profit by imitating them from day to day.

XII. *On bishops.*

The sacred canons define that no one is to be elected as bishop except one who has first lived religiously in the sacred orders. Now they decree that only the diaconate and presbyterate are to be called sacred orders, because the primitive Church is described as having had only these, and only of these have we the precepts of the apostle. Yet, since subdeacons also administer to sacred altars, when the moment demands, the canons permit them to be elected bishops, but only very rarely and with the permission of the Roman Pontiff or metropolitan, provided he be of tested religion and proved knowledge. To bishops in a special manner belong the consecration of basilicas, the anointing of the altar, and the making of chrism, the imposition of the hand, and the common benediction over the people. He himself distributes the above-mentioned offices and ecclesiastical orders; he himself blesses sacred virgins. For while everyone has precedence in individual cases, he is the foreordainer in all.

No bishop should consecrate another as bishop without the consent of the metropolitan, nor should the metropolitan ordain a bishop without at least three bishops being present, all other bishops who are in the same province giving their consent. When indeed one is ordained, two bishops place and hold a copy of the Gospels over his head and above the top, and while one pronounces benediction over him all the remaining bishops who are present touch his head with their hands. His head is anointed with holy ointment, since all sanctification rests in the Holy Spirit whose invisible virtue is both signified and conferred in the ointment itself of holy chrism. When ordaining, the pontiff imposes the hand. The deacon reads the gospel selection; the notary writes the letter of confirmation. Finally both the ordainer and the ordained should celebrate mass at the ordination itself. And this form, indeed, for consecrating pontiffs has been handed down by the holy Fathers.

XIII. *On archbishops.*

But when an archbishop has to be admitted to office, all bishops of the same province should convene at the metropolitan seat in order that he may be admitted to office by all. For it is proper that he himself who has to preside over all those should be elected and consecrated by all those, otherwise the consecration is judged void. Now it is established that within three months of his consecration an archbishop send to the apostolic see to set forth his faith and receive the pallium, because he is judged to be of greater importance than a bishop. For an archbishop is over bishops and carries a pallium.

XIV. *On the highest pontiff.*

Since the apostolic see is preferred to all churches in the world, and it cannot have a metropolitan above it, the cardinal bishops without doubt perform the duty of the metropolitan who conduct an elected priest to the apex of the apostolic column. Now when the election has been made, if by chance accident or some violence interferes so that he who was elected cannot be enthroned according to custom, nevertheless the elected, as it is established, as pope should hold the authority of ruling the Holy Church and of disposing its faculties.

XV. *On the other offices which are in the clergy.*

These are orders and ministries of clerics. Yet these are divided into pontifical authority, into the duty of the archdeacon, and into the responsibility of the head chamberlain and of the treasurer.

XVI. *On archdeacons.*

The archdeacon gives orders to subdeacons and levites, and these ministries belong to him. The responsibility of parishes and ordination and disputes are a part of his care. He himself advises the priest on repairing diocesan basilicas; he inquires into parishes with the order of the bishop, into ornaments or properties of basilicas, or of parishes. The deeds of ecclesiastical liberties the same refers to the bishop; money collected from communion he himself receives and delivers to the bishop; and he dispenses certain other ministries of episcopal providence under the bishop as in part a counselor in the problem when examining ecclesiastical cases.

XVII. *On the head-chamberlain.*

The acolytes, the exorcists, the readers, and the psalmists, that is the cantors, pertain to the head-chamberlain; also the sign to be given for the office of clerics, for probity of life, and the office of singing, of performing carefully; who of the clerics should speak the readings, the benedictions, the praises of the psalms, the offertory, and the responses; also the order and mode of singing psalms in the chorus according to the solemnity and the time; the arrangement also for conveying lights. If anything is necessary for the repair of basilicas which are in the city, he reports to the priest. The letters of the bishop for parochial days of fast he directs through porters. The clerics whom he knows to be failing he himself importunes; he brings to the notice of the bishop the aberration of anyone whom he cannot emend. He himself establishes the frequenters of the basilicas and disposes the lists. Now when the head-chamberlain is absent, that one investigates the affairs which have been mentioned above, who is rather close to him or who by erudition is decided upon for fulfilling these matters.

XVIII. *On the treasurer.*

The treasurer's duties include the porters, the arranging of the basilicas, the preparation of incense, the care of making chrism, the care of arranging the baptistery, the preparation of lights at the sacrifice and of the sacrifice.

XIX. *When and how ordinations should be performed.*

Now the holy Fathers have decreed that sacred ordinations, namely, of presbyters and of deacons should be made only at certain times, that is, on the fast of the fourth month and of the seventh and of the tenth and on the day of the fortieth beginning and of the middle fortieth, about the evening of the Sabbath, after the fast has been celebrated. When indeed the bishop arranges to make ordinations, all who wish to enter into the sacred ministry must be called to the city on the fourth holiday before the ordination itself, together with the presbyter who should present them. Then accordingly the bishop should select from his side priests and other prudent men, wise in divine law and trained in ecclesiastical sanctions, to investigate carefully both the lives and the knowledge of those to be ordained without grace of favor or desire of gain according to truth, so that thus examined carefully for three successive days finally on the Sabbath those who have been found approved are presented to the bishop for consecration. Indeed, the sacred canons have sanctioned that the benedictions of pontiffs must be celebrated only on the Lord's day.

XX. *At what age those should be ordained who are ordained.*

Indeed, regarding the age of those to be ordained the explanation of Sacred Scripture has left the following distinction, that the subdeacon should not be ordained before fourteen years and the deacon not before twenty-five and the presbyter not before thirty, so that then, if he should have been found worthy, he can be elected to the episcopacy.

XXI. *That priests are not to be ordained without a definite title.*

Now of what importance is it to say that a presbyter or a deacon should not be ordained without a definite title when, even if we should follow the perfection of ecclesiastical discipline, he ought not to be taken otherwise among the clergy?

XXII. *Of what nature men should be who are to be elected to sacred orders and of what nature not.*

Now the fathers have left us many examples concerning the life and nature of those who are elected to sacred orders. For I have decided to define what does not bar those from sacred orders who have been of proven life. Those who are made lame perhaps from the incision of doctors or as the result of sickness or who through violence are torn asunder and who not of their own accord but by chance have amputated some limb of theirs, if however it was such as not to prevent them from work of administration; and laics who know not a concubine or mistress and have not been bigamous and have lived among others without crime; freemen who have been so manumitted by their lords that they have kept over them no right or power of obedience and have lived without crime, these they have decreed can be taken among the clergy without delay. They have decreed indeed that public penitents, the criminal, the illiterate, the bigamous, the husbands of divorced women, those born of adultery, those baptized by heretics, and those who have dismembered themselves are to be kept from sacred orders and those possessed should not be received among the clergy. But they have decreed that the sons of presbyters also must not be admitted to sacred orders, except those whom either the disposition of religion or the integrity of a spiritual life commends. Indeed, they have decreed that penitents, if necessity shall urge, are classed among the porters or among the readers, so that they do not read the Gospel or the Epistle. Now if they have been ordained among the subdeacons, they grant them to be retained there, so that they do not impose the hand and do not touch sacred things. By penitents we mean those who after baptism for homicide or for various crimes or for very grave sins enduring public penitence under a hair-covering have been reconciled at the divine altar. Similarly, they do not permit foreigners and unknown men or clerics of other churches to be ordained or to be received ordained without commendatory letters from their bishops.

XXIII. *For what reason a change of the ordained can be made.*

A change of bishops from their places to other places should for no reason be made except for great utility or pressing necessity. And this indeed should not be made by themselves but on the advice and invitation of fellow-bishops and by the authority of the Roman pontiff. Similarly a change of clerics or presbyters should not be made without great discretion, with the advice and authority of their own bishops. The sacred canons also forbid a cleric to be enrolled in the churches of two cities. They testify also that presbyters, abandoning the care of the churches, should not take up a journey either for preaching or for any other purpose without consulting their bishop. They also determine what those things are which presbyters should necessarily know, namely, the book of the sacraments, the lectionary, the baptistery, compotum, the canon, the penetential, the psalter, homilies suited during the course of the year to Sundays and individual feast days, and many other things which concerning the life and intercourse of sacred orders either have been mentioned reasonably or are to be done of necessity.

PART FOUR

On Sacred Garments.

I. *On sacred garments.*

The priests and ministers of Christ should know that a special habit is assigned to those in the sacred ministry, that by means of what appears externally it may be shown of what nature they should be within. Now the ceremony concerned with vestments is a holy thing; it was taken partly from the Old Testament, partly expanded by the late Fathers. We read (Cf. Leviticus 8) that Moses placed his brother Aaron with his sons at the door of the tabernacle as a testimony to be sanctified and, washed with water, he vested him with a tunic of byssus; then he girded him with the girdle and vested him with an interior tunic and placed over it the ephod and he bound it according to the formation of the ephod and placed upon it the logion, that is the rational, on which were Doctrine and Truth; however, he placed the mitre upon his head, and upon the mitre over the forehead he put the plate of gold on which the name of God was inscribed, (Cf. Leviticus 8, 2-9). If you enumerate the aforementioned seven instruments of pontifical dress, you will find indeed the tunic of byssus, the girdle, the interior tunic, the ephod, the rational, the mitre, and the plate of gold, and, if to these you add the thigh bandages, which according to the sacred rite were bound about the thighs of the pontiff, the sacerdotal garments amount to eight.

II. *On the tunic of byssus.*

The tunic of byssus is what the Greeks call ποδήρης, that is, "reaching to the ankles," because it extends from the neck even to the ankles; this in the new priesthood is woven not only from byssus but also from linen, which modified and fitted to the members of the body shows that there should be nothing superfluous or dissolute in the life of a priest. This, on account of the species of its brilliancy, receives the name of alba which signifies the cleanness of the ministers of God. As it was written: "The fine linens are the justifications of saints," (Apoc. 19, 8). For the flesh of man acquires the cleanness, which it does not have from nature, through grace with the help of zeal, so that according to the Apostle the minister of Christ chastises his body and brings it into subjection, (Cf. 1 Cor. 9, 27), just as byssus or linen acquires the splendor which it did not have from nature through zeal and industry, being worn bright by many beatings and, as it were, by a kind of violent shaking.

III. *On the girdle.*

This vestment, that is, the linen tunic, is drawn tightly about the loins as a girdle, that the chastity of the priest may not be broken by any impulsive incentive, as it is written: "Let your loins be girt," (Cf. Luke 12, 35). For the white garment signifies cleanness, the girdle indeed continence, so that in the one spiritual life does not grow sordid, in the other it does not flow forth. This girdle in the Old Testament is found distinguished by four colors, namely, byssus, purple, hyacinth, scarlet, which men have variously interpreted as referring either to the four elements, with whose combination human nature corresponds, so that all that is man's is bound and checked from the flow of sins, or to the four principal virtues of the spirit by which on every side man should be girt and fortified.

IV. *On the linen thigh-bandages.*

This also is as a sign of the same chastity which is designated by the tunic and girdle, that together with the other sacred garments linen thigh-bandages are ordered to be applied about the loins of those entering the sacred ministry, not so much out of necessity to veil the baseness covered by the customary garments of daily use as to indicate the preservation of chastity and cleanness. And we should not think that among that earlier people men walked with the flesh of shame uncovered or unveiled, and that at length they were ordered to cover their private parts as they were about to enter sacred and revered places. But God by these words wished His ministers in sacred office to have a proper and special covering to clothe the weaknesses of the body, that by this He might show that their modesty and chastity should be unique and special, especially when they handled sacred things. Therefore the ministers of the new priesthood do not assume this special covering in sacred office, who have been charged with the daily necessity of preserving chastity as well as endowed with the power of offering daily. The ministers of the old order indeed at the time of offering the sacrifice take on the thigh-bandages which they loose again when the ministry has been fulfilled, since the old law prevented those about to handle sacred things from contact with flesh and again, when their turn was fulfilled, released them to the labour of carnal commerce. Now the two remaining garments, that is, the linen tunic and the girdle, are known to be common to the priests of the Old and the New Testaments, although the new priesthood does not require a girdle interwoven with four colors, perhaps for the sake of avoiding superstition or, influenced by lack of handicraft, remaining content with pure and simple continence.

V. *On the interior tunic.*

Next we have the fourth garment, the interior or hyacinthine tunic, which in the Old and New Testaments the pontiffs alone use. And fittingly does the pontiff put on two tunics, who should from his treasury offer the new and the old. Therefore, the second tunic is also called interior or hyacinthine, whose color imitates the appearance of the serene sky, that accordingly it may be understood that a pontiff should think more upon heavenly than upon earthly things. The proper order follows: First, in the linen tunic and girdle and thigh-bandages cleanness of flesh is expressed; then, through the inner or hyacinthine tunic cleanness of heart is signified.

VI. *On the superhumeral.*

The fifth vestment is the superhumeral which in Hebrew is called Ephot. In the Old Testament the pontiffs alone used this, distinguished by the same colors as the girdle also had been. Now under grace this vestment is common to priests as well as to pontiffs. What we said was signified in the girdle by the four colors, this very thing we find signified by the same three colors of the superhumeral. The superhumeral signifies fortitude in work and patience in labour, and accordingly it is placed upon the shoulder which carries burdens. On the superhumeral itself, on the two precious stones, one of which was placed on the right shoulder, the other on the left, the names of the twelve patriarchs had been inscribed, six on one and six on the other, because by the names of the patriarchs is understood the memory of the saints, which the priest on the right and on the left, that is, in prosperous and in adverse circumstances, should always have and carry impressed on the heart. Now our priesthood does not have the superhumeral similarly interwoven like the old, in as much as the Christian religion should be zealous for simple truth rather than for superstition.

VII. *On the rational which in Greek is called the logion.*

The rational or logion which is placed upon the breast of the pontiff follows, to show that there should be wisdom and discretion in his heart. Now on the rational doctrine and truth are placed that the pontiff in his teaching may presume to proclaim nothing but what the truth suggests, that he may not cease to approve and declare what he has imbibed from the truth. We should note of course, that the rational and superhumeral are joined together, since they should cling together and should harmonize reason and work, that what we perceive with the intellect of the mind we may fulfill by work. We should note also that the rational is not named before the superhumeral, because in the school the works of virtue precede that you may understand wisdom, as it is written: "By thy commandments I have had understanding," (Psal. 118, 104). And again:

"Things which Jesus began to do and to teach," (Cf. Acts 1, 1). Then teaching follows after the rational, lest you presume to teach what you have not first learned. With this the fact also harmonizes that on the rational itself twelve stones had been inserted with the names of the twelve patriarchs inscribed on them, since the pontiff should have the examples of the holy Fathers impressed on his memory and should regulate his deeds according to theirs.

VIII. *On the mitre which is called cydaris or tiara, and on the golden plate.*

After the other ornaments the mitre is placed upon the head of the pontiff, which by another name is called cydaris or tiara and by which the reign of the five senses that have their seat in the head is signified. Therefore, the minister who guides his life well adorns his head as Christ, since indeed as the Apostle says: "The head of Christ is God," (Cf. 1 Cor. 11, 3). Upon the ornament of the head is fittingly placed last of all a golden plate, on which is inscribed the name of God, which in Hebrew is called "ineffabile," that through this it may be signified that, just as God was the creator of all things, so also is He the Director of the universe and to His honor and glory whatever has been well dispensed by the sacred priests and ministers must be referred. Moses in Exodus (Cf. 28), therefore, has established that these garments should be eight but in Leviticus (Cf. 8), treating of the same garments, he was silent about the eighth, that is, the thigh bandages, perhaps because the law does not regulate about the generative or private parts of us who should make a voluntary sacrifice of our chastity to God, as it is written: "Concerning virgins, I have no commandment of the Lord," (1 Cor. 7, 25). And the Lord himself speaking of voluntary eunuchs added: "He that can take, let him take it," (Matt. 19, 12), as if He should say: I clothe not in thigh-bandages; I do not impose the necessity on anyone. Whoever wishes to be a priest let him clothe himself and, when he is about to enter upon sacred things, let him voluntarily take up the protection of chastity by covering his private parts. Indeed we must note that neither the hyacinthine tunic nor the superhumeral nor the rational nor the golden plate, which the pontifices alone use, that is the highest priests, are given to the priests of the lower order, but only the poderis and the mitre and the girdle with which the poderis itself is bound, that is, the byssine tunic, because to be one, they enjoy the priesthood but not in that dignity with which the priesthood is enjoyed by those who are decorated with eight garments.

IX. *On the garments of the new priesthood.*

These then are the garments which the new priesthood assumed from the Old Testament: the linen tunic, the girdle, the superhumeral, the interior tunic, the rational, and the mitre, but the pontifices alone use the interior tunic, the rational. The new priesthood does not have the golden plate. Instead the sign of the cross is now imprinted on the foreheads of the faithful, since the blood of the Gospel is more precious than the gold of the law.

X. *On the stole or the napkin.*

The following are the things that the new institution has added to the old. The stole, which by another name is called napkin, is that which is placed upon the neck of the priest to signify that he has assumed the yoke of the Lord. This descends from the neck over the front, adorns the right and left sides, to teach that the priest should be fortified by the arms of justice on the right and on the left, that is, in prosperous and adverse circumstances, as it is written: "Patience is necessary for you, that you bring back the promises," (Cf. Heb. 10, 36). And again: "He that shall persevere unto the end, he shall be saved," (Cf. Matt. 10, 22; 24, 13). Hence it is that the stole and the girdle of the poderis are gathered together by a kind of knot, because virtues are associated with virtues lest they be moved by some impulse of temptation.

XI. *On the planata or casula.*

Thus then, when the priest of the Lord has been adorned with cleanness by the tunic, with continence by the girdle, with justice by the superhumeral, with patience by the stole, finally upon all is placed the casula which signifies charity, as it is written: "I show unto you yet a more excellent way," (1 Cor. 12, 31). "If I speak with the tongues of men, and of angels, and have not charity, I am nothing," (Cf. 1 Cor. 13, 1).

XII. *On the napkin or maniple.*

Since, even when the mind is well composed and devoted to divine worship, negligence at times steals in, we must apply perpetual diligence to purge this. In this way a kind of rheum, so to speak, dropping from the eyes may be cleansed again and again. So a kind of napkin is placed in the left hand. This often touches the flowing rheum of the eyes and wipes away the bleardness of the eyes.

XIII. *On the dalmatica.*

The Levites, moreover, use another garment which is called the dalmatica. The name, in fact, is from the region where its use is first thought to have been established, but it takes its form, with sleeves added, from the colobium which the apostles and certain successors of the apostles are said to have used. Now the dalmatica, because of its width, signifies care of neighbours which through love spreads out so as to benefit the majority. Therefore, both the significance of the dalmatica among the Levites and the significance of the casula among the presbyters tend toward one end, since care and anxiety for neighbours, to be fulfilled through love, is enjoined upon both.

XIV. *On sandals and half-boots of byssus or linen.*

Now the bishops and the cardinal presbyters use sandals which are the shoes of preachers. These have a whole sole beneath, lest the foot touch the ground, but above they consist of leather perforated here and there, because the steps of preachers should be fortified below that they be not polluted by earthly things and open above that they be open to know heavenly things. That they are open in certain places signifies that evangelical preaching should not be revealed to all nor concealed from all, as it is written: "To you it is given to know the mystery of the kingdom of God, but to the rest in parables," (Cf. Luke 8, 10). For the sandals are opened where the mysteries of the kingdom of God are known. Before they put sandals on the feet, they put on half-boots of byssus or linen, extending even to the knees where they are bound. By this it is signified that they should take straight steps with their feet and should strengthen their weak knees, which have been loosed by negligence, and thus hasten to preach the Gospel.

XV. *On the staff and the ring of the bishop.*

Pontifices use staffs and rings. The staff by its straightness signifies the justice with which prelates should rule subjects. The staff has a point below, that by rebuke he may chide the rebellious; it is curved from above, that by consolation he may attract the kindly. The ring signifies the sacrament of faith, by which the spouse of Christ, the Church, is pledged, whose guardians and teachers, the bishops and prelates, bear the ring as a sign in testimony of this.

XVI. *On the pallium of the archbishop.*

Archbishops use the pallium signified by a golden necklace which they were accustomed to assume as they strove according to law. By this necklace with which the shoulders are bound, are signified the fear and the discipline of the Lord with which they should rule themselves and those subject to themselves. Indeed by the two cords from each side, that is, hanging down from the top in front and in back, the preaching of both Testaments or the love of God and neighbour is symbolized.

XVII. *On the sacred vessels.*

The following are the sacred vessels in the divine ministry, which we have briefly touched upon. The altar signifies the cross, the chalice the sepulchre, the dish the stone, the corporeal palla the muslin with which the body of Christ was wrapped.

On the Dedication of a Church.

I. *On the dedication of a church.*

After the orders which we have presented in the first part of the ecclesiastical administration we pass to a consideration of the sacraments. It seems that we must speak first about the sacrament of the dedication of a church, in which all the other sacraments are celebrated. Above in this treatise which we have set forth in general on the sacraments we made a distinction, that some sacraments were of salvation, some of administration, some of exercise; the first for remedy, the second for office, the third for practice. And indeed those which are of administration or preparation are connected with orders, since both the orders themselves are sacraments and those things also which are considered in connection with orders, such as the sacred garments and the vessels and other things of this kind. All these things, because, as has been said, they are considered in connection with the orders themselves, should not have been treated separately. Some considerations indeed demand that all sacraments be treated subsequently, for the performance and sanctification of which all these things have been set forth first as sort of instruments.

First, as has been said, we must speak of the dedication of a church, just as of the first baptism by which the church itself in a manner is baptized, that in it after a fashion men may be baptized to be regenerated unto salvation. For the first sacrament, as it were, is recognized in baptism through which all the faithful are computed among the members of the body of Christ through the grace of the new regeneration. Therefore, this comes up first for discussion. Regeneration is first symbolized in the dedication of a church; then it is exhibited in the sanctification of a faithful soul. For what is expressed visibly in a figure in this house is exhibited entirely through invisible truth in the faithful soul. For the faithful soul is the true temple of God by the covenant of virtues which is built, as it were, by a kind of structure of spiritual stones, where faith makes the foundation, hope raises the building, charity imposes the finish. But the Church herself also, brought together as one from the multitude of the faithful, is the house of God constructed of living stones, where Christ has been placed as the corner stone, joining the two walls of the Jews and the gentiles in one faith. Thus we set forth first what is shown in the dedication of the church as the form of this sacrament, that we may seek next the mystical understanding of the faith which is formed in it.

II. *Concerning these things which are carried on visibly in it.*

First, the pontiff blesses the water, mixing figurative salt, then outside he sprinkles the church itself going around it three times, the clergy and people following him. Meanwhile in the course of dedicating the church, twelve lamps are lighted within it. Then coming through each place to the door of the basilica, which for the figure of the sacrament should have been closed, he strikes its lintel with the pastoral branch, saying: "Lift up your gates, O ye princes, and be ye lifted up, O eternal gates," (Psal. 23, 7). And to this the deacon stationed within the church replies: "Who is this King of Glory?" (Psal. 23, 8 and 10). And the pontifex replies: "The Lord of hosts, he is the King of Glory," (Psal. 23, 10). Then in the third place, when the door is unlocked, the pontifex with the clergy and the people enters saying three times: "Peace be to this house," (Luke 10, 5). Then with the priests and Levites and clerics he prostrates himself for prayer for the sanctification of the house which is to be dedicated. Afterwards rising from prayer, not yet addressing the people, by saying: "The Lord be with you," (Ruth, 2, 4), he only exhorts all to pray. When this is completed, he begins from the left corner of the basilica from the east to write the alphabet over the pavement all the way to the right corner of the west and again from the right corner of the east all the way to the left corner of the west. Then he ascends to higher places and standing before the altar he invokes God to his assistance saying: "O God, come to my assistance," (Psal. 69, 2), completing the verses with the Gloria, without Alleluia.

After this he blesses water, mixing salt and ashes and making the sign of the cross three times upon it, to which mixture wine also is added. After this he dips a finger in the water and makes a cross over the four corners of the altar. Then he comes before the altar and walking around he sprinkles it in seven places, the sprinkling being made with hyssop. Then he walks around the entire church three times, sprinkling its walls within with the same water, doing this even a third time. Meanwhile a psalm is being sung: "Let God arise," (Psal. 67), with antiphonal. The antiphonal is also sung: "He that dwelleth in the aid of the most High," (Psal. 90). Then the pontiff himself goes about, crossing through the middle of the church and singing: "My house shall be called the house of prayer, etc." (Isa. 56, 7: Matt. 21, 13). And again: "I will declare thy name to my brethren: in the midst of the church will I praise thee," (Psal. 21, 23). Now when these things have been done, the pontiff takes himself to prayer, asking that all who have entered the same house to pray rejoice that they have been heard. And so when the expiation has been completed he returns toward the altar beginning the antiphonal: "I will go in to the altar of God," (Psal. 42, 4), with the psalm itself and he pours forth upon the base what is left of the water of purification. Then the altar is wiped with linen and the pontiff offers incense upon it. Afterwards he makes a cross with sanctified oil in the middle of the altar and over its four corners. Then around the church twelve crosses are anointed on the walls, three marked individually by the pontiff himself. Then returning again to the altar he offers upon it burned incense in the form of a cross and finally when the consecration has been completed the altar is uncovered of its white veils.

III. *What the mystery of the above mentioned matters is.*

Many profound mysteries lie hidden in all these things and of these we will touch upon a few which should be brought to mind. A house to be dedicated is a soul to be sanctified. Water is penance washing away the stains of sins. Salt is the divine sermon which stirs by chiding and flavors the insipid things in the heart. The threefold aspersion is the threefold immersion of purifying through water. The twelve lamps are the apostles, illuminating the church through the four parts of the world, and carrying the mystery of the cross throughout the whole world. The pontiff is Christ, the branch power, the threefold striking of the lintel the domination of heaven, earth, and hell, the question of the one inclosed the ignorance of the people, the opening of the door the removal of sin. The pontiff entering the church implores peace upon the house, because Christ on entering the world made peace between God and man. Before the sanctification of the house he prays prostrate, and Christ, humbled before the disciples and before all who were ready to believe, prayed to the Father, saying: "Father, sanctifying them in thy name," (Cf. John 17). Now rising to prayer he does not address the people, since those who have not yet been sanctified should not be given approval but should pray for themselves. The writing of the alphabet is the simple teaching of faith. The pavement is the human heart. The alphabet is described on the pavement because carnal and rude people are initiated by the first and simple teachings of faith. Escorted from the left corner of the east to the right of the west and likewise from the right corner of the east to the left of the west, he expresses the form of the cross which is impressed upon the minds of the people by the faith of the evangelical preaching, and likewise because faith was first among the Jews and afterwards passed over to the gentiles and again finally the fullness of the gentiles shall come in, then all Israel shall be saved, (Cf. Rom. 11, 25 and 26). Therefore, these two verses arranged in the sign of the cross signify the gathering of both peoples, that is, that Jacob blessing the sons of Joseph, expressing the form of a cross with hands cross-wise, placed the right hand upon the head of Ephraim and the left upon the head of Manasse, since after the earlier people were cast aside the younger were placed on the right, (Cf. Gen. 48). The cambria or pastoral branch, by which Scripture is represented, signifies the ministry of the doctors by whose zeal and preaching the conversion of the gentiles has been made and that of the Jews is to be made.

His standing before the altar and calling God to help signifies those who, after they have received a knowledge of faith, gird themselves for good works and for the struggle against invisible enemies and, because they presume less on their own strength, ask that divine assistance be present to them. In this, since the labour of those in the struggle is expressed, as it were, in the midst of sighs, and groans, "Alleluia" is not yet spoken. After this the water is blessed with salt and ashes, wine being added to the mixture of water. The water is the people, the salt teaching, the ashes the memory of the passion of Christ, the wine mixed with water Christ, God and man, wine divinity, water mortality. For thus the people are sanctified by the teaching of faith and by the memory of the passion of Christ, united with their head, God and man. After this the Church is sprinkled within with holy water, that the soul to be sanctified may be shown both within and without. The sprinkling of hyssop signifies the humility of Christ by which the holy Church is sprinkled and cleansed. The pontiff goes around the altar, by word and example showing himself common to all both by sprinkling the entire church, as it were, by purifying all and by giving care to all. On this account also he completes the work with a prayer, praying that those seeking justice there be heard, since the work of man without divine assistance can be but cannot be fruitful. Lastly, when the expiation has been completed the pontiff turns to the altar, pouring forth upon its base what is left of the water of purification, as if committing to God what is above his strength, departing at the completion of his sacred ministry.

Then the altar is wiped with linen. The altar is Christ upon whom we offer to the Father the gift of our devotion. The linen is His flesh, brought by the beatings of the passion to the whiteness of incorruption, the incense the prayers of the saints. Now the oil demonstrates the grace of the Holy Spirit whose fullness preceded on the head; then participation flowed to the limbs. From the consecrated altar twelve crosses are anointed on the walls, because spiritual grace descended from Christ upon the apostles, so that they proclaimed the mystery of the cross with the faith of the Trinity through the four parts of the world. The white covering with which the altar is covered after the consecration designates the glory of incorruption with which after the passion, when the mortality of the Jews was fulfilled, humanity was clothed, as it is written: "Thou hast cut my sack cloth, and hast compassed me with gladness," (Psal. 29, 12).

PART SIX

On the Sacrament of Baptism.

I. *On the sacrament of baptism.*

The sacrament of baptism is the first among all the sacraments upon which salvation is proven to rest. For the Lord has said regarding it: "Unless a man be born again of the water and the Holy Ghost, he cannot enter into the kingdom of God," (John 3, 5). And again: "He that believeth and is baptized shall be saved," (Mark 16, 16). These then are the things which we principally propose for inquiry on the sacrament of baptism: first, what is baptism; second, why baptism was established or why circumcision and certain other sacraments of the Old Law were changed; third, when baptism was established, and about the three times—first, when circumcision had status before baptism; finally, when baptism had status after circumcision; medially, when circumcision and baptism ran simultaneously, the one so that it was finished, the other so that it was confirmed; likewise, when men began to be bound by the precept of receiving baptism; likewise, what difference there is between the baptism of John and of Christ; likewise, what was the form of the baptism of John; likewise, what is the form of the baptism of Christ; likewise, whether anyone can be saved without actually receiving the sacrament of baptism. Much remains to be asked about all these things, but let us for the time follow up a few matters according to our ability.

II. *What baptism is.*

If, therefore, it is asked what baptism is, we say that baptism is the water sanctified by the word of God for washing away sins. For water alone can be an element; there cannot be a sacrament until word is added to the element and there be a sacrament. For the element is sanctified through word; so that it receives the virtue of a sacrament; so that, just as the element represents from some natural quality and signifies from superadded institution, thus the element from sanctification contains spiritual grace which is to be obtained through it by those to be sanctified. Now we understand the way by which the element is sanctified, so as to be a sacrament, about which it is said: "Going therefore, teach ye all nations: baptizing them in the name of the Father, and of the Son, and of the Holy Ghost," (Cf. Matt. 28, 19). Therefore, "the name of the Father, and of the Son, and of the Holy Ghost" is the word of God, through which the element is sanctified so as to be a sacrament. And rightly are those things sanctified through the word of God, which subsist created through the word of God: "For he spoke, and they were made," (Psal. 148, 4). Through word He was able to create and through word can He not sanctify? To what He gave subsistence through word do you not think that He can add grace through word? So do not wonder if, through the word of God, that is sanctified which was instituted as a sacrament for the remedy of salvation.

But perhaps your thoughts say: What is that word of God? What is this "the name of the Father, and of the Son, and of the Holy Ghost" in which we are ordered to be baptized? Should we consider this as any word and sound brought forth to human ears? If some word should be understood as the name of the Trinity, what and of what nature should the word itself be understood? If we say that this word "God" is that name, it follows that where that sound is not uttered over the water to be sanctified, there cannot be the sacrament of baptism.

What then? You immersed a man and you said: "I baptize thee in the name of the Father, and of the Son, and of the Holy Ghost." And you say to me: This man is a Christian. He was baptized in the name of the Father and of the Son and of the Holy Ghost. I immersed him three times in the water. I said when I immersed him: "I baptize thee in the name of the Father, and of the Son, and of the Holy Ghost." I, therefore, assist as a witness because this man was baptized in the name of the Father and of the Son and of the Holy Ghost.

He was baptized in the name of the Trinity. In what name? You told me that the name of the Trinity is God. This name I did not hear here when you said: In the name of the Father and of the Son and of the Holy Ghost. What name then did you wish to say? You said that you baptized in the name of the Father and of the Son and of the Holy Ghost. And you did not say that name about which you spoke. How then was the water sanctified in a name that was not said? But if you think that you said the name of the Father and of the Son and of the Holy Ghost in this, because you said: "In the name of the Father, and of the Son, and of the Holy Ghost," and that "in the name of the Father, and of the Son, and of the Holy Ghost" is to be understood thus, in as much as the name of the Father is said there where "of the Father" is said; and the name of the Son is said where "of the Son" is said; and the name of the Holy Ghost is said where "of the Holy Ghost" is said, then there are many names, not one. I have received the precept of the Lord, that I should baptize in the *name* of the Father and of the Son and of the Holy Ghost but you have baptized in many names. Father and Son and Holy Ghost are three names and the names of three, not one name nor the name of one, because the three are not one although the three are one thing. Now He himself did not say "in the names" but He said: "In the name of the Father, and of the Son, and of the Holy Ghost," because there is one name where there is one nature, one substance, one divinity, one majesty. Now this is the name whereby all should be saved, (Cf. Acts 4, 12).

Therefore, I would like you to show me where you uttered this one name of the Father and of the Son and of the Holy Ghost, and when immersing the man you said: "I baptize thee in the name of the Father, and of the Son, and of the Holy Ghost." If, then, you conceive some such thing in your mind and demand to be taught what the name of the Father and of the Son and of the Holy Ghost is in which we are baptized and obtain the remission of sins, I think that the diligence of your faith should by no means be contemned. For how can we baptize in the name, if we are ignorant of it? We cry out daily: "Hallowed be thy name" (Matt. 6, 9). But how is it hallowed in us, if we do not know it? And if we seek that a word be hallowed, let him who can, say how we ask to be saved in a word? "Save me, O God," he says, "by thy name," (Psal. 53, 3). If then salvation is in a word, those who are silent or rather are not able to speak cannot be saved because they cannot speak. Who would say this? Then we should seek the name of God in which we should be hallowed and be saved outside a word, lest by chance, if we place it in a single word, we cause scandal to truth. "In Judea, God is known: his name is great in Israel," (Psal. 75, 2). Therefore, where there is a celebrity, there there is name because the celebrity itself is a name. Someone says: Of great name is that man, and that man has a great name among the people. Perhaps because his name has many syllables, on this account his name is great. Then the name of God (*Deus*) is small because it embraces only two syllables and the name of God (*Deus*) is formed by two syllables. You see now where the magnitude of God's name is. For where the magnitude of the name is there also should we consider the name itself; if then we understand fittingly the magnitude of the name, the magnitude of the fame, and the magnitude of the celebrity, we should understand the name itself as the fame and the celebrity rather than some word or sound of a word coming to the ears. Then His fame and His celebrity itself is His name. And again His celebrity is nothing else than His faith, since through faith alone is God really known now, who is afterwards to be known by appearance. Faith in God then is the name of God through which His celebrity is now enjoyed among men, where thus far His presence is not seen by men. I think that there is no obscurity or ambiguity about his being saved in the name of God, who, in that he was able to feel about Him and by feeling believed, is justified and being justified is freed. Again, how the name of God is sanctified, when God is honoured by those by whom He is known, there is no doubt, if to Him whom we already have merited to know through faith we exhibit the reverence of chaste fear and love. How does it seem to you? If the name of God is His celebrity and faith in Him is in us are they not baptized in His name who are baptized in the Faith of the Father and of the Son and of the Holy Ghost? For this is one name and the name of one, by which the Trinity is proclaimed and the unity is not denied. Therefore, when you baptize in the faith of the Father and of the Son and of the Holy Ghost you baptize in the name of the Father and of the Son and of the Holy Ghost. And you confess this name, that is, this faith when you say: "I baptize thee in the name of the Father, and of the Son, and of the Holy Ghost," so that what is written is fulfilled: "With the heart, we believe unto justice; but with the mouth, confession is made unto salvation," (Rom. 10, 10).

But perhaps, since the Lord Jesus Christ said: "Baptize in the name of the Father, and of the Son, and of the Holy Ghost," if as the name itself the celebrity and the faith of the Trinity are to be understood, it will suffice, to complete the form of the sacrament and to perform the sanctification, to immerse the one to be baptized without the utterance of words, with faith alone. For He who said that men should be baptized in the faith of the Trinity did not teach what is said but showed what is believed. Therefore, lest perhaps in the sanctification of the sacrament the profession of faith seem to be superfluous, we should, in what is said in the name of the Father and of the Son and of the Holy Ghost, understand something more than if it had been said in the faith of the Father and of the Son and of the Holy Ghost. For "name" seems to contain much more than "faith." For faith is within and lies hidden until it begins to be named and to come into manifestation. For the name begins to be then when it begins to be named and to be celebrated so as to be known. For thus, indeed, we baptize in the name of the Father and of the Son and of the Holy Ghost, when we baptize in the confession of the faith of the Father and of the Son and of the Holy Ghost. For He himself said: "Going, teach ye all nations, baptizing them in the name of the Father and of the Son and of the Holy Ghost." Teach and baptize, and if you moisten and are silent, you moisten and do not teach. You have "baptize," but you do not have "teach." Believe, therefore, and confess; speak and immerse that those things which are to be cleansed may be washed in confession.

But perhaps you seek the exact form of the profession of faith in performing the sacrament of baptism, of what nature that should be understood. To this I think a brief reply should be made, that the form of baptizing is what the Lord Jesus Christ handed down when He sent His disciples to baptize all nations, saying: "Going, teach ye all nations, baptizing them in the name of the Father, and of the Son, and of the Holy Ghost." So, you will do rightly if you confess what He commanded. He ordered that you baptize in the name of the Father and of the Son and of the Holy Ghost. You immerse a man and you say: I baptize thee in the name of the Father and of the Son and of the Holy Ghost. Well do you follow the form of the divine institution, you do what He ordered, you profess what He instituted. But you say: What then? If by chance anyone through ignorance without consciousness of error, not keeping the form of these words, yet with full faith should baptize a man, saying: "I baptize thee in the name of the Almighty Father or in the name of the Son of God or in the name of the Holy Ghost or even as we read in the Acts of the Apostles: "In the name of our Lord Jesus Christ," (Cf. Acts 2, 38), or something else similar, which indeed as far as the expression of the word is concerned would be different from the form of speaking mentioned above but as far as the profession of truth is concerned would not be contrary, ought not the true sacrament of baptism to be established in that? A great many ways possibly to the solution of this question of yours could have been brought together from here and there, and it could have been shown that where the same faith exists diversity of words not differing from the soundness and unity of faith do not obstruct.

But in this part it seemed to me that a response should be given to your question by authority rather than by my reason. Blessed Ambrose in the book which he wrote on the Trinity says the following. Those who denied that they knew the Holy Spirit, although they said that they had been baptized in the baptism of John, were baptized afterwards because John baptized unto the remission of sins in the name of the coming Jesus, not in his own, and on this account they did not know the Spirit because they had not received baptism in the name of Christ as John was accustomed to baptize. For although John did not baptize in the Spirit, yet he proclaimed both Christ and the Spirit. Finally, when he was questioned, lest perhaps he himself should be Christ, he replied: "I baptize you in water. But He that shall come after me, is mightier than I, whose shoes I am not worthy to bear: He shall baptize you in the Holy Ghost and fire," (Cf. Matt. 3, 11). Thus, those who have been' baptized neither in the name of Christ nor with the faith of the Holy Spirit cannot have received the sacrament of baptism. And so they have been baptized in the name of Jesus Christ, and baptism was not repeated in these but renewed. For there is one baptism. Now where there is no complete sacrament of baptism, neither the beginning nor any species of baptism is considered. But it is complete to confess the Father and the Son and the Holy Ghost. If you deny one you destroy the whole; just as, if you should comprehend one in speech, either Father or Son or Holy Spirit, but in faith you should deny neither Father nor Son nor Holy Spirit, the sacrament of faith is complete. Thus too, although you say the Father and the Son and the Holy Ghost but diminish the power either of the Father or of the Son or of the Holy Ghost, the entire mystery is void. Finally even those themselves who had said: "We have not so much as heard whether there be a Holy Ghost," (Cf. Acts 19, 2), were baptized afterwards in the name of the Lord Jesus Christ and this abounded unto grace because already they knew the Holy Ghost through the preaching of Paul. Nor should it seem contrary because, although even afterwards there was silence regarding the Holy Spirit, yet there was belief in the Spirit, and what had been kept silent in word had been expressed in faith. For when the expression is in the name of our Lord Jesus Christ, the mystery is fulfilled through the unity of the name. Nor is the Spirit separated from the baptism of Christ because John baptized in repentance, Christ in spirit.

Now let us consider whether, as we read that the sacrament of baptism is complete in the name of Christ, likewise, when the Holy Spirit is mentioned, nothing is lacking to the fullness of the mystery. And let us pursue the reason why he who said one denoted the Trinity. If you should say "Christ," you have designated God the Father by whom the Son was anointed and the Son himself who was anointed and the Holy Spirit with whom He was anointed. For it is written: "This Jesus of Nazareth whom God anointed with the Holy Ghost," (Cf. Acts 10, 38). If you should say "Father," you have indicated His Son and the Spirit of His mouth likewise, since you comprehend this also in the heart. And if you should say "Spirit" you have named God the Father from whom the Spirit proceeded and the Son because the Spirit is also of the Son. Therefore, that authority may be joined with reason, Scripture indicates that we can also be rightly baptized in the Spirit, when the Lord says: "But you shall be baptized with the Holy

Ghost," (Cf. Acts 1, 3; Matt. 3, 11). And He says to the Apostles: "For we were all baptized in the body into one Spirit," (Cf. 1 Cor. 12, 13). One work, because one mystery; one baptism because one death for the world. Therefore, unity of operation, unity of proclamation which cannot be separated. Thus far do the words of blessed Ambrose explain clearly how we should feel about the correct form of baptizing.

You see, then, how in the faith of the Trinity, when the Father alone or the Son or the Holy Spirit is mentioned, the sacrament of baptism is complete and how without the faith of the Trinity, even when the three have been named together, it is imperfect. For just as whole faith is sought everywhere, so with the same integrity of faith abiding the words of salvation are varied without detriment. Yet ecclesiastical custom chose to hold this form which it received from the author of sanctification Himself, most strictly in baptizing, to be preserved according to the first institution. If anyone, by chance, should ask whether in a moment of necessity it might suffice for the complete sacrament of baptism if someone were baptized in the faith of the Trinity without the expression of words, either because the one baptizing was unable to speak or because, in the haste or in the shock of imminent danger or for some other reason, he was prevented from recalling the words while he baptized, if anyone by chance should ask this, I declare myself unwilling to pass judgment on such matters which are hidden, especially because I have not heard the name of the Trinity in this case; even if there was true faith, yet there was not confession of faith. Let these words suffice for the present on this matter, as to what the sacrament of baptism is, and on the sanctifying word.

III. *Why the sacrament of baptism was instituted.*

It now remains to show why the sacrament of baptism was instituted, and why circumcism, which is thought to have been put in its place once, was taken away or changed when baptism succeeded. For if through circumcision, just as now through baptism, sins were once similarly remitted, what necessity was there for circumcision to be changed when the sacrament of baptism succeeded it? Why should that be believed to have been of little profit when received, which is declared to have caused considerable harm when neglected? For just as it is now said through the Gospel: "Unless a man be born again of water and the Holy Ghost, he cannot enter into the kingdom of God," (Cf. John 3, 5), thus was it once said by the law: "The male, whose flesh of his foreskin shall not be circumcised, that soul shall be destroyed out of his people," (Gen. 17, 14); unless by chance it is meant that he who is not baptized should be excluded from the kingdom of God, but he who is not circumcised shall perish. Some one may wish then to understand that baptism confers something more than circumcision, because circumcision when received was able to free only from perdition but baptism is able to lead the reborn even to glory. For those ancient fathers who had received the justification of the sacrament of circumcision were indeed saved from perdition but were not led to the glory of the kingdom until He should come who, extinguishing the fiery two-edged sword by pouring forth His blood, made clear again the approach to paradise and, himself going ahead, was the first to open the door of the kingdom of heaven to all who believed in Him. In this respect, then, baptism confers more, in that it sends the reborn from this world, as they go forth, straightway to the kingdom, and this, moreover, is greater by virtue of the blood shed by Him who sanctifies the water. If, therefore, anyone should wish to say that circumcision was changed by baptism that that might be completed in baptism which circumcision was not able to complete, perhaps it will appear a fitting answer to say that what is already more through baptism is not completed from baptism but from the passion of Christ which sanctifies baptism, indeed that circumcision could have done the same, if the passion of Christ had been added to it unto the cooperation of sanctification. For in baptism, in so far in fact as it looks to the virtue of baptism, just as in circumcision, only the remission of sins is received, because, as has been said, it is granted by the Cross of Christ that the approach to the heavenly fatherland is laid open to those justified thereafter.

For another similar reason we think that the reason for changing circumcision should be set forth more fittingly perhaps and more manifestly. When we treated of the sacraments in the preceding, in a certain place we said that all sacraments were certain signs of that spiritual grace which is granted through them, that with the progress of time the signs of the spiritual graces would be made ever more and more evident and declarative so that with the effect of salvation would grow the knowledge of truth. Thus under the natural law the sacraments, tithes, sacrifices, and oblations were given that in the tithe the remission of sins might be designated, in sacrifices the mortification of the flesh, and in oblation the exhibition of good work. But this significance was obscure in the sacrament of the tithe, where man offered a part of the things which he possessed and retained a part, so that thus in that which was, he assigned to himself, what was imperfect and defective, and he imputed to God what pertained to goodness. The nine parts retained meant this: nine is a sign of imperfection, failing of the perfect ten. Now, because the sign of cleansing was obscure in the tithing, circumcision was given to demonstrate the virtue of justification more evidently when it was said to man that he should bear as a sign a portion of his flesh, not indeed superfluous but of what was superfluous in man, that by this he might know that through the sacrament of circumcision grace might clean the sign which nature carried through that part of the body. Yet since circumcision can cut off only those enormities which are without, but cannot cleanse those pollutions which are within, there came after circumcision the laver of water purging all, that a perfect justice might be signified. Again, since the earlier people who served under fear had a laborious cleansing, the sacrament of circumcision in the flesh which has pain was given them. To the new people who serve with willingness and love, the sacrament of justification in the laver of water which has a soothing purification was proposed, and thus we believe that the reason should be given for the changing of the sacrament of circumcision and the instituting of the sacrament of baptism.

IV. *When the sacrament of baptism was instituted.*

It is asked also when the sacrament of baptism was instituted; then, from what time it was unlawful to neglect it; when it was an obligation to receive it. There are indeed diverse opinions from many sources regarding this. Some say that baptism was instituted at the time when Christ, introducing the way of new regeneration to Nicodemus who came to him in the night, said: "Unless a man be born again of water and the Spirit, he cannot see into the kingdom of God," (Cf. John 3, 5). Some say that the institution of baptism began from the time when Christ after His resurrection, as He was about to ascend into heaven, sent the disciples forth to preach, saying: "Going, teach ye all nations: Baptizing them in the name of the Father, and of the Son, and of the Holy Ghost," (Matt. 28, 19). Some think that the institution of baptism began from the time when John began to baptize in the water proclaiming that he would baptize in the Spirit. Some think that in the passion of Christ, when He said: "It is consummated," (John 19, 30), all the sacraments of the Old Testament received an end and those of the New a beginning. However, we believe we can say more properly that baptism was brought forth into use first by John and then by Christ or by His disciples for a while only, lest it should differ with custom, but that it was finally instituted generally when they were sent as preachers to baptize the whole world.

Now it seems that a certain three periods must be distinguished here. For at first, before baptism, circumcision alone had status and was received unto justification without baptism. But lastly now, after circumcision, baptism alone has status and is celebrated unto salvation without circumcision. Moreover, there was a certain middle period, when both circumcision and baptism ran concurrently, the one, that is circumcision, so that it was ended, the other, that is baptism, so that it was confirmed. For it was right that those things also which had to be ended should be dismissed by no means suddenly or precipitously but gradually, so that they might be shown to have been good in their own time, and similarly, that those things which had to be begun should not be assumed suddenly unto authority but should be entered upon with delay and with seriousness, lest they should be thought, so to speak, as something foreign and suddenly introduced from somewhere disadvantageously. Thus, the former were dismissed, not cast forth, and the latter were instituted, not appropriated, so that the authority of divine counsel was preserved everywhere and human causation was advised that it should not dare to rebuke divine works. Thus, although in the passion of Christ through which all things were consummated, the status of the old figure received an end and the establishment of the new a beginning, yet even before, at some time, the new were begun unto custom and afterwards the old were tolerated for some time according to dispensation. Therefore, they both existed together at that time, whether before the passion or after, from the time when the new began until the old were afterwards forbidden.

In that middle period what was baptism with circumcision from its beginning even to the passion of Christ was circumcision with baptism after the passion of Christ, even to the time when circumcision itself began to be prohibited. For just as before the passion circumcision in its own status was received as a remedy, and even then baptism was not contemned without danger to salvation by those to whom it was preached, so after the passion baptism as if in its own status was received for salvation, and even then circumcision was not contemned without danger to salvation by those to whom its end had not yet been made manifest. After it was said: "If you be circumcised, Christ shall profit you nothing," (Cf. Gal. 5, 2), already then circumcision could not be received for salvation, just as before, after it had been said: "The male whose flesh of his foreskin shall not be circumcised, that soul shall be destroyed out of his people," (Cf. Gen. 17, 14), circumcision could not have been contemned without danger to salvation by those especially upon whom it had been enjoined. Again, just as in the beginning baptism was given by John according to the sacrament alone, to instruct those who did not know the practice of baptizing, so in the end circumcision was received by certain of the faithful with dispensation according to the sacrament alone, lest those who had been accustomed to circumcision might be scandalized.

V. *When man began to be obligated by the precept of receiving baptism.*

If then it is asked when man began to be obligated by the duty of receiving baptism, the following is proven to be consistent with truth and reason, that everyone began to be obligated by the duty of receiving baptism from the time when either after the institution he received the precept or before the institution he received the counsel of baptizing. For he who neither before was a contemner of the counsel nor afterwards a prevaricator of the precept was not to be blamed, unless perhaps someone either before or afterwards might be said to have been ignorant, to whom the notice of the divine institution would have come if his sin had not prevented. When, therefore, Christ said to Nicodemus: "Unless a man be born again of water and the Holy Ghost, he cannot enter into the kingdom of God," (Cf. John 3, 5), counsel was revealed to a friend. But when afterwards He said: "Going, teach ye all nations; baptizing them in the name of the Father, and of the Son, and of the Holy Ghost," (Cf. Matt. 28, 19), a precept was set forth for the information of all. At this time in fact the institution was made general, which from that time held everyone a debtor, because the precept of the institution came to Him himself while the apostles, messengers of the word, were preaching.

Now then regarding those who, situated afar off or placed nearby in hiding, were taken away from this life by chance without knowledge of the divine institution, it seems to me that we should have the same opinion as regarding those who, before the institution itself, were either in the prepuce or in the law, since what the times did for the one, absence performed for the other. Now if anyone wishes to be stubborn and contends that some of this kind still live in unknown regions and in remote seats of the world, who perhaps have not heard the divine mandate of receiving the sacrament of baptism, I affirm that either there is no such person or, should there be someone, if his sin had not prevented, he could have heard and known and was obligated without delay, especially when the Scripture clearly proclaims: "Their sound hath gone forth unto all the earth: and their words unto the ends of the world," (Psal. 18, 5). If then their sound has gone forth unto all the earth, in all the earth either they have been heard and their contemners are condemned or they have not been heard according to their sin, and being ignorant they are ignored and are not saved. Such is my opinion regarding the time of the institution of baptism and regarding the obligation of receiving baptism.

VI. *What the difference is between the baptism of John and that of Christ, and regarding the form of the baptism of John and that of Christ.*

Between the baptism of John and the baptism of Christ there is this difference: in the baptism of John by the dipping in water the sacrament alone was given but in the baptism of Christ with the sacrament the power of the sacrament also is received. For John dipped sinners in water and, as they confessed sins, enjoined repentance upon them; Christ baptizes and forgives sins. The one baptizing proclaimed Him who was to come and baptize in spirit, the other baptizing infuses the spirit unto the remission of sins. In the one case men were baptized in the name of one who was to come, in the other men are baptized "in the name of the Father, and of the Son, and of the Holy Ghost," (Cf. Matt. 28, 19). Therefore, in both cases as far as the external form is concerned the sacrament was the same, but as far as the effect is concerned it was not the same, since in the one case there was the sacrament alone, for there was no remission of sins, but in the other the form of the sacrament is set forth and the virtue of the sacrament also unto the remission of sins is bestowed.

VII. *Whether after the precept of baptism was given anyone could be saved without actually receiving the sacrament of baptism.*

Some either through curiosity or zeal are accustomed to inquire whether anyone after the enjoining and proclaiming of the sacrament of baptism can be saved, unless he actually receives the sacrament of baptism itself. For the reasons seem to be manifest and they have many authorities, (if, however, they are to be said to have authorities, who do not understand); first, because it is said: "Unless a man be born again of the water and the Holy Ghost, he cannot enter into the kingdom of God," (Cf. John 3, 5), and again: "He that believeth and is baptized, shall be saved," (Mark 16, 16). There are many such passages which seem, as it were, to affirm that by no means can he be saved who has not had this sacrament, whatever he may have besides this sacrament. If he should have perfect faith, if hope, if he should have charity, even if he should have a contrite and humble heart which God does not despise, true repentance for the past, firm purpose for the future, whatever he may have, he will not be able to be saved, if he does not have this. All this seems so to them on account of what is written: "Unless a man be born again of the water and the Holy Ghost, he cannot enter into the kingdom of God," (Cf. John 3, 5).

Yet if someone should ask what has happened to those who, after shedding blood for Christ, departed this life without the sacrament of water, they dare not say that men of this kind are not saved. And, although one cannot show that this is written in what is mentioned above, yet they dare not say that, because it is not written there, it is to be denied. For he who said: "Unless a man be born again of the water and the Holy Ghost," did not add: "or by pouring forth his blood instead of water," and yet this is true, although it is not written here. For if he is saved who received water on account of God, why is he not saved much more who sheds blood on account of God? For it is more to give blood than to receive water. Moreover, what some say is clearly silly, that those who shed blood are saved because with blood they also shed water and in the very water which they shed they receive baptism. For if those who are killed are said to have been baptized on account of the moisture of water which drips from their wounds together with the corruption of blood, then those who are suffocated or drowned or are killed by some other kind of death where blood is not shed have not been baptized in their blood and have died for Christ in vain, because they did not shed the moisture of the water which they had within their body. Who would say this? So, he is baptized in blood who dies for Christ, who, even if he does not shed blood from the wound, gives life which is more precious than blood. For he could shed blood and, if he did not give life, shedding blood would be less than giving life. Therefore, he sheds blood well who lays down his life for Christ, and he has his baptism in the virtue of the sacrament, without which to have received the sacrament itself, as it were, is of no benefit. So where this is the case, to be unable to have the sacrament does no harm.

Thus, it is true, although it is not said there, that he who dies for Christ is baptized in Christ. Thus, they say, it is true, although it is not said there, and it is true because it is said elsewhere, even if it is not said there. For He who said: "Unless a man be born again of the water and the Holy Ghost, he cannot enter into the kingdom of God," the same also said elsewhere: "He who shall confess me before men, I will also confess him before my Father," (Cf. Matt. 10, 32). And so what is not said there, is nevertheless to be understood, although it is not said, since it is said elsewhere. Behold therefore why they say it. They say that what is not said is to be understood where it is not said, because it is said elsewhere. If, therefore, this is to be understood in this place where it is not said, since it is said elsewhere, why is it not also to be understood similarly about faith, since it is said elsewhere: "He who believeth in me, shall not die forever," (Cf. John 11, 26). Likewise, He who said: "Unless a man be born again of the water and the Holy Ghost, he cannot enter into the kingdom of God," He himself said: "He who believeth in me, shall not die for ever." Therefore, either deny faith or concede salvation. What does it seem to you? Where there is faith, where there is hope, where there is charity, finally where there is the full and perfect virtue of the sacrament, there is no salvation because the sacrament alone is not and it is not, because it cannot be possessed. "He that believeth," He said, "and is baptized, shall be saved," (Mark 16, 16). Therefore behold, there is no doubt but that where there is faith and is baptism, there is salvation.

And what follows? "But he that believeth not shall be condemned," (Cf. Mark 16, 16). Why did He wish to speak thus? Why did He not say: "He that believeth not and is not baptized, shall be condemned," just as He had said: "He that believeth and is baptized, shall be saved?" Why, unless because it is of the will to believe and because he who wishes to believe cannot lack faith. And so in him who does not believe, an evil will is always shown, where there can be no necessity which may be put forth as an excuse. Now to be baptized can be in the will, even when it is not in possibility, and on this account justly is good will with the devotion of its faith not despised, although in a moment of necessity he is prevented from receiving that sacrament of water which is external. Do you wish to know more fully whether or not this reason is proven elsewhere by more manifest authority, although even those authorities which we have mentioned above seem so manifest that there can be no doubt about the truth of them?

Listen to something more, if by chance this matter about which you should not be in doubt can be shown you more clearly. Blessed Augustine in his book, "On the One Baptism," speaks as follows: Again and again, as I consider it, I find that not only suffering for the name of Christ can fulfil what was lacking to baptism but also faith and conversion of heart, if perhaps assistance could not be rendered for the celebration of the mystery of baptism in straitened circumstances. You see that he clearly testifies that faith and conversion of heart can suffice for the salvation of good will where it happens that the visible sacrament of water of necessity cannot be had. But lest perhaps you think that he contradicted himself, since afterwards in the book of Retractations he disapproved of the example of the thief which he had assumed to establish this opinion where he had said that the shedding of blood or faith and change of heart could fulfil the place of baptism, saying: "In the fourth book, when I said that suffering could take the place of baptism, I did not furnish a sufficiently fitting example in that of the thief about whom there is some doubt as to whether he was baptized," you should consider that in this place he only corrected an example which he had offered to prove his opinion; he did not reject his opinion. But if you think that that opinion is to be rejected, because the example is corrected, then what he had said is false, that the shedding of blood can take the place of baptism, since the example itself was furnished to prove that. For he does not say: "When I said that faith could have the place of baptism," but he says: "When I said that suffering could have the place of baptism," although he had placed both in the one opinion. If, therefore, regarding what he said, that suffering can have the place of baptism, an example has been furnished, since it is established that it is true without any ambiguity, it is clear that the example was afterwards corrected but the opinion was not rejected.

You should, therefore, either confess that true faith and confession of the heart can fulfil the place of baptism in the moment of necessity or show how true faith and unfeigned charity can be possessed where there is no salvation. Unless perhaps you wish to say that no one can have true faith and true charity, who is not to have the visible sacrament of water. Yet by what reason or by what authority you prove this I do not know. We meanwhile do not ask whether anyone who is not to receive the sacrament of baptism can have these, since this alone as far as this matter is concerned is certain: if there were anyone who had these even without the visible sacrament of water he could not perish. There are many other things which could have been brought up to prove this, but what we have set forth above in the treatment of the sacraments to prove this point we by no means think needs reconsideration.

VIII. *On the sacraments of the neophytes.*

Neophyte is interpreted as novice. One lately converted to the faith or one inexperienced in the knowledge of the religious life is called a neophyte. Those lately converted to the faith are to be instructed in the visible sacraments that through that which they see they may understand what they do not see. Men of this kind should be advised to consider that the faith is not new in which they themselves are new, since, just as from the beginning of the world at no time were the faithful and the just lacking as members of Christ, so from the beginning never have the sacraments of salvation which preceded for the preparation and for the sign of the redemption which was completed in the death of Christ been lacking. In the second age Noe guided the ark in the flood, just as Christ guiding the Church midst the floods of temptations did not permit it to be submerged. In the third age Abraham slaughtered a ram for his son who had been offered, just as God the Father offered His Word for the salvation of the world. However in this although inviolable divinity remained, humanity alone endured the pain of death. Afterwards the people of Israel were led out of Egypt through the Red Sea in a column of fire and cloud, just as the faithful of God are freed from the shades of sin, renewed through the sacrament of baptism, consecrated by the blood of Christ, following with faith Him himself in whom is both the cloud of humanity and the fire of divinity. In the fourth age in Jerusalem the temporal kingdom of the people of God is raised, prefiguring the eternal in which the Prince of Peace, the Father of the world to come, (Cf. Isa. 9, 6), will introduce His faithful to the vision of eternal peace. Now David established the beginning of this kingdom, who tried and glorified through many tribulations left the Son as the successor of peace to show that they cannot come to the quiet of future peace who in the present life have not been strong against the trials and tribulations which must be overpowered. On this account, those who are to be baptized on the Holy Sabbath of the paschal solemnity, are brought to the church on the fourth habdomada of the quadragesimal observance which furnishes us the arms of continence and on the fourth festival of the same hebdomada to be catechized and exorcised, there to hear and to be instructed as to how they are to fight against spiritual wickedness. But their baptism is postponed, even until the Sabbath of the paschal festival, while the Church considers that, in whatever respect they are called to combat in the present life, they are baptized in the hope of future rest.

In the fifth age the people are led captive into Babylon on account of their sins and again through God's mercy after seventy years, when the yoke of captivity has been loosed, they are recalled to their own land. Since the people of God, who in this life revolving in periods of seven days are subject to vanity and confusion, carry the yoke of mortality, after its end they are freed from corruption. So then from the beginning at no time were the sacraments of God lacking by which the faithful people might be nourished unto the perception of the invisible and excited unto cognition. Finally in the sixth age Christ was born of a virgin, just as on the sixth day the first man was moulded from virgin land. He himself, therefore, as if about to consummate all things, when He had come to the age of manhood, in the thirtieth year of His age was baptized by John not of necessity but by dispensation, that He might sanctify the laver for those who are to be cleansed. Thereafter, calling together the apostles as ministers of the Gospel, He began to preach the kingdom of heaven which is to come, and lastly for the consummation of all things, offering Himself to the Father on the altar of the cross as a victim for the redemption of the world, He endured death that He might take away the fear of death from those who believe in Him, and He arose from the dead that He might give hope of life and resurrection to those who die for Him. Afterwards, when about to ascend into Heaven He sent the disciples into the whole world to teach and to baptize all nations, that they might be called who should follow Him to the life, who was going before. These are the sacraments of the Christian faith, founded from the beginning, to be believed at the end, to be of benefit without end. These are the sacraments with which we imbue those who are to be catechized and we demand that the faith of those who are to be regenerated by the sacrament of the new should be merited by salutary confession.

IX. *On catechizing.*

A catechumen is interpreted as one instructed or as one hearing; for to catechize is to instruct, since those to be baptized are first instructed and are taught what the form of the Christian faith is in which they must be made safe and receive the sacrament of salvation, as it is written: "Going, teach ye all nations: baptizing them in the name of the Father, and of the Son, and of the Holy Ghost," (Cf. Matt. 28, 19). First teach, afterwards baptize. Teach unto instruction, baptize unto cleanness. Teach unto faith, baptize unto the remission of sins. Therefore, teach since you baptize him who has believed because "he that is baptized, shall be saved," (Cf. Mark 16, 16). So, this form of catechization was instituted from the earliest period of the Christian faith.

This form was then necessarily preserved, when the rule of the Christian faith was announced to adults and to those possessing intelligence before they approached the sacrament of baptism, so that either acquiescing in the faith of their own accord they were judged worthy of spiritual regeneration or being unwilling to believe they were prevented deservedly, as being unworthy, from receiving the sacrament of God. Of course, to obtain salvation the decision of man must be consulted, because the work of salvation should be voluntary. Now after the multitude of the nations entered the faith, even then the same form is preserved among those children who are born of the faithful; these also the Mother Church, provident with dispensation, does not wish to be deprived of the sacrament of salvation meanwhile, lest perhaps by the very delay they become estranged from salvation, if without receiving the sacrament of salvation they should suddenly depart from this life. Fittingly, therefore, the remedy of salvation has been provided even for them, that they whom it is agreed were alienated from God through the sin of another, may be baptized in the sacrament of faith and through the faith of another be reconciled to God. Thus it has been instituted according to this new sacrament to catechize, to exorcise, to initiate, and then to baptize children; and in these ceremonies the Church hears for the children and replies to questions and promises until they come to the years of understanding and are able to understand and to keep the sacraments of faith and charity.

X. *On exorcism.*

Exorcism from Greek is used for Latin *adjuratio.* For exorcists are those who, after opposing with divine virtue, invoke the name of the Lord Jesus over the catechumens or over energumens, that is, those who have an unclean spirit, entreating the unclean spirit to depart from them. Rightly, therefore, does exorcism follow after catechization, that the adverse power may be expelled from him who has now been instructed in the faith. For three things must be accomplished towards the reception of the new, by which the one to be baptized is, as it were, received and nourished and promoted up to the integrity of the new life. Now these are the catechisms, the exorcisms, the prayers. Thus first the one to be baptized is catechized that he may be moved to faith by the decision of his own will. Then he is exorcised that the evil power of the devil may be cast from him. Prayer is also added that grace may go before and follow after to furnish strength for free decision and to make the entire illusion of the evil spirit afar off.

The form of exorcism then is performed in this manner. First the one to be baptized is signed with the sign of the cross on the forehead, on the breast, on the eyes, on the nostrils, on the ears, on the mouth, so that the senses of the whole body may be fortified by this sign, through whose virtue all our sacraments are fulfilled and all the inventions of the devil frustrated. Afterwards blessed salt is put in his mouth, that fortified with wisdom he may be free from the noisesomeness of iniquity and furthermore may not grow rotten from the vermin of vice. Then a strong breath is blown forth that spirit may be expelled by spirit. Afterwards his ears and nostrils are touched with saliva, that by the touch of supernal wisdom his ears also may be opened to hear the word of God, and the nostrils similarly to discern the odor of life and of death. This is the sacrament of opening, which the Lord signified in the Gospel when he touched the ears and the mouth of the deaf and the dumb, saying: "Ephpheta, which is, Be thou open," (Mark 7, 34).

XI. *On those things in baptism which follow exorcization.*

Thus, when these things have been completed, the priest comes to the font. The font is consecrated in the name of the Father and of the Son and of the Holy Ghost, that the sanctity of the sacrament may be known to exist not from him who ministers but from Him who sanctifies, just as it is written: "He it is that baptizeth," (Cf. John 1, 33). Thus nothing better is given by something good, nor is anything worse received from something evil, because the sanctity of the sacrament of God is not performed by the merit of those ministering but by the virtue of the One sanctifying. There is also given to the hearers of the new life a symbol of faith in which the form of the apostolic doctrine consists. Finally the child when offered for baptism and questioned by the priest, whether he renounces Satan and all his works and all his pomps, replies through the mouths of those who carry him, so that he who was bound by another's iniquity is loosed by another's faith and confession. After the renunciation has been made, he is anointed with holy oil on the breast, that he may be fortified against the enemy, lest afterwards the enemy be able to persuade him of unclean and sinful things. He is also anointed between the shoulders, where the strength is for carrying a burden, that he may receive fortitude for carrying the burden of the Lord. Then he is asked whether he believes in God, the Father and the Son and the Holy Spirit, in one Catholic church, in the remission of sins, and in eternal life. After this response of faith, he is washed of the stains of age with a threefold immersion, and, having put on the new man, he is buried with the three-day death of Christ, as the Apostle says: "All we, who are baptized in Christ Jesus, are baptized in his death. For we are buried together with Christ by baptism into death; that as Christ is risen from the dead by the glory of the Father, so we also may walk in newness of life," (Cf. Romans 6, 4, and 5). For the threefold immersion is the threefold cleansing of thought, speech, and operation.

When the sacraments of baptism have been completed, after the one baptized has ascended from the font, he is anointed on the head with holy chrism, that by sharing in the spirit of Christ he may thereafter worthily be called a Christian, having been made a coheir of the kingdom and of the glory by the holy unction. Then there is given to the Christian a white garment, that he who darkened the splendor of the first nativity by the garments of age may with the habit of regeneration hold forth the cloak of glory. Also, after the holy anointing his head is covered with a holy veil, that he may understand that he possesses the diadem of the kingdom and sacerdotal dignity. Finally a lighted candle is put into his hand, that he may be taught to fulfil that part of the gospel where it is said: "So let your light shine before men, that they may see your good works, and glorify your Father who is in heaven," (Matt. 5, 16). Thus if he keeps the lamp inextinguishable, he will enter nuptials with the celestial spouse in the midst of the wise virgins.

XII. *On godparents.*

They are called godparents who offer children for baptism and by promising for them become as it were surety before God. These are called godparents because they offer children to be reborn to a new life and become in a manner authors of the new regeneration. With reference to these the Fathers have decided that a single godparent be admitted for baptizing a single person, that is, one only, whether man or woman, perhaps, lest spiritual relationship to which reverence should be shown, becoming diffused at random, might have become an impediment to the union of matrimony. But certain churches do not observe this custom, admitting several for the acceptance of children. This similarly has been decreed, that he who has not been baptized or confirmed may not receive another as a godchild in baptism or in chrism, that is, confirmation. But religious cannot act as godfathers and godmothers, to whom relationships of familiarity of this kind are forbidden. Godparents are surety for those whom they have received in baptism, that they may advise these, when they have come to a proper age, to guard the right faith and good conversation. Above all let them keep the Creed and the Lord's prayer and let them teach those for whose faith they have made promise.

XIII. *On rebaptizing.*

The Apostle says: "One Lord, one faith, one baptism," (Ephes. 4, 5). Thus, what is one cannot be doubled. Therefore, it has been established by the holy Fathers by a very reasonable explanation that he who is known to have received the sacrament of baptism once may by no means receive it again, whether in the Church or outside the Church, that is, by a Catholic or by a heretic or finally by one of the faithful or by an infidel. If any person of whatever condition, age, or sex has received it, provided only he has received it according to the correct form of Catholic baptism, it shall of necessity be valid and it cannot be repeated in any way. For, whatever good a man has received, why should it not be judged a good, even if he did not receive it from a good person? For it was not of him from whom he received it, or rather through whom he received it, who was not good, but of Him in whose name he received it, who being always good could not have given evil. Thus, regarding those who have been baptized by heretics in the name of the Trinity, when they return to the unity of the Church, the ancient tradition of the Fathers has established that they be not rebaptized, but that they be reconciled to the Catholic Church either by the anointing of chrism or by the imposition of the hand, just as formerly the West reformed Arians for entrance into the Catholic Church by the imposition of the hand, and the East by the unction of holy chrism. For those who have received the sacrament only externally, by the imposition of the hand receive the spirit internally. But it has pleased those who do not know that they have been baptized and have no witnesses of their baptism to be baptized without delay, because it should not be said that what is not known to have been done has been repeated.

Question is also raised about those who are baptized in mimicry, that is, in fun, whether they receive the true and full sacrament of baptism. It must be understood that it is one thing to give or to receive something in fun or jokingly and still to wish to give or to receive and to intend this in every way, namely, that what is given or received jokingly be given and be received, but another thing to do something which has the form of this in deed and yet not to wish to do this and not to intend that this be done but something else whatsoever. Where, therefore, there is the intention of baptizing, even if due reverence does not exist in the act, there is indeed the sacrament, since it is done completely and this is intended, and yet it is not without blame on the part of the agent, since what is done and intended is not done worthily. But it is quite ridiculous that where no intention of acting exists, the work be said to exist on account of a certain appearance made similar to the work, not assumed for this purpose but coming forth from something else whatsoever. Thus it is that certain ignorant persons think that those words which were instituted to perform the Eucharist, when proclaimed by any person whatsoever or in any place whatsoever and with whatever intention over bread and wine, have the effect of consecration and sanctification, as if the sacraments of God were so instituted that they admit no reason for operating but by a certain tumultuous and violent and irrational obstinacy proceed to their effect without any intention or will on the part of those operating.

I by chance had brought my son to the baths. I came to the water not to baptize but to bathe, not to give a sacrament but to wash away filth and benefit flesh. I placed my child in the water but because I wished him to be blessed and to be benefited I said by chance as I might have said in eating or in drinking, as in ploughing or in sowing,—I said: "In the name of the Father and of the Son and of the Holy Ghost." You come and you say to me that my son has been baptized. I know that he has been bathed; I do not know that he has been baptized. But if you think that he has been baptized, because when I immersed him I said: In the name of the Father and of the Son and of the Holy Ghost, then the morsel of food also has been baptized, because when I immersed it I said: In the name of the Father and of the Son and of the Holy Ghost. Behold, therefore, and consider that the work of the ministries of God should be rational and one should not forejudge on account of form alone where there is not intention of acting.

XIV. *Why baptism is celebrated in water only.*

It must be understood also that in the element of water only has it been established that the sacrament of baptism be consecrated, because this alone has full and perfect cleanness. All other liquids indeed are purified by water. And if anything has been touched by any other liquid it is washed off by water so that it be cleansed. Therefore, in water alone is the sacrament of cleanness established, as it is written: "Unless a man be born again of water and the Holy Ghost, he cannot enter into the kingdom of God." (Cf. John 3, 5).

XV. *On the form of baptism.*

The form of baptism already preceded once in the flood where, in a figure, eight souls of those to be saved were saved through the wood. Similarly also in the Red Sea where the water proclaimed baptism and the redness blood. Similarly in the water of aspersion with which the ashes of a red calf were mixed; this represented the flesh of Christ which is denoted on account of weakness by its feminine sex and is red on account of blood.

Seventh Part

On Confirmation.

1. *On confirmation.*

We read that the unction of chrism had already been established from olden times in the Old Testament, by which at that time only kings and priests were anointed. By the anointing of these that specially anointed One who was anointed before all His sharers, (Cf. Heb. 1), was prefigured as they who deserved to be His sharers in unction had shared with Him in name. For Christ is so called from chrism and the Christian is named from Christ. Therefore, ever since all began to share the name all had to receive unction because "in Christ we all are a chosen generation, a kingly priesthood," (Cf. 1 Peter 2, 9). Chrism is made of oil and balsam, because through oil the infusion of grace is designated, through balsam the odour of good fame.

II. *That the imposition of the hand is celebrated by pontiffs alone.*

The imposition of the hand, which by its usual name is called confirmation, by which the Christian is signed on the forehead with the unction of chrism through the imposition of the hands, is due to bishops alone, vicars of the Apostles, that they may mark the Christian and hand down the Spirit Paraclete, just as in the primitive church the Apostles alone are read to have had the power of giving the Holy Spirit through the imposition of the hands.

III. *On what Pope Sylvester established—that a presbyter should anoint the baptized person with chrism.*

Among the *gesta pontificalia* we read that Pope Sylvester established that a presbyter should anoint a baptized person on the head with chrism on the occasion of death, lest by any chance through the absence of a bishop and the difficulty of obtaining him it might happen that the baptized person depart from this life without the imposition of the hand, which indeed would be altogether dangerous since, just as the remission of sins is received in baptism, so the Spirit Paraclete is given through the imposition of the hand; in the one case grace is attributed unto the remission of sins, in the other grace is given unto confirmation. Now of what profit is it if you should arise from a fall, unless you be also strengthened to stand? Thus they must fear who lose the presence of a bishop through negligence and do not receive the imposition of the hand, lest perhaps they be damned, since they should have hastened while they were able. For the sake of those who in a moment of time are prevented, that unction of holy chrism has been established by which the priest may anoint the baptized on the head immediately, so that in this case it may be shown how necessary that sacrament is for salvation, when all must be so anxiously on guard lest by chance they be taken from this life without it. Now it is manifest that in earliest times all the anointing with chrism was done by the pontiffs alone. But even after the practice was established of having a priest anoint the baptized person on the head, still the signing of the forehead was reserved for pontiffs alone. For the pontiff alone can sign and anoint the forehead and give the Spirit Paraclete.

IV. *Which is the greater sacrament—imposition of hands or baptism.*

The question is also raised whether the sacrament of confirmation, that is, of the imposition of hands is a greater sacrament than baptism. But, as the sacred canons defined, both are truly great sacraments and must be considered with the highest devotion. Although the one, that is, the imposition of the hands, in that it is celebrated by highest pontiffs only, apparently should be cherished with greater reverence, nevertheless these two have been so joined in the operation of salvation that unless death intervenes they should by no means be separated.

V. *That the imposition of the hands should not be repeated, just as baptism should not, and that it should be celebrated by fastings.*

Regarding the sacrament of the imposition of hands it has been explained that it should by no means be repeated, just as baptism should not, and if by chance this should be done, the act ought to be punished by serious penitence. This also has been established, that the sacrament of the imposition of hands should not be given nor received except by persons who are fasting, if those who receive it have been of the perfect age so that being clean they may receive the gift of the Holy Spirit. For just as at two seasons, namely at Easter and at Pentacost, baptism which in general is to be celebrated only at those times should be celebrated by fasting, so also it is fitting that the gift of the Holy Spirit through the imposition of the hand should be celebrated only by fasting pontiffs, the infirm and those in danger of death being excepted.

VI. *How long those who have received the imposition of hands should be under the discipline of chrism*

Certain persons customarily ask how long they should keep the unction of chrism on the head, so that those who receive the imposition of the hand may not wash the head, except at the time of the baptistery. To these the reply can be given that the coming of the Holy Spirit should fittingly be celebrated by everyone who has received Him for so long as the coming of the Holy Spirit upon the Apostles is in general celebrated by the Church, that is seven days. And worthily so, since there are seven gifts of the Holy Spirit and the Holy Spirit came to His host among seven companions. It is worthy that each one have his day and that a banquet be prepared for each one on his day. Wisdom has one day, the intellect another, counsel another, fortitude another, knowledge another, piety another, fear another. Christ customarily gave such banquets among His hosts, as did the Holy Spirit also.

Eighth Part

On the Sacrament of the Body and Blood of Christ.

I. *On the sacrament of the body and blood of Christ.*

The sacrament of the body and blood of Christ is one of those upon which salvation principally depends and it is peculiar among all, since from it is all sanctification. For that victim who was offered once for the salvation of the world gave virtue to all the preceding and subsequent sacraments, so that from it they sanctify all who are to be freed through it.

II. *When the sacrament of the body and blood of Christ was instituted.*

Our Lord Jesus Christ Himself instituted the sacrament of His body and blood when after the supper of the old pasch, changing the bread and wine into His own body and blood by divine power, He gave it to His apostles to be eaten and He ordered that after this they should do the same in commemoration of Him.

III. *Whether at the supper He gave His mortal or immortal body.*

Certain persons are inclined to ask what the nature of the body was that our Lord Jesus Christ gave to His disciples, that is, whether capable of suffering or incapable of suffering, mortal or immortal, and other things pertaining to this question. I think, as I have professed also in other places, that divine secrets of this kind are more to be venerated than to be discussed. I think that this suffices for simple faith, if we say that He gave such as He wished and again that He himself knew the nature of what He gave. For He gave such as He wished, because He was omnipotent and was able to give all that He wished. Now He knew the nature of what He gave, because He was wisdom and He was unable to be ignorant of what it was. So he frees himself more lightly of the question and perhaps he subsists more safely within himself who does not say: He gave the mortal, lest he seem to speak against the dignity of the sacrament, and does not say: He gave the immortal, lest he be thought to believe contrary to that truth of the mortal body which was in Christ before the resurrection. Thus it is better perhaps that we presume to define neither, although on the other hand we believe that the body was one.

But if an answer must be made, then without prejudice to the truth I accede to this with greater inclination, that He be said to have given over that body incapable of suffering and immortal, insofar indeed as pertains to the sanctification of the sacrament. Now if anyone thinks that an objection must be raised on the ground that before the resurrection our Lord Jesus Christ bore a mortal body, we ourselves profess this also without doubt, that our Lord Jesus was mortal according to the humanity which He took on, because if we did not believe that He was mortal we would deny His death. Therefore, human nature in Christ was mortal, but by will, not by necessity. For from the time when human nature through grace, clean of all sin by the word of God, was joined into unity of person, it was made free from every necessity and obligation of death, so that it owed nothing to death in as much as it had no sin. Yet He endured mortality of His own free will, because He wished to endure death, and if He had not endured mortality He could by no means have died. Thus then of His own will He bore mortality, that He might taste death and thus put mortality aside. Since, therefore, He was mortal by will not by necessity, according as reason and the order of time demanded, before He put off mortality through complete death, He sometimes put it aside in part when He wished, and again He took it back when He wished, so that in this very question He proved that, in so far as He endured it, it was not of necessity, because by His power, in so far as He wished, He was able not to have it, not to endure it at all.

We read in the Gospel that, when the Lord Jesus Christ preached the word of life and invited mortals and those destined to die to live, the zealous enemy, who could not be convinced by reason, in his fury wished to destroy Him. And so, as it were, upon Him who had nothing more than the mortal, "upon Him they laid hands, and they led Him to a high mountain, that He might cast Himself thence," (Cf. Luke 4, 4 and 9). That He himself might show that He indeed was mortal, He endured being held and, that He might again show that He bore mortality and capability of suffering by will, not by necessity, He did not endure that He cast Himself down. When He was to be led, He bore patiently being held. But when He was to cast Himself down, passing mightily through the midst of them He went away. As much as He wished, He was held, and as much as He wished, He was not held. In so far as He wished and when He wished He admitted the nature of mortality. In so far as He did not wish to endure it and when He did not wish, by his power He removed this from Himself. He said: "He passing through the midst of them went His way," (Cf. Luke 4, 30). You do not think do you that Christ withdrew Himself from the hands of the enemy by struggling when He was held by them, so that passing free through the midst of them He went His way? Thus is fortitude of body alone to be praised in Him, not virtue of Godhead? It is not fitting so, but He showed Himself of what nature He wished, admitting to Himself from that which He bore of His own accord to what extent He wished.

If then Christ according to time at some period laid aside in part the nature of mortality, according to the reason of divine dispensation, before He put it off when about to live always, and again when time demanded assumed it, what wonder is it if it is said that at some time because of and by reason of time, according to something, He laid all that aside, in which, however, when time demanded He was still to suffer? If then this could have been, that He himself bore Himself in His hands and without corruption of Himself gave Himself to the disciple to be eaten, and yet He who gave and who was given, who carried and who was carried, was the same, what wonder is it if it is said that He, in that which He gave, was mortal and, in that which was given, was immortal, and yet He himself who gave as a mortal and who was given as an immortal were not two but the one Himself? How was He not given as a mortal who was taken invisibly and was eaten incorruptibly? He was taken invisibly in so far as I speak with reference to the proper form of His body, not with reference to the appearance of His sacrament. For He was taken invisibly since in that which was taken what He himself was, was not seen. For Christ was taken and the appearance of bread and wine alone was seen. On this account I say: He was taken invisibly and what He was, was not seen. If, therefore, in that which He gave, what He himself was, was seen and in that which was given what He was, was not seen, although in that which He gave He was held and crucified and in that which was given He was broken and was not divided, was eaten and was not corrupted, why do you wonder if in that which He gave He is called mortal, in that which was given He is proclaimed to have been immortal and incapable of suffering? However, may these words be such that on this subject, which lies hidden, the present prejudice may not be raised in anyone.

IV. *Whether that was the body of Christ which Judas received through the dipped bread.*

They also ask this, whether what He gave to His betrayer through the dipped bread must be believed to have been the body of Christ. He said: "When Jesus had dipped the bread, he gave it to Judas Iscariot, the son of Simon," (Cf. John 13, 26). But, as blessed Augustine says, not as some think, reading carelessly, did Judas then receive the body of Christ. For it must be understood that He had already distributed the sacrament of His body and blood to all these, where even Judas himself was, just as holy Luke very clearly relates. And then we come to this, where according to John's narrative through the morsel dipped and offered He very openly portrays His betrayer, perhaps signifying his feigning by the dipping of the bread. For all things that are dipped are not washed off but some are dipped that they may be stained. Now if this dipping signifies some good, not undeservedly did damnation follow what was displeasing to the same good. And indeed these are the words of the blessed Augustine on this question, whether Judas in the morsel received the body of Christ. Yet as a result of the fact that the Lord gave to His betrayer a dipped morsel to mark him, custom has it that the faithful should not receive the body of Christ when dipped.

V. *That the paschal lamb was the figure of the body of Christ.*

Just as at one time circumcision, in so far as it had to do with effecting the remission of sins, took the place of baptism, and the Red Sea presented a likeness and figure of the same, so the paschal lamb, whose flesh was eaten by the people and by whose blood the posts of the houses were marked, preceded in the figure of the sacrament of the body of Christ. After the truth came, the sign was taken from their midst, when indeed there was nothing in the future to be signified but something in the present to be received. Yet the figure remained as long as the thing did not yet exist, and it was exhibited first in likeness which afterwards was to be completed in truth. Egypt, the world; the devil, the destroyer; Christ, the lamb; the blood of the lamb, the passion of Christ; the house of souls, the bodies; the home of thoughts, hearts. These we dip with blood through faith in the passion, the others we dip with blood through imitation of the passion, opposing the sign of the cross within and without against adverse powers.

Finally we eat the flesh of the lamb when by taking His true body in the sacrament we are incorporated with Christ through faith and love. Elsewhere what is eaten is incorporated. Now when the body of Christ is eaten, not what is eaten but he who eats is incorporated with Him whom he eats. On this account Christ wished to be eaten by us, that He might incorporate us with Him. This is the sacrament of the body of Christ and the substance of the sacrament of the body of Christ. He, who eats and is incorporated, has the sacrament and has the substance of the sacrament. He who eats and is not incorporated has the sacrament but has not the substance of the sacrament. Just as he who is incorporated, even if he does not happen to eat, has the substance of the sacrament, although he has not the sacrament. He who takes has the sacrament, he who believes and loves has the substance of the sacrament. Therefore, it is better for him who believes and loves, even if he cannot take and eat, than for him who takes and eats and does not believe nor love or if he believes does not love.

VI. That the sacrament of the altar is also a figure as far as pertains to the appearance of bread and of wine, and is the substance as far as pertains to the truth of the body of Christ.

There are those who think that they have drawn a defence of error from certain passages in the Scriptures, saying that in the sacrament of the altar the body and blood of Christ do not truly exist but only an image of this and an appearance and figure, especially because Scripture sometimes says that what is taken in the Eucharist of the altar is the image or the appearance of that which will be received by participation with Jesus. These surely would not fall into the noose of this error, if they received the sacraments of God with right and humble faith or treated the Scriptures with fitting intelligence. But now, since in the sacraments of God they prefer their own meaning of faith in the Scriptures, they contemn holding a sane form of interpretation and it comes about that the words of truth cause them to be more befogged, until the intellect wrongly ministers error instead of truth. This, however, is not the fault of Scripture but the blindness of those who read and do not understand. And it is not the confusion of God's sacraments but the perverseness of those who presume.

Now here they have erred dangerously from so many manifest opinions and undoubted assertions, preferring certain ambiguous things and in them selecting the lie rather than the truth, not because this was said there but rather because this rather was believed by them. What then! Is the sacrament of the altar then not truth because it is a figure? Then neither is the death of Christ truth because it is a figure, and the resurrection of Christ is not truth because it is a figure. For the Apostle declares manifestly that the death of Christ and the resurrection are a figure and an image and a likeness and a sacrament and an example, saying: "Christ died for our sins and rose again for our justification," (Cf. Rom. 4, 24 and 25). And the Apostle Peter says: "Christ suffered for us, leaving you an example that you should follow in his steps," (Cf. 1, Peter, 21). Therefore, the death of Christ was an example, that we die for sin, and His resurrection was an example, that we live for justice. On this account then was it not truth? Then Christ did not truly die and did not truly rise, if His death or resurrection was not true. Far be it from the truth! For of Him it was written: "Surely he hath borne our infirmities and carried our sorrows," (Is. 53, 4). The death of Christ was true, and yet it was an example, and the resurrection of Christ was true and was an example. Why can the sacrament of the altar not be a likeness and truth? In one respect, indeed, a likeness; in another, truth.

VII. That there are three things in the sacrament of the altar: the appearance of bread and wine, the truth of the body of Christ, spiritual grace.

For although the sacrament is one, three distinct things are set forth there, namely, visible appearance, truth of body, and virtue of spiritual grace. For the visible species which is perceived visibly is one thing, the truth of body and blood which under visible appearance is believed invisibly another thing, and the spiritual grace which with body and blood is received invisibly and spiritually another. For what we see is the appearance of bread and wine, but what we believe under that appearance is the true body which hung on the cross and the true blood of Jesus which flowed from His side. We do not believe that through bread and wine the body and blood alone are signified but that under the appearance of bread and wine the true body and the true blood are consecrated, and that the visible appearance indeed is the sacrament of the true body and of the true blood, but that the body and blood are the sacrament of spiritual grace. And just as the appearance is perceived there, whose thing or substance is not believed to be there, so the thing whose appearance is not perceived is believed truly and substantially to be present there; for the appearance of bread and wine is seen, and the substance of the bread and wine is not believed, but the substance of the body and blood of Christ is believed and yet it is not discerned. Therefore, what is seen according to appearance is the sacrament and the image of that which is believed according to the truth of the body, and what is believed according to the truth of the body is the sacrament of that which is perceived according to spiritual grace.

Thus the sacrament of the altar and the Divine Eucharist in the true body and blood of Our Lord Jesus Christ is an image according to the appearance of bread and wine, in which it is perceived, and the thing is according to the truth of its substance, in which it is there believed and perceived. And again, that we now take Christ on the altar visibly, according to the appearance of the sacrament, and corporally, according to the truth of the body and blood of Christ, is the sacrament, and the image is that we should take the same Himself in the heart invisibly and spiritually according to the infusion of grace and the participation of the Holy Spirit. So the most divine Eucharist, which is treated visibly and corporally on the Altar, according to the appearance of bread and wine and according to the truth of the body and blood of Christ, is a sacrament and a sign and an image of the invisible and spiritual participation with Jesus, which is being accomplished within the heart through faith and love.

VIII. *Why Christ instituted the sacrament of His body and blood
under the appearance of bread and wine.*

The wisdom of God which manifests itself through visible things wished to show that the refection of souls is food, and He proposed flesh assumed as edible food that He might through the food of the flesh invite to the taste of Divinity. But lest again human infirmity might shudder at the touch of flesh in the taking of it, He veiled it with the appearance of the usual and principle food, and proposed that it be so taken that sense might be fostered in the one and faith might be built up in the other. For sense is fostered in the one, when it receives only the usual and customary things; while faith is built up in the other, when in that which one sees he recognizes the nature of what he does not see. So the appearance of bread and wine is proposed, that the full and perfect refection may be taught to be in the taking of the body and blood of Christ, by reason of the divinity of Christ. Now full refection is food and drink, but bread and wine are the principal substance of food and drink. And the appearance is proposed from the principal substance of refection, that He may be taken in it and through it the truth of the body and blood of Christ may be signified; just as He himself testifies, saying: "My flesh is meat indeed: and my blood is drink indeed," (Cf. John 6, 56).

Yet the Saviour himself likewise shows that this assumption of body and blood alone without the spiritual effect does not confer salvation, when He says: "It is the spirit that quickeneth: the flesh profiteth nothing," (John 6, 64). Accordingly, the virtue and the fulness of the spiritual refection which is in the body and blood of Christ is signified through the appearance of bread and wine; but it is perfected in the reception of grace by the infusion of internal and eternal refection. So, although the three are there in one, in the first is found the sign of the second, but in the second the cause of the third, in the third truly the virtue of the second and the truth of the first, and these three are in one and are one sacrament. Thus it is clear that the assumption of the most divine Eucharist is a sacrament and the image of the participation with Jesus, since that which we receive visibly as His sacrament is a sign that we should be united with Him spiritually. Now the Eucharist, that is good grace, is itself, of course, called the most divine and holy victim, since it makes people divine and makes those participants in divinity who partake of it in a worthy manner. And since truth itself is also a sign, in which the true flesh of Christ is taken under the appearance of bread, in His flesh worthily taken the reception and the participation and the society of divinity are also presented, on this account most divine, most holy, and sanctifying all things that sanctify and are holy.

IX. *Of what nature the change of bread and wine into the body of Christ is to be understood.*

Through the words of sanctification the true substance of bread and the true substance of wine are changed into the true body and blood of Christ, the appearance of bread and wine alone remaining, substance passing over into substance. But the change itself is not to be believed to be according to union but according to transition, since by no means does essence add unto increase of essence, so that through what is added that to which it is added becomes greater, but it happens by transition that what is added becomes one with that to which it is added. Nor do we say that in the bread the body of Christ is so consecrated that the body of Christ receives being from bread, nor, so to speak, that a new body has suddenly been made from a changed essence; rather we say that essence has been changed into the true body itself and that the substance of bread and wine has not been reduced to nothing because it ceased to be what it was, but rather that it has been changed because it began to be something else which it was not, and the thing itself which began to be did not receive being from it because it was bread, but it itself received its being when it ceased to be what it was. This we have distinguished rather strongly on account of those who pass judgment on faith according to their own reason, and proceeding with their own feeling strive to assert either that this alone is what is perceived or that it is such as is believed, specifically, that because the appearance of bread and wine alone is perceived the substance of bread and wine is there or, because the substance of the body and blood of Christ is believed, the appearance and quality of bread and wine are passibly in that which is perceived, as if the appearance of that whose substance is not present could not appear, or the substance of that whose form does not appear lies hidden.

X. *What those three portions signify, which are made of the body of Christ in the sacrament of the altar.*

These three portions which are made on the altar from the body and blood of Christ have a mystic signification. For the entire Church is the body of Christ, namely, the head with its members, and there are found in that body, so to speak, three parts of which the whole body consists. One part is the head itself. For the head is both head and likewise a part of the body. And so the head itself is one part of the body. Another part of the body consists of those members which immediately followed the head, and they are together with the head itself, where the head itself is. As it is written: "Wheresoever the body shall be, there shall the eagles also be gathered together," (Matt. 24, 28; Luke 17, 37). Therefore, those who already have passed from this life, whose bodies rest in the sepulchres and whose souls are with Christ, these are another part of the body and are, as it were, these two parts at the same time, namely, the head and this other part of the body.

Therefore, on the altar two parts are reserved apart outside the chalice, as it were, outside suffering, since the head itself already immortal and incapable of suffering has arisen from the dead neither to die more nor to suffer more. And similarly those who as saints have passed from this life and already glory and rejoice with their head, themselves also awaiting the resurrection of their flesh and immortality, now feel neither any pain nor suffering, and they are at the same time those two parts outside the chalice and outside suffering, since these have crossed over first. The third part is placed in the chalice, signifying those who still live in suffering until they themselves also go out of this life and pass over to their head where they neither may die nor suffer more.

XI. *That the body of Christ, when it seems to be divided, is divided according to appearance alone, but remains entire according to itself, thus entire in individual parts, just as in different places it is one and the very same.*

Do not think, when you see the parts in the sacrament of the altar, that the body of Christ has, as it were, been divided or separated from itself or as if torn limb from limb. He himself remains whole in Himself; neither is He divided nor parted. But what pertained to the mystical signification had to be shown you in appearance. Therefore, He shows you the external appearance, by which your sense is instructed, and He preserves the internal incorruption of His body, in which His unity is not divided. One part is seen and, as it were, seems to be a part, and the whole is there, and another part is seen and, as it were, seems to be another, and is the same and the whole itself. Although a third part is seen similarly, it is itself the same and the whole. The whole is here and the whole is there. Nor is it less in part than in the whole nor greater in the whole than in the part. Whatever member of the parts you make, the whole is in each.

Do not wonder. This is the work of God. If He can be one in diverse places, why can He not also be whole in individual parts? Both are wonderful but they are not false because of the fact that they are wonderful. And it is true that it is wonderful; yet let it not be wonderful because it is the work of God. It is not wonderful if the Marvelous One works marvelous things. How, you say, can one body be at the same time in diverse places? He is here, He is there. And the whole is in both places and in many places similarly. Do not wonder. He who made place made body and the place in the body and the body in place. And He who effected that one body was in one place effected as He wished, and if He had wished He would have done otherwise. For when He wishes He does otherwise, and He is just as He himself always wishes. Now since He himself made one body to be in one place, you have seen what was done and you know nothing except what you saw was done. So you marvel when you see or hear anything other than you are accustomed to see and hear. Now He himself does not marvel when He does anything other than what He is accustomed to do, since when He did that He knew even then that He could have done otherwise if He had wished. Therefore, when you begin to marvel at anything and your thoughts perhaps say to you: How can this be?, consider Him who does this and the thing will cease to be marvelous, whatever it may be. And if perhaps it shall not cease to be marvelous, yet it will not be incredible. If the doer is considered omnipotent, whatever the thing will be, it will not be impossible.

XII. *That those things which seem unworthy in the body of Christ are done according to appearance only.*

Do not be horrified that it so happens sometimes, as it customarily happens, that you see some things take place in this sacrament which will seem to be unworthy. This is so in the evident appearance only. He shows you the appearance, He preserves the truth for Himself. He exhibits to your sense the likeness of the corporeal, that your sense in all things may be trained in its own. He preserves the truth of inviolable and immortal nature for His body, lest it be corrupted in its own. If He should withdraw from likeness in something, it would not be a true sacrament, and He would betray Himself there, and He would take away room for faith and would not then be believed. But that would be seen which should not be done. And thus in so far as pertains to us He preserves through all things the likeness of corruptible food and yet in so far as pertains to Himself He does not lose the truth of an inviolable body. He seems to be gnawed to pieces and He remains uncorrupted. He seems to be affected or sullied and He perseveres unviolated. He endures that these things be done about Him, lest our sense perceive something strange, but He does not receive these things in Himself, lest His incorruptible nature lose its purity. So great is the dignity and cleanness of Christ's body that it can neither be affected by any corruption nor stained by sordidness. And so if at any time you see these things take place do not fear for Him but be solicitous for yourself. He himself cannot be injured, you can be harmed who can believe badly.

XIII. *What happens to the body of Christ and its corporeal presence after the taking of the sacrament.*

But perhaps your thoughts again ask you what happens to the body of Christ after it has been taken and eaten. Such are the thoughts of men that they scarcely wish to be quiet in these things which especially are not to be questioned. So your heart says to you: What happened to the body of Christ after I took and ate it? Then give heed. Do you seek the corporeal presence of Christ? Seek it in heaven. There is Christ sitting at the right hand of God the Father. He wished to be with you temporarily when and as long as it was necessary. He showed His corporeal presence to you temporarily, that He might raise you to the spiritual presence. So He came to you corporeally and showed His corporeal presence to you temporarily, that through it the spiritual might be found which was not taken away. Thus by taking on flesh He once came into the world and according to corporeal presence He associated with men temporarily that He might raise them to seek and find the spiritual presence. Afterwards, when the dispensation was completed, according to corporeal presence He withdrew and according to spiritual presence He remained. For that He might show that according to spiritual presence He did not withdraw, when according to corporeal presence He arranged to go away, He said: "Behold I am with you all days, even to the consummation of the world." (Matt. 28, 20).

Thus then in His sacrament now He comes temporarily to you and He is by means of it corporeally with you, that you through His corporeal presence may be raised to seek the spiritual and be assisted in finding it. When you hold His sacrament in your hands, He is with you corporeally. When you take it in your mouth, He is with you corporeally. When you eat it and when you taste it, He is with you corporeally. Finally in sight, in touch, in taste, He is with you corporeally. As long as the sense is affected corporeally, His corporeal presence is not taken away. But after the corporeal feeling in receiving fails, then the corporeal presence is not to be sought but the spiritual is to be retained; the dispensation is completed, the perfect sacrament remains as a virtue; Christ passes from mouth to heart. It is better for you that it pass into your mind than into your stomach. That food is of the soul not of the body. Do not seek in Him the custom of corporeal food. He came to you that He might be eaten, not that He might be consumed. He comes that He may be tasted, not that He may be incorporated. Augustine heard a voice from heaven, because this could not have been said or replied to him by the earthly. I am the food of the great, increase and you will eat me, not that you may change me into you as the food of your flesh but you will be changed into me. And so discern prudently what has been exhibited to the sense in the sacrament of God, what has been accommodated to the spirit, so that, if it is customary, after the reception has been completed you may feel something again. In this also the appearance according to propriety is made serviceable to the sense, that the truth of the likeness may be preserved everywhere. For if in anything, in so far as must be shown to the sense, the likeness should fail, without doubt there would be no sacrament there. But the thing itself would be betrayed and made manifest by an evident miracle, which is not fitting as long as faith holds place. After this then, if you seek the corporeal presence of Christ, seek it in heaven. Seek there where he was even before He began to be with you corporeally through His sacrament and whence He did not depart when He came to you.

XIV. *That the celebration of the body of Christ is called the mass, and when and by whom it was first instituted and why it is called the mass.*

The celebration of the mass is carried on for a commemoration of the passion of Christ, just as He Himself ordered the Apostles giving them His body and blood, saying: "Do this for a commemoration of me," (Luke 22, 19). The blessed apostle Peter is said to have been the first of all to celebrate this mass at Antioch, in which at the beginning of faith only three prayers were said, starting from that place where it is said: Therefore this oblation. The other different parts were added by the Holy Fathers afterwards at various times. Now the mass was said as if transmitted or as if a transmission, because the faithful people through the ministry of the priest who performs the duty of a mediator between God and man transmit prayers and vows and oblations to God. Even the sacred victim Himself can be called a mass because He was transmitted first, namely, by the Father to us that He might be with us, afterwards by us to the Father that He might intercede for us with the Father; first, by the Father to us through the Incarnation, afterwards to the Father by us through the Passion; now in the sacrament first by the Father to us through sanctification, by which He begins to be with us, afterwards to the Father by us through oblation, by which He intercedes for us.

Now the mass (*missa*) has been so called as some think from "sending forth," (*emittendo*) because when the priest begins to consecrate the body of the Lord the catechumens are sent outside (*emittuntur*). For when the gospel has been read, the deacon proclaims: If any catechumen is present, let him go out. Catechumens should not be present at the sacred mysteries which are not committed to any save the baptized and Christians, just as of some who bore the stamp of catechumens and not yet of the reborn it is written: "But Jesus did not trust himself unto them," (John 2, 24).

NINTH PART

On the Sacraments that have been Instituted for Practice and that All are Sanctified through the Word of God.

I. *On the sacraments that have been instituted for practice and that all are sanctified through the word of God.*

There are certain sacraments in the Church and, although salvation does not depend on them principally, yet salvation is increased from them according as devotion is exercised. Although all these cannot be enumerated at present, nevertheless we should not omit certain ones as examples of all. So of these sacraments some consist of such things as the water of aspersion, the reception of ashes, the blessing of branches and of candles, and other such things. Now others consist of deeds such as the sign of the cross, the blowing of exorcization, the spreading of the hands, the bending of the knees, and other acts of this kind. Others consist of words, like the invocation of the Trinity and whatever else is done in this manner. Now all these things are sanctified by the word of God, whether they are sanctified through the utterance of words by invoking divine power or receive the effect of sanctification through the same divine power by the exhibiting of faith alone. For where there is true faith, the word of God cannot be lacking, since the word itself is conceived by faith and operates through faith.

"All," the Apostle says, "whatsoever you do, do in the name of the Lord," (Cf. Col. 3, 17). But it is not fitting that we should understand that the Apostle ordered us in all our works to prefer words but in all our works to cling to right faith. For he operates in the name of the Lord all that he does, who through right faith knows that he can do no good without Him and, if he does anything praiseworthy, that he should not glory without Him. And he faithfully in all his work both before a deed seeks help from Him and after every deed turns all the good which he has accomplished to His praise and glory. Therefore, just as all the things that we do by faith alone even without the offering of words are said to be done rightly in the name of the Lord, so too certain sacraments are sanctified without the offering of words, through faith alone. For words themselves are sometimes sacraments; but they do not receive sanctification from other words. Yet no sacrament is sanctified without that word which, whether invoked by faith alone or by both faith and the utterance of words, accomplishes all sanctification.

II. *On the water of aspersion which is blessed together with salt.*

Alexander, the fifth Pope after blessed Peter, established that salt and water should be blessed for sprinkling the people and their habitations, following the example indeed of Elisaeus, the prophet, who, we read, had put salt into the water, so that the bitter springs might be turned into sweetness by this condiment. Therefore, with this sanctified water the faithful are sprinkled and the habitations of the faithful are cleansed of the illusion and the disturbance of evil spirits.

Now the significance of this sacrament is the following: that water signifies penitence for past acts, salt discretion and caution regarding future acts, and, if these two are mixed together, bitter conscience is turned into sweetness and the illusions and the disturbances of the demons no longer dominate it. Thus following the above mentioned institution, every Sunday we bless salt and water mixing them together, that by this sprinkling we may fortify the faithful and the abodes of the faithful against spiritual iniquities.

III. *On the reception of ashes.*

Ecclesiastical institution has it that every year at the beginning of quadragesima, which is called the head of the fast, on the fourth festival when the votive fast is undertaken, consecrated ashes are placed on the heads of the faithful, as a recollection of course of our mortality, that mortal man, who by habit of repentance and by recollection of his sins is goaded to devotion, may then also be humbled through the memory of his foundation. Therefore, it is said to him: "Remember that dust thou art and into dust thou shalt return," (Cf. Gen. 3, 19).

IV. *On blessing branches of palms and foliage.*

Ecclesiastical custom also has it that, on the Sunday which is next before the Paschal feast, the branches of palms and the foliage of trees be blessed and distributed to the people, to carry as those did, who while singing and praising with branches of palms and flourishing foliage of trees met the Lord Jesus on the same days as He ascended to Jerusalem, (Cf. Matt. 21, 8). Thus not only is it proposed that this must be done by us corporeally as they did it corporeally, but rather this is signified, that either in that or in this corporeal deed there must be spiritual imitation. For the palm is the sign of victory but the flourishing branches signify good works. So then we meet Christ in an act of praise with branches of palms and foliage, when we praise Him with good works and with action worthy of graces as the triumpher over death.

V. *Regarding the candle which is blessed on Holy Sabbath and re-garding lambs which are blessed on the Pasch.*

Pope Zozimus established that a large candle be blessed on the Holy Sabbath of the Pasch, which the deacon blesses after benediction has been received from the priest. This candle designates Christ: in the wax humanity, in the fire divinity; and as it illuminates it precedes the catechumens to baptism, just as once a column of fire preceded the children of Israel as they crossed the Red Sea, illuminating by fire and shading by a cloud, (Cf. Exod. 14, 19, 20, 24, etc.). Under the same figure according to an ancient custom, on the paschal day in the Roman Church waxen lambs are blessed and distributed to the people.

VI. *On the signs by whose sound the faithful are called together.*

The use of signs was taken from the Old Testament, where the Lord ordered silver trumpets to be made thin, by which the multitude of people ought to have been called together. In imitation of these trumpets signs were made of bronze metal in the church, to stir the hearts of the faithful that by these a sign may be given when they should come together, (Cf. Num. 10, 2, and 3). These metal vessels signify the mouths of those preaching. The metal plectra by which they are struck within that they may emit sound are tongues of the same. Now the rope is the measure of life and the mode of conversation which is set forth in

Scripture. The rope is held by the hand when Scripture is fulfilled by work. He follows the rope upwards who by the guidance of Holy Scripture is elevated to good things. He drags the rope downward who with the teaching of the same does not know to what extent he lies pressed down in evils. He is fit to call together the people of God who elevated by work shows examples of goodness and bowed by humility truly recognizes his infirmity. Therefore, the evangelical signs are more durable and are heard longer than the trumpets of the law, because the voice of the Old Testament resounded only temporarily for the Jews, but the sound of evangelical preaching went out among all nations to the ends of the world and will not cease even unto the end of time.

VII. *On curtains.*

The curtain which hangs before the sacred objects, that is, between the people and the clergy, signifies the veil of the letter by which the truth of the Gospel was still covered for those who were under the law. That curtain which is hung between the sacred objects and the Holy of Holies, that is, between the clergy and the sanctuary, signifies the veil of mortal nature, by which the secrets of heaven are still hidden from us even when placed in the state of grace. The first veil is the one which, we read, was rent at the death of Christ, (Cf. Matt. 27, 51; Mark 15, 38). The second veil will not be removed until the time of the resurrection. For this reason at the time of Quadragesima, which signifies the present life, one veil only is spread between us and the Holy of Holies, and this will not be taken away until the day of resurrection; for the letter to be sure has now been revealed but mortality has not yet been taken away, all of which, however, will have to be taken from our midst in the future, when this mortal object shall put on immortality and the corruptible shall put on incorruption. For then, when His face has been revealed, we shall go forward or rather we shall go out to contemplate the glory of the Lord, that we may know Him whom we know now through faith alone by seeing Him face to face, just as He is.

VIII. *On the other sacraments that consist of deeds.*

There are many other sacraments of the Church expressed by objects or deeds, all of which cannot be enumerated here, for there are many of them, and so this brief discussion does not include them. The breathing in exorcization signifies the virtue of the Holy Spirit by the coming of whom the evil spirit is routed and put to flight, just as it is written: "Thy wind blew and the sea covered them: they sunk as lead in the mighty waters," (Exodus 15, 10). The sign of the cross shows the virtue of Christ's passion. By this then, when the forehead is impressed, the Christian is fortified. When he is placed face to face with impending danger, opposing power is put to flight, first against arms, second against weapons; first against defense, second against attack. The beating of the breast designates compunction of heart. The breast is beaten that empty thoughts and wicked desires may be driven from the heart. The inclining of the head, the bending of the knees, or prostration, signify humility and reverence or even the asking of pardon. The spreading of the hands shows charity and the desire of good shows greatness.

IX. *On those sacraments that consist of words.*

There are likewise other sacraments set forth by the utterance of words only, and these too show varied significance. Pope Celestine established that the antiphons from the psalms of David should be sung before the sacrifice, which is called the introit. Different persons composed the collects, chiefly Galasius and Gregory. "The Lord be with you," (Ruth 2, 4), was taken from ancient practice; Boaz saluting his reapers used this salutation and the prophet in Paralipomenon salutes Asa the king and those who were with him, saying: "The Lord is with you," (2 Paralip. 15, 2). In earliest times the mass was begun with the epistle of Paul, after which the gospel followed, just as now the angelic hymn, which is recited at the office of the mass on festival days, we read was repeated first by angels, (Luke 2, 14). And what has been added to these is believed to have been appended by the blessed Hilary of Poitiers, by whom the hymn was enlarged and completed as we sing it today. Now Pope Symmachus, the fifty third pope in order, established that this hymn be sung in the church at the office of the mass on Our Lord's days and on the birthdays of martyrs.

The Italians have handed down the response which signifies operation. *Alleluia* signifies happiness. By the shout with which it is completed ineffable joy is expressed as finally about to come. A tract sometimes signifies tribulation, as *De profundis, Commovisti;* sometimes joy, as *Jubilate, Laudate.* One hundred and fifty Fathers at the Council of Constantinople composed *Credo in unum Deum* against the heresy of Macedonius, bishop of the same city, who declared the Holy Spirit a creature. Pope Sixtus established that, before the consecration and after the hymn, *Sanctus, Sanctus, Sanctus,* should be sung, the threefold repetition of which is a confession of the Trinity. It is called secret because it is said secretly, lest it become worthless. Once it was spoken with a high voice, but we read that shepherds, while they sang it in the field, having learned it by the daily practice of listening to it, were struck from heaven, and so the custom is thought to have been changed. Pope Pelagius teaches that those who, because of some dissension midst the sacred mysteries of the masses, do not celebrate the memory of the apostolic pontiff according to custom were separated from communion with the whole world. *Te igitur in primis,* this supplication and consecration holy Pope Gelasius composed for the greater part.

Blessed Gregory added *diesque nostros in tua pace disponas* and decreed that the Lord's prayer be recited over the body of Christ according to what we read in his life. *Qui pridie quam pateretur* up to *in mei memoriam facietis* the Apostles had used, and in these words they celebrated the sacrament of the body of Christ. Some say that Pope Alexander had added these. Pope Leo decided actually to call the holy sacrifice the immaculate victim. Pope Felix decreed that masses be celebrated in memory of the martyrs. Pope Gregory decreed in a canon that this be said: *Quorum solemnitatis hodie in conspectu tuae maiestatis celebrantur: Domine Deus noster in toto orbe terrarum, intra quorum nos consortium.* Pope Sergius decreed that the *Agnus Dei* should be sung at the breaking of the Lord's body.

Pope Innocent wrote to Decentius: "You declare that before the mysteries have been completed priests bestow peace upon certain people or interchange it amongst themselves, since, besides all those things which I should not reveal, peace must be disclosed as necessary, through which it is established afterwards that the people have given consent to all that is being done in the mysteries and is being celebrated in the church, and let these mysteries be shown to have been completed by concluding with the sign of peace."

Three hundred and eighteen bishops at the synod of Nicaea composed *Gloria et honor Patri et Filio et Spiritui sancto in saeculo saeculorum. Amen* against the heresy of Arius, who asserted that the Son was less than the Father, and the Holy Ghost less than both. Jerome afterwards translated this hymn from Greek into Latin for Pope Damasus and added: *Sicut erat in principio et nunc et semper.* "*Pater noster,*" (Matt. 6, 9), Christ himself handed down to His disciples. For this reason in particular is it called the Lord's prayer, in which the seven different petitions are the sacrament of a sevenfold grace. The symbol of faith, that is, *Credo in Deum,* the twelve Apostles dictated, comprised of the same number of statements, which number establishes the sacrament of apostolic faith. Blessed Athanasius composed *Quicumque vult.* And many other holy Fathers have added now some and now others in the celebration of the divine office for the glory of the Church and the instruction and the devotion of the faithful.

X. *On sacred things but not sacraments.*

There are certain other sacred things in the Church, but not sacraments, which also, although they have not the effect of grace and do not confer sanctification, are nevertheless sacred in that they pertain to holy things and are closely connected with those things which both have sanctity and confer sanctification. Of the same nature are all things that pertain to the adornment of churches or are contained among their possessions, which to some extent are holy in that they have been given over and assigned to the ministry of holy things. These then are holy, so to speak, in a simple way; but those to which these are consecrated are the holy of holies. Therefore, he who takes a holy thing from the holy performs a sacrilege. But he who dares to desecrate the holy things themselves commits an abomination. Therefore, of the same nature are the things which are called holy or sanctified by the holy, whatever the Church possesses in earthly substance, whether in money or in land, especially in tithes, which were so instituted from the beginning that they could never have been removed from the divine ministry without sin or from the use of those who serve God and have been allotted to the divine ministry. These indeed in the beginning seem to have been established rather as the form of a sacrament. But afterwards, under the written law and grace, they have been reserved for the support of the ministers of God, so that by them the devotion of those who offered them was merited and the necessity of those who received them was comforted. These, therefore, can by no means be removed lawfully from the use of the Church nor pass over into the possession of the laity whether by exchange or by donation.

Other corporeal things which the Church possesses, whether in lands or in money, as long indeed as they are possessed by it licitly, cannot be taken away without blame, but if cause and reason shall demand, by exchange or by donation they can pass over to another's possession. Therefore, just as it is rapine and violence to take away goods of this kind from a person who possesses them justly, so is it sacrilege and more than this rapine to take them from the Church when she possesses them justly. Moreover, no one can in any way usurp or retain tithes without the blame of sacrilege, except those alone for whose support they were ordained by divine institution. Therefore, there is this difference between tithes and other possessions of the Church: tithes pertain to sacred things both by institution and possession, but other ecclesiastical possessions pertain to sacred things by possession only. Thus, some possessions of the Church can be transferred to other possessors with reasonable exchange but tithes cannot be possessed by others at all; the former cannot be taken away, the latter cannot be transferred. In the former there is sacrilege, if they should be taken away; in the latter, if they should be transferred. But the bishops should be the dispensers of tithes and other ecclesiastical possessions, that they may distribute them reasonably to those who serve the Church, and if any of these tithes by chance sometime be accommodated for the support of those who do not serve in ecclesiastical offices but yet in secret have been bound to divine service, indulgence is not an obligation, provided that this be of the portion of the poor, not of the sustenance of clerics. For in what is due the ministry the worker is worthy of his pay, and he does not sustain well the one in need who defrauds the one in service.

Tenth Part

On Simony.

I. *Why simony is so called and what simony is.*

Simony received its name from Simon Magus who left to posterity a fatal example of this evil. For simony is the desire to procure spiritual grace by money. When this is done, both he in truth who sells and he who buys are struck by the same sentence, since they are proven liable to the blame of the same guilt.

II. *On the authors of simony.*

The contagion of simoniac heresy once flourished in Balaam who, when the price of divination was proposed, sought to curse the people of God, (Numbers 22). Then we read that two destructive authors of this heresy arose, the one under prophetic, the other under apostolic doctrine. First Giezi is seen to be the master of the sellers (Cf. 4 Kings 5), then Simon is seen to be the author of the buyers, (Cf. Acts 8). But, as it is said, the followers of these, just as they are not different in error, are thus not distinguished in damnation.

III. *On those who buy or sell spiritual things.*

Those who buy or sell sacred orders are set down as convicted without mercy, because surely they are unworthy of sacred orders who are proved to have sinned in the sacred orders themselves. We read that those who come from the heretics into the unity of the Church have sometimes been received in their own orders, since some heretics in receiving orders did not err, but there was another cause and doctrine which impeded their faith. But the heresy and sin of the Simoniaci is their very ordination. Therefore, rightly are they not received in their orders, since they sinned in their very orders. But it must be known that those who are unwittingly ordained by Simoniaci, since they do not think that these Catholics are Simoniaci, receive spiritual grace through their ministry, if they do not become participants in their error of which they had not been conscious. Now those who offer money for obtaining spiritual grace, even though ordained by Catholics, are Simoniaci.

But you say to me: How can one ordained by a Simoniacus through the imposition of the hand receive the gift of the Holy Spirit? How can a Simoniacus give what he has not, even if he is thought a Catholic? Hear how. Just as an adulterer, just as a fornicator, just as a drunken or avaricious person can give what he does not have, so the Simoniacus can give what he does not have and can truly give to those who are worthy to receive. For the giving is done through his ministry, not through his merit. Thus grace is given to those, who are not participants in his error and are not conscious of his guilt, through him; it is not given by him. The minister is wicked but a good bestower; nevertheless he is a minister. Just as a heretic or any other evil minister is evil, and yet is a minister, evil in that he has error or malice, a minister in that he has office; so the Simoniacus, (for he himself is also a heretic, although not in faith but in deed), is an evil minister and yet is a minister; evil in that he is a Simoniacus, a minister in that he was ordained to office; evil in that he gave a price, a minister in that he received an order and an office.

But you say to me: How was he able to receive an order or an office who gave a price? Hear how. Unto destruction, unto perdition! He was able to buy an office; he was not able to receive grace. Yet since he received and holds the office, through his ministry indeed grace and the office are given to the good. From the evil indeed no grace but the office alone is received, and yet it is received although unto his destruction who receives evilly, just as unto his destruction who gave evilly.

IV. *On those who by buying corporeal things in the Church buy spiritual things with them and in them.*

Now there are certain things in the Church and, while they are bought for a price, participation in spiritual dignity is also received along with corporeal benefit. Where indeed someone is known to sell or buy one of two things, he is proven to have left neither one unsold or unbought. But you tell me: How can this be? I bought food and clothing in a church, I did not buy the church. I bought a log; I bought it for supply; I bought only corporeal things; I bought nothing spiritual, nor did I wish to do so. Tell me then: Who assigned you a place in the chorus, in the *capitulum*? If you did not buy these things, how do you possess them? Who gave these to you? But, you say, I received these free; I bought the others. These have been given free. You speak well. You bought a sheep and did not buy the wool, but received it free. Yet if you had not bought the sheep, you would not have had the wool. You gave a price for a tree, that you might eat its fruit free. Very cleverly did you think to enter upon a ridiculous falsehood.

See then how you do not buy what you would not have had, if you had not given a price. Either you confess that you bought this equally or, if you did not buy it, do not take what is not yours. But you say to me again: What then? Can I not buy a log from the Church and procure the material for corporeal sustenance at a price without the sin of simony? Behold I have my estates or my money with which I could have been sustained and have lived, but perhaps I fear the violence of princes or the fraud of relatives or something else. Perhaps also I consider failing old age or bodily weakness. I see that I myself cannot dispose of my property as is expedient and serve my own advantage. I come to a church; I commend my property to it and I commit the care of my life to it, that it may nourish and sustain me and minister assistance to me from my own; and, lest perhaps I be defrauded in some way, I demand that a certain and determined ration be established for me, such as, for example, anyone of those receives who serve the Church, who have been inscribed in the title of the church. I demand that a ration be furnished for the use of daily fare, just as anyone has who is in the Church, who lives by the Church, and serves the Church. The Church gives and concedes that to me, receiving mine and returning hers, rather dispensing mine, not hers, to me. You ask then what conclusion is to be drawn from this. I reply to you briefly, that if you make the Church the dispenser in your life or leave Her as your heir after death, neither do I wish nor am I able to stop you. And if She feeds you from your own or for your own, the care is not sin, the necessity not iniquity. Thus meanwhile, that you may seek and receive nothing, corporeal necessities are granted you; the commerce of iniquity is denied.

V. *On the fact that corporeal things alone are sold.*

Now it happens sometimes that the possessions of the Church or other ecclesiastical corporeal goods are given away or sold by evil prelates, and are thus alienated from the Church's use. To this class the crime of simony does not seem to belong, although grave sin is not lacking. For how great the iniquity is, is manifest: those who were appointed to build and protect churches contribute to their destruction and to the dissipation of the goods that belong to them, especially if what is taken away is such as can never licitly pass over to another's use, as, for example, the tithes which were established from the beginning for the sustenance of those only who serve the tabernacle. So, what else is the transferring of those things to the laity than the taking of the sacred from the sacred? Thus, then, if every sin is given a fitting name, no evil is done in the judgment of equity.

ELEVENTH PART

On the Sacrament of Marriage.

I. *On the sacrament of marriage.*

Although all sacraments took their beginning after sin and on account of sin, we read that the sacrament of marriage alone was established even before sin, yet not as a remedy but as an office. Now in marriage these things must be considered and discerned first: the origin and the institution, together with the manner and its causes, and its variation according to time and place and rites.

II. *On the origin of marriage.*

The author of marriage is God. For He himself decreed that there be marriage, when He made woman as an assistance to man in the propagation of the race. Adam also knowing in spirit for what use woman had been made, when she had been brought to him, said: "This now is bone of my bones, and flesh of my flesh. Wherefore a man shall leave father and mother, and shall cleave to his wife: and they shall be two in one flesh," (Cf. Gen. 2, 23 and 24). And Christ also in Cana of Galilee, (Cf. John 2), not only by corporeal presence but also by the exhibition of a miracle consecrated nuptials. All this shows that marriage is from God and is good.

III. *On the twofold institution of marriage and on the twofold cause of the institution.*

The institution of marriage is twofold: one before sin for office, the other after sin for remedy; the first, that nature might be multiplied; the second, that nature might be supported and vice checked. The first institution proposed marriage in a compact of love, that in it might be the sacrament of the society which exists in the spirit between God and the soul. But it proposed the office of marriage in the mingling of flesh that in it might be the sacrament of the society which was to be in the flesh between Christ and the Church. The second institution sanctioned marriage in a compact of love that through its goods what belonged to weakness and evil in the mingling of flesh might be excused. Now the office of marriage in the mingling of the flesh conceded that in it besides the multiplication of the genus of those generating weakness might be supported.

But the Apostle indicates why the sacrament of marriage was instituted, (1 Cor. 7), where he shows that a man is the image of God and through this in some way a woman bears the stamp of the rational soul. Likewise God himself, the institutor and the ordainer, shows why the office of marriage was first instituted, when He says: "Increase and multiply and fill the earth," (Cf. Gen. 1, 28). Now the office of marriage is this, that the mingling of flesh was established before sin not for the remedy of weakness but for the multiplication of progeny; after sin, blessed Augustine testifies that the very same was conceded as a remedy for weakness, saying: The weakness of both sexes inclining toward the ruin of shamefulness is rightly supported by the honor of marriage, so that what was office for the sound is remedy for the sick. Likewise the very same Augustine testifies in his book, On the Conjugal Good, that in marriage, marriage itself is one thing and is the sacrament of something else, and that the office itself of marriage is one thing and the sacrament another, saying: In marriage there seems to be some good, not only because of the propagation of children but also because of the natural association between the different sexes. Otherwise it would not indeed be called marriage in the case of old people, if either they had lost children or had not begotten them, among whom, even if the ardour of the flesh has disappeared, the order of charity nevertheless flourishes. Likewise he says: In nuptials the sanctity of the sacrament flourishes more than the fruitfulness of the womb. Wherefore, some who do not understand these words: "That woman cannot attain to the sacrament of Christ and of the Church, with whom carnal commerce is known to have taken place," think that the sacrament of marriage cannot exist where carnal intercourse has not taken place. For they do not know that the office of marriage in the intercourse of flesh typifies that union which was made between Christ and the Church through His assumption of flesh, and thus the sacrament of Christ and of the Church could not be where carnal commerce had not been. Yet true marriage and the true sacrament of marriage can exist, even if carnal commerce has not followed; in fact the more truly and the more sacredly it can exist, the more it has nothing in it at which chastity may blush but has that of which charity may boast.

For marriage itself is a sacrament just as also the office of marriage is known to be a sacrament. But marriage, according as it is worthy, is a sacrament of that society which exists in spirit between God and the soul. The office of marriage indeed is a sacrament of society, which is in the flesh between Christ and the Church. It is written, he says: "They shall be two in one flesh," (Gen. 2, 24), and if two are in one flesh, indeed there are not two but one flesh. "This is," as the Apostle says, "the great sacrament in Christ and in the church," (Cf. Ephes. 5, 32), to which sacrament woman cannot attain with whom carnal commerce is known not to have taken place. Yet she can attain to another sacrament, not great in Christ and the Church but greater in God and in the soul. Why? If that which is in the flesh is great, is not this much greater which is in the spirit? He says: "It is the spirit that quickeneth: the flesh profiteth nothing," (John 6, 64). If then that is great which is in the flesh, surely that is much greater which is in the spirit.

If God is rightly called betrothed by Sacred Scripture and the rational spirit is spoken of as betrothed, surely there is something between God and the soul of which whatever exists in marriage between male and female is the sacrament and the image. And perhaps, to speak more specifically, the very association which is preserved externally in marriage by a compact is a sacrament and the substance of the sacrament itself is the mutual love of souls which is guarded in turn by the bond of conjugal society and agreement. And this very love again, by which male and female are united in the sanctity of marriage by their souls, is a sacrament and the sign of that love by which God is joined to the rational soul internally through the infusion of His grace and the participation of His spirit. Therefore, the bond of flesh, which before sin was office in marriage and after sin was granted in the same as a remedy, is thus joined in both ways to marriage so that it is with marriage, is not marriage of itself. For even before it there is true marriage and without it marriage can be holy; then indeed, if that were not present, less fruitfully; but now, if it should not be present, more sincerely. For the fact that after sin the bond of flesh is admitted in marriage is rather a matter of indulgence and compassion, lest the vice of concupiscence, which took root in human flesh after sin, might pour forth disgracefully into every excess, if it could never have been received licitly.

IV. *What marriage is.*

Some have thought that marriage should be defined in these words: marriage is an agreement between male and female that preserves their individual association in life. To this definition one should add "legitimate," because, if the agreement between male and female has not been legitimate, that is, made legitimately and between legitimate persons, then marriage cannot be consecrated. Now we call those persons legitimate in whom no reasonable cause can be established why they cannot mutually confirm the pact of marriage. Now I say, "in whom no reasonable cause can be shown," because, even if by chance such a cause exists but is hidden and concealed and not yet acknowledged by the judgment of the Church, in so far as the judgment of the Church is concerned, the marriage pact can neither be prohibited from taking place nor, after it has taken place, can it be weakened so as not to last. For what is entirely hidden, in so far as the judgment of the Church is concerned, should be said not to be, since as far as accomplishing or preventing something is concerned, it does not differ from what does not exist.

Now the first institution excepted only two persons, that is, father and mother, from the contract of marriage, where it asserted that man would leave father and mother that he might be able to cleave to his wife, in these words: "Wherefore a man shall leave father and mother, and shall cleave to his wife," (Gen. 2, 24). It is manifest that those who are left on account of this are not sought after for this. So the first institution excepted only these two persons. Among all the rest it forbade no woman to anyone for contracting the sacrament of marriage. Afterwards there came a second institution which was made by law and excepted certain other persons, either for the dignity of nature or for the increase of chastity. And thereafter that began to be illicit by prohibition which had been granted by nature, wherein indeed, if the prohibition is not ignored culpably, ignorance is excused in the transgression. The virtue of the sacrament is not prohibited as long as the transgression of the precept is not clear. Now although what was prohibited has begun to be established, yet what was done cannot be established or be lawful, because what is done manifestly against injunction is not judged to be legitimate or true.

There will be some perhaps who think that ignorance cannot accomplish so

much that, as a result of it, a pact between persons of this kind should be called
a marriage, to whom the union of marriage would be justly prohibited, if the
cause which lies hidden were known. I ask these what should be thought of
children born from a union of this kind, whether they are to be judged legitimate
or illegitimate. But if it seems hard that children be called illegitimate, because
their parents for some hidden reason have been joined illicitly but according to
the judgment and the concession of the Church legitimately, they must concede
that that union from which they have been born, as long indeed as the cause was
hidden, was legitimate, even if they argue justly that it was illicit.

  For not everything that is done illicitly is not done because it is done illicitly,
since what is done must surely be said to be done, although in that it is so done,
it may rightly be said to be done badly. Now if what is done and what is done
illicitly may indeed be known to be done, yet not be known to be done illicitly,
ignorance indeed can temper or excuse the blame, so that the act becomes legitimate
in that it is done, although ignorance cannot cause the act to be done without
blame in that it is so done. If then children are according to some standard
legitimate, the union also from which they take their existence is according to some
standard legitimate. But if the union itself is according to some standard rightly
called legitimate, it is not clear to me why the marriage also should not properly
be so named according to this same standard. For there is no great contention
about a name where the same opinion is felt about the truth. Therefore, except
for reasons of this kind, in which either on account of horror or baseness it seems
that consideration should be given to chastity, in all other cases I think that this
opinion should be held, that if in any union offence is caused by chance through
ignorance, as long as this is hidden and the marriage was performed legitimately
in the judgment of the Church, we can by no means tolerate its being called
illegitimate.

So let no one put up to me the case of a brother and sister or other cases of
this kind, in which the reason of ignorance does not admit excuse. They are not
permitted to offend in matters of this kind, because in what they do ignorance
should give excuse. Deeds of this kind belong to horror, not to reason, in which
even if there should be ignorance, yet shame and modesty do not avoid confusion.
It is another matter to speak of those things about which the Apostle says: "Let
no temptation take hold on you, but such as is human," (1 Cor. 13). For in what
it is human to err, ignorance of error can excuse the blame. Thus then we think
that they should be called legitimate persons, according to the judgment of the
Church, in whom no cause exists for which what is to be done can be justly prohibited or when it has been done be weakened. But as long indeed as this is so,
what is, is said to be legitimate. Now if anyone asks how that can be legitimate
according to the judgment of the Church which according to divine judgment is
not legitimate, I indeed think that both are legitimate. Yet I think that it is

especially called legitimate according to the judgment of the Church, because according to the judgment of the Church there is nothing in it because of which it should not be called legitimate; however, according to divine judgment, in what was manifest to the judgment of the Church, there is something which was not legitimate marriage; that is, there is something in it, hidden indeed to the Church but known to God, and if this were likewise manifest to the Church, the marriage would not be legitimate. Now then it is excused through ignorance, so that it is legitimate before God as before man as long as it is unknown, because before man indeed nothing is reprehended in this, yet before God what is reprehensible, even if it has blame, is nevertheless not charged to reprehensible confusion. And these persons of the Church, indeed, we think are legitimate according to the judgment of the Church.

Moreover, we believe that to be a legitimate consent which is made for what it should be made. For those who consent only to the mingling of the flesh, in view of such a consent cannot still be called consorts. For both fornicators and adulterers do this, from whom the phrase, conjugal chastity, is recognized to be far removed. Therefore, that is another thing consent to which between male and female sanctifies marriage. Now what else are we to call this but that association which God the Creator established from the beginning between male and female, when after forming woman from the side of a man He associated her with this same man? For since she was given as a companion, not a servant or a mistress, she was to be produced not from the highest or from the lowest part but from the middle. For if she had been made from the head, she would have been made from the highest and she would seem to have been created for domination. But if she had been made from the feet, she would have been made from the lowest and she would seem to have been subjected to slavery. She was made from the middle, that she might be proved to have been made for equality of association. Yet in a certain way she was inferior to him, in that she was made from him, so that she might always look to him as to her beginning and cleaving to him indivisibly might not separate herself from that association which ought to have been established reciprocally.

This association then is marriage, which is consecrated by a compact of mutual agreement, when each by voluntary promise makes himself debtor to the other, so that thereafter he neither passes over to association with another, while the other is living, nor disjoins himself from that association which is established reciprocally. With reference indeed to consent in this association, if the consent to carnal mingling is also joined in the first compact, joined by the obligation of this mingling they are thereafter reciprocally constrained. But if perhaps in the compact of marriage on both sides by equal vow the consent of flesh is remitted, thereafter those joined are not reciprocally bound as debtors for this. For what was dismissed by equal consent of both and confirmed by vow cannot afterwards justly be exacted by either, and yet even so the sacrament of marriage stands firm, and just as its virtue is not achieved by the union of flesh when it is present, so it cannot be destroyed when this union is absent. So such an agreement is believed to preserve the individual association in life, in as much as it was made that the mutual association which was initiated reciprocally through it, as long as either lives, may never more suffer separation. He then who wishes to define marriage can say that marriage is a legitimate consent, that is, between legitimate persons and legitimately made on the part of male and female, to observe an individual association in life. In this consent, indeed, the commerce of carnal copulation by equal vow is not forbidden to be nor is it praised when not about to be.

V. *When marriage begins to be.*

Now if anyone asks when marriage begins to be, we say that from the moment when such a consent as we have defined above has been made between male and female, immediately from that moment marriage is and even if the joining of flesh follows afterwards nothing more is contributed to the marriage with reference to the virtue of the sacrament. Therefore it is established that, if man or woman after such a consent should pass over to association with another, even if the mingling of flesh should follow there, nevertheless he will have to return to the former association in which the sacrament of marriage was sanctified and after which the second copulation is judged altogether illicit. But you say to me: Someone promised or by chance swore to someone that he at an agreeable time would marry her and she similarly promised or swore that she would wed him. Meanwhile, by mutual agreement, one or both passed to association with another; he took another wife and she wed another husband. What must be done then? On account of the former promise must the compact of the second agreement be severed? But consider that it is one thing to do and quite a different thing to promise. He who promises does not yet do; but he who does, already does what he does. In him who promises, if he does not do what he promises, there is falsehood. But in him who does, even if he repents after the deed, nevertheless what has been done has been completely done. He then who has promised that he would take a wife, nevertheless has not yet taken a wife, and she who promised that she would wed, has not yet wed; there was still no marriage but there should have been. But afterwards he took a wife and she wed a husband, there was already marriage on both sides, and what has been done cannot be dissolved, even if what was promised was not fulfilled. Therefore, the preceding lie must be corrected by penitence, but the following marriage must not be dissolved.

Now this is not so when there is no promise by mutual consent, as has been described above, that the sacrament of marriage will take place, but there is a confirmation through witnesses of the consent in person, since after such a consent whatever has followed in another's association, even with the mingling of flesh or with the procreation of children, will have to be entirely void. But certain men think that what was done afterwards should stand, because in this case more seems to have taken place, where after consent even the mingling of flesh has followed. But why should that stand in which more has been done, if all that has been done has not been done justly? If that is judged a marriage afterwards, because in it carnal copulation has taken place, which did not take place in an earlier case, then if a third shall follow after that, someone will say that this should be judged better than the second, because in it perhaps carnal copulation has taken place more often than in the second. But reason does not admit this. Therefore, whatever should be admitted with another, man or woman, whether by consent or by coition after conjugal consent, which sanctifies marriage, this will belong to the stain of incest and adultery not to the sacrament of marriage.

But you say: If after the first consent to the conjugal pact there is marriage straightway, what then does that authority mean which says that a legitimate marriage is made only by those who seem to have power over this woman; and let her be sought from those by whom the wife is guarded, and let her be betrothed by her nearer relatives, and let her be endowed according to the law, and in her time in a priestly manner as is the custom let her be blessed by the priest with prayers and oblations, and he says certain other things which he adds in this manner. Otherwise what have been assumed must not be called marriages but adulterous cohabitations or defilements or fornications, rather than legitimate marriages. But it should be understood at this point that they are not legitimate, that is, that they are not made according to the institution of the laws which establish that consorts be betrothed in this manner. For what he adds afterwards, that they are presumed adulterous or defilements rather than legitimate marriages, he straightway tempers in a subsequent sermon, saying: Unless perhaps one's own will should support and legitimate vows should assist.

There, therefore, where one's own will and legitimate vow assist, even without all these other things there can be legitimate marriage. For if marriage cannot be where these things are not, neither can baptism be where the consecration of the font has not preceded the catechising and exorcization of baptizing, and where the unction of oil and chrism do not follow. But just as baptism can be without these, although these should be with baptism, so too marriage can be without those, even there where those things should be in marriage and with marriage. For blessed Ambrose testifies that marriage does not consist of coition but of consent, and coition does not consist of consent, since just as there can be consent without coition, so too coition can be without consent, if perhaps on both sides a plan of chastity and continence has been agreed upon. He says: Not the deflowering of virginity but the conjugal pact makes marriage. Again he says: Coition does not make marriage but consent and if this be lacking all things even with coition itself are made void. Isidore also says that consorts are more truly so called from the first faith of the betrothal, although as yet conjugal copulation between them is unknown.

But perhaps this may seem to be contrary to what we said above, that marriage is sanctified in marital consent. For if marriage begins from the first faith of betrothal, since the faith of the betrothal seems to precede in the promise of future consent, when marriage is said to begin from this faith, without doubt the consent itself of matrimony also is proven to go before. But if we should understand the pact and promise of future matrimony as the betrothal itself, then surely we fittingly receive the faith of betrothal as the fulfilment of a promise and the maintenance of a pact. From this surely, since marriage consists of the forementioned consent, it worthily takes its beginning, because in that the faith of the betrothal and of the promise which had been made on both sides regarding future marriage is fulfilled, the sacrament of marriage is accomplished in marital consent. But we conjecture that the name of betrothal in the very expression of the word does not signify the consent itself to marriage, by which matrimony is confirmed, but the betrothal and the promise of future consent, because to promise is not to give or to do but to promise. Therefore also the Apostle says: "For I have espoused you to one husband, that I may present you as a chaste virgin to Christ," (2 Cor. 11, 2). But if we should understand the name of betrothal in the contract of matrimony, then fittingly do we receive the faith of betrothal as the consent to mutual association which is called marriage.

Therefore too Augustine says of the mother of the Lord that from the first faith of betrothal she was called the wife of Joseph, whom he had not known by coition and was not to know. And likewise Ambrose says: She who was betrothed to a man received the name of wife. For when marriage is begun, then the name of marriage is assumed; and in these words, just as it was said above, if we accept betrothal as this, when marriage is sanctified by marital consent, rightly is marriage itself said to begin then and the name of spouse said to be assumed. But if we understand betrothal as when the future consent for performing marriage is promised, then indeed is marriage said to begin in what precedes marriage; and from this time also she who is to be wife, on account of those matters with which marriage is begun, is marked by the name of wife. But let opinion on these things and on things of this kind be as it pleases, provided only that marriage before the attestation of the legitimate consent, in which each gives himself over to the other for the association of the conjugal pact, be not believed to be true and thereafter not to be imperfect.

Do you wish to know what I mean? When he says: I receive you as mine, that hereafter you may be my wife and I your husband, and she says similarly: I receive you as mine that hereafter I may be your wife and you my husband, either they say this or something else like this, in which, even if they do not say this, yet they understand this. Or if they do not say this, because perhaps elsewhere words are not employed but the deed is carried out, nevertheless they do this. He marries her, receives her, just as is the legitimate custom of taking wives. When therefore, as is the custom, they say this or consent to it between themselves, this is what I wish to say, thereafter they are consorts, whether they have said this and have agreed to this between themselves in the presence of legitimate witnesses, as they should, or perhaps alone, apart and in secret, with no one witnessing and being present as they should not; nevertheless they are consorts completely, and thereafter, unless some cause for parting arise, they cannot be separated from each other licitly, even if on account of the secret consent, if they should deny the deed, they could not be refuted.

VI. *On those who marry secretly or after they have married do some fearful things contrary to marriage.*

But you say: What then must be done about people of this kind who have come together secretly, if afterwards either one or both, denying the deed, should pass over to association with another? A certain man took a wife secretly without the presence of witnesses, marital consent alone being confirmed between the two, as customarily happens sometimes, avoiding for some reason another's notice; afterwards, when a short time has intervened, before he has proven the secret consent by manifest deed, he repented of the deed and dismissed her whom he had taken as wife in this way; he married another with distinguished pomp openly in the church, perhaps with parents giving her away; he accomplished the marriage with the blessing of the priest; he begot children. That former wife comes to the church, interrupts the judgment, demands justice, explaining that an injury was done her secretly. He denies it, and there are no witnesses who can prove what is hidden. Here you ask what should the Church do, since on both sides something improper seems to be occurring. For in that woman who tells the truth indeed, credence is placed without legitimate testimony, but yet it is hidden and what she says is not proven on account of her word alone; and on account of what is uncertain and hidden what is certain and manifest is destroyed; then any man or woman will be able to trump up whatever he or she should wish against any man or any woman that credence may be placed in them in a similar way. If this should be admitted, great confusion will result. And thereafter nothing will stand firm in the Church. But if to preserve the authority of the Church the marriage which was made first is broken and the adultery which was assumed in the second is confirmed, there is something serious, since not only is liberty granted but necessity also is placed upon the man to remain in his sin. Here then you seek advice.

I perhaps am not going to say what is preferable to you, but we should not be ignorant of such evils any further. If anyone should think that to avoid evils of this kind such a consent which is proven by no testimony nor is confirmed by the mutual confession of the doers is invalid, and that marriage cannot by any means rest on it, he more easily avoids the unfitting. For it is also possible, as has been said above, that concealed agreements are not marriages but adulterous cohabitations or defilements, unless one's will has supported it and legitimate vows have assisted in it. So some think that agreements of this kind, which are made in secret, do not sanction marriage, unless the same parties themselves who consented to each other in secret both voluntarily profess the same consent on their part openly, since then indeed one's own will supports and legitimate vows assist when they both profess openly what they did of their own free will in secret. If anyone then in this manner says that marriage can be begun secretly indeed, but not unless it is confirmed more briefly by the manifest confession of both, he avoids many evils; but the approbation of the majority supports the following: whether such an agreement has been made manifestly or secretly between legitimate persons, it is judged a perfect sacrament of matrimony.

But if we must establish this to be true, we are obliged to consider how we should give answer to the aforesaid question. There is no doubt but that what cannot be proven to the Church, the Church itself cannot judge. But again there is no doubt but that what was done by the legitimate and manifest judgment of the Church cannot be rescinded without legitimate and reasonable and manifest cause. Reason presses us. This woman says that with mutual consent she entered upon marriage with that man. But what she says, she herself cannot prove and the Church cannot approve what has not been proven. Therefore, because of what is hidden, what is manifest cannot be undermined. Accordingly, the Church must judge that the second union which was performed legitimately in the judgment of the Church should be valid. But you say: What then must be done for this woman who seeks her husband from the Church, but cannot have him because she cannot prove what was hidden? Perhaps, when she shall see that she cannot have her husband, she will wish to marry another, and will come to the Church demanding either that her own husband be returned to her or that she be permitted to marry another. In this case then, you ask, what should the Church do? Because the Church cannot return the former husband, shall She concede a second? But how can the Church concede a second husband to her who confesses that her own still lives? She herself says: My husband lives. And yet she presumes to seek to marry another. Therefore, you say: This woman must be forced into continence. So indeed; since she did not wish to guard against negligence, it is just that she endure punishment. Why did she not marry openly? If in the first place when marrying she belittled having the testimony of the Church, for what reason does she now solicit the judgment of the Church? Therefore, she herself has obligated herself. Thus let her endure the punishment of negligence now, that she may become an example of correction and a caution to other women, lest they presume likewise.

To be continent is not a sin nor is it impossible, even if it is difficult. If then women do not wish to be continent, let them beware against marrying in secret. Let them marry where they can have witnesses, if they cannot have consenting husbands. But if they do not wish to avoid fault, let them endure punishment. Whoever then wishes to accept marriage, let him consider first that when he has accepted it he must endure its law. Whoever seeks what pleases him, must endure this, if in it or because of it the result should be even that which oppresses. So the Church does not permit a woman who confesses that she has married one man to go over to other nuptials while he is living. Even if later it should happen that the very same man, after the celebration of the second nuptials, should return to her and, repenting of his deed, should confess that he has sinned and should wish to return to his former wife, bearing witness with her to the truth of the first compact, the Church does not accept his testimony, because his word changed and he bore testimony against himself and took faith away from himself in both cases. What the Church herself has done, she cannot rescind without legitimate cause, but she decrees that the second should be valid, lest hidden things be injurious to the manifest. And so that woman whom, according to the judgment of the Church, he is known to have married legitimately, the Church adjudges to that man as his legitimate wife.

But you say: So then, if the judgment of the Church should stand, since hidden things cannot be injurious to the manifest, what must that man do for his soul who, while his wife is living, is forced to cleave to another whom he can neither dismiss, lest he seem to go counter to the precept and judgment of the Church, nor hold without scruple of conscience; who, while the former still lives, he knows has associated with him illicitly contrary to divine justice and institution? If then such a person as this should take refuge with the Church seeking the counsel of salvation, what will the Church say to him? Listen and understand what the Church can say to him. If the Church should say to him that he should dismiss the second, whom he took publicly, and return to the former, whom he just now confesses that he took as his wife contrary to his first testimony, and the Church in this shall receive his testimony, all thereafter who shall hold their wives as objects of hatred will make up and falsify that they had married others first in order that they may be separated from those whom they hate, and thus the law of matrimony will have nothing stable in it, but at random everywhere according to the will of everyone it will be dissolved. Therefore, the Church cannot say anything else to him than that he should keep faith with the marriage which was confirmed by his testimony.

But you say: His cause is for his soul; he seeks counsel for salvation; for on both sides he sees danger, and whichever of the two he selects, in this he does not find it. If he remains, he acts contrary to conscience; if he departs, he acts contrary to obedience. Therefore, he does not seek now whether he should depart, but, if he does not depart, whether it is expedient to remain. He sets forth his conscience and he seeks counsel for salvation. What will the Church say to the man who confesses sin and seeks counsel? If the Church should say to him that he should remain, after he has revealed his sin, that is to say, as it seems, that he should abide in sin. But if she can say neither this nor that, as it seems, the way of salvation cannot be pointed out to such a man. But again this is very abhorrent to Christian faith, that anyone should be said to be such that he cannot, if he has truly repented, be saved in whatever danger he may be. There are many things which could have happened in this manner. One says that he had an affair with the sister or the mother of his wife. Another confesses that he took another wife first, and many other horrible things which man's wretchedness either makes up falsely or commits truly. And it is true indeed that many horrible things are done by men in their evil desires, so blinded that they do what they should not, and these evils are so great that they scarcely admit counsel, unless God who gave the law should offer grace and mercy. For all flesh will not be justified by the law in His sight. Just as once a curse of the law pressed upon all who were under the law, and there was no one who could have avoided the malediction, since there was no one who could guard against prevarication, until the Legislator himself came and took away the malediction through grace and, lest malediction and prevarication should always reign, changed even the law itself through the same grace, so too now man, with his sin and malice pressing, sometimes comes to the necessity of sinning, and he cannot endure the law, unless he incurs the malediction of prevarication; God commutes the law for him through mercy and grants that the penitent can be saved, who surely would not be saved, if he were judged without mercy through the justice and rigour of the law.

Perhaps I do not reply to you according to your thought. It is according to mine not according to yours that I speak. I can do nothing else. What my mind suggests to me, I profess. If I should say anything else, I would speak contrary to my conscience and opinion. Whoever judges for himself, to you I speak from my heart. The sinner comes to me and sets forth his conscience to me seeking counsel for salvation. What shall I say to him? If I shall say: Withdraw to the former, I make him disobedient to the Church, his mother, and by his example I encourage others to dismiss their legitimate wives, and, when they hold them in hatred, to make up whatever shall please them, and to lie to the Church that they may have the liberty of withdrawing from them because they do not love them. And if the Church should accept and suffer this, a great evil would come, and all, either men their wives or women their husbands, would dismiss according to their pleasure, and for one man many would be damned, and this should not so happen. Some have thought that they have given deep consideration to this, not consulting their neighbour's good, saying, as often as by chance something of this kind happened, that the Church should do both, namely, in secret advise the penitent to withdraw from a union of this kind and publicly force him, as he separates, to remain. This indeed would not be to seek a neighbour's salvation but, as it were, to wish to free him from danger. My conscience does not persuade me to say this to him. He asks me what he must do; he shows his danger; he exhibits his necessity; he testifies that he is prepared for whatever he shall be ordered. I have no confidence in myself; I say to him that he should go to God.

Lord, you have given the law through your servants as you wished and through whom you wished, and behold we your servants are under the law; you the Lord, passer of the law, are not under the law. What you established when you wished and as long as you wished, you can when you wish and to whom you wish indulge without guilt of prevarication. For there will be no blame indeed because there is remission on the part of one who is indulging or presumption on the part of one who is acting. You then, O Lord, have ordered through your servants, through whom you have spoken, and you have disposed your Church so that a man, while his wife is living, should not cleave to another. I had a wife and while she was living I cleaved to another. Behold now, I cannot bring it about that this be undone. But you can bring it about that this be not done unto damnation. You likewise ordered, O Lord, that we should obey your Church, just as you, for it takes your place on earth, and that we should not scandalize one of your little ones, and you have said that he who spurned the law of your Church would not be obedient to you. Behold, I, wretched on account of my sins, have come into a contradiction; I have fallen into a snare of necessity, so that I cannot go out without sin. If I remain, my conscience accuses me before you for my secrets, in which I acted against your disposition. If I withdraw, I shall be disobedient to your Church, and I shall scandalize not only your little ones but also your great servants who in this case do not know what is hidden but wish what is just, and my conscience accuses me for my manifest actions in which I acted contrary to your order. I then, who am placed in difficulty and am surrounded on all sides by danger, implore your mercy, prepared for all that you order, if you will permit me to know this. If you shall say: Depart, I do not remain. If you shall say: Remain, I do not depart. For I know that whatever is done at your command cannot be evil, whatever that shall be. For yours is the power from which all that has pleased you is good. Whomever you indulge is not imputed; whomever you impute is not indulged.

If then, O Lord, you shall order that, putting aside scandal of the Church and contemning the mandate of my masters whom you gave me and whom you ordered me to obey, I give heed to you rather than to a man whom I should not heed except on account of you, nor do I wish to do so contrary to you; if then you so order, O Lord, I do not wait upon man. Now if you wish to spare your little ones or to preserve the authority of your Church for the salvation of the many, I indeed for my sins am in your judgment. But yet I know that you are kind and merciful and that you can, if you should wish, not impute necessity, if you should receive and have the will. Therefore, I prefer to fall into your hands than into the hands of men, since power is present with you and pity is not lacking. Man cannot change the law. The law does not dominate you, since you are the founder and the Lord of the law. Man judges deeds, not the will; you are indulgent toward deeds on account of the will. Therefore, confiding in your mercy I commit the secret deeds of my necessity to you, not presuming on account of fear of you to cause scandal to the Church, because I hope that you may be able through pity to ignore my offense against you, since I do not presume to offend a neighbour, lest in my neighbour I offend both my neighbour and my God.

Thus it seems to me, as often as secret things in some necessity torment the conscience, and especially if they should be of such a nature that the dispensation of institution admits indulgence, since what is contrary to nature and without sin could never have been done, they do not receive remission unless they shall have had correction. Therefore, in hidden things of this kind in which there is prevarication of a temporal institution, not of natural precept, it seems to me that those things which lie hidden should never prejudice the manifest and especially those which cannot be changed without grave scandal; rather it is more expedient that in manifest affairs scandal should be guarded against and regarding hidden things recourse should be had to grace and mercy; moreover, it can be brought about that what at any time is done against institution out of necessity to avoid scandal, because it is hidden and cannot be proven and thereby avoided, through mercy should not be imputed to one who repents and grieves. "The husband hath not power of his own body, but the wife. And in like manner the wife hath not power of her own body, but the husband," (Cf. 1 Cor. 7, 4). Therefore, man or woman by sinning can bring it about that he or she lose power in the body of another, but he or she cannot bring it about that he or she take away from the other power of their own body, in so far as rests with them. It is possible to lose what belongs to one's right; what is not one's own, one cannot take away. Thus then, if at some time he should bring it about that he cannot rightly exact his debt in the body of another, yet he does not bring it about that he can rightly deny the debt of another in his own body.

Now the question is raised regarding those who say that, after the conjugal pact or before, they had carnal intercourse with sisters and mothers or certain other relatives in line of kinship, what must be done if it can be proved with legitimate testimony that this was done. I indeed, as long as it could be done reasonably, for the sake of preserving the peace of this kind of marriage couch, would avoid testimonies and proofs. But if the affair should become entirely manifest, then indeed, to avoid the horror of the deed and scandal, I would urge that a separation take place, but in such a manner that both be forced to remain in continence, since indeed the sacrament of marriage should not be broken on either side, even if the deed of carnal intercourse should be raised in opposition. If someone, however, should ask how a woman who has not sinned can be forced into continence against her will, he should see that this too is of the misery of the flesh, and he who does not check himself from its voluptuousness in prosperity is worthy of bearing its pains also in adversity. As for this woman who says now that she cannot restrain herself, what would she do, if her husband were oppressed by a long and continuous or even perpetual sickness? Him then whom she would not have deserted while lying in languor of body she should not desert now when he repents of iniquity. Or, if perhaps she does not wish to sustain the condition of flesh, let her not subject herself to the law of the flesh, and let her not accept towards pleasure what she does not wish to endure towards affliction. And these matters indeed regarding the hidden consent of marriage or regarding other things which are hidden in it or are if possible to be concealed or to be dreaded had to be mentioned by us. Therefore, we confess that, as has been said, marriage is sanctioned in marital consent, and whatever else, after it has been legitimately performed, is done against it cannot stand, if this consent alone can be proved by legitimate testimony. Therefore, after we have shown what marriage is and on what ground it is to be said that marriage should be valid, we must now treat in a fitting manner of the blessings of marriage.

VII. *That there are three blessings that accompany marriage, namely, faith, hope of progeny, sacrament.*

There are in the main three blessings that accompany marriage, namely, faith, hope of progeny, sacrament. In faith care is taken that there be no lying with another woman or with another man outside the conjugal bond. In hope of progeny care is taken that progeny be expected devoutly, received lovingly, nourished religiously. In the sacrament care is taken that the marriage be not broken and that the man or woman dismissed be not joined with another for the sake of progeny. These are the blessings which marriage places over against that concupiscence of the flesh which still remains in the flesh of sin, without which the mingling of flesh cannot take place. For, as blessed Augustine says, the good of marriage in some manner limits and modifies the evil of the disobeying members, so that carnal concupiscence becomes at least conjugal chastity.

Now this good occurs as a remedy against that evil in two ways, when it restrains that ardor of immoderate lust from unrestrained coition by limiting it under the definite law of one compact, and when it excuses this ardor which would by itself be evil, through the blessings attached to itself. Yet it does not effect that evil not exist at all but that it be not damnable; indeed on account of this good that evil is made venial; for unless it were evil, it would not have need of being excused. And again unless it had a remedy, it would have to be imputed. But if marriage had no good in itself, it could not be a remedy against evil. Now the blessings themselves that are in it excuse the evil which is not sought by it but is tolerated in it, so that that is not imputed to damnation which necessity imposes and the will does not exact. Likewise Augustine says to Valerius: Not only fecundity of which the fruit is in progeny and not only chastity whose bond is faith but also the sacrament of marriage is commended to the married faithful. The essence of this sacrament is that those joined legitimately are not separated as long as they live.

VIII. *Whether or not these blessings are inseparable from marriage.*

If the faith of marriage is not to know another coition outside marital coition, and the violation of this faith is to commit adultery, it is clear that this blessing so clings to marriage that, if it should indeed be present, as a result of it the marriage would be commended the more, but, if it should not be present, the sacrament of marriage nevertheless would not be annihilated. For as for her who is an adulteress, she is not a wife because she is an adulteress; rather, if she were not a wife, she could not be an adulteress. For there is no adultery except when the faith of the legitimate couch is violated, and surely when this is done, a sin is committed; the sacrament is not made void. Similarly, if hope of progeny is in this, that progeny is awaited devotedly, received lovingly, nourished religiously, there is no doubt that this blessing also cannot always be present in every marriage or in all consorts. For how is progeny hoped for by those who either by a mutual vow maintain continence or from the weakness of age can no longer generate? And so these two, that is, faith and hope of progeny, so accompany marriage that when indeed they are present, in the one case marriage appears more pure, in the other more fruitful, but when they are not present, marriage is proven either more blameworthy or less fruitful, and yet it does not cease to be marriage. But the sacrament seems to be so inseparable that without it marriage cannot exist at all.

So Augustine* says: To so great an extent is the nuptial contract the essence of the same sacrament that it is not made void by separation, since while the husband by whom a woman has been left is living, she commits adultery, if she shall marry another. So great a strength of the marriage bond means this, that it would not be so strong unless a certain sacrament of some greater essence were added, which remains unshaken because, though divorce intervene, the nuptial compact is not abolished, so that they are consorts even though separated. For since the two are different, marriage which rests on legitimate association, and the office of marriage

---

*The material throughout these sections on marriage quoted as from St. Augustine is for the most part from the *De Bono Conjugali.*

which rests on mingling of flesh, in the one indeed, that is marriage, is the sacrament, but to the other, that is to the office of marriage, faith and hope of progeny seem to belong; one, that is faith, so that through it illicit mingling of flesh may be guarded against, the other, that is hope of progeny, that on account of it licit mingling of flesh may be exercised. Just as the office itself of carnal intercourse can be absent from marriage, so too marriage itself can exist without these things which belong to the office of carnal intercourse, although, as it is said, if it should lack faith, it would be less pure, but if it should lack hope of progeny, it would be found less fruitful. For faith has fruit in the chastity of conjugal virtue. Hope of progeny has fruit in the use of fecundity.

Now marriage in marital association itself is a sacrament and on this account, just as the association itself is not divided while both live, so too the sacrament of conjugal association, as long as the marriage exists, is not separated from it. And in this marriage indeed the sacrament externally is undivided association; the essence of the sacrament internally, charity of souls burning mutually and perseveringly. The sacrament externally belongs to Christ and the Church, the essence of the sacrament internally to God and the soul, so that just as in the coition of the flesh we have mentioned the sacrament of Christ and the Church, so also in the compact of the association we show the sacrament of the same. So, this has been said, that it may be shown that sometimes marriage exists without faith and without hope of progeny, but it can never exist without the sacrament, although the sacrament sometimes is found to exist where the sanctity of the sacrament is shown not to exist.

For blessed Augustine says that the sacrament of marriage can be common to all nations, but the sanctity of the sacrament does not exist except in the city of our God and on His holy mount. One can easily see how true this is, if he considers what has been said above. For we said above that in marriage a twofold sacrament existed: one in carnal intermingling, the sacrament of that association which exists between Christ and Church; the other in conjugal association, the sacrament of that association which exists between God and soul; or also which was the sacrament of Christ and the Church in the association of marriage; indeed the sacrament of God and the soul in conjugal love. Whether then the sacrament of marriage is accepted in this way or in that, the sacrament of marriage is rightly said to be common to all nations, but the sanctity or virtue of the sacrament does not exist except in the city of our God and on His holy mount, that is, it is said to exist in faith and charity, namely in Holy Church and between the faithful. Now they have the sacrament of marriage who with mutual consent come together to preserve indivisably and mutually that association which was established by God between male and female. Indeed they alone possess the sanctity of this sacrament, who through faith have been made members of Christ, and through charity have been united to God internally by the mind and devotion.

IX. *On those who live incontinently in marriage and take more care to satisfy lust than to generate progeny.*

Blessed Augustine so speaks about those who overcome by weakness and lust are subservient to such incontinence: Nuptials do not force that coition to take place which is not performed for the sake of progeny, but they obtain forgiveness if on the other hand it is not so excessive that it interferes with the time which is due to prayer and is not changed to that practice which is contrary to nature. For coition, which is necessary for the sake of progeny, is blameless provided only it be nuptial. But it behooves a consort not to exact what proceeds beyond that necessity, for it follows not reason but lust, but to render that to a consort lest he or she commit fornication. But if both subject themselves to such concupiscence, they perform a deed which does not belong to nuptials, of which sin nuptials are not the exhorter but the deprecator. Indeed conjugal glory is chastity in begetting and faith in rendering the carnal debt. This is the work of nuptials which the Apostle defends against all sin, saying: "If thou take a wife, thou hast not sinned. And if a virgin marry, she hath not sinned," (Cor. 7, 28). But immoderate progression is conceded according to indulgence. An unbelieving wife is not an obstacle even to the sanctity of marriage but rather is the believer of assistance to the unbeliever. Therefore the Apostle says: "The unbelieving husband is sanctified by the believing wife, etc." (Cf. 1 Cor. 7, 14).

X. *For what reason the ancients had several wives at the same time.*

About this blessed Augustine speaks similarly as follows: In ancient times, when the mystery of our salvation was still veiled, the just contracted marriage in the office of propagating, not overcome by lust but induced by piety, since they could contain themselves much more easily and desired so. Yet they enjoyed wives and one man was permitted to have several whom he kept more chastely than some men of our time keep one, as the Apostle conceded out of indulgence. For they possessed them in the work of generating, not in the vice of desire. The same one says in his book On Virgins: It was not a sin for the just ancients to enjoy several wives, nor did they do this contrary to nature, since they did it not for the sake of being wanton but of begetting, nor contrary to custom, since at the time such things were being done, nor contrary to precept since no law forbade it. But as the same Augustine testifies elsewhere, it serves the good of nuptials more for one man to be joined with one woman rather than with many, and this the divinely made union of the first husband indicates in order that nuptials may have their source where the more honorable example was noted.

Likewise the same one says: Just as the merit of patience is not unlike in Peter who suffered and in John who did not suffer, so the merit of continence is not unlike in John who experienced no nuptials and in Abraham who generated sons.

For both the celibacy of the one and marriage of the other according to the division of times did service for Christ. But John had continence in deed, Abraham in appearance only. Now the chastity of celibates is better than the chastity of nuptials, of which Abraham had one in practice, two in appearance. For he lived chastely as a married person, yet he could have been chaste without marriage, had it then been fitting. Likewise the just man, although he desires to be dissolved and to be with Christ, (Cf. Philip. 1, 23), yet he takes nourishment not because of the desire to live but because of the office of counseling, that what is necessary for others may remain. Thus having intercourse with women by right of marriage was a matter of duty for holy men, not a matter of lust. For what food is for the salvation of man, coition is for the salvation of race, and both are not without carnal pleasure which, however, must be limited with restraining temperance, and cannot be lust reduced to natural practice. Now what illicit food is in sustaining life, fornicating and adulterous coition are in seeking progeny, and what, on the other hand, immoderate appetite is in licit food, that venial coition is among consorts.

XI. *Whether that is to be called marriage which can at some time be dissolved.*

Some say that what admits separation at some time is not marriage at all. For they find certain authorities and words of Holy Scripture set forth by the Holy Fathers according to which this seems to be construed. For blessed Augustine says in his book, "De Bono Conjugali": In this respect is the nuptial compact the essence of a certain sacrament, that it is not void by separation, since, as long as the man who abandoned her lives, she commits adultery if she should marry another. And likewise he says: Though divorce may intervene the nuptial agreement is not abolished, and consequently they are consorts even when separated. On account of assertions of this kind those men think that marriage should not be spoken of where that exists which at some time admits division and separation in such a way that when separated the partners may not mutually be called consorts. But on the other hand it is not clear to me how they can prove that this which pertains to the virtue of the conjugal sacrament, for the preservation of an undivided association by both as long as both live, was not marriage for the reason that it could be dissolved at some time. For if they say that this is not marriage for the reason that this does not have those things which pertain to marriage, let them bear in mind that the statement, whenever made, that undivided association pertained to marriage was true, because marriage, when it is indeed where it should be, ought to have this. For this is of marriage and marriage exacts or rather confers this, in so far as lies in it. Just as it is of baptism to confer remission of sins, so also is the statement, whenever it is made, true that baptism confers the remission of all sins, and just as it is the virtue of the sacrament of the body of Christ to confer association with and participation in Christ, so also the statement is true that the reception of the body of Christ confers spiritual participation in Christ; yet he who falsely receives the sacrament of baptism does not receive the remission of sins, and he who unworthily eats the body of Christ by no means on this account merits spiritual participation in Christ. If then we say truthfully that these things pertain to those sacraments, and yet we shall sometimes find those sacraments without them, and not because they are without them do these things pertain any less, when, indeed, the sacraments are where and among whom they should not be, is it remarkable if we say that undivided association pertains to marriage, although on the other hand we find marriage without that, when indeed it is where it should not be and among whom it ought not to be?

But if they say that the sacrament of marriage does not exist because it does not have this which it should have, when it is where it should not be, they should say similarly that the sacrament of baptism is not true with the false and the false is not truly baptized because it does not operate remission of sins there, and that the true body of Christ is not that which is received unworthily because there spiritual participation in Christ is not conferred. Let them understand then that as often as spiritual effects of this kind are attributed to divine sacraments, the virtue of the sacraments themselves is expressed; in which indeed it is not shown what it is to be according to the vice of those who abuse the sacraments of God, but rather what can be done from them according to the efficacy of the spiritual grace in them, provided that they do not remain in the depravity of those who abuse. He then who said that marriage had this effect surely meant to say that marriage should have this effect, in so far as lies in it, if it is where it ought to be. Now if by chance it is not where it ought to be, there is no wonder if it is deprived of that which it ought to have. But not for this reason, however, is the sacrament less true, while it exists, although it is less useful to him in whom it is. Thus we think that certain marriages can truly be called marriages, as long as they are held valid according to the judgment of the Church, but afterwards, as legitimate causes arise, they are rightly dissolved, that is, if afterwards contrary to the prohibition of the Church they are held with stubborn presumption and are judged illicit and illegitimate copulations.

Yet we do not think, as I have said above, that this opinion should be held about all. For after an excuse for the horror has been formed, none will be able to retain the name of being legitimate. The situation is different regarding those where there is venial sin, as for example, if anyone within the seventh or sixth or possibly even the fifth degree, ignoring the line of relationship, should commit defilement, which indeed would not be so much against the natural or ancient legal institution as against the subsequent precept of the Church. We read that blessed Gregory permitted the English who had been recently converted to the faith, lest perhaps they be frightened at the Christian religion, to join marriage by way of dispensation within the fifth degree of consanguinity; consequently it is clear that those things, which sometimes admit dispensation so that they are manifestly done licitly, have excuse even if they are done through ignorance without concession. And thus perhaps matters of this kind, as long as they lie entirely hidden, are thought to be excused more properly because of ignorance, whereas, when they have been made manifest, they are not to be tolerated, because they are against precept. Now these things have been said against those who think that a marriage which at some time can be dissolved, cannot be called a marriage.

XII. *On those who think that even between any illegitimate persons whatsoever mutual consent makes a proper marriage.*

Others no less precipitously are borne in their opinions to the opposite assertion, to such an extent that they say that illegitimate persons of any kind who have belonged to any profession or order, when like consent has been mutually given, are consorts. They think that neither priests who have professed continence nor high priests nor monks nor holy virgins are to be excepted from this law. They similarly, moreover, have certain words of Scripture by which they believe that they fortify and confirm their opinions. And, if this could be fittingly done, certain words of this kind have been said in which it could be fittingly understood. But they, to whom the teaching of the Word of God has been committed, should not judge so that, for the sake of confirming some one thing, they withdraw from the sense of all. The whole should not follow the part but the part should follow the whole. And if by chance a part is found discordant with the whole, either it must be adapted, if possible, or, if not, it must be rejected. For a withdrawal is made better from a part than from a whole. But it is best if both the part and the whole are retained.

These then are the things which they adduce for the approval of their assertion. Blessed Augustine in his book "De Professione Sanctae Viduitatis" so speaks: If chastity is preserved in the marriage bond, damnation is not feared. But in the continence of a widow and of a virgin the excellence of a greater gift is sought. When this is sought and elected and offered as the debt of a vow, then it is damnable not only to take nuptials but even, if one is not wedded, to wish to wed. For to show this, the Apostle did not say: "When they have done these things in wantonness, they marry in Christ, but they wish to marry." "Having damnation," he says, "because they have made void their first faith," (Cf. 1 Tim. 5, 11 and 12), although not by marrying but by wishing; not because the nuptials of such are judged damnable but the deceit of the plan is damned; the broken faith of the vow is damned; not the reception of an inferior good is damned but the fall from a superior good. Finally such are damned not because they entered upon marital faith rather late but because they made void the first faith of continence. And after a little he says: Furthermore those who say that the nuptials of such are not nuptials but rather adulteries, do not seem to me to consider sharply and diligently enough what they say, for the similarity of the truth deceives them. For since those who do not wed according to Christian sanctity are said to elect the marriage of Christ, some conclude from this, saying: If while her husband is living she who marries another is an adulteress, just as the Lord himself explained in the Gospel, then while Christ lives, whom moreover death will never dominate, if she who had elected His marriage weds a man, she is an adulteress.

Those who say this are sharply moved indeed but little do they note how great an absurdity follows this argument. For although a woman in a praiseworthy manner, even while her husband is living, with his consent vows continence to Christ, yet according to the reasoning of these men no woman should do this lest, (and this it is improper to think), she commit adultery with Christ whom she marries while her husband is still alive. And after a little he says: Now through this rather slightly considered opinion by which they think that marriages do not exist with women who have fallen from the holy plan if they should marry, no little evil results so that wives are separated from husbands, as if they were adulteresses not wives. And when they wish to return these who have been thus separated to continence, they make the husbands of these women true adulterers when they have married other women while their own wives still live. Wherefore I cannot say indeed that, if women who have fallen from a better resolution should marry, we have adulteries not marriages. But plainly I should not hesitate to say that lapses and falls from the more holy chastity which is vowed to God are worse than adulteries.

And thus indeed blessed Augustine says: And the authority seems manifest and the reason evident about which there can be no doubt. But behold, let us say and so let us believe that, if women who have fallen from the design and profession of continence should wed, we have true marriages and marriages of this kind can by no means be broken. What then? Should we not believe similarly and in the same manner about the other sex, that if men having fallen from the design and profession of continence take wives, we should regard the marriages as true and valid to the extent that they cannot by any means be broken although they cannot be defended against blame? Well then, let us say that it is so and that we should so believe and hold. We have no reason by which we can diminish or weaken such evident reason and authority. We are held by necessity so to feel and to hold. Behold what follows. If this should be promulgated and men should hear that the Church so holds, that men who have fallen from the design and profession of continence, if they should enter marriages, cannot be separated nor can the Church force them to return to keep the design of continence, then nothing can be stable and valid. No order or state, finally no vow or profession, will be able to keep men from relaxing the reins of unchasteness and rushing into their desires, either when they have begun to loathe the good in which they are, seeking liberty, or when they have been tempted by chance with respect to evil, in which they are not yet, hastening to fulfil their pleasure.

Thus all order will be dispersed and the beauty of the Christian religion will be reduced to nothing and great infamy will succeed. I speak according to the weakness of our time. Who then will stay in the state or profession of religion, if he shall begin to be pressed by the torments of his flesh, as nature mortal and subject to corruption is accustomed to suffer, and if his thoughts shall say to him: You will not be able to resist so violent a passion, such burnings and surgings of your desires, which not for today or tomorrow or for three days or four or eight days or even for the span of one month or one year have declared war on you but as long as you live upon earth, as long as you will be able to feel, will not leave you, will not spare you, will not give you peace or rest, will always oppress your intention, will avert your thought so that you can never raise a free mind or pure will to God?

Behold then that you both lose this world and do not acquire the future. It would be better at least for you to avoid these torments indeed than to perish entirely and to experience no good. God sees that you suffer against your will, you endure unwilling, you assent when forced. Perhaps He will have regard for the violence of your passion and taking pity will grant pardon to your digression, especially when the Apostle says, "It is better to marry than to burn," (1 Cor. 7, 9). And let everyone have his wife to avoid fornication. For the Apostle well knows human weakness and so he did not say: Let them have because it is permitted them, and let them not have because it is not permitted them but let everyone have; it is better that he who cannot contain himself marry than be burned.

It is better that he accept the weakness licitly than that he always be burned by vice unto passion. For the Lord himself says: "He that can take, let him take it," (Matt. 19, 12). He knows that I cannot take this word to remain continent. When I thought I could, I gladly proposed and still will I gladly persevere in the same if I could endure. But I am not strong enough to endure the impulse of raging nature; I cannot sustain the ardour of burning concupiscence. Accordingly I do what I can. I go and take a wife; I accept my weakness, grieving indeed because I am forced to descend from a higher good but yet not despairing entirely since I descend to what was granted. I prefer to be saved in an inferior good than to run risk in the highest. And if possibly there is some blame, I descend because I do not hold to my design, I shall do penance, and I shall placate God with satisfaction. There will be nothing hard or difficult provided only I can escape this passion and avoid that death in which I am held living.

Who would not bestir himself by reasoned thoughts of this kind, and be encouraged when he begins to be afflicted and to burn under the goads of his flesh, if he should know what is permitted and what can be done? There is salvation for those who do this, and the Church does not force those who so look back but permits them to live as they are and decrees that their marriages are legitimate. Who does not prefer, when he has been in grave temptation, to repent for many years and to pay any satisfaction whatsoever provided only he may be able to enjoy his vow and his wish and to fulfil his desires licitly? What then shall we say? We dare to attest openly that, even if by chance we cannot deny that it has so been stated here and that these words must be so understood, nevertheless, especially in these times when men are prone to vices, it is by no means expedient so to hold and to do. And perhaps someone may wish to say that these statements were made regarding those times when men were more ashamed to sin, when it was possible for the shameful things of prevarication alone to check the wavering, and those placed in temptation from falling from the design and vow of sanctity, when men were more terrified at this, because they realized after a fall a return to the purity of the former excellence was no longer open. Perhaps someone may wish to say that thus the Church at that time according to the state of the time should have held and did hold that whoever after the vow and profession of continence descended to conjugal coition should remain as they were and contracts of this kind should not be broken. Perhaps someone may wish to say that according to the judgment and permission of the Church at that time marriages of this kind were valid, but that afterwards, when men began to abuse such confession and permission, the Church on account of imminent dangers changed the practice and altered her opinion, and thus now there are no marriages of this kind on account of the prohibition and the institution of the Church according to which licit or illicit marriages all are judged valid and dissolvable. If anyone should say these things, perhaps he will seem to have made a point.

We find no fault with any of all the things that permit the truth to remain undisturbed. But if anyone should understand that these things have been said about those who vowed the purpose of secret continence and offered their vow to God alone without the attestation of men, and that these men, if afterwards they should break their vows and wish to descend to conjugal association, cannot be prohibited by the Church, because she did not accept their profession and did not enjoin observance of continence upon them; therefore, if anyone thinks that such widows or virgins, who after their vow of continence descend to marital coition, have damnation indeed, that is, do a damnable thing not because they marry but because they break their vow, not on account of the lower good which they seek but on account of the higher good which they leave, indeed that thus on account of violated faith they have damnation but that they are in every respect consorts and should not be separated, it is certain, as we have said above, that these things which cannot be proven to the Church cannot at all be judged by the Church. Therefore, regarding these things which have been established as true, if we accept them as spoken fittingly in the sentiment mentioned above, nothing more remains of the question, why we do not approve matters spoken truly and to be held for a useful purpose. For it is certain that those who, after a concealed vow of chastity and design for continence, not yet confirmed by manifest profession, return to the experiences of the flesh can by no means be prohibited by the Church, and the Church itself does not abjudicate coition of this kind, if ever it happens but confirms that it is lawful and that hidden things should not be prejudicial to the manifest.

But if anyone wishes to speak against this, saying that those women who have married Christ spiritually cannot thereafter have husbands while He lives, his assertion is rightly reproved by the reason mentioned above. In this way regarding those things which are manifestly false or secretly true it will be permitted to everyone to feel according to his own measure. But to me it is more commendable if we should succeed in discovering that which both preserves the truth and does not disprove authority, especially of so great a man toward whom we should be well disposed even at this time when we cannot feel what he himself felt. Let us say then as much as we can say according to the truth, that either this was said according to the time when it should have been done thus, or that this was said only according to those who after the hidden vow of continence return to the experiences of the flesh and become consorts, whom the Church cannot separate because, although the deed is established as manifest here, what was hidden there cannot be proven. Yet in these matters the guilt of desecrated faith in some respect is called worse than adultery, since through the one there is sin against man but through the other sin against Christ?

Now it is different regarding those who after a vow, even with public profession under the testimony of the Church, have bound themselves with God and perhaps also, what is greater, have been consecrated to the moral purity of continence. Of these we say truly that after such a purpose and such a vow confirmed with manifest profession, they cannot descend to the conjugal compact, and that, if possibly they should attempt this sometime, they should be recalled severely, not as consorts but as fornicators and violators of spiritual chastity, to repair and to preserve the pristine integrity of their purpose strictly. Now if, after this rash daring has been attempted, they should wish to persist and should scorn to abandon the illicit union upon which they have entered contrary to the obligation of their first profession, as disobedient and contaminated by the uncleanness of unspeakable fornication they must be cut off from the communion of the Church with a sentence of just severity; by no means are they to be admitted to repentence unless they withdraw themselves from the intercourse of this infamous association. And this is perhaps what those words mean, already known to almost all for their ambiguity.

For Innocent the Pope, whose authority in the Church of Christ is celebrated, thus speaks. He says that those who marry Christ spiritually and are veiled by the priest, if they should marry publicly or be corrupted secretly, must not be permitted to do penance, unless he with whom they had joined themselves has departed from this life. For if this procedure is maintained among men, that she, who after dismissing her husband has passed over to another, be held as an adulteress and be conceded no opportunity for making repentance, unless the other has died, how much more also should she who had joined herself with the immortal spouse? There is no doubt, therefore, but that we are discussing here those who in their purpose of continence even under manifest profession have been consecrated to preserve chastity. Of these, therefore, they say that if after such a purpose they should pass over to carnal nuptials, they should not be admitted to repentance, unless he with whom they had joined themselves, that is, the fornicator or the adulterer, has departed from this life, that is, from such intercourse. For in this state they cannot offer repentance and as long as they shall remain in it, they cannot be saved.

Certain men wish him with whom these women had joined themselves to be interpreted as Christ, to whom they had vowed themselves before for the purpose of continence, and as if it should be said on the condition that the second person to whom they pass over is not judged legitimate, unless first he with whom they had joined themselves before should die. For if among men this procedure is maintained, that as long as the former lives the second cannot be legitimate, surely it is established that where the former cannot die at all, the second cannot by any means be legitimate. And in this way, by some such reasoning as this, it is proven that these women who with profession of continence have been consecrated as spouses of Christ can no more pass over to carnal marriages. Surely in this demonstration indeed there is not a compelling reasoning throughout, but a fitting similarity according to something by which the spouses of Christ are taught that if on the carnal couch such great faith is exacted, much more devotion and more sincere love is due the spiritual. There are those who think that this was said with a view to terror, others refer it to public repentance, which on account of rigour in instilling fear, it seems, must sometimes be denied, so that, while a sinner is cast out according to dispensation, fear of falling is increased for those who stand, and humility of rising in those who lie down. I reject none of those things which are not contrary to the truth. Anything may be said, provided only what is permitted is believed.

This is a summary. Now if anyone, after the vow of continence has been made, should pass over to carnal nuptials, if indeed his vow should be hidden, the Church cannot prohibit him from marrying. And if afterwards he regrets the deed, the Church can neither repel a penitent for secret deeds from counsel of salvation nor on account of hidden things dissolve those which are manifest. Now if those who have confirmed their purpose by public profession and vow, should then wish to pass over to the laws of carnal compact, by no means does the Church permit them, and if perhaps they should presume to enter upon these nuptials contrary to the purity of their purpose and their profession, the Church with due strictness dissolves them as illegitimate and contrary to the sanctity of marriage. Thus the Church holds. Thus should we hold, both who follow the institutes of the Church and who believe that whatever was established by her at the dictation of the Spirit of God and judged worthy of reverence is salutary; even if on other occasions it should be shown that at some time it was not so and that now it is otherwise than it was, yet we should not consider, as if it were done with some levity, that now it is held otherwise and is instituted otherwise than it was, but that it was fitting then and was so salutary that it should be held so and so ordered, but that now times are different and something different is fitting or necessary for human salvation.

XIII. *On the marriage of unbelievers.*

Certain men think that the association of pagans or unbelievers is not marriage, although it was made legitimately according to the manner of a divine institution. For they say that that should not be called legitimate which was made without faith. But I meanwhile can think of no way by which they can deny that the association of unbelievers made according to divine institution is marriage, unless perhaps they should wish to say similarly that that is no sacrament of baptism which the heretic gives or receives because neither he who gives nor he who receives is a believer. And by this reasoning they may contend that the sacraments of God cannot extend to the participation of unbelievers, if unbelievers cannot have the sacrament of marriage, or that the sacrament of marriage alone should be called more excellent than all the rest, if this alone cannot be shared outside the faith. An unbeliever can have the sacrament of baptism; an unbeliever cannot have the sacrament of matrimony; therefore the unbeliever can have the sacrament of baptism which especially possesses the sign of faith, but the sacrament of matrimony, which is not so much a sign of faith as of nature, not so much a judgment of virtue as an instrument of propagation, a believer and an unbeliever cannot have equally.

But, they say, when the unbeliever has received the sacrament of baptism he has received it because, although he was an unbeliever in some respect, yet he received the sacrament itself according to the true form of faith. Otherwise, unless he had received that according to the right form of faith, surely he would not have received it whether he had been a believer or unbeliever. So, since in receiving this he was not contrary to faith, he was able to receive it, although in one respect he was not faithful. And I say that, when an unbeliever takes a wife for the propagation of children, he preserves the faith with the marriage couch, loves and guards his companion and, while she lives, does not pass over to the company of another, although he is an unbeliever in some respect, because for example he does not believe, yet in this he does not act either against faith or against divine institution. But authority, they say, says that marriages of this kind are not true. So it says that all things which are without faith, even if they are true according to appearance, are not true unto salvation and, if they are true according to the form of the sacrament, yet they are not true according to the effect of virtue and of spiritual grace. Thus too regarding certain other sacraments it has been said that they are not true, since they are participated in by unbelievers. They are unworthily handled not only by unbelievers but also by depraved believers and by those who act perversely.

Regarding the sacrament itself of the body of Christ authority says that the body of Christ which the schismatic prepares is not true. And again another authority says that they err who think that the words of the priest make the body of Christ and not life, and many expressions are found in this manner. It is worthy that we venerate in every respect the words of the saints in so far as we can and that we believe that whatever has been said by them is true, in whom and through whom the Spirit of truth has spoken. So we say that the truth of the sacraments of God is twofold, namely, one in the sanctification of the sacrament, the other in the spiritual effect. For the truth of the sacraments is said to be the virtue and the spiritual grace which is received in themselves and through the sacraments themselves, and they who receive the sacraments of God unworthily cannot receive this truth. And so in this manner sacred Scripture sometimes says that the sacraments of God are not true for those who receive them unworthily for the reason that by only handling the sacraments externally they do not attain to the truth of those sacraments which consists in spiritual grace.

Thus then the sacraments of God are in themselves always true, in so far as pertains to that sanctification which is made through the word of God, and for those who treat and receive them unworthily they are not true, at least in so far as pertains to the participation of spiritual grace which is received in them. Thus then the true body of Christ is not that which the schismatic prepares because, since the body of Christ is a sacrament of unity, in it surely the schismatic does not prepare unity for himself who separates himself from unity itself. In similar manner those who think that the words alone of the priest suffice for the consecration of the body of Christ and that good life and conversation are not necessary on his part in order that this may be made for him and made for his utility which through him is the sacrament of God, whoever indeed thinks this errs, because the sacraments of God and the flesh of the Lamb remaining in sin do not sanctify, although through their ministry the sacraments are made for the sanctification of others. So then we say also regarding the sacrament of marriage, that in some respect with them it is rightly said not to be true or valid or holy, who having only the sacrament or not believing rightly or living wickedly do not merit to receive its truth, that is, its virtue and spiritual effect.

Blessed Augustine says that the sacrament of marriage is common to all peoples but that the sacredness of the sacrament exists only in the city of our God and on His holy mount. He says likewise: When the Gospel began to be preached, at first He found pagans joined with pagans as consorts. Likewise he says: If the Lord admits fornication as the only cause for dismissing a wife, and prohibits a pagan marriage being dismissed, (Cf. Matt. 5, 32), the consequence is that paganism should not be subject to fornication. What is it then, they say, that the blessed Ambrose says: that the marriage is not ratified in God's sight? Dismissal on account of God is not a sin if there is association with another. Likewise blessed Gregory says that dismissal for the sake of God is not a sin, if there is union with another. For injury to the Creator dissolves the law of matrimony. But behold how they prove that a marriage of this kind does not exist, because, he says, it was said: A marriage without God is invalid, and because it was said again: Injury to the Creator dissolves the law of matrimony. Therefore, he says it was not a marriage because he says it was not ratified, and because he said that the injury to the Creator dissolved the law of matrimony. But notice that in this he said rather that there was marriage, and he affirmed this marriage but not as valid. In similar manner he who said that injury to the Creator broke the law of marriage asserted that marriage existed there and that it had law, and this law surely would stand firm and would not be denied without sin, unless it were dissolved for some greater intervening cause. For if there was no law there before, why was it necessary especially to excuse those who withdraw from that law by breaking it? If even he who was dismissed seemed blameworthy, unless he were excused for some greater cause, how would he not rightly be accused who dismissed without cause? Now then since the debt of the conjugal sacrament was true, it could not at all have been denied without cause. For the husband owes the wife and the wife the husband that the one depart not from the other, and if by chance one should depart, the one who is deserted should nevertheless keep the law and debt of marriage inviolate.

But there is a greater cause of God against which no cause should stand. When this is harmed, nothing contrary to it is due anyone. In every cause, he who opposes this cause, loses his right; under it and according to it we owe certain things, contrary to it nothing. Your wife says to you: You have become a Christian; I shall not follow you; since you do not worship idols, since you have cast aside the rite and custom of your parents, I am going to another or, if I am not going to another, I am not now going with you. I do not recognize you as a husband unless you deny Christ. Pay attention to this. The injury to the Creator broke the law of marriage. You owe her nothing more. She who did injury to her Creator lost her right. It had not been permitted you to desert her, if she had not lost her right in you. She had power over your body, and it was not permitted you to take from her what was her own, until she herself wished to take from the Creator what was His own. Now after she wished to do injury to her Creator, she rightly lost her right.

You should do the same thing regarding father, regarding mother, regarding brother and sister, regarding sons and relatives, finally regarding your soul. For to all these you owe something but before God, not contrary to God. Behold your father or your mother or brother or sister or even your soul is on one side, and someone says to you: I love this; I seek this; I note this. I come to obtain this, to acquire this, to accomplish this. Come after me; agree with me; cooperate with my will; favour my desire. Your God stands on the other side and He says to you: I reject this; I detest that malice; that sin does not please me; do not give consent; it is evil; you should not do that. Attend rather to me; submit to me; come after me; follow what I urge; follow whither I precede; your father cries out to you on the contrary: Son, how do you desert me? I begot you; I brought you into this life; I fostered and nourished you; I trained you in habits and discipline. Your God says on the contrary: He indeed begot you but when he begot you, he received from mine what he gave you. He ministered to you generating substance from what is mine, but he was not able to give you life after generation. I, since it was ministered to you by me from mine through him, alone vivified without him; I gave you your life. I also gave my death. Your father did not die for your sake, but I died for you, that you might live in me. He should not precede me in cause, who was not able to go first in grace and in benefit. Therefore, you should not hear him against me; you should not follow him in that which displeases me. You owe him nothing except on account of me from whom you could have received nothing, unless it had been given by me.

This I say; to this pay attention. If at any time some such thing should happen, whether father or mother or brother or sister or wife or children, still more I say, even if our soul should wish to avert us from our God, we should not listen to it or give heed to it or follow its desires. The Gospel cries out to us: "Whoever does not dismiss father and mother, brothers and sisters, mother and sons, but yet even his own soul on account of me is not worthy of me," (Cf. Luke 14, 26; Matt. 10, 37). All piety is impiety there where you are pious toward becoming impious. You see, therefore, that no cause can stand against the cause of God; moreover, there is no cause at all which is opposed to Him who alone is the highest. For this reason dismissal on account of God is not sin, if there is union with another. For injury to the Creator dissolves the law of matrimony. "If the unbeliever depart, let him depart. A brother is not under servitude in such cases," (Cf. 1 Cor. 7, 15). He would be under servitude, if either he were taken unwillingly or were held involuntarily. He owes nothing to her, whether he departs or remains. He who did injury to the Creator lost his law. If then the unbeliever departs, let him depart; it is nothing to us. The believer is not forced, obligated, as it were, by some debt, either to follow the one who departs or to endure him who scorns. He is not subject to servitude; he is free to do what he wishes; only in the Lord let him take a wife, if the person is a man; if a woman, let her so marry. Let him select what association he wishes; he is not held now by the debt of the earlier association whose law was loosed on account of the injury to the Creator. And indeed this injury to the Creator not only excuses the believer then when, dismissed on account of God by the unbeliever, he is joined with another without blame, but also excuses then when the believer himself, choosing by preference a faithful association, indeed abominates with Christian devotion cohabitation with an unbeliever, who wishes it but refuses to receive the faith. For whether the unbeliever departs or elects to remain he who had become a believer owes her nothing. No one can force him from doing what he wishes. The injury to the Creator looses the law of matrimony. The unbeliever cannot now exact anything from him because she has lost her due in him. After she scorns to render what she owes to the Creator, the faithful person already has cause for which he can justly deny even that which he owed before and which he still would have owed indeed, if he had not a cause that intervenes and resolves the debt.

Therefore, the believer is free, if he wishes to choose a believing companion; no one can prohibit him. Yet if he suffers an unbeliever who is willing to live with him, he does a work of perfection to the benefit of his neighbour. So says the Apostle: "The unbelieving husband is sanctified by the believing wife; and the unbelieving wife is sanctified by the believing husband," (Cf. 1 Cor. 7, 14). If then a believer suffers an unbeliever who consents to this, to live with him so that he makes a believer from an unbeliever, whether he does this or not, in so far as in him, he wins the soul of his brother and fulfils a work of piety. But if he does not wish to suffer it, abhorring her infidelity, a brother is not subject to servitude toward a person of this kind. No one can force him, if he wishes, from deserting an unbeliever nor can anyone prohibit him, even if he should wish, from joining himself with a believer. In an unbeliever who casts out faith there is a sin whose fault breaks the right of matrimony, so that now he cannot exact by right that which, if it were exacted by a believer, could not be denied without injury. For the fault of the unbeliever releases the believer from the debt just as contrariwise the justice of the believer binds the unbeliever to the debt.

And so the believer does not sin if he marries another, since he was released from the law of matrimony toward the unfaithful, but the unbeliever, even when deserted without blame, does not seek association with another, whom the law of matrimony and the debt of the conjugal pact still binds to the faithful one. Therefore, the believer cannot be called an adulterer, if he is joined with another. But the unbeliever, even though abandoned, incurs the crime of adultery, if he copulates with another. Thus if the believer checks himself, even from that which is permitted, in order to avoid danger to his neighbour, he does a more perfect work. And yet by no means can he be forced to this, since it is not a work of debt but a function of charity, just as blessed Augustine says in his book, "On Adulterous Marriages." The Lord does not prohibit the separation of the believer from the unbeliever, since it is not unjust toward Him; however, the Apostle does prohibit it, on the counsel of charity, not only lest the dismissed be scandalized but also because, when they have fallen into strange unions bound by adulterous ties, they may with the greatest difficulty be released from the unfaithfulness. And so the unbeliever commits adultery, if he associates with another, since he was not released from the debt of the prior pact.

But you say: Behold the unbeliever or whoever, pagan or Jew, is made Christion, by freedom of faith deserts the wife whom he had first, because she does not wish to follow him to faith; he marries another believer; the first wife seeing that she has been spurned marries another binding herself by an adulterous tie. It happens that afterwards filled with remorse she begins to abhor her unfaithfulness, comes to the faith, is made Christian. What should be done about this woman? She cannot contain herself. She begs the Church that either she receive her husband or be permitted to marry another. What will the Church say to her? If the Church returns her husband to her, the Church breaks the marriage which was confirmed by Christian sanctity, and makes him an adulterer when, in the lifetime of his wife whom he as a believer married legitimately as a believer, he joins with another, which is by no means permitted to be done. Therefore, the Church does not return her husband to her. What then will She say to her? If She should tell her to marry another She seems to make her an adulteress, whom while not yet freed from the law of a living man She permitted to join in marriage with another. Therefore, there seems to be nothing else left except for the Church to force this woman to preserve continence, who seems to have been bound by her sin so that she can neither have her own nor another. But if the Church does this, it can happen that that woman is scandalized and, abhorring the Christian faith, reverts to infidelity. Other women also or men established in infidelity, whose husbands and whose wives already have passed over to the faith and who themselves having been deserted entered upon marriages with other believers, when this becomes known, might fear to come into the Christian faith, and there might follow the loss of many who will avoid the faith because either they do not wish or they cannot be continent. Finally, if this woman after receiving the grace of baptism is adjudicated for previous sin, grace seems to have been imperfect; all that preceded in sin does not seem to have been washed away by the laver of regeneration, and it does not now seem to be true that the old have passed and all have been made new, (Cf. 2 Cor. 5, 17). Because of these things this woman seems to have been freed after she received the faith and put on the sacrament of liberty and newness, so that thereafter she is not held by the debt of the earlier union. For it is just that whomever injury to the Creator bound, reverence and faith should now absolve. On this account the Church does not prohibit people of this kind, if they should not wish to preserve continence, from joining others in matrimony.

Now it can be asked if it should happen that he who first came to the faith did enter upon a conjugal union until the other who had remained in infidelity should follow him, what the Church should do about a case of this kind. But there is no doubt that such persons, after they have been made one in the faith, if they do not wish to contain themselves, should return to the marriage itself, and again with Christian devotion come together to pay the debt of the earlier marriage upon which they had entered not without the institution of the Creator. This also can be asked, if, the one who came first to the faith, being bound by marriage to a believer, he who remained in infidelity with her, to whom he had joined himself with an adulterous connection, should likewise follow into the faith, whether the Church should tolerate their remaining together after receiving the faith, since when established in infidelity they had been wrongly joined. But with the same grace intervening and destroying all the old, nothing prevents them from remaining rightfully together in Christ, who had been wrongly associated outside the faith of the Christ. It can be asked also about those who, established in infidelity, marry relatives or any others at all with whom they could not have associated under the Christian law, if both should happen to come into the faith together, whether the Church could tolerate a union of this kind. But here is another reason,—because the grace of baptism destroys the blame, not the nature. In baptism what is human in our nature is sanctified; what is guilt in our sin is absolved. Therefore, the Christian religion should not yield when there comes to its judgment that which could have been begun indeed outside it, but should not be tolerated within it. These matters in truth which have been mentioned above must be weighed in similar manner for both sexes, whether indeed a man before his wife or a woman before her husband should enter upon the faith of Christ.

XIV. *On consanguinity and the degrees of consanguinity.*

In the first degree, in the higher line are included father and mother; in the lower line, son and daughter; to whom in addition no others are joined. In the second degree, in the higher line are included grandfather and grandmother; in the lower line, grandson and granddaughter; in transverse line, brother and sister; which persons are doubled. For the grandfather and grandmother are received as well from the father as from the mother. These persons also in subsequent degrees similarly according to the essence of those who subsist in any degree are doubled in the order itself. These persons in the second degree are called twofold, because the grandfathers are two, paternal and maternal. Likewise there are two kinds of grandchildren, whether born from a son or a daughter. Brother and sister come transversely, that is, either brother of a father or brother of a mother, who are called either uncle on the father's side or uncle on the mother's side, who also themselves are doubled in this order. In the third degree above come grandfather once removed and grandmother once removed; below, grandson once removed and granddaughter once removed; obliquely, son or daughter of brother and of sister; uncle and aunt on the father's side, that is, brother and sister of the father; uncle and aunt on the mother's side, brother and sister of the mother. In the fourth degree above come the grandfather twice removed and the grandmother twice removed; below, the grandson twice removed and the granddaughter twice removed; obliquely, the grandson and granddaughter of a brother and of a sister; the brother of a father's brother's son or daughter, and the sister of a father's brother's son or daughter, that is, the son or daughter of an uncle on the father's side; the son of a mother's sister's son or daughter, the daughter of a mother's sister's son or daughter, that is, the son or daughter of an uncle on a mother's side and of the aunt on the mother's side; the son of a father's sister, daughter of a father's sister, that is, son or daughter of an aunt on the father's side. Likewise there are cousins who are born from two sisters. To these there are added the great-uncle on the father's side and the great-aunt on the father's side, that is, brother and sister of the paternal grandfather; great-uncle on the mother's side, great-aunt on the mother's side, that is, brother and sister of the paternal grandmother as well as of the maternal grandmother. In the fifth degree indeed above come the grandfather thrice removed, the grandmother thrice removed; below, the grandson thrice removed, the granddaughter thrice removed; obliquely, the grandson once removed, the granddaughter once removed of a brother and of a sister, of a brother of a father's brother's son or daughter, of a sister of a father's brother's son or daughter, of the son of a mother's sister's son or daughter and of the daughter of a mother's sister's son or daughter; son or daughter of the son or of the daughter of brothers and sisters; son of a cousin, daughter of a cousin, that is, of a great-uncle on the father's side, of a great-aunt on the father's side; son or daughter of a great-uncle on the mother's side or great-aunt on the mother's side. To these there are added: the father's brother twice removed, the father's sister twice removed; there are brother and sister of a paternal grandfather once removed; brother of a grandmother once removed, sister of a grandmother once removed. These last are brother and sister of a paternal and maternal grandmother once removed and of a maternal grandfather once removed. This discription cannot be made clear in other degrees than in those in which it has been pictured nor in other words.

In the sixth degree above come the grandfather four times removed and grandmother four times removed; below, the grandson four times removed, the granddaughter four times removed; obliquely, the son and the daughter of a great-grandchild of a brother and of a sister, of a brother descended from a father's brother, of a sister descended from a father's sister; sons descended from a father's sister and daughters descended from a father's sister; sons descended from a mother's sister and daughters descended from a mother's sister; grandson, granddaughter of a great-uncle and of a great-aunt on the father's side; grandson, granddaughter of a great-uncle and of a great-aunt on the mother's side; son or daughter of a nearer cousin, who are called cousins. To these there accrue laterally, the son or the daughter of a great-grandfather's brother, of a great-grandmother's sister; grand-uncle twice removed on the father's side, grand-aunt twice removed on the father's side, (these are brother and sister of the paternal grandfather twice removed); grand-uncle twice removed on the mother's side, grandaunt twice removed on the mother's side, (these are brother and sister of the paternal and maternal grandmother twice removed and of the maternal grandfather twice removed). These things also cannot be explained further than the author himself has discussed them.

In the seventh degree those who are related in direct line above and below are not called by the names of the former but in transvere line there are included: grandson thrice removed, granddaughter thrice removed of brother and of sister; sons and daughters of a cousin. Seven grades of succession have been established because further through the nature of things neither can names be found nor can life be prolonged for those who succeed. In these seven degrees all names of relationship are included, beyond which no affinity can be found nor succession propagated more.

Why consanguinity is guarded even to the sixth degree. While consanguinity breaking itself off gradually with the orders of progeny will drag itself out to the last degree and will cease to be relationship, again the law by the bond of matrimony seeks this and in a manner calls it back as it flees. Now on this account has consanguinity been established unto the sixth degree of descent, that just as in six ages the generation of the world and the status of man is completed, so the propinquity of relationship is terminated within so many degrees in this manner. Let son and daughter, which is, brother and sister, be the stock itself. After these have been separated from each other, from the root of that stock come forth these twigs: grandson and granddaughters, first; grandson and granddaughters once removed, second; grandson and granddaughter twice removed, third; their son and daughter, fourth; the latter's son and daughter, fifth; and the last's son and daughter, sixth.

We have decreed that everyone observe his progeny until the seventh generation and as long as they know that they are related by affinity we prohibit their entering upon conjugal union. If they should do this, let them be separated.

Pope Gregory.[*] *How the degrees of consanguinity are to be computed.*

Bishop Alexander, servant of the servants of God, to all bishops and clerics

[*]Decret. Grat., ed. Friedberg, I, II, cols. 1271-1274.

and also to the judges established throughout Italy, health and apostolic benediction. The Apostolic See has received a question, lately arisen, regarding the degrees of consanguinity, since some unskilled in the laws and canons believe and strive to number the same degrees of relationship contrary to the holy canons and ecclesiastical custom, affirming in a new and unheard of error that full brothers or sisters are mutually in the second generation, their sons or daughters in the fourth, their grandchildren or granddaughters in the sixth, computing progeny in such a manner and terminating it in a sixth degree of this kind. Then they say men and women can contract nuptial laws between themselves, and to confirm a profane error of this kind they assume in their argument the secular laws which the Emperor Justinian promulgated regarding the successions of kindred, relying upon which they strive to show that brothers have been counted in the second degree, their sons in the fourth, grandsons in the sixth. Thus terminating the genealogical series they strive by a kind of perverse shrewdness to disturb the reckoning of the Holy Fathers and the ancient computation of the Church, which has been handed down to us. We indeed under God's favour strove to discuss this question in a synod held in the Lateran consistory, having called together for this work bishops and clerics and judges of the different provinces.

Finally after the laws and the holy canons had been investigated for a long time, we found distinctly that for one reason and another one computation was made on the part of the laws and another on the part of the canons. In the laws indeed mention of the degrees themselves has been made for no other reason than that heredity or succession may be transferred from one person to another between kin. Therefore, since heredities cannot be transferred except only from one person to another, on this account the secular emperor took care to fix the individual degrees in the individual persons. Since indeed nuptials cannot take place without two persons, on this account the sacred canons establish two persons in one degree. Yet it will be manifest that both computations, if they should be attentively and carefully examined, meant the same and are the same in sense and come to the same end. For Justinian did not define in his laws to what degree consanguinity itself persists. As a matter of fact, the canons have numbered no generation beyond the seventh. Indeed after the sixth degree had been determined the emperor added to the laws themselves. Thus far let it suffice to have shown how degrees of relationship are counted; for from these it is easy to understand how we should count further degrees. For when a person has been generated he adds a degree.

Behold in these brief words it is shown clearly that such degrees as these men compute should not only be enumerated to the sixth but even beyond, since he decrees that beyond the sixth further degrees should be enumerated. For when he says further degrees, he clearly indicates that there are not only six degrees but when the six are finished that others should be enumerated. Therefore, that the laws may be truthful and the canons be true, let us say this, that truth indeed holds that consanguinity is not terminated in the sixth degree of this kind but is terminated according to the canons in the seventh degree. For both computations, as we have said above, are concluded in one end. For two legal degrees effect one canonical degree. Thus brothers, who according to secular laws are said to be in the second degree, according to the canons are counted in the first; sons of brothers, who there are counted in the fourth degree, are here computed in the second; grandsons indeed, who there are computed in the sixth, are here enumerated in the third. Thus then, those who in the laws are inscribed in the eighth and in the tenth, in the canons are defined as in the fourth and in the fifth. And in this way regarding the rest, it must be understood that those who according to the canons are said to be in the sixth or the seventh degree, according to the laws are received in the twelfth or fourteenth. For if canonically and in the usual manner they are counted in the seven degrees, all the names of relationships are retained, beyond which neither consanguinity is found nor are names discovered nor can succession be asked for more nor be recorded in the memory by any generation.

Lest indeed in this computation of consanguinity ambiguity henceforth possibly remain, we have thought that some other enumeration should also be completed in this disputation than that which some men make. For there are indeed those who do not begin to count genealogy from brothers but from their sons, that is, from children of a father's brother and of a mother's sister, saying that sons of brothers should be computed in the first generation, since brothers stand as a kind of stock from which the other branches come forth. But this computation of degrees, if it should be well understood, will possibly be different in meaning from that which we set forth above.

From the third book of Institutions, sixth chapter, (1-9), on the degrees of relationship.

In this place it is necessary to set forth how degrees of relationship are counted. In this matter we should be especially advised that one relationship is counted above, another below, another transversely, which is also called laterally. The higher relationship is of parents, the lower of children; transversely of brothers and sisters of those men or women who are born from these, and consequently uncles and aunts on the father's side, uncles and aunts on the mother's side. And indeed relationship above and below begins from the first degree. But that which is counted transversely is from the second degree.

In the first degree above are father and mother; below, son and daughter; in the second degree above, grandfather and grandmother; below, grandson and granddaughter; transversely, brother and sister; in the third degree above, great-grandfather and great-grandmother; below, great-grandson and great-granddaughter; transversely, son and daughter of brother and sister, and consequently uncle and aunt on the father's side and uncle and aunt on the mother's side. *Patruus* is brother of the father whom the Greeks call πατρῷος or πατράδελφος. *Avunculus* is the brother of the mother who among them is properly called μητρῷος and in general is spoken of as θεῖος. *Amita* is the sister of the father; *matertera* is the sister of the mother who as is evident above is called θεία. In the fourth degree above is the grandfather twice removed and grandmother twice removed; below, the grandson twice removed and granddaughter twice removed. Transversely are grandson and granddaughter of brother and sister and consequently great-uncle and great-aunt on the father's side, that is, brother and sister of a grandfather; likewise, great-uncle and great-aunt on the mother's side, that is, brother and sister of a grandmother;* cousins, that is, whoever are born either from brothers and sisters. But some rightly think that these are properly called *consobrini,* who are generated from two sisters, as it were, *consororini,* but that those who are generated from two brothers should properly be called *fratres patrueles.* But if daughters were born from two brothers, they are called *sorores patrueles.* But those who are generated from brother and sister should properly be called *amitini.* The sons of an aunt on the father's side you call *consobrini,* if she should be your aunt on the father's side; likewise, the sons of your aunt on the father's side you call *consobrini* and you call them *amitini.* In the fifth degree, above are the father and the mother of grandparents twice removed; below, the children of grandchildren twice removed. Transversely are great-grandson and great-granddaughter of brother and of sister and rightly great-granduncle and great grandaunt on the father's side, that is, brother and sister of a great grandfather; and great-granduncle and great-grandaunt on the mother's side, that is, brother and sister of great-grandfather; likewise, *fratris partruelis, sororis patruelis, consobrini et consobrinae, amitini et amitinae filius, filia, propior sobrinus, sobrina.* These are the son and the daughter of a great-uncle and great-aunt on the father's side and of a great-uncle and great-aunt on the mother's side. In the sixth degree, above are grandfather thrice removed, grandmother thrice removed; below, grandson thrice removed and granddaughter thrice removed; below, grandson thrice removed and granddaughter thrice removed; transversely, great-grandson and great-granddaughter of brother and sister, and rightly great-granduncle and great-grandaunt on the father's side, that is, brother and daughter of great-grandfather; likewise the son and daughter of *sobrinus* and *sobrina* who are born from brothers or sisters, *patrueles* or *consobrini* or *amitini.*

To this extent let it suffice to have shown how the degrees of relationship are counted. For from these it is easy to understand how we should also count de-

---

*The passage beginning in our translation with "who as is evident above" through "brother and sister of a grandmother" is omitted from our manuscripts but included in the text of Migne's Patrologia Latina.

grees further. For every person generated always adds a degree so that it is much easier to reply in what degree anyone is than to denote him with the proper term of relationship. But the degrees of consanguinity on the father's side are also counted in this way. But since the concealed truth is better impressed upon the minds of men by faith than through the hearing, on this account we have thought it necessary after the narration of the degrees to inscribe them also in the present book, in order that adolescents may be able to obtain the most perfect teaching both from hearing and from seeing.*

From the letter of John, Bishop of Constantinople.

Pope Gregory† being asked by Augustine, bishop of the English people, in what generation the faithful should join in marriage, thus wrote back by way of direction. A certain law in the Roman state permits that either brother and sister or the son and daughter of two full brothers or of two sisters marry. In as much as we have learned by experience that in such a marriage progeny cannot flourish, on this account it is necessary that the faithful be legitimately joined with each other in the fourth or fifth generation. John likewise says: But a long time afterwards when asked by Felix, the governor of Messina in Sicily, whether he wrote to Augustine that marriages among the English contracted within the fourth generation should by no means be dissolved, the most humble father Gregory among other things gave such a reason. As to what I wrote to Augustine, bishop of the English people, your disciple indeed, as you recall, you should know that I wrote with the greatest certainty to him and the English people, who had lately come into the faith, on the marriage of kin in a special manner, not in general, lest the people by fear of rather austere treatment withdraw from the good which they had begun.

Wherefore also every Roman state is a witness to me. I did not write these mandates to them with the intention that after they had been established in the faith with firm root, if they should be found below proper consanguinity, they should not be separated, or below the line of affinity, that is, up to the seventh generation, they should be joined, but because first they should agree with them on the kind of things that are illicit, while they were still neophytes, and they should instruct them by word and by example, and what of these things they may do afterwards they should reasonably and faithfully exclude. For according to the Apostle who says: "I gave you milk to drink, not meat," (Cf. 1 Cor. 3, 2), we conceded that these things be held to those times only, not to later times as if fixed beforehand, lest the good which had been planted with root still weak should be pulled up, but that some little might be made strong and be protected

---

*The passage beginning with "But since the concealed truth" through "from hearing and from seeing" is omitted from our manuscripts but included in the text of Migne's Patrologia Latina.

†Greg. M., Epist. 11. 64.

even unto perfection. These matters, therefore, have I, John, caused to be touched upon briefly on this account, that those who on the occasion of a new dispensation plead for illicit marriages contrary to this very learned man should realize that he in general did not agree to marriage within the fourth generation but rather graciously and at the same time temporarily permitted it.

Pope Zachary,* from the first chapter.

From men who speak about parts of Germany I have learned that until divine grace guided them to the religion of Christianity, Pope Gregory of blessed memory had given them licence to marry within the fourth generation; this indeed we do not doubt was not permitted Christians, whenever in truth they should know themselves, but while uninstructed they were to be invited into the faith.

The same, from the fifth chapter.

Let no one dare to join in marriage with himself a cousin, granddaughter, step-mother, wife of a brother or one of his own relationship or whom kinship has included. If anyone should enter such a nefarious marriage as this and persist in it, let him know that he has been involved in the bonds of anathema of apostolic authority and let no priest give him communion. If indeed he should be converted and separated from such a union, let him submit himself to worthy penance such as the priest of the locality shall determine.

The decree of the younger Gregory.†

If anyone should take the wife of his brother in marriage, let him be anathema. If anyone should take his step-mother or his daughter-in-law, let him be anathema. If anyone should take in marriage someone of his own kin or whom kinship possessed, let him be anathema.

Bede,‡ in his history of the English.

To Augustine who asks whether two full brothers each ought to take as wives sisters who were born in distant relationship from them, Gregory replies: By all means may this be done. For nowhere in Sacred Scripture is anything found which seems to contradict this union.

The reply of Gregory to Augustine. (Chapter 37. 5).

To have intercourse with a step-mother is a grave misdeed, since in the law it is written: "Thou shalt not uncover the nakedness of thy father," (Levit, 18, 7). For the son cannot uncover the nakedness of his father. But since it is written: "They shall be two in one flesh," (Gen. 2, 24), he who shall presume to uncover the nakedness of his step-mother who was one flesh with the father, surely he

---

*Cf. Mansi, vol. 12, 384b.
†Cf. Mansi, vol. 12, p. 263, cap. V, VII, IX.
‡Bede, Hist. Eccl. 1. 37. 4.

shall uncover the nakedness of the father. For a brother to have intercourse with a kinswoman is also prohibited, since through an earlier union she was made the flesh of the brother, for which cause also John the Baptist was beheaded and consumed by holy martyrdom.

XV. *On affinity.*

Gregory,[*] the servant of the servants of God, said to Venerius Caralitanus: To the wisdom of your zealous brotherhood, loving brother, I return the thanks which I owe, since you have sought what you should have and have rendered me happy. Wherefore with pleasure do I reply to what has been asked. You have decided to consult the Apostolic See as to whether a woman joined by nuptial union with an unrelated man belongs to his kin, whether when he has died the same kinship remains, or if under another husband the words of kinship are dissolved, or whether progeny that has been conceived can legitimately pass over into union with the kin of the first husband. For the word of the Lord is forceful and strong, lasting, persevering, unchangeable, not momentary, not transitory. Now Truth of itself says that the word of God is God: "Heaven and earth shall pass away, but my words shall not pass away," (Luke 21, 31; Matt. 25, 35). Before God appeared in the flesh among men, under His inspiration Adam said: "Wherefore a man shall leave father and mother, and shall cleave to his wife: and they shall be two in one flesh," (Gen. 2, 24). And the Lord has not contradicted this.

Finally when Truth arose from earth upon earth and appeared invisible among humanity, it was asked if man was permitted to leave his wife. He prohibited and forbade that this be done, and only fornication should exclude marital union. Wherefore He at once proclaimed publicly the same opinion which before the ages when remaining with the Father, the Word inspired in Adam, He himself confirming what man himself proclaimed: "Wherefore a man shall have etc." If they are made one flesh, how will any relative of theirs be able to belong to one if he does not belong to the other? And we must by no means believe that this can be done. For when one has died, affinity is not destroyed in the survivor nor can another conjugal union dissolve the affinity of the former union. But it is not pleasing that the progeny of the second union pass into association with the first affinity, in as much as the word of the Lord is forceful and strong and as the Prophet said in these words: "For he spoke and they were made: he commanded, and they were created. He hath established them forever, and for ages of ages; he hath made a decree, and it shall not pass away," (Psal. 148, 5 and 6).

Can He not by His word and precept make two into one flesh, both male and female, who has not ceased to make an innumerable multitude of both sexes one

---

[*]Decret. Grat., ed. Friedberg, I, II, cols. 1286-1287.

with Himself, just as the Truth by Himself says: "And not for them only do I pray, but for them also who through their word shall believe in me; that they all may be one, as thou, Father, in me, and I in thee; that they all may be one in us"? (John 17, 20 and 21). If anyone with rash daring and sacrilege seek relationship in the dead, believing that he dissipates the words of kinship under another husband or that progeny conceived in a second marriage is associated legitimately with the earlier relationship, this person denies that the word of God is vigorous and strong. And he who seeks so easily and so swiftly to dissolve, does not believe that the word of the Lord remains forever. Behold the land made and put together from four places separated by long intervals, imagine a body of any shape or immensity that you may wish.

From the Council of Matisco*

Surely the consanguinity which is to be observed in a particular man, this indeed according to the law of nuptials is to be guarded in the relationship of the wife; since it is established that these two were in one flesh, we must believe the relationship of both to be common to them, as it is written: "They shall be two in one flesh," (Gen. 2, 24).

From the Council of Cabillonum.†

We also forbid that anyone in the fourth or fifth or sixth generation be joined further in marriage. Now when after the interdict has been made this shall be found, let it be separated.

XVI. *On spiritual relationship. Nicolaus‡ to Solomon, Bishop of Constantium.*

Your Sanctity inquires of us whether any man can have spiritual god-mothers, one after the other, in which matter your Brotherhood should remember that it has been written: "They shall be two in one flesh," (Gen. 2, 24). Thus, since it is established that a husband and wife are made one flesh through intercourse, it remains surely that the man is established godfather to that woman by whose marriage the wife seems to have been assumed as godmother; and it is clear, therefore, that a man cannot be joined in coition with that woman who was his godmother, with whom the same had been one flesh.

The same to Charles,§ Archbishop.

If anyone should fornicate with a spiritual godmother, he is struck, as you know, with the blows of anathema. Now similarly, we teach to strike him also who has perpetrated the crime of fornication with her whom he received from the sacred font of baptism, or with her whom he held before he was bishop when

---

*Idem, col. 1267.
†Idem, col. 1269.
‡Idem, col. 1102-1103.
§Idem, col. 1158.

he was anointed with sacred chrism. However, if he had her as a legitimate wife, let him not be forced to dismiss her.

From the Council of Cabillonum.*

It has been said that some women through indolence but others through deceit, in order to be separated from their husbands, hold their own children before bishops for confirmation. Wherefore we have thought it worthy that, if any woman through indolence or through some deceit should hold her own child before a bishop for confirmation, on account of her falsity or deceit she should do penance as long as she lives, but let her not be separated from her husband.

From the Council of Maguntia.†

On that matter about which you inquired, whether he who took his little daughter as wife, and about him who married his spiritual mother, and about him who baptized his own son and whose wife took him from the font for the purpose of dissolving the marriage, whether afterwards they should be able to remain in such a union, regarding such we must answer as follows. If anyone should take his little daughter or spiritual mother in marriage, we judge that they should be separated and struck with severe penance. Now if legitimate consorts, one or both, should purposely bring it about that they take their child from the font for the purpose of effecting a divorce, we give the following advice. If they should be willing to remain unmarried, it is good, but if not, a severe penance should be enjoined upon the plotter and they should remain together, and, if the falsifier of the marriage should survive, he should be treated roughly with a very severe penance and he should remain without hope of marriage.

On the Council of Tribur.‡

He who has a spiritual godfather, whose son or daughter he received from the laver of the holy font, and the wife of the godfather is not godmother, let it be permitted him, when his godfather has died, to take his widow as wife, if they have no relationship of consanguinity. For what reason, indeed? Can they not be joined whom no carnal proximity or spiritual generation separates in this? Likewise in similar manner, he who has a spiritual godfather is not prohibited from becoming his son-in-law, provided it be with that daughter whom he himself did not take from the holy font. Also the sons or daughters of spiritual parents, that is, of godparents, born before or after compaternity, can be joined legitimately, with the exception of those persons for whom they are godparents, because no one can take as wife the spiritual daughter of his father, although he

---

*Idem, col. 1097.
†Idem, cols. 1097-1098.
‡Idem, col. 1103.

is not prohibited from receiving as wife the daughter of him who is godfather of his godfather, if she was not daughter of his father.

XVII. *What difference there is between blood relationship or consanguinity and affinity and spiritual union.*

There are three things, that is, consanguinity, affinity, and spiritual union, in which the law has been proclaimed for the marriage of Christians. Consanguinity is between those who are joined according to line of descent. Affinity is between those who indeed are not joined by descent and yet are associated through the medium of descent. For example: The son of my brother is related to me by blood; his wife, who is not of my descent through him who is of my descent, is made a relative of mine by marriage and I of her. He, therefore, who takes a wife from another relationship makes her relatives related to him by marriage, and there is between the woman and the relatives of the man or between the man and the relatives of the woman not consanguinity indeed, but affinity, in which just as in consanguinity the contract of marriage is prohibited. In consanguinity marriages are forbidden even to the seventh degree. Yet some Scriptures seem to terminate the prohibition in the sixth degree but some others in the seventh.

For in that statement that up to the seventh degree unions are not permitted to be made the phraseology is ambiguous. For it can also be so understood that they are indeed prohibited up to the seventh degree but in the seventh they are permitted or that the seventh degree is the last in which they are prohibited and after that they are permitted. Some have classified children in the first degree, grandchildren in the second, great-grandchildren in the third, grandchildren twice removed in the fourth, grandchildren thrice removed in the fifth, grandchildren four times removed in the sixth, grandchildren five times removed in the seventh. In this manner the seven degrees are contained in the prohibitions. Now those who say that mother and father are the root of generation but establish son and daughter as the stalk of generation, they are of the opinion that the first degree should be computed in grandchildren, according to which proposition that degree which in the former disposition was seventh, in this is shown to be sixth. A degree of consanguinity, however much it be extended up and down, does not admit conjugal union, as from son to mother and all who are above, that is, grandmother, great grandmother, etc., and from mother to son and all who are below, that is, grandson, greatgrandson, etc., similarly, from father to daughter or from daughter to father above and below is it considered. Wherefore between those who descend laterally, the degrees of consanguinity are computed in matrimony. Some wished to terminate affinity in the fifth degree. Others have judged that it should be observed to the seventh degree, just as consanguinity should.

Now spiritual union or relationship is guarded in this way. No one can take a godmother or spiritual daughter as wife. In a similar manner a woman cannot be wife to her godfather or spiritual son. The son also is forbidden to have as wife the godmother of his father or his spiritual daughter. And similarly a daughter cannot be wife to the godfather of her mother or to her spiritual son. In the council of Tribur it is granted that a man when his godfather has died may marry the wife of that one, if she is not his godmother. And if this is true, similarly the woman, when the godmother has died, can marry the husband of that one, if he is not her godfather. Yet this in some localities is found to have been prohibited.

XVIII. *Whether the ruse called substitution dissolves marriage.*

We have heard that sometimes, when certain ones betroth women unknown in appearance, certain other worthless persons were substituted by trickery, in which case indeed, if afterwards those who suffered the trick, since they did not do what was done, intentionally, should not wish to offer their assent, by no means do we believe that the marriage should be valid. For it is established that it was done according to intention, nor can they be constrained to carry out what they neither intended when they did it, nor wished when they knew it.

XIX. *Whether the condition of slavery, if it be unknown,*
afterwards dissolves marriage.

It is also asked whether, if any woman should marry a slave, thinking him a free man, or a free man should wed a maid servant thinking her free, afterwards, when the fraud has been detected, the marriage should be dissolved. And there are those who think that this deception must be judged otherwise than the former. For since here the error is not in the person but in the state of the person alone, on this account they think that the sanctity of her marriage should prejudge the matter. But perhaps this would more befit the truth and the peace in which God has called us, that where the ignorance of the one is shown not to be culpable, the trickery of the other is not permitted to stand for the harm of the innocent one in that which he seized by fraud.

TWELFTH PART

On Vows.

I. *On vows; whether they are different.*

Regarding vows, I do not pay my vow. You have demanded and I indeed am forced to pay what I have promised. Stealing a little leisure midst frequent occupations, I have briefly touched upon but not fully carried out what you asked. You ask about vows, whether they bind those who promise them with equal obligation and the same necessity. If I wished to give reply only to your question and also for your edification, I could have replied briefly that no one obligation exists in all vows. But since I do not doubt that you did not move the question but rather sought edification, in so far meanwhile, according to circumstances, as ability and reason have prompted, I have tried to satisfy your devotion.

II. *On the five ways in which the mind treats what must be done.*

There are five ways in which the human mind is accustomed to treat what must be done: by thought, by will, by deliberation, by promise, and by vow. It is one thing to think about something and another to wish that about which you have thought. For you can think about what you do not wish but you can wish only when that pleases about which you have thought. But sometimes it happens that what pleases according to delight does not please according to reason, and that not yet does the mind acquiesce with reason to the point that it does what delights. And there is indeed in the delight itself a kind of will, as it were, to the deed, but in the reason, however, there is not yet an intention of doing. Now if the intention should follow after the will, so that the mind supports assent in what delights, it is still bound either to blame, if the thing is evil, or to merit, if it is good.

Now all this which is of thought, is also of will and is of purpose, is entirely in itself and unto itself, whether it be good or evil, and is contained only in itself and, in so far as it is in itself, to this extent it is contained. Now when also the promise shall follow after the purpose, then he who promises begins to be obligated against another, and he becomes the debtor of his promise for the preservation of truth toward his neighbor. If indeed what he promised is good, he is debtor because it is good and because he promised. Now if what he promised is evil, he is not a debtor in that what he promised is evil. Yet he is responsible, because he presumed to promise what he was unable to fulfil without blame. Lastly, there follows the vow in which something more seems to be contained by the promise.

III. *What making a vow is.*

For a vow is a kind of attestation of a spontaneous promise which more properly is referred to God alone and to those things which are God's. To take a vow indeed is by attestation of a spontaneous promise to obligate oneself to God and to establish oneself as debtor. For he who promises simply, pledges that he will do something, but he who vows bears witness to his promise and affirms the promise itself, wherein, in so far as it is a promise, he is held; in so far as there is attestation, he is obligated. Now some vows are hidden before God and in the presence of God; others are manifest before God in the presence of man. A broken hidden vow is a sin. But a manifest broken vow is a sin and a scandal. In the one there is offense against God, but in the other there is sin also against neighbor. But if you wonder what vows should by all means be kept, and what likewise can be passed over or even changed without blame, I accept this first distinction.

IV. *What vows should not be kept.*

Scripture says: "The vows of fools are to be broken," (Cf. Ecclesiastes 5, 3). Surely we know that the vows of fools are those that are either made with reference to evil or are made badly with reference to good. For example: If anyone should vow to kill someone or to do something else in which there might be blame, the vow would be with reference to evil and it would be evil and on this account would not have to be dissolved. And in this the first blame was to vow; the second would be to perform it, if it should be fulfilled. Similarly a vow made with reference to good, if it should not be done well, is counted among the vows of fools which are to be broken. Now it is not done well, even if that vow is with reference to good, in cases where either what is not permitted or what is not expedient is vowed. A woman, when her husband does not consent or rather forbids, is not permitted to take the vow of continence. It is not expedient for anyone in fasting or in any other deed to propose to do something beyond his strength and his power. Therefore, all these are counted among the vows of fools which are either perverse or illicit or indiscreet. Now when a good is vowed and is vowed well, certain vows are of such a kind that by dispensation they allow an exchange, but some are such that they permit no making of recompense at all.

V. *What vow admits no exchange.*

Do you wish to know what vows those are which permit no exchange? Perhaps you who seek authority do not believe me, if I should wish to set forth some one thing out of all. Yet there is a certain vow which admits no exchange. For there cannot be dispensation where there can be no making of recompense. Dispensation indeed is the designation of a loss; it signifies how great the damage is in it. But it is foolish to sustain a loss voluntarily, when no gain follows. Now when a loss is voluntarily born in a small thing that a gain may result in a greater thing, this is called dispensation and this dispensation is good. Well then, how can a loss be well sustained voluntarily in that by which nothing greater can be acquired. There is one vow, if you wish authority, which does not accept exchange. I do not speak but truth speaks. And if I speak, I speak after truth and I speak according to truth, that man will not give exchange for his soul, (Cf. Matt. 16, 26). But perhaps you will reply and will say that what truth has not mentioned it will not give, but what exchange will man give for his soul? Behold then, he did not affirm but questioned. You reply, if you can, what exchange man will give for his soul. You see manifestly that there is one vow which does not accept exchange nor admit dispensation.

If you vow, moreover, because you vow, for you cannot be good unless you make this vow, render this which you have vowed and render the very thing which you have vowed, because if you should wish to render something else, it is not accepted for that, whatever that might have been. "Vow ye, and pay to the Lord your God," says the Psalmist, "all you that are round about him bring presents," (Psal. 75, 12). What presents? "Bring to the Lord, O ye children of God: bring to the Lord the offspring of rams," (Psal. 28, 1). Perhaps these are the presents which the Psalmist orders us to vow and to pay: rams and the offspring of rams. When he says: Vow etc., to whom the presents? Hear what follows. "Even to him who taketh away the spirit of princes: to the terrible with the kings of the earth," (Cf. Psal. 75, 12). How was this applicable, that after he had said: Pay to the Lord your God presents, He should straightway add: Who taketh away the spirit of princes, unless because He wished to signify the spirit as the presents? But if He takes away the spirit of princes, will He not be able to take away your spirit? Therefore, pay voluntarily lest you lose unwillingly. Vow and pay to the Lord your God; all ye that are round about Him bring presents to the terrible and to Him who taketh away the spirit of princes, to the terrible with the kings of the earth. See therefore, brother, what it is that we should vow and pay to the Lord our God.

But if afterwards we do not wish to vow or after the vow to pay, yet we cannot retain. If we pay, He will receive; if we do not pay, He will destroy. If we pay, He will remunerate for what was given; if we do not pay, He will condemn for what was not given. For if we pay, we give what is ours and it is computed unto justice but if we do not pay, we retain what is another's and it is accounted unto blame. He says: "He that loveth his life shall lose it," (John 12, 25), "and he that shall lose his life for me, shall find it," (Matt. 10, 39). He saves for himself, who contributes to Me and he who retains for himself loses. Therefore, vow and pay. If you vow your life, pay your life. Do not think that you can pay your money for your life. For this would be to vow more and to pay less and would not be an equal payment of recompense. If you give your own to God, yourself to the devil, there is no equal division. If you offer rightly and do not divide rightly, have you not sinned? For a life is worth more and money less. "Is not the life more than the meat: and the body more than the raiment?" (Cf. Matt. 6, 25; Luke 12, 23). If life is more than meat, surely it is more than money, because meat is more than money. For money is given on account of meat, and if there is not meat what would money be? For whatever confers more and benefits more, it is necessary for this very thing to be more. If, therefore, you vow life, do not give money for life, because if you do this you do a fraud, vowing more and paying less. You can give your money with your life, you cannot for your life, unless perhaps you shall so wish to give your money for your life that your life, when given, may become more acceptable. For that, with that he is loved; for that, without that he is not received. Do not therefore think that for your life, that is, in exchange for your life, you can give your money, because He would not receive your money so given, and you could not save your life so retained. Thus both the money would be lost and the life not saved. This then is one vow that does not receive payment by way of recompense.

VI. *What vows permit change.*

All other vows admit change according to place and time and cause. You have vowed gold; you can pay silver because what is less in value can be greater in weight. You have vowed your travel to the Lord; He admits change, if by chance it be more expedient, which can happen, for you to remain in your country and in your home. For if in the one case you can pay something being so able, whether with respect to labor of work or devotion of virtue or utility of administration, you can give an exchange. You have vowed a fast and here there can be an exchange, if by chance this that can happen is inexpedient. I mention still another example. You have promised to serve God in some place, either in habit or in some association. I say that even all this can have exchange, since the place can be destroyed and men die and the habit can be changed. Do you think that you lose your life on this account, if some place is laid waste or if men die? Only let that not be done on your part, which is done in them, nor let that remain in you which should have been done by you. You are not in danger where you are not at fault. Do what you can and as much as you can, and that is sufficient for you. No more is exacted from a good will than as much as is possible.

Now if you shall vow some of these things or something similar, which either can be taken away from the unwilling or changed by the willing, and indeed you can fulfill what you have vowed, exchange of your vow is not in your will, even if you see something greater or better to be done which you might do. Indeed dispensation can be effected regarding you, but should not be effected by you. For truly, in so far as is in you, you owe that very thing which you vowed and nothing else. You are not permitted to exchange one thing for another but your dispenser and master; if He shall wish and shall know that it is expedient, permission is granted to receive another thing. If the same is given by you, it was due; if another thing is received by Him, there is indulgence. For He is called a dispenser, because according to utility and the fruit of recompense He can with sound and reasonable exchange weigh out to all subjects, certain things different from the first and other than those which had been proposed. Therefore, just as your vow depends upon your will, so the change of your vow depends upon His power. In the one case the good that delights can be operated through you, but in the other you ought to consult Him as to what is more expedient.

Now there is still something more which it seems should be added to what has been said. Behold you have vowed the virginity of your flesh to your Lord God;

I say that you should pay what you have vowed. You are not permitted to look back, so that thereafter you may descend to the experience of the flesh. I say to you therefore: Pay what you owe. You are not permitted to pay anything else for this, if it is possible to pay this. But what do we do? Behold you have vowed, and you have not kept your vow because you have lost virginity. You cannot pay virginity more; you cannot give what you do not have. Once virginity has been lost, it can no more be repaired or regained. Now what shall you do? What shall you pay to the Lord your God for your virginity, which you vowed and after the vow lost? Is there something else which can be paid for this, so that the debt may be paid and so great a vow fulfilled? If there is nothing else which may be paid for this, there is no salvation for those who vowed this and cannot pay it after it was lost. Then shall we dare to cut off the bridge of mercy for people of this kind? Let him who dares, say this? I neither presume nor wish to do so. Let him beware who should wish to say this, lest perhaps he raise a danger for himself. Therefore, there is another thing which you can pay for your virginity, if you have lost it. What other thing? Pay your penance. Pay your humility. For virginity of the flesh pay humility of the heart. For broken flesh break your heart. You owed humility of itself, even if you had had virginity. And yet if you cannot pay virginity, pay humility for that, and it will suffice for itself as well as for that.

Behold how great is the virtue of humility. Humility is the ally of virginity and virginity is the ally of humility; and virginity, if humility is absent, cannot satisfy God. But even if virginity be absent, true humility, if it be possessed, can satisfy God. There is, therefore, something which you may pay for your virginity, if you cannot pay that, and the means by which you may satisfy God, even if you do not offer this. So shall I say anything further about your life? Lose your life so that you can no longer pay this. And behold if anything is left to you which you can pay for this. Therefore, I have said to you that this is one thing for which no exchange can be given. If this alone cannot be given, unless you shall pay this, whatever you shall give, you do not satisfy. If you pay this, whatever you shall not give, you do not offend.

THIRTEENTH PART

On Vices and Evil Works.

I. *On vices and evil works.*

Sacred Scripture mentions seven capital or principal or original vices which are called capital or principal or original because they are the source and the beginning and the origin of all the rest. Indeed all the others arise from these seven vices. Now this seems to be the difference between sins and vices, that vices are corruptions of the soul, out of which, if they are not checked by reason, sins, that is, acts of injustice arise. Now when consent is offered to the temptation of vice, there is an act of injustice which is called a sin. So vice is the weakness of spiritual corruption, but sin arising from corruption through consent is an act of iniquity. And so vice without consent is weakness, to which in so far as there is weakness mercy is due, but in so far as it is checked from an act of iniquity a reward and a crown are due. With consent indeed vice becomes a fault wherein in so far as it is vice it is evil, in so far as it is voluntary it is worthy of punishment. Therefore, there is vice in corruption but sin in action. But an act of sin is performed with consent alone, even if there should be no deed without, because what is of iniquity is fulfilled through vicious consent in the will alone, even then when it is restrained externally against its will from performing that which it wishes. For it does what is entirely its own, and anything more it does not do is not its own, nor is the fact that it does not do more, from itself but contrary to itself. Thus work is judged in the consent, to which indeed that work which is external adds so much in malice as it inflames the movement itself of the will which operates within to malice. Thus then vices are the origin of sins from which are born the works of iniquity. These indeed, as it has been said, without consent have punishment because they are corruption but with consent they have blame because they are voluntary. For in so far as they are original, punishment is exercised in them. In so far as they are voluntary, punishment is due them.

Now these are: first, pride; second, envy; third, anger; fourth, despair; fifth, covetousness; sixth, gluttony; seventh, lust. Of these, three despoil man; the fourth scourges him when despoiled; the fifth ejects him when scourged; the sixth seduces him when ejected; the seventh subjects him to slavery when seduced. Pride takes God from man; envy takes his neighbour; anger takes himself; despair scourges him when despoiled; covetousness ejects him when scourged; gluttony seduces him when ejected; lust subjects him to slavery when seduced. The rational soul in its health is a solid and sound vessel having no corruption, and when vices come into this they vitiate and corrupt it in this way: it is puffed up by pride, is made dry by envy, is made noisy by anger, is broken by despair, is dispersed by covetousnss, is corrupted by gluttony, is crushed by lust and reduced to mud. Pride is love of one's own excellence. Envy is hatred of another's felicity. Irrational anger is disturbance of the mind. Depair is sadness born from confusion of the mind, or weariness and immoderate bitterness of the spirit by which spiritual enjoyment is extinguished, and by a kind of beginning of desperation the mind is overthrown within itself. Covetousness is the immoderate appetite to possess. Gluttony is the immoderate appetite to eat. Lust is the excessive desire to experience pleasure, that is, the longing for coition beyond measure or burning beyond reason. There are two kinds of pride, one internal, the other external. Pride is internal, boasting external. Pride is in elation of the heart; boasting is in ostentation of work. Pride in that it pleases itself despises the testimony of another. But boasting, that it may please itself the more, seeks the testimony of another. Thus boasting counterfeits itself by fawning smoothness; pride shows itself truly cruel in inflation. For pride desires to be feared, boasting to be loved, and yet both in that they seek perversely what is pleasing to themselves, although in different ways, are persuaded to glorify themselves inordinately. If anyone then should compute pride and boasting under one member, he will find seven capital vices from which all sins, that is, the acts of iniquity and the works of injustice, arise.

Now some sins are called venial, others mortal. The venial are those which neither can easily be avoided, so as not to be committed sometimes, nor do they possess much viciousness or great harm if they are performed. Those are called mortal which either induce great harm or inflict viciousness, in which either God or neighbor is much offended or he himself who does them is defiled. Such are homicides, adulteries, perjuries, thefts, and those similar sins which are added to these or are contain in these, as rapines, sacrileges, incests, and other such sins. Venial sins are such as light and transitory anger, laughter of this kind, which happen without deliberation on the part of the doers or incautiously from negligence or precipitously from weakness.

II. *On virtues and good works.*

As we have said above that vice is one thing and sin another which proceeds from vice itself, so we understand that virtues are one thing and words of justice another which arise from them. For virtue is, as it were, a kind of sanity and integrity of the rational soul whose corruption is called vice. Truly a work of justice is in the movement of the rational mind which advances according to God, arising from a conception of the heart and proceeding outside even to the completion of the corporeal act. Many virtues are enumerated in the Scriptures, especially indeed those which in the Gospel are disposed under the same category, as it were, as kind of antidotes or sanities against the corruption of the seven vices.

First is humility; second, clemency; third, remorse of mind; fourth, desire of justice; fifth, mercy; sixth, cleanness of heart; seventh, internal peace of mind. Therefore, a man lying in sins is sick; the vices are wounds; God is the physician; the gifts of the Holy Spirit are antidotes; the virtues are sanities; the beatitudes are joys; for through the gifts of the Holy Spirit vices are made sound. The soundness of vices is the integrity of virtues. The sound man operates; operating he is remunerated. Thus good works follow after the virtues, and from virtues the works themselves arise.

Six works of mercy are especially enumerated by the Lord in the Gospel, (Cf. Matt. 25, 35). The first is to feed the hungry; the second, to give drink to the thirsty; the third, to take in the stranger; the fourth, to cover the naked; the fifth, to visit the sick; the sixth, to go to the incarcerated and imprisoned. For in these necessities all the trouble of life is either comprehended or figured in which, whoever has compassion for his neighbour on account of God, merits mercy from God in his own necessity.

III. *On fear and love.*

Indeed there are two movements of the heart by which the rational soul is impelled to do everything which it does. One is fear; the other, love. When these two are good, they effect all good. For through fear evils are avoided; through love goods are practiced. But when they are evil, they are the cause of all evils. For through evil fear there is a recession from good, but through evil love evils are accomplished. There are then these two gates, as it were, through which death and life enter, death indeed when they are opened to evil but life when they are drawn back to good.

IV. *What fear is.*

Fear is the affect of the mind by which it is moved to give way to a superior; for by love it approaches, by fear it recedes. If man had persisted in justice, of his will he would be subject to the better. But now of necessity he is subject to the stronger. This is that punishment of fear from which we call it servile, when he who was unwilling before to be subject to the better is now of necessity subject to the stronger. And this punishment, indeed, charity sends forth when he makes the subjection voluntary. The more charity grows, the more the will grows; the more the will grows, the more the necessity decreases. And now with perfect charity he loves voluntarily unto better reverence; he does not fear unwillingly unto stronger punishment.

They ask about Christ the man, how He had fear of the Lord. But it is easy to show how He was voluntarily subject to His superior, the Father, in so far as He was man, and with spontaneous reverence gave way to Him whom He knew as superior, saying: "The Father is greater than I," (Cf. John 11). Therefore, just as one love, when there is movement of the mind naturally, receives different names according to its different qualities and is sometimes called cupidity, when for example it is for the world, but charity, when indeed it is for God, so the one fear, when there is movement of the mind naturally, according to the different ways by which it is possessed and operated, is on the other hand signified by different names.

V. *On the four fears.*

Holy Scripture indeed discerns four fears: servile, mundane, initial, filial. Servile fear is to abstain from evil to avoid punishment, while the evil will is retained. Mundane fear is to abstain from good to avoid punishment, while the good will is retained. Initial fear is also to check evil thoughts to avoid punishment with perverse deed. Filial fear is to cling firmly to the good because you do not wish to lose that. Of these four fears two are evil, that is, the servile and the mundane but two are good, that is, the initial and the filial. Servile fear dreads the punishment which is inflicted by man, and on this account suffices also to cease from evil work, because it attends to the eye and does not fear the charge of conscience, wishing to please man. Mundane fear indeed, not seeking to please man but fearing to displease, imagines what is not; it is as false in denying truth as the other is deceitful in concealing falsehood. And both offend truth, the one because it denies out of timidity what is, the other because it simulates out of perversity what is not.

Initial fear indeed, since it is busy in avoiding that punishment which God threatens, sees that it by no means is sufficient unto itself for keeping itself from illicit actions, since to Him who looks at the heart it is not enough for approval, if the action should be innocent, but the thought of the heart also must appear sincere and unpolluted before His eyes. Therefore, since it fears to displease Him who sees the whole unto perfect innocence, it considers it necessary to cleanse the whole before Him. And this fear is called initial, because under this through good will both virtue take a beginning and vice an end. However, perfection does not yet exist, since, while one thing is being done and another is intended, the good itself is not loved for its own sake. Then charity is added and enters through that fear which, while it shows what we should flee, in some way causes us to seek danger and to desire assistance. Therefore, the heart turns to God, so that in some way for His sake it flees to Himself, that is, while it avoids having Him angry, it is eager to have Him propitious. This fear is followed by filial fear which is born from succeeding charity, so that the fear itself is nothing else than the unwillingness to lose the good already tasted in charity. And this fear indeed has something added to the punishment, in that we walk in uncertainty, and the changeable state of life can still incline to either side. But when there will be no change, then there will be no punishment from the uncertainty of suspicion. And then fear will be in some way without fear, when we shall be certain about stability, and yet we shall not cease to exhibit reverence to the Creator.

VI. *On charity.*

Holy Scripture commends a twofold charity to us, namely, of God and of neighbour; charity of God, that we may love Him so as to rejoice in Him; charity of neighbour, that we may love him not so as to rejoice in him but with him in God, that is, so as to love God on account of Him, Himself, but our neighbour on account of God. Now God must be loved on account of Himself for the reason that He himself is our good. Now our neighbour must be loved on account of God for the reason that with him our good is in God. We love the One that we may go to Him and rejoice in Him. We love the other that we may run with him and arrive with him. The One as joy, the other as an ally of joy; the one as rest, the other as a consort of rest.

What is it to love God? To wish to possess Him. What is it to love God on account of Himself? To love Him on this account, that you may possess Him. What is it to love our neighbour on account of God? To love him on this account, because he possesses God. Just as we love man on account of justice, that is, because he possesses justice, and just as we love man on account of wisdom, that is, because he possesses wisdom, so we love man on account of God, that is, because he possesses God, or if he by chance does not yet possess Him, because he is going to possess Him or that he may possess Him. And so on account of God we love man whom surely we would not love on account of God, if we did not love God. Just as when I love man on account of wisdom I love him on this account, because I love wisdom itself, and surely I would not love man, if I did not love wisdom, the very thing on account of which I love him; so, when I love my neighbour on account of God, I love him, because I love God; on His account I love my neighbour himself, whom surely I would not love, if I did not love God on account of whom I love him.

Thus then, if I love well, I also love the good. For I do not love well unless I love the good, and unless I love the good on account of nothing else but goodness. If then I love well, I love so. How? A friend in God and an enemy on account of God. What is it to love a friend in God? To love because he possesses God. Not in his riches, not in his fortitude, not in his beauty, but in his justice, in his sanctity, in his goodness. For those things, although they are from God, can be loved with the exclusion of God; and often when they are loved, they turn and pervert the mind of those who love themselves, so that they do not love God. God is to be loved for them, because, when they are given, they are given by Him and they are His gifts, but the neighbour is not to be loved in them, because they are not his virtue, nor do they make a man good, even if they should abound, nor evil, if they should be lacking. But goodness makes a man good, and justice just, and truth true. And when those are present, God is present because God is goodness and justice and truth. On this account man must be loved in goodness and in justice and in truth. And when he is loved in these, he is loved in God, because God is goodness and justice and truth. If therefore, we love good and we love well, we are good. For nothing makes us good except good love and love of good.

Now if we are good we have no friends except the good and no enemies except the evil because if we are good, we love nothing except the good and we hate nothing except evil. Now if we have good friends and evil enemies, we should indeed love friends in their goodness, that is, because they are good. But as for enemies, since we cannot love them in goodness because they are not good, nevertheless we should love them that they may have goodness and be good. And in all these nothing but goodness is loved, when nothing is loved except on account of goodness. In similar manner when God is loved, He is loved on account of Himself, because He is not from another, nor is anything else from Him himself, which is loved in Him himself. When indeed a neighbour is loved, he is loved not on account of himself, but on account of God; the one, that is a friend, because he possesses God; the other, that is an enemy, that he may possess God; and in all these nothing is loved but God, because there is nothing else but God which is loved in the one, because it is, and is loved in the other, that it may be.

Therefore, when God is loved and when the neighbour is loved, it is God who is loved. Why then did Scripture say that you should love both God and neighbour? If you love God in God and love God in neighbour and you love nothing else in neighbour than in God, why are there two precepts of charity? For if God is loved in both cases, one thing is fulfilled in both, nor would it have been ordered that the work be doubled with reference to one work. It would have sufficed if he had said: "Thou shalt love the Lord thy God," (Deut. 6, 5; Matt. 22, 37). For everything is in this. For he who truly loves God, loves everywhere. If He is truly loved, He is loved wherever He is found: in Himself, in neighbour, within and without, both up and down, far and near. If honey is sweet, the honey-comb also is sweet. If you love honey, you love also the honey-comb, the receptacle of the honey. But when honey is loved, it is loved because in itself it is sweetness. When indeed the honeycomb is loved, it is loved because there is sweetness in it. Honey is loved on account of itself. But the honey-comb is loved on account of the honey, and if you should happen to see the honey-comb not having honey, you see the receptacles where the honey should have been, and you grieve that they are empty; you are not pleased because they are dry, and you desire that the honey which you love be there, and if it shall come there, you love it the more.

Thus love thy God because He himself is sweetness and goodness and truth. "But thou shalt love thy neighbour," (Cf. Matt. 19, 19; 22, 39), because he is the receptacle of sweetness, of goodness, and of truth, and if you find in him what should have sweetness and goodness and truth, love those things in him and love him on account of those things. But if you find him bare of His goods, grieve because you see the receptacle empty; wish that His goods come to him and enter him, that he may be made good, having His goods without which he cannot be good. Therefore, love God because He is goodness. Love your neighbour because he is good from goodness, or if he is not good that he may be good who can be good. For those indeed who cannot be good are not to be loved, nor are they neighbours but strangers and separated and foreign. "Give not," it says, "thy honour to strangers, and thy years to the cruel. Lest strangers be filled with thy strength, and thy labours be in another man's house," (Prov. 5, 9, and 10).

These then are strangers and foreigners greatly removed and become far distant, to whom return to good is open no more, namely, the evil spirits and wicked men damned with evil spirits. Why should we love them no more, because they have fallen irreparably from that good on account of which everyone is loved who is loved well? Never does the Scripture tell us that we should love evil spirits nor those men who have already been damned with evil spirits. For they are not neighbours but removed and strangers to us. Now we should love our neighbours not strangers, that is, men not evil spirits, and those men who either through goodness have not withdrawn or through freedom of choice can return. For they are not at all far distant who, although they have gone away, can still return. These are neighbours whom we should love, either in God, if they have not withdrawn, or on account of God, if they can return. When we love these, either we love God in them, because they are good, or we love and long for God in them, since they can be good which they are not.

On this account there are two precepts of charity, namely of God and of neighbour, so that through charity of God you love the good itself; through charity of neighbour you do not envy with reference to your neighbour the good which you love. You were able to love something and not love it with reference to your neighbour; you were able to wish to have something, yet not to wish that your neighbour have that; yet in God you could not. For you could not love God unless you also loved your neighbour, because God cannot be loved with envy and hatred; yet, because in other things you were able to do this, that you wish something and not wish it with reference to your neighbour, it is clear that you understand that you must do both, although indeed you cannot do one without the other. Although they are together, yet they are two, love of God and neighbour, and they should not on this account have been confused in precept, although they cannot be separated in action. Therefore, the precepts of charity are two, one by which we are ordered to love God, the other by which we are commanded to love neighbour.

VII. *Why there are not three precepts of charity.*

But you say: Why were not three precepts of charity given, that man similarly love himself, just as he is ordered to love God and neighbour? But consider how superfluous it would be to order that this be done, to do which man has been so prone of himself that either he could not or would not give it up, even if it were prohibited. Therefore, man should not have been ordered to love himself, but it was to be feared and to be avoided that he love himself too much. This indeed was innate in nature, that he could not hate himself, according to which no man hated his own flesh, (Cf. Ephes. 5, 29), whose advantage desire, which is innate in nature, loves inseparably and always detests and flees what is adverse to it. Yet since some question seems to exist as to why man is not ordered to love himself as he is ordered to love God and his neighbour, we should consider if by chance in these two mandates in which there is a discussion of the love of God and neighbour this also is contained, which either must be commanded man or be done by him for loving himself.

In man there are two: soul and body, spirit and flesh. God made both and man received both from God. Now that which is from God is all good, and that which is good must all be loved. Thus man should love all the good from God, which he has received from God, because he would be ungrateful to goodness, if he did not love the good which is from it. Therefore, he does well when he loves his body, but in this way, if he loves well, that is, if he loves in Him in whom it must be loved. Similarly, when he loves his soul, he does well. And he does better when he loves his soul than he does when he loves his flesh, and so much better as the soul is better than the flesh. And so in both he does well, when he loves both well. For the body must be loved unto necessity, the soul indeed must be loved unto goodness. Flesh must be loved that it may be fostered against corruption; the soul must be loved that it may be guarded against iniquity. Yet if the necessity of one should be at stake and it should be necessary for the other to suffer, it is better for the flesh to endure corruption than for the soul to perform an iniquity. Both, therefore, must be loved but, nevertheless, that which is better must be loved more. But although both were to be loved, yet it was not necessary to order that both be loved. For, since through the affect of nature love of his flesh was in man sufficiently, he did not have to be called upon by precept to have that, but he had rather to be restrained from having it too much. The Apostle says: "Make not provision for the flesh in its concupiscences," (Rom. 13, 14). Indeed man loved his flesh before sin through affect of nature unto necessity, but after sin through the vice of concupiscence he is now inclined to love to excess; so he needs no precept in this respect, where through himself he is willing, even if he be not advised, but rather prohibition and threat lest he rush headlong, if he be not restrained. Thus then love of flesh did not have to be placed in a precept, and it was established regarding this that it was possessed sufficiently, even if not ordered.

Regarding the love of soul indeed the question can be asked whether it was established in a mandate, and if man has this mandate to love his soul, whether it is to be understood as different from those two mandates which were distinguished above in love of God and of neighbour, or as the same as those. For what is to love the soul, except to love its good; for just as he is said to love his flesh who loves the good of that and seeks its advantage, and just as he is said to hate it, who seeks zealously and sustains voluntarily the things that are adverse and harmful to the flesh, so too he is said to love his soul who loves those things that are good and healthful to it and that cooperate to its good and benefit its salvation. But those who love the things that harm it, do not love it. He says: "He that loveth iniquity hateth his own soul," (Psal. 10, 6). You love envy and blows and wounds, and you say: I love my flesh; what kind of love? You do not cease to harm and afflict it and you say you love it. If you love it, love its good. If you love it, do good to it, if you can; desire to, if you cannot. This is to love, to do well, and to wish good. He who persecutes, hates; he who fosters, loves. If you wish to love me, love me thus; otherwise, if you persecute friends, you foster enemies. I prefer to have you as an enemy than a friend. We call it love when good is loved, advantage is desired, salvation is sought. He who does this loves. Now if this is to love, he surely loves his soul, who loves its good and loves what is good for it.

Now what else is the good of the rational soul than God? If then the true good of the soul is God, he surely loves his soul who loves God, because he loves the good of his soul. For what did you think was said to you when you were told that you should love God? Perhaps you thought you were told to love God, just as you love your neighbour, your relative, friend or companion. For how do you love Him, unless you do so because you desire good for Him; you both desire and do if you can, and you do as much as you can, if you love as much as you can. For you do as much as you love. If you are able as much as you love, you do as much as you love. Now if you are less able, yet you do as much as you can. But if you are more able and love less, you do as much as you love. What then? Do you think that you were so ordered to love your God, that you do or desire good for Him, and not rather that you desire that good? You do not love Him unto His own good, but you love Him unto your own good, and you love that good of yours. For you do not so love Him unto your own good that your good is apart from Him, and He is not your good. You so love Him unto your own good that He whom you love is your own good. For if you wish to love Him unto His own good, what good can you give Him which you have and He himself has not, you who have all that you have from Him? You forget to tell Him: "Thou art my God, for thou hast no need of my goods," (Psal. 15, 2).

What then will you give Him who has all that you have and has more than you have? You are poor; He is rich. In this world the poor give to the rich, and those who have more can receive what they have not from those who have less, for those who are richer have more, yet those who have not all can receive what they do not have. Your God possesses other riches. What you have less, He has more; and what else you have, He has entire. How then do you love Him? What will you give Him? But you say: Although I cannot give, yet I can desire. I wish that good result for Him. Indeed my power is small and slight with reference to Him, but my affection and love is rich toward Him. What I cannot do, I can wish for. Indeed I would do, if I could, but since I cannot, I do what I can. What do you do? I love my God. How do you love? I desire, you say, good for Him. What good can you desire for Him, who cannot find good outside Him? God is the highest good, and in Him is all good, and He is all good.

What do you desire for Him who has all, possesses all? Do you desire good for good, right for justice, sense for wisdom, increase for perfection? You are moved by unnecessary piety. Pity rather yourself. He has enough. Do you wish to make Him better who is best?

Therefore, when you love God, you love for yourself. It is your good that you love, and you love for your good, because He is your good whom you love. When you love justice, for whom do you love? For Him or for you? When you love wisdom, when you love truth and goodness, for whom do you love? For them or for you? When you love the light which is pleasing and delightful to the eyes, for whom do you love? For them or for you? Thus is your God. When you love Him, understand that He is your good. What is to love, unless to desire and to wish to have and to possess and to enjoy? If it is not had, to wish to have it; if it is had, to wish to retain it, although true good can never be loved except when it is had nor can it be had except when it is loved. Those goods which are without are often loved when they are not had, and when they are had, they are sometimes despised. Not such is the good which is God. If He is loved, He is had; if He is loved, He is enjoyed; He is present for love. If you can love, you can have. If you can give this, you receive this. Nothing else is sought for Him nor is one thing given for another.

VIII. *That he loves purely and freely who loves God on account of himself.*

But perhaps you will be mercenary, if you love God and serve Him in order to receive a reward from Him. Some foolish persons say this and are so foolish that they do not understand themselves. We love God and we serve Him, but we do not seek a reward, lest we be mercenary; we do not even seek Him. He will give if He wishes but we do not seek. For to such an extent do we cut off our hands from every reward that we do not even seek Him whom we love. For we love with pure and gratuitous and filial love; we seek nothing. Let Him consider if He wishes to give anything; we seek nothing. We love Him but we do not seek anything; we do not even seek Him whom we love. Hear the wise men. We love Him, they say, but we do not seek Him. That is to say, we love Him but we do not care about Him. I as man would not wish to be loved thus by you. If you should so love me that you did not care about me, I would not care about your love. You should see if it is worthy for you to offer God what man would worthily reject. How, they say, are we not mercenary if we love God on this account, in order to receive a reward from Him. This is not to love freely, nor is this love filial but of a mercenary and of a servant, who seeks a reward for his service.

Those who say this do not understand the virtue of love. For what is to love except to wish to have Him? Not anything from Him but Himself, that is, freely. If you should seek anything from Him, you would not love freely. But now you do not seek something in exchange for the fact that you love, and yet you seek something and you yourself desire in Him what you love. Otherwise you would not love, if you did not desire. But one thing is for Him, another in Him. If you love something for Him, you are mercenary; if you love in and love Him, you are a son; even if you consider that life eternal is something else and different from the good itself which is God, and to obtain it you give so much service, your service is not pure nor your love free. Those sons of Zebedee who sought the seat on the right and on the left in His kingdom considered something else foreign and different from that good, and to obtain this they clung for some time, until rebuked and changed they recognized the truth and corrected their purpose. For they thought that God would have to be served for what He himself was not, because they did not understand that He himself was good which alone should be loved on account of Him, and whatever must be loved besides Him must be loved on account of Him, and this indeed is love the more fortunately, the more ardently it is loved.

He who loves this loves himself because he loves his own good, and he loves truly because he loves true good. Scripture did not say that you should love yourself lest by chance you should err and should think that you must be indulged and be eager for those external things, which are advantageous and pleasing to your flesh, and lest you should believe that you ought so to love yourself and so to take occasion from Scripture as to foster your own flesh and to neglect your soul. On this account it did not say to you that you should love yourself, lest you should understand this wherein you should love more, and neglect that wherein you might perish more dangerously. Therefore, it did not say to you that you should love yourself, nor was it altogether silent when it said that you should love your God. For when you love your God, you love your good and the better good and the good of the better. And when you love your good, you love yourself.

IX. *On the measure of loving God.*

Now Scripture makes clear to us how much we should love our good which is God, when it says: "Thou shalt love the Lord thy God with thy whole heart, and with thy whole mind, and with thy whole soul," (Cf. Deut. 6, 5; Matt. 22, 37); as if it said: I do not order you to love so much, but indeed that you love God as much as you are able; so much are you to love. Your power shall be your measure. The more you love, the more you have. And the more you have, the happier you are. Therefore, extend and force yourself as much as you can, that all that is in you may be fulfilled, even if the whole which is in Him is not taken. Do not fear as if He should fail you, if your capacity should be too great. However strong you shall be, you shall never be as strong as He is. If you were so strong, you would be so great. But now you grow in Him; you cannot equal Him. Therefore, grow and profit. The greater you will be in good, the better you will be. If you were the highest, you would be the best. Now since you cannot be the highest, you can be in the highest. And this is great for you and from this you are great, if you are in the highest; surely the greater you are, the higher you are.

But you ascend when you love. You proceed upward in charity because charity leads upward, just as the Apostle says: "Still I show you the higher way," (1 Cor. 12, 31). Ascend therefore while you can. Now is the time to increase and perfect. Afterwards when all shall be consumed, you will stand in that to which you will come, and this will be your highest in Him above whom you will pass no more. But it will not be His highest in which you may stand on this account, as if you would not find more with which you may grow. Therefore, ascend while you can as much as is possible; never can you ascend too much, where you can never ascend entirely on your part with your whole heart and your whole soul and your whole mind, so that your whole may be filled from Him, even if His whole is not taken by yours. He fills the whole in you and superabounds in Himself. If the vessel does not fail, the oil suffices. Your heart is the vessel; His love is the oil. As long as you have a vessel, He does not cease to pour in oil, and afterwards, when you no longer have a vessel, He still has more oil. Therefore, do not spare Him; take as much as you can; love as much as you are equal to, since He does not fail. Love with your whole heart and your whole soul and your whole mind, that is, with your whole intellect and your whole affection and your whole memory; as much as you understand, as much as you know, as much as you are equal to, so much do you love. Let the whole be filled with knowledge; let the whole be affected by love; let the whole be held by memory. As much as you are illumined, so much should you be affected, so that the whole is sweet, whatever comes from Him into knowledge and memory. If the whole is rightly proven, why should not the whole be loved? Therefore, as much as He deems worthy to become known to us, let all be loved by us. All that we can take, let us love, and as much as we can.

X. *On the measure of loving neighbour.*

On the love of neighbour Scripture says to us: "Thou shalt love thy neighbour as thyself," (Cf. Matt. 22, 39; Levit. 19, 18). This mandate then we surely fulfil, if that good which we desire for ourselves we also desire truly for him. For in what we rightly love ourselves, we should without falsehood love our neighbour, whether unto necessity of body or unto salvation of soul, and in so far as we can reasonably do so we should aid him. Now some ask if that which was said, namely, "as thyself," is to be understood only according to likeness or also according to equality. For if we are ordered to love our neighbours only as much as ourselves, a kind of scruple seems to arise from this, which we cannot lightly explain. Behold there are two, one of whom must perish. Option is given one to select whichever he wishes of the two things, one of which cannot be avoided at all. If rather he elects his own salvation, he loves his neighbour less. If rather he elects the salvation of his neighbour, he loves God less than neighbour, since he wishes to be separated from Him on account of his neighbour.

But possibly someone may say that equal love cannot make a choice, that it wished both equally and equally does not wish both, nor can it prefer one to the other of things which stand entirely alike in love. Thus then someone possibly may struggle to avoid this objection. But what do we say? If I should love some one man as much as myself, should I not love two or three or four more than myself? Thus questions of men come and disturb the men themselves with their considerations. For they say: What is better must be loved more. Let us set three men here, one on this side and two on that. I say that it is necessary either for this one or these two to perish. Tell me then which you choose, who love your neighbour as yourself? It is better for one to perish than two, since it is better for two to be saved than one. On this account, you say, I choose rather that one perish and two be saved. Therefore, you wish that those two be saved rather than this one. Then do you not love that more which you chose by preference? Thus you say: By all means do I love that more.

Behold then what follows. You confessed above that you love, or if you do not love, you should love your neighbour as yourself. If then you love that one as much as yourself, and again if you love those two more than this one, surely you love those two more than yourself. And if you love those more than yourself, as it seems, you love those more than God, on account of whom you wish to be separated from God, so that you do not have God nor love God, and perish that they may be saved. And perhaps someone will think that Moses had a love of this kind, who, opposing himself to God in His anger, for the salvation of his neighbours said: "If you do not dismiss from them this trespass, strike me out of the book that thou has written," (Cf. Exod. 32, 31 and 32). And the Apostle wished to be an anathema from Christ for His brethren, (Cf. Rom. 9, 3), that they might be saved in Christ. And possibly someone may believe that this also pertains to the love of God, that we love Him so much as to desire rather that His glory be amplified in others than confined to us, and thus, for the salvation of many, our destruction should be desired by us, that many rather may be saved and we perish than that many perish and we be saved.

But consider that the order of love is not such that man loves his neighbour before himself, whose love he is ordered to take and to form from his own when it is said: Thou shalt love thy neighbour as thyself. For if he loves his neighbour as himself, how does he love his neighbour when he does not love himself? For if he loves his neighbour as himself, surely he desires and wishes for him that which he does for himself. Now if he desires that this happen to him which he does for himself, how does he desire his salvation who wishes his own perdition? Thus he should first love himself well that afterwards according to himself he may love his neighbour also. Now if he wishes to ruin himself in order to have his neighbour safe, the love was not ordained since man can give no exchange for his soul. For God requires this first from you, that you give your soul to Him, then that you add the rest. If you should wish to give anything for this, it is not accepted unless you give this also. First this, the rest with this. So I do not say two or three or four men, but you should not love the whole world against your own soul. For if you love something more than your own soul, surely you are proven to love this same thing more than God, because you love your own soul only in this, that you love its good which is God. Therefore, first love your own soul by loving the good of your own soul. Then love also your neighbour as yourself by loving the good for him which you love for yourself. For to love him is to love good for him. For you could love his good, even if you did not love for him. For you could love for yourself or for someone else and not for him, and thus you would not love him, since you would not love it for him, although you would love the good. You could love his horse, garment, house and farm, money, fortitude, beauty, or his wisdom, although you would not love him, since you would love for yourself not for him. So you would be able to love his good for yourself and yet not love him, because you would be loving for yourself not for him. Yet you would not be able to love true good for yourself, unless you loved and desired that for your neighbour.

Therefore, Scripture distinguished this love according to that love which is in others and about other good things, first ordering man to love God, intending surely that he should love himself in Him, since to love himself is the same as to love his good and to love his good is the same as to love for himself, that is, to wish and to desire that. For since everyone who loves his good loves for himself, and again since everyone who loves God loves his own good, it is established surely that no one loves God who does not love Him for himself. And everyone who loves, loves for himself because he desires and wishes to have whom he loves; likewise he loves for himself because not everyone who loves the good of another, loves him whose good he loves, since he does not love for him the good that he loves. Scripture has distinguished for the human mind, according to those things which are sometimes found divided in human affairs, that which divine things have inseparable, saying to man that after he loved God he should love his neighbour also, not because he could do one without the other, but lest he might think he could. First then it said that he should love God, and in this it said that he should love Him for himself, since everyone who loves his good loves for himself. Since indeed not everyone who loves the good of another loves for him whose good he loves, after love of God straightway he added love of neighbour, that this man might desire for his neighbour by loving him, what he desires for himself by loving God.

Therefore, let no one think according to that which has been said: Thou shalt love thy neighbour as thyself, that he should love every single man as much as himself and two or three or four more than himself. For if he loves himself as much as he loves his good, and he loves his good as much as he loves his God, it was fitting that he should love a neighbour as much as God, if he should love him as much as himself. Thus he is not told that he should love him so much but that he should love him in that he loves himself, and what he desires for himself, he should desire for him. For this is to love someone as himself, to desire and to wish for him what he wishes for himself; he desires good first indeed for himself, then for him. For he does not love him as himself, unless first he should love himself. And indeed in corporeal goods which sometimes are so constrained that what is possessed by one alone cannot pass to the use of another, unless it shall all withdraw from him by whom it is possessed, if, with gratuitous charity and on account of greater remuneration of a spiritual good or on account of love, a man should not extol himself beyond his due, he is not forced to expend anything upon his neighbour, which is due without necessity. For he owes nothing to his neighbour except after that and according to that which he owes himself. And so when he cannot do both, let him do first what should be done first. For as regards the rest, if effect is lacking, affection suffices. And perhaps to show this affection Moses according to the written book sought to be destroyed and Paul for the brethren desired to be made anathema by Christ, not because they wished to lose God on account of man but because they did not wish, if it could be done, to possess God without the neighbour whom they loved. For affection spoke and, as it were, secure regarding love, it threatened with separation the loved one and the loving in the sweetness of love, not because it loved His separation but because it desired the union of the other. Now in that he loves the good of his neighbour and loves the good for his neighbour, he loves his own good and he loves for himself, because the good of his neighbour is a good for himself, if he loves and desires that for him which is good for him. For true good is not possessed with envy and is possessed more happily with charity.

But you say: That which is the greater good must be loved the more, but the greater good is that two be saved rather than one. Wherefore, if the desire that I should prefer should be granted, I would choose that many be saved rather than I alone. Here then you do not consider what is the greater good for me, that I alone should be made safe and many perish rather than that I alone perish and many be saved. Now what is the greater good for me must be loved more by me, since it was implanted in me first to love my own good, that especially which is true good and after that and according to that to love the good of my neighbour. According to me and after me I owe him something; before me and contrary to me nothing. Otherwise this would not stand: Thou shalt love thy neighbour as thyself, if holding myself as an object of hatred I should love him. Thus in this way there are only two precepts of charity: first, concerning love of

God in whom man truly loves himself; second, concerning love of neighbour in whom he loves his neighbour as himself.

XI. *Whether charity once possessed is lost.*

Certain men wish to say so much about charity that they begin to praise charity contrary to truth, and yet there is no praise of charity where there is injury of the truth. They say that charity is such and has such great virtue that without it all the other virtues, although in some way they can exist inclined toward good according to the affection of nature, cannot, however, have the merit of eternal recompense with God. For what is done without charity is not done on account of God, and what is not done on account of God, God, if He wishes, does not have to remunerate, even if what is done is according to some good. For the good of nature is not of grace, in nature but not above nature. What therefore is good according to nature alone is in nature alone and is at once its merit and reward. And so what is done without charity, in nature alone, does not pertain to that reward which is in God above nature. It is clear, therefore, that by performing good he does not merit the highest good except him above who performs that good which he does on account of the highest good. You wish to merit God, do what you do on account of God. Therefore, they say this regarding charity, that it is the virtue of all virtues and those virtues please on account of it, and without it, even if they were good in some respect, they could nevertheless not be good for obtaining the highest good.

All these statements about charity we gladly accept as a good beginning of a true definition. But something else follows which indeed joins with truth, so that it proceeds with truth and is received for it, although it is itself false. But we discern light from darkness, and we deride the obscure which intrudes upon the light and thinks that it stands with the light. For if charity is light, surely error and foolishness are darkness. For where there is charity, there is clarity, and there is no one in it who proceeds feeling his way. For he who is in charity either walks or sees or stands or does not presume beyond what he sees. As long indeed as he is in the light, whether he stand or walk, he cannot err, since he sees where he is. Now he who by his presumption casts himself headlong where he does not see, loses clarity since he has not charity, and wherever he proceeds further, all is error. Thus these men lie about charity in their ignorance of it, since they should not have presumed in that which they were unable to see. They say that charity once possessed thereafter never more is lost. Therefore, I ask them whether they themselves have never lost charity, and would that they had not lost charity for the reason that once having possessed it, they had retained it. But I fear that they have not lost it rather for the reason that they never possessed it.

Now if they have never possessed nor experienced it, how do they presume to assert what they do not know? Now if at some time they had had charity, they still have the very charity which they had, since according to their opinion they were unable to lose it once they had it. Now if they have charity, they walk according to charity and do not perform iniquity. Now if they perform iniquity, they have not charity. For if he who loves the world and the things which are in the world, fails to love God, how much more does not he who loves iniquity fail to love God? "He that loveth iniquity hateth his own soul," (Cf. Psal. 10, 6). He who hates his soul does not love himself, or, if he loves himself, loves badly, since he loves according to the flesh alone. Now he who does not love himself does not love his neighbour as himself. "For he that loveth not his neighbour whom he seeth, how can he love God whom he seeth not?" (Cf. I. John 4, 20). Therefore, let those who sometimes perform iniquity say how they have charity. Or, perhaps, will they say that they themselves do not perform iniquity, but the sin does which dwells in them?

For there were some foolish men of this kind who did not understand the reason for man's existence, and thought that certain sins even with deliberation were perpetrated in this manner, so that man could truly say about them, "It is not I who perform them, but the sin which dwells within me;" they did not consider that man himself does not operate this fact, that he feels concupiscence, because concupiscence belongs necessarily to corruptible life; he himself alone operates that he consents to concupiscence because it is of the will. If, therefore, they operate iniquity through their own will, surely they do not have charity. And what will they say? Let them confront their own conscience and let them moderate their own knowledge. Let the conscience be humbled lest their knowledge be puffed up. Therefore, let them not presume about justice, lest perhaps through the presumption of false justice they lose the knowledge of truth. They say that he who once has charity, thereafter cannot lose it, that is to say, he who is good cannot be evil. Why then similarly shall we not say that he who is evil cannot be good, if we say that he who now is good cannot be evil? For he who has charity is good, and he who has not charity is not good. If then the good man who has it cannot lose it, neither can the evil man who does not have it acquire it, and if this shall be established to be the truth, he who stands must not fear, and he who is fallen must not hope.

Are we in time where all things whirl around in uncertainty, and do you make eternity for me from time? Scripture says that man never continueth in the same state, (Cf. Job 14, 2). And do you contend for some reason that he who stands never falls? Why then is it said: "He that standeth, let him take heed lest he fall,"? (Cf. 1 Cor. 10, 12). Would that it were true, if, however, it were just, that everyone who is good could not be evil. But this life now should not have this, in which the evil are expected to become good and the good are proven if they incline not to iniquity. Outside this life indeed there are the evil who cannot be good, and there are certain good who similarly cannot be evil, since the former are bound by malice, the latter confirmed by grace. But in these also nature, which of itself is changeable, by no means operates necessity, since in some, as it is said, not nature but malice constrains the changeableness of nature to the worse; in the others also not nature but grace confirms the same changeableness of nature to the better. Therefore, those who are evil there cannot be good. Similarly those who are good cannot be evil. For this is of eternity and of unchangeableness, that there can be no transition from one to another. But here, as long as there is living by change, both the good can be evil and the evil good. And if someone should happen to be found so good that he is always good, yet the same one himself who is good can be evil, as long as he who is evil can be good. For both truly live under time, and the foundation of both is one in time.

But you say: What then does authority mean which says: "Charity never falleth away,"? (1 Cor. 13, 8). Hear what. You perhaps understand it so, that from the time when it was once had, it could no more be lost. Scripture did not mean to say this but something else, which you indeed did not understand rightly because you did not examine Scripture well. What then? What does that Scripture mean? "Now," he says, "there remain these three: faith, hope and charity," (Cf. 1 Cor. 13,13). What is "now?" This is "in this life," as long as what is not seen is believed, and what is expected is hoped for, and what is loved is desired. Now when this life shall receive an end, and all facts shall be manifest, what will be hidden which is believed when there shall be nothing which is not seen manifestly? What then can be hoped for in the future when all things will be present and will be destined to be? It is said that if you see, there is not hope, (Cf. Rom. 8, 24), and again: "For what a man seeth, why doth he hope for?" (Rom. 8, 24). Therefore, you will not believe there. I do not say that you will be unfaithful, but you will not believe because you will know. Similarly I say that you will not hope there, and yet I do not say you will despair but I say you will not hope, because having all that you hoped for you will expect nothing in the future. Similarly, do I say now that you will not love there? Then when you still did not have, did you love, and will you not love when you will have? Far be it! On the contrary, much rather will you love then, when you will see whom you will love and you will have whom you will see. For this love is not such that when absent He is loved, and when present He is disdained. Therefore, you will love even then and you will love much more, and charity will remain when faith and hope will be no more. Therefore, this means what is said: Charity never falleth away, since it is had here and is retained there, whether prophecies shall be made void or tongues shall cease or knowledge shall be destroyed. For all these things are only in life; even that knowledge of ours which now is, then will not be, not because there will be none then, but because it will be different. Therefore, all these things will fall away with life itself, since they do not remain afterwards, when He who is believed will be seen and He who is hoped for will be had.

Now charity never falleth away, in so far as it is here and will be there, and love will never have an end, just as examination will never have an end. Just as we shall never be separated from contemplation, so shall we never be freed from love but always shall see and always shall love. Thus then charity never falleth away because it always remains. For he did not say that it falleth away from none, but it never falleth away because it does not remain in all, and yet it always remains in whom it remains. For if it does not remain always, because it does not remain in all, then neither faith nor hope remain here, because they do not remain in all. For many have withdrawn from faith and hope which are unto God, and have deserted the faith and the hope which are unto God, and have deserted the faith and the hope which they had begun to have; and faith and hope fall away from them even in this life. Yet not on this account was that which was said less true. These three now remain, namely, faith, hope, and charity. If then faith and hope which fall away sometimes from certain ones, yet remain here, because, since they remain in some, they definitely never fall away here, then similarly charity which sometimes falls away here from certain ones nevertheless remains always because, although it shall fall from someone, yet it never indeed falls away because it always remains in some. For it does not perish, if it perishes in me and it perishes for me. Nor is it destroyed, if it is made void by me and is destroyed in me, since that which does not remain for me remains for another.

But again you say: If those who are to be evil and to perish can have charity sometime, how is charity called a special fountain in which a stranger does not share. For those who perish are strangers and do not pertain to us nor to that which is ours. If then they are strangers, how can they share in that which is specially ours? It is a marvel. For if those who were at some time foreign became neighbours by drawing near, why similarly cannot they who are neighbours become foreigners by drawing away? For if those who are distant can draw near, they who are near can also draw away. Those who draw near are reconciled; those who draw away are alienated. Now if those who have been reconciled are neighbours, then those also who have been alienated are foreigners, but as long as they were neighbours they were not foreigners, just as those who were foreigners, before they were reconciled, were not neighbours. And those who were neighbours, as long as they were neighbours, shared in the special fountain. And similarly, those who were foreign, as long as they were foreign, did not share in the special fountain. Now when those who were foreign began to be neighbours, they began to share in the special fountain, and similarly those who were neighbours, after they began to be alienated, ceased to share in the special fountain. And the special fountain always remains, in which the foreigner does not share. For a foreigner cannot share, and yet he who is a foreigner can be a neighbour. An evil person cannot have charity, but he who is evil can be good. When he begins to be good, he begins to have charity, and when he ceases to be good, he ceases to have charity; never can anyone have charity except the good because no one can have charity and at the same time be evil.

You say again: If at some time charity once possessed is lost, what does Scripture mean: "He that is a friend loveth at all times,"? (Cf. Prov. 17, 17). For if he that loves is a friend, and he that is a friend loves at all times, surely he that loves, loves at all times, but he that loves at all times never loses charity. If then Scripture is true and he who loves, loves at all times, he who once has charity never loses that. Thus it seems to you: There are many such things that can be deduced in some way; but it is nothing great if you say something, but it is if you understand what you say, whether it should so be said. He who is a friend always loves. This is true, that a friend always loves, and an enemy always hates, and yet he who is a friend can be an enemy and hate, and he who is an enemy can be a friend and love. As long as he is a friend he loves, and as long as he is an enemy he hates. Now there are certain men, not true friends, who in prosperity pretend that they love, and in adversity are proven for what they are. On account of men of this kind it is said that a true friend always loves, that is, not only in prosperity but also in adversity, that is, always. For he is not a true friend, even when he seems to be a friend, who according to time waivers and moves toward either side after fortune. He is not such, who loves always, who loves man not money, a friend not gain. For he who loves on account of money alone, loves as long as money abounds; when money fails, love fails, and he is not a friend now who seemed to be a friend. On the contrary he who was not a friend before but was thought to be is now proven manifestly neither to be nor to have been a friend. Therefore rightly is it said to him: He who is a friend loves always. If you have been a friend in prosperity, love in adversity. For what you may have loved in prosperity, you show in adversity. For if you have loved a friend and he still is, love him. Why should love cease, when what is loved is not taken away? Now if you have loved fortune, you now have not what you love, since fortune departed and man alone remained. This he wishes for himself, which has been said: He who is a friend always loves. You still approach as if to bring something greater to prove that charity once possessed does not withdraw.

You show the complete tunic of Christ which was unable to be torn even when Christ was able to suffer. The body of Christ was wounded and yet the tunic of Christ was not torn. It is a great thing which you bring forward if you understand well. For what is the tunic of Christ but the Church of Christ, and what is the integrity of the tunic but the unity of the Church? "Behold how good and how pleasant it is for brethren to dwell together in unity," (Psal. 132, 1). What is unity? "Abide in my love," (John 15, 9). Therefore, charity is the unity of the Church. And Scripture says: Those who are in the unity of the Church cannot perish. This is what you wish to say: Those who are in charity cannot perish. Whether you name it charity or unity, it is the same, since unity is charity and charity is unity. Those, therefore, who are in the unity of the Church are always in charity and those who are in charity cannot perish at all. The truth is manifest. No faithful one contradicts. No one can perish in charity. There one cannot perish but from there one can go forth. He who remains there fears no perdition. Let him beware lest he go forth. Perdition is not for those placed within, just as salvation is not for those who are outside. He who begins to go forth begins to perish. Now when placed outside he returns to charity; he is being prepared for salvation.

What more do you ask? Perhaps you will wish that another unity of the Church be interpreted about which you can truthfully say that no one will perish in it, because no one will go forth from it. For unity is of the predestination of which it is said: "The Lord knoweth who are his," (Cf. 2 Tim. 2). And it is true that all who are in this unity will be saved, since of those who have been foreseen unto life none will perish. For just as Scripture says: "And whom he predestinated, them he also called. And whom he called, them also he justified. And whom he justified, them he also glorified," (Rom. 8, 30). Those then are the ones who love God to whom "all things work together unto good, to such as, according to his purpose, are called to be saints," (Cf. Rom. 8, 28). For those who according to his purpose, are not called and who are not predestinated to the life, although at some time they love God temporarily, do not persevere even to the end in the love of God. And these on account of this, when charity has been lost perish, since when they have fallen into iniquity they do not rise again to charity. Now they are predestinated after they have begun to love God or love perseveringly, so that they do not fall from love, or when they have fallen from love rise to it again lest they perish.

What does it seem to you? Do you not believe it to be so, as I say? Perhaps the Apostle who says this will not suffice for you. Therefore, not because you so think must what the Apostle says be so understood. He did not wish to place all who love God in the number of those for whom all things work together unto good but only those who according to His purpose are called to be saints. The truth is manifest, unless you wish to deny it impudently. But you will say perhaps that what the Apostle says, should not be so understood: We know that to those who love God all things work together unto good, to such as according to His purpose are called to be saints. You say then that it is not to be understood so, as if through that which he added, "to such as according to His purpose are called to be saints," He wished to determine those for whom, loving God, all things work together unto good, but rather that the same ones themselves all of whom love God according to His purpose are called to be saints. Thus then perhaps you will think that the words of the Apostle are to be understood nor will you believe me, if I shall wish to say that this has been charged to you, that all are not predestinated who love God at some time, because they do not remain in that which they love.

The words of Augustine are these: If you do not believe me, believe him that you may believe me. Nay, you should not believe me but truth. Hear then what the Apostle says, says Augustine when he said: We know that for those who love God all things work together unto good. Knowing that some love God and do not remain in that good even unto the end, he added immediately, "to such as according to His purpose are called to be saints." For these in this, that they love God, remain until the end. And those who deviate from this temporarily return and carry on until the end what they began to be in the good. Here you have manifestly the fact that some possessing charity temporarily, because they do not persevere in that to the end, fall and perish, and again some who fall from it temporarily, since they rise again, are preserved and saved. Some indeed, since they never fall from this, persevere even to the end in their fervour, and they carry on the devotion of charity once received.

What do you seek more manifest? If you do not see this, what do you see? How were they able at some time to have true charity, who were not to persevere in it? It is a marvel. Therefore, faith was not faith which at some time ceased to be faith. Why do you not say similarly that never was he white who at some time ceased to be white? Do you not believe that that is said to have been in him at some time who at some time is spoken of as having ceased to be that? For what one never was, he never ceased to be. Wherefore, he who ceased to love at some time, it is established indeed that he loved before he ceased to love. But you say, it was not true love which existed temporarily. Therefore, neither was it true hatred which existed temporarily. Nor was he truly white, who was white temporarily. Who would say this? Therefore, it was true love and truly did it exist as long as it existed, even if in some measure it was not true in that it ceased to be, when indeed it truly was not. If then you say that that was not true love which at some time ceased to be love, understand this, that when love ceased to be, there was not true love, since in the very fact that it waivered and failed so as not to be love, it began to be and received such that presently it was not true love as it was before.

XII. *Whether all love of God is to be called charity.*

Perhaps you will say what some of this kind say that those who do not love God perseveringly have indeed love of God but have not charity in as much as they think that not all love of God is to be called charity but that alone which perseveres unto the end. But if anyone should wish to say this, I do not find any reason or authority by which he can prove it, unless perhaps on this account he thinks that love means one thing and charity another, because he thinks that the Latin word means one thing and the Greek the other. Holy Scripture says to us that love is charity and that love of God is always good. It does not say to us that because one loves he loves well, and that because this one loves, he acts evilly.

Augustine says that the Apostle knew that certain men loved God and did not remain in good even unto the end, and he calls love of God good even in those who are not to remain in that, and these found any number of kinds of charity in the manner of the foolish declamations of paint dealers on market days. They say that it must not be understood of all charity that charity when once possessed is not lost but only of the perfect charity. And if I ask those men what that perfect charity is, they do not say anything to me in reply except "that which is not lost." For they do not dare to speak about that except to talk about the perfection of charity which will be possessed in the future, lest they be convicted of speaking unnecessarily about that which does not pertain to this life. Therefore, they do not find here the perfect charity which they mention except "that which is not lost." And again when they wish to mark what that charity is which is not lost, they find nothing to say except "that which is perfect." Thus they make a circle turning themselves around since they have not a place of escape.

Finally they are involved in such a cloud of error that, while they contend tenaciously that charity once possessed cannot be lost, they begin to assert that it is retained by certain men who with deliberation perpetrate not only minor sins but also criminal and damnable ones. They say that the adulterer and homicide David had the charity of God when, serving lust, he gave free rein to turpitude in violating his neighbour's wife, and, to cover this same turpitude by cruel betrayal, he put that innocent and just man himself out of existence, whose couch he had foully violated. Let them tell me where charity was then, doing no harm where the innocent is oppressed, not seeking what are his own when what belong to another are raped. Let them show me here, if they can, the love which is the fullness of the law, where even the precepts of the law are violated and the law of nature is corrupted. The law says: "Thou shalt not kill. Thou shalt not commit adultery. Thou shalt not covet thy neighbor's wife," (Cf. Rom. 13, 6; Exod. 20, 13-17; Deut. 5, 17-21). If charity is here, fullness of the law is here. If fullness of the law is, how can there be prevarication? If they say that one who does such things had charity, why do they not also say that in doing this they committed no sin since Scripture says: "Whosoever is born of God, sinneth not," (Cf. 1 John 5, 18), and since again it is said elsewhere: "Have charity and do whatever you wish"? For if this is true, that those who do such things can retain charity, when it is granted those who have charity to do whatever they please, surely it is proven that whatever they have done is no sin. Therefore, let them go with their charity and do whatever they wish, since they have great defenders, some indeed who defend by saying that they do not lose charity, but others who concede that they do whatever they wish with charity.

But they say: If David by sinning lost charity, how then is that true which is written about himself, that "the spirit of the Lord did not recede from David from that day forward," (Cf. 1 Kings 16, 13). For if charity receded, how did the spirit of the Lord remain, as if indeed the spirit of the Lord were not able to remain according to many other things, even if it should recede according to the gift of charity? Does it not remain in those or with those whom, as they fall, it guards lest they perish, but whom, as they stand, it does not guard lest they fall? "When the just shall fall, he shall not be bruised, for the Lord putteth his hand under him," (Cf. Psal. 36, 24). What then? If the Lord was present to him standing, why did he fall? And if He was not present with him as he fell, why was he not bruised? For if He were held, he would not be had. Likewise, if His hand were not put under, he would be bruised. Therefore, he was not bruised, because he fell upon His hand. If His hand had fallen upon him, he would have been bruised. He says: "And whosoever shall fall on this stone, shall be broken: but on whomsoever it shall fall, it shall grind him to powder," (Matt. 21, 44). The Lord then did not place His hand upon the one lying down, that He might oppress him, but He placed it under him that He might raise him up. He placed it under that by assisting He might restore him; He did not place it upon him that by judging He might condemn. And so the spirit of the Lord did not recede from David, since it was with him that it might bring him back as he went away and justify him when repentant, and possibly it was with him and not in him. It was with him unto protection but it was not in him unto justice. For then David was not just when he was laid low in so grave a sin, nor did that then pertain to him which was written: "The just man falls seven times in a day and yet he does not lose the name of just," (Cf. Prov. 24, 16). On this account, therefore, the spirit of God, although it was then with David that by sinning he might not perish, by no means however was it so that he could sin without damnation.

Similar is that which they deny and try to assert about Peter, that even then he had not lost the charity of God when on being questioned he denied that he knew Christ. For they do not notice what is written: "No man, speaking by the Spirit of God, said Anathema to Jesus. And no man can say the Lord Jesus, but by the Holy Ghost," (Cf. 1 Cor. 12, 3). But if by chance they should wish to say that Peter indeed then had the spirit of God inwardly in his heart, but he did not say what he spoke outwardly in the spirit of God, let them hear what is written: "Out of the abundance of the heart the mouth speaketh," (Cf. Luke 6, 45). Therefore, that spirit spoke outwardly in the mouth which dominated within in the heart. He who ruled the heart moved the tongue. But perhaps they will say: The spirit of God indeed receded but charity remained. Consider whether truth suffers this statement. The Apostle says: "The charity of God is poured forth in our hearts, by the Holy Ghost, who is given to us," (Rom. 5, 5).

We have not charity except in so far as we have the Holy Spirit, and do you say that with the Holy Spirit receding and absent charity remains? And they say: What then? No spark of piety, no affection of love remained in David and in Peter when the one overcome by the trouble of carnal concupiscence, the other indeed crushed by the fear of impending death in some manner both sinned unwillingly. On the contrary, both sinned voluntarily, since, if they had wished, both would not have sinned. But since they loved themselves more than God they fulfilled their own wills rather than God's. Flesh persuaded one thing and God ordered another, and they elected rather to obey the flesh than the Creator. If they had wished, they would have contemned the will of the flesh, and they would have preferred the will of the Creator. But not yet did they imitate the good Master who taught and said: "Father, not my will but thine be done," (Cf. Luke 22, 42). And it can be that they wished the will itself of the flesh, whose violence they felt, either to be nothing or not to be so violent. Yet because they consented to the same as it tempted and harassed, they acted only willingly, since they wished to offend the Creator rather than to endure the trouble itself and the harassing, which they would not have done at all had they not wished. Therefore, in this they willingly did that which the flesh wished; that which the Creator wished they did not wish, since, if they had wished that, they would not voluntarily have consented to do the other. For when, of two things which cannot be done at the same time, one is chosen by the will, without doubt the other is proven to be not in the will. In this will, therefore, by which they chose against God to consent to the flesh surely they by no means had the charity of God, although in that they suffered great violence in temptation, they can have some excuse in their sin.

But regarding the affection of piety which sinners of this kind sometimes seem to have, when at the same time they consent to sin and yet, in some manner, in the sin which they do not forsake, they do not cease to be affected by a kind of grief, we must nevertheless be on our guard by all means, lest it be thought worthy of the name of charity or love of God. For if in those who are turned from iniquity to justice there remain certain affections and loves of past evils which, however, for those established in good purpose are not imputed unto iniquity, why similarly in evil purpose also should not certain affections of a lost or corrupted good be said to survive sometime, since they can exist without purpose of good will, from practice or nature but without this very purpose cannot have the merit of justice? For this one thing is indeed the purpose of the will or the consent of the mind arising from the will, for which alone is there judgment with God, and this alone, if it is good, is not unto evil whatever is in man, whether it be good or evil; likewise, if it is evil, it is not unto good whatever is left, whether good or evil. Therefore, they should have looked back upon this eye from which alone the whole body shines, who establish the merit of man in affections of any sort such as we see exist in the incredulous and iniquitous sometimes, either from nature or experience.

Superstitious questions were sufficiently able to receive an end for these, if, however, they were able to receive an end. But now they ask, and they always ask, and they never find. They question whether David and Peter should have been damned, if they had died in their sins before repentance. Would that they could see what answer this question deserves. For why should they not have perished, if they had died in their sins? But, they say, they could not have perished, since they were predestinated unto life. Why, I say, similarly were they unable not to sin, since they were foreknown to be about to sin? For if predestination cannot be impeded, neither can foreknowledge indeed be deceived. Now if foreknowledge of sinning does not bring on necessity, neither does predestination of damnation take away possibility. You still wish to hear what Augustine says, since you do not believe me. Hear who they are who love, and who they are who will persevere, and what unity of love is, and what unity of predestination is. "We know that to them that love God, all things work together unto good, to such as, according to his purpose, are called to be saints," (Rom. 8, 28); however, the purpose does not belong to those who are predestinated and foreknown but to God. Thus, furthermore, are all things so that even if some of them deviate and also go astray, He causes this very situation to be of benefit to them unto good, that they return more humble and more experienced.

If any one of these perishes, God is deceived and is overcome by human vice. But no one of these perishes, since by no means is God overcome or deceived. These are sealed according to Timothy, where, when it was said that Hymeneus and Philetus subverted the faith of some, it was presently added: "But the sure foundation of God standeth firm, having this seal: the Lord knoweth who are his," (2 Tim. 2, 19). Of these is the faith which operates indeed through love, or does not fail at all, or, if there are some whose faith fails, it is repaired before this life is ended and when the iniquity which had intervened has been destroyed, perseverance is destined even to the end. Now those who are indeed not to persevere and so are to lapse from Christian faith and communion, so that the end of this life finds them such, without doubt not even at that time, when they lived well and piously, are they to be reckoned in the number of these. For they have not been separated from the mass of perdition by the prescience and predestination of God, and on this account have not been called according to His purpose and have not been chosen. But they are called among those of whom it is said: "Many are called," not among those of whom it is said: "But few are chosen," (Cf. Matt. 20, 16). And yet who would deny that they are chosen when they believe and are baptized and live according to God? Clearly they are said to be chosen by those who do not know what they are to be, not by Him who knows that they have not the perseverance which leads the chosen to the blessed life. And He knows that they so stand that He has foreknowledge that they will fall.

Here, if I am asked why God did not give them perseverance, who gave that love by which they lived in a Christian manner, I reply that I do not know. And let them reply, if they can, why God, when they were living faithfully and piously, did not then snatch them from the dangers of this life, lest malice change their understanding and lest fiction deceive their souls; whether He did not have this in His power or did not know their future evils. Surely none of these things is said except most perversely and most insanely. Of such men John says: "They went out from us, but they were not of us. For if they had been of us, they would no doubt have remained with us," (Cf. John 2, 19). And what else does he say than that they were not sons even when they were in the profession and in the name of sons, not because they pretended justice but because they did not remain in it? For he did not say: For if they had been of us, they would indeed have had true, not fictitious justice with us. But if they had been of us, he says, surely they would have remained with us. Surely they were in good, but, since they did not remain in it, that is, did not persevere even until the end, they were not, he says, of us even when they were with us. That is, they were not of the number of sons, even when they were in the faith of sons, since those who are truly sons are foreknown and predestinated and are called according to His purpose so that they are elected. For not the son of promise but of perdition perished. And because of this none of the predestinated ends this life changed from good to evil, since he has been so ordained and given to God with this purpose, that he may not perish but have eternal life. Of these John says: We know that everyone who is born of God does not sin. David sinned gravely, but because being born of God he belonged to the society of God's sons, he did not sin even unto death but merited pardon by repenting. Of this sin unto death indeed, the same John reminds us earlier in these words: "There is a sin unto death," (Cf. 1 John 5, 16). And straightway he added: "We know that whosoever is born of God, sinneth not," (1 John 5, 18).

FOURTEENTH PART.

On Confession.

I. On confession.

Great is the malice of man. No one when he wishes to act evilly seeks authority, but when we tell men that they should do good deeds and that they should confess the evils which they have done, they say to us: Give authority. What Scripture orders that we confess our sins? If then Scripture does not command us to confess our sins, answer now, if you have Scripture, what sins it orders us to keep silent. If then you do not wish to confess because you have no authority for confessing, why do you wish to keep silent when you have no authority for keeping silent? Yet since you seek authority, receive authority. An ancient law orders you to confess your sins and sends men to priests to confess their sins, that they may receive pardon. There then the prevarication of the law is abolished by confession and by oblation, when there was still a shadow and the confession of the crime had still to fear the punishment rather than to expect mercy. If this authority does not suffice, hear Scripture saying manifestly somewhere: "He that hideth his sin, shall not be justified," (Cf. Prov. 28, 13). For what is to hide unless to keep silent and not wish to confess? For those who make their crimes manifest through the impudence of acting wrongly do not merit justification but damnation. Therefore, evils must be covered in so far as pertains to the impudence of a wrong deed and must be revealed through the humility of confession.

Do you wish still to know the danger of silence and the utility of confession? The Psalmist says: "Because I was silent my bones grew old; whilst I cried out all the day long," (Psal. 31, 3). And again: "I have acknowledged my sin to thee, and my injustice I have not concealed. I said I will confess against myself my injustice to the Lord: and thou hast forgiven the wickedness of my sin," (Psal. 31, 5). See then and consider, if you keep your sins silent, they grow old; if you confess, they are pardoned. If you say: Behold I speak my sin but to God, not to man. I follow Scripture. That says to me that I should confess my sin to God; it does not send me to man in whom there is no salvation, but it brings confession where it promises remission. "I said I will confess against myself my injustice to the Lord and thou hast forgiven the wickedness of my sin," (Psal. 31, 5). What does man do? Hear what he does. Was that not man who said: "Son, thy sins are forgiven thee," (Cf. Mark 2, 5), and it is true that that was a man who said this. On this account those who saw that he was a man but did not know God, murmured among themselves saying: "Who is this that forgiveth sins also?" (Luke 7, 49). For they knew that it belonged to God to forgive sins but they did not know that what was God's, man had received from God and that man indeed had what he had in so far as he was man for this reason, because he had received it. In so far indeed as He was God, he had this very thing and had not received it.

Now on this account He wished to receive at some time in humanity what He always had in divinity, that He might approach His neighbour man in this which belonged to man and that in this very thing which belonged to man He might show to man what belonged to God. For in this very thing which belonged to man He was joined to man as a friend. But in that which belonged to God He operated more powerfully in man. On this account he said: "That you may know, he says, that the Son of man has power of forgiving sins on earth, He then said to the paralytic: 'Arise and walk,'" (Matt. 9, 6). He showed what they were able to see, that through this they might believe what they were unable to see. On this account then God was made man, that to converse with man He might show Himself a neighbour and a friend, that in one and the same person man both might find his own kind to whom he would faithfully reveal his own weakness, and that believing in God above man he might not be diffident to the remission of his sins received from Him. Then that the grace of dispensation might be multiplied more abundantly, the God-man made the men who were pure men sharers in His power, that they might fulfill His office by receiving the confession of penitents and might exercise His power by forgiving the sins of those who repent and confess. He says: "Receive ye the Holy Ghost. Whose sins you shall forgive, they are forgiven them; and whose sins you shall retain, they are retained," (Cf. John 20, 22, and 23). Therefore, Christ the man gave to His disciples who performed His office upon earth the power of forgiving sins.

But you say perhaps: Why did not Christ similarly give men a precept to confess their sins, just as He gave the disciples power to forgive the sins of those who confessed them? Hear why Christ wished that your confession should rise from yourself that it might not seem as if extorted or forced. He enjoined that His office which pertained to Himself must be carried on by His disciples; so that in the manner of physicians they might receive the sick who came to them and heal them. Therefore, He said to the physicians that they should cure but He did not say to the infirm that they should go to the physicians to be cured. He wished this, as it were, to be certain, that the sick should seek salvation gladly and offer themselves to be cured, if they should find physicians. On this account He advised the physicians alone, for his own sickness advises the infirm sufficiently nor has he need of precept if he suffers pain. Yet the physicians themselves afterwards, since they found the sick negligent in their own cure, stirred them up by their admonition to seek salvation and moved them by precept.

The apostle James says: "Confess your sins one to another: pray one for another, that you may be saved," (Cf. James 5, 16). What is "one to another?" To each other, man to man, not only man to God, just as that true confessor says: "I said, I will confess against myself my injustice to the Lord and thou hast forgiven the wickedness of my sin," (Psal. 31, 5), but to man on account of God. For he does more who humbles himself to a servant on account of the Lord than who humbles himself to the Lord himself. On this account, "Confess your sins one to another." What is "one to another?" Not only everyone to everyone but "one to another," that is, between yourselves, men to men, sheep to shepherds, subjects to prelates. Those who have sins to those who have power to forgive sins. Indeed it was due that you should go to Him who is above you when you intend to make confession, but now for the disposition of forgiveness it is granted that you confess your sins to yourselves in turn, between yourselves. He indeed who would alone receive confession should not make confession, since He would not have sins, but these who receive the confession of sins and dismiss the sins of those who confess them have the necessity of confessing their sins to Him that sins may be forgiven those who repent and confess. On this account, therefore, confess your sins one to another and pray one for another. For what? That you may be saved. What is "confess that you may be saved?" That is, you would not be saved, unless you should confess. This perhaps you did not wish to hear, because you seek shadows and conceal your crimes so that you are not justified.

What is said does not please you, that those who do not wish to confess their sins cannot be saved. On this account, perhaps, you try to twist the statement of the apostle to something else, so that it may be understood indeed to have promised salvation to those who confess their sins but not to have denied justification to those who do not confess. Hear then. Augustine says: No one can be justified from sin, unless he shall first confess sin. Likewise Bede, on the same letter of James from which we took testimony above, says: Without confession sins cannot be forgiven. But here there should be this distinction, that we confess daily and slight sins to equals, to one another, in order that we may in turn be saved by prayers; furthermore, that we relate the uncleanness of more serious leprosy to the priest and seek to be justified according to his decision. Behold how the testimonies of truth agree. There is a certain common penitence in the Church which we make daily in turn, in which prayer, poured forth mutually for daily and lighter sins, we obtain indulgence and remission. But we disclose the guilt of more serious blame by special confession to the priest and according to his advice when the gift of satisfaction has been offered, we obtain the remission of sin.

But you say: If no man can be saved unless he confesses his sins, what is the meaning of these words which are found: Tears wash away a crime which it is a shame to confess by mouth. For certain words of this kind are found and they seize men with rejoicing, not because they seek truth in them, but because they wish to defend their malice by means of them. For they say: Why do you destroy us, why do you straiten us? Our deeds should cause us shame; modesty does not permit us to speak; we blush to confess what we have done but what we can we do; we offer a contrite and humble heart; we grieve at that which we have done evilly; we shed tears; we punish the guilt by maceration of the flesh. Why do you seek words when there are good deeds? We have Scripture which consoles us and says: Tears wash away a crime which it is a shame to confess by mouth. We do not excuse the malice but we spare the shame. What then we are ashamed to say to man we say to God who does not reproach.

Therefore, on occasions of this kind men seek an excuse for their lethargy and try to pervert Scriptures, because they themselves are perverted. But why? If Scripture says: "Tears wash away a crime which it is a shame to confess by mouth," did it say so on this account: If you are ashamed to confess, would it suffice if you should only bewail your sin, even if you should not confess? Isn't it much better for you to understand that Scripture wished rather to say this, that tears offered with the deepest contrition of heart can wash even those sins which cannot be confessed without shame and disgrace? What then? If tears wash away shameful sins, must there be silence where divine assistance is more necessary? Nay, much more must there be confession there, that the humility of confession may aid the tears of contrition. Similarly, when it is said to you: "If you are ashamed to tell your sin to man, you should tell it to God who reproaches not," it is not said to you: "If you are ashamed to tell it to man, you should not tell it to man but to God." But God's clemency is shown you, who is so gentle and sweet to all who take refuge with Him, that you should not fear anything improper from Him, although your sins have been such that it happens that you cannot make them manifest to man without shame. For in this about which you are ashamed when you speak to man, you should not be ashamed when you speak to God, because He does not reproach him who speaks but condones him who confesses. Speak therefore to man, that advantageously you may be confounded temporarily in his presence, that this confusion may afterwards bring you glory and furnish confidence, lest you fear reproach when you begin to be made manifest in God's presence. But lest perchance your thoughts should say to you: "If it is so serious to reveal sins to man and if we are so ashamed before men, what shall we do before God whose majesty we cannot avoid and whose judgment we cannot escape," lest then you should despair by considering God so, God's clemency toward those who repent and confess is shown you in that He condones those who regret all sins and does not reproach those who confess.

Thus then receive what has been said. Tell God who does not reproach, as if He said: Even if you blush before man, you should not blush before God, since God is more kindly than man and more gentle and sympathetic with the wretched, so that He does not reproach. And so according to this measure it is not said to you that you should not tell your sins to a man but that even in those things of which you should be ashamed in the presence of man you should confide in the piety of God. Still you offer in opposition those tears of Peter of which you read; you do not read of a confession. Tears wash away a crime which it is a shame to confess by mouth. These tears then you offer not because you like remorse but because you avoid confession. You say then that you read of the tears of Peter; you do not read of satisfaction. You have heard that he wept but you have not heard what he said. On this account tears wash away the crime which it is a shame to confess by mouth.

What then? You think that this is said to you, that because Peter is read to have wept he is not read to have confessed. If you weep, you do not confess. Is it not much better for you to understand that this rather is demonstrated here, that if tears were of such avail there where they had not confession of mouth, how much more, if they should be true, do they avail now when with contrition of heart they have confession of mouth? For this is demonstrated to you when it is added: First there must be weeping, afterwards confessing. Since this tends to truth of confession, that you should first feel remorse, afterwards you should confess. For some indeed, just as they are imprudent in action, so they are shameless in speech, who, since they do not see their disgrace in action, have no shame in speech, to whom indeed it is said by the prophet: "Thou hadst a harlot's forehead, thou wouldst not blush," (Cf. Jer. 3, 3). These sometimes without any feeling of compunction, without any attraction of fear or love of God, to fulfill custom alone, bring themselves to tell their sins, thinking that they for the utterance of words only are absolved from the debt of their sins and to these it is rightly said: First there must be weeping, afterwards confessing. For in the confession of sins man should be ashamed, so that he may humbly realize what he has done and yet not be so ashamed that he is silent. That woman sinner knew this well who even came that she might show that she was unwilling to hide her sins, and yet she stood not before but behind, that she might show that the shame of her disgrace attended her. On this account rightly is it said that first there should be weeping, afterwards confessing.

II. *On penance and the fruit of penance.*

One penance is exterior, another interior. Exterior penance is in the affliction of the flesh. Interior penance is in the contrition of the heart. Through exterior penance the blame of a small deed is punished. Through interior penance the blame of a depraved will is amended. The measure of the correction is to be weighed according to the extent of the crime. "Bring forth," he says, "fruit worthy of penance," (Cf. Matt. 3, 8; Luke 3, 8). For the fruit of penance is one thing, penance itself another. Just as a tree is one thing and its fruit another, so is penance one thing, its fruit another. Penance is grief for something committed in the past, when you grieve that you have done what is evil. When, therefore, you reject and condemn your evils, you have penance, but when, with satisfaction following, you both punish and correct your evils, you have the fruits of penance. If what you have done displeases you, you do penance. If you follow up and punish what you have done, you perform the fruits of penance. Penance is disapprobation of the deed; the fruit of penance is the correction of the crime. But since the measure of the correction is to be weighed according to the measure of the blame, you should perform worthy fruits of penance. If the affliction in the correction is less than the delight was in the sin, the fruit of your penance is not worthy.

But you say to me: How can I know when my penance is worthy? Because you cannot know this, you must always repent. You can give satisfaction, you cannot do too much. It is better that you do more than less. On this account be solicitous, give satisfaction, pay attention, expend zeal, that blame may be with and devotion without end. Nevertheless, that a sinner may be consoled in conscience, a method and a measure of exterior penance has been laid down, in order that, when it has been fulfilled or perfected, you may begin to have confidence and by a kind of holy presumption in the hope of divine mercy you may be confident about the indulgence and the remission of your sins, and more truly so as you have fulfilled the enjoined penance the more sincerely.

III. *On those who do not fulfil penance in this life.*

But perhaps after silent consideration by yourself you may reply: How, you say, can I be certain of indulgence on account of the penance and satisfaction enjoined by man, even if I shall have studiously completed it, when man himself to whom I confess my sins often either from ignorance does not know or from negligence does not consider the nature of the satisfaction which according to the method and measure of the crime, he should enjoin upon me? To this I reply to you briefly: Because if man does not know, God knows. Yet do what is ordered you. Be obedient in that which is ordered you. Let God see your devotion, even if man does not worthily allay your affliction. You cannot perish, if you shall be found devoted. But I am deceived, you say, thinking that I have given satisfaction, when I have not done sufficient. He enjoined me to do so much and ordered me no more. Behold I have done all thoroughly and I have not done enough. I go to God as if secure, thinking that I have done enough for Him when I am still held obligated, since I have not done enough. Why then, you say, has it happened that I do not have such a priest as to tell me what he should? Hear why. This has happened because on account of your sins you have deserved to have evil, since, if you were judged strictly, you had deserved this also, that you have nothing. Scripture says: "Who maketh a man that is a hypocrite to reign for the sins of the people?" (Job 34, 30). It says: "And I will make thy tongue stick fast to the roof of thy mouth and thou shalt not be as a man that reproveth, because they are a provoking house," (Cf. Ezech. 3, 26). For that you may know that your malice did this, see where your devotion was. For if you had had perfect devotion, even if no one gave advice, you would nevertheless have been able to cease. But now your laziness and negligence sought a fitting time, not correction. And God saw this and gave to you according to your heart, so that you did not find what you did not seek to receive.

Yet I do not say that you should despair at this, even if it should happen that a man who applies a medicine externally to cure the wounds of sins offers something which is not adequate. Often what is done externally to a less degree, operates more efficaciously internally. In a small work there can be a great devotion. "A man looks upon the face, but God beholdeth the heart," (Cf. 1 Kings 16, 7). And to say the least it is a great thing, if in this life you should be able to begin, even if you should not complete the task. For even after death there is a certain fire called purgatorial, where they are purged and cleansed who began to correct themselves in this world but did not complete the task. Now those who did not wish to begin their correction in this life cannot consummate it there. Those who are permitted to begin their correction here, even if they are not permitted to complete it, have the completion of their correction reserved for them there. Nevertheless, it is safer in every respect that you should strive both to begin and complete it here, so that nothing may remain for you to suffer or to do there. It is hard to feel those torments even for a little. Thus, it is safer in every respect for you to begin and complete what you should do here. But if you cannot complete this here, nevertheless, if you have begun it, do not despair; you will be saved, "yet so as by fire," (Cf. 1 Cor. 3, 15). Indeed you will burn until the combustible material which you carry shall have been consumed. But you will be saved, since there has remained in you the foundation of God's charity.

IV. *Whether penance can be repeated.*

There are some who say that for those who have relapsed into previous sins there is no longer place for forgiveness, because certain passages of Scriptures seem to deny the approach to salvation to those who, after accepting penance, return to their former sins. And indeed there are certain statements of this kind in which this is not truly said but seems to those who do not understand well to have been said.

The Apostle Paul in that letter which he wrote to the Hebrews spoke as follows: "It is impossible for those who were once illuminated, have tasted also the heavenly gift, and were made partakers of the Holy Ghost, have moreover tasted the good word of God and the powers of the world to come, and are fallen away to be renewed again to penance, crucifying again to themselves the Son of God, and making him a mockery," (Heb. 6, 4-6). And again he says: "For if we sin wilfully after having the knowledge of the truth, there is now left no sacrifice for sins," (Heb. 10, 26). And again we find it written elsewhere, that there is no place for a second penance. But whether these or other such writings or expressions of Catholic men be found on this subject, by no means must we think that those who had right wisdom wished to imply that, into whatever sins men have fallen, they could not, indeed, have repented, if they were looked upon with divine mercy, or that they could not obtain pardon, if they were struck with true repentance. For the Catholic faith does not accept this at all, because He who said: "I say not to thee, till seven times; but till seventy times seven times," (Matt. 18, 22), meant that He does not oppose in such circumstances a second or a third or any true repentance at all. Therefore, what has been said, that it is impossible for those who have fallen after the illumination of grace and the tasting of the celestial gift and the participation of the Holy Spirit to be renewed again unto repentance, must indeed be understood thus, that they were able to fall by themselves but they cannot rise by themselves, and so it is impossible for them, but not for God. Just as it has been written: "A wind that goeth and returneth not,"

(Psal. 77, 39). Concerning the way of perdition it has been said that all who enter by it will return no more, since man indeed can go to evil by himself but cannot return by himself, unless he be aided by grace and with this aid be renewed unto repentance. Indeed then what has been written must be understood thus, that it is impossible for those who have fallen to be renewed unto repentance and that that prophecy which was so uttered: "The virgin of Israel is cast down," (Cf. Amos 5, 2),—He will not add: "That the virgin of Israel may rise again," in which similarly some have strayed from right understanding,—has been expressed fittingly in these words which have been used.

For since St. Jerome has set forth some ambiguous words on this passage, some, who more gladly take from the Scriptures material of error rather than of edification, try to construe that the fallen cannot be restored. For he says that although God is all powerful, He cannot make a virgin from one corrupted. He himself could see whatever he wished to say; I do not depart from the purity of the Christian faith. Truth is one. I hear the Apostle saying: "Though an angel preach another gospel, let him be anathema," (Cf. Gal. 1, 8). Nevertheless I so feel that he wished to say something, even if I do not know what he wished to say. However, it is thus good for me to feel that he has spoken the truth, even if possibly he could have said what he said more competently and more clearly. I shall try to interpret the words of the Catholic man according to Catholic truth.

Yet if this is understood about the corruption of the flesh, it is foolish to feel thus, that man can vitiate his flesh, that God cannot heal it. If this is understood about the corruption of the heart, similarly it is also foolish to say that man can sin, that God cannot justify, and that man can justify only so far as he can sin. Now if God is said to be unable to do this, because it has been done and what has been done cannot be undone, since what is true cannot be false and He cannot do this, because he cannot act against truth since, if He could act against truth, He could act against Himself who is truth, what weight has this phrase more than if it were said about something else which has been done and now cannot be undone, even if what has been done can be emended, so that the fact that it has been done does not harm what has been done? It is certain that he who falls can rise again and not only rise again but also rise again better than he was when he fell. Many have fallen and have arisen better than they were before they fell, even better than they would have been if they had not fallen, because they were permitted to fall for the very purpose that they might be taught by their mishap and ruin and be made better. Yet no one after a mishap has arisen or could have arisen better than he might have been even if he had not fallen and all these goods which he performed now by rising he might have performed by standing.

On this matter it can be said, in some respect, that no one who falls can recover to a greater extent than the whole, that which he loses by falling, because no matter what thereafter he shall add unto correction or unto recovery he cannot by any means do it so that he would not have been better, if he had all these and yet had not fallen. On this account no one in hope of correction ought to sin, since what is once lost is itself not recovered to a greater degree, since whatever shall be added afterwards by way of reparation does not itself belong to what was lost but is something else in place of it, and surely there would be more if both existed together. And this cannot be done because, just as past times return no more, so what has once been done can no more be undone. If, therefore, you are a virgin, guard diligently what you have. Do not sin in hope; do not fall as if you are to rise again better. Whatever you should do afterwards, you cannot nevertheless do without your being better, if you did this and were a virgin. Thus perhaps in this manner it is fittingly understood that the virgin of Israel fell, and he will not add, "so that the virgin of Israel may rise again, and that where there were a thousand, there will be a hundred, and where a hundred, ten in the house of Israel." If we say that those who have fallen in this way cannot be renewed unto penance, perhaps we say nothing unfitting, nor do we shut off the way of indulgence to penitents, but we show the danger of falling. For if it is a great thing to rise again sometime, surely it is greater never to have fallen. If it is a good thing to have been healed, it is better never to have been corrupted.

There is still another meaning which we can understand with the same truth in the above-mentioned statement; whether with equal fitness I do not know. It is impossible, he says, for those who were once illuminated, and who tasted the gift of God (and the rest which he added), after falling away, to be renewed again to penance, and as if he were adding the cause why men of this kind cannot be renewed to penance, he speaks of their crucifying again and making the Son of God a mockery. Therefore, they cannot be renewed again in this, because they cannot have another cross and another death of the Son of God, not because pardon will be denied to those who repent but because Christ will not die again for those who sin. Therefore, guard your salvation, for which Christ died once. If you shall lose it, you will not be able to have another Christ to die for you, or another death of the same Christ. Christ says to you: Preserve your salvation; I have died once for it. If you shall lose it, I cannot die again, yet by the same death I can render it lost again. But I do not want you to do me an injury, since if, by sinning voluntarily, you again lose your salvation which was acquired by my death, in so far as is in you, you compel me to be crucified again and to die again. I offered my flesh as a victim that those who repent of sin might acquire pardon, not that those who sin voluntarily and who persist in sin might be justified. Therefore, those who repent for sin have in it a victim of expiation. Now those who remain voluntarily in their sins have, as a result of this, no reason for salvation. Indeed this victim was given them that through it they might be expiated on repenting for sin, but now indeed the victim itself is not left them that through it they may be justified while persisting voluntarily in sin. Therefore, let them not think that that victim belongs to them when they sin voluntarily, since to those who sin voluntarily no victim is left for sin, because they cannot usurp for themselves what was so offered that it might benefit those who repent of sins, not those who remain in sins. Thus one truth having been manifested, another also became clear.

Now as to the statement that there is no place for a second repentance, some wish to understand the following: that all this life is a place of repentance for man the sinner. Those who wish to do penance here have the place, since this place was given to men for repentance. Now those who do not wish to do penance here, even if they should wish to do penance in another life, will not be able to do so in such a way that their penance will have fruit, since it has no place. Therefore, the first repentance in this life has a place. The second repentance after this life has no place, nor do they have fruit even if they have pain. Some understand this phrase regarding public repentance, which they say cannot be repeated because of the rigor and the punishment, that men may not contemn the sacraments of God. But let everyone, in so far as he shall be able, understand according to truth. I mean him who said that there is no place for a second repentance because man should have one repentance as long as he lives, so that he always grieves regarding past sins and guards himself against the future, and never returns to sins which he has once dismissed. He who does this does what he should do. He who does otherwise, that is, who returns to past sins, so that after he has sinned as long as he wishes he returns again to repentance and after a first does a second repentance, does what he should not do and yet he does not do badly in that he repents, but he does badly in that he does not persevere in repentance. As for him who has thus said that there is no place for second repentance, I think that he has found an easier solution and has without scruple avoided the troublesomeness of the question.

V. *On those who repent at the very end.*

Some ask what must be thought of those who persevere in their sins even to the end of their lives, and who nevertheless, at the very end terrified at the threat of death, are stung by conscience and repent, and with all their hearts seek mercy and indulgence, even if prevented at the moment of death they cannot render satisfaction. Briefly, because it seems to me best, I absolve. I think that man, as long as he lives in this life, just as he can do evil, so too he can emend if he should do so, and never at any time, even at the very end and at the moment of death, is the repentance of man fruitless, if it be true. I hear Scripture saying: "At whatever hour the sinner shall grieve, he shall be saved," (Cf. Ezech. 18 and 33). It does not say, if he shall grieve two days or two years before death but at whatever hour he shall grieve, he shall be saved. Therefore, do not place a time on the mercy of God, lest perhaps your justice be turned against yourself. Do not lay down a law which is not of benefit to you. Sinner, love mercy, since if you do not love it, you do not deserve it.

Yet under this hope you must not sin without concern because you are promised salvation, if you should be converted at the end. For although even then forgiveness is promised you, if you shall repent truly, yet you are not promised that you must repent truly then. It is very difficult for repentance to be true then, when it comes so late. When pain binds the limbs and grief oppresses the sense, a man can scarcely think of anything else. Therefore, if you wish to be secure, do penance while you are sound. While your mind is free, exercise it in its own work. Repentance, which seems to have been forced, should be strongly suspected. It is easy for a man to think that he does not wish the power which is not given him. Possibility best tests the will. If you do not do what you can manifestly, you show what you do not wish. Now although repentance is more secure at the time of health, yet it is better late than never. Fear before the end, lest you delay to repent; at the end rest that you may even then look back. But if then by chance you see that the time of good work is not at hand for you, yet go forth in firm hope with the pledge of good devotion. The repentance of the thief was very late, but indulgence was not late. See how quickly he received what he delayed so long to seek. "A contrite and humbled heart our God will not despise," (Cf. Psal. 5, 19), because He desires not the death of the sinner but that he turn from his way and live, (Cf. Ezech. 33, 11).

VI. *That good will alone suffices, if the opportunity for operating is not given.*

If, therefore, you have good will, do not despair. The angels call down from heaven: "On earth peace to men of good will," (Cf. Luke 2, 14). They did not say: Peace to rich men or to noble men or to powerful men or to men able to do many things. If they had said this, you would not have to fear because all these things can be absent even from the unwilling, and similarly be present to those who do not love. Will can be absent from no one but him who wishes it. The will is such a thing as can neither be given to nor taken away from the unwilling. Therefore, the will of man is the power of God. And on this account the will is of man, because to will is in the power of man and no external violence that occurs can take the will from man, nor can infirmity, nor any adversity, nor poverty take will from man, unless man himself should wish it. Work can be taken from man; even when he himself does not wish, will cannot. It is not in himself when he can but is in himself when he wishes, even though will is not from himself when he wishes, since for himself to wish is a good from God. Yet it is said to be in man himself when he wishes, because externally there can be no preventing of man's wishing. For this, that he may wish, nothing is sought outside; all is in himself that is necessary to do this. He seeks nothing outside himself that he may have wishing in himself. On this account to wish is in himself, to be able is not in himself, unless something outside is applied to unfold the will, of which thing the proper presence or absence at any time is not in man's power. Therefore, when he does not wish good, no one is blamed but himself. But when he cannot, if indeed he wishes, impossibility is not imputed to him on account of will, but if he does not wish on account of impossibility, the will is not excused. Therefore, the entire merit is in the will. As much as you wish, so much you deserve.

But you say: If to wish alone is merit and if the merit of man consists of will alone, why then does he do work? I have the will and that suffices for me. What work is it necessary to perform, if work does nothing? But you cannot have will without work, when you are able to perform works. There is no will, if it does not do what it can. Now if it cannot perform, it itself suffices for itself and has its merit on account of itself, in which it alone pleases because it is good.

But you say again: If all merit is in will and nothing more is from work, even when the work itself is with will, why then is work required, if for the merited work of man nothing is added or taken away? Hear why. After the will work is also required for the reason that by the work itself the will may be increased. Such is the heart of man that by its work it enkindles the more either to love goodness, if it is right, or to love malice, if it is evil. Thus in two ways the affection is nourished by work so that it increases and is greater, so that with difficulty it can be brought about that the will is not increased by its own work. Therefore, to whatever extent the will increases, to such an extent merit increases, and to such an extent the work either benefits the will unto good or harms unto evil, as it exercises by enkindling the will unto the affection of goodness or malice. And if by chance it shall happen that there is as much will in him who does not perform works as in him who carries on work, where the will is the same, merit cannot be dissimilar.

But you say again: If all merit is in the will, then not good work but only will is rewarded. See how you wish to understand this. For in some respect this is also said truly, that the will of man is alone rewarded whether for good or for evil. And again it is said fittingly that work and will are rewarded, and also man himself, who wills and works, is rewarded according to will and work. The will is said to be rewarded because merit depends on it. And work is said to be rewarded because on it the cause or occasion of meriting depends. The will is rewarded according to work; the work is rewarded according to will. The will is rewarded according to work because in work it merited that it should please. Work is rewarded according to will because from will it accepted that it should please. The will pleases because it itself is good and in itself is justice which pleases. Work pleases because it is from good will, and the sign of justice and goodness which is in the will pleases. The will pleases according to that which is in itself; work pleases according to that from which it is. Therefore, just as it is justice alone according to which both the will and the work of the will please, so there are not two but there is one retribution by which both the will and the work of the will are rewarded.

Therefore, there is one retribution by which man is said to be rewarded because it is given to him, and the will is said to be rewarded because it is given according to it. And work is said to be rewarded, in which the will itself deserves to please. Even when it does not operate, the will pleases in this, that it wished to operate and from the work itself it pleases, even when it cannot do this. Therefore, the will always pleases according to the work, and man never pleases except according to the will. Yet when man pleases according to the will, he pleases because the will itself pleases. Now when the will pleases on account of the work, it does not so please as if the work pleases on account of itself and the will on account of the work, since the will pleases rather on account of itself and the work on account of the will. But the will is said to please on account of the work, because the will is of the work and that which pleases is from the work. For to wish is always to wish for something, and man pleases because he wishes for something on account of just will which is from something, and it is just, because it is from what it should be. And it is such as it should be. Thus then all merit is in the will, even if it is with regard to work; whether this work be or not, there is nothing less in the will except perhaps in this, that the will itself would be greater, if the work be done. If then you wish to have great merit, have great will, great trust. You deserve as much as you wish.

They who are unequal in resources can be equal in will. Zacheus gave much who was rich and had much. That widow who sent two mites had little and gave little and yet she gave as much as Zacheus. She had less resources but had equal will. If you notice what they gave, you will find different values; if you notice from what source they gave you will find equal values. Now God does not weigh how much is given but from what it is given. If then where more and where less is given, merit is not different, if the will be held equal in both cases, then where something is given and where nothing is given there cannot be different merit, if the will be held equal in both cases. On this account I have said to you that you should not despair if the resources are lacking to you. Let good will be present. To the extent that you wish, to this extent do you merit. Therefore, effect a great will, if you wish to have great merit. Well did that sinner know this who, since she had much to be forgiven, did not bring much substance but much love. Much against much. If much iniquity were redeemed with much money rather than with much charity, the rich would be more fortunate than the poor, and they would, without concern, sin as much as they wished and as long as they wished. For in themselves would be the redemption of their sins. Whenever they wished they would give money and have justice. But now God does well, since God placed our redemption in Him where no one, unless he himself wishes, can lack it. They can love equally, both the rich and the poor, even if they cannot give money equally. Love much, if you wish that much be forgiven you. He said: "Many sins are forgiven her, because she hath loved much," (Luke 8, 47). He loves more who is forgiven more. There seems to be something contradictory here. For if many sins are forgiven him by God because he loved much, love seems to be before remission, and again if he loves more who is forgiven more, remission seems to be prior to love. For thus it is said: A certain creditor had two debtors; the one owed much, the other little. And whereas they had not wherewith to pay, he forgave them both. Which therefore of the two loveth him most? And he answered: I suppose that he to whom he forgave most, (Cf. Luke 7, 41-43). Here remission seems to be first and love after. For on this account is He loved much, because much is forgiven.

Afterwards He adds, showing why He made this proposition. He says: "Dost thou see this woman? I entered into thy house, thou gavest me no water for my feet; but she, after I had entered, with tears washed my feet, and with her hairs hath wiped them," (Cf. Luke 7, 44). And afterwards He says: "Wherefore I say to thee: Many sins are forgiven her, because she hath loved much. But to whom less is forgiven he loveth less," (Luke 7, 47). These statements do not seem to be consistent, because He said that he loves more who is forgiven more, and that this man has been forgiven much because he has loved much. In this, therefore, the likeness does not seem to be fitting, unless perhaps He should so speak, that in this it appears that much is forgiven the man, because he has loved much, since he who is forgiven the more, loves the more. He says: Many sins are forgiven him because he has loved much. Many sins are forgiven him. And by what means do I prove this or how do I show this, that many sins are forgiven him? He says: In this, because he has loved much. Great love is a mark of great remission. For he loves more for whom more is forgiven. For a debtor is he to whom more is forgiven, that he may love more. And if he loves more, he does what he ought and he shows that he has received much in this, that he returns much. Thus then this woman, very courteous, very zealous, very devout, loves much because she knows that she has received much. Many sins are forgiven her because she has loved much. If anyone then so wishes to understand what has been said: "Many sins are forgiven her, because she has loved much," it will not be unfitting.

But perhaps the following seems to some to pertain more to the truth; that we should so understand that love here, by which the woman sinner inflamed with a desire for health began to love the Saviour from whom she believed that she had salvation; because she knew that there was much for which she hoped she was to be forgiven by Him, on this account she loved much. Not yet had she heard: Thy sins are forgiven thee. Still, what the woman desired to obtain, she demanded, and yet, as if she had already received it, she loved her Giver from whom she did not doubt that she would receive what she sought. On this account He says: "Thy faith hath made thee safe," (Luke 7, 50). For because she believed, she loved; because she loved she merited. On this account, thy faith hath made thee safe. From this faith began; salvation began. But you did not know that I attracted you to me through faith and love, that I might pardon the many sins of him who believes and loves. Now you perhaps did not think of this. That you may know and be consoled, I now say: Thy sins are forgiven thee. Who is forgiven more, loves more. Some love after they receive; but you, before you received, loved because you believed that you would receive. On this account "thy faith hath made thee safe, go in peace," (Luke 7, 50). See now how much charity does; how much good will does. Therefore do not fear. If good will should not be lazy, pardon will not be tardy.

VII. *That man judges work; God weighs the will.*

There are two things: the will and the work of the will. God weighs the will; man judges the work. But again there are some hidden works which are not known; some doubtful which are not discerned; some manifest, that is, either so evil that they cannot be hidden or so good that there can be no doubt about them. The hidden and the doubtful are reserved for divine judgment. Now those which are manifest, if they are good, are judged through approbation, but they are not judged through retribution, since their reward and recompense are reserved for the future. God wished that evils be judged and punished in this world, lest, if the judgment of these should be reserved for the future, all judgment be exercised not for correction but for damnation. For this reason men have been established as judges in place of God, that they may examine and punish the faults of those subjected to them, so that at the end when God shall come as judge He may be able to save those whom He subjected to human judgment for correction and who have been corrected. Therefore, judgments have been given, that is, against different sins for their expiation; mode and measure of corrections and of satisfactions are set forth with reasonable definition; and a penitential book has been written in which antidotes of spiritual medicine, as it were, are proposed, where physicians of souls may receive what may be applied to the disease of sin for the healing of sick minds.

VIII. *On the remission of sins and whether priests who are men can forgive sins.**

Certain men try to ascribe the power of forgiving sins to God alone, and they

---

*Hugh of St. Victor accurately analyses the nature of sin and attacks Abelard's error as to the indifferent character of all acts in themselves apart from the will of the doer. However, he is wrong in his teaching of the reviviscence of previously pardoned mortal sins after a fall, as he sets it forth in this chapter.

by no means admit that man can be made a participant in it. And for confirmation of this assertion they adduce the cleansing of that leper whom the Lord first restored to health through Himself, and then sent him thus to the priests, not that the cleaning might be accomplished by their power but only that it might be confirmed by their testimony. In similar manner now in the Church of today they say that the ministeries of the priests have no more power than as a kind of sign only, that he indeed who is first absolved by the Lord through contrition of heart within, afterwards is shown to have been absolved by them through the confession of the mouth. Now they wish to prove that sins are forgiven only in the contrition of the heart before the confession of the mouth and they do so by that prophetic testimony which is expressed thus: "At whatever hour the sinner shall grieve he shall be saved," (Cf. Ezech. 18 and 33). And elsewhere: "Because while you still speak I shall say: Here I am," (Cf. Isaias 58, 9). And the Psalmist says: "I said I will confess against myself my injustice to the Lord, and thou hast forgiven the wickedness of my sin," (Psal. 31, 5). However, after contrition of heart confession of mouth is also necessary, because, if anyone, even after obtaining pardon for sins, shall neglect to confess these same sins of his, as if a contemner of a divine institution, although he may not be held as a defendant for the sins which are already forgiven, he will nevertheless be a defendant for contempt, or perhaps because the sins themselves presently return to the stubborn, which before were forgiven him who was humbled by the sting of conscience. In this way, therefore, they prove that men by no means have the power of forgiving sins but that this belongs to God alone, just as even in the Gospel the Jews murmuring against the Lord because He said to the paralytic: "Thy sins are forgiven thee," (Cf. Mark 2, 5; Luke 5, 20), said that God alone could dismiss sins.

But perhaps those who say this about the absolution of sins, that everyone is bound by sin, do not consider with sufficient care. For the sinner is bound in two ways. He is bound by obduracy of mind; he is bound by the debt of future damnation. For as long as the grace of God is with man, man is free and ready to act well. But when the grace of God is taken away through sin, straightway the mind itself is impeded internally by its obduracy. This obduracy or blindness of the mind is interior darkness by which man for his sin is held impeded in the present world, and unless he shall be freed of them in this life, afterwards with hands and feet bound he will be cast into exterior darkness. But since no one after the fall of sin would be able to rise by his own power, unless divine mercy going before gratuitously should rouse him, on this account it is necessary that God, when we are to be quickened to repentance, out of mercy alone with no previous merit on our part, return His grace which He justly took away from us when we sinned, in order that approaching grace may stir our heart from the torpor of infidelity and from the death of sin; thus as soon as we are struck to repentance by it as it operates and as soon as we are freed from the bonds of torpor, then also by its cooperation we may, as we repent, deserve to be absolved from the debt of damnation. This is well noted in the raising of Lazarus from the dead, whom the Lord himself through Himself first absolved internally from the bond of death, but ordered him when quickened externally to be released from the ministry of the apostles.

For thus in the holy Church now He quickens internally and arouses the dead from sins through grace alone to remorse and He orders them, quickened by confession, to go forth, and thus then as they confess through the ministry of the priests He absolves them from the exterior bond, that is, from the debt of damnation. Now the debt of damnation is well called an external bond, since it pertains to exterior darkness which he is unworthy to avoid who in this life does not merit to be freed from interior darkness. But, they say, as for the priest you do God harm by attributing to him the power of forgiving sins, which befits God alone. I do not make priests gods; the divine word which cannot lie calls priests gods. It says: "Thou shalt not speak ill of the gods, and the princes of the people thou shalt not curse," (Exod. 22, 28). These indeed contrary to the precept of the law detract from the gods, since they wish to take away the power conferred divinely. Nor indeed did I attribute to priests the power of forgiving sins. He attributed divine power to men who made gods of men. But yet just as He himself of Himself is God, so too by Himself whenever He wishes He can forgive sins without human cooperation. Those indeed who are not gods of themselves, except when He, from whom they are thus which they are, operates in them and through them and cooperates with them, cannot forgive sins. Therefore, just as God alone is good and yet it does not follow that they are not good, even those who serve God, and just as God alone does marvelous things and yet it is said of the just man: "For he did marvelous things in his life," (Ezech. 31), so also God alone forgives sins, even then when the priest forgives by Him and through Him.

For He himself does in man this which man does through Him, and it must not be said that man does nothing there because God does through him, but rather that he does much better and much more truly because God does through him. So it is that He says to Peter the chief of the Apostles: "And I will give to thee the keys of the kingdom of heaven. And whatsoever thou shalt bind upon earth, it shall be bound also in heaven: and whatsoever thou shalt loose on earth, it shall be loosed also in heaven," (Matt. 16, 19). He did not say: Whatsoever you shall loose, that is as they say, shall declare loosed, was loosed, but will be loosed, because the statement of heaven does not precede Peter's statement but follows it. Now lest you think that this was granted to Peter alone, hear what He says to all the Apostles and thereby to all the successors of the Apostles and to those who function in place of the Apostles. He says: "Receive ye the Holy Ghost. Whose sins you shall forgive, they are forgiven them; whose sins you shall retain, they are retained," (John 20, 22, and 23). Where did He say: If you shall declare, it was? Never did He say this but He did say: If you shall do, it shall be. Let them hear, then, and understand whose sins you shall forgive, etc., to whom this was said, before it had been said: Receive ye the Holy Ghost, whose sins you shall forgive, etc., lest either what was given might be believed contemptible or what they received and operated might be thought to proceed from human power.

It is no wonder then if men can forgive sins, since they receive power to do this not from their own but from divine power, and for God to grant this to men is nothing else than for God to do this through men. Now what they oppose regarding the cleansing of the leper least of all supports their opinion, since if a sinner is to be believed as absolved before confession because the leper was cleansed before demonstration, in the same way the sinner after remorse should not go to the priest to bewail his sin but to show his justice, since he was sent to the priests not to receive health but to show health and this the Christian faith entirely abhors. Therefore, if the marvel which the Lord worked is shown the priests not on account of reverence for the office but as a reproach, what other than contempt is generated for the new priesthood even in spiritual care? But that also which they say: "At whatever hour the sinner shall grieve, he shall be saved," I think was said especially about those who after living all their lives in sin repent at the end and abandon sins, when now in this life they cannot have time for satisfaction. To these it is said, lest indeed in any way they despair about forgiveness, since even then, if they have truly repented, they can obtain mercy. For that is "at whatever hour," namely, even at the very end, even at the moment of death, if the sinner shall grieve, that is, shall be converted with full contrition of heart, he shall be saved from eternal damnation, as if it were said in other words: At whatever hour in the present life the sinner shall truly repent, he shall not perish in the future life.

But if someone should contend that what was said, namely, "he shall be saved," was not said about the salvation which is assigned in the future absolution of sinners but rather about that which is pardoned in the present, nevertheless it is not necessary for us to say that the sinner is absolved of all debt immediately from the moment when he begins to grieve until he has obtained all the remedy which God established for obtaining pardon. Now this is the remedy: that he repent with the heart and confess his sin with the mouth. When the debtor has done this, there will not be more damnation, even if satisfaction remains to be paid for sin. But if by chance a sinner truly repents, but when the moment of death intervenes he cannot go to confession, I declare confidently that in him the highest priest completes what the mortal could not, and before God indeed the deed stands which the man truly wished but was not able to fulfill, since contempt did not exclude confession but necessity prevented it. Furthermore, if what has been said: "At whatever hour the sinner shall grieve, he shall be saved," is accepted with respect to the present salvation, it must be understood as if it were said thus: The salvation of the sinner begins then when he truly grieves for his sins, which salvation, however, is fully accomplished at the time when he also confesses by mouth what he grieves. Likewise what is said: "While still you speak, I shall say, Here I am," (Cf. Isaias 58, 9), can be accepted fittingly thus: that God is present first through grace to sting the heart to repentance; then that He is present to assign the forgiveness of sins to him who confesses.

Finally, here is what they set up in opposition from the Psalmist. I have spoken: I shall confess etc. Saint Gregory asserts regarding the sin of thought that it was said only in accordance with these words. Often merciful God washes away the sins of the heart more quickly because He does not permit them to pass out into works. Therefore, it is rightly said by the Psalmist: I have spoken: I shall confess etc. And a little later he shows how easy forgiveness beyond this is in the case of him who, while he still promises to seek what he promised to seek, brought it about that because his sin did not reach the point of deed, his repentance did not arrive at the point of punishment, but contemplated affliction cleansed his mind which iniquity, only contemplated, had truly defiled. But if anyone wishes to accept this about any sin, yet let him know that sin is one thing, the impiety of sin another. For the impiety of sin is most rightly accepted as obduracy of the heart which is first removed in remorse, so that afterwards in confession the sin, that is, the debt of damnation, may be absolved. But whether the above-mentioned authorities are explained in this or any other way, we confess with probability that the priests of God in the Church have the power of binding and loosing, a power signified not perfunctorily and by an unusual kind of language but truly granted by God to those to whom it was said: Whose sins you shall forgive, they are forgiven them; and whose sins you shall retain, they shall be retained.

But perhaps someone will say in opposition that priests bind many in the Church who are not bound before God, likewise free many who remain in guilt and thus it will not be true whose sins you shall forgive etc. But it must be known that often Holy Scripture speaks in such a way about some things that it seems to pronounce what is going to happen thereafter and yet expresses its virtue rather than the happening, since it shows not what must happen but what can happen. For example Scripture says in a certain place: "He that believeth and is baptized shall be saved," (Cf. Mark 16, 16), and yet we know that many believe and receive baptism, who afterwards are condemned through the exigency of their sins and do not arrive at eternal salvation. Likewise in another place it says: "He that eateth my flesh and drinketh my blood, hath everlasting life, and will not come to judgment but will pass from death to life," (Cf. John 6, 55), and yet Paul says that whoever shall presume to eat the body of the Lord unworthily and to drink the chalice, eateth and drinketh judgment to himself, (Cf. 1 Cor. 11, 27 and 29). Everywhere then rather the virtue of the sacraments is expressed, and it is not signified that any at all who partake of it must be saved by it, but that they can be saved, as if it were said: So great is the virtue of baptism that whoever receives it faithfully and devoutly can through it attain eternal salvation. Likewise so great is the virtue in the taking of the body and blood of Christ that through it whoever shall receive worthily can obtain eternal life. In similar manner I think that this has been said: Whose sins you shall forgive etc., as if it were said more plainly: So much power do I attribute to you in loosing and in binding sins that whoever shall merit to be bound by you cannot be loosed before me and whoever shall merit to be loosed by you is not bound now before me. Let men hear, let sinners understand that help is granted them by God, judgment is again being prepared. Perhaps they do not yet presume to address God. They have men as priests functioning in place of God with whom meanwhile they can plead their cause without danger. Let them love intercessors and let them fear judges.

But perhaps someone asks again why it is necessary to seek men as cooperators with God to loose the sins of men, as if He were not able to fulfill what He wishes by Himself. But most certainly we should know that, in abolishing sins, by no means does human cooperation support God. Yet we know man is made a co-operator because the salvation of the sinner is accomplished more fittingly in this way. For what are sins but wounds, as it were, and what is penance but medicine? And we know that in healing wounds of the flesh, unless a proper remedy is applied to the pain, by no means does the effect of the cure follow. Since then every sin is committed through pride, it is necessary for all repentance to be tempered through humility, in order that obedience may crush disobedience and the devotion of humility suppress the swelling of elation. Therefore, it is very fitting that we who have been insolent to God by sinning be suppliants also to the servants of God by repenting to men, and that man who did not need a mediator to preserve the grace of God be unable now to recover it except through man as a mediator.

For this too is most salutary for the sinner, that he learn how far he has receded from God by sinning when he returns to God with such difficulty by repenting, because he is also made more cautious in the future when the way to remission is not opened without the grave labor of repenting. Therefore, let the sinner bewail and sigh and let him fear and tremble quite anxiously for his sin; let him go about apprehensively; let him seek helpers and intercessors; let him prostrate himself humbly before man who humbly did not wish to stand before the Creator, in order that in this deed even he may in some way cry out to God and say: See, Lord, and consider and notice what I do. I know indeed, O Lord, and I confess that to be unwilling to be subject to you was damnable elation, but now on your account I beg that my being prostrate before man be not a despised devotion. Great is that which I have taken away and not small is that which I return. O how sweet and pleasing is the mercy of our God! He himself works all our good in us and as a jesting father among sons He so does all that it seems as if He were doing nothing. Behold the sinner filled with remorse grieves, sighs, weeps, confesses his guilt, asks for pardon, begs for mercy, and all this is believed to be as if from man. But who, I ask, does this, if not He who rules within and moves the heart of man to do this?

I beg that it be not burdensome, if I shall set forth a brief example of this thing. A certain father expelled an insolent son as if with great fury, that being thus afflicted he might learn to be humble. But when he persists in his insolence, by a kind of secret dispensing of advice the mother is sent by the father in order that, not as if sent by the father but as if led of her own accord by maternal love, she may go and soften the obstinate one by feminine gentleness, bend the insolent one to humility, vehemently declare the father as angered, yet promise that she will intervene, promise pardon, suggest counsel for salvation, persuade to seek intercessors, say that the father cannot be placated except by great prayers; moreover, she asserts that she will take up the cause of the defendant and promises that she will bring the entire affair to a good end. See, I beg, if our cause is not thus carried on. God the Father, as it were in anger, expelled the sinning son at whom, however, in the design of His good will He was not angered. But, because human weakness is not able by itself to arise from the fall, mother grace is sent to the heart of the sinner; a priest is sought as an intercessor, that God who was not angered may be placated. What shall I say? "Who is wise, and will keep these things; and will understand the mercies of the Lord?" (Psal. 106, 43). For has that which has been done been done superfluously because God was not changed from being angered to being propitious? Far be it! But it must be done so, since otherwise the guilt of our crime cannot be expiated. It must be done so, because God orders that this also be demanded of Him which He desires to give. It must be done so, because, although in God according to design there had been no anger against us, yet in us according to guilt anger remained and, while this is abolished with due satisfaction, so to speak, God is not reconciled to man but man is reconciled to God.

Now regarding sins, whether they return or not from the time when they have been once forgiven, I judge indeed that meanwhile we must not assert but must fear. Yet whether this is or is not true, by what justice this takes place or does not take place, awaits the work of another treatise for this reason especially, because certain testimonies of the divine Scriptures are read which have been set forth ambiguously on this subject, so that even from them some absurdity seems to arise which surely ought not to be discussed with a light or a transitory consideration.

IX. *On the question whether sins return after they have once been dismissed.*

There are many questions on the part of men. As long as there is life, there is questioning. For he who seeks has not yet found what he seeks, and yet he seeks because he has lost what he seeks, and if he has not lost it, because he perhaps never had it, yet as long as he seeks he shows that he does not yet have what he seeks. Therefore, as long as we live we hold it necessary always to seek, because not yet do we have all that we should have. Now what is this which we should seek but truth and goodness? If we had these perfectly, we should have to seek nothing more, because if by chance there were anything more, it would be added, even if it were not sought. He says: "Seek yet first the kingdom of God and his justice, and all these things shall be added to you," (Matt. 6, 33; Luke 12, 31). The kingdom of God is truth; justice is His goodness. If you seek these two as you should, all others are added freely.

Why then do you labour to seek those things which you can have freely? If you seek these without those, either you do not have or if you have, you do not have usefully. If you seek those without these, you have those unto salvation and these unto usefulness. All these things, he says, will be added unto you. These are many; those are few. For there are two there; here many will be found, and yet those two are of more value than all these. Do not look upon the greater but upon the better. Do not pay attention to the quantity, but weigh the value. Seek few that you may find many. Therefore, these are the only things that men should seek, truth and goodness. And would that they were as zealous to seek goodness as they are found curious to seek the truth. In some way it is customary for all to seek the truth, even for those who do not love goodness. For to such an extent do all wish to know the truth that no one is found who wishes to be deceived. Many seek truth without goodness but the ally of truth is goodness. Truth does not come gladly without goodness or if it comes, it does not come from those parts and from that region where salvation is. Men seek whether their own sins return to them after they have once been forgiven. They wish to know this and they are unwilling to beware of this.

Why then do they wish to know that of which they are unwilling to beware, unless because curiosity attracts them when goodness does not delight? They seek this on the chance that they may be told that it is not so. They hang on the messenger of their own sluggishness on the chance that some may tell them what they wish to hear. They seek as if for truth, not that they truly love truth itself, because they do not love goodness, but they wish this to be the truth which they themselves wish. On this account then they seek on the chance that they may receive a response which they themselves prefer to hear, and, if by chance anyone shall come as a witness of the truth to say the truth contrary to their wish, they are not stirred up but are consternated and are crushed in mind because they have not heard what they wished to hear. Therefore, truth replies to them according to their malice, either as they wish, that they may err more, or as they do not wish, that they may despair more. Nevertheless, since this very question must be asked on account of those who are aroused and are making progress regarding truth, it is not absurd to ask what the human conscience, if as is usual it is struck by some consideration, should answer itself in this part of our subject.

Thus then it is asked whether the sins which have once been forgiven the penitent are again charged to him. Possibly he who said that this should not be expressed but should be feared will judge more securely. For it is better sometimes to fear in hidden matters of this kind which cannot be known without danger to salvation than to give any definition. Therefore, let someone mention this which must be feared and not expressed. I think that for him who can correct his own thought so that this may suffice for him this is enough, and that perhaps it is more expedient for him to seek no more. As for him indeed who is hard pressed and is disturbed in mind and cannot stand here so that he proceeds no further in the search, I think that that person ought to be satisfied in so far as it can be done with saving reverence for secret things.

Behold then you who wish to be certain whether those sins return any more which have once been forgiven; let us see then and discuss what disturbs you. My sins, you say, have been forgiven. I wish to know if they should be charged against us more. What then does it seem to you? To me, you say, it does not seem that sins which have been forgiven should be charged anew. Otherwise God seems changeable, who does not hold to his decision and so easily changes His judgment. How does He change? You say: He changes in this, because when he first pardoned my sins He said that He would not require them more of me. For He would not have pardoned them, unless he had said this. But now He requires them again and demands of me for punishment the sins which He had previously forgiven. On this account I say that if God is said again to charge the sins which He once forgave, He is pronounced changeable and His work variable which should always be constant. Therefore then, since this cannot be, it seems to me that sins which have once been forgiven by God should by no means be charged further. If by chance it shall seem so to you, you will also confirm yourself in this way so as not to fear your danger.

But tell me now how you understand this statement of yours, that your sins are forgiven you. For if you do not understand how they recede, you do not understand how they return; rather, if you do not understand how they are present, you do not understand how they recede or how they return. What then is said when God is said to charge sins? If it is said that when he charges to the sinner He is angry, then when He pardons the sins of him who repents He is placated. If then we say that God sometimes is angered and afterwards placated, how will you be able to deny that He changes in this very fact? When then He charges and when He pardons, He charges and He pardons not by change of

Himself but by change of you. He charges sins when He judges a sinner worthy of punishment. He pardons sins when He judges a penitent worthy of forgiveness. And in both cases He himself is the same. You change from one thing to another, now a sinner through blame, now a just man through repentance. He himself is not changed but remains the same always, and standing in that which He is unchangeably, He sees and discerns that which you have been made variably, whether evil from good or good from evil. And when He sees you a sinner, He charges your sins to you since He discerns you such as He punishes worthily, but when He sees you repenting He pardons you your sins, since He discerns you such as He spares justly.

Now all these things He himself works immutably, since both when you cease to be a sinner through repentance, He himself still does not cease to know what you are, and when you begin to be just He himself does not begin to know what you begin to be, since even before you began He knew what you were going to be, and when you cease to be what you were He himself nevertheless is not ignorant of what you were. Therefore, you should not so understand, as if God changed when you change, but that He is said to charge your sins to you because He discerns you as worthy of His anger and indignation, but afterwards to pardon the same sins when He recognizes you as worthy of forgiveness and mercy. If then this is the charging of sins, being guilty through blame, and the pardoning of sins is being made just through repentance, why are sins not said to revert to man when man himself reverts to sins? But you say to me: When I revert to sins, I so revert that I do something similar to that which I did before but not the very thing which I did before. And if I do the same, it is the same in likeness, not the same in truth, the same because it is similar to that, not the same because it is that, a similarity of action but not one action. If, therefore, I am said to be obliged to undergo punishment for past sins because after the former were forgiven I return to commit similar sins, I confess it to be rightly thus, if in this manner I am said to be punished for those sins, just as I am said to commit them. But if I am said to commit the first evils anew only because I do certain other evils similar to those, in like manner when I am said to have to undergo punishment for those, reason persuades that nothing else must be understood than that I must undergo punishment for these sins which I afterwards committed similar to the former.

But this was not in the question, but whether indeed the guilt is doubled after the forgiveness of the first sin, if the sin itself is sought again, when that blame which had been forgiven returns to the following sin. For example: A certain man has done penance with his whole heart for having committed homicide, and he obtained forgiveness. It happened afterwards that he committed homicide. Behold, this man has committed two homicides or rather homicide twice. For thus it is expressed in proper language more fittingly and more specifically. For homicide is a certain single evil indeed, just as adultery and theft and fornication are individual evils, just as charity and patience and chastity are individual virtues. And he who loves two men, does not love with two loves but with one charity and one love. Thus then did this man commit homicide twice; in the first case by repenting he obtained forgiveness; in the second case at some time after receiving forgiveness he again committed homicide. Now this man afterwards died without repentance and he was condemned for his sins. It is asked then regarding this man whether he should be punished for that homicide for which he did penance and received forgiveness. And if it is so declared, it is not evident by what justice this is done. For if he is punished for the fact that he sinned and did not emend, the justice is manifest.

Now if what had been pardoned is sought again, there is either true injustice or hidden justice. In this then it should be shown by what justice man is punished a second time for that which had already been forgiven. Thus perhaps in this respect it may seem to you that you ought to object. Speak then now. Does it seem just to you that on account of a subsequent penance a preceding fault which was charged should be pardoned and not similarly on account of a subsequent fault that a preceding fault which had been forgiven should be charged a second time? If an added virtue closes the open wound of sin, does not an added fault open a closed wound? If good works which live die through blame and the dead are vivified again through justice, why similarly are not evil works which are excused through virtue charged again through blame? Do you wish repentance to be so strong that the sins which were charged be pardoned and do you not wish the blame to be so strong that what were pardoned be charged? Was the following repentance able to excuse the preceding blame so as not to harm at any time the blame which had been charged, and is the following blame unable to nullify the preceding repentance so that it would be of no benefit that it was at one time praised? If the sentence can rest on your judgment, you will seek the convenient rather than the just. Accursed is the man who makes his part lower. On this account you make your part good. And you judge well according to your part. Perhaps it would be well for you, if the sentence of truth followed your judgment. Never with yourself as judge would you be condemned. But I fear lest by chance while you wish for something other than the truth, the truth do something other than you wish. For the truth rather than your will should be fulfilled.

You say that what has been pardoned should not be charged a second time. Then similarly what has been charged should not be pardoned, if what has been pardoned should not be charged a second time. If repentance, because it pleases, effects that charged malice be pardoned, does not also contempt, because it displeases, similarly effect that pardoned sins be charged? If the humility of repentance makes you worthy of not being punished even for those sins which were charged, does not the contempt and transgression or sin make you worthy of being called to punishment even for those sins which were pardoned? Do you not consider that the more often grace is given, so much the more wretched is gratitude judged? Behold there are two men; one offends more often and, as he prays and intercedes more often, forgiveness is granted; the other living innocently and always obeying humbly the will and the power of the presiding Lord has nothing for which he may intercede. Now it happens afterwards, as it can happen, that both offend in a similar sin. Tell them which of these is judged the more guilty, if not he who after so much grace is proven ungrateful? The laws punish second crimes more severely and opened wounds are with greater difficulty brought to health, and you say that the nature and number of preceding sins make no difference with the guilt of subsequent sins? If first evils which had been excused through later goods are not revived unto guilt through subsequent evils again, then are not first goods which had been made dead through later evils revived unto merit through subsequent goods again? "Judge rightly, ye sons of men," (Cf. Psa. 1. 57, 1).

If you judge one way for yourself, another way against yourself, you are not a just judge. You should love justice so much that you do not love yourself contrary to it. They are men of learning who transform causes and change the truth on account of convenience. Justice does not approve such men. "Lord," it says, "I know not learning; I will enter into the powers of the Lord, O Lord, I will be mindful of thy justice alone," (Cf. Psal. 70, 15). This is a just decision in which justice alone is so regarded that nothing is placed before justice. Make then a just decision, if you wish your goods already dead through blame to be revived again through justice. Do not be angered and do not think that an injury is done you, if your evils already excused through repentance are charged against you again on account of your malice. But God, you say, said concerning my evils, when I did penance, that He would charge them to me no more. Similarly also God said regarding your goods, when you sinned, that He would reward them no more. If then on account of God's words one should stand so that the former may no more be charged, why similarly should not the word "God" stand so that the latter may be rewarded no more? You want God to lie for your convenience. But when you feel that you are being harmed, you labour to preserve His truth. Why then do you do this unless because you love yourself perversely and do not love God?

Now He himself rightly loves your truth and justly condemns your wickedness. Yet since you think that you take an argument from God's words and you hold forth His promise to defend your iniquity, let Him himself reply to you how much confidence you should have, when you act evilly, because He promised you forgiveness when you repented before, and similarly if you do well whether you should despair because He extended death and perdition to you when you acted evilly before. The Lord speaks through the prophet, saying: "Thou therefore, O son of man, say to the children of thy people: The justice of the just shall not deliver him, in what day soever he shall sin: and the wickedness of the wicked shall not hurt him, in what day soever he shall turn from his wickedness; and the just shall not be able to live in his justice, in what day soever he shall sin. Yea, if I shall say to the just that he shall surely live, and he, trusting in his justice, commit iniquity: all his justice shall be forgotten, and in his iniquity, which he hath committed, in the same shall he die. And if I shall say to the wicked: Thou shalt surely die: and he do penance for his sin, and do judgment and justice, and if that wicked man restore the pledge, and render what he had robbed, and walk in the commandments of life, and do no unjust thing: he shall surely live, and shall not die. None of his sins which he hath committed, shall be imputed to him: he hath done judgment and justice, he shall surely live. And the children of thy people have said: The way of the Lord is not equitable: whereas the way of the wicked is unjust," (Cf. Ezech. 33, 12-17). Behold then that you should not on this account presume, if you should sin, because pardon was promised you when you repented before, nor on this account should you despair if you do well, because death and damnation were threatened you when you sinned.

God responds to you about your own, not about His own. He indicates your merit to you; He does not reveal His counsel. He says to him who does ill, you shall die. He says to him who does well, you will live. What is it to say: "You shall die," unless you shall be damned? And what is it to say: "You shall live," unless "you shall be saved?" Now what is it to say: "You shall be damned," unless to judge you worthy of damnation? And what is it to say: "You shall be saved," unless to pronounce you worthy of salvation. Therefore, He says to you that yours is what is owed you, what is to be in so far as pertains to your merit, not in so far as pertains to His counsel. For it is just that He should reply to you about your own and propose this to you which seems to pertain to you. Thus He commanded the Ninivites according to their own merit, not according to His own counsel, saying: "Still for forty days will He sojourn at Nineve," (Cf. Jon. 3, 4). Thus also He required their merit and thus it was to be according to their merit. He looked to this and to that also which was spoken to Ezechias: "Take order with thy house, for thou shalt die, and not live," (Isa. 38, 1). For thus in so far as it was to pertain to Himself and that it might be destined to be so, He exacted what was in Himself. For such was his weakness that he could live no more, unless he were assisted from some source and obtained the power from some source. Therefore, in so far as pertained to them, what was said was to be, although it might be delayed and dispensed otherwise by Him by whom it was said. Thus then when it is said to you on sinning, "You shall die," your merit is expressed, just as when it is said to you on doing well, "You shall live," your due is announced.

And yet when the expression seems to be changed, it is not changed on account of Him who speaks but on account of you for whom it is said, because you change and do not remain the same, nor do you deserve that the same thing be always said to you. Therefore, do not be confident on account of God's words, if you do ill, because when you change toward Him His words are changed toward you. Also, He says, if I shall say to the just that he shall truly live and he, confident in his justice, shall do iniquity, all his justices shall be forgotten. If all his justices shall be forgotten, then both his penance and his humility and the other goods which he has performed shall be forgotten. Now if repentance is surrendered to forgetfulness, how is the blame excused? Therefore, if repentance is destroyed, the blame which had been forgiven on account of repentance must be born again. And justly did grace not remain with him who, after receiving grace, stood off ungrateful, but he himself changed that grace, because he did not wish to be the same toward it. See what the gospel, (Cf. Matt. 18, 24 ff.), says to you about the wicked and ungrateful servant for whom, when he asked his Lord, all sins had been forgiven but, because he was unwilling to have mercy toward his fellow-servant through the spreading out of justice, whatever was forgiven through the leniency of grace is demanded of him again. Rightly then is it said that when we are unwilling to forgive the debts of those who sin against us, rightly is that also exacted again which we rejoiced was forgiven us. And justly so. Because blame was forgiven a sinner, grace was not a debt. If anyone of his free will will cast the grace aside which has been gathered, it is surely just that it be of no benefit to him to have received grace.

But you say to me: If, after penance has been performed, former sins are again charged anew against the sinner, where is the statement that no good can be unrewarded? Behold, a certain good is here, namely, the repentance of this man which was good as long as it was true, and that good does not have any reward because his sins are charged against this man, as if he had never performed penance. Either that repentance was not good or if it was good, show its reward. What then? Does not the remission of sin seem to you to be a great reward? When this man performed repentance, his sin was forgiven him. As long as that man repented, his sin was not charged to him. As long as there was merit, the reward remained. Did you wish to give this liberty to men, that when they had given merit and received reward, again whenever it pleased them, they might do away with the merit and retain the reward? This exchange would not be just. Unjustly would you act against God, if you would thus give your own and receive His, so that you might take yours away and retain His. If you gave yours and received His, if you take back yours, He himself wishes to have what is His. Does it not seem so to you?

Perhaps you say that the way of the Lord is not just and you will think contrary to the truth, because you do not understand the truth. How, you say, will that stand which is written: "God will not judge twice on the same thing," (Cf. Nahum 1), if those which had been forgiven are required again for punishment? Hear how God does not judge twice on the same thing, since the sin which is shown to have been destroyed through worthy satisfaction, is by no means charged by Him for punishment. But this, you say, which was destroyed by satisfaction is required again for punishment. On this account it is required, because satisfaction is indeed not something which is offered for the release of that. As long as satisfaction remained, forgiveness remained and was not punished, after sin had once been forgiven. Now satisfaction ceased when malice was repeated, since this too pertained to satisfaction, that the deeds should be corrected and when corrected be not repeated. So after the blame returned, already in a measure it was not the same, since the one sin began to be under charge twice. Now since blame returned, the punishment also returned, which indeed would surely not have been sought again if the blame had not returned. When blame came, punishment followed. When blame was corrected, punishment was taken away; when blame returned, punishment also returned. One against one and two against two, not one against two nor two against one. This is justice. As much as is placed aside, so much is replaced. What does it seem to you? Reply, if you can. Now if you cannot reply, do not contend but intercede. It is not expedient for you to enter into judgment with God. Therefore, seek mercy that you may be able to carry justice.

On the Anointing of the Sick.

I. On the anointing of the sick.

There are three kinds of holy oil. The first is the oil of anointing. The second is the oil of the principal chrism. The third is the oil which is called the oil of the sick. Chrism is the name in Greek, unction in Latin. And yet although all oil is sanctified to make unction, not all oil is called of the principal chrism but only that by which the principal unction is performed, which also is called chrism in a special sense. For chrism is oil mixed with balsam with which the heads of kings and pontiffs are anointed, by which too the priest anoints the baptized on the head, just as likewise the pontiff by the imposition of the hands anoints those to be confirmed on the forehead.

Thus this oil mixed with balsam is called chrism or oil of the principal unction.

For this unction which is made by chrism is called the principal unction, because in it the Paraclete is principally given. Wherefore too on account of the abundance of grace, it contains two liquids mixed, namely oil and balsam; the oil of conscience, the balsam of fame; the oil by which the conscience within is pricked, the balsam by whose odor the neighbours outside are sprinkled; the oil within for peace with God, the balsam without for example with neighbour. There is another oil which is called the oil of unction by which the catechumens and neophytes are anointed on the breast and between the shoulder blades to receive the sacrament of baptism. The third kind of oil is that which is called the oil of the sick which belongs to the present sacrament.

II. *When and by whom the anointing of the sick was established.*

The sacrament of the anointing of the sick is read to have been established by the Apostles. For James the apostle writing in his letter so speaks: "Is any man sick among you? Let him bring in the priests of the Church that they may pray for him, anointing him with holy oil. And if he be in sins, they shall be forgiven him, and prayer will save the sick," (Cf. James 5, 14-16). In this it is shown that this sacrament was established for a twofold reason, namely, for the remission of sins and for the alleviation of sickness. Wherefore it is established that he who receives this unction faithfully and devotedly merits through it without doubt to receive both in body and in soul alleviation and consolation, if, however, it is expedient that he be alleviated in both. But if perhaps it is not expedient for him to have health and strength of body, without doubt by the reception of this unction he acquires that health and alleviation which is of the soul.

III. *Whether this sacrament can be repeated.*

Certain men ask whether the anointing of the sick can be repeated, since baptism, confirmation, and certain other sacraments once received are not repeated anew. But indeed no reason occurs to me why this sacrament cannot be repeated fittingly. For he who is baptized is baptized that he may be a Christian. Now he who has become a Christian once, cannot not be a Christian any more, even if he becomes evil, because he can be an evil Christian, and yet not cease to be a Christian, even if he ceases to be good. Furthermore he who has been baptized once is not baptized again, even if he be converted from evil to good. Now he who is anointed with oil is anointed that sins may be forgiven him and his illness alleviated. But he who is justified can sin again and he who is healed can be ill again. Now he who is made a Christian, since he cannot lose the sacrament of the name which he has, cannot receive it. Not so is the sacrament of anointing.

It is a sort of special medicine for the body and soul, mitigating and healing its languors. For oil heals ailing members. Thus oil is of benefit in curing both. If the illness does not return, the medicine is not repeated. Now if the illness cannot be checked, why should the medicine be prohibited? If anointing cannot be repeated, neither can prayer be repeated. For both are mentioned there. He says: "Let them pray for him, anointing him with holy oil; and if he be in sins, they shall be forgiven him; and prayer will save the sick," (Cf. James 5, 15 and 16).

But perhaps you will say that anointing pertains only to the remission of sins and prayer pertains only to the alleviation of the body because it is said: Prayer will save the sick. Turn anywhere. But you say that anointing confers the remission of sins and prayer the alleviation of sickness. I confess that it is true, yet in such a way that you do not deny the opposite, that anointing confers the alleviation of the body and prayer the remission of sins. Both proceed to both. Both operate and both operate in two ways and both cooperate with each other and both have one effect. Since they are not divided in the sacrament, they are not separated in the virtue of the sacrament. Yet since the anointing heals the pain of the members and seems to be of benefit more against the illness of the body, on this account perhaps he said: "Prayer will save the sick," that you may understand both in both and may not think that anointing pertains more to the health of the body than to the remission of sins. First the soul is cured, afterwards the body is healed. On account of the corruption of the soul the body is enfeebled. On this account to obtain soundness of body the soul must be cured first. And if by chance the body does not convalesce to its earlier health, there is no danger if only the soul shall receive its soundness.

Why then should it be denied that the sacrament of anointing can be repeated upon the sick to recover health again and again, and to obtain the remission of sins again and again, when it cannot be denied for the same soundness of body and similarly for the remission of sins that prayer ought to be repeated again and again? And that we may show the same in the sacraments, who would say that man once purified by the water of aspersion cannot be sprinkled again, and what is more important, when the sacrament of the body and blood of Christ has once been received he should not receive it again? But if by chance you think a response should be given to this, that a body once consecrated is not blessed anew in the same sacrament, nor is the blessing of aspersion repeated again and again in the same water, behold that, similarly, the same oil after one consecration is not sanctified again by another benediction or consecration, and yet just as he who has already received the sacrament of the body of Christ by no means is prohibited on this account from receiving it again, so he who has received the sacrament of unction, if it should be necessary and cause or devotion demand, is not forbidden rationally from receiving it again.

Sixteenth Part

On the End of Man and on Those Who Seek that End.

I. *On the dying.*

Scripture says: "Blessed are the dead, who die in the Lord," (Cf. Apoc. 14, 13). They die in the Lord who dying in the flesh indeed are yet found living in the Lord. What is "in the Lord?" In faith and hope and charity. For through these there is living in that life by which there is living in the Lord. There is a certain life by which the body lives from the soul and there is a certain life by which the soul lives in God, now indeed by faith, hope, and love, afterwards however instead of faith and hope by contemplation, with love remaining. Therefore, it cannot harm the soul, if the body loses its life, since the soul does not lose its life, but persists in faith and hope and charity. Let no one, therefore, say to me: Those who have little faith and little hope and little charity are not saved. I do not measure. Let them grow as much as they wish; the greater, the better. Yet I do not dare condemn them, however little they are. From the moment they are born from God, they are sons of God. Do you think that God will save His great sons and will condemn His small ones? Scripture says to me: "Your eyes have seen my imperfection, and in your book all will be inscribed," (Cf. Psalm 138, 16). If all, then both small and large.

What is "your eyes have seen"? They have approved. What is "they will be inscribed in the book"? They will be saved. Then the imperfect also will be saved. For those who are imperfect are something and they are some; they are placed in the number and they are written. Those who are nothing are none, nor do those who have nothing have to be written or numbered. Therefore to everyone that hath shall be given and he shall abound, (Cf. Matt. 25, 29). To everyone that has merit a reward will be given. He did not say: To him that hath great merit, a reward will be given and to him that hath small merit it will not be given, but to everyone, he says, that hath shall be given and he shall abound. Therefore, also he who has small merit, when he receives reward, will have enough, although he will not have so much as he who will have great merit. He alone is excluded from receiving the reward who has nothing of merit. All, therefore, who die in the Lord are blessed, because after the merit of virtue they come to the reward of blessedness.

II. *On the departure of souls.*

Many questions are asked, if, however, all should be asked which can be asked. Men ask about the departure of souls from bodies, how they depart, and whither they proceed on departing, or whither they proceed when they have arrived, what they find or what they perceive or endure. But all these things ought to be feared rather than asked. Therefore, since they are hidden, let them not be asked or be found but let them be feared. For who can be secure proceeding into uncertainty? Now this alone should not be uncertain, that an evil death cannot follow a good life. For an evil death is nothing but that alone which evils follow. Therefore, whoever wishes to die well, let him live well since those things which come after death are weighed against these, and according to these which precede before death in life are they repaid. There is merit to the very point of death but after death there is reward. Midway is death with which the day of the Lord begins, the day of man receives an end. On his day man is left to himself to do what he wishes. But on the day of the Lord man is not now in his own power but in the power of that to which he comes to be rewarded. On this account it is man's duty to be zealous in disposing well only that which is committed to him, but that which is not committed but promised him, he should leave to the decision of Him by whom it should be fulfilled.

Many ask about the departure of souls, how they go out from bodies, whether for example in this way, so that essentially and locally they go forth that they may begin to exist outside, as if cut off, or whether "to go" out means only this for them, that they withdraw themselves from the animation of bodies, and gathering, as it were, to themselves, they cease from the quickening of bodies so that they subsist on themselves. For example: When this corporeal breath is exhaled, it goes out of the body and begins essentially and locally outside the body, while before it was essentially and locally contained within the body. When indeed the bark begins to dry on a tree, the moisture goes out from it and is contracted toward the inner portions, and it does not go out so that it is outside but remains more within, in whatever is within, whether in the wood or in the medulla, so that it is not in the bark itself. Yet it goes out entirely from the bark, so that it is no longer in the bark nor does it go out, as if poured out toward the exterior portions, but goes out, as if gathered toward the interior. And if by chance the moisture again goes forth from its interior, so that it pours out again into the bark, that bark again flourishes, since the moisture in it is in its life. Thus they ask about the soul when it goes out from the body, whether for it "to go" means only this, that it withdraws itself to itself with regard to the quickening of the body, and in this very respect is not in the body, in that it ceases to quicken the body.

For in this respect it seems that in a measure it is outside all body, because subsisting alone in itself it is not poured forth for the quickening of the body. When indeed it is not in a body, it is not in a place, because place exists only in a body. Now when it is outside a body, it is also outside a place, because between itself and a body there is no place, and it is equally distant from all body since between itself and all body there is no body. If indeed between itself and all body there is no body, it is established surely that between itself and all body there is no place, since there is no place where there is no body. When then it is outside all body, as far as pertains to place it is equally near all body because, if when placed outside a body it were nearer one body and farther removed from another, there would surely be space between it and the body. If there were space, there would be place; if there were place, there would be body. Now if between itself and all body there were a body, there would be body without a body, which cannot be. Thus they say that the soul neither recedes through a body from a body nor is added through a body to a body, and on this account neither moves from place so as to withdraw from a body which is in a place, nor moves from a place so as to be added to a body which is in a place. For between every place and that which is in no place there is no place. And therefore they think that it is said that the spirit created in time indeed moves because it is changeable, but it does not move in place because neither does it move in place by withdrawing from a body which is in place, nor does it move in place by being added to a body which is in place. For it does not move in place when it recedes from a place, nor again does it move in place when it is added to a place. Even when, being placed in a body, the soul moves the body locally, yet it itself does not move locally. For if it is thought to move locally because it is in a body which moves locally, why similarly should not wisdom be said to move locally, since it is in the heart which moves locally. For if it is said that through the soul wisdom is in the heart, when the soul through the body moves locally is said to move locally, why also through the soul moved locally should not wisdom which is in the soul be said to move locally? If indeed reason does not prove this, that wisdom is said to move locally, although nevertheless it is in the soul, why will the soul be said to move locally, although it is in the body which is perceived to move locally? By such reflection they prove that the spirit does not move locally, although it is in the body which moves locally, but that it moves temporally, since being subject to vicissitude it changes from one thing to another. But in hidden things we should not be too curious, lest perhaps we presume more than we can.

What is the way of the spirit? God who made it knows. But we do not know how it comes nor comprehend how it recedes. When this corporeal breath is drawn in, it enters corporeally and locally; now when it is exhaled, it departs corporeally and locally. But the nature of the spirit is one, of the body another. When the soul was first given to man, God breathed into his face the breath of life, (Cf. Gen. 2, 7). And who can say how God breathed the soul into the body to vivify it, whether He sent it in, after creating it outside for vivification, or, because He made it there where he placed it and ordered the vivification created within to proceed, there was no other breathing than the vivifying itself? If then it is not known how it is breathed upon, how can it be known how it is exhaled? God breathes upon; man exhales. God sends; man sends back. By the same way by which it is sent when it is added, it is sent back when it withdraws. This one thing we know, that when the soul recedes the body dies and the very separation of the soul is the death of the body. It suffices for us to know this, that it withdraws. It is possible to examine fully how it withdraws.

We have, however, learned from many examples that on the departure of souls there is at hand the presence of evil or good angels who according to merits either carry them to torments or lead them to rest, but we also know that the souls themselves, when still placed in the body before departure, have sometimes foreknowledge of many things which are to be upon them, whether from the response of their interior consciousness or through revelations made externally. We know also that the souls which have sometimes been snatched away and again returned to the bodies have narrated certain visions and revelations made to them either about the torments of the impious or about the joys of the just, and yet in all these they have recited nothing except either the corporeal or something similar to the corporeal, namely, rivers, flames, bridges, ships, houses, groves, fields, flowers, black men, white men, etc., such as are customarily seen and had in this world, either to be loved unto joy or to be feared unto torment, also that they, when loosed from bodies, are taken by the hands, guided by the feet, suspended by the neck, shipped, cast headlong, and other things of this kind which can by no means happen except to corporeal nature. If we believe that all these things exist there thus visibly and corporeally, besides other incongruous things that arise, we confess truly that the souls themselves even separated from bodies are bodies composed of members in the likeness of bodies and yet distinct.

I indeed should not conceal what I have heard on this matter. A certain brother of approved testimony narrated to me that he had heard his abbot affirm this to be true, that when on a certain occasion he proceeded to visit certain brothers who lived at some distance, on the road as is usual he accepted hospitality at a certain place where he learned that a famous event had taken place a few days before among the inhabitants of that place. A certain foreigner, going to Saint James to pray, lodged at the place. In the night, as is the custom with travelers, he arose before daybreak and going out of the village came to a forest which was near it. There, by chance having been separated from his companions, as is usual at the parting of a road he began to go aside. When he had proceeded rather far, he met a certain man of venerable appearance and countenance and, when questioned by this person as to who he was or where he came from or where he was going, declared his name, likewise his country and the cause of his journey. That man maintains that he himself is Saint James to whom he is travelling, and that he knew all long before. Presently he praises his devotion for having come, as it were, with good pleasure and gratefulness; he commends his good purpose, saying that a great prize is being prepared for him and that his reward is already not far off. After this, while many words are being exchanged here and there, he finally sets forth the miseries and pains of this life, of what nature and how great they are, how quickly all that is cherished here flees and in like manner how without delay all that is feared or bemoaned passes on. In the midst of these and other happenings of this kind, by reasonable persuasion, as it were, he gradually injects into the mind of the traveler, who suspects nothing sinister, a contempt of life and takes away fear of death. Finally he proves that no virtue is really more advantageous than to hasten to depart from this life and, if no other way be granted, to strike death bravely with his own hand, and not to permit himself to be held long in these woes, who does not doubt that joy has been prepared for him. Why prolong the story? Deceived, he gives assent to the treacherous persuasion, and stabbing himself cuts his own throat. His comrades seek him for a long time in the byways and finally find him dead; they bring back the lifeless corpse to the village which they had left, and, since the host at whose house he had remained that night seemed probably to have knowledge of this crime, they summon him under a false charge to the same punishment. When he perceived that his innocence was endangered without cause and he implored with the innermost devotion of the heart that divine assistance attend him, behold!, suddenly he who had died arose, and, explaining what had happened to all who stood by and marveled, he absolved the innocent man. He reported that he had been led to torments by the same evil angel by whom he had been persuaded to kill himself, but that while he was being led a man of shining countenance, (now he said that he was Saint James), came to meet them as they went and snatched him off to heaven and brought him to the throne of the judge; there, when prayers had been poured forth for him, he obtained permission to return to life again. He affirmed that he saw many thousands of angels, and yet on being questioned about their state and appearance he said that there was nothing like them in this world by which he could have expressed that quality which he had seen in them, unless perhaps fire and light, but that it itself was greatly different by far; that he indeed remembered but could by no means express what he had seen.

Indeed we wished to recall this lest it seem a marvel if, when souls have departed from bodies, certain signs similar to the corporeal are presented for the demonstration of the spiritual, which, unless they were seen in and through such a corporeal likeness would by no means be mentioned by these same souls when returned to bodies, living in bodies, and knowing only corporeal things. For although being stripped of bodies there, they were able in one way to see those things; yet they would not be able to tell us in another way; those things would always remain hidden and that would not exist which might be told us about those things by those who return, unless it were shown according to these things to those who depart and see. Now whether the souls which depart from here, never more to return, see and perceive those things in this manner, is entirely doubtful except (and this seems more probable) that those souls which when living in bodies are affected by corporeal images through the delight of visible things, on departing from bodies suffer torments there in the same images. For they do not entirely get rid of corporeal capacity to suffer when, after the images of corporeal things have been impressed by the experience of wicked delight, they go out wrapped and covered up. Indeed those souls which, while remaining here, sought to cleanse and deprive themselves of the same delights and fantasies of thoughts, later, there, after they have gone out of their bodies, do not feel the punishment and torments in these bodies, because they are incapable of suffering in any way in this very respect, since they bring with themselves nothing worthy of punishment.

III. *On the punishments of souls.*

Certain men think that souls can be tortured by corporeal punishments only through bodies and while remaining in bodies. Therefore they believe that souls freed from bodies sustain only those punishments which conscience, the accuser within, inflicts. But it is most truly proven by testimony on the authority of the Sacred Scripture and Catholic faith that souls even before the reception of bodies are tortured by corporeal and material fire. For if corporeal fire is said to have been prepared for demons who are spirits, what wonder is it if souls without bodies are tortured by corporeal fire? But how, they say, can souls without bodies suffer from corporeal things? Behold, we say: We do not know how this can be done. Is it not, therefore, true that we do not know how it is? Yet what wonder is it if souls without bodies suffer? If they are harmed when they are struck down clothed with bodies, why would they not be harmed if they should be struck down bereft of bodies? If they can be affected when between themselves and that by which they are affected there is that medium through which they are affected, is it not entirely probable that they would be much more affected when they are joined immediately with that by which they are affected?

Yet we must not seek everywhere to try to believe by reason what we are commanded to believe. Sacred Scripture, the teacher of our faith, tells us this. What more do we seek? Let us accept, let us not contradict. Blessed Gregory says that they are ardent in this, that they see themselves ardent. What else do you want? Do you think as he says, that souls are ardent in this, that they see their own ardor? In other corporeal things is it not so that whoever sees fire feels the ardor? What then is that vision of the soul by which it feels all that it sees or, if not all, certainly that which looks to punishment? Or is it because the sense of the soul when it goes out through the body perceives in different ways because it perceives through different instruments and does not perceive with corporeal sense certain things established at a distance because the sense of the body does not suffice to perceive those instruments? For sense fails there where the instrument no longer suffices. Therefore, those senses which have instruments of greater sufficiency have greater force in perceiving. The eye sees things placed at a distance; the torch indeed can feel only the things immediately connected. If the instrument of touching were equally as penetrating as that of seeing, touch would perceive the things established at a distance equally with sight. What then? When there will be no diversity of instruments, why will not every sense be equal, so that, for example, it would be the same there to see as to touch, to touch as to feel pain? But this must be understood only regarding those who can be affected by torments, because on going out from here in the corruption of vices they take with them capacity for suffering.

Yet not because we say that the sense of the soul is affected from a distance, do we on this account place between corporeal punishments and the soul itself certain regions of space, as it were, since the soul which in its own nature is extended by no dimension, wherever it is present, is also proven to be present in sense through itself. For since in itself there is no place, between itself and place there is no place. But since, as it is said, all these things cannot be investigated by human reason, let us make the mind strong in these things which an unhesitating faith proves, namely, that sinful souls which have not corrected blame in this life have punishment after this life. Although we do not understand how those have feeling, what difference does it make as long as they do have feeling no less for this reason, even if it is beyond our understanding? What they suffer from is of no consequence but rather how much they suffer, since the force of pain is established not in the torment but in the feeling of the sufferer. For what benefit would it be even if the material of the tormenting elements outside were absent and yet the pain of the sufferers within were no less on this account? So why do you fear fire and flame unless because you fear to be burned? But if wounds and blows did not give pain, who would fear arms or weapons? Behold, therefore, that all these things from which pain can be are feared only because of pain itself. Take away the feeling of pain; there is nothing that you fear. God then was able even without material elements to give the feeling of pain to souls which were to be tortured. But it is fitting for them to be punished, indeed, without bodies in those elements in which they sinned before, just as in the elements themselves they were perversely delighted; indeed afterwards with bodies just as in the elements themselves through bodies they acted wickedly.

IV. *On the places of punishments.*

Just as God prepared corporeal punishments for torturing sinners, so too He distinguished corporeal places for the corporeal punishments themselves. For since those works of His which are outside should be not only instruments but also proofs of those things which He operates visibly, on this account He distinguished the torments of the wicked and the joys of the just also in corporeal places. The infernal region is the place of torments. Heaven is the place of joys.

For well is the place of torments down and the place of joys up, since blame also presses downward and justice raises upward. The greatest torments have a place in the lowest region, the greatest joys in the highest. Now the medium goods and evils are in the middle place, that is, they are mixed in this world.

The infernal region is said to be the lower region prepared in the lowest part of the land for the punishment of those to be damned. And yet regarding this it is by no means certain in what part of the land it is placed, that is, whether within a hollow of the land or outside in some region of its circumference, although indeed it seems more probable that it is placed within the earth as a kind of prison or workhouse for the shades. In this infernal region they say that there is inextinguishable fire and, that this might burn always and not lack nourishment, provision was made from the beginning of the world for the torment of demons, and in this fire indeed evil men also are to suffer eternal punishment together with the demons, since they, when placed in this life, agreed with these unto blame. To this infernal region the souls of those defiled which have departed from their bodies are thought to be driven straightway, just as conversely those of the perfect and just and of those departed this life purged are believed to be guided straightway without delay to heaven where according to His humanity Jesus Christ sits in glory on the right hand of the Father, as it is written: "Wheresoever the body shall be, there shall the eagles also be gathered together," (Matt. 24, 28; Luke 17, 37).

Now there is another punishment after death which is called purgatory. In this those who have departed from this life with certain faults but are just and predestined for life are tormented temporarily so as to be purged. And its location has by no means been determined, except that by the many examples and revelations of the souls which have been placed in punishment of this kind it has been shown very often that that punishment is exercised in this world; perhaps it will be more probable to believe that individual souls are punished especially in those places in which they committed the sin, as has often been proven by much evidence. Indeed if there are any other places for these punishments they are not easily assigned. Blessed Augustine shows from the Letter of Peter how the apostate angels falling to the lowest places of this world have been driven out until the last damnation which will be on the day of judgment. For what Peter calls "the prison of the lower hell," (Cf. 2 Peter 2, 4), Paul is shown likewise to have called "darkness," saying: "The rulers of the world of this darkness, the spirits of wickedness in the high places," (Cf. Ephes. 6, 12). Now we understand this prison or this darkness to be this air. Therefore also they are called aerial powers just as the evil spirits themselves are bound before the day of the last judgment according to one aspect, in so far, indeed, as they are constrained by the consciousness of future damnation, and according to another aspect they are freed, in so far, for example, as being released meanwhile from the greatest torments of hell they are permitted to be free to tempt men according to the direction of divine dispensation.

Now regarding hell, where that eternal fire is prepared for those to be tortured, blessed Gregory in his book of dialogues testifies that in his judgment it is more probable, as we have said, to believe it to be under the earth on account of Scripture which says: "Neither in heaven, nor on earth, nor under earth was anyone found who was able to open the sealed book," (Cf. Apoc. 5, 2 and 3). Now not unfittingly can it be asked whether the souls of those to be damned, that is, of those who among the impious and the most wretched were by a certain measure of living lower in malice, are straightway on departing from the bodies snatched to the places of hell or indeed are meanwhile separated from those severer torments of hell in certain other penal places, according to the hidden dispensations of God; thus in truth just as the good who are detained with faults in certain habitations, that they may not straightway ascend to the joys of heaven, so too no less the evil when they depart from this world, although to be damned, yet when certain lighter punishments have been disposed of according to the mode or measure of their faults, they do not straightway descend to the torments of hell.

For regarding the perfectly good, there is no doubt but that they go forth and pass straightway to joys. Similarly also regarding the very evil, there is no doubt but that they go from this world and descend without delay to the torments of hell. Regarding the imperfectly good also, it is certain that now in the meantime because of certain punishments they are indeed kept from the joys to come even until full purgation. Regarding the imperfect or less evil it is not certain where they are now, until at the time of the universal resurrection when the bodies have been received they descend to those torments where they are always. For they are said to be kept away from those torments because they are less evil; they cannot be believed to be kept from them for a similar reason, because they are to be damned. For what does the delay do, where there can be no emendation or purgation? But since this is entirely hidden, by no means should we explain it rashly.

V. *On the nature of the torments of hell.*

Now it seems very worthy of question, whether indeed only fire is prepared for the torture of the damned, for the reason that Truth mentions only this, saying: "Depart from me, you cursed, into everlasting fire," (Cf. Matt. 25, 41). For since punishments and tortures in this life proceed not only from fire but also from other elements, why should not the punishment of the damned there also consist of other elements as well as fire. For regarding the tortures of the wicked it is written: "They pass from the snow waters to excessive heat," (Cf. Job 24, 19). And again somewhere: "Their worm shall not die, and their fire shall not be quenched," (Isa. 66, 24). For if one wishes the worm to be with reference to the remorse alone of the sinner's conscience, and on this account indeed think that corporeal fire should be understood as the worm, yet not corporeal but spiritual, what does this which is written elsewhere mean: "The vengeance on the flesh of the ungodly is fire and worms"? (Cf. Eccli. 7, 19). For if then fire is believed corporeal, because it is vengeance on the flesh, why similarly is not the worm called corporeal, since it is said to have been prepared for vengeance on the flesh? Because of considerations of this kind no one thing can be defined lightly. Yet he who might say, therefore, that the vengeance on the flesh of the ungodly would be in a worm and in fire, since the ungodly, in that he also lived evilly in the flesh, will also be tortured in the flesh through fire and in the spirit through the worm of conscience, will understand surely that the worm will not die in the eternal torture of the conscience and that the fire is not to be extinguished in the flesh. But how shall we interpret "the snow waters" and "excessive heat" to which the impious are said to pass alternately for torture? Or perhaps only this is to be understood about that punishment, that now they are tormented in spirit before the day of final judgment in order to pass through a variety of torments to that one and highest punishment in which, as they subsist without end, so also they subsist without change. For the last punishment of the damned, as it is believed not unfittingly to be greater than all punishments, so too not unreasonably is it thought to be in that torment which is sharper than all others and more vehemently excruciating. This, therefore, perhaps alone will be so that it can always be the highest, since whatever would be exchanged for that would be diminished from it.

Yet there were some who, as has been said, thought that the torments of hell should be understood spiritually only and not corporeally, for the reason that certain words of the Scriptures are found which, as it were, seem to assert this. For certain Scriptures say that the substance of the lower things is spiritual, not corporeal; moreover, the gnashing of teeth and the weeping of souls should be understood as spiritual; also the flames and torments should not be understood as corporeal but are to be thought spiritual. Those who are not rooted in the faith waver because of the ambiguities of such words. For what was the necessity then of believing the torments of hell only spiritual, since the substance of infernal things has been called spiritual and not corporeal? For what are the infernal but wicked spirits which fell from the highest to the lowest through sin and are suppressed through punishment, whose substance surely even after sin is said to be not corporeal but spiritual, since, although the will in them has changed through malice to something else, yet the nature even afterwards has remained the same. Also now among the infernal the substance of the damned souls is rightly said to be not corporeal but spiritual, since now freed from bodies the souls are detained there in torments in spiritual nature alone. And so what is said about them in Holy Scripture according to the nature of corporeal things is worthily believed to be understood not corporeally but spiritually. For if what they themselves are is not body but spirit, what is in them is to be understood not as corporeal but spiritual. In this manner then truly the substance of the infernal is thought to be spiritual and not corporeal. But the statement that if we accept the weeping of souls and gnashing of teeth in a spiritual sense, we should also believe the flames of torments in themselves as not corporeal but spiritual, can indeed be so understood, if the torments of souls which are believed to be generated from corporeal flames are understood to take place in them not corporeally, that is, through the medium of bodies.

There are many other things which either have been said ambiguously or can be said ambiguously. But the truth of things is one thing, the truth of words another. We should not on account of the multitude of words deviate from the simplicity of believing. Augustine says in his Enchiridium that the time which is placed between the death and the final resurrection of man contains souls in hidden abodes according as each one is worthy either of rest or of tribulation. Therefore, the abodes of souls are hidden nor can man define that which he cannot know. Likewise of what nature that fire of hell is to be understood and how incorporeal spirits or souls freed from bodies can be tormented by fire, the authority not only of Christian faith but of Holy Scripture does not explain.

That the corporeal fire of hell will torment not only bodies but also spirits. *

Hell, which has also been called a pool of fire and sulphur, will be corporeal fire and will torment the bodies of the damned, both of men and of demons, the solid bodies of men, the airy bodies of demons, or only the bodies of men along with their spirits, but demons, spirits without bodies, clinging to corporeal fires by assuming punishment, not in receiving life. For although we do not say that incorporeal spirits can be afflicted by the punishment of corporeal fire in ways however marvelous but true, if the spirits of men, themselves also truly incorporeal, were able to be enclosed within corporeal members even then, will they then also be able to be bound insolubly with the bonds of their bodies?

If the incorporeal spirit of living man is held in the body, why after death, when the spirit is incorporeal, is it not also held by corporeal fire? For we say that the spirit is held by fire so that it is in the torment of fire by seeing and feeling. For it suffers fire by that very means by which it sees, and, because it sees that it is being consumed, it is consumed. Thus it happens that a corporeal thing burns an incorporeal one, while from the visible fire invisible ardor and pain is taken, so that through the corporeal fire the incorporeal mind is tortured also by the corporeal flame. After a little he says: When then the Truth shows that the rich

---

*The following passage is from St. Augustine's City of God, 21. 10.

sinner is condemned to fire, will any wise man deny that the souls of the false are held by fires?

*That the fire of hell will shine to some extent and will not shine to some extent.**

That flame, the avenger of vices, has cremation and has not light. There fire does not shine unto consolation, and yet, that it may torture the more, it shines unto something. For while the flame makes light, the evil are to see also with themselves their followers in the torment through love of whom they sinned, so that a view of those whose life they had loved carnally contrary to the precepts of the Founder afflicts them with an increase of their own damnation. Just as fire knows how to burn unto solace for the elect and yet does not know how to burn unto punishment, so on the other hand the flame of hell by no means shines for the evil unto the grace of consolation, and yet it shines unto punishment so that for the eyes of the damned fire of punishment does not glow with any clarity, and it shows how the evil are tortured unto the accumulation of pain.

That the fire of hell was so created from the beginning that it needs no nourishment.†

The justice of the all powerful, with foreknowledge of the future from the very origin of the world, created the fire of hell which began to be once in the punishment of the evil but even without fire-wood never ended its burning. For corporeal fire, in order that it can be fire, needs corporeal kindling wood, and when it must be preserved, without doubt it is sustained by the piling up of wood, nor is it strong enough to exist unless kindled and to subsist unless replenished. But on the other hand the fire of hell, since it is corporeal and corporeally burns the evil confined in it, is neither kindled by human endeavor nor sustained by wood, but once created lasts inextinguishably and needs no kindling and lacks no ardour. Well then is it said of the wicked: "A fire that is not kindled shall devour him," (Job. 20, 26).

Of what nature are the purgatorial fires in this life and of what nature afterwards.‡

In this mortal life indeed we confess that there are certain purgatorial punishments by which they are not afflicted whose lives are not made better thereby or rather are made worse thereby, but the purgatorial punishments are for those who when restrained by them are corrected. All other punishments whether temporal or eternal are applied according as each one is to be treated by Divine

*The following passage is from the Moralia of Gregory the Great.
†Likewise from the Moralia of Gregory the Great.
‡The following passage is from St. Augustine's City of God, 21. 13, 14, 16.

Providence, indeed whether for sins in the past or for those in which he still lives who is being punished, or for exercising and declaring virtues through men and angels whether good or evil. But some suffer temporal punishments in this life only, others, after death, others both now and then, yet before that most severe and last judgment. But all who endure temporal punishments after death will not come into those everlasting punishments which are to be after that judgment. We confess that for some what is not remitted in this world is remitted in the future, that is, lest they may be punished by the eternal punishment of the future world. Now very rare are those who pay no penalties in this life but only after this. Yet we ourselves both know and have heard that there have been some who up to decrepit old age have not even felt a little fear, as long as they have lived, although the life itself of mortals is all punishment. For lack of wisdom or ignorance is judged no small punishment, and it is fittingly judged so as to be avoided that through painful punishments boys are forced to learn some trade or literature, and to learn that that to which they are driven by punishments is for them so penal that sometimes they prefer to endure the very punishments by which they are compelled to learn rather than to learn.

Now who would not be horrified and prefer to die, if there should be proposed to him either death through punishment or infancy again, which indeed, since it begins not from laughter but from tears, in a manner prophesies this light, what evils it unwittingly is entering upon? They say that Zoroaster laughed only when he was born. Yet that monstrous laugh did not portend anything good for him. For he is said to have been the inventor of the magic arts. Now he died overcome in war by Ninus the king of the Assyrians. But so great is the mercy of God toward the vessels of mercy which He has prepared for glory that even the first age of man, that is, infancy, which is subject to flesh without any resistance, and the second which is called childhood, when reason has not yet taken up the battle against vices and lies almost under the power of all vicious delights, since, although it is now able to talk and so seems to have passed infancy, not yet is the infirmity of mind in it capable of precept, if it should receive the sacraments of the Mediator, these infants and children, even if they should end their lives in these years, translated, that is, from the power of darkness into the kingdom of God, not only should not be prepared for eternal punishmnts but they should not endure those purgatorial punishments after death. For spiritual regeneration alone suffices so that after death whatever carnal generation brought with death may not stand in the way.

Now when they have come to the age which now accepts precept and can now be subject to the power of the law, war must be taken up against the vices, and it must be waged sharply lest it lead to damnable sins and, if indeed they have not yet been strengthened by the habit of victories, more easily are they conquered and do they withdraw. But if they are accustomed to conquer and to command, they are overcome with laborious difficulty. But this war would never exist at all, if human nature had persisted through free will in that integrity in which it was made. Now indeed human nature, as an unfortunate, fights with itself which as a fortunate did not wish to have peace. Now there are very few of such felicity that from the approach of adolescence itself they commit no damnable sins, either in passions or in crimes or in the error of some nefarious impiety, but with great liberality of spirit check whatever could be damned in them because of carnal delight. Many indeed, after the precept of the law had been received, although before they had been overcome by prevailing vices, becoming violators of it, thereafter take refuge with assisting grace, through which by repenting rather bitterly and by fighting rather vehemently they become first subject to God and thus, with the mind placed over the flesh, become victors.

Therefore, whoever desires to avoid eternal punishments, let him not only be baptized but also let him be justified in Christ, and thus truly let him pass from the devil to Christ. Nothing is placed in a building before the foundation. We shall discover, therefore, who can be saved by fire, if first we shall have found what it is to have Christ in the foundation. Thus, if any Christian loves a harlot and cleaving to her is made one body with her, he indeed does not have Christ as a foundation. Now if anyone loves his wife according to Christ, who doubts that he has Christ in the foundation? If indeed this is so according to this age, if carnally, if in the disease of concupiscence, just as even the nations who ignore God, the Apostle grants this also according to mercy, rather Christ through the Apostle. Therefore, this one also can have Christ in foundation. For if he places no such affection and pleasure before Him, although he builds upon wood, hay, stubble, Christ is the foundation and on this account he will be saved through fire. For the fire of tribulation burns out the pleasures of this world and earthly loves which are indeed not damnable on account of conjugal union. "He that loveth father or mother or son or daughter more than me is not worthy of me," (Cf. Matt. 10, 37). But he who loves these relatives so carnally that nevertheless he does not place them before Christ the Lord, if he shall be brought to the point of temptation, he will be saved through fire, since it is necessary that pain so burn him by loss of them as love had cleaved to them. And this building will be harmful for him who has built because he will not have what he built up and he will be tormented by the loss of those in whom he was indeed delighted to find enjoyment. Behold in the words of the Apostle the man building upon this foundation, namely, precious stones, gold, silver, (Cf. 1 Cor. 3, 12). "He that is without a wife," he says, "is solicitous for the things that belong to the Lord, how he may please God," (1 Cor. 7, 32). Behold another building upon wood, hay, stubble, (Cf. 1 Cor. 3, 12). "Now he who is joined in matrimony," he says, "is solicitous of the things that are of the world, how he may please his wife," (Cf. 1 Cor. 7, 33). "The furnace trieth the potter's vessels, and the trial of affliction just men," (Eccli.

27, 6), "and the fire shall try every man's work, of what sort it is, if any man's work abide," (Cf. 1 Cor. 3, 13 and 14). For it remains that everyone be solicitous how he may please God, (Cf. 1 Cor. 7, 32). "What he hath built thereupon, he shall receive a reward," (Cf. 1 Cor. 3, 14), that is, of what he was solicitous, this he shall take. "If any man's work burn, he shall suffer loss," (Cf. 1 Cor. 3, 15), "since what he had loved he will not have, but he himself shall be saved," (Cf. 1 Cor. 3, 15), since no tribulation moved him from the stability of that foundation, "if, however, as by fire," (Cf. 1 Cor. 3, 15). For what he did not have without illicit love, he does not lose without burning pain.

Behold, as it seems to me, fire has been found to damn no one of these but to enrich one, to injure the other, to test both. Indeed he wished that there be no punishments after death except the purgatorial, since the elements air, water, and fire are higher than the lands. According to someone of these let that which has been contracted by earthly thought be cleansed by expiatory punishments. Therefore the pagan poet says: "Some are spread out empty suspended in the winds; for some an infectuous crime is washed out under a vast flood or is burnt out by fire." (Vergil, Aeneid, 6, 740-743). Indeed they think it unjust that one should be condemned with eternal punishment for sins, however great, perpetrated in a very short period of time, as if the justice of any case ever sees to it that every man is punished for as long a period of time as the admitted time for which he was punished. Should everyone have to be punished in chains as long as he did that for which he deserved to be bound, although most justly the servant who either harassed or struck the Lord by a very quickly passing word or stroke pays punishments of years in chains? So what the Lord, through his prophet, said would be accomplished, surely will be accomplished regarding the everlasting punishment of the damned: "Their worm shall not die, and their fire shall not be quenched," (Cf. Isa. 66, 24). Indeed some claim that both of these, fire and worm, pertain to the punishments of the soul, not of the body because it is written: "As a moth doth by a garment, and a worm by the wood, so the sadness of a man consumeth the heart," (Prov. 25, 20). Truly there are those who do not doubt that the punishments both of the soul and of the body will be in that suffering, namely the burning of the body by fire, but they affirm that in some way the soul is eaten by the worm of sadness. And yet this is said rather credibly, because surely it is absurd that pain either of body or of soul would be lacking there. Yet I think it easier to say that both rather than neither pertain to the body. For it is read in the Old Testament: "The vengeance on the flesh of the ungodly is fire and worms," (Cf. Eccli. 7, 19). It could have been said more briefly: The vengeance on the ungodly. Why then was it said, "the flesh of the ungodly," unless because both, that is, the worm and the fire, will be the punishment of the flesh?

How then is that true, they say, which our Christ says: "In what measure you shall mete, it shall be measured to you again," (Cf. Mark 4, 24), if temporal sin is punished by eternal torment? Nor do they consider that the same measure has not been named because of the equal space of time but because of the exchange of evil, that is, that he who has done evils may suffer evils. For the Lord spoke regarding judgments and condemnations. Moreover, he who judges and condemns unjustly, if he is judged and condemned justly, receives in the same measure, although not that which he gave. For by judgment he has acted and by judgment he suffers; although he has done with condemnation what is wicked, he suffers what is just. Nor is there anyone who is of the opinion that the torments of the guilty ought to end as quickly as the homicide, adultery, or sacrilege or any other crime was done. Not by length of time but by the magnitude of the iniquity and wickedness must it be measured.

VI. *On taking care of the dead.*[*]

And it must not be denied that the souls of the dead are relieved by the piety of their living, when the sacrifice of a mediator is offered for them or alms are given in the Church. But these things benefit those who while they lived merited that these things be able to benefit them later. For there is a manner of living, neither so good that it does not require these things after death, nor so evil that these things do not benefit it after death. For there is such a way of living with respect to the good that it does not require these, and there is such again with respect to evil that it cannot even on possessing these be benefited when once it has passed from this life. Therefore all merit is made ready, by which anyone after this life can be relieved or oppressed. But let no one when he has died hope to merit before God what he has neglected here. Therefore, those things which the Church repeats for commending the dead are not opposed to that apostolic opinion according to which it is said: "For we all shall stand before the judgment seat of Christ that each one may receive according to those things which he hath done through the body, whether it be good or evil," (Cf. 2 Cor. 5, 10), because each one prepared this merit for himself when he lived in the body, that these things can be of benefit to him. For they do not benefit all. And why not all except on account of the difference of the life which each one has led in body? Therefore, when sacrifices whether of the altar or of whatever alms are offered for all the baptized dead, they are acts of grace for the very good, propitiations for those who are not very bad; as for the very bad, even if they are of no assistance to the dead, they are consolations of some sort to the living. Now in the case of those to whom they are of benefit, they are of benefit either for this, that there may be true remission, or certainly that damnation itself may be made more tolerable.

---

[*]The following passage is taken from St. Augustine's Enchiridium, 110. 29.

VII. *To whom there may be benefit after death or how that is of benefit which is done for them.**

Thus there is a certain mode of life not so bad that the bounty of alms, by which even the lack of just deeds is sustained, is of no benefit toward obtaining the kingdom of heaven. And friends are made, who by means of these alms take them up into the eternal dwellings; they are not of so good a life that it alone would be sufficient for them to obtain such great blessedness, unless they obtain mercy by the merits of those whom they have made friends. Moreover, I constantly marvel that there is found even in Vergil this sentiment whereby the Lord says: "Make unto you friends of the mammon of iniquity, that they may receive you into everlasting dwellings," (Cf. Luke 16, 9). For when that poet described the Elisian fields where they think that the souls of the blessed live, he placed there not only those who by their own merits were able to come to those abodes but went on to say: Whoever made others mindful of themselves by meriting, (Vergil, Aeneid, 6, 664), that is, who propitiated others and made them mindful of themselves by propitiating; moreover, as if that were said to them which is repeated by the mouth of the Christian when every humble Christian commends himself to each of the saints and says: "Be mindful of me" and causes him to be so by propitiating.

But what this mode of life is and what these sins are which impede the arrival into the kingdom of God in such a way that nevertheless they obtain indulgence by the merits of saintly friends, it is most difficult to discover, most dangerous to define. I surely, even to this time, have not been able to succeed in an investigation of these matters, from which I might give satisfaction. Now in truth while the mode of venial sin, even if it persists, is not known, surely zeal for advancing into better things by praying and watching more vigilantly is employed, and the care of making holy friends with reference to the mammon of iniquity is not spurned. But this liberation which is effected whether by his own prayers or by the intercession of saints brings this about, that he is not sent into everlasting fire in such a way that, after he has been sent, he may not after whatever time be released from there.

The same.

Let us not think that we reach the dead for whom we have care, unless we solemnly supplicate for them by sacrifices, either of the altar or of prayers or of alms, although they are not of benefit to all for whom they are made but only to those for whom while living it is prepared that they be of benefit. But since we do not distinguish who they are, we should perform works for all the regenerated, in order that no one of those may be omitted to whom these benefits can and

---

*The following passage is taken from the City of God of St. Augustine, 21. 27.

should come. For these things will better be superfluous to those for whom they are neither an obstruction nor a benefit than be lacking to those for whom they are a benefit. Yet everyone does this more diligently for their relatives which may similarly be done for them by their own. Now whatever is applied to the human body is not an aid to health but an office of humanity, according to an affection by which no one ever holds his own flesh as an object of hatred. Therefore, it is right that he who can, should take care for the flesh of his neighbour when the neighbour, who was accustomed to take care, has departed from this world.

VIII. *On obsequies.**

The care of the funeral, the establishment of the tomb, the pomp of obsequies are the solaces of the living rather than assistance for the dead. If an expensive tomb is of some benefit to the wicked, a cheap one or none at all will be an impediment to the good. The crowd of servants displayed elaborate obsequies for the rich man clad in purple, but much more excellent ones in the sight of the Lord did the ministry of angels furnish for that ulcerous poor man; they bore him not into a marble tomb but to the bosom of Abraham.

IX. *On the sacrifice for the dead.*†

If sins are not insoluble after death, the sacred oblation of the saving victim is accustomed to give aid to the souls of many even after death.

X. *To whom it is a benefit.*‡

But it must be known that holy sacrifices are of benefit to those dead who by living well here have gained that the good deeds which are performed by them here for themselves should benefit them even after death. For this sacrifice in an extraordinary way saves the soul from eternal death. It represents sacramentally to us the death of the only begotten, who indeed "rising again from the death dieth now no more, and death shall no more have dominion over him," (Cf. Rom. 6, 9), yet He in Himself living immortally and incorruptibly for us is immolated again in this mystery of the holy oblation. For His body is taken here; His flesh is divided with salvation for the people; His blood is shed not upon the hands of unbelievers but in the mouths of believers. Therefore then let us consider of what nature this sacrifice is for us, which as our oblation always imitates the passion of the only-begotten Son. For who of believers can have doubt that at the very hour of the sacrifice at the voice of the priest the heavens are opened, that at that mystery of Jesus the choruses of angels are present, that the lowest associate with the highest, that the earthly are joined with the heavenly, that one also is made from the visible and the invisible?

---

*Aug., Cur. Mort., 2. 4.
†The following passage is taken from the Dialogues of Gregory the Great, 4. 58.
‡Likewise from the Dialogues of Gregory the Great, 4. 57.

XI. *Whether souls know what things are being done in this world.*

Some ask about souls freed from flesh, whether they have cognition of those things which are done in this life, especially the souls of those who already in the joy of their Lord and in His hidden face enjoy the representation of true light. They also add that about the souls of saints which many bring into question, whether they hear the prayers of suppliants and, when they are invoked to intercede, whether the prayers of those who beseech ever come to their cognition. It is difficult to judge about matters of this kind. For how can we who can neither grasp nor investigate that knowledge which they have about us be certain in our knowledge about them? This one thing is certain, that the souls of the saints, established in the secrecy of divine contemplation, know as much of the things that are done outside as is considered to be of benefit either for their joy or for our help. We seek intercessors before God. What more do we wish? Do you fear perhaps, lest they who always pray do not pray? How will they not pray for you when you pray, who nevertheless do not cease to pray when you do not pray?

But they do not hear you speak, and I pour forth words to the wind as I speak to those who do not hear and do not understand. Well let us say this. The saints do not hear the words of those who beseech, nor is it connected with their blessedness to know these things which are done outside. Well let us say, they do not hear. Does not God hear? Why then do you labour to investigate what they hear and how much the saints hear to whom you pray, when God himself hears for whom you pray? He himself sees your humility who will reward your devotion. Yet as for "if they hear" and "how much they hear" what is to hear except to know? For the light is one thing in which they both hear unto perceiving and see unto knowing. And in this, if anything is done outside by chance which now meanwhile they do not hear or do not see, it is a mystery of dispensation, not a detriment to felicity. Yet some of the holy Fathers are found to have said something like this, as if there were nothing in creation which they do not see who see Him who sees all things. I do not presume to judge more than this alone, that they see as much as it has pleased Him whom they see and in whom they see.

SEVENTEENTH PART

On the End of the World.

I. *On the time of Christ's coming at the very last.**

On the coming of the Saviour who is expected at the end I dare not enumerate the times, nor do I think that any prophet on this matter has determined the number of years, but that the belief prevails which the Lord himself expresses:

---

*From St. Augustine to Esycius, Epist. 197.

"No one can know the times which the Father hath put in his own power," (Cf. Acts 1, 7). Therefore to compute the times, that is "chronous," that we may know when the end of this world or the coming of the Lord is, seems nothing else to me than to wish to know what He himself said that no one can know. Surely the fitting moment of that time will not be indeed before the Gospel is preached to the whole world for a testimony to all nations. For a very clear opinion on this matter is read on the part of the Saviour who says: "And this Gospel of the kingdom shall be preached in the whole world, for a testimony to all nations, and then shall the consummation come," (Matt. 24, 14).

What is "then shall it come" unless "it will not come before"? How much after it may come is uncertain to us. Yet surely we should not doubt that it will not come before. If then it is hidden when as the Church fructifies and grows the whole world will be filled from sea to sea, without doubt it is hidden when the end will be. For it will not be before. "Then that wicked one shall be revealed," that is Antichrist, "whom the Lord Jesus Christ shall kill with the spirit of his mouth," (Cf. 2 Thess. 2, 8).

II. *On the last tribulation.**

Then shall Satan be freed from his custody and he shall go forth to seduce the nations which are in the four corners of the land; Gog and Magog, the interpretation of whose names we find to be: Gog, house; Magog, from the house, as if the house and he himself who went forth from the house. Therefore, they are the nations in which, we understood above, the devil was included as in an abyss, and he himself by some means lifts himself up from them and goes forth, so that they are "the house" and he "from the house."

III. *Why the devil is now bound.†*

The binding of the devil is the fact that he is not permitted to exercise all the temptation that he can, either by force or by craft, to seduce men to his side by violent force or by fraudulent deceit. And this, if it were permitted for so long a time and amid the great weakness of the people, would cast down very many of the faithful such as God does not wish to suffer this and would prevent their believing, and lest he do this, he was bound. For he shall be loosed then, when the time is short. For it is read that he will rage during three years and six months with all his strength and the strength of his own, and they will be so strong, with whom he must wage war, that they cannot be overcome by this great attack and trickery on his part. Now Satan will be freed at the end of the world, that he may see how great an adversary the City of God has overcome with great glory to its redeemer, helper, liberator.

---

*The following passage is from the City of God of St. Augustine, 20. 11.
†Aug., D. C. D. 20. 8.

IV. *Why he will be freed at the very last.*

Now, as it has been said, Satan will go forth into open persecution; he will rush forth from the lurking places of hate. For when the last judgment is near, this will be the last persecution which Holy Church shall suffer throughout the whole world, namely, the whole city of Christ persecuted by the whole city of the devil, however great it shall be, both upon earth. Accordingly the apostle says: "The charity of many shall grow cold and iniquity shall abound," (Cf. Matt. 24, 12). Accordingly Daniel says: "And there will be a time of tribulation such as never was from the time a nation was born upon earth even until that time," (Cf. Dan. 12, 1).

V. *For how long will the last tribulation be.**

This last persecution by Antichrist will be for three years and six months. For Christ will not come to judge the living and the dead, unless there shall come first His adversary, Antichrist, "whom the Lord Jesus shall kill with the spirit of his mouth," (Cf. 2 Thess. 2, 8).

VI. *On the coming of Elias and Henoch.†*

Then Elias the Thesbite shall come, "before the coming of the great and famous day of the Lord who will turn the heart of the father to the son, and the heart of man to his neighbour, lest perchance I come and strike the earth to its depth," (Cf. Mal. 4, 6). It is most celebrated in sermons and in the hearts of the faithful that through this Elias, a great and wonderful prophet, and by the law placed in him, on the last day before the judgment the Jews will believe in the true Christ, that is, in our Christ. For not unfittingly is it hoped that he himself will come before the Judge, the Saviour, since not unfittingly is he believed to be living even now. For he was snatched up from human affairs by a fiery chariot, (Cf. 4 Kings 2, 11), as Holy Scripture most clearly testifies. Therefore, when he shall come to set forth the law in a spiritual sense, which the Jews now know in a carnal sense, he will turn the heart of the father to the son, that is the hearts of the fathers to the sons. For thus will the heart of the fathers turn to the sons, when the understanding of the fathers will be led to the understanding of the sons, and the heart of the sons to their fathers, until they too will agree with what their fathers believe.

VII. *On the quality of the person, judge.‡*

"When the Son of man shall come in his glory, and all his angels with him, then shall all nations be gathered together before him," (Cf. Matt. 25, 31, and 32).

---

*Aug., D. C. D. 20. 13.

†Aug., D. C. D. 20. 29.

‡The following passage is taken from the work, on the Trinity, by St. Augustine, 1. 13. 28-29.

For even the Jews who, persevering in evil are to be punished at that judgment, as it is written elsewhere, "shall look upon Him whom they have pierced," (Cf. Zach. 12, 10; John 20, 37; Apoc. 1, 7). For since the good and the evil are to see the judge of the living and the dead, without doubt the evil will be able to see Him only according to the form by which He is the Son of man, but yet in the splendor in which He shall judge, not in the humility in which He has been judged. For Christ is not to be seen again on the cross. But without doubt the wicked will not see that form of God in which He is equal to the Father. For they are not clean of heart. "For blessed are the clean of heart, for they shall see God," (Matt. 5, 8). Otherwise, if the Son of God shall appear as judge even to the wicked, in the form in which He is equal to the Father when He is to judge, what is it that He promises for His great lover, saying: "I shall love him and I shall show myself to him."? (Cf. John 4).

Therefore, the Son of man shall judge, yet not according to human power but according to that by which He is the Son of God. And again the Son of the God shall judge, yet not appearing in that form in which God is equal to the Father but in that by which He is the Son of man. And so both can be said; the Son of man will judge and the Son of man will not judge, so that what He says is true: "When the Son of man shall come, then shall all nations be gathered together before him," (Cf. Matt. 25, 31), and the Son of man shall not judge, so that what He says is true: "I do not judge and I seek not my own glory; there is one that seeketh and judgeth," (Cf. John 8, 50). For according to the statement that at the judgment not the form of God but the form of the Son of man will appear, the Father himself will not judge. For according to this it is said: "Neither doth the Father judge any man, but hath given all judgment to the Son," (Cf. John 5, 22). Now regarding what is said: "The Father hath given to the Son to have life in himself," (Cf. John 5, 26), surely it is not said that the Father does not judge any man. For according to this, that the Father begot the Son equal, He judges with Him. Therefore, according to this it has been said that at the judgment not the form of God but the form of the Son of man will appear, not because He will not judge, who hath given all judgment to the Son, when the Son says of Him: "One that seeketh and judgeth," but it has been said thus: "The Father judgeth not any man, but hath given all judgment to the Son," as if it were said: No one will see the Father at the judgment of the living and the dead, but all will see the Son, since the Son of man is such that He can be seen even by the wicked, when they shall look upon Him whom they have pierced. Therefore, He has given all judgment to the Son, because the judge shall appear in the form of the Son of man, and this form is not of the Father but of the Son, and not in that of the Son in which He is equal to the Father but in which He is less than the Father, in order that at the judgment He may be visible to the good and to the evil.

Now when the evil shall see the judge, He will not appear good to them, since they will not rejoice before him in heart, but "then shall all the tribes of the earth strike themselves," (Cf. Matt. 24, 30). In the number, indeed, of all the evil and the faithless, that vision of the Son of man will not be a good thing for the wicked who shall be sent into everlasting fire, nor will it be the highest good for the just. For He still calls them to the kingdom which was prepared for them from the beginning of the world. For just as He shall say to the one: "Depart into everlasting fire," (Cf. Matt. 25, 41), so He shall say to the others: "Come, ye blessed of my Father, possess you the Kingdom prepared for you," (Cf. Matt. 25, 34). And just as the one shall go into everlasting burning, so the just shall go into life everlasting. "Now what is this eternal life except that they may know thee, the only living God and Jesus Christ whom thou has sent"? (Cf. John 17, 3). But now in that about which He speaks to the Father, "which I had, before the world was made, with thee," (Cf. John 17, 5), then will He give the kingdom to God and the Father, that the good servant may enter upon the joy of his Lord.

VIII. *On the swiftness of judgment.**

In an atom says the Apostle, that is, in an instant of time that cannot be divided, "in the twinkling of an eye," (Cf. 1 Cor. 15, 52), that is, with the highest speed, and "at the last trumpet," that is, at the last signal which will be given that these things be fulfilled. "For," he says, "the trumpet shall sound and the dead shall rise again incorruptible and we shall be changed," (1 Cor. 15, 52). Therefore, we ought to think of this change as being without pause, since all, both the just and the unjust, are to rise again. But just as the Lord says in the Gospel: "They that have done well, unto resurrection of life; they that have done evil, unto the resurrection of judgment," (Cf. John 5, 29), calling eternal punishment, judgment, just as in another place: "He that doth not believe, he says, is already judged," (Cf. John 3, 18). Furthermore, those who have arisen unto judgment will not be changed into that incorruptibility which can suffer neither punishment of pain nor corruption. For that belongs to the faithful and the saints. These indeed will be tormented by perpetual damnation, because "their fire shall not be quenched and their worm shall not die," (Cf. Isa. 66, 24). And those uncorrupted by this indeed shall rise again with soundness of members but destined still to be corrupted by the pain of punishments when they shall hear: "Depart into everlasting fire, which was prepared for the devil and his angels," (Matt. 25, 41). Of this evil report the just will have no fear.

IX. *On the same.*†

And as the ray of our eye does not reach nearer objects more quickly, and more distant ones more slowly, but traverses both intervals with equal speed, so when

---

*The following passage is taken from a work of St. Augustine to Consentius, Epist. 205. 14-15.

†Cf. Aug. Epist. 102. 1. 5.

in the twinkling of an eye, as the Apostle says, (Cf. 1 Cor. 15, 52), the resurrection of the dead takes place, it is as easy for the omnipotence of God and for His ineffable will to raise all bodies recently dead as those which fell a long time ago.

X. *On the same.**

At the unexpected coming of the Lord, the judgment which, it was thought, would be very slow, will be very swift, because it will convict consciences themselves without flow of speech. "For inquisition shall be made," as it is written, "into the thoughts of the ungodly," (Cf. Wisdom 1, 9). And the Apostle says: "Thoughts accusing or defending, in the day when God shall judge the secrets of men according to my gospel, through Jesus Christ," (Cf. Rom. 2, 15 and 16). Thus also shall the Lord be a witness, who must be considered swift, when without delay He shall recall to memory the reason for which He convicts and punishes the conscience.

XI. *On the order of rising again.*

The prophet Isaias says: "The dead shall rise again, and they who were in sepulchres shall rise again," (Cf. Isa. 26, 19). Therefore, the Apostle says: "For the Lord himself shall come down from heaven with commandment, and with the voice of an archangel, and with the trumpet of God: and the dead who are in Christ, shall rise first. Then we who are alive, who are left, shall be taken up together with them in the clouds to meet Christ, into the air, and so shall we be always with the Lord," (1 Thess. 4, 15 and 16). These words of the Apostle show very clearly that the resurrection of the dead will occur when Christ will come indeed to judge the living and the dead. But it is usually asked whether those whom Christ will find living here, whose persons the Apostle has transformed in a figure to himself and to those who were living in his time, will never die at all or at the very moment of time when they will be taken into the air with those rising again in the clouds to meet Christ, they will pass with wonderful swiftness through death to immortality. If then we believe that the saints who will be found living when Christ comes and will be taken off to meet Him, will in the same carrying off go out of their mortal bodies and will presently return to the same immortal objects, we shall experience no difficulties in the words of the Apostle, either where He says: "That which thou sowest is not quickened, except it die first," (Cf. 1 Cor. 15, 36), or where he says: "We shall all rise again or we shall all sleep," (Cf. 1 Cor. 15, 51), because they will not be quickened by immortality, unless they die a little while before, and through this they will not be strangers to the resurrection which they precede by sleep, however brief it may be but still be something.

---

*Cf. Aug., D. C. D. 20. 26.

XII. *How what has been written: "He shall judge the living and the dead,"*
is to be understood.

That He will judge the living and the dead is accepted in two ways, whether
we understand by "the living" those whom His coming will find not yet dead
here but still living in this flesh, but by "the dead" those who before He comes
have gone out or will go out of the body, or we understand by "the living" the
just and by "the dead" the unjust, that the just will judge, the unjust will be
judged.

XIII. *On the resurrection of bodies, how or of what nature they will rise again.*

There are some who, considering that the spirit is freed from the flesh, that
the flesh is turned into decay, that decay is reduced to dust, that dust is resolved
into elements so that it is not seen at all by human eyes, despair that the resurrection can take place. And while they look upon dry bones, they distrust that
these bones can be clothed with flesh and grow again into life. Those who do not
have faith in the resurrection from obedience should certainly have this from
reason. For what does the world in the elements imitate daily if not our resurrection? For through daily revolutions the temporal light itself seems to die, when
the shades of night come upon it and that which was seen is drawn away, and
daily it seems to rise again when the light which was taken away from the eyes
with the repression of the night is restored. For through the revolutions of the
seasons we perceive that the trees lose the greenness of their leaves and cease from
the production of fruits. And behold, suddenly, from a drying log, as it were,
as if a kind of resurrection were happening, we see leaves break forth, fruit grow
large, and the whole tree become clothed with quickened beauty. But behold, I
grant the resurrection, yet I seek the effect of the resurrection. For I believe that
I shall rise again but I wish to hear of what nature I shall be. For I must know
whether perhaps I shall rise in something else, subtle or ephemeral, or in that body
in which I remain. But if I shall rise in an ephemeral body, then I shall not be
the one who rises. For how is it true resurrection if the flesh cannot be true?
Therefore, clear reasoning suggests that, if the flesh will not be true, without
doubt the resurrection will not be true. For a true resurrection cannot be said to
exist where what has fallen does not rise. So also, our Redeemer showed His
hands and side to the disciples who doubted His resurrection. He offered them
his bones and flesh to handle, saying: "Handle and see: for a spirit hath not flesh
and bones, as you see me to have," (Luke 24, 39).

Now then regarding the resurrection of the flesh, that it will not be as some
have arisen and died again, but just as the resurrection of Christ himself into
eternal life, I do not find how I can present any brief discussion and satisfy all
the questions which are usually raised about this. Yet by no means should a

Christian doubt that the flesh of all who have been born, are being born, and have died will rise again, and will die. Therefore, the first question arises regarding abortive fetuses, which indeed are born in the wombs of mothers but now so born that they can indeed be reborn. If we should say that those who are already formed will rise again, surely what is said can be tolerated. As for unformed abortions, who would not be more inclined to think that they perish just as seed which has not been conceived? But who would dare deny, even if he would not dare affirm, that resurrection will bring this to pass, that whatever was lacking to the form will be completed, and this will not be so done if the perfection is that which was to be added in time, just as there will not be the vices which were added in time, in order that neither in that which the days were destined to bring forward as apt and fitting, nature may not be defrauded nor be defiled in that which the day should bring forward as adverse and contrary to nature, but that will be made whole which did not yet exist and that which had not yet been vitiated will be restored wholly?

XIV. *On abortions and monsters; whether they rise again and of what nature they are.*

Question on this matter which is subject to dispute is usually raised extremely carefully by the very learned, and I do not know whether it can be discovered by men at what point man begins to live in the womb, whether there is a kind of hidden life which appears, while there are not yet signs of life. For it seems excessive impudence to deny that the infants lived which are cut out limb by limb and cast out of the wombs of pregnant women for this reason, lest they kill the woman also, if they be left there dead. Now surely man begins to live from the time when he can indeed die. Indeed, wherever death could have happened to him I cannot find how the dead man does not belong to the resurrection of the dead. For it will not be denied that monsters which are born and live, however quickly they may die, do not rise nor is it to be believed that they will rise again vitiated and not rather corrected and emended in nature. For God forbid that the creature which was born with double members recently in the Orient, about which the most beloved brothers who saw it have related and blessed Jerome the presbyter has left a description, God forbid, I say that we should think that one double man and not rather two men, which would have been the case if twins were born, will rise again.

So also the rest, all of which individually are offspring and by having some extreme deformity more or less are called monsters, will be recalled at the resurrection to the form of human nature so that as individual souls they may obtain their own individual bodies with nothing clinging to them, even whatever has been born clinging to them, but each one apart, individually bearing his own members for which the completeness of the human body will be fulfilled. Earthly material from which the flesh of mortals is created does not perish before God, but into whatever dust or ashes it is resolved, into whatever breath or breezes it disperses, into whatever substance of other things or elements themselves it is converted, into the food and flesh of whatever animals or men it withdraws and is changed, to that human soul which animated it in the beginning so that it was made man and grew, at the moment of time it will return.

XV. *On the manner of the resurrection.*

It is promised that the remaking of all members not only from the earth but also from the most secret recess of the other elements, wherever the fallen bodies have withdrawn, shall at the moment of time be granted and completed. And so the earthly material itself, which becomes a cadaver when the soul departs, at the resurrection will not so be restored that those materials which fall away and are turned into the various species and forms of other things, although they return to the body from which they fell away, must also return to the same parts of the body in which they were. Otherwise, if all that hair returns which so many cuttings removed, if there returns to the nails whatever extensive and unsightly trimming took away from the whole, deformity occurs in the minds of those who think of this and so do not believe in the resurrection of the flesh. But just as, if a statue of some malleable metal were either melted in fire or pounded into dust or fused into a mass and the artificer should wish to restore it again from the quantity of that measure, it would make no difference regarding its whole what particles of the material were restored to each member of the statue, provided, however, when restored it took back all from which it had been built, so God the Artificer in marvelous and ineffable fashion will restore with marvelous and ineffable quickness from the whole out of which our flesh had been constituted.

Nor will it have anything to do with the integrity of the thing whether hairs return to hairs or finger nails to finger nails or whatever, if these had perished, is changed into flesh and is recalled to other parts of the body, as long as the providence of the Artificer takes care lest anything unfitting be done. Nor is it of consequence that the individuals coming to life again have different statures, because they had been so when living, or that the thin be restored to life again with the same thinness or the fat with the same fatness. But if this is in the plan of the Creator, that the peculiarity and likeness of each be preserved in his own image, but that in the other goods of the body all things be restored equally, the material will be so modified in each one that nothing will perish from it, and what was lacking to some He may supply who was able to make whatever He wished from nothing. Now if in the bodies of those rising again there will be a reasonable inequality, just as there is among voices which combine in song, this will be done for each from the material of his own body, which both returns man to the gatherings of the angels and brings nothing unsuitable to their senses. For thus none of these things will be there, but whatever will be, will be fitting, since it will not be there, if it will not be fitting.

XVI. *An example of the things mentioned above.**

For if a man, an artificer, can produce a statue, which for some reason he had made deformed, and render it very beautiful, so that nothing of the substance but only the deformity perish, and if he cannot cut off and separate from the whole anything in that earlier form which stood out improperly and did not fit in with the uniformity of the parts out of which he had made the statue, but can so scatter and mix all that he does not cause deformity or diminish quantity, what must we think about the Omnipotent?

XVII. *That the bodies of the saints will rise again without blemish and incorruptible.†*

Therefore, the bodies of the saints will rise again without any blemish, without any deformity, as well as without any corruption, weight, difficulty. And there will be great felicity in these because they have been called spiritual, although they shall without doubt be bodies not spirits. But just as now the body, which now is body and not soul, is called animal, so then the body will be spiritual, yet the body will not be spirit. Furthermore in so far as pertains to the corruption which now aggravates the soul (Cf. Wisdom 15) and the vices with which the flesh lusteth against the spirit (Cf. Gal. 5, 17), then there will not be flesh but body, since there are also said to be bodies in Heaven. Therefore it is said: "Flesh and blood will not possess the kingdom of God," (Cf. 1 Cor. 15, 50). And as if explaining what he has said, he adds: "Neither shall incorruption possess corruption." (Cf. 1 Cor. 15, 50). What he first called flesh and blood, this he later called corruption, and what he first called the kingdom of God, this he later called incorruption. Now in so far as pertains to substance, even then there will be flesh. Therefore, after the resurrection the body of Christ was called flesh. Thus the Apostle says: "It is sown a natural body, it shall rise a spiritual body," (1 Cor. 44), because so great will be the harmony of flesh and spirit that, while the spirit vivifies the subject flesh without the support of any insatiable desire, nothing from ourselves will oppose ourselves but, just as we shall suffer no enemy outwardly, so we shall not suffer ourselves as enemies within.

---

*Cf. St. Augustine's City of God, Book XXII.
†Cf. the Enchiridium of St. Augustine.

XVIII. *That infants will not rise again in that stature in which they died.**

What then shall we say about infants, except that they shall not rise again in that smallness of body in which they died. But what was to accrue to them rather slowly, they shall at this time receive by that marvelous and very swift work of God. For in the opinion of the Lord where He says: "A hair of your head shall not perish," (Cf. Luke 21, 18; Act. 27, 34), it is said that what was, shall not be lacking, but it is not denied that what was lacking shall be present. Now the dead child lacked perfect quantity of body. For perfection is lacking to the infant, at least the perfection of corporeal magnitude which, when it has been added, does not permit of a taller stature. Thus all have this mode of perfection, so that they are conceived and born with it, but they have it in reason, not in mass, just as all the members are indeed hidden in the seed, although some are still lacking to infants, such as teeth or anything else of this kind. In this way, set in the corporeal material of every single one in some manner, what does not yet exist seems, so to speak, to be marked, rather, what is hidden but will exist or rather will appear with the approach of time. In this manner then the infant is indeed either short or tall, who shall be short or tall.

It remains therefore for everyone to receive his measure, such as he had in his youth, even if he died an old man, or such as he was to have had, if he died before, so that the bodies of the dead may rise again neither before nor beyond youthful form, but at the age of strength even to which we know that Christ came. For the most learned men of this age also have defined youth to be around thirty years, and say that when this has been terminated by its proper expanse man veers towards the failings of a more sober and sensitive age, and that thus it was not said unto the measure of the body or unto the measure of stature but unto the measure of the age of the fulness of Christ, (Cf. Ephes, 4, 13).

XIX. *That all will rise again in the same stature which indeed they had or were to have had in the perfect or youthful age.†*

That which the Apostle says: "predestinated to be made conformable to the image of the Son of God," (Cf. Rom. 8, 29), can be accepted as follows, that just as He is made conformable to us in mortality, so we are made conformable to Him in immortality. Now if we are admonished in these words regarding the form in which bodies are to rise again, just as that measure was understood, so also is this conformation to be understood, not of quantity but of age. Thus all will rise again as great in body as either they were or were destined to be at the youthful age. But if indeed anyone contends that each one will rise again in that kind of body in which he died, one should not quarrel with him in tedious contradiction.

---

*Cf. the City of God of St. Augustine.
†Cf. Book XXII of the City of God of St. Augustine.

XX. *Whether the bodies of the wicked will rise again with their vices and deformities.*

Whoever indeed from that mass of perdition, which was made through man, are not freed at first by the one mediator of God and man, some surely will rise again, each one with his own flesh, but in order that they themselves may be punished with the devil and his angels. What is the need of labouring to inquire whether indeed they themselves rise with the vices and the deformities of their bodies, whatever deformed and vicious members they bore in them? For the uncertain condition and beauty of those whose damnation will be certain and everlasting should not weary us. Let it not disturb us how they can have an incorruptible body, if it can suffer pain or how corruptible, if it cannot. For there is no true life except where there is happy living, nor true incorruption except where health is uncorrupted by pain. Now where the unfortunate is not permitted to die and, so to speak, death itself does not die, and where perpetual pain does not bring to an end but corruption itself afflicts and is not ended, this in Holy Scriptures is called the second death, (Cf. Apoc. 20, 6 and 21, 8). Yet the first would not have happened to man, by which the soul is forced to leave the body, nor the second by which the soul is not permitted to leave the penal body, if no one had sinned. Indeed the mildest punishment of all will be for those who, besides the original sin which they have born, have added nothing thereto, and in the rest which they have added each one will have the more tolerable damnation there, the less iniquity he will have here.

XXI. *How earthly bodies will abide in heaven.*

It is necessary, some say, that natural weight either hold earthly bodies on earth or force them to earth, and on this account they cannot be in heaven. Indeed those first men were in a wooded and fruitful land which received the name of paradise, and thus they adduce proof regarding the weight of the elements. For they have learned from the master Plato, for example, that the two greatest and extreme bodies of the world are joined and kept together by two media, namely, by air and water. And on this account, they say, since earth turning here upward at first, water upon the earth second, air upon the water third, the heavens upon the air fourth, there cannot be an earthly body in the heavens. For at proper moments, that they may retain their order, their elements are balanced. Behold with what arguments the human weakness which vanity possesses opposes the omnipotence of God.

What, therefore, are so many earthly bodies doing in the air, when the air is third from the earth, if perhaps He, who through the lightness of feathers and wings gave to the earthly bodies of birds the power to be borne in the air, will not be able to give to the bodies of men made immortal the power by which they can also live in the heavens? For although when bearing the weights, as it were, of earthly bodies we are accustomed to feel that the greater the quantity is the greater is the weight, yet the soul bears the members of its flesh lighter when they are in robust health than when they are thin in languor. And although when sound and strong he is more burdensome for others who carry him than when thin and sick, yet he himself is more agile in moving and carrying his own body when he has more bulk in good health than when he has very little strength in sickness and hunger. Even in possessing earthly bodies, although still corruptible and mortal, the weight of quantity is not so strong but the kind of constitution. And who will explain with words how much difference there is between the present health of which we speak and the future immortality? And so philosophers do not disprove our faith in the weights of bodies. For thus turned upward, here is land first, water second, air third, heavens fourth, so that above all is the nature of the soul. For Aristotle even said that it was a fourth body and Plato that it was none. If there were a fifth, surely it would be superior to the rest. Although in truth there is none, it surpasses all by far. What then does it do in an earthly body? What does it, more subtle than all, do in this mass? What does it, lighter than all, do in this weight? What does it, swifter than all, do in this slowness? Thus through the merit of so excellent a nature as this can it not be effected that its body be raised to the heavens? And since the nature of earthly bodies is able now to press souls downward sometimes, will not souls also be able to raise earthly bodies upward?

Finally, if the order of the elements is so disposed that according to Plato the two extremes, namely, fire and land, are joined by two media, namely, by air and water, and the heavens obtain the highest place but this land the lowest, as it were, the foundation of the world, on this account the land cannot be in the heavens. Why is fire in the land? For according to this, by this reason, the two elements, land and fire, should have been in their proper places, in the lowest and in the highest, so that just as what is of the lowest does not wish that it could be in the highest, so what is of the highest could not be in the lowest. Therefore, just as they think that there neither is nor will be a particle of earth in the heavens, so we should have seen no particle of fire on earth. Now indeed not only is fire on the earth but it is also under the earth in such a way that mountain peaks cast it forth, in addition to the fact that we see fire on earth among the benefits of man, and we see it rise from the earth, whenever it rises from both wood and stone which are without doubt earthly bodies. Why then do they not want us to believe that the nature of earthly bodies, at some time made incorruptible, will be suitable to the heavens, just as now corruptible fire befits this earth? So they make no assertions about the weights and the order of the elements, whereby they could prescribe to the all-powerful God how He might make our bodies lighter and of a nature that would enable them to dwell in heaven.

XXII. *Of what nature the judgment will be.*

We must understand a certain divine force which will bring it about that one's works, whether good or bad, are all recalled to the memory of everyone and with marvelous speed are perceived by the mind's eye, so that knowledge may accuse or excuse the conscience, and thus at the same time all and each individually may be judged. This truly divine force has received the name of book. For in it in some manner is read whatever is recalled by the doer.

XXIII. *That God uses our conscience as a witness for judging us.**

When the Judge comes, the conscience of each one will be brought in to give testimony. Then all sin is brought back before the eyes, and the mind is tormented above the fires of hell more severely by its own fire.

We must consider again and again of what nature we shall be on the day of judgment, to be offered to the view of the purest angels and to render to the eternal Judge an account from the books of conscience. For when all trials have been removed, it is certain that on that day man must be set up before himself, and his soul must be shown to himself in the mirror of his heart, and witnesses must be offered against it, not from somewhere outside but from within himself, and no extraneous things will have to be added, but well known testimonies, his own works.

XXIV. *How God judges in the present.†*

God judges at this time not only universally over the race of men and demons, that they may be wretched on account of the merit of first sins, but also over the particular works of individuals which they carry on by free will. For we know not by what judgment of God that good man is poor, that evil one is rich; this one rejoices who, we are convinced, should have been tortured for his profligate character; there goes out from the court not only the unavenged but also the condemned, the innocent, either oppressed by the iniquity of the judge or crushed by false testimonies; on the other hand his wretched adversary not only unpunished but even sentenced behaves insolently; the wicked is very strong, the good wastes away in languors; the most sober minded youth are brigands; even those who were unable to harm anyone by a word are afflicted by various atrocities of diseases; infants important for human life are snatched away by premature death, and he who, it seems, should never have been born, lives a very long life full of crimes, is raised to high honors, and shades of obscurity conceal the man without complaint; and other things of this kind.

---

*Cf. the Morales of Gregory the Great.
†Cf. the City of God of St. Augustine.

XXV. *On the same.**

Now since not only the good are in evil and the evil in good, which seems unjust, but also for the most part evils result for the evil and goods come forth for the good, more inscrutable are the judgments of God and unsearchable are His ways, (Cf. Rom. 11, 33). Now when we shall come to that judgment of God, which time indeed is usually called the day of judgment and sometimes the day of the Lord, not only whatever will be judged then but also whatever has been judged from the beginning and whatever is to be judged up until that time will appear to be most just; when this also will be made manifest, how it is brought about by the just judgment of God that now so many and almost all just judgments of God are hidden from the senses and minds of mortals, although indeed in this matter it does not escape the faith of the good that what is hidden is just.

XXVI. *On the same.†*

Although the divine judgments are very well concealed as to why in this life sometimes affairs go badly for the good and well for the evil, they are more concealed then when affairs go well here for the good and badly for the evil. For when affairs go badly for the good and well for the evil, it is perhaps understood as follows, that if the good have been delinquent in any respect they receive herein the reward of being freed more fully from eternal damnation, and the evil find herein the good things which they do according to this life, so that they are brought into the next world for torments alone. So also is it said to the rich man burning in hell: "Son, remember that thou didst receive good things in thy lifetime, and likewise Lazarus evil things," (Luke 16, 25). But when affairs go well here for the good and badly for the evil, it becomes very uncertain whether the good receive good things on this account, that being urged on to some extent they may grow better or by a just and hidden judgment they may receive the remuneration of their works here, so as to be deprived of the rewards of the next life; and whether adversities strike the evil on this account, that they may ward off eternal punishments or their expiation may begin here so that some time it may lead to the completion of the last torments of hell.

XXVII. *On the same.‡*

God judges man in this life in two ways, because either through present evils He already begins to inflict ensuing torments or He abolishes ensuing torments by present scourgings.

---

*Cf. the City of God of St. Augustine.
†Cf. the Morales of Gregory the Great.
‡Cf. Book VIII of the Morales of Gregory the Great.

XXVIII. *Where the saints will be corporeally, when the world will burn.*

Perhaps someone is asking if, after judgment is made, this world will burn before a new heaven and a new land is put in its place, where the saints will be at the very time of its conflagration, since having bodies they must be in some corporeal place? We can reply that they will be in the higher places where the flame of the conflagration will not ascend, just as the water of the flood did not. For they will have the kind of bodies that will enable them to be wherever they wish to be. But those made immortal and incorruptible will not fear the fire of that conflagration, just as the corruptible and mortal bodies of those three men were able to live unharmed in the fiery furnace, (Cf. Dan. 3).

EIGHTEENTH PART

On the State of the Future Life.

I. *On the renewing of the world.*

When they have been judged who are not inscribed in the Book of life and have been sent into eternal fire, I think that no man knows what the fire will be like and in what part of the world or land it will be, unless perhaps the divine spirit will disclose it to someone. Then the shape of the world will be destroyed by the conflagration of worldly fires, just as the flood was made by the inundation of worldly waters. Thus as He said, by that worldly conflagration the qualities which were in harmony with our corruptible bodies will perish within by burning, and the substance itself will have those qualities which, by a marvelous change, befit immortal bodies, so that indeed the world renewed for the better is openly accommodated to men also renewed for the better in flesh.

II. *How the eternal punishment of the evil will benefit the good.*

The unjust will surely burn to some extent so that all the just in the Lord may see the joys that they receive and in those may look upon the punishments which they have evaded, in order that they may realize the more that they are richer in divine grace unto eternity, the more openly they see that those evils are punished unto eternity which they have overcome by His help.

III. *That the good will see the evil, not the evil the good, and on the second death.*

Those who will be in punishments do not know what is going on within in the joy of the Lord, but those who will be in that joy know what is going on without in the exterior shades. For there will be none but everlasting death, when the soul will neither be able to live by not having God nor to be free from the pains of the body by dying. At first, death drives the soul unwilling from the body;

the second death holds the soul unwilling in the body. By both deaths this is possessed in common, that what the soul does not wish regarding its body, this it suffers.

IV. *That the evil will always live for this purpose, that they may always die.*

A soul placed there has lost being blessed and has not lost being. Thus it is always forced to suffer death without death, failure without failure, and end without end in order that it may have immortal death and unfailing failure and endless end.

V. *That eternal fire will not torture all equally.*

The unlikeness of those who suffer abides even in the likeness of the sufferings, and although under the same torment, the virtue and the fault are not the same. For just as under the one fire gold glows, chaff smokes, and under the same threshing sledger stalks are crushed, grains cleaned, and dregs are not confused with oil, because they are pressed by the same weight of the pressing beam, so one and the same crushing force tests, purges, and clarifies the good; damns, lays waste, and exterminates the evil. But there is not so much difference in the nature of the things which one suffers but in the nature of everyone who suffers.

VI. *On the same.*

By no means must it be denied that even the eternal fire itself according to the diversity of merits, however evil, will be lighter for some, severer for others, whether its force and ardour are varied according to the punishment worthy of each, or it itself burns equally but is not felt with equal annoyance.

VII. *On the same.*

Indeed there is one fire of hell but it does not torment all sinners in one way. For in the case of each one as much as fault demands, to such an extent will punishment be felt there. For just as in this world many stand under one sun and yet they do not feel the ardour of the same sun equally, since one burns more and another less, so there in one fire, there is not one mode of burning, since what a diversity of bodies experiences here, a diversity of sinners experiences there, so that they do not have dissimilar fire and it burns the same ones differently as individuals.

VIII. *How it is just that eternal punishment be paid for a temporal sin.*

How then is it true, they say, which your Christ says: "In what measure you shall mete, it shall be measured to you again in the same," (Cf. Matt. 7, 2; Mark 4, 24), if temporal sin is punished by eternal suffering? They do not notice that the same measure has been mentioned, not because of equal space of time but because of the change of evil, that is, that he who has done evils should suffer evils. For the Lord was speaking regarding judgments and condemnations. Furthermore, he who judges and condemns unjustly, if he is judged and condemned justly, received in the same measure, although not that which he gave. For by judgment he acted and by judgment he suffers. Although he has done damnation which is unjust, he suffers damnation which is just. There is no one who grants that the torments of the guilty must be ended as quickly as the homicide was committed, or adultery, or sacrilege, and does not grant that any crime whatsoever must be measured not by length of time but by the magnitude of the iniquity and impiety.

IX. *On the same.*

Christ says: "In what measure you shall mete, it shall be measured to you again," (Cf. Mark 4, 24; Matt. 7, 2), that is, what you shall do, you shall suffer, not that if he shall do a defilement he may suffer a defilement, but what he does to the law by this sin, this the law may do to him, that is, since he took out of his life the law which prohibits such things, the law also takes him from the life of men which it rules. Likewise He says: "Judge not, that you may not be judged. For with what judgment you judge, you shall be judged," (Cf. Matt. 7, 1 and 2). Then if they shall judge with unjust judgment, shall they be judged with unjust judgment? Far be it! For there is no injustice in God, but thus is it said: In what judgment you shall judge, in that you shall be judged, as if it were said: In what will you shall benefit, in it itself you are freed, or in what will you shall do evil, in it itself you shall be punished. For according to the nature of wills, not according to spaces of time, whether done rightly or done sinfully, they will be measured. Otherwise to cast down a tree is held a greater sin than to kill a man. For the one is done after long delay, with many strokes; the other with one stroke, in the shortest time. For in this opinion there is the same measure for this alone, that what is preeminent be not preeminent for him. And so that he himself is judged will be eternal, although that he has judged could not have been eternal. Therefore, in the same measure, although not for eternal malfactions, eternal punishments will be meted out so that, since he wished to have the eternal enjoyment of sin, he may find the eternal severity of punishment.

X. *On the same.*

I would like to know how it is just that sin which has been committed with end be punished without end. Gregory says: This would be said rightly, if the severe Judge did not weigh the hearts of men but the deeds. For the unjust sinned with end, because they lived with end. For surely they would have wished, if they had been able, to live without end, that they could have sinned without end.

For they who never cease to sin while they live show that desire always to live in sin. Therefore, it pertains to the great justice of Him who judges that they never are free from punishment who in this life did not wish to be free from sin.

XI. *How the devil is now being tormented and how he will be tormented in the future.*

As for the ancient enemy bound by the bonds of his iniquity, there is one thing which he suffers now, another which he will suffer at the end. For since he has fallen from the order of inmost light, he now confounds himself within the darkness of horror. But afterwards he will be involved in this bitterness, since punishments not only of all kinds but also without end are being prepared for his pride. And this punishment of his indeed receives its beginning then when the severe judge finally comes.

XII. *On the same.*

Now after the death of the flesh there is prepared by the hostile devil a death of another kind, in which he exalts very proudly in the eternal fire of Tartarus, where spirits not only with earthly but also with ephemeral bodies can be tortured.

XIII. *That after the damnation of the wicked, the saints recognize more fully the grace of God.*

Therefore, while bad angels and men remain in eternal punishment, the saints will then know more fully what a blessing grace has brought them.

XIV. *That, after the evil have been damned, the saints will enter upon eternal life.*

For just as He will say to the wicked: "Depart into everlasting fire," (Cf. Matt. 25, 41), so will He say to the just: "Come, ye blessed of my Father, possess etc.," (Cf. Matt. 25, 34). And just as the former will go into eternal burning, so the just will go into eternal life. Now what "is eternal life except that they may know thee," He says, "the only true God, and Jesus Christ whom thou has sent?" (Cf. John 17, 3). But now in that glory about which He speaks to the Father, "which I had had, before the world was, with thee," (Cf. John 17, 5), then will He give over "the kingdom to God and the Father," (Cf. 1 Cor. 15, 24), that the good servant may enter "into the joy of his Lord," (Cf. Matt. 25, 23).

XV. *How the just will not then have pity for the evil.*

And what does it mean that they are saints, if they will not pray for their enemies, whom they shall see burning, to whom it is said: "Pray for your enemies,"?

(Cf. Matt. 5, 44; Luke 6, 35). They pray for their enemies at the time when they can turn their hearts to fruitful repentance and save them by conversion. For what else must we pray for enemies but for this as the Apostle says: "That God may give them repentance to know the truth, and they may recover themselves from the snares of the devil, by whom they are held captive at his will,"? (Cf. 2 Tim. 2, 25 and 26).

Likewise on the same.

May what you say be pleasing. And how will there be prayer for those then who indeed can by no means be changed from iniquity to works of justice?

Thus the same reason exists why there is no prayer then for men who have been condemned to eternal fire, and this now is also the reason that there is no prayer for the devil and his angels destined to eternal punishment. What now is also the reason that holy men do not pray for faithless and wicked men who have died, unless indeed because, for those whom they know have already been destined to eternal punishment, they shun the merit of their prayer being brought to naught before the sight of the just judge? But if the living just have not pity for the unjust who are dead and damned, when they themselves also know that they still bear for their own cause something that may be judged, then they regard the torments of the unjust the more severely, as more closely and more firmly they now cling to justice itself stripped of every vice of corruption. For thus the force of severity engrosses their minds through this, that they cling to the most just judge, so that whatever does not agree with the strictness of that eternal law does not please them at all.

XVI. *On the vision of God.*

If you ask whether God can be seen, I reply: He can. If you ask, how I know, I reply: Because in the most true Scripture it is read: "Blessed are the clean of heart: for they shall see God," (Matt. 5, 8). If you ask how it is that He is called invisible, if He can be seen, I reply that He is invisible by nature. But He can be seen when He wishes, just as He wishes. For He has been seen by very many, not just as He is, but in such an appearance as it please Him to appear. What is it then that the same authority says: "No man hath seen God at any time," (Cf. John 1, 18) and that the Apostle says explaining more clearly: "Whom no man hath seen, nor can see."? (1 Tim. 6, 16). How then did Abraham see God, or did Isaac, Jacob, Job, Moses, Michaeas, Isaias, and if there are any others of whom the most truthful Scripture testifies that they saw God, if no one has seen God at any time, nor can see Him? A great question is this: how it is not contrary that so many ancients saw God, if no one has seen God at any time, whom no man has seen nor can see.

Surely it cannot be refuted, as Ambrose says, that either the Father or the Son or the Holy Spirit, (if however there is a vision of the Holy Spirit), are seen under that appearance which His will chooses, not nature forms. For we have also accepted the Spirit seen as a dove and so: No one has seen God at any time because no one has seen that fulness of God which dwells in God; no one comprehends it with mind or eyes. Therefore, Moses says to God with whom he spoke "face to face, as friend to friend. If I have found favour in thy sight, show me thyself," (Cf. Exod. 33, 11 and 13). What then, was He not himself? If He were not Himself, he would not say to Him: Show me yourself but show me God. And yet if he perceived His nature and substance, much less would he say: Show me thyself. Therefore, He himself was in the appearance in which He had wished to appear, but He did not appear in His proper nature which Moses desired to see. For this is promised to saints in another life. Therefore we have the reply to Moses: "It is true that no one can see the face of God and live" (Cf. Exod. 33, 20), that is, no one while living in this life can see Him just as He is. For many saw, but what the will chose, not what nature formed. If you ask how the truly accursed Cain saw Him, when he was questioned and judged by Him about his crime, or even the devil himself when he came with the angels that he might be present before Him, (Cf. Job. 1, 6), if blessed are the clean of heart, for they shall see God, I reply that it is not fitting indeed that even they should see God who sometimes hear the words uttered by Him. For they did not see Him, who heard Him when He said to the Son: "I have both glorified it and will glorify it again," (Cf. John 12, 28). However, it is not to be wondered if at some time even the clean of heart do not see God in the appearance which His will has caused, His nature lying hidden and invisible and remaining unchangeable by itself.

If you ask whether even at some time, as it were, He can be seen, I reply that this has been promised to His children of whom it is said: "We know that, when he shall appear, we shall be like to him: because we shall see him as he is," (1 John 3, 2). For it is not asked how God is seen in that appearance in which He wished to appear in this world to certain men, but how He is seen in that kingdom where His children will see Him as He is. For then their desire will be satiated in good things. For the unworthy will not see God, of whom it is said: "Let the wicked be taken away lest he see the glory of God," (Cf. Isa. 26, 10), to whom also it shall be said: "Depart into everlasting fire etc." (Cf. Matt. 25, 41). But God promised that He would show His lovers one God with the Father, not as He was seen in this world in the body by the good and the evil. For at the future judgment when He shall come in the same way as He was seen going into heaven, that is, in the same form of the Son of man, they will see the same form to whom He shall say: "I was hungry and you gave me not to eat," (Matt. 25, 42), "for the Jews also shall look on him whom they pierced," (Cf. John 19, 37; Zach. 12, 10), not that form of God in which "he thought it not robbery to be equal with God," (Cf. Philip.

2, 6). In that form of God will they then see God, who will see Him as He is. And they will not see Him because they have been poor in spirit in this life, because gentle, because mournful, etc., but because they are clean of heart, since He will be seen by the clean heart, who neither is seen in place nor is sought by corporeal eyes nor is circumscribed by sight nor is held by touch nor is heard by speaking nor is felt by approach.

XVII. *What is the difference between seeing and believing.*

We say that there is this difference between seeing and believing, that things present are seen, things absent are believed. Indeed it is perhaps enough if by those things present we understand in this place the words which are at hand for the senses either of soul or of body. Therefore too, when words are uttered they are called present. For just as I clearly see this light by a sense of the body, so too I see my will because it is at hand to the senses of my spirit and is present within me. If anyone indeed indicates his will to me, whose face and voice are present to me, yet since the will which he indicates to me escapes the sense of the body and of my spirit, I believe, I do not see. Or if I think that he lies, I do not believe, even if by chance it might be as he says. Therefore, those things which are absent from our senses are believed, if what is offered as proof for them seems sufficient. And not because I have said that those things are believed which are absent from our senses could they so be accepted as to be placed among those things which we have seen and are certain of, because they are not present then when they are recalled by us. For they are not classed among the things believed but among those seen and so they are known, not because we had faith in other witnesses but because we recall without doubt and know that we have seen them. Therefore, our knowledge is established from things seen and believed, but in those things which we see or have seen we ourselves are the witnesses. But in those things which we believe, we are moved to faith by other witnesses, when of those things which we neither recall having seen nor see, signs are given either in words or in letters or in any documents whatever, on seeing which the unseen things are believed. Now not unfittingly do we say that we know not only those things which we have seen and see but also those which we believe by proper testimonies and witnesses.

Furthermore, if we do not say unfittingly that we know, those things also which we believe have thereby been made most certain, so that we may be said to see with the mind the things rightly believed, even if they were not present to our senses. Thus when it is said to man: Believe that Christ has risen from the dead; if he believes, consider what he sees, consider what he believes, and distinguish each. He sees a man whose voice he hears and the voice itself is placed among seen corporeal things, according to what we have said above. These two are witness and testimony, one of which pertains to the eyes, the other to the ears. But perhaps he confirms this witness by the authority of other witnesses, namely, of Divine Scriptures, or of any others by which he is moved to faith. The Scriptures have to do with impressions on the body: on the eyes, if one reads them; or on the ears, if one has heard them. This, therefore, I do not show in such a way that it be held seen or perceived by a sense of the body or the soul, and yet I do say something which must indeed be either true or false but is seen by neither of these two; it remains only that it either be believed or not believed. But if it is confirmed by the clear authority of these Scriptures, specifically which in the Church are called canonical, it must be believed without any doubt.

Indeed in other witnesses or testimonies in which we are persuaded to have some credence, you may either believe or not believe according as you consider that I either do or do not possess what causes trust in him who advises of these things. For if we did not believe at all those things which we have not seen, that is, have not felt in present appearance either by mind or body, nor have learned from Holy Scripture either by reading or by hearing, how would we learn that there are cities where we have never been or that Rome was founded by Romulus or, to speak of things closer to us, that Constantinople was founded by Constantine? How, finally, would we learn what parents had begotten us, from what fathers, grandfathers, and ancestors we were born? For indeed although we know most of such things, yet we did not learn them by any sense, by their presence, like the sun, like the will of our spirit, or the authority of canonical eloquence, as the fact that Adam was the first man or that Christ born in the flesh and having suffered rose again, but we learned them when others referred to them, about whose testimony in this kind of things, at least we thought that there should be scarcely any doubt.

You have learned sufficiently, in my opinion, from this preamble of mine what it is to see either by mind or by body and how believing differs from this, which indeed is done by the mind and is seen by the mind, since our faith is clear to our mind. But yet what is believed by the same faith is absent both from the sight of our body, as the body is absent in which Christ arose, and from the sight of another's mind, as is your faith from the sight of our mind; although I believe that it is in you, when I do not see with the body what you cannot nor with the mind what you can, just as I can see my faith which you cannot.

XVIII. *On the corporeal and spiritual visions in the future.*

It is hard to say that saints will have such bodies then that they cannot close and open their eyes when they wish, but it is harder to say that whoever closes his eyes will not see God there. For if the prophet Eliseus, absent in body, saw his son Giezi receiving gifts which were given him by Neaman the Syrian, (Cf.

4 Kings 5), whom the famous prophet had cleansed of the vileness of leprosy, and the wicked servant thought that he had done this secretly while the master was not watching, how much more will the saints in that spiritual body see all things, not only if they close their eyes but also even when they are absent from this place in body?

XIX. *Whether our thoughts there will be changeable.*

Furthermore, the word which gives an outward sound is a sign of the word which shines within, to which the name of word is more appropriate. For that which is uttered from the mouth of flesh is the voice of the word. And the word itself is spoken on account of that from which it was assumed, in order to appear externally. The same in the same a little afterwards.

Accordingly that word of God is uttered in such a way that His thoughts are not spoken, lest there is believed to be something changeable in God; what He accepts now receives form so that it is word or so that the word can lose form and be twisted in some formless way. And a little afterwards we read: Indeed God's thoughts are also mentioned in Holy Scripture but in such a manner of speech that anger and forgetfulness are predicated of God, and as for there being a property of God, there is none. And a little afterwards we read: And then indeed in the eternal life, surely our word will not be false, since neither shall we lie nor be deceived. Perhaps also our thoughts will not be changeable going from some things to others, but we shall see all knowledge together at one glance.

Nevertheless when this shall be, if this shall be, the creature will be formed which was formable so that nothing will be then lacking to the particular form to which it should have arrived, but yet it will not have to be made equal to that simplicity where something not formable is formed or reformed, but the form neither unformed nor formed is itself there, eternal and immutable substance.

XX. *Of what nature and how great will be the future joy and blessedness.*

How great will be the joy where there will be no evil, where no good will lie hidden? He will be void of the praises of God, who will be all things in all. The same one says in the same work: Surely where the spirit wishes, there forthwith will be the body. Nor will the spirit wish for anything which it can call neither spirit nor body. True glory will be there where no one will be praised by the error or adulation of him who praises. True honour which will be denied to no one worthy, will be conferred on no one unworthy. But no one will go around to Him where no one will be permitted to be unless worthy. True peace will be there where no one will suffer anything adverse either from himself or from another. The reward of virtue will be He himself who gave virtue and to him He promised Himself, than whom nothing can be better and greater.

For what else is it that He said through the prophet: "I shall be their God, and they will be my people," (Cf. Jeremias 30, 22); unless I shall be him from whom they will be satiated; I shall be whatever is honorably desired by all, namely, life and salvation and food and plenty, glory and honour, peace and all goods? For so is that also rightly understood which the Apostle says: "That God may be all in all," (Cf. 1 Cor. 15, 28). For He himself will be the end of our desires, who will be seen without end, will be loved without aversion, will be praised without weariness. This office, this affection, this act will surely be common to all, just as life eternal itself. But also what are to be the grades of honours and glories according to the merits of rewards, who is prepared to consider, much less to say? Yet that they shall be is not to be doubted, and so too that blessed city will see a great gift in itself, because no inferior will envy a superior just as the other angels do not envy archangels.

So will no one wish to be what he did not receive, although he be bound by the most peaceful bond of concord to him who did receive, as the eye does not wish to be in the body what the finger is, although the peaceful bond of the whole part contains both members. And thus one will have a gift less than another in such a way that he has this gift also, that he does not wish for more.

XXI. *That true blessedness consists of three things.*

Our being there will not have death; our knowing there will not have error; our loving there will not have offense.

XXII. *That for the saints in the future the memory of the past will conduce not to pain but to joy.*

Therefore free-will will be a property of that city, one in all and inseparable in each, freed from all evil, filled with all good, enjoying without cease the pleasure of eternal joys, forgetful of sins, forgetful of punishments, yet not therefore so forgetful of its liberation that it is ungrateful to its liberator. Thus, in so far as pertains to rational knowledge, it will be mindful of its past evils, but in so far as pertains to the sensation of him who experiences, utterly forgetful. For even the most experienced physician knows all the diseases of the body as they are known by science, but as they are felt in the body he does not know most of them which he himself has not suffered. So then there are two knowledges of evils, one by which they do not escape the power of the mind, the other by which they cling to the senses of him who experiences them. For in one way all vices are known through the knowledge of wisdom, in another way through the very bad life of the universe. Thus also there are two oblivions of evils. For in one way the erudite and the learned, in another way the tried and the sufferer forget them; the one if he neglects experience, the other if he is bereft of misery. According to this oblivion which I have placed in a lower plane, the saints will not be mindful of past evils. For they will be so free of all evils that the evils are thoroughly wiped away from their senses and yet the power of knowledge, which will be great in them, will not only avoid their past but also those of the damned in eternal misery. There we shall call and we shall see; we shall see and we shall love; we shall love and we shall praise. Behold what will be in the end without end!

GENERAL INDEX

Abelard, his *Introductio ad Theologiam*, x, 38 f.n.; 416 f.n.

abortions, on abortions and monsters; whether they rise again and of what nature they are, 458f.

Abraham, 187ff.; 217ff.; 296; 342f.; 470.

acolyte, on acolytes, 264.

Adam, which sinned more, Adam or Eve, 124f.; 149; 187; 325.

administration, on the distribution of ecclesiastical administration, 253ff.; that every ecclesiastical administration consists of three things, that is, orders, sacraments, precepts, 257.

affinity, on affinity, 365ff.; what difference there is between blood relationship or consanguinity and affinity and spiritual union, 368f.

Alexander, Pope, 320; 359.

Alexandria, 261; 316.

allegory, 5.

altar, that the sacrament of the altar is also a figure as far as pertains to the appearance of bread and of wine, and is the substance as far as pertains to the truth of the body of Christ, 308.

Ambrose, St., 214ff.; 331f.

angels, 74ff.; in the beginning angels were created, 75; of what nature were angels when they were first made, 77f.; in what they were created similar and in what dissimilar, 80; on their threefold power, 80f.; on their threefold knowledge, 81f.; that they were founded perfect according to the first perfection, 82; whether they had foreknowledge of their future lot, 82; of what nature they were founded, good or evil, just or unjust, happy or wretched, 83f.; on their free will, 84f.; on the aversion and fall of the evil angels, and on the conversion and confirmation of the good angels, 86; how God turns all the will and power of the angels to the order and disposition of His own will, 88f.; that God restrains the will and the power of the evil angels in four ways, 89; orders of angels, how many were founded by God in the beginning, 90f.; names of angels, 92; the ministries of the angels, 93; that angels were made so that they were instructed from within, men from without, 137f.

anointing, on the anointing of the sick, 430ff.; when and by whom the anointing of the sick was established, 431; whether this sacrament can be repeated, 431ff.

Antichrist, 452; 453.

Antioch, 261; 314.

Apostle, the, 165; 249; 256; 263f.; 316; 325f.; 332; 342; 355; 363; 386; 396; 397f.; et passim.

Aquileia, 261.

archbishop, on archbishops, 269f.

archdeacon, on archdeacons, 270.

arithmetic, 5.

Arius, 210; 320.

arts, all arts are subservient to divine wisdom, 5.

Asa, 319.

ashes, on the reception of ashes, 316f.

aspersion, on the water of aspersion which is blessed together with salt, 316.

astronomy, 5.

Athanasius, blessed, 320.

Augustine, bishop of the English people, 363ff.

Augustine, St., ix, 210ff.; 218f.; 306ff.; 314; 325; 332; 339ff.; 353; 396; 397; 400; 404; 443ff.; 449f.; 451f.; 464ff.

Balaam, 322.

baptism, on the sacrament of baptism, 282f.; what baptism is, 283ff.; why the sacrament of baptism was instituted, 288ff.; when the sacrament of baptism was instituted, 290f.; when man began to be obligated by the precept of receiving baptism, 291f.; what the difference is between the baptism of John and that of Christ, and regarding the form of the baptism of John and that of Christ, 292; whether after the precept of baptism was given anyone could be saved without actually receiving the sacrament of baptism, 293ff.; on those things in baptism which follow exorcization, 298f.; why baptism is celebrated in water only, 301; on the form of baptism, 310f.; which is the greater sacrament — imposition of hands or baptism, 303.

Bede, 364; 404.

being, how both are eternal, foreknown being and future being, 36f.

beings, what is the first cause of the foundation of rational beings, 31.

[477]